# THE ILLUSTRATED

# Encyclopedia of

# Scotland

First published in Great Britain in 2004 by
Lomond Books
36 West Shore Road
Granton
Edinburgh EH5 1QD

Produced by Colin Baxter Photography Ltd

Copyright © Colin Baxter Photography Ltd 2004

A CIP catalogue record for this book is available from the British Library

ISBN 1-84204-028-6

Printed in China

Photographs and illustrations copyright 2004 by: **Front cover from left to right:** MSP office window © Adam Elder/Scottish Parliament;
Falkirk Wheel © Fintray Fine Frames; Robert Burns © Scottish National Portrait Gallery; Ladderback chair and wall stencils, The Hill House © Colin Baxter
**Back cover from top to bottom:** Eilean Donan © Colin Baxter; Billy Connolly © Reuters/Corbis; North Sea oil rig © Colin Baxter;
City Chambers, Glasgow © Colin Baxter; Forth Bridge © Colin Baxter; Thistle illustration © Julianne Irvine

Whilst we have made every effort to trace all copyright holders, we shall be glad to learn of any instances where acknowledgement is due.

**Front cover photographs from left to right:** Scottish Parliament office window; Falkirk Wheel; Robert Burns; Ladderback chair and wall stencils
**Back cover photographs from top to bottom:** Eilean Donan Castle; Billy Connolly; North Sea oil rig; City Chambers, Glasgow; Forth Bridge

# THE
# ILLUSTRATED
# *Encyclopedia of*
# *Scotland*

### EDITED BY
### ISEABAIL MACLEOD M.B.E.

## LOMOND
**EDINBURGH ▪ SCOTLAND**

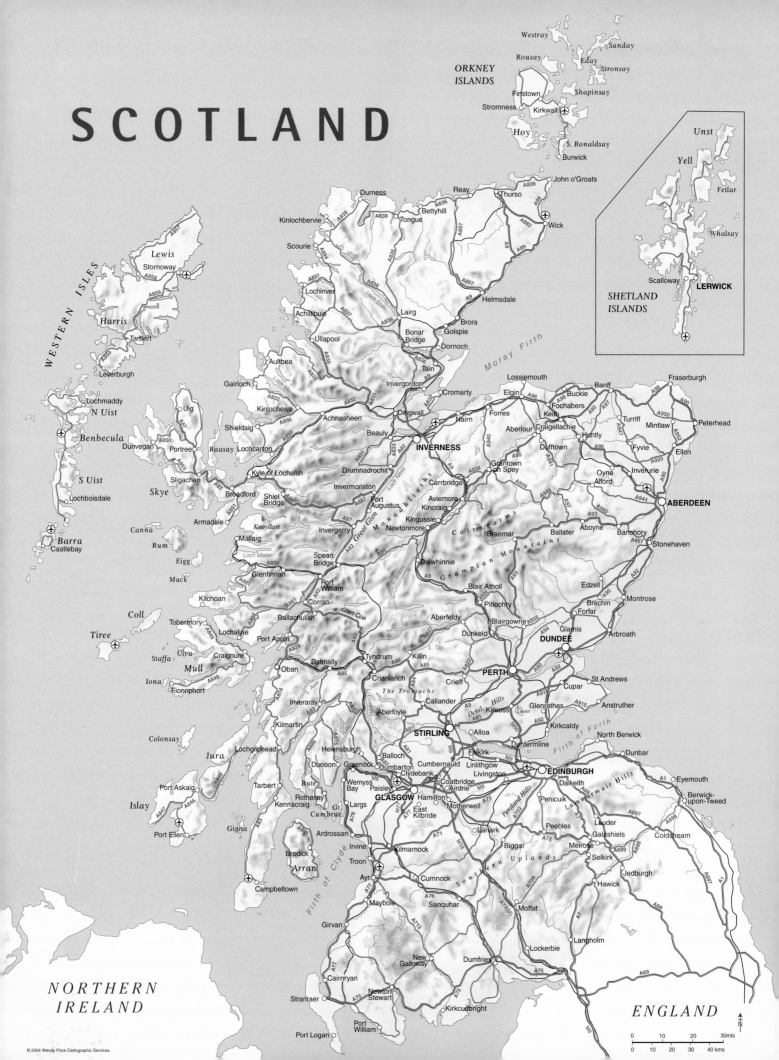

# SCOTLAND

ORKNEY ISLANDS

Westray
Rousay
Sanday
Eday
Stronsay
Finstown
Shapinsay
Stromness
Kirkwall
Hoy
S. Ronaldsay
Burwick

John o'Groats
Reay
Thurso
Durness
Bettyhill
Tongue
Wick

Kinlochbervie
Scourie

Unst
Yell
Fetlar
Whalsay
Scalloway
LERWICK
SHETLAND ISLANDS

WESTERN ISLES

Lewis
Stornoway

Harris
Tarbert
Leverburgh

Lochinver
Achiltibuie
Lairg
Bonar Bridge
Helmsdale
Brora
Golspie
Dornoch

Ullapool

Aultbea
Gairloch
Invergordon
Tain
Cromarty
Lossiemouth
Elgin
Buckie
Banff
Fraserburgh

Lochmaddy
N Uist
Benbecula
Dunvegan
S Uist
Lochboisdale

Uig
Shieldaig
Kinlochewe
Achnasheen
Dingwall
Nairn
Forres
Aberlour
Craigellachie
Fochabers
Keith
Turriff
Mintlaw
Peterhead

Portree
Raasay
Lochcarron
Beauly
INVERNESS
Huntly
Dufftown
Fyvie
Ellon

Barra
Castlebay

Skye
Sligachan
Broadford
Kyle of Lochalsh
Shiel Bridge
Drumnadrochit
Invermoriston
Fort Augustus
Carrbridge
Grantown on Spey
Oyne
Alford
Inverurie
ABERDEEN

Canna
Rum
Armadale
Knoydart
Invergarry
Kingussie
Newtonmore
Aviemore
Kincraig
Braemar
Ballater
Aboyne
Banchory
Stonehaven

Eigg
Muck
Mallaig
Spean Bridge
Dalwhinnie
Grampian Mountains

Glenfinnan
Fort William
Corran
Blair Atholl
Edzell
Brechin
Montrose

Coll
Kilchoan
Tobermory
Lochaline
Ballachulish
Port Appin
Glen Coe
Aberfeldy
Pitlochry
Dunkeld
Blairgowrie
Glamis
Forfar
Arbroath

Tiree
Staffa
Ulva
Mull
Iona
Fionnphort
Craignure
Oban
Dalmally
Tyndrum
Killin
DUNDEE

Crianlarich
The Trossachs
Callander
Crieff
PERTH
Cupar
St Andrews
Anstruther

Colonsay
Inveraray
Aberfoyle
Ochil Hills
Kinross
Glenrothes
Kirkcaldy

Kilmartin
STIRLING
Alloa
Dunfermline
North Berwick
Dunbar

Jura
Lochgilphead
Helensburgh
Balloch
Falkirk
Linlithgow
Livingston
EDINBURGH
Dalkeith
Eyemouth

Islay
Port Askaig
Tarbert
Bute
Dunoon
Greenock
Dumbarton
Clydebank
Cumbernauld
Coatbridge
Airdrie
Penicuik
Peebles
Lauder
Galashiels
Coldstream
Berwick-upon-Tweed

Port Ellen
Gigha
Rothesay
Gt. Cumbrae
Largs
GLASGOW
Hamilton
East Kilbride
Motherwell
Lanark
Biggar
Melrose
Selkirk
Jedburgh
Hawick

Ardrossan
Irvine
Kilmarnock
Cumnock
Sanquhar
Moffat
Lockerbie
Langholm

Brodick
Arran
Troon
Ayr
Maybole

Campbeltown
Girvan

NORTHERN IRELAND

Cairnryan
New Galloway
Dumfries
Stranraer
Newton Stewart
Kirkcudbright
Port William
Port Logan

ENGLAND

Moray Firth
Firth of Forth
Firth of Clyde
Southern Uplands
Lammermuir Hills
Pentland Hills
Cairngorms
Monadhliaths
Great Glen
Loch Ness
Loch Shin

0    10    20    30mls
0    10    20    30    40kms

© 2004 Wendy Price Cartographic Services.

# CONTENTS

PHYSICAL MAP OF SCOTLAND 4

INTRODUCTION 6

HOW TO USE THE ENCYCLOPEDIA 6

LIST OF CONTRIBUTORS 7

ACKNOWLEDGEMENTS 7

A - Z ENTRIES 8-393

FEATURED ENTRIES

ABERDEEN 9

BURNS 61

CLANS 77

CLEARANCES 78

DICTIONARIES 108

DUNDEE 120

EDINBURGH 130–3

EDUCATION 136

FISHING INDUSTRY 147

FOOTBALL 151

GLASGOW 162–4

GOLF 170

IMMIGRATION 195

JACOBITE RISINGS 201

LANGUAGE 220

LAW 223

LIGHTHOUSES 229

LOCAL GOVERNMENT 233

MACKINTOSH, CHARLES RENNIE 255

MOUNTAINEERING AND HILLWALKING 278

NEWSPAPERS 288

OIL AND GAS 293

PLACE NAMES 303

PRESBYTERIAN CHURCHES 307

RAILWAYS 312

REGIMENTS 315

RUGBY 327

SCOTTISH ENLIGHTENMENT 336

SCOTTISH PARLIAMENT 340–1

STIRLING 358

WEIGHTS AND MEASURES 382–4

WHISKY 388

APPENDICES

Local Authority Area Maps 394-5

Calendar of Annual Festivals 396

Scottish Societies and Organisations 397

Further Reading 398-400

# INTRODUCTION

*The Illustrated Encyclopedia of Scotland* aims to give an overview of the country in a wide perspective: its varied landscapes, its towns and their buildings, its past and more particularly its present, but above all its people, and their occupations and pastimes. It is not of course possible to cover all these aspects in depth in one volume, but we have tried to include the most important and interesting facts.

Other Scottish reference books published in recent decades have treated many topics in greater depth. The aim of this book is to provide a wide range of facts in a highly accessible form. Some broader topics are treated in greater detail, and for additional information there is a classified list of further reading, mainly readily accessible works, on p.398. Further lists will be found at the back along with maps of local-authority areas which, with the names of local authorities in the text, should help to clarify the complications of radical changes to local government in Scotland in 1975 and 1996.

Though we now live in a post-industrial age, for two centuries until recently, industry was a dominant factor in Lowland Scotland. We have tried to reflect this, especially in entries for towns and larger companies, which usually indicate their later history up to the present.

Descriptions of castles and mansion houses, some within the entries for towns and villages, are a mirror not only of the landowning aristocracy of earlier days, but also of the industrialists and business people of later times. Again we have tried to indicate their current use; see for example Broughty Castle (under **Broughty Ferry**).

*Iseabail Macleod, General Editor*

# HOW TO USE THE ENCYCLOPEDIA

Entries are in strict alphabetical order of the entry word, ignoring hyphens and spaces:

> **Galloway**
> **Galloway cattle**
> **Galloway, George**
> **Galloway House**
> **Galloway, Janice**
> **Galloway, Jim**
> **Galloway, Mull of**
> **Galloway, R(h)inns of**

People are entered under the name or title by which they are most likely to be known:

> **Argyll, Archibald Campbell, 2nd Duke of**
> **MacDiarmid, Hugh** (pen name of **Christopher Murray Grieve**).

Where there are alternative forms of a name, for example a Gaelic and an English, the second is cross-referred:

> **Donnchadh Bàn** (Duncan Ban Macintyre) Gaelic poet ...
> **Macintyre, Duncan Ban** see **Donnchadh Bàn**

Place names are usually given in full:

> **North Uist**
> **Lower Largo**

with a cross-reference at the second element, for example

> **Uist** see **North Uist, South Uist**.

Ben, Glen, Loch and Strath are given under these elements:

> **Ben Lomond**

> **Strathspey**

but rivers appear under the name:

> **Spey** The second-longest river in Scotland ...

Gaelic names are given where possible for the Gaelic-speaking and recently Gaelic-speaking areas:

> **Lewis** or **Isle of Lewis** (Gaelic **Eilean Leodhais**) ...

People with the same name are listed chronologically, regardless of title or sobriquet:

> **Macleod, Norman** (1780-1866)
> **Macleod, Revd Dr Norman** ('Caraid nan Gaidheal' 'friend of the Highlanders') (1783-1862)
> **Macleod, Norman** (1812-72)

Words which have their own entry are picked out in bold type when their mention in another entry gives helpful additional information:

> **Haddo House** Mansion in Aberdeenshire, near **Ellon**, with extensive and well laid out gardens. It was built by William **Adam** in the 1730s ...

Population is given for towns and for some islands, from the 2001 census.

Measures are given in metric, followed by the imperial equivalent. Many are given in approximate form, simply to give an idea of distance. Old Scottish measures are treated under Weights and Measures on pp.382-4.

# CONTRIBUTORS
# AND ACKNOWLEDGEMENTS

**General Editor:** Iseabail Macleod

**Editors:** Stuart Bathgate, Clare Crawford, Flora Johnstone and Helen Kemp

## CONTRIBUTORS

**Agriculture:** Gavin Sprott, former Keeper, Department of Social and Technological History, National Museums of Scotland

**Archaeology:** Dr Anna Ritchie, archaeological consultant

**Architecture:** David Walker, Emeritus Professor, University of St Andrews, Dictionary of Scottish Architects Project

**Art:** Philip Long, Senior Curator, Scottish National Gallery of Modern Art

**Education:** Professor Lindsay Paterson, Moray House School of Education, University of Edinburgh

**Engineering/Landscape:** Iain Macleod, Professor of Structural Engineering, University of Strathclyde

**Fishing:** Angus Martin, historian and poet

**Food/Drink:** Catherine Brown, food writer

**Gardens/botany:** Robert J Mitchell, Honorary Curator, St Andrews Botanic Garden

**Geology:** John McManus, Professor Emeritus of Geography and Geosciences, University of St Andrews

**History, Medieval:** Dr Alastair MacDonald, Department of History, University of Aberdeen

**History, Modern:** Bruce Lenman, Professor Emeritus of Modern History, University of St Andrews

**Industry/Transport/Commerce:** John R Hume, Honorary Professor, Universities of Glasgow and St Andrews

**Law/Local government:** Dr Peter G B McNeill, retired sheriff

**Literature (Scots and English):** Alan MacGillivray, President, Association for Scottish Literary Studies

**Local Government:** J W L Lonie, director, Scottish Language Dictionaries

**Measures:** Dr Allen D C Simpson, Research Fellow, National Museums of Scotland

**Medicine:** Professor Michael Moss, University of Glasgow

**Music:** James Porter, Professor Emeritus, University of California, Honorary Professor, University of Aberdeen; Ewan McVicar, storyteller and song-writer; Piping: Robert Wallace, Jeannie Campbell, College of Piping, Glasgow

**Parliament:** Dr Roland Tanner, formerly School of History, University of St Andrews

**Place names:** Ian Fraser, Department of Celtic and Scottish Studies, University of Edinburgh

**Religion/Gaelic literature:** Professor Donald Meek, Department of Celtic and Scottish Studies, University of Edinburgh

**Sport/popular culture/media:** Stuart Bathgate, Chief Sports Writer, *The Scotsman*

## ACKNOWLEDGEMENTS

We are very grateful to all the above and also to the following for valuable information: G W S Barrow, Emeritus Professor of Scottish History, University of Edinburgh; Robert Black, Professor of Private Law, University of Edinburgh; John Burnett, National Museums of Scotland; Alan Carswell, National War Museum of Scotland; Hugh Cheape, National Museums of Scotland; Professor Emeritus Alexander Fenton, European Ethnological Research Centre; Douglas Gifford, Professor of Scottish Literature, University of Glasgow; Professor Douglas M Henderson, Queen's Botanist in Scotland; R D S Jack, Professor of Scottish and Medieval Literature, University of Edinburgh; Revd Finlay Macdonald, Principal Clerk, General Assembly of the Church of Scotland.

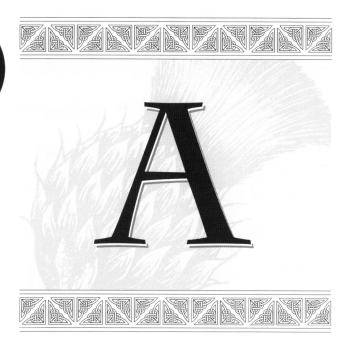

A

**Abbotsford** Pioneer Scots baronial mansionhouse on the River **Tweed**, 3km (2mi) west of **Melrose**, built (1816–23) by Sir Walter **Scott** to the design of the English architect William Atkinson. It is open to the public and contains Scott's collection of historical relics, including **Rob Roy**'s gun and **Montrose**'s sword, and his library of more than 9000 books.

**Abbotsinch** see **Glasgow** (airport)

**Abercorn** Hamlet on the south side of the Firth of **Forth**, 5km (3mi) west of South Queensferry and the site of the first bishopric in Scotland, 681. A decorated doorway with a fine tympanum is all that survives of a 12th-century church. The present 16th-century church, dedicated to St Serf, was restored in 1893. The Hopetoun aisle was designed by Sir William **Bruce** in 1708, and contains one of the finest laird's lofts in Scotland. The gatehouse contains a superb collection of Anglian and later sculpture, including a fine hogbacked gravestone.

**Abercromby, Sir Ralph** (1734–1801) Soldier, b. Menstrie, Clackmannanshire. After studying law in **Edinburgh** and Leipzig, he took part in the Seven Years' War. He declined to serve in the American War but held commands in the Low Countries, the West Indies, Ireland and Scotland after 1793. In 1801 he led an expedition that, after an opposed landing at Aboukir Bay, defeated the army Napoleon had left in Egypt in 2 battles. He died of wounds received at the Battle of Alexandria, after securing the first British military victory in the wars of the French Revolution.

**Aberdeen** see p.9

**Aberdeen Football Club** Founded 1903, their home ground is Pittodrie, to the northeast of the city centre. Although one of the most successful provincial clubs in the 1940s and 50s, they did not really come into their own until the 1980s, when managed by Alex **Ferguson**. They then became not only Scotland's leading team, but one of the best in Europe, a status confirmed by their victory over Real Madrid in the final of the Cup Winners' Cup in 1983. Their recent history has not been so successful, but they have been constantly in the Scottish Premier league. Their nickname is 'The Dons'.

**Aberdeen, George Gordon, 1st Earl of** (1637–1720) Lawyer and politician. Appointed a Lord of Session in 1680, he became Lord President of the **Court of Session** in 1681 and Lord Chancellor in 1682. The Aberdeen earldom was created for him in the same year. He strongly supported the Act of Union of 1707.

**Aberdeen, George Hamilton-Gordon, 4th Earl of** (1784–1860) Politician, b. Edinburgh. After serving as ambassador to Austria he entered politics. He was Foreign Secretary (1841–46) and Prime Minister (1852–5) but resigned shortly after the outbreak of the Crimean War, which he did not support. He made many agricultural improvements to his **Haddo** estate. A keen philo-Hellenist, he was described by Byron in *English Bards and Scotch Reviewers* as 'First in the cat-fed phalanx shall be seen/The travell'd thane, Athenian Aberdeen'.

**Aberdeen and Tremair, John Campbell Gordon, 7th Earl and 1st Marquess of** (1847–1934) Liberal politician, b. Edinburgh. After serving as Lord Lieutenant of Ireland in 1886 and 1906–15, and Governor General of Canada 1893–98, he was created 1st Marquess of Aberdeen in 1915. He married Ishbel Maria **Marjoribanks**, a pioneer in social improvements. Together they published 2 books of reminiscences, *We Twa* (1925) and *More Cracks with We Twa* (1929).

**Aberdeen-Angus cattle** An important hardy black hornless breed of beef cattle that was developed in northeast Scotland in the early 19th century. The breed was first shown in 1829 and the Aberdeen-Angus Society was established in 1879. Aberdeen-Angus beef is an industry standard for quality.

**Aberdeen Canal** Opened in 1807, it connected **Aberdeen** with **Inverurie**, terminating just to the south of the latter, at the confluence of the Rivers **Don** and Urie. It was heavily used for the export of grain and the import of coal and building materials until it was superseded in 1854 by the Great Northern Scottish Railway Company, which used part of the canal bed for its tracks.

**Aberdeen District** see **Aberdeen, Grampian Region**

Aberdeen (pop. 189,707) Scotland's third-largest city, on the east coast, 92km (57mi) northeast of **Dundee**, between the mouths of the Rivers **Dee** and **Don**, now the main administrative and commercial centre of northeast Scotland. Formerly a royal **burgh**, county of city, and county town of **Aberdeenshire**, in 1975 the City of Aberdeen became a district of **Grampian Region**, and also its headquarters. Since 1996 Aberdeen City has been a unitary authority; see **local government**. By the 13th century it was an important trade and fishing centre. It developed into a major commercial port and in the 19th century shipbuilding was an important part of the economy. The decline in these industries in the middle of the 20th century was offset by the discovery of North Sea oil in the late 1960s when the city became the major centre for servicing the offshore oil fields. The busy harbour also has the terminal for the ferry service to Shetland. In the late 19th and early 20th centuries, its long beach made it a popular holiday resort.

The city had an extensive trade in finished granite, which was also used for many of the buildings, giving it the nickname 'Granite City'. Other important industries were cotton, linen, engineering, comb-making and paper-making. The centre of the city is built largely on a series of road viaducts spanning the deep valleys of minor watercourses. Its main street, Union Street (1801–07) is a remarkable piece of urban planning soaring over the old town. The Assembly Rooms were built by Archibald **Simpson** in 1820, in neo-Greek style with a massive Ionic portico; the Music Hall by James Matthews was added to the north in 1858. A granite columnar screen by John Smith (1830) fronts the St Nicholas Kirkyard, which has many interesting tombs. The St Nicholas Kirk dates from the 12th century, and was divided into two churches at the Reformation; both were later rebuilt: West St Nicholas by James **Gibbs** (1851–5) and East St Nicholas by Archibald **Simpson** (1835–7). Towards the northeast end of Union Street is the Town House, whose 17th-century core is largely masked by a flamboyant Flemish-Gothic extension by **Peddie & Kinnear** (1868–74). Nearby stands the Mercat Cross (1686), justly described by Lord **Cockburn** as 'the finest of its kind in Scotland'. On Rosemount Viaduct is a trio of imposing public buildings: the Public Library by George Watt (1891), St Mark's Church by Marshall **Mackenzie** (1892), and His Majesty's Theatre by Frank Matcham (1904–8). Mackenzie also supplied the flamboyant design for Marischal College (see **Aberdeen University**). Aberdeen's many museums and art galleries include Aberdeen Art Gallery and Museum, in Schoolhill, designed by Marshall Mackenzie (1895 and 1905), and Aberdeen Maritime Museum, in Shiprow (1996); the building includes the 16th-century Provost Ross's House, restored in 1954 by the **National Trust for Scotland**. Provost Skene's House, now a museum, also dates from the 16th century; it later belonged to Sir George Skene, provost 1676–85. Other points of interest include the **Bridge of Dee**, built in the 1520s by Bishop Gavin Dunbar. Its seven arches span 122m (400ft). Just beyond it lies the extensive Duthie Park, opened in 1883, with the David Welch Winter Gardens, the UK's largest.

Old Aberdeen, originally a separate burgh, now a northern suburb, contains the medieval Bridge of Balgownie, and the Cathedral Church of St Machar, a twin-towered granite building dating mainly from the 15th century; the nave and tower are still in use as a church and the ruined transepts are in the care of **Historic Scotland**. It also has the main campus of **Aberdeen University**. The main campus of **Robert Gordon's University** is in the city centre. The city's international airport is at **Dyce**, 9km (6mi) to the northwest.

*Union Street, Aberdeen.*

*Coats of arms, Marischal College, Aberdeen University.*

**Aberdeen Press and Journal** see **Press and Journal**

**Aberdeenshire** Former county in northeast Scotland; see maps on pp.394–5 and **local government**. The county town was **Aberdeen**. In 1975 it became part of **Grampian Region** and was divided into the districts of Banff and Buchan, Gordon, Kincardine and Deeside, and the City of Aberdeen.

**Aberdeenshire Council** Local authority in northeast Scotland created in 1996 from the **Grampian Region** districts of Banff and Buchan, Gordon, and Kincardine and Deeside; the pre-1975 county covered a smaller area; see maps on pp.394–5 and **local government**. The administrative centre is **Aberdeen** and other towns include **Fraserburgh**, **Peterhead**, **Stonehaven**, **Inverurie** and **Huntly**. Farming and fishing are important in the east while the mountainous west is sparsely populated. The main rivers are the **Dee** and the **Don**.

**Aberdeen University** Scotland's third university, founded in 1495 by William **Elphinstone**, Bishop of Aberdeen, as King's College, on the authority of a bull of the Borgia Pope Alexander VI. The Chair of Medicine was founded by **James IV** and it remains a medical teaching centre. King's College Chapel, in the main campus in Old Aberdeen, was begun in 1500, and has a fine crown tower, original choir stalls and a unique pre-Reformation altar-top. Marischal College was founded in 1593 as a more radically Protestant alternative to the very conservative King's College by George Keith, 5th Earl Marischal of Scotland (c.1553–1623). Its early 20th-century building in Gothic style is the second-largest granite building in the world (after the Escorial in Madrid). It houses the Marischal Museum (open to the public). The 2 colleges amalgamated in 1860 to form the modern

University of Aberdeen. The Aberdeen campus of the Northern College of Education has recently been integrated into the University's Faculty of Education. The University now has 14,000 students. The Cruickshank Botanic Garden, a 4-hectare (11-acre) public garden, is primarily used for teaching and research in the University. It contains a wide variety of trees and shrubs, alpine, herbaceous, bulbous, and 'peat-loving' plants.

**Aberdour** (pop. 1524) Small commuter and tourist town, former **burgh** on the Firth of **Forth** in **Fife**. The substantial remains of the medieval Aberdour Castle are now in the care of **Historic Scotland**; it has a fine terraced garden and **doocot** and was once the home of the Earls of **Morton**. The 12th-century parish church of St Fillan, with 16th- and 17th-century alterations, became ruinous but was restored in 1926. Offshore is **Inchcolm** Island. Just to the north is The Murrel; see **Deas, Francis William**.

**Aberfeldy** (pop. 1748) Small town on the River **Tay**, 9km (6mi) downstream from **Loch Tay**, close to the geographical centre of Scotland. Its bridge over the Tay was designed by William **Adam** and built in 1733 as an important link in the military roads of General **Wade**. The town is now an important tourist centre. There is a distillery with a visitor centre, a restored early 19th-century water mill on a 400-year-old site, and a recreation centre.

**Aberfoyle** Village, 13km (8mi) southwest of Callander, in the **Queen Elizabeth Forest Park**, a tourist centre for the **Trossachs**. It features as 'the clachan of Aberfoyle', in Sir Walter **Scott**'s *Rob Roy* as the meeting place of **Rob Roy** and Bailie Nicol Jarvie.

**Aberlady** Village on Aberlady Bay in **East Lothian**, 10km (6mi) southwest of **North Berwick**. Until the 19th century it was the port for Haddington but is now mainly a commuter village for Edinburgh. Its Victorian parish church has a 15th-century tower. To the northeast is the 16th-century Luffness House with later additions and to the southwest Gosford House, home of the Earl of Wemyss and March, designed in the late 18th century by Robert **Adam**, and dramatically aggrandised by William Young, 1887–91. Some 2km (1mi) to the east is the Myreton Motor Museum. Aberlady Bay is a Nature Reserve frequented by wintering seabirds and waders.

**Aberlemno** Village in Angus, 8km (5mi) northeast of **Forfar**. In the churchyard is a Pictish cross-slab, about 2m (6ft) high, sculpted on one side with a cross and animals and on the other with a battle scene (thought to be **Nechtansmere**). Nearby, on the B9134 between Forfar and Brechin, are 3 other Pictish carved stones, including another great cross-slab. They are all in the care of **Historic Scotland** and are covered in winter.

**Aberlour,** in full **Charlestown of Aberlour** Small planned town on the River **Spey**, 20km (13mi) south of **Elgin**. It was built in the early 19th century by Charles Grant of Wester Elchies on an ancient ecclesiastical site dedicated to St Drostan. St Drostan's Well still stands in the grounds of the Aberlour Distillery. Shortbread and biscuits from Walker's bakery are known worldwide.

**Abernethy** Village near the junction of the Rivers **Earn** and **Tay**, 5km (3mi) west of Newburgh, the site probably of a Pictish monastery. The Abernethy Round Tower, 22.5m (74ft) high (in the care of **Historic Scotland**), is one of only 2 round towers in the Irish style that survive in Scotland (see also **Brechin**); the upper part dates from the 11th century but the base is earlier, and it may have been the lookout tower for a monastery. Beside it is a fragmentary Pictish symbol stone. Overlooking the village are the extensive remains of a timber-laced Iron Age fort, Castle Law, which was excavated at the beginning of the 20th century. Among the finds was a bronze brooch dating from the second half of the 1st millennium BC. At Carpow, to the northeast, are the remains of a Roman fortress and naval base near the south bank of the Tay. In 1072 **Malcolm III** made a submission to William the Conqueror following William's invasion of Scotland. Malcolm's son Duncan, later **Duncan II**, was taken to England as a hostage to ensure that Malcolm agreed to regard William as his overlord.

**Abernethy Forest** Woodland in **Strathspey**, 10km (7mi) south of **Grantown-on-Spey**.

**Abertay University** Founded as the Dundee Technical Institute in 1888, it became a university in 1992. It has 5600 students, and specialises in computing technology, especially computer games and biotechnology.

**Abington** Village on the River **Clyde**, 18km (11mi) southwest of **Biggar**, at the junction of the roads from Carlisle to Glasgow and Edinburgh, with a service station on the nearby M74.

**Aboyne** (pop. 2067) Small town on the River **Dee**, 16km (10mi) west of **Ballater**, now mainly an opulent commuter town for **Aberdeen** and a tourist centre. It was also known as Charlestown of Aboyne after its 17th-century founder Charles Gordon, Earl of Aboyne. Its medieval castle was enlarged in 1671 and 1801, and reduced to its nucleus in 1975. It contains the Formaston Stone, dating from between 800 and 1000, with the Celtic mirror symbol and an **ogham** inscription. The Aboyne Highland Games, held in September and dating from 1867, are among the most popular. The Loch of Aboyne, 2km (1mi) to the northwest, has waterskiing facilities.

**academy** The term, borrowed from Ancient Greek, to describe a school established in the later 18th century where subjects such as English, modern foreign languages and mathematics were taught rather than the classical curriculum favoured by the grammar schools. The first was probably established in Perth in 1760. Later, and especially in the 20th century, the term became a common name for any school that provided post-primary courses; see also **high school**.

**accordion** The core instrument of Scottish country dance bands. Some Scottish players of this bellows-driven free-reed instrument prefer a button keyboard, others a piano keyboard.

*Aberlady Bay, East Lothian.*

*No. 6 Charlotte Square, Edinburgh, designed by Robert Adam, now the official residence of the First Minister.*

The recordings of virtuosos Jimmy **Shand** and lesser known Will Starr have contributed to the international popularity of Scottish country dance. Currently Sandy Brechin is an accordion player who is much admired.

**accused** In Scots **law**, in criminal cases, equivalent of English defendant.

**Achamore Gardens** see **Gigha**

**Acharacle** (Gaelic **Àth Tharracaill**) Village at the southwest end of **Loch Shiel**, a tourist centre for the surrounding area. From here Charles Edward **Stewart** sailed up Loch Shiel in 1745 to raise his standard at the head of the Loch.

**Achavanich Standing Stones** Unusual arrangement of standing stones near Latheron, Caithness. About 35 of the original 54 stones survive in an elongated U-shape, perhaps aligned on the setting of the moon and dating from about 2000 BC.

**Achiltibuie** (Gaelic **Achd-ille-bhuidhe**) Crofting village spread along the north shore of Loch Broom, 16km (10mi) northwest of **Ullapool** (much further by road). There are stunning views

across the **Summer Isles**, at the mouth of the Loch. The Hydroponicum is a complex of soil-free glasshouses where semitropical plants are grown. Achiltibuie Smokehouse, 8km (5mi) northwest, is open to the public and visitors can see fish being prepared for smoking.

**Achnabreck Cup and Ring Marks** see **Kilmartin**

**Achnashellach** see **Loch Carron**

**Achray** see **Loch Achray**

**Act of Union** see **Union of Parliaments**

**Adair, John** (d.1722) Surveyor and map-maker. In the early 1680s he was commissioned by the Privy Council of Scotland to chart the River **Forth** and to survey 'the shires', and in 1703 published the first part of his *Description of the Sea Coasts and Islands of Scotland*; the second part was never published. He was made a Fellow of the Royal Society in 1688.

**Adam, James** (1731–94) Architect, b. Edinburgh. The third son of William **Adam**, after studying in Rome he was in partnership with his older brother Robert in London. Together they published *The Works in Architecture of Robert and James Adam* (1773, 1779, 1822).

**Adam, John** (1721–92) Architect. Eldest son of William **Adam**, he inherited his father's practice and contracting interests. He designed the Royal Exchange in **Edinburgh**, now the City Chambers (1753–61), and **Dumfries House** (1754–59) with his brother Robert. His own simple style is best represented by Moffat House (1761), now a hotel. He was a partner in the **Carron** Ironworks, but his life was clouded by a series of financial misfortunes.

**Adam, Robert** (1728–92) Architect, b. Kirkcaldy. The second son of William **Adam**, he studied in **Edinburgh** and Rome and became the most famous of them, establishing the neoclassical style in Britain, and is often regarded as the foremost British architect of his day. He spent much of his career in London and was architect to George III (1762–98), resigning to become MP for Kinross-shire. His finest buildings in Scotland include Charlotte Square, Register House and Old College, all in Edinburgh, **Culzean** Castle in Ayrshire and **Mellerstain** House in Berwickshire.

**Adam, William** (1689–1748) Builder and architect, b. Kirkcaldy. His 4 sons all became architects and joined the firm that he established; see James **Adam**, John **Adam** and Robert **Adam**. His buildings include **Arniston House**, **Duff House**, the **House of Dun** and the remodelling of **Hopetoun House**, which was completed by his sons, John and Robert. As a contractor his firm built many military fortifications, notably the masonry of **Fort George** after the 1745 **Jacobite** Rebellion (built after his death).

**Adamnan** or **Adomnan** (c.625–704) Irish monk, probably from Donegal, who joined the **Iona** community in the 670s and became abbot in 679. In the 690s he wrote *Vita Columbae*, a 'life' of his predecessor, **Columba**. He also wrote *De Locis Sanctis*, an account of the Holy Land, dictated to him by a Frankish bishop and one of the earliest accounts of the Holy Land produced in Europe. In the great debate on the timing of Easter and other issues, he was an advocate of the Roman position.

**Adamson, John** see **Adamson, Robert**

**Adamson, Patrick** (1537–92) Minister, b. Perth. After two years as minister of Ceres, Fife, he travelled to France and Geneva. He became chaplain to the Regent **Morton**. As Archbishop of St Andrews from 1575, he was favoured by **James VI**. As a supporter of divine right monarchy and episcopacy, he clashed violently with Andrew **Melville**. He died deposed and poor.

**Adamson, Robert** (1821–48) Pioneer photographer, b. St Andrews. He was taught the techniques of photography by his doctor brother, John (1809–70), influenced by Sir David **Brewster**. He set up a studio in **Edinburgh** in 1843 and went into partnership with David Octavius **Hill** to produce a series of high-quality photographic studies, using the calotype process.

**Aden Country Park** (pronounced 'aaden') Large park on a former Aberdeenshire estate, 16km (10mi) west of **Peterhead** between the villages of Mintlaw and Old Deer. As well as an arboretum and many recreational facilities, it contains the North East of Scotland Agricultural Heritage Centre, giving a picture of the country life of the area.

**Admirable Crichton** see **Crichton, James**

**Adomnan** see **Adamnan**

**advocate** A lawyer, a member of the Faculty of Advocates, who formerly had the sole right to plead in the **Court of Session** and the **High Court of Justiciary**, equivalent to English barrister. Since 1990, solicitor advocates have also been allowed to appear in these courts. In Aberdeen solicitors are known as advocates.

**Advocates' Library** see **National Library of Scotland**

**Aed** or **Aodh** A personal name that eventually became Hugh. It was the name of several early kings: 1. (d.777) son of Eochaid and King of **Dal Riata**. 2. (d.839) King of Dal Riata. 3. (d.878) son of **Kenneth mac Alpin** who ruled for only a year before being killed by **Giric**, son of Donald.

**Aedan** (d. c.608) King of **Dal Riata**. Son of Gabrain, a former King of Dal Riata, **Adamnan** claimed he was inaugurated by **Columba** on **Iona** c.574. He developed Dal Riata's independence from its Irish mother kingdom. In 603 he led a large force against Aethelfrith, the Anglian king of Bernicia, but was defeated at Degsastan.

**Aeneas Silvius** see **Piccolomini**

**Affric** (Gaelic **Afraig**) River that rises in the Five Sisters of **Kintail** and flows northeast through Glen Affric to join the River Glass at Fasnakyle. It has been dammed to supply water to the Affric-Beauly Hydroelectric Scheme. See also **Glen Affric**, **Loch Affric**.

**Afton Water** River that rises in the hills of southern Ayrshire and flows north through Afton Reservoir to join the River **Nith** near New Cumnock. Robert **Burns** describes it in his song, 'Flow Gently, Sweet Afton'.

**Agricola, Gnaeus Julius** (AD 37–93) Roman Governor of Britain (76–84). He invaded Scotland in 79 and built camps in the Forth-Clyde valley and campaigned as far as the northeast. In 84 he defeated the Caledonii at **Mons Graupius**. He was the father-in-law of the Roman historian Tacitus, who wrote his life.

*Newhaven fishwives photographed by David Octavius Hill and Robert Adamson.*

**Aidan, St** (d.651) Monk from Iona. He became Bishop of Northumbria in 635 and established his seat on the tidal island of Lindisfarne where he also established a monastery. With King Oswald he Christianised Northumbria.

**Aikman, William** (1682–1731) Artist, b. Cairney, Forfarshire, son of the Sheriff of Forfarshire. He studied with Sir John de **Medina** in **Edinburgh**. After a period spent in London and Rome he returned to Edinburgh in 1711, succeeding Medina as Scotland's pre-eminent portrait painter. From 1723 until his death he lived in London. Among his works is a portrait of the poet Allan **Ramsay** (1722, **Scottish National Portrait Gallery**), his friend from youth.

**Aikwood** Tall rectangular tower house of the Scotts near **Selkirk**, built 1602 with square turrets at the diagonally opposite angles. Restored for Sir David and Lady **Steel** (1991–2). Also known as Oakwood until recently.

**Ailort, Loch** see **Loch Ailort**

**Ailsa Craig** The smallest of the islands in the Firth of **Clyde**, lying 17km (10mi) west of **Girvan**. Formed of granite, it has a circumference of 3km (2mi) and reaches a height of 340m (1114ft), making it a prominent seamark. It is popularly known as 'Paddy's milestone' as it is roughly halfway between **Glasgow** and Belfast. On its eastern side are the ruins of a castle and a **lighthouse**. On the north coast is the quarry from which granite is obtained to make curling stones. It has large populations of sea birds, notably gannets, guillemots and puffins.

**Airdrie** (pop. 36,998) Former iron-founding, cotton-weaving and coal-mining town in Lanarkshire, 17km (11mi) east of **Glasgow**. It was planned as a market town in the late 17th century and grew as the road system was developed, and more rapidly after the opening of the railways in the 1820s. Its iron-founding firms closed in the 1970s. It is now mainly a dormitory town for nearby **Coatbridge** and Glasgow.

**Airth** Village 7km (5mi) north of **Falkirk**, a former royal **burgh** and now a dormitory town. It was a port in medieval times, but silting of the River **Forth** ended its use as a port. Its medieval castle, later enlarged, is now the Airth Castle Hotel. To the northwest is Dunmore Park, which contains the Pineapple, a remarkable folly in the shape of the fruit, bearing the date 1761, now in the care of the **National Trust for Scotland**. It is leased to the Landmark Trust for letting as a holiday home.

**Airthrey Castle** see **Stirling University**

**Albany, Alexander Stewart, Duke of** (c.1454–85) Second son of **James II**. An opponent of his elder brother, **James III**, he fled into exile in 1480. Allied to Edward IV, he returned with an English invading army in 1482 but was unable to take lasting advantage of James's chronic political difficulties. Further attempts to intevene in Scotland failed, and while in France in 1485 he was accidentally killed while spectating at a tournament.

**Albany, Dukedom of** Title created in 1398, for nearly 300 years bestowed on Scottish princes, usually the king's second son. Later, Charles Edward **Stewart** styled himself Count of Albany and gave his illegitimate daughter, Charlotte, the title of Duchess of Albany. The brothers of the Hanoverian kings George I and George IV were given the title, and the last holder was a grandson of Queen Victoria.

**Albany, John Stewart, Duke of** (1481–1536) b. France, son of Alexander, Duke of **Albany**. Although he considered himself to be French, he was Governor of Scotland following the death of his cousin, **James IV**, from 1515 to 1524. He pursued a pro-French policy in diplomacy but, hampered by long absences in France, was unable to maintain harmony domestically among noble factions.

**Albany, Murdoch Stewart, Duke of** (c.1362–1425) Son of Robert, Duke of Albany. He was taken prisoner at the Battle of **Homildon Hill** in 1402 and was kept in the Tower of London until 1415. He succeeded his father as Governor of Scotland in 1420 during the captivity of **James I** in England but his rule was less capable than that of his father. Although he negotiated James's release, in 1424 he and his family were imprisoned. Albany, 2 of his sons and his father-in-law were executed.

**Albany, Robert Stewart, Duke of** (c.1340–1420) Third son of **Robert II**, he became Guardian of the Kingdom in 1388, replacing his older brother, who reigned as **Robert III** from 1390. Made Duke of Albany in 1398, his influence remained strong during his brother's reign and the challenge to his authority posed by the king's son, David, Duke of Rothesay ended with the latter's imprisonment and probable murder in Albany's custody in 1402. The great survivor of Scottish medieval politics, Albany thereafter wielded power in the realm until his death. From 1406, when **James I** began his captivity in England, Albany was styled Governor of the Kingdom.

**Albion Motors Ltd** Company founded in **Glasgow** in 1899 by T Blackwood Murray and N O Fulton to make motor cars. The firm speedily moved into commercial-vehicle manufacture, and expanded during World War I to produce motor transport for the war effort. By concentrating on quality the firm survived the interwar eclipse of the Scottish motor industry. It lost its independence in 1950, when it was absorbed by Leyland Motors Ltd. The residue of the business still operates in Scotstoun, Glasgow as Albion Automotive, making components for commercial vehicles.

**Alder, Ben** see **Ben Alder**

**Aldie Castle** Tall rectangular tower house of the Mercers of Aldie, 8km (5mi) southwest of **Kinross**. Built 1464 and remodelled with angle turrets in 1585, a lower L-plan wing was added in the 17th century. It was restored 1939–60 by I G **Lindsay**, who pioneered the minimum intervention approach to castle restoration.

**Alexander I** (c.1078–1124) King of Scots (1107–24), b. Dunfermline. Fifth son of **Malcolm III** and **Margaret**, he succeeded his brother **Edgar**, but was forced to tolerate the rule of his younger brother **David**, who succeeded him, in southern Scotland. A vassal of Henry I of England, Alexander looked south for ecclesiastical influences, for instance in staffing his Augustinian foundation at **Scone**. He did defend the bishopric of **St Andrews** against English claims of supremacy. He married Sybilla, an illegitimate daughter of Henry I, but had no legitimate children.

**Alexander II** (1198–1249), King of Scots (1214–49), b. Haddington. He succeeded his father, **William I**, at the age of 16. Exploitation of civil war in England early in his reign did not bring lasting Scottish control of the English North and the **Tweed-Solway** border line was agreed in 1237. At home, the rival MacWilliam claimants to the crown were eliminated and royal control was consolidated and expanded in the peripheries of the realm. Alexander died on **Kerrera** attempting to conquer the **Hebrides**, under Norwegian rule at the time.

**Alexander III** (1241–86) King of Scots (1249–86), b. Roxburgh. He succeeded his father, **Alexander II**, at the age of 8. After a troubled minority his reign was tranquil in domestic politics and featured amicable relations with England. The **Hebrides** were

*King Alexander III of Scotland, seated on King Edward I of England's right hand, at a gathering of the English Parliament, c. 1270.*

acquired from the Norwegian crown after the Battle of **Largs** and the resulting Treaty of **Perth**. He died near **Kinghorn**, presumably after a fall from his horse. A succession crisis followed, his children by his first wife, Margaret, daughter of Henry III, having predeceased him. His daughter, Margaret, had married Eric II of Norway and died giving birth to the child now heir to the throne, **Margaret, Maid of Norway**.

**Alexander, Walter, and Co Ltd** Company founded in the 1920s by Walter Alexander, a pioneer of motor-bus services in central Scotland. His company had a monopoly of services in the area by 1939. The company established a bus body-building works at **Camelon**, initially to serve its own needs, and this became the largest of its kind in Scotland. The bus business became part of the nationalised Scottish Bus Group after World War II, but the body-building works remained independent. It has thrived, and now has an international business as Transbus Alexander.

*Robert Burns's cottage, Alloway, Ayrshire.*

**Alexander, Sir William, Earl of Stirling** (c.1567–1640) Poet and politician, b. Menstrie Castle, Clackmannanshire. Educated in **Stirling**, **Glasgow** and Leiden, he accompanied the 7th Earl of Argyll on the grand tour and became tutor to Prince Henry, son of **James VI**. In 1621 James granted him a charter to establish a colony called Nova Scotia, now a province of Canada. He was Secretary of State for Scotland from 1616 until his death. In 1632 he built the elegant mansion now known as Argyll's Lodging in Stirling. His works include *Aurora* (1604), a collection of sonnets and songs, and the tragedies *Darius* (1603) and *Julius Caesar* (1607).

**Alexander, William** (1826–94) Writer, b. Chapel of Garioch, Aberdeenshire. Originally a farm worker, he became a journalist after losing a leg in an accident. He became editor of the *Aberdeen Free Press* and wrote a novel, *Johnny Gibb of Gushetneuk* (1871), which features the people, places and the Scots language of his native Northeast.

**Alexandria** (pop. 14,150) The largest town in the Vale of Leven, on the River Leven, 5km (3mi) north of **Dumbarton**. Its main businesses were bleaching, calico-printing and turkey-red dyeing. The Argyll Motor Company operated in an ornate building from 1906 until 1914; the office block is now a shopping centre. Nearby is the Antartex Village where sheepskin and leather goods are made and sold.

**Alford** (pronounced 'a-ford') (pop. 1394) Small town on the River Don, 37km (23mi) west of **Aberdeen**, in the centre of the fertile Howe of Alford. It developed when it became a railway terminus in 1859, and though the railway closed in 1966, there is a short narrow-gauge railway and a transport museum. At the Battle of Alford in 1645, **Covenanting** forces were defeated by the Marquis of **Montrose**.

**Allan, David** (1744–96) Artist, b. Alloa. Studied in **Glasgow** at the Foulis Academy and in Rome, under the influence of Gavin **Hamilton**. He worked in London from 1777, moving to **Edinburgh** in 1780. In his painting he moved away from portraits and, in particular, 'conversation pieces' (informal family group portraits), towards scenes of ordinary Scottish life, a genre he pioneered in this country; notable examples are *The Highland Dance* (1780, on loan to the **National Galleries of Scotland**) and his illustrations for Allan **Ramsay**'s *The Gentle Shepherd* (1788).

**Allan, Sir William** (1782–1850) Artist, b. Edinburgh, where he studied as well as in London, before sailing to Russia in 1805. His subsequent experiences, which included shipwreck, patronage from the Polish and Russian aristocracy, and travels across Russia and Turkey, provided with him exotic subject matter for his art following his return to Edinburgh in 1814. He later painted scenes from Scottish history, e.g. *The Murder of David Rizzio* (1833, **National Galleries of Scotland**), and enjoyed an influential career as Master of the Trustees' Academy and Limner to the Queen in Scotland.

**Allardice** or **Allardyce** Stepped L-plan castle on a terrace high above the Bervie Water, to the northwest of **Inverbervie**. First mentioned in 1297, it was the seat of the Allardice family until 1854.

**Alloa** (pop. 18,842) Administrative centre of **Clackmannanshire** Council and former county town of Clackmannanshire; former coal port on the River **Forth**, 9km (6mi) east of **Stirling**. The town was begun in the late 15th century by the Erskine family who, as Earls of **Mar**, have held the lands around it ever since. By the 1770s it was exporting a third of Scotland's coal but the harbour silted up and was filled in in 1951. It was second only to **Edinburgh** as a centre of the brewing industry. Its present industries are glass-making and other light manufacturing.

The recently restored 15th-century Alloa Tower was the home of the Earls of Mar for 4 centuries and is now managed by the **National Trust for Scotland**.

**Alloa Glass Works** Company founded in 1750 by Lady Frances Erskine of Mar. During the 18th century it made both bottles and window glass. It was re-equipped in the 1820s, with 2 new glass cones, one of which survives. The **Distillers' Co** Ltd took over the works in the 20th century, and operated it as United Glass Ltd. This firm rebuilt the works on a massive scale in the early 1970s, to make glass bottles for the Scotch **whisky** industry. It is now owned by the Diageo Corporation.

**Alloway** Village 4km (2mi) south of **Ayr**, now a residential suburb. It was the birthplace of Robert **Burns** in 1759, and the cottage where he was born (built by his father) is now a museum of his life and work. Many sites in the area are mentioned in his poem *Tam o' Shanter*: the Auld Brig o' Doon to the south; Alloway Old Kirk, a ruin in Burns's day, features as the place where the warlocks and witches dance. Burns's father, William Burnes, is buried in the churchyard. The splendid monument by Thomas **Hamilton** beside the Brig o' Doon was built 1820–3. There is a large modern visitor centre.

**Almond, River** River in **West Lothian** that rises west of Whitburn and flows northeast to join the Firth of **Forth** at **Cramond**. In its lower reaches it powered a series of ironworking mills from the 18th to the early 20th century.

**Almond, River** River in Perthshire that rises in the hills behind the southern shore of **Loch Tay**, and flows east through Glen Almond and then southeast through the **Sma Glen** and again east to join the River **Tay** just north of **Perth**.

**Almondell and Calderwood Country Park** see **East Calder**

**Alness** (pop. 5696) Small town on the north shore of the **Cromarty Firth**, 5km (3mi) west of **Invergordon**, on the River Alness, noted for its angling. Its 18th-century church incorporates medieval remains. In recent decades it has expanded with housing for oil-related developments at Invergordon. It has 2 distilleries, **Dalmore** and Teaninich. Nearby is the Black Rock of Novar, a ravine roughly 3km (2mi) long. To the west on Cnoc Fyrish is a spectacular monument in Indian style, commissioned in the 18th century by the local landowner, General Sir Hector Munro of Novar, to relieve unemployment.

**Alsh, Loch** see **Loch Alsh**

**Alva** (pop. 5201) Town 4km (3mi) north of **Alloa**, one of the towns that lie in the Devon valley along the base of the **Ochil** Hills,

often known as the Hillfoots. In the 19th century the river provided power for woollen mills. There is a visitor centre devoted to the local woollen industry. Alva Glen, north of the town, is known as the Silver Glen as silver was mined here in the 18th century. Walks and gardens have been laid out in the lower reaches and there is a fine waterfall at its head.

**Alyth** (pop. 2383) Small market town, 8km (5mi) northeast of **Blairgowrie**. The Alyth Burn provided water for the former **linen** textile industry. In the churchyard is the arcade of a pre-Reformation church dedicated to St Moluag. To the northeast is Barry Hill, with the remains of a vitrified British fort, traditionally said to be the place where King Arthur's wife, Guinevere, was imprisoned by the Picts and Scots.

**Am Bodach** see **Bodach, Am**

**Amisfield Tower** Late 15th- early 16th-century tower house, to the north of **Dumfries**, remodelled with richly turreted upper-works in 1600 by Sir John Charteris, whose family had been settled there since the 12th century. It is the finest of its type and date in the region.

**Amulree** Village on the River Quaich, 14km (9mi) southwest of **Dunkeld**. Drove routes from the west, north and east met here before the descent down the **Sma Glen** to **Crieff**. A military road built by General **Wade** in the 1730s bypassed the village.

**Anchor Line** Shipping concern founded in 1852 in **Glasgow** by Nicol and Robert Handyside and Thomas Henderson. The company went through several changes of ownership, and operated on many routes. It was particularly associated with services from Glasgow and Liverpool to North America and India. The last passenger service from Glasgow to Bombay was in 1966.

**An Comunn Gaidhealach** see **Comunn Gaidhealach, An**

**Ancram, Michael (Michael Andrew Foster Jude Kerr, Earl of Ancram)** (1945– ) Conservative politician and advocate, b. London. He became Conservative MP for **Berwick** and **East Lothian** (1974), then **Edinburgh** South (1979–87) but anti-Conservative feeling in Scotland led him to stand for Devizes (1992– ). He was Under Secretary then Minister for Northern Ireland (1993–97) and then shadow Foreign Secretary.

**Ancrum Moor, Battle of** Battle fought in 1545 near the village of Ancrum, 5km (3mi) northwest of **Jedburgh**, this was one of the last Scottish victories in Border warfare. The Earl of Angus's victory helped to inspire resistance to Henry VIII's **Rough Wooing** of Scotland.

*Ian Anderson, founder of the rock group Jethro Tull.*

**Anderson, Arthur** (1792–1868) Shipping magnate and philanthropist, b. Shetland. A former fish curer, he was pressganged and served in the Royal Navy before joining a London firm of shipping agents as a clerk. He rose to be a partner and expanded the firm into commissioning its own ships and in 1840 setting up a shipping line, the Peninsular & Oriental Steam Navigation Co. (P&O), of which he became chairman. He became MP for **Orkney** and **Shetland** in 1847 and inaugurated various institutions to benefit Shetland, including in 1862 the Anderson Education Institute, now Anderson High School, in **Lerwick**.

**Anderson, Ian** (1947– ) Rock musician, b. Dunfermline. In 1967 he formed the progressive rock group Jethro Tull, which had its greatest commercial successes in the 1970s, e.g. *Thick as a Brick* (1972), and still performs. Anderson has also recorded solo albums, e.g. *Walk Into Light* (1983).

**Anderson, John** (1726–96) Scientist, b. Roseneath. A minister's son, he studied in **Stirling** and at **Glasgow University**, where in 1756 he became Professor of oriental languages and in 1760 Professor of natural philosophy. He was interested in practical applications of science and allowed working men to attend his lectures in their ordinary clothes. James **Watt** used his model of a Newcomen engine for his experiments on the separate condenser. His works include *Institutes of Physics* (1786), which went through 5 editions in 10 years. He bequeathed the bulk of his estate to establish Anderson's College, which became the core of the later **Strathclyde University**.

**Anderson, Joseph** (1832–1916) Archaeologist, b. Arbroath. As Keeper of the **National Museum of Antiquities of Scotland** in **Edinburgh**, he was highly influential in the early development of archaeology in Scotland. With J R Allen, he wrote *The Early Christian Monuments of Scotland*, which is still an essential resource today.

**Anderson, Sir Robert Rowand** (1834–1921) Architect, b. Edinburgh. He studied law, but became a pupil of John Lessels and worked for Sir George Gilbert Scott before setting up a practice in **Edinburgh**. His works include the Gothic **Scottish National Portrait Gallery** and the early Italian Renaissance McEwan Hall and Medical School in **Edinburgh University**, as well as many churches. He was a founder of the **Royal Incorporation of Architects in Scotland** and initiated the systematic recording of Scottish buildings.

**Anderson, Tom** (1910–91) Fiddler, b. Eshaness, Mainland Shetland. He preserved and disseminated the Shetland style of fiddle-playing through teaching among many others Aly **Bain**, organising fiddle groups, collecting hundreds of tunes, and composing over 500 tunes.

**Anderson, Willa** see **Muir, Willa**

**Anderson's University** see **Strathclyde University**

**Andrew, St** The apostle of Christ who was martyred at Patras in Greece. There is a legend that some relic relating to him was brought to Fife by St **Rule** in the 8th century and there was a Pictish cult of St Andrew there. He was later adopted as the patron saint of Scotland; his cross, a **saltire**, first appeared on the seal of the Guardians in 1286. See also **St Andrews, St Andrew's Day, Athelstaneford**.

**Aneirin** or **Aneurin** (fl. later 6th century) Bard of post-Roman Britain, who composed the set of heroic elegies known as *The Gododdin*, the earliest known poetic work emanating from what is now Scotland. He speaks of himself as being one of those personally involved in the disastrous expedition celebrated in the elegy, in which the Celtic army was defeated by the Anglian forces of Bernicia. See also **Gododdin**.

**Angus** Local authority on the east coast of Scotland created in 1996 as Angus Council, from the Angus District of **Tayside Region**, with somewhat altered boundaries. The pre-1975 county (formerly Forfarshire) covered a slightly larger area; see maps on pp.394–5 and **local government**. The administrative centre **is Forfar** and other towns include **Arbroath**, **Montrose**, **Kirriemuir**, **Brechin** and Monifieth. The eastern coastal plain is mainly agricultural. To the west are the **Sidlaw Hills**. The area has many ancient relics.

**Angus (King of Picts)** see **Unuist**

**Angus, Archibald Douglas, 5th Earl of** (c.1449–1514)
Magnate who was a central player in the execution of **James III**'s 'favourites' at **Lauder** in 1482 and the subsequent imprisonment of the king. His nickname 'Bell the Cat' derives from later accounts of this episode. Although he served as **James IV**'s Chancellor, he remained a maverick figure and was in captivity for much of the reign.

**Angus, Archibald Douglas, 6th Earl of** (c.1489–1557)
Magnate who succeeded his grandfather, the 5th Earl. He married **James IV**'s widow **Margaret Tudor** and was active in the turbulent politics of **James V**'s minority, representing pro-English interests and vying for power with the Earl of **Arran**. When James took personal charge of government in 1528 Angus fled to England where he stayed until after James's death. Henry VIII's **Rough Wooing** alienated Angus on his return in 1543, and he was in command at the Scottish victory at **Ancrum Moor** and a leader at the defeat at **Pinkie**.

**Angus, Archibald Douglas, 8th Earl of** (1555–88)
Grandson of the 6th Earl, he succeeded his father, David, at the age of 2. He was made a ward of his uncle, James Douglas, 4th Earl of **Morton**, Chancellor for **Mary, Queen of Scots**. He took part in Scottish politics, supporting his uncle, until the latter's execution in 1581, when he fled to England. He returned in 1585 following the **Ruthven Raid** and as a strong Presbyterian became involved with the struggles of the Reformation.

**Angus, Marion** (1866–1946) Poet, b. Aberdeen. She published several collections of poems, mainly in Scots and sometimes influenced by the ballad tradition.

**Annan** (pop. 8930). Town near the mouth of the River **Annan**, a former royal **burgh**, 24km (15mi) east of **Dumfries**, which developed round a castle of the Bruce family that figured in the **Wars of Independence** but of which nothing now remains. An encounter at Annan in December 1332 forced Edward **Balliol** to temporarily flee south of the border. Annan was for many years a significant port. It also had an early cotton-spinning industry. Between Annan and Kirkpatrick Fleming is Annan Activities, a leisure park with facilities for many sports. **Chapelcross** nuclear power station is nearby.

**Annan, James Craig** (1864–1946) Photographer, b. Hamilton. Son of the photographer Thomas **Annan**, he studied chemistry and natural philosophy, before joining the family firm, T & R Annan. Studied photogravure in Vienna and was one of the first to use the Kodak snapshot camera. An important figure in the international Pictorial movement in photography, he was the first President of the International Society of Photographers.

**Annan, River** Rises on the **Devil's Beeftub** and flows south past **Moffat**, Lochmaben and then southeast past **Annan** to enter the Solway Firth just south of Annan.

**Annan, Thomas** (1829–87) Photographer, b. Fife. Began his career as a lithographer and became interested in photography in 1855, co-founding a photographic studio in **Glasgow**. Through his association with David Octavius **Hill**, he established a reputation as a photographer of works of art, but is best known for his photographs of the slums in the centre of Glasgow before their demolition.

*The Old Vennel, off the High Street, Glasgow, photographed by Thomas Annan.*

**A**

**Annandale and Eskdale** see **Dumfries and Galloway Region**

**Anne of Denmark** (1574–1619) Queen consort of **James VI**, b. Jutland. Second daughter of Frederick II of Denmark, she was married by proxy to James VI in 1589. James went to meet her in Norway and they arrived in Scotland in 1590. She bore him 7 children, the eldest of whom, Henry, died at the age of 18, and Charles succeeded his father as **Charles I**. Baptised a Lutheran, she converted to Roman Catholicism in the early 1600s.

**Anstruther** (pop. 3154) Small town and resort in the **East Neuk of Fife**, 14km (9mi) south-southeast of **St Andrews**. It became a **burgh** for **Pittenweem** Priory and was made a royal burgh in 1587, formed from the amalgamation of two older settlements separated by the Dreel Burn, Anstruther Easter and Anstruther Wester. St Adrian's at Anstruther Easter is a fine externally unaltered church of 1634, and Anstruther Wester Church (now a church hall) has a 16th-century steeple. Formerly a major port for herring fishing, Anstruther has a fine harbour by Alan Stevenson 1866–77, extended in the early 20th century. Boat trips run from here to the Isle of **May** nature reserve. It now has the **Scottish Fisheries Museum**, near the harbour, founded in 1969, giving a picture of Scotland's **fishing** industry from the earliest times.

**An Teallach** see **Teallach, An**

**Anti-burghers** see **Presbyterian Churches**, p.307

**Antiquaries, Society of** see **Society of Antiquaries**

**Antonine Wall** The most important Roman fortification remaining in Scotland. It was built in the reign of Emperor Antoninus Pius in the 2nd century AD, as part of a frontier system against the northern tribes, and abandoned in the 160s, when Hadrian's Wall in the north of England became the effective frontier once again. It extended 60km (37mi) from the River **Clyde** at Old Kilpatrick to the River **Forth** at Carriden. The wall was mainly made of sods on a stone foundation but in the east parts were made of clay. It was garrisoned by soldiers based in forts made of turf and timber positioned approximately every 3km (2mi). Visible remains include lengths of stone foundation and a bathhouse at **Bearsden**, Bar Hill Fort near **Kilsyth**, a fort and stretch of wall at Rough Castle near Bonnybridge, wall and ditch near Watling Lodge, **Falkirk**.

**Aodh** see **Aed**

**Aonach Beag** Mountain in **Lochaber**, a **Munro** (1236m/4054ft) with splendid views across to **Ben Nevis**, a short distance to the west.

**Aonach Mòr** Mountain in **Lochaber**, a **Munro** of 1221m (4006ft), 2km (1mi) north of **Aonach Beag**. On its western slope is Scotland's highest skiing centre, Nevis Range, with a gondola operating year-round to carry skiers and climbers halfway up the mountain.

**Appin** Mountainous district in Argyll, bounded by **Loch Linnhe**, Glen Creran and **Loch Leven**. The Strath of Appin forms a natural pass between **Loch Creran** and Loch Laich, an inlet of Loch Linnhe. The Gaelic form of the name, Apuinn, means 'abbey land', referring to an early monastery on **Lismore**. Appin was formerly Stewart country. The main settlement is Port Appin, where the 18th-century Airds House is now a hotel. See also **Appin murder, Castle Stalker**.

**Appin murder** The murder at Lettermore, between **Ballachulish** and Kentallen, on 14 May 1752, of Colin Campbell of Glenure ('the Red Fox'), factor for the Duke of **Argyll**, on his way to evict tenants from lands held by **Jacobite** chiefs. James Stewart of the Glens was tried, found guilty and hanged for the crime, his body left suspended from a tree in the area as a warning to others. Local tradition attributed the murder to a Stewart of Ballachulish. Robert Louis **Stevenson** used the event to good effect in his novel *Kidnapped*.

**Applecross** (Gaelic **A' Chomraich** meaning 'the sanctuary') Remote village on the **Inner Sound** on the west side of the peninsula between Loch **Kishorn** and **Loch Torridon**. In AD 673 St **Maelrubha** founded a monastery here, the only traces of which are a cross-slab by the churchyard gate and some fragments in the church. The Applecross peninsula, which belonged to the Mackenzies, had no road until the late 18th century, when one was built from Kishorn over the **Bealach na Ba** ('Pass of the Cattle'); its summit at 625m (2053ft) makes it one of the highest roads in Scotland, involving steep zigzag turns. Another road around the north of the peninsula to **Shieldaig** was completed in 1976.

**Arbroath** (pop. 23,474) Industrial town and port 25km (15mi) northeast of **Dundee**. Arbroath Abbey was founded in 1178 by **William I**, the Lion; its substantial remains are now in the care of **Historic Scotland**. The famous 'Declaration of Arbroath' is a letter of 1320 to Pope John XXII espousing the cause of Scottish independence. Purportedly from the barons of Scotland, but in reality a product of **Robert I**'s chancery, the declaration remains the subject of much scholarly dispute. On 11 April 1951, the Stone of Scone, or **Stone of Destiny**, was found here

A

after its theft from Westminster Abbey. The abbey thrived until 1606, after the **Reformation**, but thereafter succumbed to decay. Arbroath was made a royal **burgh** in 1599, its fortunes founded mainly on farming, fishing and related industries, with linen and engineering developing later. Its linen industry was second only to **Dundee**, specialising in sailcloth. Other industries included textile machinery and fan and machine-tool making. Until recently it had 2 yards building and repairing wooden fishing boats. Hospitalfield House was built between 1850 and 1890 to his own design in Scottish **baronial** style by Patrick Allan Fraser on the remnants of an earlier house, which was the model for 'Monksbarns' in Sir Walter **Scott**'s *The Antiquary*. He aimed to encourage the arts and included an art gallery, and the house is now an arts centre in the care of Angus Council. Arbroath Museum, based in the Signal Tower, the shore station for the **Bell Rock** lighthouse, features displays devoted to the lighthouse as well as the fishing community and life in Arbroath generally.

**Arbroath smokie** A haddock beheaded and gutted, but unsplit, lightly salted and hot-smoked; originally produced at **Auchmithie**, but now a speciality of **Arbroath**.

**Arbuthnot, John** (1667–1735) Physician and satirist, b. Arbuthnott, Kincardineshire. The son of an Episcopalian clergyman, he took his medical degree at **St Andrews** in 1696 and settled in London. He was elected a Fellow of the Royal Society in 1704 and was appointed physician extraordinary to Queen Anne in 1705. He became a friend of Jonathan Swift and other wits, including Alexander Pope. He wrote medical as well as satirical works, including an essay on diet (1732) and his most famous work, *The History of John Bull* (1712), which established that character as the typical Englishman.

**Arbuthnott** Northeast village 4km (2mi) northwest of **Inverbervie**. St Ternan's Church, founded in 1297, has a 2-storeyed lady chapel, or Arbuthnott Aisle, built 1500, restored 1896. James Leslie Mitchell (Lewis Grassic **Gibbon**) is buried in the kirkyard, and there is now a Lewis Grassic Gibbon Centre in the village. To the west above the Bervie Water and its tributary is Arbuthnott House, remodelled 1682–95, with a symmetrical pedimented west front formed 1755–57.

**Archer, William** (1856–1924) Drama critic, translator and playwright, b. Perth. Trained as a lawyer in **Edinburgh**, he never practised. Instead, in 1875 while still a student he began writing editorials for the *Edinburgh Evening News*. Following a trip

*Arbroath smokies.*

around the world he settled in London in 1878, working as a drama critic. He became a friend of George Bernard Shaw and championed the work of Ibsen, some of whose plays he also translated. He wrote several plays, the most successful of which was *The Green Goddess* (1923).

**Archers, Royal Company of** see **Royal Company of Archers**

**Ard, Loch** see **Loch Ard**

**Ardblair Castle** see **Blairgowrie**

**Ardeer Works** Company founded in 1871 by the British Dynamite Co Ltd to exploit Alfred Nobel's patents for explosives manufacture. It developed in 1877 into Nobel's Explosives Co Ltd, which became one of the constituents of **Imperial Chemical Industries Ltd** when it was founded in 1925. After World War II silicones and nylon were made here. The works still operates, but on a much-reduced scale.

**Ardersier** Village, also called Campbelltown, on the inner **Moray Firth** 3km (2mi) southeast of **Fort George**. It was formerly the southern terminal of a ferry to Chanonry Point on the

**A**

**Black Isle**, which was an important link to the north. In 1623 the Campbells of **Cawdor** obtained a charter to build a **burgh** of barony but their plan was never fully realised, and the village later became dependent on the garrison at Fort George. From the 1970s to the 1990s employment was provided by a platform-construction yard for the North Sea oil industry, situated to the east of the village.

**Ardestie and Carlungie Earth Houses** Good examples of Iron Age store-houses, to the north of **Dundee**. The earth house (or souterrain) was subterranean, lined with stones and roofed at ground level. Traces of the adjacent dwelling houses are visible at Ardestie. In the care of **Historic Scotland**.

**Ardfearn Nursery** Specialist nursery for alpines and rare plants, set up at Bunchrew to the west of **Inverness** by horticultural adviser and broadcaster Jim Sutherland.

**Ardfern** see **Loch Craignish**

**Ardgour** (Gaelic **Àird-ghobhar**) Mountainous district between **Loch Linnhe** and **Loch Shiel**. There is convenient access by the **Corran** ferry across the narrows of **Loch Linnhe**; otherwise the road takes a lengthy route by **Fort William** and round **Loch Eil**. To the west of Corran is the Georgian Ardgour House, seat of the MacLeans of Ardgour who owned the district from the 15th century.

**Ardkinglas** Estate at the head of **Loch Fyne**, with a fine arboretum, with one of the largest silver firs in the country. Ardkinglas House, Sir Robert **Lorimer**'s finest house, was built in 1906 for Sir Andrew Noble of the Tyneside armaments firm Sir W G Armstrong, Whitworth and Co.

**Ardlamont Point** Headland between the **Kyles of Bute** and **Loch Fyne**. To the northeast is Ardlamont House, built for the Lamont family in 1920, replacing an earlier building. Ardlamont was the scene in 1892 of the 'Ardlamont Mystery', the still-unsolved murder of 17-year-old Cecil Hambrough. His tutor, Alfred John Monson, was tried but the case was found not proven.

**Ardnamurchan** (Gaelic **Àird nam murchan**) Long peninsula stretching from **Loch Moidart** and **Loch Sunart** to the east to Ardnamurchan Point, the most westerly point of the British mainland. Ardnamurchan **Lighthouse**, built in 1849 by Alan Stevenson with granite from Erraid, is 36m (144ft) high and since automation has become a visitor centre.

**Ardoch Roman Camp** Well-preserved remains of a very large Roman fort, to the north of the village of **Braco** (10km/6mi northeast of **Dunblane**). Excavations in 1896–7 produced evidence of a sequence of earthworks, including a permanent camp for a legionary garrison. The camp was originally established by Agricola in the 1st century and was in use again as late as the time of Septimius Severus in the early 3rd century.

**Ardrishaig** (pop. 1315) Small town and port in **Argyll** on the western shore of Loch Gilp, 3km (2mi) south of **Lochgilphead**. At the southern end of the **Crinan Canal**, it developed quickly after the building of this waterway. Its harbour was used by herring-fishing boats and is now used for shipping timber from Argyll forests.

**Ardrossan** (pop. 10,750) Town and port on the Firth of **Clyde**, 20km (12mi) west of **Kilmarnock**. It was established as a planned town in 1805 by the Earl of Eglinton and developed rapidly later in the century with the use of seagoing steamboats and ferry connections to **Arran**. It was also an important port for the export of coal and iron, and had an oil refinery for most of the 20th century. It is still the ferry port for Arran. On a hill overlooking the sandy beaches of Ardrossan Bay stand the ruins of Ardrossan Castle, which probably dates from the 13th century and figured in the campaigns of William **Wallace**. It was destroyed by Cromwell.

**Ardtornish** (Gaelic **Àrd-tòrranais**) Locality on the peninsula of **Morvern**, on the mainland side of the Sound of **Mull**. At Ardtornish Point are the ruins of Ardtornish Castle, a 14th-century seat of the **Lords of the Isles**. The fanciful Treaty of Westminster-Ardtornish (1462) stipulated that John, Lord of the Isles and the 9th Earl of Douglas would cooperate with English efforts to conquer southern Scotland and partition the northern part of the realm between them. Ardtornish Estate has established gardens around the Grade A-listed Ardtornish House, which contains self-catering properties.

**Arduaine Garden** Eight-hectare (20-acre) garden overlooking Loch Melfort, 32km (20mi) south of **Oban**. Now in the care of the **National Trust for Scotland**, it is noted for its woodlands, rhododendrons, magnolias, azaleas and herbaceous perennials that flower throughout the year.

**Ardunie Roman Signal Station** Part of an early Roman frontier-system some 4km (2.5mi) southwest of **Perth**. Ardunie was one of a series of watch-towers along the Gask Ridge, set at intervals of roughly 1km on the line of a former Roman road. Visible is the ditch that surrounded a 2-storey wooden tower. In the care of **Historic Scotland**.

**Ardverikie** Large elaborate Victorian shooting lodge on the south shore of **Loch Laggan**, visited by Queen Victoria and Prince Albert. It has been used by the BBC for the filming of the TV series *Monarch of the Glen*.

**Ardvreck** (Gaelic **Àird-bhreac**) Ruined 16th-century castle, seat of the MacLeods of Assynt, on a rocky promontory on the north side of **Loch Assynt**, 18km (11mi) east of Lochinver. It was here that **Montrose** was captured in 1650 after his defeat at **Carbisdale**.

**Argathelians** Term used to describe the supporters of the interest of the Dukes of **Argyll** in the electoral politics of 18th-century Scotland. Before the rise of the **Dundas** predominance they and their **Squadrone** rivals were the main political groups in Hanoverian Scotland.

**Argyll** or **Argyle** (Gaelic **Earra Ghàidheal** 'coastland of the Gaels') Former county on the west coast; see map on p.395. It was the second-largest county by area (after **Inverness-shire**), stretching from the **Ardnamurchan** peninsula in the north to the Mull of **Kintyre** in the south and including more than 90 islands. In 1975 the southern part of the county became the **Argyll and Bute** District of **Strathclyde Region**, while **Arran** became part of Cunninghame District, and the northern part became the **Lochaber** district of **Highland Region**; see maps on pp.394–5 and **local government**. Historically the name represented an even greater area, reaching as far north as **Loch Broom**, consisting of North Argyll, Mid-Argyll, centred on **Loch Awe**, and South Argyll.

**Argyll, Archibald Campbell, 8th Earl and Marquis of** (1598–1661). He succeeded his father, the 7th Earl, in 1638. Provoked by **Charles I**'s plans to attack his lands, he became a leader of the **Covenanters'** Revolution. Despite being created a marquis by Charles I in a gesture of appeasement in 1640, he supported the decision to ally with the English opponents of Charles to prevent the king winning the English civil war. **Montrose** undermined Argyll's grip on Scotland by catastrophically defeating him in battle, and he was marginalised by his refusal to accept the **Engagement** alliance with Charles I. His recovery of power after their defeat spared Scotland an immediate Cromwellian invasion. After the execution of Charles I, he came to terms with the royal cause and took part in the coro-

*Ardvreck Castle, Assynt.*

nation of **Charles II** at **Scone** in 1651. However, he sat as an MP in the Commonwealth parliament in 1658, and this ambivalence led to his execution for treason after the restoration of Charles II in England. His marquisate died with him.

**Argyll, Archibald Campbell, 9th Earl of** (1629–85) Son of the Marquis of Argyll, unlike his father he was an enthusiastic royalist in the 1650s but after his father's execution he was imprisoned for 2 years. On his release he managed to have his title recognised, apart from the marquisate, and his estates reinstated. In 1664 he became a member of the Scottish privy council and in 1667 had oversight of the troubled **Highlands**. His power base in **Argyll** in the west antagonised the king and other nobles, especially the Duke of York, later **James VII** and **II**. Unhappy with the ambiguous and self-contradictory Test Act, he was tried in 1681 for taking it only in so far as it was consistent with itself, and imprisoned. With the help of his stepdaughter, Sophia Lindsay, he escaped and became involved in the Duke of Monmouth's machinations after the death of **Charles II**. In 1685 he attempted an invasion of Scotland on Monmouth's behalf but was captured and executed without a second trial.

**Argyll, Archibald Campbell, 3rd Duke of** (1682–1761) b. Petersham, Surrey. Son of the 1st Duke, best known as the Earl of Islay, he succeeded his brother, the 2nd Duke, just before the 1745 **Jacobite Rising**. After a brief army career he entered politics and in 1706 became one of the commissioners for the Union of 1707. Created Earl of Islay, he was chosen as one of the 16 representative peers of Scotland. He was wounded at **Sheriffmuir**. From the

**A**

premiership of Sir Robert Walpole to that of Henry Pelham, he became the first great Manager of 18th-century Scotland, using a combination of Campbell power and government patronage to dominate Scottish politics. He rebuilt the castle and town of **Inveraray** and died without legal issue, the title going to a cousin.

**Argyll, George Douglas Campbell, 8th Duke of** (1823–1900) Politician, b. Ardencaple Castle, Dunbartonshire. Second son of the 7th Duke, he succeeded his father in 1847 and immediately took his seat in the House of Lords. He became a member of the Cabinet in Lord **Aberdeen**'s coalition government in 1853 and thereafter served as a minister until 1874, being out of office for only brief periods when the Conservatives were in power. As Secretary of State for India (1868–74) he initiated decentralisation of decision-making. His great interest in science and Scottish education led to the Education Act of 1872, and he wrote several books on scientific subjects and on religion.

**Argyll, John Campbell, 2nd Duke of** (1678–1743) Soldier and politician. Eldest son of the 1st Duke, whom he succeeded in 1703, he was created an English peer with the titles Baron Chatham and Earl of Greenwich for his support of the Union of 1707. He took part in the War of Spanish Succession (1706–1709) and was Commander in Chief of British forces in Spain (1711). After the peace of Utrecht in 1712 he was made Commander in Chief of the forces of Scotland and Governor of **Edinburgh Castle** and in 1715 led Government forces against the **Jacobite** uprising at **Sheriffmuir**. As leader of the **Argathelians** he later was an influential figure in Scottish politics. He became Duke of Greenwich in 1719.

**Argyll and Bute Council** Local authority on the west coast created in 1996 by the amalgamation of the former Argyll and Bute district of **Strathclyde Region**, taking in part of **Dumbarton District** and including the islands of **Bute**, **Mull**, **Islay**, **Jura**, **Colonsay**, **Tiree** and **Coll**; see maps on pp.394–5 and **local government**. The administrative centre is **Lochgilphead** and other towns include **Helensburgh**, **Dunoon**, **Oban**, **Campbeltown** and **Rothesay**. Industries include agriculture, fishing, tourism and whisky distilling.

**Argyll and Sutherland Highlanders** A regiment of the British army formed in 1881 by the amalgamation of the 91st Argyllshire Highlanders and the 93rd Sutherland Highlanders. The Argyllshire Highlanders was originally raised in 1794 by Duncan Campbell of Lochnell. In 1872 it was renamed 91st Princess Louise's Argyllshire Highlanders. The 93rd Highland

Regiment was raised in 1799 by General Wemyss, renamed Sutherland Highlanders in 1861. They united in 1881 as Princess Louise's Sutherland and Argyll Highlanders and later Argyll and Sutherland Highlanders (Princess Louise's). It has taken part in many actions, notably in France, Italy and Malaya in World War II and later in Palestine, Korea and Northern Ireland. A threat to disband it in 1971 was withdrawn following a massive petition to retain it. It recruits mainly from Argyll and west central Scotland and its regimental museum is in **Stirling** Castle.

**Argyll Forest Park** A forested and mountainous area in Argyll in the northern part of the Cowal Peninsula, between **Loch Long** and **Loch Fyne**.

**Argyll Highlanders** The 74th Highlanders, an infantry regiment raised in 1778 to serve in America. It was disbanded in 1783.

**Argyll's Bowling Green** Informal name for the mountainous area between **Loch Goil** and **Loch Long**; now part of the **Argyll Forest Park**.

**Argyllshire Gathering** Founded 1871 and held annually in **Oban**, it is one of the oldest of **Highland Games**. It is one of the two major solo piping competitions, awarding the Highland Society of London Gold Medal for **Piobaireachd**, and former winners of the Medal compete for the Senior Piobaireachd trophy.

**Argyll Wildlife Park** A wildlife park in Argyll, 3km (2mi) southwest of **Inveraray**, that contains many examples of indigenous animals and birds and some introduced species living in natural surroundings. The animals that can be seen include foxes, wild cats, badgers, buzzards and owls.

**Arisaig** (Gaelic **Àrasaig**) Village on the west coast, 11km (7mi) south of **Mallaig**, that also gives its name to the surrounding area. The village lies at the head of Loch nan Ceall, on the 'Road to the Isles', the road between **Fort William** and Mallaig and on the railway between the two. From the village there are fine views of the **Small Isles** and the Inner **Hebrides**. The area is particularly associated with Prince Charles Edward **Stewart** as he arrived on the Scottish mainland at **Loch nan Uamh** in 1745 and escaped from there in 1746. During World War II, Arisaig House, until recently a hotel, housed the Special Operations Executive, which trained agents to be dropped in occupied Europe. A summer ferry runs from Arisaig to **Eigg**, **Muck** and **Canna**.

**Arkaig, Loch** see **Loch Arkaig**

**Arkinholm, Battle of** The site on the River **Esk** near **Langholm** of a battle on 1 May 1455 when the 3 brothers of the 9th Earl of **Douglas** were defeated by an army of other leading

Border families. Only the youngest escaped to join his brother in England. It was part of the downfall of the **Black Douglases**.

**Arkle** (Gaelic **Arcuil**) Mountain ridge in Sutherland, 8km (5mi) southeast of Rhiconich, that reaches a height of 787m (2581ft).

**Armadale** (pop. 8958) Town in West Lothian, 11km (7mi) southwest of **Linlithgow**. It grew rapidly in the late 19th century when 'Paraffin' **Young** pioneered the use of mineral oils extracted in the area. It developed important brick-making and steel-founding industries. It now has light industry and is a dormitory town for **Falkirk** and **Edinburgh**.

**Armadale** Settlement on the **Skye** side of the Sound of **Sleat**, with a ferry to **Mallaig** (now summer only). The ruins of the 19th-century Armadale Castle, seat of the Macdonalds of Sleat, now contain the Clan Donald Centre. In the surrounding woodland there is a 19th-century collection of exotic trees.

**Armour, Jean** (1767–1834) A stonemason's daughter, b. Mauchline, Ayrshire, whom Robert **Burns** met and fell in love with in 1784. Jean's father was against their marriage and she had 2 sets of twins (three of whom died) by Burns before their marriage, which was regularised by the Kirk Session in Mauchline in August 1788. She had 4 more children after their marriage, one of whom was born after Burns's death. She also took in Burns's daughter by the Dumfries barmaid, Anna Park.

**Armstrong, Johnnie** Legendary freebooter of the **Borders**, he became the hero of many Border ballads, one of which was published by Allan **Ramsay** in his *Evergreen*. The real 'reiver' was either John Armstrong of Gilnockie, who was hanged in 1530, or the John Armstrong known as 'Black Jock', who was executed in 1531. A marker at Carlanrig, 15km (9mi) south of **Hawick**, purports to mark the mass grave of the Laird of Gilnockie and his men, hanged without trial by King **James V** in 1530.

**Armstrong, William** see **Kinmont Willie**

**Arnisdale** Village on the north shore of **Loch Hourn**. The River Arnisdale runs down Glen Arnisdale to enter Loch Hourn just south of the village.

**Arniston House** Seat at Gorebridge, Midlothian, of the once powerful Dundas of Arniston family, an outstanding example of the work of William **Adam** (1726), incorporating parts of an older building as well as later additions. It contains an important collection of furniture and Scottish portraiture and is open to the public.

**Arnol** Village near the northwest coast of **Lewis**, 5km (3mi) west of Barvas. To the north is **Historic Scotland**'s **Black House** complex.

*Jean Armour, wife of Robert Burns.*

**Aros Experience** see **Portree**

**Arran** (Gaelic **Arainn**) (pop. 5058) Island in the Firth of **Clyde**, halfway between **Ayrshire** and the Mull of **Kintyre**, mountainous in the north and Lowland in character in the south. It is 32km (20mi) long and 15km (9mi) broad and its highest point is Goat Fell (874m/2866ft) from which there are views to mainland Scotland and the **Hebrides**, England, Ireland, and the Isle of Man. The Arran hills provide excellent walking and rock climbing. The chief town is **Brodick**, on the east coast, and other centres are Lamlash and Whiting Bay. A road runs all round the island and a 'string' road across the island connects Brodick with Blackwaterfoot on the west coast. The main industry is tourism, as Arran is a popular holiday resort with ferry connections to **Ayrshire** and **Kintyre**, but there is also fishing, farming and cheese-making. Arran Aromatics, 1.5km (1mi) north of Brodick, manufactures body-care products and has a visitor centre, as has nearby Arran Brewery, which produces real ales. There is now a malt-whisky distillery at **Lochranza**. Prehistoric remains include stone circles on Machrie Moor and a small fort at Torr a' Chaisteil (both in the care of **Historic**

Scotland). **Robert I** was on Arran prior to launching his campaign on the mainland in early 1307 which was to witness his first military successes.

**Arran, James Hamilton, 2nd Earl of** (c.1516–75) Magnate, who succeeded his father in 1529 and in 1542, after **James V**'s death, was chosen to be Governor of Scotland for the infant **Mary, Queen of Scots**. At first he supported pro-English policies (see **Rough Wooing**) but soon turned towards France and was made Duke of Chatelherault in 1550. By the time **Mary of Guise** took over the regency in 1554 there was a substantial French military presence in Scotland. During Queen Mary's personal rule Arran was sidelined by her marriage to **Darnley** in 1565, revolted and was exiled. The murder of Darnley, Mary's marriage to **Bothwell**, and the appointment of **Moray** as regent altered his attitude and he protested his loyalty to Mary. On his return to Scotland he was arrested and imprisoned until after Moray's assassination in 1570. During the civil war that followed he continued to support the Queen's Party until 1573 when he acknowledged **James VI**'s authority.

**Arran, James Hamilton, 3rd Earl of** (1537/8–1609) Eldest son of the 2nd Earl, his father gave him as hostage to Cardinal **Beaton** in 1543 and in 1546 he was detained in the Castle of **St Andrews** as a hostage by the murderers of the cardinal. He was released on the surrender of the castle to the French the following year. He went to France, and in 1550 was apppointed to the command of the Scots guards there. After he converted to Protestantism in the late 1550s, an order was made for his arrest but he escaped to Geneva. His Protestant zeal for a time neutralised the weak resolution of his father, who, under his advice, became reconciled to some of the Lords of the **Congregation**. He successfully conducted resistance to the French in **Fife** and was present at the siege of **Leith**. In 1560 he was a candidate for marriage with Elizabeth and in 1561 with **Mary, Queen of Scots**. He was imprisoned in 1562 for involvement in a plot to kidnap Mary and, having become insane, he spent the later years of his life in confinement.

**Arran, James Stewart, Earl of** (d.1595) Courtier, second son of the 2nd Lord Ochiltree, father-in-law of John **Knox**. He became a mercenary and served in the army of the states of Holland against Spain. Plausible, able and unscrupulous, after his return to Scotland he was appointed in 1580 a gentleman of the chamber and also made captain of the guard and tutor to his cousin, the insane 3rd Earl of **Arran**. In December 1580 he was

made use of by Esmé Stewart, Duke of Lennox, to accuse the Earl of **Morton** before the privy council of the murder of **Darnley**. The reward for this was recognition in 1581 as the legitimate head of the Hamiltons (his father's mother having been the only child of the 1st Earl of Arran by his first wife). After the **Ruthven Raid**, he became **James VI**'s trusted adviser and was made Chancellor in 1584. He was overthrown in 1585 after the extreme Protestant lords returned from exile.

**Arrochar** Tourist and climbing centre at the head of **Loch Long**, 2km (1mi) west of Tarbet, **Loch Lomond**. Nearby to the northwest are Ben Arthur ('the **Cobbler**', which has excellent rock climbing), and Ben Ime and Ben Narnain, both **Munros**. To the southwest is the **Argyll Forest Park**. The proximity of Arrochar to Loch Lomond was used to good effect during the Viking invasion of Scotland in 1263 (see **Loch Long**).

**Arrol, Sir William** (1839–1913) Engineer and industrialist, b. Houston, Renfrewshire. He began his working life at the age of 9 in **Coats**' thread factory in **Paisley**. In 1853 he was apprenticed to a blacksmith. Ten years later he set up his own boiler-making business and in 1872 set up a large ironworks. The works undertaken by his companies include the second **Tay** Railway Bridge, the **Forth Railway Bridge** and Tower Bridge, London. The firm also developed hydraulic machinery. He was a Liberal-Unionist MP for South **Ayrshire** (1892–1906).

**Arthur's Oon** see **Stenhousemuir**

**Arthur's Seat** see **Edinburgh**

**Ascherson, Charles Neal** (1932– ) Journalist, b. Edinburgh. He began his career in 1956 as a reporter for the *Manchester Guardian* before joining *The Scotsman* in 1959 as Commonwealth Correspondent. In 1960 he became Foreign Correspondent for *The Observer*, reporting from Asia, Africa and Central Europe. He rejoined *The Scotsman* in 1975 as Scottish Political Correspondent. He went freelance in 1979 but was Senior Assistant Editor and political columnist for *The Independent on Sunday* (1985–89). His books include *The Polish August* (1981), *Black Sea* (1996) and *Stone Voices: The Search for Scotland* (2002).

**Asquith, Margot** (née **Emma Alice Margaret Tennant**) (1864–1945) Daughter of the industrialist Sir Charles **Tennant**, b. The Glen, Peeblesshire. His money and her innate wit ensured her great social success when she 'came out' as a debutante in 1881. In 1894 she became the second wife of the politically and socially ambitious Liberal politician Herbert Asquith and soon established herself as a hostess, particularly when he became Prime Minister (1908-16) but she refused to moderate her flamboyance during World War I. Though personal relations with Asquith were difficult, she was a fanatical defender of his political reputation until her death. She wrote several books, including 2 volumes of autobiography.

**Associated Presbyterian Churches** Church group formed in 1989 following a division in the **Free Presbyterian Church**. Differences came to a head after the suspension of a minister, Alexander Murray and an elder, Lord Mackay of Clashfern.

**Associates, The** Rock group comprising Dundonians Billy McKenzie and Alan Rankine, successful in both the singles and album charts in the early 1980s, thanks largely to McKenzie's vocal range and eerie stage presence. Their hits included 'Party Fears Two' and 'Club Country'.

**Association for Scottish Literary Studies** Literary organisation founded in 1970 to promote interest in and awareness of the languages and literature of Scotland. Its publications include an annual collection of new Scottish writing, an annual volume of older Scottish literature, a Scottish Studies review, and study guides to literary works for schools and colleges. It also organises a number of conferences yearly.

**Assynt** Mountainous coastal district in the southwest of **Sutherland**. The main village is **Lochinver**. In 1993 the Assynt Crofters' Trust succeeded in buying their land through a new law which gives a right to buy to those who work the land. See also **Ben More (Assynt), Loch Assynt**.

**Athelstaneford** Village in East Lothian, 4km (3mi) northeast of **Haddington**, that takes its name from Athelstan, a king of the Northumbrians, and his legendary defeat here by the Picts led by **Unuist**. His army was allegedly inspired to victory by the appearance in a cloud formation of **St Andrew**'s white **saltire** against the blue sky. The Flag Heritage Centre, in a restored 16th-century **doocot**, commemorates the event. John **Home** was minister here for a time and Sir David **Lyndsay** is thought to have been born nearby.

**Athole** see **Atholl**

**Atholl** or **Athole** Large area in Perthshire, at the southern end of the **Grampian** Mountains, including the Forest of Atholl, a large deer forest. The main settlement is **Blair Atholl**, which has the Atholl Country Life Museum.

**Atholl, John Murray, 2nd Marquis and 1st Duke of** (1660-1724) Politician, b. Knowsley, Lancashire. A convinced Whig, his support of William of Orange and the Hanoverian succession led to political preferment, e.g. as Secretary of State and Lord High Commissioner, 1696-8, and many titles: the dukedom of Atholl in 1703 was just one of many. After the accession of Anne, he became a privy councillor and Lord Privy Seal. He was a supporter of the **Darien** Scheme but opposed the Union of 1707. He supported George I during the **Jacobite Rising** of 1715.

**Atholl, John Stewart, 4th Earl of** (d.1579) Courtier. As a devout Catholic, he was opposed to the Reformation Parliament in 1560. He was made a privy councillor in 1561 and became a close adviser to **Mary, Queen of Scots** (1565-97). Following the murder of **Darnley**, he supported her abdication but later worked for her restoration. In 1578 he was made Chancellor of Scotland. He was an opponent of Regent **Morton**.

**Atholl, Katharine, Duchess of** (née **Katharine Marjory Ramsay** of Bamff, Perthshire) (1874-1960) Politician. In 1899 she married the Marquis of Tullibardine, later the 8th Duke of Atholl. She was Unionist MP for Kinross and West Perth (1923-38) and was the first woman Conservative politician to become a minister. However, she joined Churchill in opposing the 1935 Government of India Act, and also opposed tacit British support for Franco in the Spanish Civil War. She was ousted as Conservative candidate in 1938 because of her opposition to the Munich agreement and defeated by her supplanter in a bitter by-election. Thereafter she became involved in working with refugees. Her publications include *Women in Politics* (1931) and *Searchlight on Spain* (1938).

**Atholl brose** Dish of honey, **whisky** and **oatmeal**, sometimes with other ingredients. It is said to have been invented by an Earl of Atholl who was reputed to have doctored a well with it in 1476, thus capturing the **Lord of the Isles**.

**Atholl Highlanders** The 77th Highland Regiment, an infantry regiment raised by the Duke of Atholl in 1778. It served in Ireland but when later ordered to the East Indies the soldiers refused to embark because of a breach of the terms of enlistment. It was disbanded in 1783, but the name is now used by the Duke of Atholl's own regiment at **Blair Atholl**, the only private army in Britain.

**Atkinson, Kate** (1951- ) Novelist and short-story writer, b. York. Educated at **Dundee University**, she now lives in **Edinburgh**. Her first novel, *Behind the Scenes at the Museum*, won the Whitbread First Novel Award and the overall Whitbread Book of the Year in 1995. Other novels are *Human Croquet*

## MUSÉE DE LA VIEILLE ALLIANCE FRANCO-ÉCOSSAISE "AULD ALLIANCE"

TÉL. : 48.81.50.00

de PÂQUES à la TOUSSAINT

## AUBIGNY-SUR-NÈRE (Cher)

### CHATEAU DES STUARTS

*A poster celebrating the 'Auld Alliance'*
*between Scotland and France. It was issued to mark the*
*twinning of Aubigny-sur-Nère with Haddington.*

(1997) and *Emotionally Weird* (2000) and her short-story collection, *Not the End of the World*, was published in 2003.

**Attadale** Settlement, railway station, house and garden near the head of **Loch Carron**, Wester Ross. The 8-hectare (20-acre) garden has restored rhododendron borders containing unusual shrubs, and a drift of meconopsis and primulas; and sunken and kitchen gardens. Recently a new Japanese-style water feature has been added.

**Auchincruive** Estate to the northeast of **Ayr**, site of the West of Scotland Agricultural College, founded in 1902, later the National College for Food, Land and Environmental Studies. From 1930 it was based in Auchincruive House (now restored and known as Oswald House).

**Auchindoun Castle** see **Dufftown**

**Auchindrain** An ancient joint-tenancy township, 8km (5mi) south of **Inveraray**, which was the last in Scotland to survive. After its lands were sold for forestry in 1963 it was turned into a folk museum. The stone-built houses, byres and outbuildings and surrounding lands look as they would have done at the end of the 19th century.

**Auchinleck** (pop. 4116) Former coal-mining town in **Ayrshire**, 5km (3mi) northwest of **Cumnock**. Auchinleck House, 5km (3mi) to the west, was built in 1757–61 by Alexander Boswell, Lord Auchinleck, the militant Whig father of James **Boswell**. Dr Johnson, an arch-Tory, was entertained here in 1773 and had a famous dispute with his host, provoked by an image of Oliver Cromwell.

**Auchmithie** Former fishing village in **Angus**, 5km (3mi) north-east of **Arbroath**, original home of the **Arbroath smokie**. It appears as 'Musselcrag' in **Scott**'s *The Antiquary*.

**Auchterarder** (pop. 3549) Small town in **Perthshire**, a former royal **burgh**, 12km (8mi) southeast of **Crieff**. There is little trace now of the medieval royal castle in which **Mary of Guise**, widow of **James V** and Regent, negotiated the Treaty of Perth in 1559. After the Battle of **Sheriffmuir** in 1716, the town was destroyed by the retreating **Jacobites** so that the army of the Duke of **Argyll** could not shelter in it. The town was rebuilt and became a weaving centre. St Kessog's well was said to have curative properties. The Gleneagles Hotel and golf courses are nearby. Auchterarder Heritage tells the history of the town and area. It was said to be 'the largest village in Scotland'.

**Auchterlonie, Willie** (1872–1963) Professional golfer and clubmaker, b. St Andrews. He won the Open in 1893. In 1935 he became honorary professional to the **Royal and Ancient Golf Club**.

**Auchtermuchty** (pop. 1932) Small town, former royal **burgh**, in the Howe of Fife, 7km (4mi) south of **Newburgh**. It had weaving and a distillery and, later, iron-founding and engineering. The site of a Roman camp is on the east side of the town.

**Audubon, John James** see **MacGillivray, William**

**Auld Alliance** The term for the understanding, social and cultural as well as political, that existed between Scotland and France from 1295 until the **Reformation**. During the Middle Ages alliance with France and opposition to England was the dominant foreign policy strategy of the Scottish state.

**Auldearn** Village 4km (2mi) east of **Nairn**, on the ridge between the **Findhorn** and **Nairn** rivers. In 1645 it was the scene of a battle in which **Montrose** defeated the **Covenanters** under General Hurry, said to have been the most tactically brilliant of Montrose's battles.

**'Auld Lang Syne'** Name of a song by Robert **Burns** often sung at the end of social gatherings and at midnight on **Hogmanay**.

**Auld Lichts** see **Presbyterian churches**, p.307

**Auld Reekie** see **Edinburgh**, p.130

**Aultbea** see **Loch Ewe**

**Average White Band, The** Soul/funk group, mainly comprising musicians from the **Dundee** area. Their 1973 debut album *Show Your Hand* received scant recognition, but its successor, *AWB*, was successful on both sides of the Atlantic, and spawned the US No 1 single 'Pick Up the Pieces'. Rocked by the death of key member Robbie McIntosh in 1974, the group returned with a third album, *Cut The Cake*.

**Aviemore** Village on the River **Spey**, 18km (11mi) northeast of **Kingussie**. Originally the site of an inn on a **Wade** military road, it developed in the 19th century with the opening of the railway to Inverness (via **Forres**) in 1863. It became a junction in 1897 when the present direct line to Inverness was opened. The Aviemore Centre, of hotels, shops and leisure facilities, was built in the 1960s and is now being redeveloped, and the village is a focus for skiing and other outdoor sports in the **Cairngorms**. The Strathspey Steam Railway is an additional tourist attraction; see **Boat of Garten**.

**Avoch** (pronounced 'auch') Former **fishing** village on the south shore of the **Black Isle**, 3km (2mi) southwest of **Fortrose**. Nearby are the ruins of the 12th-century Ormond Castle.

**Avon** (pronounced 'aan') River that rises in the **Cairngorms** and flows through Loch Avon, east down Glen Avon and then north to join the **Spey** near **Aberlour**.

**Avon** River that rises near **Cumbernauld** and flows east, then northeast and northwest to join the **Forth** at **Grangemouth**.

**Avon Water** River that rises near **Galston** in Ayrshire and flows northeast past Strathaven and **Larkhall**, then north to join the **Clyde** near **Hamilton**.

**Awe** River that flows from the northwest end of **Loch Awe** through the Pass of **Brander** into **Loch Etive** near **Taynuilt**.

**Ayala, Pedro de** Spanish envoy to court of **James IV** whose report of his stay gives a flattering account of Scotland and its king.

**Ayr** (pop. 47,962) Town on Ayr Bay, on the Firth of **Clyde**, at the mouth of the River Ayr, 19km (12mi) southwest of **Kilmarnock**, former royal **burgh** and county town of **Ayrshire**, now administrative centre of **South Ayrshire** Council. It has varied industries and relies heavily on tourism. Its historically important harbour is still used for the export of coal from the Ayrshire opencast sites. In the 1650s Cromwell's Model Army built a citadel, and the Auld Kirk of Ayr dates from the same period. The Auld Brig of Ayr dates from 1491, and the splendid steeple of the Town Buildings was built 1827–32 by Thomas **Hamilton**. Robert **Burns**, born in nearby **Alloway**, has strong associations with the town, and is commemorated in a statue in Burns Statue Square. Ayr Racecourse is the home of the Scottish Grand National. Ayr Gorge Woodlands, by the River Ayr, is a semi-natural woodland dominated by oak and some coniferous plantation.

**Ayrshire** Former county on the Firth of **Clyde**, historically divided into Cunninghame in the north, Kyle in the middle and Carrick in the south. **Ayr** was the county town. In 1975, it became part of **Strathclyde Region** and was divided into the districts of Kilmarnock and Loudon, Cumnock and Doon Valley, and Kyle and Carrick. See maps on pp.394–5 and **local government** and see also **East Ayrshire, North Ayrshire, South Ayrshire**.

**Ayrshire cattle** Breed of dairy cattle developed in Ayrshire in the late 18th century, derived from a cross between local stock and north of England shorthorns. The rich creamy milk was once widely used to make **Dunlop** cheese.

**Ayton, Sir Robert** (1570–1638) Courtier and poet, b. Kinaldie Castle, near St Andrews. Educated at **St Andrews University**, he then embarked on a continental tour and studied law in Paris. He returned to Britain in 1603, bringing with him a Latin poem addressed to **James VI**, newly crowned James I of England. He was welcomed at court, became a gentleman of the bedchamber and private secretary to Queen Anne. On the death of James in 1625 he became secretary to **Charles I**'s queen, Henrietta Maria. He also wrote poems in English and he has been called 'the Father of the Cavalier lyric'.

**Aytoun, William Edmonstoune** (1813–65) Poet and lawyer, b. Edinburgh, a descendant of Sir Robert **Ayton**. He contributed to *Blackwood's Magazine*, and in 1845 he became Professor of Rhetoric and Belles-Lettres at **Edinburgh University**, proving to be a very popular lecturer. In 1852 he was made Sheriff of **Orkney**. He is remembered for his poetry, often humorous, and for translations.

B

*The Piper to the Laird of Grant, painted in 1714 by Richard Waitt;*
*Castle Grant, near Grantown-on-Spey, is in the background (see bagpipes).*

**Ba, the** see **handba**

**Bac Mor** see **Treshnish Isles**

**Badenoch** (Gaelic **Baideanach**) District along the upper reaches of the River **Spey** between the Grampian and Monadhliath ranges, seized by **Robert** (Bruce) from the **Comyns**. Its main town is **Kingussie**.

**Badenoch and Strathspey District** see **Highland Region**

**Badenoch, Wolf of, Alexander Stewart, Earl of Buchan** (c.1343–c.1405) Son of **Robert II**, he was given the overlordship of **Badenoch** and was made lieutenant of the north. His aggressive style of lordship, and in particular his burning of **Forres** and **Elgin** in 1390, earned him his nickname.

**BAE Systems** Part of the British Aerospace group, since 1999 the owner of the former **Yarrow** and **Fairfield** shipyards on the River **Clyde** and of the Barrow-in-Furness shipyard of Vickers Shipbuilding and Engineering Ltd. It has a virtual monopoly of warship and fleet auxiliary vessel construction in Britain, building both for the Royal Navy and for foreign navies.

**bagpipes** A wind instrument with a blow pipe, a **chanter** for melody and usually 2 or 3 drone pipes, 'blown' by inflating a leather bag by mouth (Highland bagpipes) or underarm bellows (Lowland and Border bagpipes). Though closely associated with Scotland it is a very ancient instrument, and used in different forms in many countries throughout the world. The versatility of Highland bagpipe music is evidenced by its use as a rallying call to battle, as a lament for the dead, and as cheerful music for dancing. There are two basic styles: *ceòl beag* (Gaelic, meaning 'small music'), in the forms of march, **strathspey**, **reel**, jig, hornpipe; and *ceòl mór* (Gaelic, meaning 'great music') or **pìobaireachd** (anglicised as 'pibroch'). The latter is considered to be one of the great musical art forms of Europe. Because of its emotive sound the Highland bagpipe is now used around the world as a ceremonial instrument and it enjoys a high standard of performance and level of popularity in many countries.

**Bailey, Sir Edward Battersby** (1881–1965) Geologist, b. Marden, Kent. An important figure in the mapping of the Central Highlands, especially **Argyll**, he was Professor of Geology in **Glasgow University** and later Director of the Geological Survey of Great Britain.

**bailie** An officer of a **barony** (until the 19th century); a municipal officer and magistrate second in rank to the **provost**, since 1975 only a courtesy title used by certain authorities.

**Baillie, Lady Grizel** (née **Hume**) (1665–1746) Songwriter, daughter of Sir Patrick **Hume**, a **Covenanter** (an opponent of the restored Stewart monarchy). She helped to conceal her father, initially by feeding him when he hid in the family vault under Polwarth Church, and spent some years in exile until the Revolution of 1688–9. Her best-known song is 'Werena my heart licht I wad die'. She married George, son of Robert **Baillie** of Jerviswood. Her household book, published in 1911, provides a detailed picture of daily life in the period, partly at their new Borders home of **Mellerstain**.

**Baillie, Dame Isobel** (1895–1983) Soprano, b. Hawick. Her singing talent recognised at an early age, she worked in a music shop before her debut with the Hallé Orchestra in Manchester. Continuing her studies in Milan, she first appeared on the London stage in 1923, and sang with many of the century's finest conductors.

**Baillie, Joanna** (1762–1851) Poet and playwright, b. Bothwell, Lanarkshire. She moved to London in her early twenties and her poetry includes *Fugitive Pieces* (1790), *Metrical Legends* (1821) and *A Collection of Poems* (1823). She wrote mainly in English, but also occasionally in **Scots**. Her first plays were not successful, but *The Family Legend*, produced in **Edinburgh** in 1810, was a brief success. Her close friend, Sir Walter **Scott**, greatly admired her writing, but her reputation has faded. There is an elaborate monument to her in Bothwell churchyard.

**Baillie, Robert, of Jerviswood** (1634–84) Covenanter, b. Lanarkshire. A supporter of Monmouth's plot against the Catholic **James VII** and **II**, he was arrested in London, returned to

*Aly Bain.*

Edinburgh for trial and hanged. His son George married Lady Grizel Hume; see **Baillie**, Lady Grizel.

**Baillieston** Village to the east of **Glasgow**, now a suburb of the city. Developed in the 19th century with the industries of weaving and coalmining, largely populated with refugees from the Irish potato famine.

**Bain, Alexander** (1818–1903) Philosopher and psychologist, b. Aberdeen. Leaving school at 11, he worked as a weaver and continued his education through the Aberdeen Mechanics Institute. He received a bursary to study at Marischal College, where he was an outstanding student. He published *The Senses and the Intellect* (1855) and *The Emotions and the Will* (1859), and founded the journal *Mind* in 1876. As Professor of Logic and English at **Aberdeen University** (1860–80), his works included English textbooks which were influential in methods of teaching grammar.

**Bain, Aly** (1946– ) Musician, b. Lerwick, Shetland. Perhaps the finest modern fiddle player in the Scottish tradition, Aly Bain was taught by the renowned Tom **Anderson**. He was a founder member of Boys of the Lough and has worked with Phil **Cunningham** since 1988 and also as a solo artist.

**Baird, Sir David** (1757–1829) Soldier, b. Newbyth, East Lothian. Served for many years in India, leading the attack on Seringapatam in 1799. He captured the Cape of Good Hope from the Dutch in 1806, and replaced Sir John **Moore** in command after the latter's death at Corunna, in which battle Baird lost an arm.

**Baird, Sir Dugald** (1899–1986) Gynaecologist. Promoter of medical advances, he developed a cervical cancer screening programme in Aberdeen in 1960; he supported the concept of free choice in abortion, and had significant input into the 1967 Abortion Act, declaring that women should have 'freedom from the tyranny of excessive fertility'.

**Baird, Edward McEwan** (1904–49) Artist, b. Montrose, where he remained for most of his career. His paintings are distinguished by their meticulous realist technique and, in his most notable works, by their strange compositions, influenced by the artist's interest in early Renaissance art and in particular by Surrealism.

**Baird, John** (1787/8–1820) Weaver, b. Condorrat, Dunbartonshire. One of the 'radical martyrs', in 1820 he became captain of a group of radical rebels. He was joined by Andrew **Hardie** and they were defeated by government troops at Bonnymuir, near **Falkirk**. Both he and Hardie were convicted of high treason and hanged.

**Baird, John Logie** (1888–1946) Pioneer of television, b. Helensburgh. Trained as an electrical engineer, his poor health led to a move to southern England, where he demonstrated the first television picture in 1926. The BBC used his systems from 1929–37, but finally adopted the EMI-Marconi system. His research projects included colour television and stereophonic sound, and also secret signalling and fibre optics, but were cut short by his continuing ill health and financial troubles.

**Balbirnie House** see **Markinch**

**Balcarres Castle** Large castle in the **East Neuk of Fife**, at Colinsburgh to the north of **Elie**. It has belonged to the Lindsay family, recently the Earls of Crawford and Balcarres, since the late 16th century. The original house was much extended in the 19th century.

**Balcaskie** Late 17th-century house to the northwest of **Pittenweem**, Fife, the first house of Sir William **Bruce**, who remodelled it in towered symmetrical form and built the great terraced gardens focussed on the **Bass Rock** across the Firth of **Forth**.

**Balcomie Castle** Partly ruined castle near **Crail**, Fife, seat of the Learmonth family. In June 1538, **Mary of Guise** was entertained there after landing at Fife Ness on her way to be married to **James V**.

**Baldred, St (Bealdhere)** (d.756) Northumbrian anchorite who had a cell on the **Bass Rock** in the early 7th century and is associated with **Tyninghame** and other Lothian churches.

**Balerno** Village on the Water of Leith to the southwest of **Edinburgh**. Once a rural community, it became an important paper-making centre and is now a dormitory village for Edinburgh.

**Balfour, Sir Andrew** see **Royal Botanic Garden**

**Balfour, Arthur James, 1st Earl of Balfour**
(1848–1930) Politician. Succeeded to the family estate in East Lothian in 1856, and became Conservative MP for Hertford in 1874. His uncle Robert Cecil, Lord Salisbury, being Prime Minister, he rose rapidly, as Secretary for Scotland 1886, Leader of the Commons 1892–3, and Prime Minister from 1902–6. He continued to hold senior offices, was Foreign Secretary to Lloyd George and authored the Balfour Declaration of 1917, pledging support for Zionists' aims for a home in Palestine.

**Balfour, Isaac Bayley** (1853–1922) Botanist, b. Edinburgh. Son of John Hutton **Balfour**, he was Professor of Botany at **Glasgow** and Oxford, before following his father as Regius Keeper of the **Royal Botanic Garden Edinburgh** and Professor of Botany in Edinburgh. He developed the Garden much as we know it today, especially with the flood of new plants collected by several plant collectors in southeast Asia, in particular by George **Forrest**, whom he sponsored.

**Balfour, Sir James, of Denmylne and Kinnaird**
(1600–57) Historian, b. probably near Newburgh, Fife. He was appointed **Lord Lyon** in 1630 and contributed to the systematic recording of Scottish arms and bearings. He is best remembered for his collection of charters of Scottish monasteries (now in the **National Library of Scotland**). The substantial ruin of his castle can still be seen near the main road just to the southeast of Newburgh.

**Balfour, Sir James, of Pittendreich** (d.1583) Lawyer and politician. Compiler of a collection of ancient statutes and precedents, he was a skilled exploiter of the confused political situation of his day. Implicated in the murders of Cardinal **Beaton** and Lord **Darnley**, he still became president of the Court of Session in 1567.

**Balfour, John** see **Sharp, James**

**Balfour, John Hutton** (1808–84) Botanist, b. Edinburgh. He began as a doctor but developed his interest in botany, founding the Botanical Society of Edinburgh (now of Scotland) in 1836. He became Professor of Botany at **Glasgow University** and later at **Edinburgh**, with the double appointment of Regius Keeper of the **Royal Botanic Garden Edinburgh**, which he greatly expanded.

**Balfron** Village on the Endrick Water to the northwest of Glasgow, north of the **Campsie Fells**. In the 19th century it had a large cotton mill; now it is mainly a commuter village. It was the birthplace of the architect Alexander 'Greek' **Thomson**.

**Balgonie Castle** Great courtyard castle in Fife, above the River **Leven**, to the southeast of **Markinch**, now mainly roofless. Dominated by the tall 15th-century tower built by the Sibbalds, it was greatly enlarged by the Earls of Leven between 1635 and 1706. Partially restored, it is now open to the public and used for functions.

**Balintore** A village with harbour and pleasant beaches on Tarbat Ness, on the **Moray Firth**. It was formerly known as Abbotshaven, the current name, from Gaelic *bail' an todhair*, bleaching village, dating from its participation in the flax industry. It was formerly a centre for commercial salmon fishing.

**Ballachulish** (Gaelic **Bail' a' chaolais**) Village at the mouth of **Loch Leven**, Argyll, on either side of the narrows, where a car ferry operated until the opening of a bridge in 1975. It was prosperous in the 18th and 19th centuries for its slate workings, the largest in Scotland. A centre of Episcopalianism, a **Gaelic** version of the Prayer Book is preserved at the Episcopal church. A unique Early Iron Age oak wood figurine was found in a peat bog here in 1880 (now in the **Museum of Scotland**). See **Appin murder**.

**ballads** In early medieval times songs written for dancing to, ballads became simple poems or folksongs that told a story and, until they attracted the attention of historians and folklorists,

*John Logie Baird demonstrating his television system.*

*John Balliol depicted with symbolic broken crown, sceptre and sword in the mid 16th-century* Forman of Luthrie Armorial.

were passed on in an oral tradition. The ballads of southern Scotland reached a wider public in Sir Walter **Scott**'s *The Minstrelsy of the Scottish Border* (1802–3). Later collectors found an even richer tradition in the Northeast, evident in the Scottish component of the American scholar F J Child's 10-volume *English and Scottish Ballads* (1882–98). In the early 20th century Gavin **Greig**, along with J B Duncan, made a huge collection from the area, and from the 1950s, the School of Scottish Studies in **Edinburgh** University continued this collecting tradition with tape-recorders, thus enabling them to record the music as well as the words. This research brought to light another rich seam among the travelling people, notably in east Perthshire. Some ballads have links in the various areas of Scotland and indeed, like 'Lord Randal', internationally, while the origins of others are marked by their subject matter, such as 'The Battle of Otterburn' and 'Kinmont Willie' in the **Borders**, and 'The Battle of Harlaw' in the Northeast. Others, such as 'The Wife of Usher's Well', may overlap into Northumbrian territory. See also **bothy** ballads.

**Ballantrae** A village at the mouth of the River Stinchar, near **Girvan**, once famous for smuggling. Above it is the ruin of Ardstinchar Castle. Though not the location for Robert Louis **Stevenson**'s *Master of Ballantrae*, Stevenson did visit the village; unfortunately the locals threw stones at him because of the peculiarity of his costume. It has a small harbour, used in summer by inshore fishing boats.

**Ballantrae, Lord** see **Fergusson, Sir Bernard**

**Ballantyne, James** (1772–1833) Printer, b. Kelso. A friend of Sir Walter **Scott**, he set up a printing company in **Edinburgh** with an investment from Scott. Later his brother John (1774–1821) ran an unsuccessful publishing and bookselling business attached to the firm. The printing company was brought down by the collapse of publisher Archibald **Constable**, which also led to the bankruptcy of Scott.

**Ballantyne, R(obert) M(ichael)** (1825–94) Children's author, b. Edinburgh, nephew of James **Ballantyne**. Inspired by the success of his reminiscences of his 7 years with the Hudson's Bay Company, Ballantyne began to write for children, swiftly finding success with *The Young Fur Traders* (1856) and his best-known book *Coral Island* (1858) and producing often more than a book a year until his death.

**Ballater** A small town on the River Dee near **Balmoral**, with close royal associations since being a favourite of Queen Victoria. A tourist resort of long standing after the establishment of a spa at nearby Pannanich in 1760 by **Jacobite** Colonel Francis Farquharson, it developed rapidly after the opening of a railway from **Aberdeen**. The Ballater **Highland Games** are held annually in August.

**Ballindalloch** Village on the River **Spey**, northeast of **Grantown-on-Spey**, dominated by its largely 16th-century castle, ancestral seat of the Grants. It has a notable malt-**whisky** distillery, Cragganmore. Nearby Inveravon Kirkyard has 3 Pictish stones.

**Ballinluig** Small village on the River Tummel, where the road from **Aberfeldy** meets the main road from **Perth** to **Inverness**. Nearby are a small stone circle and some standing stones.

**Balliol, Edward** (c.1283–1364) Son of John **Balliol** and claimant to the Scottish throne. Briefly successful in reclaiming his father's crown after victory at **Dupplin** Moor in 1332, he was increasingly reliant on English military aid. He surrendered the southern counties of Scotland to Edward III, but failed to establish lasting authority in the rest of the kingdom and resigned his claim to the English king in 1356.

**Balliol, John** (c.1250–1314) King of Scots 1292–96. After the death of **Margaret, Maid of Norway**, Balliol's claim to the throne was adjudged strongest by Edward I in the **Great Cause**, where English claims to overlordship were also asserted. Balliol's rule was hampered by the English king's demands and the Scots allied with France against Edward in 1295. There is no evidence that Edward chose Balliol as king because he thought he would be pliable, although King John may have been politically side-lined by the Scots in the crisis of 1295. In 1296 Edward marched on Scotland and dethroned Balliol, who was eventually allowed to retire on family estates in Northern France.

**Balliol College** Probably the oldest college of Oxford University, it began as a house leased for poor scholars by John Balliol, father of John **Balliol**, King of Scots, sometime before 1266. After his death in 1269 his widow **Devorguilla** formalised the arrangement, providing an endowment, statutes and the college seal.

**Balloch** (pronounced 'ball*och*'.) Village on the River Leven at the south end of **Loch Lomond**; a focus for trips on the Loch. For many years in the 20th century it had large silk-printing works. It now has Loch Lomond Shores, a visitor centre at one of the gateways to the **Loch Lomond and the Trossachs National Park**. Balloch Castle (1809) was designed by Robert Lugar in castellated Gothic style; it houses the visitor centre for the Balloch Castle Country Park.

**Balloch** (pronounced 'ba*loch*'.) Village to the east of **Inverness**, now a dormitory area for the city.

**Ballochmyle** see **Catrine, Mauchline**

**Balmacara** (Gaelic **Baile Mac Carra**) Village and estate in the care of the **National Trust for Scotland** on the Kyle-Plockton promontory opposite **Skye**. Includes Lochalsh Woodland Garden.

**Balmaclellan** Village to the northeast of **New Galloway**, with a small steep-sided motte.

**Balmaha** Boating centre on the southeast shore of **Loch Lomond**, near Drymen. In the 19th and early 20th century it had a small chemical works.

**Balmerino Abbey** On the south bank of the River **Tay**. Founded about 1227 by **Alexander II** and his mother for Cistercian monks from **Melrose** and rebuilt after English raids in 1547, it was destroyed in the

Reformation and is now a romantic ruin (in the care of the **National Trust for Scotland**).

**Balmerino, Arthur Elphinstone, 6th Lord** (1688–1746) **Jacobite** who fought in the 1715 Rising, escaped to France, was pardoned and returned. Despite his age he joined Prince Charles Edward **Stewart** in 1745, was captured at **Culloden** and beheaded on Tower Hill. The manner of his death earned him a place in Scottish hearts; at the block he said 'If I had a thousand lives I would lay them down in the same cause' and then put on a Scotch bonnet, saying he died a Scotchman.

**balmoral** A kind of round flat cap similar to a **Kilmarnock** bonnet with a pompom on the crown and a band, worn to one side, sometimes with a feather.

**Balmoral** Castle and 9713-hectare (24,000-acre) estate on the River **Dee**, personal property of the Queen; it was leased from 1848 and bought for his family in 1852 by Prince Albert. The Scottish **baronial** castle, replacing a 16th-century home of the Gordons, was designed by Prince Albert and architect William Smith (1853–5). Queen Victoria was passionately attached to the estate, and her faithful servant John Brown is commemorated in nearby Crathie old kirkyard.

**Balquhidder** Small village on Loch Voil, north of the **Trossachs**, lands of the MacLarens and scene of their persecution by the MacGregors, but famous for its association with **Rob Roy** MacGregor, who with his wife and 2 of his sons is buried in the kirkyard of the ruined old kirk.

*Balmoral Castle.*

The Battle of Bannockburn, 1314, *by William Hole, 1899.*

**Balvenie** Distillery at Dufftown, near **Elgin**, founded in 1892 and still owned by William Grant. Balvenie is one of the few single malts to be supplied by its own maltings, using largely home-grown barley, coppersmith and cooperage. Beside the distillery is the ruined medieval Balvenie Castle, originally of the Comyns (in the care of **Historic Scotland**).

**Banavie** Village near **Fort William**, on the **Caledonian Canal**, famous for the series of 8 locks called Neptune's Staircase.

**Banchory** (pop. 6034) Small town on the River **Dee** 29km (18mi) southwest of **Aberdeen**, now mainly a prosperous commuter town, famous for leaping salmon in the gorge of the River Feugh. It was formerly a resort for convalescents; Somerset Maugham was cured of TB here. Until recently it had lavender cultivation.

**Banff** (pop. 3991) Town on northeast coast, a former royal **burgh** and county town of **Banffshire**. Its massive old castle, a royal residence in the 12th century, is almost completely destroyed, partly built over with a new 'castle' in the mid 18th century. However, some fine 17th- and 18th-century buildings remain. It has a pre-**Reformation** mercat cross, a fine Tolbooth Steeple and Town House and, nearby, **Duff House**. It was an important

port and its harbour was enlarged both by John Smeaton and Thomas **Telford**, but it was supplanted as a port by **Macduff**.

**Banff and Buchan District** see **Grampian Region**

**Banffshire** Former county in the northeast, noted for its agriculture, fishing and distilling industries; in 1975 it became part of the districts of Banff and Buchan, Gordon and Moray of **Grampian Region**, and from 1996 part of **Moray** and **Aberdeenshire**. See maps on pp.394-5 and **local government**.

**Bank House** Garden in Glenfarg, to the south of **Perth**, really two gardens in one. The enclosed garden is meticulously managed on organic principles, with three distinct seasonal plantings and the effective use of colour and form. The garden opposite has a water feature and 'ying and yang' flower beds, while beyond there is an arboretum and pond.

**banknotes** The Scottish chartered and joint-stock banks pioneered the use of notes in small denominations, in a reputable way, in the mid 18th century when gold for coinage was scarce. The **Royal Bank of Scotland**, the **Bank of Scotland** and the **Clydesdale Bank** still retain the right to issue their own notes, a jealously guarded privilege.

**Bank of Scotland** Founded in 1695, it prospered as a monopoly until the early 18th century, when the **Royal Bank of Scotland** was founded. It is one of the three Scottish banks permitted to issue banknotes. In 2001 it merged with Halifax plc; the new group name is HBOS plc. Its Head Office is at the top of the Mound in Edinburgh and also contains a Museum.

**Banks, Iain** (1954– ) Novelist, b. Dunfermline. Two prolific novelists in one man, as Iain M Banks, writer of prizewinning science fiction, including *Consider Phlebas* (1987) and *Feersum Endjinn* (1995), and as plain Iain Banks, writer of humorous and sometimes cruel stories such as *The Wasp Factory* (1984), *The Crow Road* (1992), *Complicity* (1993) and *Whit* (1995).

**Bannatyne, George** (1545-1608) Antiquary and anthologist, compiler of the substantial collection known as the Bannatyne Manuscript (now in the **National Library of Scotland**). It includes otherwise unrecorded works by Robert **Henrysoun**, William **Dunbar** and Sir David **Lyndsay** in addition to many minor poets.

**Bannen, Ian** (1928-99) Actor, b. Airdrie. Early success with the Royal Shakespeare Company led to a career in film, mainly in supporting roles, as in *Flight of the Phoenix* (1965), *Hope and Glory* (1987), *Waking Ned* (1998). He played **Robert the Bruce**'s father in *Braveheart* (1995). Television appearances included Dr Cameron in *Dr Finlay's Casebook* (1993-96).

**Bannerman, Helen Brodie** (née **Boog Watson**) (1862–1946) Children's author, b. Edinburgh. From 1889 to 1918 she lived in India, and there wrote *The Story of Little Black Sambo* (1899) based on illustrated letters she had sent to her children, followed by several similar titles.

**bannock** Round flat cake, usually of **oat-**, **barley-** or pease-meal (but softer than an **oatcake**), baked on a **girdle**. See also **Selkirk bannock**.

**Bannockburn** Village to the south of **Stirling**, site of the battle fought 23–24 June 1314, when a substantial English army, headed by Edward II, on its way to raise the siege of Stirling Castle, was defeated by the Scots under **Robert I**. The victory did not bring the Anglo-Scottish wars to a close, but did greatly aid King Robert's efforts to establish his domestic authority in Scotland. The precise site is not known, but the battle is commemorated at the Bannockburn Heritage Centre (in the care of the **National Trust for Scotland**). Nearby is the Borestone site, believed to be where the king's standard at the battle was fixed in a stone. Bannockburn House was the headquarters of Prince Charles Edward **Stewart** on his retreat in 1746; while there he became ill and was nursed by Clementina **Walkinshaw**, who became his mistress. From the late 18th century the village had textile manufacture and in the 19th William Wilson and Co were important suppliers to the hugely expanded market for **tartan**.

**Baptist Churches in Scotland** There have been Baptist congregations in Scotland since the 17th century. In the 19th there were various Baptist associations and in 1869 the Baptist Union of Scotland was formed.

**Barbour, Hamish** see **Gray, Muriel**

**Barbour, John** (d.1395) Poet, scholar and churchman. He was archdeacon of **Aberdeen** from 1356, studied in Oxford and Paris and later became an officer of the exchequer to **Robert II**. Much of his poetry has been lost, but his great poem *The Bruce*, recording the careers of **Robert I** and Sir James **Douglas**, survives, and gives a keen insight into chivalry in a Scottish context.

**Barbreck House** Impressive late Palladian mansion in **Argyll**, on the Barbreck River near the head of **Loch Craignish**. It was built in 1790 by Major General John Campbell after he bought the family estate back from forfeiture.

**Barcaldine Castle** Near **Loch Creran**, to the northeast of **Oban**, built 1601–9 by Duncan **Campbell of Glenorchy** and restored at the turn of the 20th century by Sir Duncan Campbell.

**Barclay, Andrew, Sons and Co Ltd** Company founded as a general engineering business in **Kilmarnock** in 1847, it later specialised in mining machinery and in industrial locomotive building. In 1970 it was taken over by Hunslet of Leeds, also locomotive builders. It is now owned by Telfos Holdings plc, and makes shipbuilding machine tools as well as building and overhauling railway locomotives and rolling stock.

**Barclay, Hugh** (1828–92) and **David** (1846–1917) Architects, brothers, b. Glasgow. They won the competition for the giant municipal buildings in **Greenock** (1875), never completely finished. School specialists, they designed Glasgow Academy (1878) and many other classical schools in **Glasgow**. David built the Royal College of Science and Technology, Glasgow, now The Royal College Building of **Strathclyde University**.

**Barclay, Robert** (1648–90) Scottish Quaker, b. Gordonstoun, near Elgin. His marriage was the first Quaker wedding in Scotland, and he published many works defending Quaker beliefs. Although repeatedly imprisoned he gained the protection of the Duke of York (later **James VII** and II) and travelled to Germany with William Penn and George Fox.

**Barclay-Allardice, Robert** (1779–1854) 'Pedestrian' and soldier, b. near Stonehaven. In the summer of 1809, some years after his retirement from the army, he performed the feat of walking 1000 miles (1609km) in 1000 consecutive hours.

**bard** From Gaelic meaning 'a poet', now referring to a poet in general. In ancient Gaelic society, the bard had an important role in the household of the clan chief, a professional, often a hereditary post (see **MacMhuirich**), with a long rigorous training in a bardic school. They produced rule-bound poetry, for example praising the chief, exciting to battle.

**Barke, James** (1905–58) Novelist, b. Torwoodlee, near Galashiels, wrote realistic accounts of the effect of industrialisation on Scotland, his major novel being *The Land of the Leal* (1939). He also wrote fictionalised novels about Robert **Burns**, as well as a carefully researched edition of Burns's *Poems and Songs* and of *The Merry Muses of Caledonia*.

**barley** Long a major crop in Scotland, it is still a popular feature of Scottish cooking, for example of broth, as well as an essential ingredient of Scottish beer and **whisky**. In earlier times, a hardy 4- or 6-row form was grown, known as bere or bear, and also as bigg. It is not as productive as modern barley, but will mature in a northern climate. It is still grown in small quantities in the Northern Isles, and is the base for bere-meal bannocks, an **Orkney** delicacy. Barley and bere are more easily malted for ale and **whisky** production than ground; ale was thus once an important nutritional element in the Scottish diet.

**Barlinnie** The last of Glasgow's 19th-century prisons, it is now mainly used for remand and short-stay prisoners, though in the 1980s it was home to a rehabilitation unit which had some success with prisoners such as Jimmy **Boyle**.

**Barnbougle Castle** see **Dalmeny**

**Barns-Graham, Wilhelmina** (1912–2004) Artist, b. St Andrews. Recognised for her abstract paintings and drawings based on the landscape, which she began to produce in the 1940s when she went to St Ives in Cornwall; she continued to live there and in **St Andrews**.

**baron** In Scotland, a landowner who held his land directly from the Crown, even if a commoner.

**baronial,** or **Scottish baronial** Of an architectural style characterised by numerous turrets, crow-stepped gables etc, used especially for country houses from the 1840s, and later for Edinburgh **tenements**.

**baron court** Court held by a **baron** in his **barony**, a form of local government used from the 16th century. The baron, who held his land of the crown, or his depute the baron baillie, presided over a court formed by the tenants. Among its functions it settled disputes over land use, and upheld fair shares of common resources such as grazing, fuel and timber. The earlier extensive criminal and civil jurisdiction of the baron court was massively reduced by the **heritable jurisdictions** Act in 1748.

**barony** The land owned by a **baron**, in tenure directly from the Crown by which the baron had judicial and administrative powers. See also **regality**.

**Barr, A G and Co** Company founded as an aerated water business in the east end of **Glasgow** in 1889 by R F Barr and Co, who had a similar business in **Falkirk**. The firm made a wide range of flavoured drinks, of which their 'Iron Brew' proved

the most popular. Imaginatively marketed as 'Irn Bru' it is now one of the world's most popular soft drinks.

**Barra** (pop. 1078) Southernmost large island of the Outer **Hebrides**, about 80km (50mi) from mainland Scotland; it is barren but attractive, with beautiful white sand beaches and some prehistoric remains. The main port is Castlebay, from which there is a ferry to **Oban** and **Lochboisdale** in **South Uist**, and there is an air connection to **Glasgow** and **Benbecula**. As with South Uist, the majority of the population is Roman Catholic. The island and its castle **Kisimul** were part of the clan lands of the MacNeils. The island people suffered greatly during the Highland **Clearances**. Barra was the location for the film *Whisky Galore* (1948), and is the burial place of the book's author, Sir Compton **Mackenzie**. Barra Head, with its **lighthouse**, is on **Berneray**, the most southerly island of the **Hebrides**.

**Barra Castle** Courtyard castle in Aberdeenshire, to the southwest of **Old Meldrum**, mainly built 1614–18 by George Seton, tutor and Vicar of Meldrum, remarkable for the completeness of its walled gardens and inner and outer courts.

**Barrhead** (pop. 17,244) A manufacturing town near **Paisley**, established with the 18th-century textile trade, and diversifying into sanitary ware in the 19th century. The large Shanks works (latterly Armitage Shanks) closed in 1992.

**Barrie, Sir J(ames) M(atthew)** (1860–1937) Novelist and dramatist, b. Kirriemuir, Angus. His early works were of the **Kailyard** school, including his most successful novel (later dramatised) *The Little Minister* (1891). An unsuccessful marriage and a fierce devotion to his mother may have developed his interest in attractive women with children, from which stems his most famous work, the play *Peter Pan* (1904). Other successful plays include *The Admirable Crichton* (1902), *What Every Woman Knows* (1908), *Dear Brutus* (1917) and *Mary Rose* (1920). Although his writing often reveals an appreciation of the artificiality of social mores, it is frequently diluted by sentimentality and conventionality.

**Barrier Act** Act passed by the **General Assembly** of the **Church of Scotland** in

*Barr's Irn Bru can.*

*The Bass Rock, Firth of Forth.*

1697 whereby any acts affecting the rules and constitution of the church are submitted to the **presbyteries** and only passed when a majority of these approve them.

**Barrow, Geoffrey Wallis Steuart** (1924– ) Historian, b. Leeds. Professor of Medieval History, Newcastle University and Professor of Scottish History in the Universities of **St Andrews** and subsequently **Edinburgh**, he is best known for his masterly work on **Robert I**, *Robert Bruce* (1965, 1988). Other distinguished works on medieval Scotland include *The Kingdom of the Scots* (1973), *The Anglo-Norman Era in Scottish History* (1980), *Kingship and Unity: Scotland 1000-1306* (1981). He has edited the charters of the kings of Scots from **David I** to **William I**.

**Barry** Village near **Carnoustie**, with a fine golf course, sited on the Buddon Ness. A 19th-century water mill, in use until 1982, has been restored by the **National Trust for Scotland**. There is an important army training camp at Barry Buddon.

**Barry, James** (c.1795–1865) Doctor Barry had a long and distinguished career as a military doctor in the British colonies after graduating from **Edinburgh** in 1812, culminating in appointment as Inspector General of British hospitals in Canada. An autopsy revealed the doctor to be a woman, for which reason she was denied a military funeral. Her original name may have been Miranda Stuart.

**Bartholomew, John George** (1860–1920) Cartographer, b. Edinburgh. His father John Bartholomew (1831–93), a publisher and map engraver, enrolled him in the family firm, where he published atlases and developed a system of indicating contours by colour. The firm continued to produce maps, especially their half-inch series, until the 1990s. They also produced the cartography for the *Times Atlas*.

**Barton, Andrew** (d.1511) Merchant and privateer. Barton and his 2 brothers, with the encouragement of **James IV**, energetically attacked foreign shipping. It may have been John Barton who allegedly sent 3 barrels of Flemish pirates' heads to King James; Andrew was eventually killed in a skirmish with 2 English ships.

**basket-hilted broadsword** Single-handed sword, with a tapering blade about 90cm (3ft) long with a single cutting edge, evolved in the late 17th and 18th centuries into the main weapon of the Highland clansmen, usually supplemented by a defensive targe. Named from the unusually elaborate guard for the swordsman's hand, it should not be confused with the **claymore**. Its use was protracted by adoption by the regular Highland regiments of the British army.

**Bass Rock** Small island in the Firth of **Forth** off **Tantallon**, East Lothian, about 110m (313ft) high and 1.5km (1mile) in circumference, a volcanic outcrop, part of a chain including **Edinburgh** Castle Rock. Originally an early Christian retreat (St **Baldred** had a cell there), the rock was later used as a fortress and prison, notably for **Covenanters** after 1671 under **Charles II**. After **Killiecrankie** the rock was held by **Jacobites** for 3 years on behalf of **James VII and II**. It is now a sanctuary for many sea birds, with a large gannet colony. See **North Berwick**.

**Bathgate** (pop. 15,068) An industrial town between **Edinburgh** and **Glasgow**, based on weaving in the 17th century, moving to shale oil and coal in the 19th century. A commercial vehicle plant was established here by the **British Motor Corporation**, but it closed in 1986. The town is now a centre for distributing cars to dealers throughout Scotland. More recent developments include electronics, but the Motorola mobile phone plant closed in 2001.

**Battlefield Band, The** Innovative group which blends traditional Scottish music with other idioms, named after the Glasgow district of Battlefield. Formed in the early 1970s, the band has undergone many changes of personnel.

**bawbee** Specifically a copper coin, originally equal to 6 pennies Scots; from the 18th century a halfpenny and later a general term for money.

**Baxter, Sir David** (1793–1872) Textile manufacturer and philanthropist, b. Dundee. He joined the family linen-manufacturing company, which through innovation and business acumen became one of the largest in the world. He donated widely, giving the Albert Institute and Baxter Park to **Dundee**, and co-endowing the Bell-Baxter school in **Cupar**.

**Baxter, Jim (James Curran)** (1939–2001) Footballer, b. Fife. Played for **Rangers** 1960–4 and capped for Scotland 34 times, he also played for Nottingham Forest and Sunderland. He did not fully realise the potential that many spectators saw in him.

**Baxter, Stanley** (1926– ) Actor and comedian, b. Maryhill, Glasgow. His career began as a stage manager, but he swiftly moved into acting, in the 1950s into radio, and into television in the 1960s. He was often paired with, or pitted against, Jimmy **Logan**. He moved to London in 1959 and continued his stage, film and television work, culminating in the *Stanley Baxter Picture Show*s of the 1970s and 80s. He was also a fine pantomime dame. Now retired, he occasionally voices *Maisie the Cat* for children's television.

**Baxters of Fochabers** Company founded in 1868 as a jam-making concern. It diversified into making other food products, including high-quality tinned soups, in the late 20th century, and now employs some 900. It opened a visitor centre in 1987, which has proved very successful.

**Bay City Rollers, The** Pop group from Edinburgh, immensely popular with a young female audience in the mid 1970s. Expertly marketed, they briefly provoked the type of hysteria once associated with the Beatles. Their hit singles included 'Remember', 'Summerlove Sensation' and 'Give A Little Love'.

**Bealach na Ba** Spectacular but narrow and hair-raising pass carrying the road from **Kishorn** to **Applecross** on the northwest coast. The name means 'pass of the cattle'.

**Bean, Sawney** Mythical cannibal. The story of Sawney Bean is focused on his alleged hideout in a cave on Bennane Head, **Ballantrae** near Girvan, where he and his huge incestuous family preyed on passing travellers. Despite anxiety over the number of missing persons in the region, it was only when one victim escaped from the Beans' clutches that an armed troop, personally led by **James I**, discovered the cave and the cannibals. The Beans were executed horribly at Leith. The story is sometimes dated in the reign of **James VI**, and as the earliest references to it are from the 19th century, it is clear that it should be taken with a pinch of salt.

**beann** see **ben**

**bear** see **barley**

**Beardmore, William** (1856–1936) Shipbuilder, b. Greenwich, London. Expanding his father's firm, he became one of the largest employers on the River **Clyde**, taking over shipyards, steelworks and the Arroll Johnston vehicle plant. During World War I he was a major armaments supplier. Despite apparent success the company began to fail, and struggled on in a reduced form until 1975. Beardmore sponsored Shackleton's 1907 Antarctica expedition, and a glacier was named after him.

**Bearsden** Suburb to the northwest of **Glasgow**, it had a brief spell as a **burgh** until 1975, but is now part of East Dunbartonshire. It contains some good sections of the **Antonine Wall**, and other Roman remains including a fine Roman bath house, in the care of **Historic Scotland**.

**Bearsden and Milngavie District** see **Strathclyde Region**

**Beaton, David** (c.1494–1546) Statesman and churchman, nephew of James **Beaton**, b. Balfour, Fife. He spent time at the French court negotiating the marriages of **James V**, and was given French citizenship. Made commendator of **Arbroath** in 1524, in 1538 he became a cardinal and in 1539 succeeded James Beaton as Archbishop of **St Andrews**. He established himself as regent on the death of **James V** and, although arrested, regained sufficient favour to become Chancellor. A pillar of the Catholic, pro-French party, he was assassinated both for political reasons and in revenge for the burning of Protestant George **Wishart**.

**Beaton, James** (c.1480–1539) Statesman and churchman, uncle of David **Beaton**. Archbishop of **Glasgow** and later **St Andrews**, he served as Chancellor and was a regent during **James V**'s minority. A supporter of close ties with France in the struggles of the minority, Beaton's role was less prominent during the king's personal reign from 1528. He opposed the reformed religion and burned Patrick **Hamilton** as a heretic.

**Beaton, James** (c.1523–1603) Churchman, nephew of David **Beaton**. The last Roman Catholic Archbishop of **Glasgow**, from 1551 until 1560, when he went to Paris and removed the treasures and archives of Glasgow Cathedral to France. He later acted as a Scottish diplomatic presence in the French court.

**Beaton, Mary** see **'four Marys'**

**Beaton family** In Gaelic Mac Beatha, meaning 'son of life', Scotticised as MacBeth and later as Beaton. (They should not be confused with the Lowland Beatons (see above), whose name came from Béthune in France.) From the 14th to the early 18th century, a family of hereditary doctors in the **Highlands** and Islands, in the tradition of the **Gaelic** learned orders, they became physicians to the Kings of Scots and to several clan chiefs. There were 2 divisions of the family, in the islands and on the mainland, each with branches. They left behind a large body of Gaelic manuscripts. The Beatons of Pennycross in **Mull**, who became physicians to the MacLeans of Duart, are commemorated by the Beaton Cairn and Cross at Pennyghael in the south of the island.

*Beinn Eighe.*

**Beattie, James** (1735–1803) Poet, philosopher and essayist, b. Laurencekirk. He was Professor of Moral Philosophy at **Aberdeen** at 25, and he challenged the views of David **Hume** in his *Essay on Truth* (1770) and wrote a number of largely forgotten poems, including the two-volume *The Minstrel* (1771–74). He also published lists of Scotticisms to help people to avoid them in efforts towards the use of English.

**Beattie, Johnny** (1926– ) Comedian and entertainer, b. Glasgow. One of Scotland's foremost comedians, he has also had stage and film roles, for example in *The Big Man* (1990). In 2002, he celebrated 50 years in show business with sell-out one-man shows at the **Edinburgh International Festival**.

**Beattie, William Hamilton** (1840–98) Architect, b. Edinburgh. He came of a large firm of builders and designed Craiglockhart Poorhouse, later hospital (1867–90), in **Edinburgh**, one of the largest projects of its period. His later free Renaissance work in Edinburgh includes Jenners department store (1893–1903) and the North British (now Balmoral) Hotel (1895–1902), a colossal project for which he made a European study tour.

**Beattock** Village to the south of **Moffat**, best known for its proximity to Beattock Summit, at 314m (1029ft) the highest point on the Glasgow to London railway line, and for many years a base for locomotives assisting trains to reach the summit.

**Beaufort, Joan** see **James I**

**Beauly** Market town and river near **Inverness**, whose name may derive from French *beau lieu* 'beautiful place'. Its priory was founded in 1230 and has been in ruins since the **Reformation**; now in the care of **Historic Scotland**. Nearby Beaufort Castle, seat of the Frasers of Lovat, was destroyed by Cumberland after **Culloden**; its successor was rebuilt in massive **baronial** form by James Maitland **Wardrop** (1880–6).

**Beauly Firth** Inlet of the sea stretching from the mouth of the River Beauly at the town of **Beauly** eastwards to **Inverness**, where it opens into the **Moray Firth**.

**beinn** see **ben**

**Beinn a' Ghlo (Ben-y-Glo)** Mountain near **Blair Atholl**, a group of 3 **Munro** summits of which the highest, Carn nan Gabhar, is 1116m (3661ft).

**Beinn an Dothaidh** Mountain, a **Munro** (1002m/3287ft) at **Bridge of Orchy** near Rannoch Moor, with a view over the Moor and the Black Mount.

**Beinn Chaluim (Ben Challum)** Mountain, a **Munro** (1025m/3363ft) at the head of **Glen Lochay**, overlooking **Tyndrum**.

**Beinn Dorainn** Mountain, a **Munro** (1076m/3530ft) next to **Beinn an Dothaidh**, the subject of 2 well-known Gaelic songs by **Donnchadh Bàn**.

**Beinn Eighe** Seven-peaked **Munro** near Torridon, centre of the first National Nature Reserve in Britain (1951). Covering 4047 hectares (10,000 acres) of immensely varying altitude, it has populations of red deer, pine martens, Scottish wild cats and eagles.

**Beinn Fhada (Ben Attow)** Mountain, a **Munro** (952m/3123ft) near Morvich in **Kintail**. Beinn Fhada is also the name of one of the Three Sisters, mountains in **Glencoe**.

*Alexander Graham Bell.*

**Beinn Fhionnlaidh** Name of 2 mountains, both **Munros**, one (1005m/3297ft) at the head of Glen Cannich, near **Glen Affric**, and the other (959m/3146ft) to the west of **Glen Etive**.

**Beinn Ghlas** Mountain, a **Munro** (1103m/3619ft) on the shoulder of Ben Lawers, near **Loch Tay**. The Beinn Ghlas wind farm was opened in 1999.

**Beinn Mheadhoin** Mountain, a **Munro** (1182m/3878ft) in the **Cairngorms**, overlooking Loch Etchachan.

**Beinn Mhor** see **Five Sisters of Kintail**

**Beith** (pop. 6346) A town to the southwest of **Paisley**, once a centre of the textile industry, later Scotland's largest centre of furniture manufacture. In the 18th and early 19th century it was a clearing house for smuggled goods.

**Beith, John Hay** see **Hay, Ian**

**Belhaven, John Hamilton, 2nd Lord** (1656–1708) Agricultural improver and leading opponent of the Act of Union of 1707 in the Scottish Parliament, along with Andrew **Fletcher of Saltoun**.

**Bell, Alexander Graham** (1847–1922) Inventor, b. Edinburgh. Moved to Canada in 1870 and then to the USA. His experiments in telephony led in 1875 to telephone transmission, and the Bell Telephone Company was set up in 1877. However, the US courts decided in 2002 that the telephone was invented by Antonio Meucci, who demonstrated his invention in 1860. Bell's other inventions include the photophone and a number of aeronautical innovations. He founded the journal *Science* in 1883.

**Bell, Andrew** (1753–1832) Teacher and minister, b. St Andrews. As chaplain to the East India Company in Madras, he devised an education system whereby older pupils in the Madras Male Orphan Asylum helped to teach the younger ones. Known as the 'Madras system', this approach became popular particularly in English schools. On his death he left a large bequest to be used for a number of educational purposes, including the founding of Madras College, **St Andrews**, and Bell-Baxter, **Cupar**, schools which operated according to his principles. His bequest also founded the first university chairs of education in the English-speaking world, at **Edinburgh** and **St Andrews Universities**.

**Bell, Arthur Kinmont** (1868–1942) **Whisky** manufacturer and philanthropist, b. Perth. Son of Arthur Bell, who started blending whiskies in the mid 19th century, though they were not called 'Bell's' until the end of the century. A K Bell ran the domestic side of the business, while his brother Robert dealt with overseas trade.

**Bell, Sir Charles** (1774–1842) Surgeon. A pioneer in the field of neurology, he was the first to distinguish between the motor and sensory nerves of the brain. Bell's palsy, a type of facial paralysis, is named after him.

**Bell, Henry** (1767–1830) Engineer, b. Torphichen Mill, Linlithgow. In 1812 he launched the *Comet* on the River **Clyde**, the first passenger steamer in Europe; it ran a regular service between **Greenock** and **Glasgow**.

**Bell, J(ohn) J(oy)** (1871–1934) Writer, best known for *Wee MacGreegor* (1902), an entertaining account of the family life of a **Glasgow** boy in the early 20th century.

**Bell, Patrick** (1799–1869) Inventor, b. Auchterhouse, near Dundee. Over 1826–8 he developed the world's first successful reaping machine. The lack of mechanical skill in the countryside put it ahead of its time. The design shaped Cyrus McCormick's successful reaper in the US.

**Bellany, John** (1942– ) Artist, b. Port Seton, East Lothian. While a student, Bellany began making large-scale allegorical paintings, most frequently inspired by his experience of growing up in a fishing village. Influenced in the 1960s by the German artist Max Beckmann and by a visit to the former concentration camp at

Buchenwald, Bellany has developed a deeply personal symbolism, often rendered in bold colour and with a forceful use of paint, to produce works on themes of universal human significance.

**Belle and Sebastian** Rock group from Glasgow, founded in 1996 by Stuart Murdoch and Stuart David. Militantly non-macho, they gained a reputation for fey, laid-back performances and wistful songs. Their first album, the limited-edition *Tigermilk*, was followed by the greater commercial successes of *If You're Feeling Sinister*, *The Boy With The Arab Strap*, and *Fold Your Hands Child, You Walk Like A Peasant*.

**Bellenden, John** (c.1495–c.1547) Cleric and writer. He translated Livy and Hector **Boece**'s *Chronicles of Scotland*, good examples of early prose in **Scots**.

**Bell Rock** Also known as Inchcape Rock, a half-tide sandstone reef lying off the coast of **Arbroath**, a major danger to shipping trying to enter the Firths of **Tay** and **Forth** from the north. Its **lighthouse** was built by Robert Stevenson in 1808–11.

**Bells Cherrybank** Garden in **Perth**, home of the Scottish collection of over 900 varieties of heaths and heathers. Now owned by Scotland's Garden Trust, who are developing the adjacent site to become Scotland's showplace garden.

**Bellshill** Town between **Glasgow** and **Motherwell**. An industrial centre originally based on coal and steel, now relying on more diversified activities.

**Beltane** Pre-Christian festival celebrated in early May, usually on the 1st, to mark the beginning of summer. Fires were lit on hilltops, especially in the **Highlands**, and the name was also applied to midsummer fire festivals. Many still gather on this date on Arthur's Seat, **Edinburgh**, to wash their faces in pre-dawn dew, regarded as having magical properties.

**belted Galloway** see **Galloway cattle**

**Bemersyde** see **Haig, Douglas**

**ben** Scots word for a mountain, often found in place-names, from Gaelic *beinn* (often found in the genitive plural form *beann*).

**Ben Alder** (Gaelic **Beinn Eallar**) Mountain, a **Munro** (266m/3765ft) in Inverness-shire towering above **Loch Ericht**. It is associated with the **Jacobite** Ewan **MacPherson** of Cluny, who hid out on its slopes after the 1745 Rising.

**Ben Attow** see **Beinn Fhada**

**Benbecula** (Gaelic **Beinn nam Faoghla**) An island of the Outer **Hebrides** between **North** and **South Uist**, to both of which it is joined by a causeway. There is an air connection to **Glasgow**, **Stornoway** and **Barra**. It is very flat, and networked with a large number of inland lochs. Its principal village is Balivanich (Gaelic Baile a' Mhainich), and historic remains on the island include Dun Buidhe and Borve Castle. It is the site of major defence installations.

**Ben Bhraggie** see **Golspie**

**Ben Challum** see **Beinn Chaluim**

**Ben Cruachan** see **Cruachan**

**Benderloch** (Gaelic **Meudarloch**) Agricultural peninsula, north of Connel near **Oban**, between **Loch Creran** and **Loch Etive**. There is a complex of Iron Age fortifications, partly vitrified, on a hill nearby.

**Ben Hope** Mountain, the most northerly **Munro** (927m/3040ft), to the southeast of **Loch Hope**.

**Beinn Làir** Mountain (860m/2821ft) in Wester Ross, to the west of the head of Lochan Fada, and above **Loch Maree**.

**Ben Lawers** (Gaelic **Beinn Labhar**) Mountain, a **Munro** (1214m/3984ft) on the north shore of **Loch Tay** between **Killin** and **Aberfeldy**. Rare alpine plants grow on its slopes. The peak and southern slopes were bought by the **National Trust for Scotland** in 1950. From the summit there are views extending from the Atlantic Ocean to the North Sea. The area is popular with hillwalkers.

**Ben Ledi** (Gaelic **Beinn Lidi(dh)**) Mountain (879m/2883ft) on the west bank of Loch Lubnaig, 7km (4mi) northwest of **Callander**. Its proximity to the **Central Belt** makes it a popular walking area.

**Ben Lee** Mountain (445m/1460ft) on **Skye**, above Loch Sligachan to the west of Peinchorran.

**Ben Line** A shipping line established by William Thompson (d.1889) in **Leith** in 1825. William Thompson and Co began to name all its ships with the prefix 'Ben' in the late 19th century. Renamed Ben Line in 1919, it remained successful for many years. It was liquidated in 2000.

**Ben Lomond** (Gaelic **Beinn Laomainn**) Mountain on the east shore of **Loch Lomond**, north of Rowardennan. At 973m (3192ft), it is the most southerly **Munro**. It lies within the **Loch Lomond and the Trossachs National Park** and is a popular destination for weekend hillwalkers.

**Ben Loyal** (Gaelic **Beinn Laoghail**) Mountain (764m/2506ft) in Caithness, on the west side of **Loch Loyal**, 8km (5mi) south of Tongue. Its isolated position and striking shape make it a landmark over a wide area.

**Ben Lui** (Gaelic **Beinn Laoigh**) Mountain, a **Munro** (1130m/3702ft) 11km (7mi) east of **Dalmally**, part of a 3-peak ridge.

**Ben Macdui** (Gaelic **Beinn Macduibh**) Mountain in the **Cairngorms**, highest of the region's 4 highest peaks, a **Munro** 1309m (4295ft).

**Ben More** (Gaelic **Beinn Mór**, meaning 'big hill') Name of several Scottish hills. Three are **Munros**: Ben More in Perthshire (near **Crianlarich**) (1174m/3851ft), Ben More Assynt in Sutherland (998m/3273ft) and Ben More in **Mull** (966m/3168ft). Ben More Coigach in Wester Ross, however, is simply the highest hill in its area at 743m (2437ft).

**Benmore Botanic Garden** Garden near **Dunoon**, a specialist garden of the **Royal Botanic Garden** in **Edinburgh**, specialising in rhododendrons, conifers and Chilean and Bhutanese plants.

**Bennachie** Prominent group of hills in Aberdeenshire, 11km (7mi) west of **Inverurie** surrounded by woodland. The highest point, the Mither Tap (518m/1700ft), has an Iron Age fort on its summit.

**Ben Nevis** (Gaelic **Beinn Nibheis**) Highest mountain in the British Isles at 1344m (4408ft), a **Munro**, its huge mass rises steeply above Glen Nevis, to the southeast of **Fort William**. There was a weather observatory on the summit from 1883 to 1904, and the ruins of the building can still be seen.

**Ben Wyvis** (Gaelic **Beinn Uais**) Mountain, a **Munro** to the north of **Strathpeffer**, 1046m (3432ft) high.

**Ben-y-Glo** see **Beinn a' Ghlo**

**bere** see **barley**

**Bernard of Arbroath** (d.1331) Churchman and statesman. Chancellor to **Robert I** and Abbot of **Arbroath**, he was later made Bishop of the Isles. His role in the drafting of the **Declaration of Arbroath** is unclear; and he is not to be confused with Bernard de Linton, a different person.

**Bernera** (Gaelic **Bearnaraidh**) A small village near **Glenelg** with a (now ruined) barracks built by General **Wade** as part of his road-building project in the 18th century. The barracks was later used as a refuge for local victims of the **Clearances**.

**Bernera** Two islands, Greater and Lesser Bernera, off the west coast of the Island of **Lewis**.

**Berneray** Island, with a small population, between **Harris** and **North Uist**, to which it is now linked by a causeway. There is a ferry to **Leverburgh** in **Harris**.

**Berneray** A small island to the south of **Barra**, the most southerly of the Outer **Hebrides**, with the Barra Head lighthouse on its summit.

**Bernicia** Anglian kingdom in northeast England, which extended north to the **Forth** in the 6th century. It was sometimes joined with its southern neighbour Deira and was later called Northumbria. The Angles ruled what is now southeast Scotland until their defeat at **Carham** in 1018 by **Malcolm II** confirmed the incorporation of **Lothian** into his kingdom.

**Bervie** see **Inverbervie**

**Berwick cockle** A kind of fawn- and red-striped boiled sweet with a mild peppermint flavour, originally made in **Berwick-upon-Tweed**.

**Berwickshire** Former county on the southeast coast, bordered on the southeast by the River **Tweed**. In 1975, with reduced area, it became the Berwickshire district of **Borders Region**. Since 1996 it has been part of **Scottish Borders** local authority. Most of the area is agricultural, including the fertile **Merse**. See maps on pp.394-5 and **local government**.

**Berwick-upon-Tweed** Formerly a **burgh**, sacked by Edward I during **Wars of Independence**, it changed hands many times and finally came under English rule in 1482. It has kept up strong Scottish connections, as in its Scottish League football club. See also **North Berwick**.

**'Betty Burke'** see **Stewart, Prince Charles Edward**

**Bidean nam Bian** Mountain, a **Munro** near **Glencoe**, at 1150m (3766ft) the highest peak in Argyll.

**Biggar** Handsome market and weaving town near **Lanark**, once a royal **burgh** commanded by (now ruined) Boghall Castle, home of Mary Fleming, one of **Mary, Queen of Scots'** 'four Marys'. It still has many of the features of a medieval town, including narrow wynds, remnants of strip farming, and a 16th-century parish church. It also has a historic gasworks in the care of **Historic Scotland**, and an important museum enterprise created in the late 20th century. Biggar Park has a series of merging feature gardens from Japanese style to rock bank leading to woodland plantings and an 18th-century walled garden, with a fine collection of old roses and herbaceous plants.

**Binns, House of the** Between **South Queensferry** and **Linlithgow**, a Georgianised 17th-century house with 15th-century portions and impressive 17th-century plasterwork, once home of General Tam **Dalyell**, anti-**Covenanter**, and now of his descendant Tam **Dalyell**, MP. (In the care of the **National Trust for Scotland**.)

**Birgham, Treaty of** The agreement to marry **Margaret, Maid of Norway**, the child Queen of Scots, to Prince Edward of England (Edward II) was made at the small village of Birgham north of the **Tweed** in 1290. The death of Margaret before the marriage could take place deepened the Scottish succession crisis, leading to the **Wars of Independence**.

**Birnam** Village near **Dunkeld** on the River **Tay**, laid out in the 1850s by Sir William Drummond with a picturesque **baronial** hotel and boarding houses. When a branch railway from **Perth** was opened, it was the first rail-connected Highland resort. It is famous as the site of Birnam Wood, whose apparent move to Dunsinane (**Malcolm III**'s soldiers carried branches cut from the Birnam trees) was the sign of **Macbeth**'s imminent defeat in Shakespeare's play. The Beatrix Potter Centre celebrates the fact that the author holidayed in this area and is reputed to have written *The Tale of Peter Rabbit* here.

**Birsay** Hamlet at the north tip of the mainland of **Orkney**, site of an early palace of the earls of Orkney, rebuilt by Earl Robert **Stewart** in the 16th century, and now roofless. The tidal island Brough of Birsay is studded with a mixture of Norse and early Christian ruins. Both are in the care of **Historic Scotland**.

**Bishopbriggs** (pop. 23,118) Now a commuter town for Glasgow, it developed in the 19th century around the sandstone quarries supplying Glasgow builders, and later became a mining centre. In the 20th century it became home to publishers **Blackie** and later **Collins**.

**Bishops' Wars** Two wars between **Charles I** and the forces of the **Covenanters**. In the first (May–June 1639), there was a standoff and Charles made substantial but insincere concessions in the Pacification of **Berwick**. In the second (August–September 1640) the Scots invaded England to force the King's hand and secured the Treaty of Rippon in 1641, gaining financial concessions which compelled Charles to summon an English parliament to secure funds.

**Bisset, Baldred** (fl. 1300) Canon lawyer and historian. A graduate of Bologna, he was responsible for the Scottish 'pleading' to the pope in 1301 which sought to deny Edward I's claims of suzerainty. A justification of the long and independent history of the Scots was offered. Similar themes were taken up in the later Scottish chronicle tradition and in the Declaration of **Arbroath** of 1320.

**Blà Bheinn (Blaven)** Isolated mountain, a **Munro** (928m/3045ft) on the Isle of **Skye**, an outlier of the **Cuillins**, with an excellent view of the main Cuillin ridge.

**Black, Adam** (1784–1874) Publisher, b. Edinburgh. After working for a bookseller, he started his own bookshop in 1807 and, with his nephew, a publishing business, A & C Black, in 1817. He bought the rights to the *Encyclopaedia Britannica* and later to the novels of Sir Walter **Scott**. Since 1848 the firm has published *Who's Who*. In 1889 it moved to London and is currently owned by Bloomsbury.

**Black, Sir James Whyte** (1924– ) Pharmacologist, b. Uddingston, near Glasgow. A lecturer and researcher, and later Professor of Analytical Pharmacology at Cambridge, he won the Nobel Prize for Medicine in 1998 for developing the drugs propranolol (for heart problems) and cimetidine (for treating duodenal and gastric ulcers).

**Black, Joseph** (1728–99) Chemist and physician, b. Bordeaux, France. He was educated in Belfast, **Glasgow** and **Edinburgh**. He succeeded William **Cullen** first as Professor of Anatomy and Chemistry in **Glasgow University** and later as Professor of Medicine and Chemistry at **Edinburgh University**. His scientific investigation included the discovery of carbon dioxide and the development of the theory of latent heat.

**Blackadder, Dame Elizabeth** (1931– ) Artist, b. Falkirk. Like her tutor William **Gillies**, she has invariably found her subject matter in the world around her (she has travelled widely in the company of her husband, the artist John Houston), producing landscapes, portraits, and still lifes in oil and watercolour; she has become particularly well-known for the latter. The characteristic thoughtful mood and delicate draughtsmanship of her art elevates it beyond the ordinary, and she is distinguished as the first woman to be elected both a Royal Academician and Royal Scottish Academician; she was appointed Queen's Limner in Scotland in 2001.

**'Black Agnes'** (c.1320–69) Countess of Dunbar, famous for defending Dunbar Castle against an English siege in 1338. The colourful details about the incident offered by Scottish chroniclers should be treated with caution.

**Black Book of Clanranald** see **Clanranald, Black** and **Red Books of**

**Black Book of Taymouth** see **Taymouth, Black Book of**

**black bun** A very rich spicy fruit cake, baked in a pastry crust, eaten at **Hogmanay**. Also called Scotch bun.

**black cattle** General name for several different breeds that were prominent in the cattle trade from the 18th century onwards. These include one of the **Galloway** breeds (as distinct from the Beltie or Belted Galloway), the **Aberdeen-Angus** (descended from the Buchan Hummlie or hornless, and Angus Doddie), and the **Highland** breed, which before the 19th century was often enough black until 19th-century fashion bred up the familiar red Highlanders.

*A black house on the Isle of Lewis in 1878, with a broch in the distance.*

**'Black Dinner'** Name given to the banquet held in the Old Parliament Hall of **Edinburgh Castle** in 1440 at which William, 6th Earl of **Douglas** and his brother, still young children, were executed on the order of Chancellor Crichton in the presence of the boy King **James II**, breaking the hold of the Douglases over the crown.

**Black Douglases** A branch of the Douglas family (see also **Red Douglas**) whose most prominent early figure was the original 'Black Douglas', Sir James (1286–1330), friend and greatest captain of **Robert I**, who earned the epithet with the ferocity of his raids (or perhaps by his swarthy colouring). He took Bruce's heart on a crusade, but died fighting in Spain. Others in this line include Archibald 'the Grim', William (murdered at the '**Black Dinner**'), William the 8th Earl, and James the 9th.

**Black Dwarf, The** A novel by Sir Walter **Scott**, published in *Tales of my Landlord* (1816), set in the reign of Queen Anne and featuring a dwarf betrayed in love who becomes a recluse. His solitary life leads to rumours of supernatural powers, but he is eventually revealed as a force for good.

**blackface sheep** First known as the Linton, and now often as the Blackie, this small hardy breed is the commonest of hill sheep, and spread northwards from the **Borders** during the 18th century, displacing the native grey and whiteface breeds. The wool is coarse but tough, and is the basis of **Harris Tweed**.

**Blackford** Perthshire village to the southeast of **Auchterarder**, once famous for its brewery, in existence since at least 1488, when **James IV** tasted the ale. The village was burned in 1716, after **Sheriffmuir**, by the retreating **Jacobite** army. It now has the Tullibardine distillery and the Highland Spring water-bottling plant.

**Blackgrange** Large complex of **whisky**-maturing warehouses, and blending and bottling plant, at Cambus, Clackmannanshire established by The **Distillers' Co Ltd** in the 1970s. It replaced outmoded small warehouses all over Scotland, and some of the smaller bottling plants. It is by far the largest site of its kind, and contains the biggest stock of Scotch whiskies in the world.

**Blackhall, Sheena** (1947– ) Poet and story-writer, b. Aberdeen. She has produced many collections of prose and verse, much of it in Northeast Scots, including *A Hint o' Granite* (1992) and *Back o' Bennachie* (1993), *Wittgenstein's Web* (1996), *Singing Bird* (2000) and *A Boorich o Fowk* (2003).

**Black Hill** Archaeological site above the River **Clyde** to the west of **Lanark**, including a Bronze-Age burial cairn and an Iron-Age fort. (In the care of the **National Trust for Scotland**.)

**Black Hill** Hillfort near Abington, South Lanarkshire, apparently constructed in two separate periods.

**black house** (Gaelic **taigh dubh**) Typical of the **Highlands** and Islands until the early 20th century, a cottage designed to withstand severe weather and wind. It has low double drystone walls with a core of earth, rounded corners, and a thatched roof roped and weighted down. Smoke from the fire escaped through a hole in the roof. A restored example is at **Arnol**, Isle of **Lewis** (in the care of **Historic Scotland**). The name comes from the contrast it made with the new whitewashed cottages which began to appear in the 19th century (in Gaelic *taigh geal*).

**Blackie, John** (1782–1874) Publisher, founded the firm of Blackie & Son in **Glasgow** in 1809. It became renowned as a children's, schoolbook and technical publisher, but its lists were taken over by other firms in 1993.

**Blackie, John Stuart** (1809–1905) Classical scholar, b. Glasgow. A regular contributor to *Blackwood's Magazine*, and a translator from German, especially of Goethe's *Faust*, he was a Professor of **Humanity** at **Aberdeen University** and later of Greek at **Edinburgh**. An advocate of Scottish nationalism and university reform, he helped endow a chair of Celtic studies at Edinburgh University.

**Black Isle** (Gaelic **An Eilean Dubh**) Broad fertile peninsula between the **Cromarty Firth** to the north and the **Moray** and **Beauly Firths** to the south.

**Black Mount** (Gaelic **Am Monadh Dubh**) A stretch of high moorland between **Rannoch** Moor and **Glen Etive**, crossed by the road from **Tyndrum** to **Glencoe**.

**Blackness** A village on the Firth of **Forth**, near **Linlithgow**, once a substantial sea port. Its restored 15th-century castle was used as a **Covenanters'** prison. (In the care of **Historic Scotland**.)

**black strippit ba** A kind of round black- and white-striped boiled sweet, with a strong peppermint flavour, a bull's eye.

**Black Watch** (Gaelic **Am Freiceadean Dubh**) Raised as 6 independent companies of infantry in 1725 to maintain order in the **Highlands** after the **Jacobite Rising** of 1715. In 1739 these were combined into the 43rd Regiment of Foot, renumbered 42nd in 1751. Its dark tartan and original role gave it its name; its motto is 'Wha daur meddle wi' me'. It has served in most British campaigns and is now known as the Black Watch (Royal Highland Regiment). It recruits from east central Scotland.

**Blackwater** Name of several rivers in Scotland, one of which, to the north of **Rannoch Moor**, was dammed to form the Blackwater Reservoir, providing power for the aluminium works at **Kinlochleven**, now supplying the Lochaber Aluminium Smelter at **Fort William**, with the surplus going to the National Grid.

**Blackwaterfoot** Small village on the southwest coast of the Isle of **Arran**, a popular holiday resort. Nearby is the 'King's Cave', a supposed hideout of **Robert I**. 5km (3mi) to the north is the stone circle of Machrie Moor.

**Blackwood, William** (1776–1834) Publisher, b. Edinburgh. He opened a bookshop in 1804, after an apprenticeship as a bookseller, and his company published John **Galt** and James **Hogg** and, in partnership with John **Murray**, Byron and Shelley. He founded *Blackwood's Magazine* as a Tory rival to the Whig *Edinburgh Review*. J G **Lockhart** and John **Wilson** were early assistant editors and regular contributors. The magazine was published from 1817 to 1980, and continually featured major writers, including James **Hogg**, George Eliot, John **Galt**, Neil **Munro** and John **Buchan**. Its early issues were distinguished by satirical criticism of Whiggery and by popular poets such as Keats and Wordworth, and from 1822–35 featured the *Noctes Ambrosianae* written by John **Wilson**. Its literary quality was not however maintained during its later years.

**Blaeu's Atlas** Scotland takes up one volume of the *Atlas Major* published in 1654 by the Dutchman Jan Blaeu (d.1673), featuring 49 maps prepared by Timothy **Pont** and revised by Robert **Gordon of Straloch**, supplied with local details by Sir John Scot.

**Blair, Hugh** (1718–1800) Minister, writer and critic, b. Edinburgh. As well as minister at St Giles', he was the first Professor of Rhetoric and Belles-Lettres at **Edinburgh University**. His sermons and lectures had a high reputation in his day, which failed to survive much beyond his lifetime.

**Blair Adam** Large but irregular quadrangular house of the **Adam** architect family, 6km (4mi) south of **Kinross**, its nucleus a house built in 1733 for William **Adam**'s factor. William's son John planned a new house but it was never built. It was remodelled from 1805 for Lord Chief Commissioner William Adam.

**Blair Atholl** (Gaelic **Blàr an Athoill**) Estate village in beautiful scenery at the join of the Rivers Tilt and Garry to the north of **Pitlochry**, a popular holiday destination. Nearby is **Beinn a' Ghlo**.

**Blair Castle** Seat of the Dukes of **Atholl**, near **Blair Atholl**. Comyn's Tower, built by John **Comyn** of **Badenoch**, dates from about 1269. The castle was occupied by the Marquis of **Montrose** in 1644 and in 1689 by Claverhouse; the latter's body was brought here after **Killiecrankie**. It was attacked, unsuccessfully, by the **Jacobite** Lord George **Murray** while garrisoned by Hanoverian troops in 1746, making it the last castle in Britain to be besieged. Its damaged roofs were drastically simplified after 1745, but the interior was palatially fitted out in 1751–57. The roofs were rebarionalised by David **Bryce** (1869–71). (Now owned by a trust and open to the public.)

*Blair Castle, Perthshire.*

**Blair Drummond** Safari and leisure park on an estate near **Stirling**, with a breeding programme for endangered species. Blair Drummond House was rebuilt as a dramatic baronial pile by James Campbell Walker in 1868–72; it is now one of the Scottish Camphill communities.

**Blairgowrie** Town on the River Ericht in the fertile area in Perth and Kinross, from 1929–75 forming a **burgh** with the adjacent **Rattray**. It is famous for raspberry growing, and had an important **linen** and **jute** industry. One of the mills, Keathbank, is now a visitor centre. It is a gateway to the skiing area in **Glenshee**. To the northwest is Newton Castle, early 17th century Z-plan, private home of the Chief of Clan MacPherson. To the west is Ardblair, a 16th-century L-plan castle.

**Blairs College** Roman Catholic seminary near **Aberdeen**, formed by the merging of two earlier seminaries. It was founded in 1829 when John Menzies of Pitfodels donated his estate to the church, and was a training place for boys and young men intending to enter the priesthood. The college closed in 1986, but the buildings continued to be used by the Catholic Church as a retreat until the estate was sold in 1994.

**Blake, George** (1893–1961) Novelist, b. Greenock, which he fictionalised as Garvel in many of his novels. A journalist, first at the Glasgow *Evening News*, then in London, he joined publishers Faber and Faber in 1930, managing their interests in Scotland from 1932. His major work is *The Shipbuilders* (1935), about the effect of a shipyard closure on the community, but all his books carry a convincing feel of location and character.

**Blane, St** A 6th-century Celtic saint born on the island of **Bute**. He founded a church at **Dunblane**, now the site of the cathedral. At Kingarth, at the south end of Bute, are the ruins of a 12th-century Romanesque chapel dedicated to him, within an earlier monastery.

**Blantyre** Village near **Hamilton**, Lanarkshire, developed in the late 18th century for cotton-spinning, it later became a coal-mining centre. The Blantyre Pit Disaster in 1877, caused by an underground explosion, was one of Scotland's worst, killing 207 of the 235 miners on the shift. Blantyre was the birthplace of explorer David **Livingstone**, whose home is now a museum.

**Blaven** see **Blà Bheinn**

**Blind Harry** (fl. 1470–92) Poet. Author of *The Wallace*, a long heroic poem about William **Wallace**, which, though highly untrustworthy historically, has done much to shape the modern vision of Wallace as a national hero. Little is known about Blind Harry, though payments to him appear in the accounts of **James IV**, and he is mentioned by William **Dunbar**.

**Blind Harper** see **Clarsair Dall**

**'Bluidy Mackenzie'** see **Mackenzie, Sir George, of Rosehaugh**

**BMK** Carpet makers of **Kilmarnock**, with origins in the firm of Thomas Morton in the 1830s, when the town was the centre of the Scottish carpet industry; it became first Blackwood and Morton, and then BMK. Like the major Glasgow carpet firms it suffered badly from foreign imports in the 1960s and 70s. The much-reduced business was taken over by Stoddarts of Elderslie in 1992, and that firm, the last of its kind in Scotland, has moved its remaining business back to Kilmarnock.

**Board of Trustees for Manufactures and Fisheries** Founded belatedly in 1727 with money promised to Scotland in the 1707 Act of **Union** to support the development of manufacturing industry, especially linen, and fisheries. It inspected linen and stamped it if it was of appropriate quality, encouraged technical innovation by funding the immigration of foreign specialists and gave capital grants to help develop the capital-intensive parts of the industry, especially in the finishing trades such as bleaching. It also funded schools and awarded grants for innovations. By the mid nineteenth century businessmen in the linen trade had shaken off a supervision they no longer needed and the **British Fisheries Society** had taken over other aspects of its work.

**Boar of Badenoch** (Gaelic **An Torc**) One of two hog-backed hills above the Pass of **Drumochter** (739m/2425ft); the other is named the Sow of Atholl (Gaelic *Meall an Dòbhraichean* 'hill of the watercress') (803m/2635ft).

**boatbuilding** Mainly in wood, it was until the late 20th century a widespread and locally important Scottish industry. The largest customer was the fishing industry, much of which continued to prefer wooden boats to steel until the 1980s, but a variety of pleasure craft and ships' lifeboats was also made, especially on the **Clyde**. Latterly the largest centres were at **Buckie**, Macduff and **Arbroath**. The industry still survives, on a much-reduced scale, making small craft in wood and fibreglass.

**Boath Doocot** A 17th-century doocot on the site of a 12th-century castle motte, it overlooks the site of the Battle of

**Auldearn**, near **Nairn**. (In the care of the **National Trust for Scotland**.) Boath House was designed c.1830 by Archibald Simpson in neo-Greek style.

**Boat of Garten** (Gaelic **Coit Ghartain**) A holiday resort on the River **Spey** between **Aviemore** and **Grantown-on-Spey**, centred on **golf**, walking and skiing. It was called after the ferry that preceded its bridge. The village now has a station of the **Strathspey Steam Railway**. See also **Loch Garten**.

**'Bobbing John'** see **Mar, John Erskine, 11th Earl of**

**Bochanan, Dùghall** see **Buchanan, Dugald**

**Bodach, Am** Mountain, a **Munro** (1034m/3392ft) in Mamore Forest, 3km (2mi) north of **Kinlochleven**.

**Boddam** Small village on the northeast coast, 4km (2mi) south of **Peterhead**, with granite quarries. Boddam Power Station was set up in the 1970s with oil-fired generators and later gas was added. It is the largest supplier of power for the north of Scotland.

**Boece, Hector** or **Boethius** (c.1465–1536) Historian, b. Dundee. First Principal of King's College, **Aberdeen**, he wrote Latin lives of the bishops of Mortlach and Aberdeen, and his masterwork, also in Latin, the very unreliable *Chronicles of Scotland* (1526), translated by John **Bellenden** (1536).

**Bogle, George** (1746–81) Honourable East India Company servant, b. Bothwell, Lanarkshire. He went to India as a writer in the service of the Company, befriended by Warren Hastings, the first Governor General of British India. In 1774 he was sent from Calcutta as the first British envoy to the Panchen Lama, the second most important dignitary of Tibet. He established good relations with him, and had two daughters by a lady who may have been a niece of the Panchen Lama. At his premature death in Calcutta, she was provided for in his will as his widow. Friends brought the two girls back to Scotland and they married into local laird families in Ayrshire.

**Bonar Bridge** Village at the head of the **Dornoch Firth**, at the entrance to the Kyle of Sutherland. The original **Telford** bridge was built in 1811–12 and replaced the crossing at **Meikle Ferry**. The present elegant bridge was built in the 1970s.

**Bonawe Ironworks** (Gaelic **Bun Atha**) Ironworks of 1753 on the south shore of **Loch Etive** at **Taynuilt**, the best-preserved of its date in the UK, now in the care of **Historic Scotland**. The charcoal furnace took advantage of the substantial woods in the area at the time. The modern village of Bonawe is on the north side of the loch (near a later granite quarry).

**Bonchester Bridge** Small village near **Hawick**, with a substantial and complex fort on nearby Bonchester Hill, occupied over a long period from very early times till at least the 2nd century AD.

**bondager** In the **Lothians** and eastern **Borders**, a woman farm worker, once hired as part of a family unit. Her work at the various harvests was deemed to pay the rent of the house. Latterly bondager referred to a woman out-worker. Bondagers had distinctive clothes, particularly the hats designed to shield them from the dust of the fields.

**bonds of manrent** Undertakings by men of lesser status to adhere to a lord in return for protection. Such arrangements served to bolster the power and influence of lords, but could also provide a framework for peaceably settling disputes at a local level.

**Bone, Sir Muirhead** (1876–1953) Artist, b. Glasgow. Along with Sir David Young **Cameron** and James **McBey**, Bone is recognised as one of the most important British printmakers of the first part of the 20th century. He excelled as a draughtsman, specialising in complex architectural subjects, and produced perhaps his best work as an official artist during both world wars.

**Bo'ness** Once Borrowstounness, a town on the east coast of the Firth of **Forth**, it was one of the major sea ports of Scotland until the end of the 18th century, but declined with the development of **Grangemouth**. It had an iron-smelting works (Kinneil) and an important coal-mining industry. It has impressive warehouses and a working railway museum. One end of the **Antonine Wall** is at Bridgeness, nearby. Kinneil House, in the care of **Historic Scotland**, has 17th-century wall paintings. James **Watt** experimented on his steam engine in a workshop behind the house.

**Bonnie Dundee** see **Dundee, John Graham of Claverhouse**

**Bonnie Earl of Moray** see **Moray, James Stewart, Earl of**

**Bonnie Prince Charlie** See **Stewart, Prince Charles Edward**

**Bonnymuir** See **Baird, John**, and **Hardie, Andrew**

**Bonnyrigg** A 19th-century industrial, and former colliery village near **Edinburgh**.

**Book of Common Order** The service book adopted in 1562 by the newly formed **Church of Scotland**, later known as *Knox's Liturgy*. It was translated into Gaelic in 1567 by John **Carswell**, with significant changes reflecting the authority of the Earl of Argyll.

49

*Folio 16v from the* Book of Deer.

**Book of Deer** A 9th-century liturgical manuscript, written mainly in Latin and now in the library of Cambridge University, that contains St John's Gospel and parts of other Gospels. It is important for its **Gaelic** *notitiae* (notes), written in the 11th and 12th centuries, recording land grants which give an insight into law and society at the time. It was probably compiled at the Cistercian Deer Abbey, 16km (10mi) west of **Peterhead**, of which only ruins remain, in the care of **Historic Scotland**.

**Book of the Dean of Lismore** James Macgregor, Dean of Lismore, and his brother Duncan compiled this anthology of Gaelic poems (dating from the early 14th century to the first quarter of the 16th) between 1512 and 1542. Rediscovered in the 18th century, it showcases the wide range of early **Gaelic** verse, written in a spelling based on the **Scots** of its time.

**Books of Discipline** Two documents drawn up by the policy-makers of the **Reformation**. The *First Book* (1560) promulgated the constitution of the church, its financial structure and the funding of education and relief of the poor. The *Second Book* (1578) proposed the replacement of an episcopal system by a Presbyterian one.

**Boothby, Sir Robert John Graham, Lord** (1900–86) Politician, b. Edinburgh. Conservative MP for East Aberdeenshire 1924–58. From 1926–9 he was Parliamentary Private Secretary to Winston Churchill. During World War II he was forced to resign from parliament because of involvement in Czechoslovakia and he joined the RAF. From 1948–54 he was a member of the Council of United Europe. A prolific and candid commentator on public affairs, he caused scandal, not least by his long affair with Lady Dorothy Macmillan, wife of Sir Harold Macmillan, and by his friendship with the Kray twins.

**Borders** The area along the Scottish side of the Scottish-English border. During the later Middle Ages the area witnessed much Anglo-Scottish conflict, resulting in the development of a highly militarised society. Cattle raids and feuds were prevalent long after national war diminished, but the romanticised image of the **reiver** should be treated with caution. There is a strong **ballad** tradition, celebrating the area's violent past. Sir Walter **Scott**'s writings, powerful in creating regional myths, and his residence at **Abbotsford** helped to make the Borders one of the first large-scale tourist areas in Scotland. It is largely rural; the formerly strong textile industry has declined drastically in recent years. See also **Borders Region**, **Scottish Borders Council**.

**Borders Region** One of the 9 regions forming the upper tier of local government from 1975 to 1996, formed from the former counties of **Peeblesshire**, **Selkirkshire**, **Berwickshire**, **Roxburghshire** and part of **Midlothian**. It consisted of Berwickshire, Tweeddale, Roxburgh, and Ettrick and Lauderdale Districts; see maps on pp.394-5, **Scottish Borders Council** and **local government**.

**Border Television** see **Scottish Television**

**Bòrd na Gàidhlig (Alba) (The Gaelic Board (Scotland))** Government organisation set up in 2003 to oversee and stimulate **Gaelic** development in Scotland, by creating a National Plan for Gaelic and providing funds to initiate significant projects. It is based in **Inverness**.

**Boreraig** see **MacCrimmon**

**Boreray** (Gaelic **Borroraidh**) see **St Kilda**

**Borestone** see **Stirling**

**Borland, Christine** (1965– ) Artist, b. Darvel, Ayrshire. Recognised internationally for her art in a wide variety of media, which has progressed from an interest in forensics and criminology, to more recent work investigating human genetics. She was short-listed for the Turner Prize in 1997.

**Borrowstounness** see Bo'ness

**Borthwick Castle** Near Gorebridge, Midlothian, the largest and one of the least altered tower houses in Scotland, dating from 1430 and reoccupied in the 20th century. It is famous for the escape of the Earl of **Bothwell** and **Mary, Queen of Scots**, disguised as a boy, pursued there by Morton and his rebels after their runaway marriage in 1567. It is now a hotel.

**Boston, Thomas** (1676–1732) Theologian, b. Duns, Berwickshire. Son of a **Covenanting** minister, he became a minister in the **Cameronian** tradition. Of his large body of writing he is best remembered for *Human Nature in its Fourfold State* (1720).

**Boston, Thomas** (1713–67) Minister, b. Ettrick. A son of Thomas **Boston** (above), he followed his father into the ministry, but a call to **Jedburgh** in 1755 was prevented by the Crown, and he formed a separate congregation. He later became a co-founder of the **Relief Church**.

**Boswell, James** (1740–95) Lawyer and man of letters, b. Edinburgh. Characterised by his self-centredness, his womanising and his fascination with famous people (he managed to meet many, including Voltaire and Rousseau), he was also a remarkable writer and kept a secret, self-regarding diary, which was published only in the 20th century. He practised at the Scottish bar for many years, but spent considerable periods of time in London, particularly in the company of Samuel Johnson, whom he persuaded to accompany him to Scotland for the trip described in *Journal of a Tour to the Hebrides* (1785) and whose *Life* he published in 1791, often regarded as one of the great biographies of all time. The *Tour* and Boswell's diaries reveal a fierce pride in his Scottish heritage alongside a longing for the cosmopolitan attractions of London, to which he finally moved in 1786.

**Bothwell** Now a dormitory town for **Glasgow** and the **Lanarkshire** conurbation, in earlier times significant for the only bridge over the River **Clyde** besides Glasgow. This was the scene of the Battle of Bothwell Brig in 1679, when the troops of Monmouth and Claverhouse defeated the **Covenanters**. Bothwell Castle, though in ruins, is one of Scotland's largest, having been the English base in the west during the **Wars of Independence**. Finally recaptured by the Scots in 1337, it was owned by the Black Douglases until the 19th century, apart from a brief period when it was granted to Patrick Hepburn, Earl of Bothwell. In the care of **Historic Scotland**. The parish church incorporated the choir of a collegiate church.

**Bothwell, Francis Stewart, 5th Earl of** (1563–1612) Nephew of James, 4th Earl of **Bothwell**, he gained the earldom in 1581, and was related to the Earl of **Moray**. A loose cannon in political terms, he mounted challenges to **James VI**, even raiding the Palace of Holyroodhouse. Bothwell was also accused, and convicted, of witchcraft, but avoided serious penalty. After he joined forces with the Earl of Huntly the campaign became a rebellion and Bothwell was exiled in 1595.

**Bothwell, James Hepburn, 4th Earl of** (c.1535–78) Third husband of **Mary, Queen of Scots**. Earl of Bothwell and High Admiral from 1556, he supported **Mary of Guise**. Appointed a privy councillor by Mary, Queen of Scots he was swiftly imprisoned on suspicion of plotting to kidnap her, but was restored to favour after her marriage to **Darnley**. After Darnley's murder in 1567, which Bothwell probably arranged, and a trial that acquitted him, Bothwell 'kidnapped' Mary, now pregnant, and after a swift divorce from his first wife, married the Queen at Holyrood. Mary was almost immediately captured at **Carberry Hill**, and Bothwell fled, reaching Norway, where he was imprisoned. His marriage to Mary was annulled in 1570. Meanwhile Bothwell was imprisoned in Denmark, where he died insane.

**Bothwell Brig, Battle of** see **Bothwell**

**Bothwell Castle** see **Bothwell**

**bothy** A rough hut used for temporary accommodation by shepherds, salmon fishermen and mountaineers; also refers to living quarters for workmen, especially unmarried farm workers on east-coast farms, often a separate building in the farmyard. The word probably derives from Gaelic *bothan*, a hut. The term is also applied to buildings used by industrial workers to eat their meals. The songs of the Northeast farmworkers, adding greatly to the rich store of folksongs, are often known as bothy ballads.

**Bough, Sam** (1822–78) Artist, b. Carlisle, began his career as a scene painter, moving to Scotland and living in **Glasgow** before settling in **Edinburgh**. He excelled as a landscape artist, his early, more highly finished, topographical views giving way to a more fluid style as his interest grew in the atmospheric effects created by light and changing weather. Amongst his most impressive works are his paintings in oil and in watercolour (a medium in which he was particularly skilled) of the east-coast fishing villages, which he depicted under romantically lit skies.

**Bower, Walter** (c.1385–1449) Historian, b. Haddington, East Lothian. Abbot of **Inchcolm** from 1418, he continued and expanded John of **Fordun**'s Latin *Chronica Gentis Scotorum*, updating it from 1383 to 1437. The complete work, the *Scotichronicon*, is a magnificent source for the history of later medieval Scotland; it was published in the 1980s and 90s in a scholarly edition with English translations.

**Bowhill** Near **Selkirk**, the seat of the Dukes of Buccleuch, a plain classic mansion mainly by William **Burn** (1831), with a fine collection of furniture and paintings. (Open to the public.)

**Bowling** Near **Dumbarton**, the point where the **Forth and Clyde Canal** joins the River **Clyde**, once a centre of shipbuilding and distilling. Nearby is Dunglass Castle and a stretch of the **Antonine Wall**.

**Bowmore** Largest village on **Islay**, on the east shore of Loch Indall, established in the late 18th century. Its church, built at the same period, is distinctive for its round shape, said to prevent the devil from hiding in corners. Its distillery, founded in 1779, produces one of the great Islay malt whiskies. It has a visitor centre.

**Boyd, Mark Alexander** (1563–1601) Poet, soldier, traveller and physician to Henry IV of France. He wrote fine Latin verse, and the famous Scots sonnet, 'Fra bank to bank, fra wood to wood I rin'.

**Boyd, William** (1874–1962) Educationalist, b. Riccarton, Ayrshire. A graduate of **Glasgow University**, he founded the university's Education Department in 1907 and lectured there until 1945. He was an influential and radical figure in the reform of secondary education. His *History of Western Education* (1921) was an important academic study.

**Boyd, William** (1952– ) Novelist, born and brought up in West Africa of Scottish parents, he was educated at Gordonstoun, **Glasgow University** and Oxford. His novels have won many awards and prizes, notably *A Good Man in Africa* (1981), *An Ice-Cream War* (1982), *The New Confessions* (1987), *Brazzaville Beach* (1990) (which gained a Scottish Writer of the Year Award), *Armadillo* (1998) and *Any Human Heart* (2002). There are Scottish elements to be noted in many of his novels, whatever their location and subject.

**Boyd Orr, John, Lord** (1880–1971) Biologist, b. Kilmaurs, near Kilmarnock. First director of the United Nations Food and Agriculture Organization, he won the Nobel Peace Prize in 1949 for his achievements in fighting the problems of world food supply. His research pioneered studies in animal and human nutrition. He was the first director of the **Rowett Research Institute**.

**Boyle, Jimmy** (1944– ) Reformed criminal, now artist and writer, b. Gorbals, Glasgow. His youth was spent in remand homes and prison for a variety of crimes, and his later membership of a violent gang led to several charges of murder, on the third of which he was imprisoned in **Barlinnie**. A rehabilitation programme there led him to develop an interest in sculpture and writing. Since his release he has worked to help young offenders. His publications include the autobiographical *A Sense of Freedom* (1977) and a novel, *Hero of the Underworld* (1999).

**Boyle family** Artists, Mark Boyle (1934– ) b. Glasgow; Joan Hills (1936– ) b. Edinburgh; Sebastian (1962– ); Georgina (1964– ). From an early interest in theatre and Performance Art, Mark Boyle and Joan Hills, later helped by their children (working collectively as Boyle family) have developed an art that involves making replicas of randomly selected areas of the world's surface. Their aim is to produce work that shows the world as it is in reality, without any artistic interpretation.

**Boys' Brigade** Christian youth organisation founded in **Glasgow** in 1883 by Sir William Smith (1854–1914). It now has groups worldwide.

**Braco** Planned village between **Crieff** and **Dunblane**. Nearby is the **Ardoch Roman Camp**.

**Brady, Ian** (1938– ) Murderer, b. Glasgow. With Myra Hindley he tortured and murdered 5 children, burying most of them on Saddleworth Moor in the Pennines, which led to the label the 'Moors Murderers'.

**Braemar** (Gaelic **Braigh Mharr**) Popular **Deeside** holiday resort at the junction of the River Cluny with the **Dee**, in summer for the scenery, in winter for skiing. The annual Braemar Gathering dates in its present form from 1832, with royal patronage from 1848. The Invercauld Arms now covers the spot where the standard was raised by the Earl of **Mar** for James VIII in 1715. Braemar Castle, built in 1628 by the 7th Earl of Mar and later the home of the Farquharsons, was converted to a Hanoverian barracks in 1748. (Open to the public). There is a splendid episcopal church by Sir Ninian Comper (1899–1907).

**Braeriach** (Gaelic **Am Bràigh Riabhach**) Mountain in the **Cairngorms**, second of the region's 4 highest peaks, a plateau-topped **Munro** (1296m/4248ft).

**Braes** (Gaelic **a' Bhràigh**) District in the north of **Skye**, where a crofters' rebellion against the injustice of the **Clearances** culminated in 1882 in violent confrontation with police from **Glasgow**, often known as the Battle of the Braes. It was much publicised and thus a major factor in the setting up of an inquiry the following year, which eventually led to the Crofters' Act of 1886 and the setting up of the **Crofters' Commission**.

**Brahan Seer** (Gaelic **Coinneach Odhar**, 'sallow Kenneth') nicknames of Kenneth Mackenzie, a shadowy 17th-century figure of the **Inverness** area, employed by the Earl of Seaforth at Brahan Castle near **Dingwall**, he was famous for his second sight and oddly accurate prophecies (apparently including the coming of **railways** and the building of the **Caledonian Canal**). He came to an unpleasant end in a barrel of burning tar after revealing to Lady Seaforth that her husband was with another woman in Paris.

*James Braid, 5 times winner of the Open between 1901–10.*

**Braid, James** (1870–1950) Golfer, b. Earlsferry, Fife. An outstanding amateur player, he turned professional in 1893 and won the Open 5 times between 1901 and 1910. He later became a golf-course designer.

**Brander, Pass of** (Gaelic **Am Brannradh**) Pass between Ben **Cruachan** and **Loch Awe**, along a narrow arm of the loch where it flows into the River Awe, the scene of a failed ambush on **Robert I** in 1308.

**Branklyn Garden** Small garden in **Perth**, once described as the best garden under 2 acres in Europe, with fine collections of alpines, rhododendrons and herbaceous plants, developed by Dorothy and John Renton from 1922. (Bequeathed to the **National Trust for Scotland** in 1968).

**branks** Restrictive bridle for controlling livestock. Hence an iron headpiece used as an instrument of human punishment, it severely restricted movement and speech. More spiteful models included spikes which could pierce the tongue and cheeks if the victim moved.

**Branxholm Tower** Castle on the River **Teviot** near **Hawick**, seat of the Scotts of Buccleuch (and still owned by the Duke of Buccleuch). It was burned by the Earl of Northumberland in 1532, and after further damage was rebuilt as a mansion later that century. It features in Sir Walter **Scott**'s *Lay of the Last Minstrel*.

**Braveheart** Film on the life of Sir William **Wallace** (1995), with Mel Gibson as Wallace. Its historical inaccuaracies did nothing to detract from its immense popularity, and it proved a boost to the Scottish tourist trade and roused interest in Scottish history.

**Braw Lads** see **Galashiels**

**Braxfield, Robert Macqueen, Lord** (1722–99) Judge, b. Lanark. He became Lord Justice Clerk in 1778. Remembered for facility in the **Scots** tongue, his severity towards prisoners (he allegedly told a man he had sentenced to death that he would be 'nane the waur o' a hanging'), and as the model for Adam Weir in R L **Stevenson's** *Weir of Hermiston*.

**Breadalbane** (Gaelic **Bràghaid Alban**, upland of Alba) Large area of mountains and lochs in the central **Highlands**, bounded by **Atholl** in the north, **Strathearn** and Menteith to the south, and **Lochaber** to the west.

**Breadalbane, John Campbell, 1st Earl of** (1635–1717) Chief of the Campbells of Glenorchy, a wily politician who tried to bribe other Highland chiefs to persuade them to accept, as he had, or at least to stop opposing the accession of **William II and III** and Mary. As an old man his political disappointments made him a half-hearted supporter of the 1715 **Jacobite** Rising.

**Brechin** (pop. 7199) Hilly town, a former royal **burgh**, on the River South **Esk**, 12km (7mi) to the west of **Montrose**, with many buildings of the local red sandstone. In 1296, in nearby **Stracathro** churchyard, John **Balliol** formally renounced the Scottish crown to Edward I of England. Brechin Cathedral, 13th-14th century, restored 1898-1902, has an early round tower similar to the towers of refuge of Gaelic Ireland (in the care of **Historic Scotland**), and some important early sculpture. Brechin was an important centre of linen manufacture, and had 2 malt-whisky distilleries. Close by is Brechin Castle, remodelled as a symmetrical classical house by Alexander Edward 1696–1708 for the Earl of Panmure, now the home of the Earl of Dalhousie.

**Bremner, Billy** (1942-97) Footballer, b. Stirling. Played in midfield for Leeds United 1959-76, captaining them regularly, and managed them 1985-8. He won 54 caps for Scotland. Fiery and rebellious early in his career, he matured into a strong and reliable player. His statue stands at Leeds United's ground in Elland Road.

**Brendan, St** (486-578) Irish saint with a strong influence on the Gaelic church who visited the **Hebrides**, according to the Latin *Navigation of St Brendan*. It seems that he may have met St **Columba** on **Iona**.

**Bressay** Small island off Lerwick, **Shetland**, providing shelter to the harbour, and featuring a mysterious echoing cave. Gardie House was built in 1724.

**Brethren** Religious movement of largely independent groups with lay leadership and adherence to strict evangelical practices. In 1848 in England they divided into 'Open' and 'Exclusive', the former often known as Plymouth Brethren. There were groups in Scotland, both 'open' and 'close', from the 1830s and from the 1870s their influence grew in industrial and fishing communities, especially in the Northeast.

**Brewster, Sir David** (1781-1868) Physicist, b. Jedburgh. Although trained for the ministry, his interests lay in scientific pursuits and he invented the kaleidoscope in 1816; in 1818 he was awarded the Rumford medals for research into the polarisation of light. He also worked on improving light projection in **lighthouses**, and was an enthusiast for the new art of photography. He became Principal of the United College at St **Andrews University** in 1838 and Principal of **Edinburgh University** in 1859.

**brick and tile manufacture** Important in Scotland from the early to mid 19th century until the 1980s. Tiles were used primarily for field drainage, but also for roofing. During the 19th century bricks were used extensively for industrial building and, often behind stone facing, for house-building. After World War I most new housing was brick-built, leading to rapid expansion, but in the 1970s and 1980s demand collapsed just as swiftly.

**Bride** (or **Brigid, Brigit, Bridget**), **St** Name of several female saints of the early Gaelic church. Thought to have begun as a pagan goddess, St Brigid of Kildare was a 6th-century Irish saint, with a feast day on 1 February (known in Gaelic Scotland as *Là Féill Brighde*), but many others of the name are recorded, and celebrated in place-names: there are numerous Kilbrides in the west of Scotland.

**Bridei mac Beli** see **Brude**

**Bridei mac Máelchú** see **Brude**

**Bridge of Allan** (pop. 5046) Small town, now virtually a suburb of **Stirling**, with elegant 19th-century buildings dating from its period as a spa resort. The Strathallan Games are held here each summer. On its edge is the campus of **Stirling University**.

**Bridge of Earn** Village on the River **Earn**, 6km (4mi) south of **Perth**. It grew in the 19th century because of the mineral springs at nearby Pitkeathly. In World War II a hospital was built on the site of a World War I army camp and it continued in use until 1997, latterly much reduced in size.

**Bridge of Orchy** Village at the top of Glen Orchy, below **Beinn an Dothaidh** and **Beinn Dorainn**, with nearby a few remnants of the **Caledonian forest**, much having been cut down in Victorian times.

**Bridge of Weir** (pop. 4635) Commuter town to the west of **Paisley**, once famous for its cotton mills and later for its leather factories. The town is in 2 sections: Bridge of Weir proper and the more residential Ranfurly. Nearby is Quarriers' Village; see William **Quarrier**.

**Bridget** see **Bride**

**bridie** see **Forfar bridie**

**Bridie, James** (pen name of **O(sborne) H(enry) Mavor**) (1888–1951) Dramatist and doctor, b. Glasgow. A prolific writer and strong supporter of Scottish theatre; he helped to found the **Citizen's Theatre** in **Glasgow** in 1943. His plays still performed include *The Anatomist* (1931), about Dr Robert **Knox** and **Burke** and Hare, and *Dr Angelus* (1947).

**Brigadoon** Sentimental story of a Scottish village under a curse by which it only appears for one day in a century, made into a musical in the US in 1947 by Alan Jay Lerner and Frederick Loewe. Often regarded as a stereotype of romantic American views of Scotland. The name comes from the Brig o **Doon** in **Burns** country in Ayrshire.

**Brigid, Brigit** see **Bride**

**Brisbane, Sir Thomas** (1773-1860) Astronomer and soldier,

B

b. Largs. After a distinguished career in the army overseas he was Governor of New South Wales from 1821-5, where he catalogued over 7000 stars. Brisbane, capital of Queensland (once part of NSW), takes its name from him.

**British Aluminium Co Ltd** Company established in 1895-6 to make aluminium using the Heroult process, which required large quantities of electricity. The company's first works was at **Foyers**, on Loch Ness, and had its own hydroelectric plant. It closed in 1967. In 1907-9 they built a larger works at **Kinlochleven**, and in 1924-9 a third one at **Fort William**. At a time when electricity from the grid was cheap a fourth works was built, in 1968-71, at **Invergordon**, but rising prices caused its closure in 1981. Kinlochleven closed in about 2000, but energy from its power station is now transmitted by the grid to Fort William. The company also has a rolling mill in **Falkirk**, and had an alumina works in **Burntisland** (later Alcan).

**British Fisheries Society** A joint stock company founded in 1786 to promote communications and infrastructure of the fishing industry, it invested in fishing villages at **Ullapool**, **Tobermory**, Lochbay in **Skye** and Pulteneytown, now part of **Wick**. In the early 19th century it had advice and participation from Thomas **Telford**, notably in the building of the harbour at Pulteneytown. The society continued until 1893.

**British Linen Company** An association formed in 1746 to promote and finance the Scottish linen industry, it soon offered banking facilities at its offices throughout Scotland, becoming the true pioneer of branch banking, though the **Bank of Scotland** had made earlier experiments. Part of the Bank of Scotland since 1971.

**British Motor Corporation** Amalgamation of several English motor vehicle makers. In the early 1960s the corporation was persuaded by government to build a large truck and tractor plant at **Bathgate**, to alleviate the unemployment in the area caused by the closure of the shale-oil industry and the rapid contraction of the coal-mining industry. It was too far from markets and from components makers to be a success, and it closed in 1986.

*The Ring of Brodgar, Stenness, Orkney.*

**British Petroleum** Scotland's only surviving oil refinery, at **Grangemouth**, which was originally founded in 1919 by Scottish Oils to refine Persian crude oil produced by the Anglo-Persian Oil Co Ltd. The latter company, renamed the Anglo-Iranian Oil Co, greatly extended the Grangemouth refinery between 1949 and 1963, from 1954 under the name of British Petroleum, then owned by the British Government. The refinery still operates, and with its associated petrochemical plants, forms what is now Scotland's largest industrial complex.

**Broad Cairn** Mountain, a **Munro** (998m/3274ft) above **Loch Muick**, Aberdeenshire.

**Broadford** (Gaelic **An t-ath leathann**) Village on the Isle of **Skye**, west of **Kyleakin**. Nearby is the ruined farmhouse of Coirechatachan, where Dr Johnson much appreciated the hospitality.

**broch** Circular drystone tower or fortified residence, with hollow walls, peculiar to the Northern and Western Isles and the adjacent mainland. Most appear to date from the 1st century BC and the 1st and 2nd centuries AD. The largest and best preserved is at **Mousa**, Shetland. They were once, erroneously, thought to have been built by the **Picts**. See also **Glenelg**.

**Brodgar, Ring of** Large stone circle near Stenness, Orkney, with nearly half of its original 60 stones still standing. It is encompassed by a rock-cut ditch with two opposing entrance-causeways. Part of a ceremonial complex with the Stones of **Stenness** stone circle and **Maes Howe** burial mound. (In the care of **Historic Scotland**.)

*George Mackay Brown.*

**Brodick** (Gaelic **Breadhaig**, locally **Tràigh a' Chaisteil**) (pop. 621) Small town on east coast of the island of **Arran**, the landing place for the ferry from **Ardrossan**. Brodick Castle, on the site of a Viking stronghold, at one time a seat of the Dukes of Hamilton, dates from the 14th century, with later additions; it was remodelled by James Gillespie **Graham** 1844–46. The garden was restored and developed by the Duchess of Montrose after World War I with plants from southeast Asia and South America. Rhododendrons collected by George **Forrest**, George **Sherriff** and others are prominent, while the ancient walled garden contains roses, herbaceous plants and annuals. (In the care of the **National Trust for Scotland**.)

**Brodie, William** (d.1788) Edinburgh town councillor, Deacon of Wrights and Masons, and burglar, son of the important furniture maker Francis Brodie. After leading his double life successfully for some time he was betrayed by an accomplice over a burglary of the Excise Office in Chessel's Court, fled to Amsterdam, but was returned to **Edinburgh** for trial. Ironically he was executed on a gallows which he had designed. R L **Stevenson**'s *Dr Jekyll and Mr Hyde* was partially inspired by his story.

**Brodie Castle** Near **Forres**, seat since the 12th century of Brodie of Brodie, a massive tower house built in 1567, enlarged in the 17th century and again by William **Burn** in 1824, with a fine collection of paintings. (In the care of the **National Trust for Scotland**).

**Brookmyre, Christopher** (1968– ) Crime fiction writer,

b. Glasgow. After working as a journalist in London, Los Angeles and **Edinburgh**, he published *Quite Ugly One Morning* (1996), which won the First Blood Award as the best first crime novel of the year. He has followed this up with other novels, including *Boiling a Frog* (2000) and *A Big Boy Did It and Ran Away* (2001). His novels feature the disreputable investigator, Jack Parlabane.

**Brora** Village on the Dornoch Firth, now a small holiday resort with a good sandy beach, formerly boasting the most northerly coal mine in Scotland, worked intermittently from 1529 to 1974. Its woollen mill closed recently. Two substantial **brochs** stand on the outskirts. Just to the north is the Clynelish distillery, dating from the 19th century, but in a modern building from the 1960s.

**brose** A dish of oatmeal with boiling water or milk stirred into it, with the addition of salt and a little butter, long a staple food in Scotland. It was sometimes made with water from boiled vegetables (**kail** brose, **neep** brose), and it was also made with peasemeal (pease brose).

**Brough of Birsay** see **Birsay**

**Brougham, Henry, 1st Baron Brougham and Vaux** (1778–1868) Lawyer and politician, b. Edinburgh. In 1802 he helped found the *Edinburgh Review*. As Lord Chancellor, in Earl Grey's Whig ministry, he helped with the passage of the English and Scottish Reform Bills. He achieved a number of reforms, working for the abolition of slavery, and for national education. In English law he achieved changes to the law of libel and the law of evidence, and helped to establish the central criminal courts.

**Broughton** Village on Biggar Water, near **Peebles**. The elegant tower house Broughton Place was designed by Sir Basil Spence (1938) and built on the site of the home of Sir John **Murray**. There is a small museum devoted to John **Buchan**, whose father was minister here.

**Broughty Ferry** Suburb of **Dundee** with the benefit of a sandy beach, an independent **burgh** until 1913, and once the retreat of the 'jute princes' of the city. The 15th-century Broughty Castle, rebuilt as a coastal defence artillery fort in 1861, still dominates the area. In the care of **Historic Scotland**, it now houses a Dundee city museum of whaling and wildlife.

**Brown, George Douglas** (1869–1902) Novelist, b. Ochiltree, Ayrshire. He completed only one novel before his early death, *The House with the Green Shutters* (1901). Published under the name of 'George Douglas', it is a strongly realistic and perhaps partly autobiographical story which challenged the sentimental traditions of the 'Kailyard' school.

**Brown, George Mackay** (1921–96) Poet and author, b. Stromness, Orkney. Ill-health interfered with his education, though he eventually achieved a degree at **Edinburgh**, but his talent as a poet was supported by Edwin **Muir**. His poetry shows a strong appreciation of the landscape and traditions of **Orkney**, with religious and mystical overtones. His short stories and novels cover similar topics. His novels include *Greenvoe* (1972), *The Golden Bird* (1987), *Vinland* (1992), and his last novel, *Beside the Ocean of Time* (1996), was short-listed for the Booker Prize.

**Brown, Gordon** (1951– ) Politician, b. Edinburgh. After working as a lecturer and journalist he became Labour MP for Dunfermline East in 1983 and a close associate of John **Smith**. He became Chancellor of the Exchequer in 1997.

**Brown, John** (1722–87) Theologian, b. near **Abernethy**. Self-educated, he had many occupations, including spells as a pedlar and teacher, before becoming minister of **Haddington**, East Lothian and later Professor of Divinity at **Glasgow University**. His *Self-interpreting Bible* was very popular.

**Brown, John** see **Balmoral**

**Brown, John and Co Ltd**
Sheffield steelmakers, in the late 19th century suppliers of armour plate and steel forgings to the **Clydebank** shipbuilding yard of J and G Thomson, later owned by the Clydebank Engineering and Shipbuilding Co Ltd. When that firm failed in 1899, Browns took over the business. Under their management the yard developed steam turbine propulsion (the Brown Curtis turbine), and built a series of very large fast turbine-propelled vessels, including the *Lusitania*, *Aquitania*, *Empress of Britain*, *Queen Mary*, *Queen Elizabeth* and *Queen Elizabeth II*. The Clydebank yard became part of **Upper Clyde Shipbuilders** in 1968, and when that company was liquidated in 1971 it was sold for oil-rig building to the Marathon Manufacturing Co, an American concern.

**Browne, Ronnie** see **Corries**

**Broxburn** Town on the **Union Canal**, near **Livingston**, once an important centre of the **shale**-oil mining industry, and with some shale bings still remaining, but now generally light industrial.

**Bruar, Falls of** Three magnificent waterfalls on the Burn of Bruar as it descends to the River **Garry**, near **Blair Atholl**. Robert **Burns** wrote a 'Humble Petition of Bruar Water' to encourage the Duke of Atholl to afforest the banks.

**Bruce, Sir David** (1855–1931) Microbiologist, b. Australia of Scottish parents, brought up and educated in Scotland. Having previously identified the tsetse fly as the source of sleeping sickness, while serving in the Royal Army Medical Corps in World War I he discovered the bacteria *Brucella*, cause of brucellosis in cattle and undulant fever in humans.

**Bruce, Edward** (d.1318) Brother of **Robert I**, and an effective lieutenant in the **Wars of Independence**. From 1315 he led campaigns in Ireland which undermined the English lordship there and opened a second front in the Anglo-Scottish war.

*The* Queen Elizabeth *being launched from John Brown's shipyard on the Clyde, September 1938.*

English rule was lastingly disrupted, although Edward's aspiration to be king of Ireland was ended by his defeat and death near Dundalk.

**Bruce, Sir George, of Carnock** (d.1625) Mine-owner who pioneered the under-sea mining of coal at the Moat Pit, **Culross**, in the early 17th century. He also developed salt-boiling there, and the making of iron **girdles** for baking **scones, oatcakes** etc, a product of which Culross had a monopoly for many years. He lived in the 'Palace' in Culross, and his burial aisle is attached to the parish church.

**Bruce, George** (1909–2002). Poet, b. Fraserburgh. He worked as a teacher and a BBC arts producer. His collection includes *Sea Talk* (1944), *Landscapes and Figures* (1967) and *Pursuit: Poems 1986-98* (1999), which won the Saltire Book of the Year award. Though he wrote mainly in English, he made considerable and vigorous use of his native Northeast **Scots**. *Today Tomorrow: Collected Poems 1933-2000* appeared in 2001, with a cover by John **Bellany**, and *Through the Letterbox*, a book of haikus, illustrated by Elizabeth **Blackadder**, was published in 2003.

**Bruce, James** (1730–94) Explorer, b. Kinnaird, near Dundee. In 1768 he began his exploration of Abyssinia, reaching the source of the Blue Nile in 1770, which he believed to be the source of the Nile itself. His other findings, though largely accurate, were considered by his readers to be fictitious; when he wrote on his experiences, he was known as 'the Abyssinian liar'.

**Bruce, Marjory** (d.1316) Daughter of **Robert I**, married to Walter **Stewart**, mother of **Robert II**, the first of the long line of Stewart kings. She is buried in **Paisley** Abbey.

**Bruce, Robert** see **Robert I**

**Bruce, Sir William, of Kinross** (1630–1710) Architect, b. Blairhall, near Dunfermline. He introduced classical architecture to Scotland after 1660. As King's Surveyor and Master of Works he rebuilt the Palace of Holyroodhouse in **Edinburgh** 1671–9. He designed his own great residence of Kinross House and the original **Hopetoun House**.

**Bruce, The** see **Barbour, John**

**Brude** (d.693) (**Bridei mac Beli**) (d.693) A King of Picts, who in 685 defeated the Northumbrians and killed King Ecgfrith at Dunnichen Moss or **Nechtansmere** near Forfar. This encounter halted Anglian expansion beyond the River **Forth**.

**Brude (Bridei mac Máelchú)** (d. 584) A King of Picts, whom St **Columba** met in 565 at a fortress near **Inverness**.

**Bruichladdich** Village on **Islay**, on the west shore of Lochindaal.

Its independently-owned distillery, built in 1881, produces 2 single-malt whiskies, Bruichladdich and Port Charlotte.

**Brunanburgh, Battle of** A major invasion of southern Britain by the Scots, under **Constantine II**, and their British and Norse allies was defeated in 937 by Athelstan, King of Wessex. The latter had penetrated Scottish territory as far as Dunnottar near **Stonehaven** in 934; and the Brunanburgh campaign was a concerted effort to check the expansive energies of Wessex.

**Brunton, Mary** (née **Balfour**) (1778–1818) Novelist, b. Orkney. She married a minister and lived in Bolton and **Edinburgh**. She died in childbirth. Her novels, *Self-Control* (1811), *Discipline* (1814), and *Emmeline* (1819), reveal, as the titles suggest, strong moral and didactic purposes, but her skill as a storyteller is undoubted.

**Bryce, David** (1803–76) Major Victorian architect, b. Edinburgh. As a classicist he designed the former headquarters of the British Linen Bank and the remodelling of the **Bank of Scotland**, both in **Edinburgh**. Following William **Burn**, he was a major exponent of the Scottish **baronial** revival, designing Fettes College, Edinburgh, Edinburgh Royal Infirmary, Tollcross House, **Glasgow**, Torosay Castle on **Mull**, and many other country houses. He also designed churches, such as St George's West, Edinburgh and **Langholm** Parish.

**Bryden, Bill** (1942– ) Theatre and television director and playwright, b. Greenock. A director at the National Theatre 1975–85, he directed an applauded version of *The Mysteries*. Skilled at large-scale productions, he wrote and directed *The Ship* for Glasgow's European Year of Culture in 1990, and *The Big Picnic* (1994), depicting the story of a Scottish regiment in World War I. With his company Promenade Productions he has produced many plays for BBC Radio. For television he directed John **Byrne**'s *Tutti Frutti* (1987). His own plays include *Willie Rough* (1972) and *Benny Lynch* (1974).

**Buachaille Etive** (Gaelic **Buachaille Éite**) Buachaille Etive Mor (1022m/3353ft) and Buachaille Etive Beag (958m/3143ft), the 'great' and 'small herdsmen of Etive' are mountains, **Munros,** to the southeast of **Glencoe**.

**Buchan** The area of Aberdeenshire forming the northeast 'snout' of Scotland, between the Rivers **Deveron** and **Ythan**. For many years it was the feudal property of the earls of Buchan. It is a rich farming area, especially for beef cattle, and its largest towns, **Peterhead** and **Fraserburgh**, have historically been significant fishing ports. The Buchan dialect is often regarded as one of the strongest and most distinctive forms of **Scots** (see **language**).

**Buchan, Alexander** (1829–1907) Meteorologist, b. Kinnesswood, near Kinross. He developed the 'Buchan spells' theory (that the British climate has 'spells' of warm and cold weather related to times of the year).

**Buchan, Elizabeth** or **Elspeth**, née Simpson (1738–91) Religious leader, who founded a fanatical sect, known as Buchanites, in **Irvine** in 1784, declaring that she was the Woman of Revelations xii.

**Buchan, Isabella, Countess of** Wife of John Comyn, Earl of Buchan, she represented the traditional role of Earls of Fife (her brother was the current earl, absent at the court of Edward I) by enthroning **Robert I** at **Scone** in 1306. For this action Edward I had her imprisoned in a cage at **Berwick**.

**Buchan, John, 1st Baron Tweedsmuir** (1875–1940) Author and politician, b. Perth. Although having fingers in many pies – law, publishing, journalism – he produced 30 novels and numerous short stories. Intermittent illness gave him time for some of this writing. His first really successful novel was *The Thirty-Nine Steps* (1915), which introduced his occasional hero Richard Hannay, later appearing in *Greenmantle* (1916) and *The Island of Sheep* (1936). Much of his writing is in the thriller genre, though he also wrote historical novels such as *Witch Wood* (1927), but it is all characterised by a fine depiction of countryside and terrain and a strong imperialist attitude. Buchan also wrote biographies of Sir Walter **Scott** and the Marquis of **Montrose**. In 1935 he was appointed Governor-General of Canada. His time there inspired his last, and best, novel, *Sick Heart River* (1941). There is a museum to him in **Broughton**.

**Buchanan, Dugald** (Gaelic **Dùghall Bochanan**) (1716–68) Gaelic poet and evangelist, b. Strathyre, near **Callander**. A travelling preacher, he worked on the first Gaelic New Testament and wrote mainly religious poems, following, and sometimes translating, Isaac Watts.

**Buchanan, George** (c.1506–82) Humanist scholar and religious reformer, the foremost Latin poet and dramatist of his age, b. near Killearn in Stirlingshire, where there is a monument to him. Appointed tutor to the future Earl of Moray in 1537, he had to flee the country after charges of heresy were levelled against his satire on friars. In 1561 he returned to Scotland and became classical tutor to **Mary, Queen of Scots**, but was alienated from

her by the murder of **Darnley** in 1567, writing an accusatory pamphlet alleging her involvement. In that year he became moderator of the new General Assembly of the **Church of Scotland**. In his latter years he was tutor to the young **James VI**, and also wrote a large but inaccurate history of Scotland.

**Buchanan, Jack** (1891–1957) Actor and entertainer, b. Glasgow. He began his career with a song-and-dance routine on stage in 1912, and first appeared on film in 1917. His Broadway debut was in 1924, and he subsequently appeared in a number of Hollywood films, including *Brewster's Millions* (1935).

**Buchanan, Ken** (1945– ) Boxer, b. Edinburgh. British lightweight champion 1968–71 and 1973–4, European champion 1974–5 and World Boxing Association champion 1970–2, he retired in 1983.

**Buchanites** see **Buchan, Elizabeth**

**Buckhaven** see **Methil**

**Buckie** (pop. 8059) Large harbour town on the south coast of the Moray Firth, a former **burgh** and once a busy fishing port and centre of boatbuilding. It has a malt-**whisky** distillery, Inchgower.

**Buick, David Dunbar** (1854–1929) Inventor and motor engineer, b. Arbroath. Taken to the United States by his parents when he was 2, he became a resourceful inventor, but quickly became obsessed by the motor car. The Buick Manufacturing Company produced superb cars, but Buick's designs were not financially viable and he left in 1904. He died in poverty.

**Bullers of Buchan** Impressive chasm, probably a collapsed cave, on the coast near **Peterhead**, its name probably comes from the Norman-French 'to boil', referring to the wild rush of the sea through the archway.

**Bunessan** (Gaelic **Bun Easain**) Harbour village in the west of **Mull**, famous for its granite quarries, and a naval base during World War II.

**Bunnahabhainn** Distillery near Port Askaig on **Islay**, founded in 1881, producing a single malt **whisky**, which also contributes to the Famous Grouse blend.

**burgess oath** see **Presbyterian churches**

**burgh** A town with privileges of trade and self-government conferred by charter. Royal burghs derived their charters direct from the Crown, burghs of **regality** and burghs of **barony** from a feudal superior (lay or ecclesiastical). Royal burghs were a separate estate in the **Scottish Parliament**, and the burgh was a unit of **local government**, along with the counties. Their powers were increased by local-government reform acts of

1833, when 13 new parliamentary burghs were formed, and modified by later statutes. Burghs were abolished in the local-goverment reorganisation of 1975.

**Burghead** (pop. 1640) Small harbour town on the Moray Firth 12km (8mi) northwest of **Elgin**, with a massive promontory fort on the clifftop, an unusual medieval well and several carved Pictish stones in the visitor centre. It was an important grain-exporting port, and later a centre for the herring-fishing indus-try. On 11 January (the old New Year), in an ancient festival known as 'Burning the Clavie', the inhabitants of Burghead carry a half-barrel of burning tar through the town in a ceremony believed to bring good luck.

**Burghers** and **Anti-Burghers** see **Presbyterian churches**

**Burke, William** (1792–1829) Murderer, b. Ireland. With his accomplice William Hare (1790–c.1860) he murdered about 16 people in **Edinburgh** between 1827 and 1828 to provide a supply of corpses for the dissection room of anatomist Dr Robert **Knox**. After Hare turned King's Evidence (he apparently died in London, a beggar) Burke was convicted and sentenced to death. His pub-lic execution was followed by dissection, and his skeleton is still preserved in **Edinburgh University**.

**Burn, William** (1789–1870) Architect, b. Edinburgh. He gained experience with Sir Robert Smirke in London and became the foremost country-house specialist of his time. Among his Scottish buildings are the Edinburgh Academy, John Watson's Hospital (now the **Scottish National Gallery of Modern Art**), and St John's Episcopal Church, all in **Edinburgh**. He also restored several churches, including St Giles' Cathedral, Edinburgh and **Dornoch** Cathedral, and built many more. He moved to London in 1844, leaving his Scottish practice to David **Bryce**.

**Burnet, Edith** see **Hughes, Edith**

**Burnet, Gilbert** (1643–1715) Historian and churchman, b. Edinburgh. Professor of Divinity at **Glasgow University** from 1669, but moved to London in 1674. His antipathy to the policies of **James VII** and **II** sent him into exile on the Continent until William of Orange's arrival in 1688. He later became Bishop of Salisbury. His works include a history of the **Reformation** and the pithy *History of my Own Time* (1723).

**Burnet, Sir John James** (1857–1938) Architect, b. Glasgow. The first Scottish architect to train at the Ecole des Beaux Arts in Paris, he designed the Clyde Trust Building in **Glasgow**, studied in the United States and designed American-influenced office blocks and department stores in Glasgow, **Edinburgh** and

London. He was selected to design the Edward VII Galleries at the British Museum in 1903–14.

**Burns, Sir George** (1795-1890) Shipowner, b. Glasgow. With his brother James he developed steam navigation on the River **Clyde** and was one of the founders of the **Cunard** shipping line.

**Burns, Robert** see p.61

**Burns Federation** see **Robert Burns World Federation**

**Burnside, John** (1955– ) Poet, b. Dunfermline. He has published several collections, including *The Hoop* (1988), *The Myth of the Twin* (1994), *A Normal Skin* (1997) and *The Asylum Dance* (2000).

**Burnswark** Hill to the north of **Ecclefechan**, Dumfries-shire, with remains of a large Bronze Age fort, and of two Roman camps on its north and south flanks.

**Burntisland** (pop. 5667) Small town on the Firth of **Forth** in Fife, former royal **burgh** and a traditional ferry port for **Edinburgh**. With its excellent harbour, it was the ferry terminal for the world's first train ferry from Edinburgh from 1848 until the opening of the **Forth Bridge** in 1890. It is dominated by Rossend Castle, where Chastelard, French admirer of **Mary, Queen of Scots**, was arrested in 1563. The early post-**Reformation** church of St **Columba** is Dutch-inspired, square on plan, with a later octagonal tower. The **General Assembly** here proposed the making of the Authorised Version of the Bible, an idea carried out by **James VI**. Aluminium products, mainly aluminium oxide for use in the smelters at **Foyers**, **Kinlochleven** and **Fort William**, was produced here from 1917 till 2003.

**Burray** Offshore island of **Orkney**, north of South Ronaldsay and linked to it and Mainland by the **Churchill Barriers**. With sandy beaches, it is a haven for birds and seals, and an excellent place for diving in clear water.

**Burrell, Sir William** (1861–1958) Shipowner and art collector, b. Glasgow. He gifted his magnificent collection of some 9000 objects, including exceptional paintings, tapestries, furniture and stained glass, to the city of **Glasgow** in 1943. The collection was eventually opened to the public in a purpose-built gallery in Pollok Park in 1983.

**Burry Man** Centre of a peculiar festival held each August in **South Queensferry**, near Edinburgh. The Burry Man wears a costume covered with burrs, carries 2 staves, and moves among the public houses, drinking **whisky**, for the whole day. He was regarded as a scapegoat whose burrs are removing the evils from the village; similar festivals formerly took place in Northeast fishing villages.

*Portrait of Robert Burns, painted after the poet's death by Alexander Nasmyth (1758-1840).*

**Robert Burns** (1759–96) Poet, b. Alloway, near Ayr. Early influence of poetry, literature and folk tales may have led to Burns experimenting with poetry despite the humdrum employment of his youth. His family moved from their smallholding at Alloway to the nearby Mount Oliphant farm, and then to another at Lochlie, near **Tarbolton**. He and his brother Gilbert then tenanted Mossgeil near **Mauchline**. While there he fathered twins on Jean Armour, whom he married in 1788, after another pair of twins was born. Meanwhile he was enjoying the society of other women, a trait for which he became well known. His first book of poems, known as the Kilmarnock Edition, and including 'To a Mouse' and 'The Cotter's Saturday Night', was published in 1786, and was hugely successful; he was lionised in Edinburgh, but failed to find a patron. In 1787 he began editing *The Scots Musical Museum*, a major collection of songs which contained many of Burns's own, and also began his platonic relationship with Agnes MacLehose. In 1788 he took the tenancy of **Ellisand** Farm, near **Dumfries**. In 1789

he became an excise officer, combining this with farming (until 1791, when the strain on his health became too great and he gave up farming and moved to Dumfries) and poetry; *Tam O' Shanter* (1791), the humorously supernatural adventure of Tam on the way home from the tavern, is one of his finest poems. His health deteriorated, and he died from endocarditis, the effect of rheumatism on the heart.

Often regarded as Scotland's national poet, his poetry covers many themes; rural scenery: 'Ye banks and braes o' bonny Doon'; rural pleasures: 'My heart's in the Highlands'; love: 'Highland Mary', 'O, wert thou in the cauld blast', 'Ae fond kiss'; friendship: **'Auld Lang Syne'**; equality: **'A Man's a Man for a' that'**, which was sung at the opening of the new **Scottish Parliament** in 1999; and nationalism: 'It was a' for our rightfu' King', 'Scots, Wha Hae'. His song collections and adaptations made an important contribution to the preservation of Scotland's musical as well as literary heritage. His writing in Scots is much more vigorous than in English, and his skilled use of the language has influenced it to this day. His collection of bawdy verse, *The Merry Muses of Caledonia*, was privately printed for himself and his friends and not openly published in the UK and US until the 1960s.

There is an elaborate mausoleum at his burial place in Dumfries, and statues worldwide. His birthday, 25 January, is celebrated as Burns Night, with a dinner of **haggis** etc and speeches, songs and recitations; the main speech is known as the Immortal Memory. Many of these events are organised by Burns Clubs. His birthplace at **Alloway** is preserved, as are his houses in Mauchline and Dumfries.

*Tam O' Shanter pursued by Cutty Sark across the Brig o' Doon, by John Faed.*

B

*Matt Busby leads the Scotland team out to play England at Hampden, 1945.*

**Busby, Sir Matt** (1909–94) Footballer and manager, b. Bellshill, near Glasgow. His playing career with Manchester City (beginning at 17) and Liverpool gave little hint of the success he would enjoy as manager of Manchester United from 1945, though he did also play for Scotland. Many of the young United team, the 'Busby Babes', were killed in an air crash in Munich in 1958, but despite his own injuries he continued to build the team, achieving the European Championship in 1968. There is a sports centre named after him in his home town.

**Bush Estate** Near **Penicuik**, Midlothian, one of the locations of the Scottish Agricultural College, it also has the Edinburgh Centre for Rural Economy. There is also a veterinary training facility for **Edinburgh University**.

**Bute** (Gaelic **Bód**) (pop. 7149) A large island in the Firth of **Clyde** separated from the mainland by the narrow Kyles of Bute, a popular holiday destination, especially for Glasgow. Until 1975, it was the name of a county, which also included **Arran** and the **Cumbraes**; see map on p.395, **local government** and **Argyll and Bute**. The chief town is the port of **Rothesay**, with a handsome basically 13th-century castle, used as a royal residence by the earlier kings of Scotland; in the care of **Historic Scotland**. To the south is Mountstuart, the great Gothic palace built by the 3rd Marquess of Bute to designs by Robert Rowand **Anderson**, 1878–86, with a marble-lined chapel, the tower of which is modelled on that of Saragossa Cathedral; the landscaped estate contains an impressive

arboretum, rock garden, an enclosed garden with southern hemisphere plants, a kitchen garden with glasshouse containing rare shrubs. It is now open to the public. There were Early Christian monasteries at Kingarth and on the island of Inchmarnock off the west coast.

**Bute, John Stuart, 3rd Earl of** (1713–92) Politician. A strong influence on George III as Prince of Wales, and later as King, an unpopular Prime Minister in 1762, after the resignation of the elder Pitt. He helped to secure the necessary but unpopular Peace of Paris in 1763, which ended the Seven Years' War, but resigned in the face of hysterical and Scotophobic attacks. He was largely responsible for the foundation of the Royal Botanic Gardens, Kew.

**Butt of Lewis** see **Lewis**

**Byrne, John** (1940– ) Dramatist, set designer and artist, b. Paisley. His artistic work ranges from record sleeve design to major paintings like *National Velvet* and *The Studio*. He has designed for the shows *The Great Northern Welly Boot Show* and *The Cheviot, the Stag and the Black, Black Oil*. His plays, beginning with *Writer's Cramp* (1977) and including the Slab Boys trilogy (*The Slab Boys*, *Cuttin' a Rug* and *Still Life* (1978)), performed at the Traverse Theatre in **Edinburgh**, made his reputation within the new wave of Scots drama. He used the techniques of the popular theatre tradition to present comedies of working life. More recently, he has written for television and film, in *Tutti Frutti* (1987), *Your Cheatin' Heart* (1989) and *Colquhoun and MacBryde* (1992).

**Byron, George Gordon, 6th Baron** (1788–1824) Poet, b. London, he was one of the major British poets of his age. Half Scots by birth and spending 6 years before the age of 10 in Aberdeen, he was proud of his Scots heritage, although he never returned to Scotland, and sometimes bitterly attacked it in verse. He managed to combine a life of elegant debauchery with adventurous travel and prolific and talented writing, but overwhelming scandal drove him from England in 1816. He befriended Shelley and spent some years in Italy, but in 1823 became involved in the Greek Revolution against the Turks and died of fever at Missolonghi. His most famous poem is *Don Juan* (1819–24), which includes the lines: 'But I am half a Scot by birth, and bred/A whole one...' (10,17–18).

**Cadboll** see **Hilton of Cadboll**

**Cadell, Francis Campbell Boileau** (1883–1937) Artist, b. Edinburgh. Along with John D **Fergusson**, Leslie **Hunter** and Samuel **Peploe**, Cadell is known as one of the **Scottish Colourists**, whose interest and direct experience of French Impressionist and post-Impressionist painting greatly influenced the development of their own art. Cadell excelled in producing stylish portraits and interior scenes, frequently set in his own New Town studio, together with paintings of the island of **Iona**, which he visited regularly throughout his career.

**Cadell, Robert** (1788–1849) Publisher, b. Cockenzie, East Lothian. He was in partnership with Archibald **Constable** & Co. 1811–25, and went on to become sole publisher of Sir Walter **Scott**'s novels.

**Cadzow, Juliet** Actor. A versatile performer on stage, film and television, she had a small role in the cult film *The Wicker Man* (1973) and was also in *Venus Peter* (1988). Her TV performances have included appearances in leading soap operas, and in recent years she has found a new audience as a regular cast member in the children's TV programme *Balamory*.

**Caerlaverock Castle** Dramatic ruin to the southeast of Dumfries, with a three-sided curtain wall and moat. It was built by the Maxwells in the 13th century and besieged by Edward I of England in 1300. Later rebuilding includes an impressive Renaissance range, built in 1638. The castle appears in Sir Walter **Scott**'s *Guy Mannering*. In the care of **Historic Scotland**.

**Caird, Edward** (1835–1908) Philosopher and social reformer, b. Greenock. Professor of Moral Philosophy in **Glasgow University** from 1866. Liberal in politics and moderate in religion, he was a British idealist philosopher who popularised the work of Hegel and Cant in the anglophone world. He championed social concern, women's rights and educational extension in the west of Scotland. He was Master of Balliol College Oxford 1893–1907.

**cairn** A heap of stones, from Gaelic *càrn*, often one used as a waymark or as a memorial. Also found in names of hills; see below.

**Cairnbulg** see **Inverallochy**

**Cairness House** Neo-classical house near the northeast coast, inland from St Combs, designed by James **Playfair** in 1791–4 for Charles Gordon of Buthlaw, a sugar planter who married a Greek princess, who never lived there. It is strongly French-influenced in its large-scale geometric forms.

**Cairngorms** Mountain range extending over 777sq km (c.300sq mi), including 4 summits over 1200m. Cairn Gorm (1245m/4084ft) itself is a popular ski centre with a funicular railway which opened in 2001. The Cairngorm Nature Reserve is the largest in Britain. A type of rock crystal found here, Cairngorm stone, is used to decorate Highland jewellery and dirks. See also **Ben Macdui**, **Braeriach** and **Cairntoul**. The name Cairn Gorm is from Gaelic meaning 'the blue hill', but the Gaelic name of the range is Am Monadh Ruadh, meaning 'the red hill(s)'.

**Cairngorms National Park** Scotland's second national park, opened officially on 1 September 2003. At 3800sq km (1400sq mi) it is the UK's largest national park, stretching from **Grantown-on-Spey** in the north to the head of the Angus glens, and from Laggan and Dalwhinnie in the west to **Ballater** in the east.

**Cairn o Mount** Summit in Aberdeenshire (450m/1475ft). The road from **Fettercairn** to **Banchory** passes over the Cairn o Mount. One of the highest roads in Scotland, it is frequently closed in wintertime. A Bronze Age burial cairn stands by the road.

**Cairnpapple Hill** Important archaeological site near Torphichen, West Lothian, which was used for burials and cremations from about 3000 to 1400 BC. In the care of **Historic Scotland**.

**Cairnryan** Village on the eastern shore of Loch Ryan, near **Stranraer**. Once a fishing village, a large military port was built there during World War II; after the war it was used to load ships for dumping surplus ammunition in a deep part of the Irish Sea. It is now a ferry terminal for crossings to Larne in Northern Ireland. Formerly known as Macherie.

C

*The Standing Stones, Calanais, Lewis.*

**Cairntoul** (Gaelic **Càrn an t-Sabhail**) Mountain in the **Cairngorms**, third of the region's 4 highest peaks, a **Munro** (1293m/4241ft).

**Cairnwell** Mountain in **Glenshee**, a **Munro** (933m/3061ft) high. A chairlift to the summit is part of the Glenshee ski centre.

**Caithness** Former county at the northeast tip of mainland Scotland; in 1975 it became a district of **Highland Region** and it is now under **Highland Council**. See maps on pp.394-5 and **local government**. The main towns are **Wick** and **Thurso**, and most people are employed in agriculture or fishing, as well as a former experimental nuclear facility; see **Dounreay**. Though so far north, Caithness is lowland in character. The Sinclairs have been Earls of Caithness since the 15th century.

**Calanais (Callanish)** Highly impressive group of standing stones on **Lewis**, erected in the early 3rd millennium BC. Avenues of stones lead from the north and south to a central circle which surrounds a burial cairn. A nearby visitor centre helps to interpret one of the most complete prehistoric sites in Britain.

**Calder** see **East**, **Mid** and **West Calder**

**Calderpark** Near Glasgow, the location for Glasgow Zoo, which operated from 1947 to 2003. The estate had previously belonged to a succession of wealthy Glasgow merchants, and coal-mining had taken place there.

**Calderwood, David** (1575–1651) Minister at Crailing, **Roxburghshire**, from 1604–19 when, as a supporter of Presbyterianism, he was banished to Holland for refusing to accept **James VI**'s reactivation of the role of bishops in the Kirk.

He returned to Scotland after 1625 and began to compile his *History of the Church of Scotland*, published in 1678.

**Caledonia** Tacitus described the people living north of the **Forth–Clyde** as Caledonii in AD 80. They may have been a leading tribe in the north. A version of the name Caledonia has survived in the place-names **Schiehallion** and **Dunkeld**. It has been used in more modern times to refer to Scotland, from **Sir Walter Scott**'s 'O Caledonia! stern and wild', to Dougie **Maclean**'s popular song 'Caledonia', and has also begun to appear as a personal name. See **Calgacus**.

**Caledonian Canal** Scotland's longest canal stretches for 96km (60mi) from **Inverness** to **Corpach**, near **Fort William**. It incorporates **Loch Lochy**, **Loch Oich** and **Loch Ness**. Built by Thomas **Telford**, it was opened in 1822. Its main use is now recreational. It has 29 locks, including the remarkable Neptune's Staircase of 8 consecutive locks, at **Banavie** near Fort William. The top gates of each chamber form the lower gates of the next chamber. This is the longest flight of locks in Scotland, and raises the canal to 20m (65ft).

**Caledonian forest** About 4000 years ago most of Scotland was covered with trees: birch and pines in the higher land; oak and ash in the more fertile lowland areas; while willow and alder grew in the wetlands. The pasturage of goats and sheep, and more recently the increase in deer numbers, have decimated the forested areas, resulting in little regrowth. Only remnants of the ancient forest remain; the once-majestic pine forest is confined to 35 relict populations while the best of the oaklands are found on **Deeside**. Recently Forest Enterprise has been trying to increase these relict populations with exclusion fencing and replanting. Still the pine woods in particular are home to an amazing array of wild life – pine martens, wild cats, crested tits, the Scottish crossbill and **capercaillie** especially.

**Caledonian MacBrayne Ltd** (operating name **CalMac**) Company formed in 1973 by the nationalised Scottish Transport Group to bring together the Caledonian Steam Packet Co Ltd and David MacBrayne (1928) Ltd. The former operated steamer services, mainly on the **Clyde**, and the latter's ships served the western **Highlands** and Islands. Northlink Orkney and Shetland Ferries

Ltd, jointly owned by Caledonian MacBrayne and the **Royal Bank of Scotland**, now operates ferry services from **Scrabster** and **Aberdeen** to **Orkney** and **Shetland**.

**Caledonian Mercury** This newspaper, founded in 1720, was for a time printed, and later owned, by Thomas **Ruddiman**, which contributed to its **Jacobite** viewpoint. In 1867, now an evening paper produced 5 times weekly, it was bought by **The Scotsman**. See also **newspapers**, p.288.

**Calgacus** (fl. c.84 AD) Military leader. Tacitus describes him as the leader of the Caledonii at the battle of **Mons Graupius**, and attributes to him an inspiring address to his army.

**Calgary** Hamlet on **Mull** with a splendid sandy beach and a pier for shipping cattle. In the 19th century many people emigrated from Mull, and Calgary in Alberta, Canada, is named after this settlement. Calgary Castle, built in 1810, is let for self-catering.

**Callander** (pop. 2754) Town lying 29km (18mi) northwest of **Stirling**. Laid out as a planned village by the Duke of Perth but mainly developed by the Commissioners for Forfeited Estates, it became a thriving Victorian tourist resort and remains a popular base for exploring the **Trossachs**. It featured as Tannochbrae in the television series *Dr Finlay's Casebook* in the 1960s.

**Callanish** see **Calanais**

**Callendar House** Mansion in **Falkirk** incorporating a 15th-century tower house which was remodelled as a French chateau by Maitland **Wardrop** in 1869–77. It belonged to the Livingstones, who became Earls of Callendar, and later to the Forbes family. It is now run by the local council as a museum and history research centre.

**Callendar Park** Callendar Park is without doubt 'the jewel in the crown' of the parks within the **Falkirk** district, covering an area of over 69 hectares (170 acres). It is renowned for its beautiful spring displays of daffodils, its spectacular early summer shows of rhododendrons and azaleas and its autumn presentation of nature's artistry in shades of crimson, brown, russet and gold. Centrepiece of the park is the magnificent chateau-style **Callendar House** museum.

**CalMac** see **Caledonian MacBrayne**

**Calvine** Village near **Blair Atholl**, by the River **Garry**.

**camanachd** see **shinty**

**Cambuskenneth Abbey** Near **Stirling**, founded by **David I** for the Augustinians c.1140. **James III** and his wife Margaret of Denmark are buried here. A freestanding tower, dating from the 13th or 14th centuries, is all that remains of what was once one of their richest foundations; in the care of **Historic Scotland**.

**Cambuslang** Now a suburb of **Glasgow**, east of **Rutherglen**, it grew up around the coal, iron and textile industries. In 1742 a large-scale evangelical religious revival took place here, attracting national attention.

**Camelon** Suburb to the west of **Falkirk**, which has bus-building on a major scale. A station on the **Edinburgh-Stirling** railway has recently been reopened. It is the site of a Roman fort.

**Cameron, Sir Alan, of Erracht** (1753–1828) Soldier, b. Erracht, near **Fort William**. After taking part in the War of the American Revolution, in 1793 he raised the 79th Highlanders (later the **Queen's Own Cameron Highlanders**). He also served in the Netherlands, the West Indies and the Iberian Peninsula.

**Cameron, Dr Archibald** (1707–53) Doctor. The younger brother of Donald **Cameron** of Lochiel, he took part in the 1745 **Jacobite Rising**. He was involved in the Elibank Plot, an attempt in the early 1750s to restore the Stewarts to the throne. He was captured on the shores of **Loch Katrine**, and was hanged, the last Jacobite to be executed for treason.

**Cameron, Charles** (Karl Karlovich) (1743–1812) Architect. Little is known of his early life other than his studies of ancient

*The Caledonian Canal.*

monuments in Rome, perhaps as a protégé of Lord **Bute**, which produced the book, *Roman Thermae* (1772). In 1779 he accepted an invitation from the Empress Catherine the Great to move to Russia, where he was the architect of major buildings in St Petersburg, including Tsarskoe Selo and the Pavlovsk, and contributed greatly to the classical style of the then Russian capital. He was dismissed in 1796, but continued to live and work successfully in Russia until his death.

**Cameron, Sir David Young** (1865–1945) Artist, b. Glasgow. Known principally for his landscape paintings of Scotland and France, Cameron was also a prolific print-maker, who, along with **Bone**, **McBey** and **Strang**, was one of the most important figures in the revival of interest in British print-making in the early 20th century.

**Cameron, Donald, Younger of Lochiel** (c.1700–48) Acting chief of the Clan Cameron. Known as 'the Gentle Lochiel', he was initially reluctant to join the 1745 **Jacobite** Rising, concerned by the lack of French support. He nevertheless led his clan to follow Prince Charles Edward **Stewart**, and was wounded at **Culloden**. He died in exile, a colonel in the French army.

**Cameron, Donald** (1810–68) Piper, b. Contin, Ross-shire. With his brother Alexander and sons Colin, Alexander and Keith he made up the Cameron School of Piping. Taught by John and Angus **MacKay** and John Ban **MacKenzie**, he won many awards.

**Cameron, Richard** see **Cameronians**

**Cameronbridge** Very large distillery in **Fife**, at Windygates, to the east of **Leven**, founded in 1824. As well as large quantities of grain **whisky**, it also produces gin and vodka and other spirits.

**Cameron Highlanders** see **Queen's Own Cameron Highlanders**

**Cameronian Regiment** Had its origins in the 26th Regiment, raised in 1689 from among the **Cameronians**, winning its first victory, defending **Dunkeld** against **Jacobite** forces, in 1690. They continued some Cameronian customs, such as appointing a **Kirk** elder to every company, and posting armed sentries outside when attending church services. In 1881 the regiment merged with the 90th (Perthshire Light Infantry) and were renamed the Cameronians (Scottish Rifles). They won 113 battle honours through World Wars I and II, and disbanded in 1968.

**Cameronians** Supporters of Richard Cameron (1648–80), an extreme Covenanting minister. They refused to accept the 1689 settlement of the church and later became the Reformed Presbyterian Church. Many of the congregations became part of the **Free Church** in 1955, but there are still congregations in **Airdrie**, **Stranraer** and **Wishaw**. See also **Presbyterian Churches**, **Covenanters**.

**Campaign for a Scottish Assembly,** later **Campaign for a Scottish Parliament** Body set up in 1980 to coordinate moves towards home rule for Scotland. In 1988 it published the **Claim of Right**, and it recommended the setting up of the **Scottish Constitutional Convention**. See **Scottish Parliament**, pp.340-1.

**Campbell, Alasdair** (**Caimbeul, Alasdair**) Gaelic writer, b. Ness, Lewis. Author of short stories and novels, including *Am Fear Meadhanach* (*The Middling Man*). He also wrote *The Ness Man* in English.

**Campbell, Archibald, of Kilberry** (1877–1963) Piper, b. Kilberry, Argyll. His teachers included John MacDougall **Gillies**, John **MacColl**, John **MacDonald**. He was one of the founders of the **Piobaireachd Society** and editor of Piobaireachd Society books 1 to 8. He wrote the *Kilberry Book of Ceol Mor* (1948). He was a judge of piping and an authority on pipe music.

**Campbell, Colin, of Glenure** see **Appin murder**

**Campbell, Colin** (1679–1726) Architect, b. near Forres, Morayshire. He played an important role in the introduction of Palladian architecture in Britain and his 3-volume *Vitruvius Britannicus* (1712, 1718 and 1725) is a key text in the process. His buildings include the Rolls House and Burlington House in London, and Mereworth Castle, Kent (based on Palladio's Villa Capri, near Vicenza).

**Campbell, Sir Colin, Lord Clyde** (1792–1863) Soldier, b. Glasgow. Rose to prominence as commander of the Highland Brigade in the Crimea, where he took a distinguished part in the British victory at Balaclava. He was also the leading British commander during the Indian Mutiny of 1857.

**Campbell, Donald** (1940– ) Dramatist and poet, b. Wick. His plays, *The Jesuit* (1976), *Somerville the Soldier* (1978) and *The Widows of Clyth* (1979), established him as one of the leaders of the new wave of Scottish theatre in the 1970s and 80s.

**Campbell, Duncan, of Glenorchy** (c.1553–1631) Known as 'Black Duncan of the Seven Castles', he significantly expanded the family's territory. His castles included, **Kilchurn** and Balloch (later **Taymouth**), and he built those of Achallader, **Barcaldine**, Edinample, **Finlarig** and Loch Dochart.

**Campbell, John** see **Breadalbane, John Campbell, 1st Earl of**

**Campbell, John** see **Argyll, John Campbell, 2nd Earl of**

**Campbell, John Francis** (Iain Og Ile) (1822–85) Folklorist, from Islay. He collected immense amounts of **Gaelic** literature, customs and folklore. Some of this was published in works including *Popular Tales of the West Highlands* (1860–2) and *Leabhar na Feinne* (1872). Much more remains in manuscript form in the **National Library of Scotland**, along with journals and sketch-books from his travels in Scandinavia.

**Campbell, John Lorne** (1906–96) **Gaelic** scholar and folklorist. He and his wife Margaret Fay Shaw amassed a huge collection of manuscripts, sound and film recordings of Gaelic oral tradition and the Hebridean way of life. His numerous publications include *Stories from South Uist* (1961) and *Songs Remembered in Exile* (1990). See also **Canna**, which he owned and where he lived for many years.

*Campbeltown, Kintyre.*

**Campbell, John McLeod** (1800–72) Theologian, b. Kilninver, Argyll. Minister at **Rhu**, Dunbartonshire, he caused controversy by his preaching on the universality of atonement and was deposed by the General Assembly of the **Church of Scotland** in 1831. He continued to preach, but without joining any other church. His best-known work is *The Nature of Atonement* (1856).

**Campbell, Nicky** (1962– ) Radio and television presenter, b. Edinburgh. After hosting music and discussion shows on BBC Radio 1 from 1987, he moved in 1997 to present current affairs programmes on Radio Five Live. Television credits have included *Wheel of Fortune* and *Watchdog*.

**Campbell, Norman** (Caimbeul, Tormod) Gaelic writer, b. Ness, Lewis. Author of short stories and novels, most notably his black comedy *Deireadh an Fhoghair* (The End of Autumn) about a Gaelic community in terminal decline.

**Campbell, Steven** (1953– ) Artist, b. Glasgow. Along with Ken **Currie**, Peter **Howson** and others, he first came to attention in the mid 1980s as part of a group whose large-scale figurative paintings earned them the name of the New **Glasgow Boys**. His paintings continue to be characterised by their highly personal symbolism and use of human figures in fantastical situations.

**Campbell, Thomas** (1777–1844) Poet, b. Glasgow. He lived mainly in London from 1803, and is particularly remembered for his war poems, which include 'Ye Mariners of England', 'Hohenlinden' and 'The Battle of the Baltic'. He also contributed to newspapers and edited *New Monthly Review* 1820–31. He was involved in the establishment of University College London.

**Campbell-Bannerman, Sir Henry** (1836–1908) Politician, b. Glasgow. A wealthy businessman, he became Liberal MP for **Stirling** in 1868, leader of the Liberal Party in 1899, and was Prime Minister from 1905. He was an ardent supporter of Free Trade and an opponent of the Boer War. Ill health forced his resignation shortly before his death.

**Campbeltown** (pop. 5144) Town to the south of the **Kintyre** peninsula, established in 1607 by the 7th Earl of **Argyll**. The Campbeltown Cross, used as a market cross, dates from 1380. There were once 34 **whisky** distilleries here, along with a flourishing **fishing** industry, but both industries have declined. Of the distilleries, **Springbank** survives; its owners, J & A Mitchell, opened the rebuilt Glengyle Distillery in 2004. A small coalfield existed to the west, worked from the early 19th century to the 1950s. A ferry service to Ballycastle in Northern Ireland has operated intermittently.

**Camperdown** see **Dundee**, p.120

**Campsie Fells** Range of hills in the **Central Lowlands**, to the north of **Glasgow**, formed on ancient volcanic rocks, popular with walkers looking for steep slopes close to the city. The highest point is the Earl's Seat (578m/1897ft). The highest road running across the area is known as the Crow Road.

*Capercaillie.*

**Campvere** see **staple**

**Candida Casa** see **Whithorn**

**Candlemas** 2 February, one of the Scottish **term days**. It was used as the name for the spring term in some of the Scottish universities. The Christian festival on that date celebrates the purification of the Virgin Mary 40 days after the birth of Christ.

**Canisp** Mountain near **Lochinver**, within the Glencanisp Forest, 846m (2775ft) high.

**Canmore** see **Malcolm III**

**Canna** (pop. 6) Island in the Inner **Hebrides**, northwest of **Rum**. It was an early Christian settlement, and remains of a Celtic nunnery can be seen. Devastating **clearances** took place here in the 19th century. In 1938 John Lorne **Campbell** bought the island, and he and his wife Margaret Fay Shaw lived in Canna House. They handed the island over to the **National Trust for Scotland** in 1981. Plans are underway to enable wider access to Canna House and its tremendous Gaelic resources.

**canntaireachd** Gaelic term (pronounced approximately '**kown-tarackhk**) for the chanting of **bagpipe** music in syllables, varying in different piping traditions, generally with the vowels representing melody and the consonants the grace-notes; also refers to a written representation of this.

**Cannich** Village southwest of **Beauly**, where the rivers Cannich

and Glass meet. As the only village in this popular hillwalking area, it is sometimes used as a base by walkers. Fasnakyle hydroelectric power station is nearby.

**Canonbie** Village on the River **Esk**, 9km (6mi) south of **Langholm**. Just 5km (3mi) from the English border, it was in the heart of the **Debatable Land** which both English and Scots monarchs found hard to govern. Johnnie Armstrong's **Gilnockie Tower**, recently restored, is nearby.

**Canongate** see **Edinburgh**, pp.130-3

**Caol Ila** Distillery near Port Askaig on **Islay**, established in 1846. As well as producing a single malt, it also contributes to blends. The name means 'Sound of Islay'.

**Capella Nova** Vocal ensemble, formed in 1982 in Glasgow by Alan and Rebecca Tavener. It specialises in early and contemporary music, including early music by Robert **Carver** and David Peebles, and contemporary works by James **MacMillan** and John Tavener. The group commissions new works from Scottish composers.

**capercaillie** or **capercailzie** Scots name for the wood grouse, a large bird of the grouse family, from Gaelic *capull coille* (horse of the wood). It became extinct in Scotland in the 18th century but was reintroduced in the early 19th; it is once more under threat.

**Capercaillie** Celtic band founded in 1984 by Donald Shaw, accordionist. It also includes Karen Matheson, considered to be one of the best Gaelic singers of her time, Charlie McKerron, fiddler, and Manus Lunny from Donegal.

**Cape Wrath** Most northwesterly point of the British mainland, with a **lighthouse** erected in 1828. Rugged cliffs and stormy seas make this a spectacular location. Much of the area has been designated a Site of Special Scientific Interest to protect the birds and plant life. The point can be reached from **Durness** by ferry and minibus.

**Capper, Stewart Henbest** (1855-1925) Architect, teacher and linguist, b. London. He studied in Heidelberg and the Ecole des Beaux Arts, Paris. He was architect for Patrick **Geddes** in the Royal Mile, **Edinburgh**, designing the brilliantly picturesque Ramsay Garden (1892). He was Professor of Architecture at McGill, Montreal (1896-1903) and at Manchester (1903-12). He spent World War I in Egypt and when he became unfit for military service he became first a military censor, and later censor to the Egyptian Ministry of the Interior.

**Carberry Hill** Near **Inveresk**, Midlothian, the site of the surrender of **Mary, Queen of Scots**, to the rebel lords on 15 June 1567. No battle took place.

**Carbisdale** Near **Bonar Bridge**, the site of a battle on 27 April 1650 between **Montrose**, fighting for **Charles II**, and the **Covenanters**. Montrose was defeated, and soon afterwards captured and executed. Carbisdale Castle, nearby, was built for the Dowager Duchess of Sutherland 1910–11, and is now a Youth Hostel.

**Cardean** see **Meigle**

**Cardenden** (pop. 4946) Small Fife town 7km (4mi) northeast of **Cowdenbeath**. It flourished in the 19th century with the coming of the railway and the expansion of coal mining. The closure of the pits in the 1960s brought much unemployment.

**Cardross** Village on the Firth of **Clyde** 5km (3mi) northwest of **Dumbarton**. **Robert I** died at Cardross in 1329, but the medieval village was much closer to Dumbarton. There was a Roman Catholic seminary here (moved from **Bearsden** in 1946), and a distinguished new building was built here in the 1960s, now already a ruin after the closure of the college. There are plans to restore it and to find a new use for it.

**Carfin** Former mining village 3km (2mi) northeast of **Motherwell**. The Carfin Grotto was created in 1922 by a group of unemployed Catholic miners as a copy of the shrine of Our Lady of Lourdes. Nearby is the Carfin Pilgrimage Centre, giving the history of pilgrimage, especially in Scotland. There is also a memorial to the victims of the Irish potato famine.

**Carfrae, John Alexander** (1868–1947) Architect b. Edinburgh. He was an innovative freestyle designer initially of the Norman Shaw school who designed Boroughmuir School (later James Gillespie's School) (1902), the Scandinavian-inspired Drummond Street School (1905) and the highly original second Boroughmuir School (1911), all in **Edinburgh**.

**Cargill, Donald** (c.1627–81) Covenanting minister, b. Rattray, Perthshire. Minister of the Barony Church, **Glasgow**, from 1655, he was ejected in 1662 because of his opposition to episcopacy. He became a field preacher and was wounded at the Battle of **Bothwell** Brig in 1679. After a brief spell in Holland, he joined Richard **Cameron**. At a meeting at Torwood, near **Stirling**, he publicly excommunicated

Charles II, and was later captured and executed for treason.

**Carham, Battle of** 1018. **Malcolm II**, assisted by Owen, King of **Strathclyde**, defeated the Northumbrians on the **Tweed** near Roxburgh and brought **Lothian** into the kingdom of the Scots.

**Carlabhagh** see **Carloway**

**Carlingwark Loch** Near Castle Douglas. Iron Age **crannogs**, or artificial island dwellings, were built in the loch. In the 18th and 19th centuries, the loch was dredged to yield marl, used as a substitute for lime in agriculture.

**Carlops** Village south of **Penicuik**, at the foot of the **Pentland Hills**. It grew up in the 18th century around the handloom weaving industry, and is now a conservation village. Witches were said to leap between 2 rocks on the edge of the village, giving it its name 'carlin's loup' or witch's leap.

**Carloway** (Gaelic **Carlabhagh**) Village on the west side of **Lewis** which includes a group of restored traditional **black houses** at Gearannan. Dun Carloway is a well-preserved example of an Iron Age **broch**. The double wall remains, showing how a stone staircase linked the different galleries. In the care of **Historic Scotland**, it has a visitor centre.

**Carluke** (pop. 13,454) Town near **Lanark**, a **burgh** since 1662. Its expansion in the 19th century was largely built around mining, brick- and tile-works and the coming of the railway. Carluke lies in a fertile fruit growing area, and a jam-making factory has been a major employer since the 1860s. It is now mainly a dormitory town.

*Dun Carloway Broch, Lewis.*

*Robert Carlyle.*

**Carlyle, Alexander 'Jupiter'** (1722–1805) Minister, b. **Prestonpans**. He was minister of **Inveresk** from 1746, and was a leader of the **Moderates** in the **Church of Scotland**. His *Autobiography*, published in 1860, gives an insight into **Enlightenment** society. He was nicknamed 'Jupiter' because of his impressive, handsome appearance.

**Carlyle, Jane Welsh** (1801–66) Writer, b. Haddington (where her childhood home is now a museum). Married Thomas **Carlyle** in 1826 and lived in London from 1834. Her home was the centre of literary society, and this is vividly portrayed in her letters, published in 1883.

**Carlyle, Robert** (1961– ) Actor, b. Glasgow. His films include *Trainspotting* (1996), *The Full Monty* (1997) and *The World is Not Enough* (1999); he has also starred in television shows such as *Hamish Macbeth* and *Looking After Jo-Jo.*

**Carlyle, Thomas** (1795–1881) Writer, b. Ecclefechan, Dumfriesshire. Married Jane Welsh (**Carlyle**) in 1826. After some years in **Edinburgh** and at Craigenputtock, near **Dumfries**, they moved to London in 1834. He became one of the most influential writers of his age, and his numerous publications include translations of German literature, as well as *Sartor Resartus* (1833–4), *The French Revolution* (1837), and *Frederick the Great* (1858–65).

**Carmichael, Alexander** (1832–1912) Folklorist, b. Lismore. He made extensive collections of Gaelic folklore and literature, including many prayers, blessings and charms. These were published in 6 volumes as *Carmina Gadelica – hymns and incantations ... orally collected in the Highlands and Islands of Scotland.* Vols 1 and 2 were published in 1900, Vol 3 in 1940, Vol 4 in 1941, Vol 5 in 1954 and Vol 6 (indexes) in 1971.

**càrn** see **cairn**

**Carnasserie Castle** see **Carswell, John**

**Carnegie, Andrew** (1835–1919) Industrialist, b. Dunfermline. He emigrated with his family to Pittsburgh in 1848. Starting work aged 13, he made his fortune in railroads, iron and steel. He gave away over £70,000,000 on philanthropic initiatives, especially libraries and trusts, including the Carnegie Trust for the Universities of Scotland, the Carnegie UK Trust (helping community development, especially rural initiatives and young people) and the Carnegie **Dunfermline** Trust (for the benefit of its citizens). His home in Dunfermline is now a museum. He bought **Skibo Castle** in 1898.

**Carn Eighe** see **Mam Sodhail**

**Carnoustie** (pop. 10,561) Popular dormitory town and coastal holiday resort south of **Arbroath**, with a championship golf course. The Open Championship was held here in 1999 for the first time since 1975. It was originally an industrial town, with linen mills, a foundry, engineering works and a fertiliser factory.

**Carnwath** Village near **Lanark** which became a **burgh** of barony in 1451. The castle motte was built by the Somervilles, landowners here from 1140. In the 17th century the land passed to the Lockharts of Lee. The north aisle of the 15th-century collegiate church survives.

**Caroline Park** see **Granton**

**Carradale** Fishing village and tourist resort north of **Campbeltown**, on the Kilbrannan Sound. Carradale House, built in 1844, was the home of Naomi **Mitchison** from 1937 to 1999. A memorial in the harbour commemorates the crew of the Carradale-based fishing vessel *Antares*, which was lost in 1990; it was salvaged and is now in the Scottish Maritime Museum in **Irvine**.

**Carrbridge** Village 37km (23mi) southeast of **Inverness**. It takes its name from the much-photographed packhorse bridge over the River Dulnain, dating from 1711. Now bypassed by the A9, the village still attracts tourists, principally to the Landmark Forest Heritage Park.

**Carrick** Area of southern **Ayrshire**, south of the River Doon. The title Earl of Carrick, once held by the Bruces through the mother of **Robert I**, has been given to the heir to the throne since the late 14th century.

**Carron Ironworks** Near **Falkirk**, founded in 1759 by Samuel Garbett, John Roebuck and William Cadell. The company was the first ironworks in Scotland to smelt **iron** using coke rather than charcoal, necessitating large supplies of **coal**. This large-scale company was hugely successful until the mid 20th century; only a fragment remains. A much-used short, light but heavy-calibre cannon produced here was known as the 'carronade'. Many of the tunnel-lining segments of the London Underground were cast at Carron.

**Carse of Gowrie** Area of Perthshire which lies south of the **Sidlaw** Hills and north of the River **Tay**, and includes Errol, Glencarse and St Madoes. The clay farmland is flat and fertile; drainage was begun by the Cistercians in the 15th century, but was completely successful only after the insertion of tile drains by early 19th-century **Improvers**.

**Carse of Stirling** Fertile, flat valley of the River **Forth** which lies around and to the west of **Stirling**. Until the 19th century it was a bog, hence the pivotal importance of Stirling and its bridge.

**Carstairs** Village near **Lanark**, known since the 19th century as a railway junction where lines from **Edinburgh** and **Glasgow** meet. Scotland's only secure psychiatric hospital was opened here in 1948 as the State Institution for Mental Defectives, now known as the State Hospital.

**Carstares, William** (1649–1715) Minister, b. Glasgow. A Presbyterian, he was imprisoned and tortured during the reign of **Charles II**, and spent time in exile in Holland. He was an influential adviser to **William of Orange**, and was 4 times Moderator of the General Assembly of the **Church of Scotland**. As Principal of **Edinburgh University** he introduced a number of important reforms.

**Carswell, Catherine** (1879–1946) Writer, b. Glasgow. Principally a journalist, her work also included two novels, *Open the Door!* (1920) and *The Camomile* (1922), and biographies of her friend D H Lawrence and of Robert **Burns**. Her work was ground-breaking among Scottish women's writing in its perception and honesty.

**Carswell, John** (c.1525–72) Bishop, b. Kilmartin. A product of bardic schools and graduate of **St Andrews**, he was rector of Kilmartin from 1551, and became Bishop of the Isles in 1567. His **Gaelic** translation of the **Book of Common Order** (1567) was the earliest printed book in Gaelic. Carnasserie Castle, near **Kilmartin**, was built by him.

**Cart, River** Renfrewshire. The Black Cart Water originates in Castle Semple Loch, and the White Cart Water flows from the East **Renfrewshire** hills through Cathcart and Pollokshaws. They join together in **Paisley**, and form a tributary to the River **Clyde**.

**Carter Bar** Road summit on the border between Scotland and England, where the modern A68 follows an ancient crossing point between the two countries. At 418m (1370ft) high, the views are outstanding.

**Carver, Robert** (1487–c.1566). Composer. The greatest Scottish composer of sacred music before the **Reformation**. He became a novice monk in 1503 and possibly went to study abroad at Louvain, where he may have been influenced by Dufay. He became a canon of **Scone** in 1511. His elaborate compositions include masses such as the 10-part *Dum sacrum mysterium* (1508–11) and the 19-part motet, *O bone Jesu* (written between 1503 and 1513). A number of his works are contained in the *Carver Choirbook* (**National Library of Scotland**).

**Caskie, Donald Currie** (1902–83) Minister, b. Bowmore, Islay. After a few years in **Gretna**, Dumfriesshire, he became minister of the Scots Kirk in Paris. During World War II he helped numerous people to escape from occupied France; for this he was himself imprisoned and sentenced to death but later reprieved. These experiences are descibed in his wartime memoir, *The Tartan Pimpernel* (1957). He returned to Scotland in 1961 and was a minister in **Ayrshire** until 1968.

**Castalian band** Group of poets and musicians at the court of **James VI**, with the king as their leader and patron. It included the poets Alexander **Mongomerie**, William **Fowler**, John Stewart of Baldynneis (c.1550–c.1605) and Alexander Hume (c.1557–1609).

C

*Castle Fraser, Aberdeenshire.*

**Castantin** see **Constantine**

**Castlebay** Main village on **Barra**, and the ferry port for the island. **Kisimul Castle** is built on a rock in the harbour. The village is overlooked by the church and by a statue of the Blessed Virgin, built on Heaval, the highest hill.

**Castle Campbell** 15th- and 16th-century castle at the head of **Dollar** Glen which belonged to the Campbells of **Argyll** and is built on the site of an earlier castle. Formerly known as Castle Gloom, its name was changed in the late 15th century. The ruined castle stands in a dramatic setting between the Burns of Sorrow and Care. Owned by the **National Trust for Scotland** and administered by **Historic Scotland**.

**Castle Douglas** (pop. 3671) Town 29km (18mi) southwest of **Dumfries**, on the shore of **Carlingwark Loch**. An earlier village known as Carlingwark was renamed by a merchant, William Douglas, who bought and developed the land in the late 18th century, building a short-lived cotton mill. The livestock market remains important to the town's economy and it is now the main market town for the east of **Galloway**. **Threave Castle** and Gardens are nearby.

**Castle Fraser** Impressive castle near **Kemnay**, Aberdeenshire, principally dating from the 16th century, including earlier elements, remodelled in its present form by John Bell in 1617–18. It was built by the Frasers and remained in the family until 1921. Now belongs to the **National Trust for Scotland**.

**Castle Grant** Known as Freuchie Castle until 1694, this castle at

**Grantown-on-Spey** was the home of the Lairds of Grant, later Earls of Seafield. It dates from the 16th and 17th centuries, with a new front by John **Adam** in 1753–6. Recently partially restored, it is privately owned.

**Castle Huntly** Tower house at Longforgan, 16km (10mi) west of **Dundee**. It was built by the Grays in 1452, and was long the principal seat of the Earls of Strathmore under the name of Castle Lyon. Much altered and enlarged, it was renamed Castle Huntly when sold to a Dundee businessman in the late 18th century. It is now one of Scotland's 2 open prisons, providing low-security accommodation for Category D male prisoners.

**Castle Kennedy** Ruined 17th-century tower house near **Stranraer** begun by John Kennedy, Earl of Cassilis. It is now owned by the Earl of Stair and is open to the public. It is also the name of a nearby village. The Castle is famous for its gardens, which are linked to those of the 19th-century Lochinch Castle by an impressive avenue of 'monkey puzzle' trees underplanted with exotic trees and many species of rhododendrons, some of which were originally collected in Sikkim by Sir Joseph Hooker. A 1-hectare (2-acre) lily pond dominates the view from the ruined castle but its walled garden is well planted with tender shrubs and herbaceous and annual plants.

**Castle Leod** Large tower house to the north of **Strathpeffer**, built 1608–16 by Roderick Mackenzie and extended in the 19th and 20th centuries. It is the home of the Earls of Cromartie.

**Castle Maoil** (Gaelic **Caisteal Maol**) Ruined medieval castle of the MacKinnons on a rocky outcrop on the coast of **Skye**, at the mouth of **Loch Alsh** to the east of **Kyleakin**. Local legend says it was built by a Norwegian princess to control the coast and to extract tolls from passing ships. The present building is probably 15th century.

**Castle Menzies** Large Z-plan tower house at Weem near **Aberfeldy**, built 1571–7. The home of the Menzies family, it was abandoned in the 20th century. It has now been restored by the Clan Menzies Society, is owned by the Menzies Charitable Trust, is open to the public and includes a clan museum.

**Castlemilk** Estate in Dumfries and Galloway, south of **Lockerbie**, on the Water of Milk. A 16th-century tower house is now ruined. The present Scots baronial mansion, built for Sir Robert Jardine (a partner in **Jardine Matheson**) in 1864, is one of David **Bryce**'s finest houses.

**Castlemilk** Housing scheme in **Glasgow** which was built on an estate purchased by Glasgow Corporation in 1938. The 19th-century mansion house, on the site of an earlier tower house, has largely been demolished. The modern housing estate was begun in 1954, and includes four 20-storey blocks of flats. When completed it had a population as large as that of **Perth**, and not one public house. Various regeneration initiatives have been launched to counter problems of unemployment and crime.

**Castle of Mey** 16th-century tower house, later altered, on the north coast of **Caithness**, overlooking the **Pentland Firth**. It was built by George Sinclair, 4th Earl of Caithness, and known as Barrogill Castle. Queen Elizabeth the Queen Mother purchased it in 1952, after her husband's death, and had it restored. She regularly spent time there until her death in 2002. The garden in the austere climate is timed for summer interest and is widely acclaimed. The castle now belongs to a charitable trust and is open to the public.

**Castle Semple Collegiate Church** see **Lochwinnoch**

**Castle Stalker** Tower house on an island at the mouth of Loch Laoich, **Appin**. It was built by Duncan Stewart of Appin c.1540. In the 17th century it was sold to the Campbells, enemies of the Stewarts, but was won back after a siege in 1685. Abandoned c.1780, it was restored in the 1960s and is privately owned.

**Castle Stuart** Large symmetrically planned house with non-identical towers, built for the 3rd Earl of Moray, 1619–25, near the **Moray Firth**, 10km (6mi) northeast of **Inverness**. It was restored in the 19th and 20th centuries.

**Castle Tioram** Built on a tidal island at the mouth of Loch Moidart, this ruined tower house has an impressive setting. It was the home of the MacDonalds of Clanranald, and dates from the 14th to 16th centuries. The **Jacobite** chief of Clanranald reputedly set fire to it in 1715,

to prevent its use by government forces. Plans for extensive restoration were recently rejected by **Historic Scotland** and by a planning enquiry.

**Castle Toward** see **Toward**

**Castle Urquhart** see **Urquhart Castle**

**Cathcart** Now a suburb on the south side of **Glasgow**, Cathcart was once a separate village. It expanded with the development of weaving and paper mills on the River **Cart**, and with the opening of the Cathcart District Railway in 1886. The Holm Foundry of G & J Weir was established at about the same time and is still one of Glasgow's largest engineering works. The ruined 15th-century tower house of the Cathcart family was demolished in 1980. Holmwood House, dating from 1857–8, was designed by Alexander 'Greek' **Thomson** for one of the local papermakers, in spectacular classical style. Conservation work has recently made interior decoration, on classical themes, more obvious; in the care of the **National Trust for Scotland**.

**Cathkin Braes** Country park on a hillside to the south of **Glasgow**, which offers outstanding views to the north.

**Catholic Apostolic Church** Founded in 1835, owing much to the teachings of Edward Irving (1792–1834), a charismatic minister who had been expelled from the **Church of Scotland** in 1833 for heresy. The church, also known as Irvingites, focussed on the Second Coming and built several massive and impressive churches. A split in 1863 led to the forming of the New Apostolic Church, which continues today in many countries, including the UK.

*Castle Stalker, Appin, Argyll.*

**Catrine** Village on the banks of the River Ayr, near **Mauchline**. In 1787 a water-powered cotton mill was established here, and the village was largely built at the same time to house the workers. This mill was destroyed by fire in 1963, but one opened in 1947 worked for a few more years. Just to the northwest is Ballochmyle House, associated with a song by Robert **Burns**.

**Catterline** Former fishing village 7km (5mi) south of **Stonehaven**. In the 1950s it gave inspiration to the artist Joan **Eardley** and other artists who lived there 1956–63. The house which she used as a studio is now used by other artists.

**Caulfeild, Major William** (d.1767) Soldier, b. Ireland. Originally working under General **Wade**, he was appointed Inspector of Roads and was responsible for building many hundreds of miles of roads and bridges throughout Scotland. Known as 'Major', he was in fact appointed Lieutenant-Colonel in 1751.

**Caw, Sir James Lewis** (1864–1950) Art historian and gallery director, b. Ayr. Author of *Scottish Painters, Past and Present* (1908), an early, comprehensive history of Scottish art. He was Curator of the **Scottish National Portrait Gallery** from 1895 and from 1907 first Director of the **National Galleries of Scotland**.

**Cawdor** Village near **Nairn**, dominated by Cawdor Castle. The land belonged to the Thanes of Cawdor from 1236, and passed to the Campbells through kidnap and forced marriage in 1511. The title 'Thane of Cawdor' was used by Shakespeare in *Macbeth*. The tower house dates from the 14th century, and was added to in later centuries. There is a series of themed gardens including white, thistle and knot gardens and a holly maze, as well as a fine collection of shrubs. It is still lived in by the Campbells of Cawdor, and is open to the public.

**ceilidh** (pronounced '**kayly**') From Gaelic, meaning 'a visit', an informal gathering among neighbours, sometimes with music, song, dancing and story. The word is now used throughout Scotland for a more organised event in a hall etc, with Scottish music and usually dancing.

**Cellardyke** Former **fishing** village in Fife, beside **Anstruther**. Also known as Lower Kilrenny. A conservation village, the harbour is little used now. The name comes from 'siller dyke(s)', possibly referring to the silvery sun glinting on fish laid on the walls to dry.

**Celtic Football Club** Established in 1888 by an Irish priest, Brother Walfrid, to raise money to counter poverty and to provide a focus for the Irish immigrant community in the East End of **Glasgow**. Celtic and its great rival **Rangers** are known as the 'Old Firm', and together they have dominated Scottish **football** for many years. Celtic's greatest moment probably came in 1967, when their team, the 'Lisbon Lions', became the first British side to win the European Cup. The club's stadium, Celtic Park or Parkhead, is situated about 3km (2mi) east of Glasgow city centre. See also **football**, p.151.

**Central Belt** The area of central Scotland, from the River **Clyde** to the River **Forth**, from the **Glasgow** to the **Edinburgh** area, taking in the surrounding industrial towns.

**Central Lowlands** Name given to the area which lies between the **Southern Uplands** and the **Highlands**. This part of Scotland has seen the greatest industrial expansion, has much fertile farming land, and is by far the most populous. It includes **Edinburgh, Glasgow, Dundee, Perth, Stirling** and **Ayr**. See also **Lowlands**.

**Central Region** One of the 9 main local authority areas forming the upper tier of local government in the 2-tier system between 1975 and 1996, formed from the former county of **Clackmannanshire**, and parts of **Stirlingshire** and **Perthshire**. It consisted of **Clackmannan, Falkirk** and **Stirling** Districts. See maps on pp.394–5 and **local government**.

**Ceol Beg** Musical group, first formed in **Dundee** in the early 1980s, incorporating **bagpipes**, harp, flute and various stringed instruments. Many of Scotland's finest traditional instrumentalists and singers, including Gary West and Rod Paterson, have been members. The name comes from Gaelic *ceòl beag*, meaning 'small music', as distinct from '*ceòl mór*', the 'big music' (or **piobaireachd**) of the bagpipes.

**Ceres** Attractive village near **Cupar**, Fife, a **burgh** of barony from 1620. The Fife Folk Museum is housed in the 17th-century tolbooth and weighhouse, and adjoining cottages. The Ceres games, held annually on the village green, are said to celebrate the return of local men from **Bannockburn**.

**Certificate of Sixth Year Studies** School courses and examinations introduced in 1968 to be taken after **Higher** Grade. They were intended to introduce pupils to the type of studying required at university. Uptake was never particularly high, and in the 1990s CSYS was absorbed into the new Higher Still programme.

**Chalmers, Dr Peter MacGregor** (1859–1922) Architect and archaeologist, b. Glasgow. Chalmers designed many fine churches, mostly in an Irish-influenced Romanesque style, notably at Kirn

(1906), **St Andrews** (1902) and Carriden (1907) but was also responsible for a number of restorations, most notably Holy Trinity, St Andrews (1907–09) and the nave of **Iona** Cathedral (1908–10). His writings include *A Scots Mediaeval Architect* (John Morvo), and *The Govan Sarcophagus*.

**Chalmers, Thomas** (1780–1847) Minister, b. Anstruther. Minister of two large **Glasgow** congregations, he was deeply distressed by poverty. He was opposed to levying poor rates, preferring to deal with the problem through organised Christian charity. He was a popular preacher and a leader of the **Evangelical** party in the Established Church. He played a prominent role in the **Disruption** (1843), and became first Moderator of the **Free Church of Scotland**.

**Chambers, Robert** (1802–71) Writer and publisher, b. Peebles. As well as working as a bookseller and publisher with his brother **William**, he wrote many notable works about Scottish history and literature, including *Traditions of Edinburgh* (1824–34), *A Biographical Dictionary of Eminent Scotsmen* (1832–4), and *Domestic Annals of Scotland* (1859–61). They also produced a weekly magazine, *Chambers's Edinburgh Journal*, later *Chambers's Journal*. Anonymously Robert published *Vestiges of Creation* (1844), prefiguring many of Darwin's evolutionary ideas.

**Chambers, Sir William** (1726–96) Architect, b. Gothenburg, Sweden of Scottish ancestry. After studying in Rome and China, he settled in London and became architect to George III. Particularly remembered as the architect of Somerset House in London, in Scotland he was responsible for Duddingston House and Dundas House (now the **Royal Bank of Scotland**), both in **Edinburgh**.

**Chambers, William** (1800–83) Publisher and writer, b. Peebles. With his brother **Robert** he established a business in **Edinburgh** initially as a bookseller and then as a publisher. They published many important reference works, including *Chambers's Encyclopaedia* (1859–68). In 1865 and 1868 he was Lord Provost of Edinburgh, and was responsible for slum clearance and improvement schemes. The publishing name still survives in Chambers Harrap, a dictionary publisher based in Edinburgh, but now part of a French publishing conglomerate.

**chanter** The pipe in a **bagpipe** on which the melody is played;

*Celtic Football Club, 'Lisbon Lions', 1967.*

a separate pipe, with no bag or drones, used for practising.

**Chapelcross** Near **Annan**, Dumfriesshire, Scotland's first nuclear power station opened in 1959 to provide plutonium for nuclear weapons. It consists of 4 Magnox reactors and a processing plant. A significant employer in the area, it is due to close between 2008–10. It is owned by British Nuclear Fuels.

**Chapelhall** Village near **Airdrie**, which grew up around iron working at the nearby Calder Iron Works and ironstone and coal mining. Monkland House, built in 1600, was used by the managers of the Calder Iron Works. It has since been demolished and replaced by a housing estate.

**Chapman** Literary magazine founded by Joy Hendry in 1972 in **Edinburgh** and still edited by her. It contains articles, fiction and poetry in English, Scots and Gaelic.

**Chapman** or **Chepman, Walter** (c.1473–c.1538) Printer. A wealthy merchant, he provided money to set up the first Scottish printing press with Andrew **Myllar** in 1507. They had premises in the Cowgate, **Edinburgh**. The only known copies of the 9 earliest books printed by Chapman and Myllar are held by the **National Library of Scotland**.

**Charles I** (1600–49) King of Scotland, England and Ireland 1625–49, b. Dunfermline. Son of **James VI** and **Anne of Denmark**,

**C**

he unexpectedly became heir to the throne in 1612 when his brother Henry died. His alienation of the Scottish, English and Irish aristocracies led to civil wars. These were ultimately triggered by the Scots **Covenanting** revolution, provoked by his political and religious innovations in Scotland. Defeated in England, Charles chose to surrender himself to the Scots army in the north of England in 1646. Negotiations between Charles and the Scots leaders proved impossible, since his only aim was to sow trouble between the Scots and the English. He would also have tried to split the Scots leadership had he remained in Scots hands. Reluctantly but sensibly, the Scots eventually handed him over to the English Parliament and went home. Charles was beheaded in London in 1649. He was the last monarch born in Scotland.

**Charles II** (1630–85) King of Scotland, England and Ireland 1660–85, b. London. He was proclaimed King in Scotland immediately after the execution of **Charles I**, and crowned at **Scone** in 1651. After being defeated at the Battle of Worcester by Oliver Cromwell, he returned to exile overseas until the Restoration in 1660. He never returned to Scotland.

**Charles Edward Stewart** see **Stewart, Prince Charles Edward**

**'Charlotte Dundas'** see **Symington, William**

**Chaseabout Raid** Campaign by **Mary, Queen of Scots** in August–September 1565 against a rebellion led by the Earl of Moray, who opposed her marriage to **Darnley**. With little support, the rebels were easily scattered, hence the name of the episode.

**Chatelard** or **Chastelard, Pierre de** (d.1563) Poet, b. France. He was infatuated with **Mary, Queen of Scots**, and was executed for hiding in her bedroom, firstly at Holyrood and then at Rossend Castle.

**Chatelherault** Now a country park, this estate near **Hamilton** belonged to the Dukes of Hamilton. (The Dukedom of Chatelherault was given to James Hamilton, 2nd Earl of Arran, in 1550.) A hunting lodge, with kennels etc and formal garden, by William **Adam** (1731–43), the main surviving features of the park of the vanished palace, were restored in the 1970s-80s by **Historic Scotland** and are open to the public. In the Low Park is the huge neo-Roman Hamilton Mausoleum, by David **Bryce** (1848–50).

**Chepman, Walter** see **Chapman, Walter**

**Cheviot sheep** Breed of sheep which was developed in the **Borders**, probably brought from the Low Countries in the Middle Ages. It became the basis of Borders textiles. The breed achieved unwitting notoriety as part of the northern Highland **Clearances**, where it developed as the larger North Country Cheviot.

**Child, F J** see **ballads**

**Children's Hearing System** System set up in the 1960s for dealing with children (under 16) in trouble, taking over most of the responsibilities of the courts for children who commit offences or who are in need of care or protection. A Reporter is appointed to decide what action, if any, should be taken in individual cases, and a Children's Panel, consisting of trained unpaid volunteers from varied backgrounds, carries out a hearing to investigate the case to make decisions about how best to intervene in the child's future; these decisions are appealable. See **Kilbrandon Report**.

**'Christis Kirk on the Grene'** Older Scots poem dating probably from around 1500 which gives a vivid description of a village festival in **Leslie**, Fife. Both **James I** and **James V** have been improbably suggested as authors. It was the forerunner of many poems of celebration in **Scots** and its complex stanza form and rhyme scheme had long-lasting influence.

**Church of Scotland** The Church of Scotland became protestant and presbyterian at the **Reformation** in 1560, but until 1690 it had episcopalian elements, some of them enforced by the monarch and government, in particular by **Charles I**. It was however established as a Presbyterian national church by Parliament in 1690, and continues thus today. In the 18th century the Church of Scotland was divided into 2 parties, **Moderates** and **Evangelicals**, and numerous groups formed their own churches; see **presbyterian churches**. The continuing dispute over patronage (appointment of ministers) led to the **Disruption** of 1843, which formed the **Free Church of Scotland**. The Church of Scotland has a network of parishes covering the whole country, and also provides many social services. Its highest court, the **General Assembly**, meets annually and is presided over by the **Moderator**. Its headquarters are in George Street, **Edinburgh**. It is often referred to informally as 'the **Kirk**'.

**Churchill Barriers** Causeways linking Mainland **Orkney**, **Burray**, **South Ronaldsay** and some smaller islands. They were originally erected during World War II to protect the deep water anchorage of **Scapa Flow**, after a German submarine sank the battleship *Royal Oak* there, with heavy loss of life.

**Churchill, Winston S** see **Dundee**

**Cináed mac Alpín** see **Kenneth mac Alpin**

**Cináed mac Duib** see **Kenneth III**

**Cináed mac Máel Coluim** see **Kenneth II**

**cist** see **kist**

From the Gaelic word *clann*, meaning children, a social group which took its name from the chief. It was not exclusively family-based but included those who owed loyalty to the chief as their landowner, and had sub-groups known as septs. The great **Highland** clan chiefs were magnates who controlled confederations, earlier by tribal authority and in the medieval period based on their feudal jurisdiction from the Scottish Crown as well as by group loyalty. Some but not all were of Gaelic origin. One theory traces the ancestry of the **Campbells** to Diarmid O'Dhuine and origins in **Argyll**, where the Duke of Argyll is still based at **Inveraray**; they became the most powerful clan with influence in Lowland as well as Highland politics. Three other branches developed, each with its own chief, but unlike many other clans, working cooperatively with Argyll. The Campbells of Glenorchy became the Earls of Breadalbane in the late 17th century; a Lowland branch became the Earls of Loudon in Ayrshire; and a Northeast branch became the Earls of **Cawdor**.

Rivalry between chiefs of branches was however much commoner, as in the case of the Macdonalds. Their progenitor, **Somerled**, was of mixed Celtic and Norse origin and their name came from his grandson Domhnull (Donald). After the ending of the **Lordship of the Isles** by **James IV** in 1492, the clan divided into several rival branches, including the Macdonalds of Sleat, powerful landowners in the south of Skye (surviving today in Lord Macdonald at Kinloch Castle, and in the Clan Donald Centre at Armadale Castle); the Macdonalds of Clanranald, a powerful branch descended from the 14th-century Ranald, son of the Lord of the Isles; the Macdonalds of Glengarry, and the Macdonalds of Keppoch. A further branch became known as 'Clan Donald South', holding lands in Islay, Kintyre and in Northern Ireland; the present McDonell Earl of Antrim continues this line.

The great confederation known as Clan Cameron, based in **Lochaber**, held together better, but its chief, Lochiel, was intermittently challenged by Cameron of Fassifern and others. The Macleods split early into two groups, known as the *Siol Thorcuil* (Family of Torquil) and *Siol Thoirmid* (Family of Norman), from the names of the two sons of their Norse progenitor, Leod. The former became the Macleods of **Lewis** and the latter of **Harris** and **Skye**. The *Siol Thorcuil* chiefs were ousted from Lewis in the early 17th century by the Mackenzies, whose chiefs became Earls of Seaforth (a Lewis sea loch), though their ancestral lands stretched from **Kintail**

on the west coast across to the east, and later further north. At times they were opposed for the chieftainship of the clan by the Cromarties. The Seaforth line died out in 1815 and and the Earl of Cromartie is now recognised as chief of the Clan Mackenzie.

Some clans were of Anglo-Norman origin, including the very powerful Gordons in the Northeast, and the **Frasers**, Lords Lovat, in eastern Inverness-shire. Some, such as the Macgregors, had no chief or feudal jurisdiction and it was very easy for them to become marginalised and criminalised, as happened in the 17th century. Clan Chattan, whose leader was the Mackintosh, was formed as a confederation in the north-central Highlands against the power of the Gordons and others.

Although clans today are known by their surnames, these only came into use at a later stage and many chiefs were known in Gaelic by patronymics indicating their ancient ancestors, eg The Duke of Argyll is known as *Mac Cailein Mór* (son of Great Colin), Lord Lovat, as *Mac Shimidh* (son of Simon). Other modern surnames derive from trades, eg Macintyre, in Gaelic *Mac an t-Saoir* (son of the joiner), or from nicknames, eg Campbell, Gaelic *Cambeul* (twisted mouth).

A similar system operated in the **Borders** and **Galloway**, based on family and name rather than feudal jurisdiction, with families such as the Armstrongs, the Nixons and the Elliotts holding considerable power, especially in medieval Border warfare. In the **Highlands**, punitive measures were taken after **Culloden** to reduce the power of the clans, and together with economic change these eroded the old system, already in decline. Nowadays clan societies worldwide, clan tartans and clan histories celebrate a more mythical notion whereby those with a common surname share a common ancestry.

*Dunvegan Castle, Skye, home of John Macleod of Macleod.*

C

*Old Smithy, Kinlochewe.*

another peak in the 1840s after the lean years of the potato famine.

While these moves can be seen in some ways as agricultural improvement, many were carried out in a brutal and inhumane fashion and were a major factor in the depopulation of the Highlands and Islands. Among the most notorious of the Clearances were those perpetrated by the Duke and Duchess of **Sutherland** and their factor Patrick **Sellar**; see **Glencalvie**, **Strathnaver**.

Later in the century sheep-farming ceased to be profitable but deer forests in the upper parts of the land brought in greater returns to the sporting estates and the need to remove tenants continued. By the late 1850s, the worst of the Clearances were over. There was considerable increase in resistance, including incidents where women (probably accompanied by men disguised as women) forcibly pushed away the boat taking a factor ashore to carry out evictions. But in most cases tenants had no redress against landlord power. Eventually strong protests, especially in **Skye** in the 1880s, led to reform of land tenure for crofters; see **Braes**, **Crofters' Commission**.

These events form a sad chapter in the long history of emigration from the **Highlands** and Islands, evoking a wide range of emotional responses, from repugnance at the forcible removal of people from their crofts to the assumption that emigration was necessary and people were being encouraged towards a better life. In the 18th century Highland landowners, mainly clan chiefs, often made efforts to prevent emigration, as the rents from their tenants were an important part of their income. During the Napoleonic Wars (1803–15) landlords saw more profit in sheep, partly due to the wartime rise in wool prices, and moved many of their tenants forcibly to coastal strips, leaving the more fertile inland areas for the sheep. There was further incentive to move people to the coast as labour was needed for the **kelp** industry. After the Wars, however, demand for kelp declined and efforts were made by many landowners to remove tenants from their land altogether; sheep were more profitable and tenants were less able to pay their rents without employment in kelp. They left for Lowland towns, England, North America and other British territories overseas. Evictions reached

*Interior of crofthouse, Shetland, 1889.*

**Citizens' Theatre** Theatre company founded in 1943 by the playwright James **Bridie** to encourage Scottish drama, housed in the former Princess Theatre in the **Gorbals** district of **Glasgow**. In recent years its innovative productions have given it international recognition, especially under the direction of Giles Havergal.

**city guard** see **town guard**

**City of Glasgow Bank** Founded in 1839, it collapsed in 1878, and lack of limited liability caused financial ruin to most of its shareholders. An investigation led to the imprisonment of 3 directors for fraud.

**clachan** Gaelic and Scots word for a village, found in many place-names. In Gaelic it often refers to the village with the parish church; equivalent to Scots **kirkton**.

**Clackmannan** (pop. 3450) Town near **Alloa**, once the county town of Clackmannanshire. There is an ancient stone in the town centre, and the name of the town comes from an old Welsh word for stone and from Manau, the name of the district. Clackmannan Tower, in the care of **Historic Scotland**, dates from the 14th-15th century. It is built on land given to the Bruces by **David II**, and belonged to the family until it was abandoned in the late 18th century.

**Clackmannan District** see **Clackmannanshire**

**Clackmannanshire** This county was Scotland's smallest. It lay to the north of the **Forth**, bordering Stirlingshire, Perthshire and Fife. In 1822 **Alloa** replaced Clackmannan as the county town. From 1975 to 1996, with a slightly larger area, it was the Clackmannan District of **Central Region**, and it is now a unitary local authority. Its administrative centre is **Alloa**. See maps on pp.394-5 and **local government**.

**Claim of Right,** 11 April 1689. A Convention of Estates – a body similar to the Parliament – declared in the Claim of Right that **James VII** had forfeited the throne, and that it should therefore be offered to **William II (of Orange)** and his wife Mary, daughter of James VII.

**Claim of Right,** 1842. Issued by the **General Assembly** of the **Church of Scotland** asserting independence from the state in spiritual matters, including the appointment of ministers. Its rejection by Parliament led to the **Disruption** of 1843.

**Claim of Right,** July 1988. Drawn up by a cross-party group, declaring Scotland's right to self-government. It led to the establishment of the **Scottish Constitutional Convention**, and was a significant step in the road towards Scotland's **parliament**.

**clan** see p.77

**Clan Line Steamers** Steamship company operating between UK and Ireland. Originating in Liverpool, from 1881 it was based in **Glasgow**. It was owned by the Cayzer family and Captain William Irvine. In 1956 the firm merged with Union-Castle to form the British and Commonwealth Shipping Ltd.

**Clanranald, Black and Red Books of** Manuscript collections made about 1670 by the MacMhuirich family, hereditary bards to the Macdonalds of Clanranald, providing one of the earliest accounts of Scotland from the Gaelic point of view. Now in the **Museum of Scotland**.

**clapshot** A dish of mashed turnip and potato mixed together with butter, salt, pepper etc, originally from **Orkney**.

**Clark, Jim** (1936–68) Racing driver, b. Kilmany, Fife. After an early career in team racing and rallying, he began Formula 2 and Grand Prix racing for Lotus in 1960, and won the Drivers' World Championship in 1963 and 1965. An outstanding talent, he held the record for the most Grand Prix victories (25) when he was killed during practice at Hockenheim in 1968. There is a museum in his memory at Chirnside, where he is buried, and a statue at Kilmany.

**clarsach** The term most often employed in Scotland for a wire-strung Highland harp, as distinct from a gut-strung harp. Music, particularly harp music, was highly valued in Gaelic society, and the clarsach player (clarsair) was a professional musician employed by the clan chief. Two surviving 15th-century Scottish clarsachs, the 'Lamont Harp' and the 'Queen Mary Harp', are displayed in the **Museum of Scotland**. There is a current revival of interest in Scottish harp music; see Alison **Kinnaird**.

**Clarsair Dall, an** (the **Blind Harper**, Roderick (Ruaraidh) **Morison**) (c.1656–c.1713) Harper to the Macleods of Dunvegan, Skye, b. Lewis. Very little of his music survives, but more of his songs. Many eminent Celtic harp players were blind.

**Clava Cairns** Also known as Balnuaran of Clava, a prehistoric burial site near **Culloden** consisting of 3 chambered cairns, each surrounded by a stone circle. Some stones have cup and ring marks. The site dates from the early Bronze Age. In the care of **Historic Scotland**. The name also refers to a class of cairns in the area, all with a circle of standing stones, a feature unique to Scotland.

**Claverhouse, John Graham of** see **Dundee, 1st Viscount**

**Clavie** see **Burghead**

**claymore** From the Gaelic *claidheamh mór*, meaning 'great sword'. A two-handed double-edged sword used in medieval

C

Highland society; also mistakenly applied to the Highland basket-hilted single-edged broadsword.

**Claypotts** Tower house near **Dundee** which was built in the mid 16th century and unusually remains unaltered. It is an impressive building, but is now surrounded by a private housing estate. Built by the Strachans, it was bought in 1620 by an ancestor of John **Graham** of Claverhouse, and was forfeited after **Killiecrankie**. It now belongs to the Earls of Home but is administered by **Historic Scotland** and has limited opening.

**Clearances** see p.78

**Cleghorn, Hugh** (1757-1834) Professor of civil history. He left his academic post in **St Andrews** in 1793, and travelled to Ceylon (Sri Lanka). It was then a Dutch territory, but Cleghorn had bought control of a Swiss mercenary regiment which was the core of its garrison and persuaded the Governor to surrender. Ceylon remained under British control until 1948.

**Cleish** Village near **Kinross**. The 16th-century tower house, which belonged to the Colvilles, became derelict in the 19th century. It has since been renovated and is privately owned. Blairadam House, home of William **Adam** and his family, is nearby and there are memorials to the Adams in Cleish kirkyard.

**Cleland, William** (1661-89) Soldier and poet. A **Covenanter**, he fought at **Drumclog** and **Bothwell Brig** before going into exile. He led the **Cameronian** Regiment in 1689, but was killed in battle with the **Jacobites** at **Dunkeld**. He is buried in Dunkeld Cathedral.

**Clements, Alan** see **Wark, Kirsty**

**Clerk, J and J** see **Coats, J and P Ltd**

**Clerk, Sir John, of Penicuik** (1676-1755) Advocate and MP. He was a commissioner for the Union in 1707 and became a Westminster MP. Interested in the arts and architecture, he built up an important collection of antiquities, on which he wrote extensively. His other great passion was for the agricultural improvement of his estates.

**Clerk Maxwell, James** see **Maxwell, James Clerk**

**Clì** (**Comann Luchd Ionnsachaidh**) (**Gaelic Learners Organisation**) Organisation, now based in Inverness, which co-ordinates **Gaelic** learner activities, promotes the status of Gaelic, and produces a quarterly bilingual magazine, *Cothrom*.

**Clifford, Sir Timothy** (1946- ) Art historian and gallery director, b. Sittingbourne, Kent. Since 1984 Director of the **National Galleries of Scotland**, and responsible for the notable acquisitions of Canova's *The Three Graces* (with the Victoria & Albert Museum, London), Guercino's *Erminia Finding the Wounded Tancred*, Botticelli's *The Virgin Adoring the Sleeping Christ Child* and Titian's *Venus Anadyomene*.

**Clisham** Mountain on **Harris** (799m/2622ft), the highest peak in the Outer **Hebrides**.

**Cloch Point** Near **Gourock**, on the rocky coast of the Firth of **Clyde** which has been hazardous to shipping for centuries. The **lighthouse** here was built in 1797 by the Clyde Lighthouse Trust and is a well-known landmark.

**clootie dumpling** A pudding made from flour, oatmeal, suet, spices, dried fruit etc, boiled in a cloot, ie a cloth, a favourite birthday treat.

**Close Brethren** see **Brethren**

**Clova, Glen** see **Glen Clova**

**Cluanie** see **Loch Cluanie**

**Clunies-Ross, George** (1842-1910) Governor of the Cocos (Keeling) islands. His grandfather John, a **Shetland** seaman, had founded a settlement in the islands in 1827, and in 1886 they were granted to George Clunies-Ross and his heirs. In 1888 he established the first settlement on Christmas Island to begin phosphate mining there.

**Cluny House Garden** Garden near **Aberfeldy**. Its steeply wooded moist conditions are ideal for growing the national collection of Petiolarid primulas and a vast array of Asiatic plants.

**Cluny's Cage** A hiding place on the slopes of **Ben Alder**, made from trees. It was used after **Culloden** by Ewen **Macpherson** of Cluny and by Charles Edward **Stewart**, and this incident features in Robert Louis **Stevenson**'s *Kidnapped*.

**Clyde, River** and **Firth of** One of Scotland's most important rivers, 170km (106mi) long, it rises in South Lanarkshire and flows northwards through **Glasgow** and into the sea, forming the Firth of Clyde, running west from **Dumbarton**, and then south between the **Ayrshire** and **Argyll** coasts, past the islands of **Bute**, the **Cumbraes** and **Arran**. With the development of direct trade with North America, especially in tobacco, in the 18th century, the river was deepened to accommodate larger ships. In the 19th century this facilitated large-scale emigrant sailings and a huge volume of manufactured exports to North America. Industries of the Glasgow, Greenock and Port Glasgow areas, including the world's leading 19th-century shipyards, grew up around the river, and steamers travelled 'doon the watter'. See also **Glasgow, shipbuilding**.

**Clydebank** (pop. 29,858) Town west of **Glasgow**, a **burgh** since 1886. Originally a village known as Barns o' Clyde, it expanded rapidly and changed its name with the coming of the major shipyard owned by J and G Thomson which later became John Brown & Co. Employment was also offered by the large Singer sewing-machine factory (closed 1979). In 1941 the area was nearly destroyed and over 1000 people died in German bombing raids, known as the Clydebank Blitz.

**Clydebank District** see **Strathclyde Region**

**Clyde Muirshiel Regional Park**

Large country park stretching down the **Clyde** coast from **Greenock** in the north to **West Kilbride** in the south and inland to Lochwinnoch,

*A pit pony at Knowetop Colliery, near Hamilton, 1958.*

where it contains the Lochwinnoch RSPB Nature Reserve. It covers a mixed area of wood, moor, wetland and coastline and has many amenities.

**Clydesdale, Ron** see **Ubiquitous Chip**

**Clydesdale Bank** Founded in 1838 with head office in **Glasgow** and a branch in **Edinburgh**. It amalgamated with the North of Scotland Bank in 1950, and has been particularly strong in western Scotland and Aberdeenshire. Since 1987 it has been part of the National Australia Bank Group. It is one of the 3 Scottish banks permitted to issue banknotes, and it is the only remaining bank with its head office in Glasgow.

**Clydesdale District** see **Strathclyde Region**

**Clydesdale horse** Breed of horse, probably a development of Flemish stock imported into Lanarkshire in the late 17th century and crossed with smaller local breeds. The Clydesdale only became recognised and started spreading from Lanarkshire at the end of the 18th century. Handsome, powerful, intelligent and gentle, it was the mainstay of most Scottish farms until replaced by the tractor after World War II. It was also used to haul heavy loads in towns. They are still bred as a hobby.

**Clynder** Village on Gare Loch, north of Rosneath.

**Clynelish** see **Brora**

**CNAG** see **Comunn na Gàidhlig**

**coal** Coal has been mined principally in central and southwestern Scotland since medieval times. During the 18th century the industry expanded rapidly as demand increased, particularly from ironworks, and as technology, transport, drainage and ventilation techniques improved. Mineworkers were serfs, like the closely associated salt-workers, tied with their whole families to the mines. The abolition of serfdom after 1800 was designed to swamp these hereditary but expensive and often militant workers with cheap contract labour. Abolishing underground work by women and children in 1842 accentuated the dependence of the males on their own employment as the source of all family income. In the 19th century there was continued expansion to service domestic and foreign markets and development in machine mining and the use of electricity underground. By 1919 Scottish coal was ceasing to be competitive. Nationalisation after World War II led to more investment but could not solve the comparative-cost problem. Coal mining continued to expand until the mid 20th century, when demand dropped and new energy sources became available. By the late 20th century massive pit closures and privatisation led to the complete collapse of a once huge industry, bringing hardship to many communities. See also **Cowdenbeath, Monklands, Newtongrange**.

**Coatbridge** (pop. 41,170) Town near **Airdrie** which grew up during the 19th century around the coal, iron and steel industries; it had the largest concentration of iron-smelting and malleable iron works in Scotland. The industrial history of the area can be explored in Summerlee Heritage Park, a museum based around the former ironworks. The Time Capsule, a leisure complex with many unusual features, attracts many visitors.

C

**Coats, J and P Ltd** The firm was founded in 1826 by James Coats at Ferguslie, **Paisley**, to make cotton sewing thread. Its business expanded dramatically after the development of practical sewing machines in the 1850s. Under the management of Thomas and Peter Coats, sons of James, the scale of manufacturing at Ferguslie was markedly increased, and mills built, behind tariff barriers, in the Americas and in central Europe. In 1890 the company amalgamated with its main rivals, J and J Clark, also Paisley-based, establishing a near-monopoly of the world trade in sewing cotton. The company amalgamated with Patons and Baldwins, makers of knitting wool, in the 1970s. The two Paisley mills closed in the early 1980s, and the remaining Scottish business is based in Newton Mearns.

**Cobbler, The** Mountain near **Arrochar**, 889m (2891ft), officially named Ben Arthur but better known as 'The Cobbler', from the idea that its 3 peaks resemble a cobbler working at his last, with his wife looking over.

**Cochrane, Archibald, 9th Earl of Dundonald** (1749–1831) Industrial innovator and impecunious landowner. When young, he served in both army and navy. He tried to develop his estate at **Culross**, Fife, by a series of industrial innovations, especially methods for distilling tar from coal. He also developed new approaches to sailcloth, alkali and white lead manufacture, taking out many patents, but failing ever to make money from his ideas. In politics he was an extreme and dogmatic Whig.

**Cochrane, Thomas, 10th Earl of Dundonald** (1775–1860) Admiral, b. near Hamilton, son of the eccentric 9th Earl. He enjoyed a promising spectacular early naval career, commanding smaller warships, and became an MP in 1806. His radical Whig views and his egotism made enemies who pounced on allegations of financial misconduct. He was cashiered by the navy, and emigrated to serve as a highly successful Commander-in-Chief of the Chilean, Brazilian and Greek navies in their wars of independence. He was eventually restored to his Royal Navy rank. He was the last British sea-dog, in the traditions of Drake and Hawkins rather than Nelson. He was also a prolific inventor, successfully inventing the use of compressed air for the construction of the Blackwall Tunnel in London and had patents for and attempted to develop gas lighting (before William Murdock), steam turbines and screw propellors for ships.

**cock-a-leekie** A soup made with chicken and leeks, traditionally in beef stock, sometimes with the addition of prunes.

**Cock Bridge** see **Lecht**

**Cockburn, Alison** (née **Rutherford**) (1710–94) Poet, from Fairnilee, near Selkirk, she married advocate Patrick Cockburn. She became a prominent figure in **Edinburgh** cultural society, and is best remembered for writing a version of the words of 'The Flowers of the Forest'.

**Cockburn, Henry, Lord** (1779–1854) Judge, b. Edinburgh. He became an advocate in 1800 and Whig Solicitor-General in 1830, and was a key figure in drawing up the Scottish Reform Bill. His detailed journals were published after his death as *Memorials of His Time* (1856), *The Journal of Henry Cockburn* (1874) and *Circuit Journeys* (1888), and give a fascinating insight into early 19th century society. His commitment to conservation is honoured in the name given to Edinburgh's Cockburn Association.

**Cockburn, John** see **Ormiston**

**Cockburnspath** Coastal village lying 11km (7mi) southeast of **Dunbar**. As the eastern end of the **Southern Uplands Way**, it attracts walkers. **Dunglass Collegiate church** dates from the 15th century and is now disused but fairly complete; in the care of **Historic Scotland**. **Torness** nuclear power station is nearby.

**Cockenzie** Former fishing village in **East Lothian**, adjacent to Port Seton. It is now dominated by the power station which opened in 1967. An early horse-drawn railway, built in 1722, carried coal from **Tranent** to the harbour here.

**Coia, Jack** (1898–1981) Architect, b. Wolverhampton, but moved to **Glasgow** as a child. In the 1930s, he designed a remarkable series of innovative brick churches with Romanesque, Renaissance and Expressionist elements. After World War II he designed a further series of churches, seminaries and schools with his partners Andrew Macmillan (1928– ) and Isi Metzstein (1928– ).

**Coigach** Peninsula in Wester Ross, northwest of **Loch Broom**. The main settlement is **Achiltibuie**. Ben More Coigach reaches a height of 743m (2438ft), and the **Summer Isles** lie just off the coast.

**coinage** see **Weights and Measures**, pp.382–4

**Coinneach Odhar** see **Brahan Seer**

**coire** see **corrie**

**Coire Cas** North-facing **corrie** which is the principal skiing area on Cairn Gorm. In 1960–1 a carpark was built here, with a road leading from Glenmore. This has become the starting point for the Cairngorm Funicular Railway. See also **Cairngorms**.

**Coire na Ciste** North-facing corrie on Cairn Gorm which is a popular skiing area. See also **Cairngorms**.

**Coldingham** Village near **Eyemouth**, with a ruined 13th-century Benedictine priory. The restored choir is incorporated into the parish church. A 7th-century religious house was destroyed and abandoned, but Coldingham once again became a religious site when the priory was established in 1098.

**Coldstream** (pop. 1813) Town on the River **Tweed** which for centuries has been an important crossing point to England; the present bridge dates from the 1760s. The bodies of many of those killed at **Flodden** were said to have been brought here for burial. The town is known for the Coldstream Guards, the regiment formed in 1650 by Oliver Cromwell as 'Monck's Regiment of Foot'. In 1658 General **Monck** assembled his troops here, and his march to London eventually led to the restoration of **Charles II** in 1660. Their history is told in a museum in the Guardhouse.

**Colintraive** Village on the shore of the **Kyles of Bute**, which is a ferry crossing point to **Bute**.

**Colkitto** see **MacColla, Alasdair**

**Coll** (Gaelic **Colla**) (pop. 164) Island in the Inner **Hebrides**, northwest of **Mull**. It is linked from Arinagour, the only village, to **Oban**. Tourists are attracted by the quiet beauty, the high levels of sunshine, and the numerous prehistoric sites. Farming and fishing also offer employment. Breachacha Castle, dating in part from the 14th century, is now an adventure-training school.

**College of Piping**. Based in **Glasgow**, it was founded in 1944 by Seumas **MacNeill** and Thomas Pearston and provides facilities for all to learn piping irrespective of means. It publishes a series of 4 tutors which are the standard textbooks worldwide, and the *Piping Times*, the only monthly piping magazine.

**Collins, William** (1789–1853) Publisher, b. Eastwood. A Glasgow schoolmaster, he set up a publishing business in 1819 in partnership with Charles, brother of Thomas **Chalmers**. They published schoolbooks and religious works, including temperance material, but most notably copies of the Authorised Version of the Bible. The firm expanded and continued under his son and further descendants, all named William Collins, until 1990 when it became part of HarperCollins.

**Collinson, Francis** (1898–1985) Composer, conductor, collector, writer on music. Research Fellow in music at the School of Scottish Studies, **Edinburgh University**, from 1951, he wrote many arrangements for folksongs, and incidental music for radio programmes. His books include *The Traditional and National Music of Scotland* (1966) and *The Bagpipe: The History of a Musical Instrument* (1975).

**Colonsay** (Gaelic **Collasa**) (pop. 108) Island in the Inner **Hebrides**, west of **Jura**, which is reached by ferry from **Islay** and

*Robbie Coltrane.*

**Oban**, and is now sparsely populated. There are standing stones at Kilchattan, and an important Viking boat burial was found at the spectacular Kiloran Bay. Colonsay House, built in 1722, is privately owned, but its exotic gardens are open at certain times. The tiny island of **Oronsay** is linked to Colonsay at low tide.

**Colquhoun, Robert** (1914–62) Artist, b. Kilmarnock. Associated in the 1940s with the London-based Neo-Romantic artists, Colquhoun's painting progressively stood apart from that group, becoming recognised for its angularity and harshness of mood, in tune with the post World War II period. He was also known for his roisterous life-style and turbulent relationship with his partner and fellow Scot, the artist Robert MacBryde (1913–66).

**Coltrane, Robbie** (**Robert McMillan**) (1950– ) Comedian and actor, b. Rutherglen. A prolific film and television actor and producer, he enjoyed early fame with the lead role in the television series *Tutti Frutti*, and more recently in *Cracker*. Films include *Nuns on the Run* (1989), *Goldeneye* (1995), *The World is Not Enough* (1999), *Harry Potter and the Philosopher's Stone* (2001) and later Harry Potter films.

**Columba, St** (Gaelic **Colum Cille**) (c.521–97) Abbot and missionary, b. Donegal. From a powerful Irish family, he established a monastic community at **Iona** in 563 as well as other foundations in Ireland and Scotland. Iona achieved a position of ecclesiastical pre-eminence in the Dal Riatan and Pictish churches and Columba and his monks played a significant role in the conversion of the **Picts**. His *Life* was written a century later by **Adamnan**, a successor as abbot of Iona. He visited the king of the **Picts** at **Inverness**, and is credited with many miracles and with spreading Christianity among the northern Picts. Columba's cult and influence was important to the Picts and Scots and also to the Angles of Northumbria. Viking attacks on Iona led to the transfer of the saint's relics to **Dunkeld** in 849. Thereafter he remained an important native saint for the Scottish royal dynasty.

**Colville, David** (1813–98) Industrialist, b. Campbeltown. His major achievement was the establishment of the Dalzell Iron Works near **Motherwell** in 1871. Responding to changing technology, he switched to steel production in 1880. The firm expanded rapidly with demand from the shipyards. See **Colvilles**.

**Colvilles Ltd** Formed in 1930 on the initiative of the Bank of England to rescue the Scottish steel industry from bankruptcy by rationalising output. It took over all the large steel companies in Scotland, with their associated ironworks, if any, with the exception of Beardmores, and by eliminating duplication of plant created a fully integrated steel industry by 1939, served by a single blast-furnace plant, at Clyde Iron Works at **Cambuslang**. In the 1950s the company was coerced by Government into building a facility for making steel strip, on a split site, part at **Ravenscraig** and part at **Gartcosh**. This expensive venture pushed the company into the red. In 1967 it was nationalised and its plant split up by the British Steel Corporation, which deliberately set out to destroy old company loyalties. During the late 1970s almost all the former Colville plants were closed, and Ravenscraig followed in 1996, ending iron-smelting in Scotland after nearly 4 centuries, and steel-making after nearly 2. Only 2 former Colville plants still survive, at Motherwell (Dalzell) and Tollcross, **Glasgow** (Clydebridge), operated by Corus, successor to the British Steel Corporation.

**Comataidh Craolaidh Gàidhlig** (Gaelic **Broadcasting Committee**) Organisation, based in **Stornoway**, which administers the Gaelic broadcasting fund of approx. £8.5 million for programmes on television and radio.

**'Comet'** Early steamboat, invented by Henry **Bell** and known as the first commercially successful steam vessel in Europe. Launched on the River **Clyde** in 1812, she regularly sailed between **Greenock** and **Glasgow**, but was wrecked at Craignish Point in 1820. A replica was built for her 150th anniversary in 1962, and is now displayed in **Port Glasgow**, where the first *Comet* was built.

**Comhairle nan Eilean Siar** see **Western Isles**

**Comhairle nan Sgoiltean Araich** Gaelic Playgroup Association, set up in 1982, providing pre-school education in Gaelic in and furth of the Gaelic-speaking areas.

**Commercial Bank of Scotland** Established 1810 in **Edinburgh**, targetting customers with smaller amounts of money who were not yet allied to a bank. Highly successful through the 19th century, it merged with the **National Bank** in 1959, and 10 years later became part of the **Royal Bank of Scotland**.

**Commissary Courts** Established in 1563, the central Commissary Court in **Edinburgh** theoretically had a monopoly of cases of divorce, marriage and legitimacy, while local commissary courts had jurisdiction over certain testamentary issues. In practice the division was less clear cut but commissary jurisdiction, rooted in medieval canon law, survived until the early 19th century.

**Commission for Highland Roads and Bridges** Commission set up by Act of Parliament in 1803 to help the Highland economy by improving communications. Over 1500km (900mi) of roads and over 1000 bridges were built between 1803 and 1821, financed partly by the government and partly by local landowners. The Commission continued the work of building and repairing until 1861. The main consulting engineer to the protect was Thomas **Telford**. See also Joseph **Mitchell**.

**Commission for Northern Lights** see p.229

**Common Riding** Name for the **Riding of the Marches** festival in certain **Border** towns, eg **Hawick**, **Selkirk**.

**Common Sense Philosophy** School of philosophy that originated in 18th-century Scotland mainly in response to the radical scepticism of David **Hume**, which threatened the delicate balance between critical thought and the strong Christian convictions of the **Moderate** clergy, who composed the great bulk of the contemporary Scottish intelligensia. Thomas **Reid** was the first to expound the ideas that became vulgarised into a theory that common sense effectively disposed of the 'absurd' extremes of corrosive scepticism. Disciples such as Dugald

Stewart and publicists like James **Beattie** spread this view and Sir William Hamilton prolonged the ascendancy of these ideas deep into the 19th century, in France and in the United States.

**commonty** Shared grazing, a standard part of pre-industrial farming. This was *naitur gerss* or 'natural' grazing, which relied on natural regeneration rather than sown grass or deliberate cultivation. The grazing on hill farms and the common grazing on croft land is the modern survival.

**Community of the Realm** This phrase, used most famously in the **Declaration of Arbroath**, referred to the corporate traditional secular and

*The Cornet (standard bearer), at the head of his mounted supporters, bears the town flag up Kirk Wynd during Langholm Common Riding, probably in the 1950s.*

ecclesiastical leaders of the country, a hierachy topped by the Crown, but much wider than just the royal family.

**'Complaynt of Scotland'** An anonymous prose work in Scots published in 1549, possibly in Paris, which sought to arouse Scottish patriotic fervour against English interference in Scotland. It was addressed to the Queen Regent, **Mary of Guise**, and shows some influence of the French writer Alain Chartier, and the Roman poet Ovid. It uses many of the conventions of medieval literature, for example, the dream, the use of pastoral setting, and the personification of abstractions: one of the main sections is the exhortation of Dame Scotia to the Three Estates to be vigilant in defence of the public good.

**Comrie** Village near **Crieff** on the River **Earn**. Positioned on the **Highland Boundary Fault**, it has recorded many earth tremors, and Earthquake House (not open to the public) contains histori-cal and modern seismographs. A torchlight procession, the Flambeaux Procession, is held here each **Hogmanay**.

**Comunn Gaidhealach, An** (The Gaelic, or Highland Association) The organisation dedicated to promoting the

**Gaelic** language and culture generally was founded in **Oban** in 1891. It is best known for organising the peripatetic annual National **Mod**, the first of which was held in Oban in 1892.

**Comunn na Gàidhlig** (Gaelic Association CNAG) Government-funded organisation, based in **Inverness**, established in 1984 for **Gaelic** development. It works closely with the Gaelic communities, particularly in educational matters, and convenes an annual 'parliament' of Gaels to discuss current issues.

**Comyn, John, of Badenoch** (d.1306) Also known as the 'Red Comyn', he supported John **Balliol** and was prominent in the resistance to English rule in Scotland. His murder by **Robert the Bruce** led to civil war. The ultimate triumph of the Bruce party led to the eclipse of what had been the most powerful family in 13th-century Scotland.

**Conan Doyle, Sir Arthur** (1859–1930) Novelist, b. Edinburgh. A doctor, he is best remembered for his fictional detective Sherlock Holmes, about whom he wrote 60 stories. The inspiration for Holmes was Conan Doyle's lecturer Dr Joseph Bell. He also wrote a number of historical novels and non-fiction works.

*Sir Sean Connery.*

**Congregation, Lords of the** Name given to the group of Protestant lords who signed the **First Bond** in 1557, opposing closer links with France through **Mary, Queen of Scots'** proposed marriage to the Dauphin. They went on to lead a rebellion against **Mary of Guise** and Roman Catholicism in 1559–60.

**Congregational Churches in Scotland** There is evidence for congregations governing their own churches as far back as the early 17th century but later congregationalism traces its history in part to various 18th-century sects, including the Glasites (see John **Glas**). The Congregational Union of Scotland was formed in 1812 and has been involved in many mergers and attempted mergers over the years. Most of it has now merged with the United Reformed Church.

**Conn, Stewart** (1936– ) Poet and dramatist, b. Glasgow. He worked for many years as a BBC producer. His poetic output includes *Stoats in the Sunlight* (1968), *Under the Ice* (1978), *In the Kibble Palace* (1987) and *Stolen Light* (1999). The plays, *The Burning* (1971), *Play Donkey* (1977), *By the Pool* (1988) and *Clay Bull* (1998) belong to the Scottish theatrical revival of the 1970s and 80s. He was appointed Edinburgh **Makar** in 2002.

**Connel** Village at the mouth of **Loch Etive**, northeast of Oban. Connel Bridge, a remarkable steel cantilever structure, was built in 1903 to take the railway to **Ballachulish** across the Falls of Lora (which is a spectacular tide race); it is now a road bridge.

**Connery, Sir Sean** (1930– ) Actor, b. Edinburgh. Rose to fame as James Bond in *Dr. No* (1962), and starred in a further 6 Bond films. Other film credits include *The Untouchables* (1987) and *The Hunt for Red October* (1990). He won an Academy Award for best supporting actor in 1987.

**Connolly, Billy** (1942– ) Comedian, b. Glasgow. Also known as 'The Big Yin.' Originally a welder in the shipyards, his career in entertainment began with folk music and his group The Humblebums. His jokes were often more popular than the music, and he became a highly successful stand-up comedian. He has starred in various television series, and won acclaim for his performance as John Brown in the film *Mrs Brown* (1997).

**Conon, River** River in Easter Ross, which flows for 19km (12mi) through Strathconon and enters the **Cromarty Firth** at Conon Bridge, just south of **Dingwall**. The Conon hydroelectric scheme utilises the power of this river and others in the area.

**Constable, Archibald** (1774–1827) Publisher, b. Carnbee, Fife. He set up a publishing business in **Edinburgh**, producing the *Edinburgh Review* from 1802 and Walter **Scott**'s work from 1803. Scott's reckless secret borrowing against future earnings and the collapse of his London agents in 1826 led to Constable's bankruptcy.

**Constantine (Castantin)** (d.820) King of the Picts from 789, and possibly also of **Dal Riata**. This was an important stage in Gaelic-speaking Scots coming to rule over a single kingdom north of the River **Forth**.

**Constantine (Castantin) I** (d. c.877) King of the Picts and **Dal Riata**. A son of **Kenneth mac Alpin**, he reigned from 862. He was engaged in conflict with Scandinavian forces for much of his reign but still tried to extend Scottish control into **Strathclyde**. He was killed in battle by the Norse of Dublin.

**Constantine (Castantin) II** (d.952) King of Alba, reigned 900–43. He fought against the Scandinavians and latterly the English kingdom of Wessex which defeated him at Brunanburh (937). It may have been in his reign that the kingdom, which attained a new level of power under his rule, became known as Alba. In 943 he abdicated as king and retired to live as a monk in **St Andrews**.

**Constantine (Castantin) III** (d.997) King of Alba. He probably seized power in 995 after the murder of **Kenneth II**. He was himself murdered 2 years later, possibly by his successor **Kenneth III**.

**Conti, Rt Revd Mario Joseph** (1934– ) Roman Catholic clergyman, b. Aberdeen. Educated at **Blairs College**, Aberdeen and the **Scots College**, Rome. Parish priest in **Wick** and **Thurso**, he became Bishop of Aberdeen in 1977 and Archbishop of **Glasgow** in 2002.

**Conti, Tom** (1941– ) Actor, b. Paisley. His film credits include *Reuben Reuben* (1983) and *Shirley Valentine* (1989).

**conventicles** Secret gatherings of **Covenanters** proscribed by the Stewart regime after the Restoration of 1660. They met for worship, often in the open air and in remote places. They were particularly common in southwestern Scotland, where many remained loyal to ministers who had been removed from their parishes. Communion was sometimes held at these unauthorised gatherings, and a watch was kept, as the punishment could be a heavy fine or death.

**Convention of Royal Burghs** Representatives of the different **burghs** had gathered together to exert influence on government and to regulate trade and commerce from medieval times. The earliest records of the Convention date from 1552, and they met in **Edinburgh** annually from 1578. It was ended by **local-government** reform in 1975.

**Convention of Scottish Local Authorities** (COSLA) Established in 1975, as part of the re-organisation of local government. Representatives of all local authorites meet together to promote and support the work of the councils. Head office is in **Edinburgh**. See **local government**.

**Cook, Robin** (1946– ) Politician, b. Bellshill, Lanarkshire. He was Labour MP for Edinburgh Central 1974–83, and has been MP for Livingston since 1983. He was part of Tony Blair's Labour government from 1997, serving as Foreign Secretary until 2001, when he became Leader of the House of Commons. He resigned from the cabinet in 2003 in protest against UK involvement in the war in Iraq.

**cookie** Semi-sweet round glazed bun made with a yeast dough. Variations include cream cookie (with whipped cream inside), iced cookie, fruit cookie (with the addition of dried fruit).

**Cope, Sir John** (d.1760) English

soldier. In 1745, as Commmander-in-Chief North Britain, he commanded the unseasoned troops which were defeated in 15 minutes by the **Jacobites** at **Prestonpans**, a battle which is celebrated in the song 'Hey Johnnie Cope'. See also **Corrieyairack Pass**.

**Corbett** Name given to Scottish hills between 2500ft (762m) and 3000ft (914m) high, with a drop of 500ft (152m) between summits. They are named after John Rooke Corbett, a member of the Scottish Mountaineering Club in the mid 20th century who compiled a list of these hills. See also **Munro**.

**Corbett, Ronnie** (1930– ) Comedian, b. Edinburgh. Best known for his 1970s television sketch show with Ronnie Barker, *The Two Ronnies*. He has starred in a number of other series, including *Sorry* (1981), and has been a regular pantomime entertainer.

**Corgarff Castle** Tower house in a remote location on the Cock Bridge to **Tomintoul** road. Built in 1530, it was the scene of a terrible massacre when in 1571 Adam Gordon of Auchidoun burnt it down. Margaret Campbell, wife of the Laird of Forbes, and over 20 members of her household were killed. The castle was used by **Montrose** in 1645, and by the **Jacobites** in 1689

*Billy Connolly, CBE.*

and 1745. After **Culloden** it became a government military post. It is in the care of **Historic Scotland**.

**corn** see **oats**

**Corpach** Village near **Fort William** which is the start of the **Caledonian Canal**. The 'Treasures of the Earth' visitor centre, with displays on geology and gemstones, opened in 1995. A large-scale paper and pulp mill operated here from the 1960s to the 1980s; the paper mill still does.

**Corra Linn** Waterfall on the **Clyde**, near **New Lanark**, with a spectacular drop of 28m (92ft). The ruins of 16th-century Corra Castle are perched on a cliff overlooking Corra Linn.

**Corran** Village on the west shore of **Loch Linnhe**, southwest of **Fort William**. A ferry crosses the loch at Corran Narrows.

**corrie** A hollow on the side of a mountain or between mountains, from Gaelic *coire*, a mountain hollow; literally a cauldron, a kettle. Often found in place-names; see below.

**Corrie, Joe** (1894–1968) Writer, b. Slamannan, near Falkirk. Starting work as a coal miner in **Cardenden**, Fife, in 1908, he wrote poems, plays and short stories inspired by socialism and the mining community. His first volume of poems was *The Image o' God and other poems* (1928). Performances of his plays *Hogmanay* and *The Shillin'-a-week man* were given to raise money for impoverished miners.

**Corries, The** Roy Williamson (1936-90) and Ronnie Browne formed this influential folk band, playing a wide variety of different instruments and recording many albums. They are best remembered for 'Flower of Scotland', written by Roy Williamson, which has been adopted as an unofficial national anthem on many sporting occasions.

**Corrieshalloch Gorge** Dramatic box canyon in Wester Ross, 61m (200ft) deep, with sheer sides. Rich plant life flourishes here, and the Falls of Measach at the head of the gorge have a drop of 46m (150ft). A 19th-century suspension bridge spans the gorge, and there is also a viewing platform. In the care of the **National Trust for Scotland**.

**Corrievrechan** (or **Corryvreckan**) (Pronounced 'corrie vrekhkan') Strait between **Jura** and **Scarba** in the Inner **Hebrides**, in which spectacular tidal overfalls (i.e. standing waves) occur when the tidal stream running westwards meets large waves coming from the west. This can be dangerous to small boats. The roar of the turbulence can be heard for several miles. The tidal effect here is often erroneously described as a major whirlpool. Many legends have formed around it.

**Corrieyairack Pass** Now a footpath, this road from **Laggan** to **Fort Augustus** was constructed by General **Wade** along an existing droving route. It is remarkable for a series of sharp zigzags as it rises. It was used by the **Jacobites** in 1745 but General **Cope** declined to assault it, retreating to **Inverness** and opening the way to **Edinburgh** for Prince Charles Edward **Stewart**.

**Corrour** Isolated railway station on **Rannoch** Moor, west of **Loch Ossian**, near the highest point of the West Highland Line. No road runs to the station.

**Cortachy Castle** Near **Kirriemuir**, Angus, this castle dates in part from the 15th century but has been added to and reduced. The main seat of the Ogilvie Earls of Airlie, it still belongs to the family.

**COSLA** see **Convention of Scottish Local Authorities**

**Cospatric** (or **Gospatrick**) Originally Earl of Northumberland, he rebelled against William the Conqueror and was forfeited in 1072. He came to Scotland and was given **Dunbar** by **Malcolm III**. His son Cospatric became Earl of Dunbar and his descendants held the earldom until 1435.

**cottar** A paid labourer, usually a subtenant, who had a cottage but little or no land and was often dependent on casual work for survival. After the agricultural revolution, the word came to mean a married farmworker living in a cottage tied to his employment.

**cotton** Cotton became increasingly important to Scottish industry from the 1780s. Merchants imported the raw material from North American colonies and the West Indies. Technological development led to the establishment of big water-powered mills such as **New Lanark**, **Blantyre**, Catrine and Deanston. In the early 19th century many steam-powered mills and weaving factories were built in and around **Glasgow**. The bleaching, dyeing and printing of cotton products took place mainly in **Renfrewshire** and the **Vale of Leven**. From the 1860s competition, mainly from northern England, and more profitable uses for capital in the West of Scotland led to the industry's decline, except sewing cotton; see **J and P Coats**.

**Coulport** Village on the eastern shore of **Loch Long**. Previously the location for a ferry across to Ardentinny, it is now the site of a Royal Naval depot for the storage of nuclear weapons.

**country dancing** see **reel, strathspey, Royal Scottish Country Dance Society**

**Coupar Angus** (pop. 2190) Town on the River Isla, northeast of **Perth**. The town is divided by a stream which, as the former boundary between Perthshire and Angus, split the town at one time into two counties. Little now remains of the Cistercian abbey which was founded here in the 12th century and was destroyed in 1559. It is now a market town, but formerly had a maltings, a tannery and a linen factory.

**Courier, The** Dundee-based daily newspaper, founded 1802. Published by D C **Thomson** it covers a large part of east central Scotland. Its sister paper is the *Evening Telegraph*.

**Court of Session** Scotland's highest civil court, formally established in the mid 16th century which sits at Parliament House, Edinburgh.

The Covenanters' Preaching *by Sir George Harvey, c.1830.*

It is headed by the Lord President, with the Lord Justice Clerk second to him, and consists of 32 judges. It is divided into the Outer House, which deals with cases of first instance, with a single judge, and the Inner House, which is mainly an appeal court, normally with 2 divisions of 4 judges each. See also **law**, p.223.

**Court of the Lord Lyon** see **Lord Lyon**

**Cousin, David** (1809–78) Architect b. Edinburgh. City Architect, **Edinburgh** 1847-78, he was primarily a classicist. With John **Lessels** he replanned much of the Old Town of Edinburgh at Chambers Street, St Mary's Street, Jeffrey Street and Blackfriars Street for the City Improvement Trust, and designed the brilliantly picturesque Free Church Offices on the Mound (1858-63) and India Buildings (1864); outwith the city he designed many handsome palazzi for the British Linen Bank.

**Coutts, John** (1699–1751) Merchant and banker, b. Dundee. He founded a banking firm in **Edinburgh** which was later taken over by Sir William **Forbes**, and was Lord Provost 1742–4.

**Coutts, Thomas** (1735–1822), Banker, b. Edinburgh. Son of John **Coutts**, he joined a banking firm in London and was influential in turning it into a leading bank favoured by politicians and nobility. Ironically this family with **Jacobite** tendency eventually became bankers to the House of Windsor.

Today the Coutts Group, an international private bank, is part of the **Royal Bank of Scotland** Group.

**Cove** Village on the east shore of **Loch Long**, south of **Coulport** and adjacent to Kilcreggan, with an interesting series of early Victorian 'marine residences', several by Alexander **Thomson**. The Linn Botanic Gardens are nearby.

**Covenant** see **National Covenant**; **Solemn League and Covenant**

**Covenanters** A term used for very different movements in 17th-century Scotland. The first Covenanters were led by the bulk of the Scots aristocracy and signed the National Covenant in 1638 opposing the religious innovations of **Charles I**. The **Solemn League and Covenant** of 1643 was an inter-governmental agreement by which the Scots government allied with the English Parliament to stop Charles from winning the civil war in England. After the Restoration of Charles II and the restoration of episcopacy in the **Church of Scotland**, the Covenanters were radical presbyterian stand-outs, especially the followers of Richard Cameron, known as the **Cameronians**. In the **Sanquhar** Declaration they went so far as to disown **Charles II** and his brother **James** (VII and II). See also **Bothwell** Brig, **Cameronians**, Donald **Cargill**, **conventicles**, **Drumclog**, Alexander **Peden**, **Pentland Rising**.

**Cowal** Between **Loch Fyne** and **Loch Long**, this peninsula is popular with tourists, particularly from **Glasgow** and the surrounding area. The main town is **Dunoon**. The area is renowned for its sailing and its scenery, and its highest peak is Beinn an Lochainn, 901m (2955ft).

**Cowdenbeath** (pop. 11,627) Town in west Fife, which flourished with the development of the coal mines in the 19th century. The closure of the pits brought high levels of unemployment. In the 1980s, a massive petrochemical processing plant was built at Mossmorran, just to the southeast of the town, but the number of permanent jobs was limited. Cowdenbeath's local football team are known as the 'Blue Brazil', and their ground is also a stock-car racing venue.

**Cowie, James** (1886–1956) Artist, b. Cuminestown, Aberdeenshire. He studied in **Glasgow**, and taught art at Bellshill Academy, and Gray's School of Art, **Aberdeen**; and latterly as Warden of Hospitalfield, **Arbroath**. Best known for his portraits (often featuring his pupils) and still lifes, his art, in contrast to much Scottish painting of the 20th century, is highly finished and academic in appearance.

**Cox, Brian** (1946– ) Actor, b. Dundee. He has acted in theatre, films, radio and television. His film credits include *Rob Roy* (1995), *Braveheart* (1995) and *X-Men 2* (2003).

**Cox Brothers** Linen and jute manufacturers, with origins in the late 18th century, when the Cox family were engaged in the hand-powered linen industry in the village of Lochee (now part of **Dundee**), where they also owned a bleachworks. In 1841 the firm of Cox Brothers was formed, and between 1845 and 1850 they built the Camperdown Works. This was enlarged in the 1860s to process **jute**, and the firm prospered supplying sandbags during the American Civil War. In the late 19th century the firm employed 14,000, and was the biggest jute company in the world. The Cox family was prominent in the development of investment trusts, especially the Scottish-American group that invested heavily in Texas. With the decline of the jute industry in Dundee, Camperdown Works closed in 1981, and lay derelict until the 1990s, when the largest block, the 'Sliver Mill' was converted to flats.

**Craig, James** (1744–95) Architect, b. Edinburgh. He designed the first phase of **Edinburgh**'s New Town, winning a competition held in 1766. He built a number of other Edinburgh buildings, including Observatory House on Calton Hill.

**Craigcrook Castle** Tower house in **Edinburgh**, built in the 16th century and owned by a number of prominent Edinburgh families and individuals, including Archibald **Constable** and Francis **Jeffrey**. It was restored in 1989 and is now used as office space.

**Craigellachie** Village near **Dufftown**, at the point where the Rivers **Fiddich** and **Spey** join. A magnificent iron bridge over the Spey was built by Thomas **Telford** 1812–15. The Speyside Cooperage, open to the public, makes oak casks for many distilleries in the area. The Craigellachie Distillery, built in 1891, and rebuilt in the 1960s, mainly contributes to blended **whisky**, and the **Macallan** Distillery is nearby.

**Craigenputtock** see **Carlyle, Thomas**

**Craighouse** see **Jura**

**Craigie** Village near **Kilmarnock**. Craigie Castle, a ruined tower house dating mainly from the 15th century, belonged to the Wallaces of Riccarton.

**Craigievar Castle** Impressive and distinctive tower house near **Alford**, Aberdeenshire, built by the Danzig merchant William Forbes in 1626, and owned by that family until 1963. It is largely unaltered, with elaborate Jacobean woodwork and plasterwork. In the care of the **National Trust for Scotland**.

**Craiglockhart** Suburb to the southwest of **Edinburgh**. Craiglockhart Hill has several interesting buildings. Craiglockhart Hydropathic, designed by **Peddie & Kinnear** in 1878–80, was used during World War I as a military hospital, where officers were treated by Dr W H Rivers for the mental effects of war; they included the poets Wilfred Owen and Siegfried Sassoon. The building later became a Catholic College of Education and is all now part of **Napier University**, as is Old Craig House, dating from 1565 and altered in the late 19th century for the Royal Edinburgh Asylum. Craighouse is a vast towered chateau designed by Sydney **Mitchell** (1889–94), originally for well-off mental patients, with chalet pavilions in its landscaped park; it too is now part of the University.

**Craigmillar** A district of southeast **Edinburgh**. To the south is the substantial ruin of 14th-century Craigmillar Castle. Built by the Preston family, it has many royal associations. John, Earl of Mar and brother of **James III**, was imprisoned and may have been killed here on his brother's orders. **Mary, Queen of Scots** came here after the murder of **Rizzio**, and it was here that **Darnley**'s murder was plotted. Now in the care of **Historic Scotland**. From the 1890s the northern part of Craigmillar was developed as a large-scale brewing 'suburb', with by far the largest concentration of breweries in Scotland.

**Craignure** Village on the east coast of the island of **Mull**, which is the main ferry port for the crossing from **Oban**. A narrow-gauge railway runs to **Torosay Castle**.

**Craik, Sir Henry** (1846–1927) Civil servant and politician, b. Glasgow. As head of the **Scottish Education Department** from 1885 to 1904, he was the leading figure in the development of educational policy. He published *The State in its Relation to Education* (1884), and was responsible for the introduction of the national **Leaving Certificate** examination. He also edited and wrote influential works of literary criticism, and after leaving his official post in 1904, he became a Unionist MP.

**Craik, Dr James** (1730–1814) Doctor, b. Kirkbean, Dumfriesshire. An army surgeon, he emigrated to America. He became friend and physician to George Washington, served in the Continental Army from 1777 and became Physician General to the United States army.

**Crail** Former fishing village on the northeast coast of **Fife** which had become a royal **burgh** by 1178. An important trading centre in medieval times, Crail had a royal castle. The altered and partly restored church dates from the 13th century, and has an 8th-century Pictish cross-slab. The churchyard is remarkably rich in late 16th-and early 17th-century monuments, and there is a 16th-century Tolbooth. Crab and lobster fishing still take place from the harbour, rebuilt in 1610 and 1728, and remarkable for its vertically coursed masonry.

**Cramond** Now a suburb of **Edinburgh**, the village of Cramond lies on the Firth of **Forth** at the mouth of the River **Almond**. It was the site of an important Roman fort, which has been excavated. A stone lioness discovered here in the 1990s is displayed in the **Museum of Scotland**. In the 18th-19th centuries ironworks operated along the river; the 18th-century houses related to them remain, as does the 1658 parish church and Cramond House, 1680 and 1760, now the church halls. Cramond Island, in the Forth, can be reached by a causeway at low tide.

**cranachan** A traditional dish made from toasted oatmeal and

*Kate Cranston photographed by Thomas Annan in the 1890s.*

cream, often with the addition of soft fruit and **whisky**; made with raspberries, it is commonly found on Scottish menus today. It is sometimes known as cream crowdie.

**crannog** A dwelling built in prehistoric to medieval times offshore in a **loch**, either on an artificial island or supported by piles driven into the bed of the loch. There are remains in several lochs and a reconstructed crannog can be seen in **Loch Tay**, at the Scottish Crannog Centre near **Kenmore**.

**Cranston, Kate** (1850–1934) Businesswoman, b. Glasgow. She opened a number of innovative and very successful tea rooms in **Glasgow**, including the Willow Tea Rooms in Sauchiehall Street, now once more in use, and Ingram Street, the original interiors of which are held by Glasgow Art Galleries and Museums. The interiors and furnishings were designed by Charles Rennie **Mackintosh** from 1900 onwards.

*Crathes Castle, Aberdeenshire.*

**Crarae** Village in Argyll, 15km (9mi) southwest of **Inveraray**. Crarae Woodland Gardens were developed by Sir George Campbell, who owned the estate from 1926. He brought in many exotic plants, and the gardens are particularly well known for rhododendrons and azaleas and a fine collection of Southern beech (*Nothofagus*). Now in the care of the **National Trust for Scotland**. Crarae was formerly an important source of granite from a local quarry, which can still be seen.

**Crathes Castle** Tower house near **Banchory**, built for the Burnett family 1553–96 with a later south wing. It remained in the family until it was presented to the **National Trust for Scotland** in 1951. The interior is remarkable for its 17th-century painted ceilings. It has fine formal gardens with yew hedges dating from 1702 while the walled garden contains a series of themed borders.

**Crawford** Village near **Abington**, Lanarkshire, which was the site of a Roman fort. Crawford Castle, built by the Lindsays in the 12th century, is now ruined.

**Crawhall, Joseph** (1861–1913) Painter, b. Morpeth, Northumberland. He was an exceptional painter in watercolour who remains widely admired for his studies of street-scenes, hunts and of the rural countryside, in which animals are the predominant subject. As a student he was briefly in Paris and he became closely connected with the **Glasgow Boys** during the formative years of the School.

**Creag Meagaidh** Mountain north of Loch Moy, 1128m (3703ft) high. A **Munro**, it forms part of the Creag Meagaidh National Nature Reserve, which was bought for the nation in 1985.

**cream crowdie** see **crannachan**

**Cree, River** Flows southeast through **Galloway** for a distance of 40km (25mi), beginning in Loch Moan and entering Wigtown Bay at Creetown.

**Creech, William** (1745–1815) Bookseller and publisher, b. Newbattle, Midlothian. His **Edinburgh** bookshop became renowned as a meeting place for lawyers and authors. He published works by Adam **Smith** and Robert **Burns**.

**Crianlarich** Village 8km (5mi) southeast of Tyndrum, particularly well-known to travellers as the meeting point of 2 railways and 3 roads. The unmanned station is the point at which the **Oban** and **Fort William** lines come together, and the roads lead to **Loch Lomond**, to Oban or to **Perth**. Until the 1960s, the Oban line continued east to **Dunblane**.

**Crichton** Ruined castle in **Midlothian**, 10km (6mi) southeast of **Edinburgh**. A late-14th-century tower house was developed into a great courtyard castle in the 15th century. The courtyard façade of the north range has diamond rustication, with Italian influence; it was built by Francis Stewart, Earl of **Bothwell**, on his return from Italy in 1581. In the care of **Historic Scotland**. Nearby is the Parish Church of St Mary and St Kentigern, originally a collegiate church built by Sir William Crichton in 1449; now in the care of a local trust.

**Crichton, James** (1560–82) Poet, b. Eliock, Dumfriesshire. Also known as 'The Admirable Crichton'. He lived in France and Italy, and has become celebrated due to exaggerated accounts of his linguistic, intellectual and athletic ability. Uncertainty surrounds his death, but he may have been murdered. Stories of his life were published in 1652 by Sir Thomas **Urquhart**, and he was the inspiration for Sir J M **Barrie**'s fictional *The Admirable Crichton*.

**Crichton University Campus** see **Dumfries**

**Crieff** (pop. 6579) Town lying 19km (12mi) west of **Perth**, which became a Victorian spa resort and still attracts tourists. It was destroyed by the **Jacobite** army in 1716. Through much of the 18th century the largest cattle market in Scotland took place here; see **drove roads**. Crieff is now a centre of pottery and glass production. Morrison's Academy, founded here in 1860, is a renowned private school. Crieff Hydro is a large opulent Victorian hotel, recently modernised throughout as a child-friendly holiday complex.

**Crinan Canal** Opened in 1801, designed by John **Rennie**, it runs 14km (9mi) from **Ardrishaig** on **Loch Fyne** to **Crinan** on the Sound of Jura, allowing boats to avoid the long and sometimes dangerous route round the **Kintyre** peninsula and becoming a link in the all-water route from **Glasgow** to **Inverness**. There are 15 locks. Previously much used by fishing and commercial vessels, the canal now attracts many yachts in summer.

**Crochallan Fencibles** Late 18th-century **Edinburgh** club, founded by William **Smellie** and attended by Robert **Burns**. It met at Douglas's Tavern in Anchor Close, and is named after a Gaelic song sung by the landlord, '*Crodh Chailein*' ('Colin's Cattle').

**Crockett, S(amuel) R(utherford)** (1859–1914) Novelist and minister, b. Balmaghie, Dumfries and Galloway. Minister of the **Free Church** at **Penicuik**, he gave up his parish for full-time writing in 1895. He wrote short stories and novels, in the kailyard style, on a wide range of themes, including historical romances set in his childhood Galloway. His publications include *The Stickit Minister* (1893), *The Raiders* (1894), *The Lilac Sunbonnet* (1894) and *The Men of the Moss Hags* (1895).

**croft** A smallholding. In the **Highlands** and Islands this was the creation of the primary **Clearances**, when people were moved to marginal land on the coasts. Nowadays this land-holding is registered by the **Crofters' Commission**, which deals with over 17,500 crofts. But the *craft* or croft was once common in the Lowlands, occupied by tradesmen, or small tenants hoping to get a first step on the ladder of tenant farming.

**Crofters' Act** see **Crofters' Commission**

**Crofters' Commission** Body established to oversee crofting. The first Crofters' Commission was set up as a result of the Crofters' Act of 1886, which sought to protect the rights of crofters, giving small tenants in the **Highlands** and Islands security and reasonable rents. This was later disbanded, but a new Crofters' Commission was established in 1955 and still operates today. Since the 1976 Crofting Reform Act (re-enacted in the 1993 Act) it has also been easier for crofters to buy the title to their **crofts**. See also **Napier Commission**.

**Croft Moraig** see **Kenmore**

**Croick Church** see **Glencalvie**

**Cromartie, Sir George Mackenzie, 1st Earl of** (1630–1714) Politician and lawyer, b. Fife. A royalist, he supported **Charles II** and **James VII**. He became Justice General in 1678, and Secretary of State in 1702, and was a supporter of the **Union of Parliaments**.

**Cromarty** Village at the entrance to the **Cromarty Firth**, with many buildings dating from the 18th century. A royal **burgh** by 1264, it became an important trading and fishing port. The birthplace of Hugh **Miller** is in the care of the **National Trust for Scotland**, and Cromarty Courthouse, built 1784, is now a tourist attraction, as is the East Parish Church, 16th century and progressively remodelled in the 18th century with a fine **laird's loft** of 1739. See also **Ross and Cromarty**.

The White Drake *by Joseph Crawhall.*

*The Cuillins and Loch Scavaig, Isle of Skye.*

**Cromarty Firth** Inlet of the sea running southwest-northeast, to the north of the **Black Isle**. The sheltered waters were used during both World Wars as a naval base. There is an oil depot at **Nigg** and from the 1970s to the 1990s it had an oil-platform building yard; there is an oil rig repair yard at **Invergordon**. A ferry runs between **Cromarty** and Nigg. A low-level bridge, part of the main A9, crosses the sea at the inland end of the Firth.

**Cromdale, Haughs of** Site, to the east of **Grantown-on-Spey**, of a battle in 1690 between the cavalry of the Williamite commander, General Hugh **Mackay**, and what was left of the army commanded by Viscount **Dundee**. Though Thomas Buchan the **Jacobite** general had reinforcements from Ireland, he was surprised and totally routed. An extraordinary Jacobite ballad, still sung, turns this defeat into a famous victory.

**Cronin, A(rchibald) J(oseph)** (1896–1981) Novelist and doctor, b. **Cardross**, near Dumbarton. He qualified as a doctor but left medicine after some years for health reasons. His first novel, *Hatter's Castle* (1931), was a great success, and issues he raised in *The Citadel* may have contributed to the creation of the National Health Service. The TV and radio series *Dr Finlay's Casebook* was based on his autobiographical stories.

**Crossraguel Abbey** Well-preserved ruin of a Cluniac monastery, near **Maybole**, Ayrshire. It was founded in the early 13th century, and rebuilt after being destroyed during the **Wars of Independence**. The patrons were the Earls of Carrick, one of whom became king as **Robert I**. Now belongs to **Historic Scotland**.

**crowdie** Refers to either: (1) a kind of soft cheese, traditionally made in the **Highlands**; (2) a dish of oatmeal mixed with cold water. See also **cranachan**.

**Crow Road** see **Campsie Fells, Lennoxtown**

**Croy** Former mining and whinstone-quarrying village near Kilsyth with a railway station on the line between **Glasgow** and **Edinburgh**. Remains of the **Antonine Wall** can be seen at Croy Hill.

**Croy** Small village 11km (7mi) southwest of **Nairn**.

**Cruachan, also Ben Cruachan** Mountain in **Argyll**, above the Pass of **Brander**, highest point is 1126m (3694ft). Cruachan Power Station, built inside the mountain as part of the **Loch Awe** Hydro-Electric Scheme, is open to the public. It is a 'pumped storage' scheme in which the turbines can either generate electricity or can pump water to the high reservoir as a form of energy storage. Such storage is particularly needed for power from nuclear reactors which cannot be shut down daily at times of low demand.

**Cruden, Alexander** (1701–70) Publisher, b. Aberdeen. From 1732 he worked as a printer and bookseller in London, and was appointed bookseller to the queen. In 1737 he published a *Concordance of the Old and New Testaments*, a revised version of which is still in print. He was on several occasions suspected of insanity and sent to an asylum.

**Cruickshank, Andrew** (1907–88) Actor, b. Aberdeen. A regular on the London stage from the mid 1930s, he found nationwide fame as the grouchy Dr Cameron, the senior partner in the 1960s TV series *Dr Finlay's Casebook*, based on A J **Cronin**'s stories.

**Cruickshank, Helen** (1886-1975) Poet, b. Hillside, near Montrose. While living in **Edinburgh** she became prominent in the literary circle of Hugh **MacDiarmid** and others. She was an active supporter of women's suffrage and Scottish nationalism. She wrote in both **Scots** and English, and drew on traditional styles in many of her poems.

**cruisie lamp** A kind of oil lamp used in former times, consisting of two boat-shaped iron bowls suspended from an iron bar on a wall. Oil, usually fish oil, was dripped by a wick from one bowl to the other.

**Cruithne** see **Picts**

**crumpet** In Scotland refers to a cake baked on a **girdle**, larger and thinner than a **pancake**, though the English meaning now tends to dominate because of the wide sale of English crumpets in supermarkets.

**Cuillin** (Gaelic **An Cuilfhionn** or **An Cuilthionn**) Mountain range whose dramatic peaks dominate the Isle of **Skye**. Including 12 **Munros**, the Cuillin are popular with climbers. The highest peak is **Sgurr Alasdair**. The Black Cuillin form the main group, and the Red Cuillin is the lower range to the east. See also **Sgurr Dearg**, **Sgurr nan Gillean**.

**Culbin** Stretch of beach and forest lying to the west of **Findhorn** Bay. Culbin Sands had been building gradually over many years when a great storm of 1694 saw the sand sweep over fields and houses, creating a desert-like landscape. The natural defences of the sand dunes had been depleted by the removal of grasses for thatch. Culbin Forest has been established by the Forestry Commission to stabilise the area. Visitors are welcome, and there is an RSPB Nature Reserve.

**Culdees** Communities of the early Irish/Gaelic church. The name comes from *Céli Dé*, meaning servants of God. They did not come under any particular monastic rule, and died out from the 12th century as the Scottish church increasingly moved closer to English and European models. Ruins of buildings originally used by the Culdees can be seen, eg St Mary of the Rock at **St Andrews**.

**Cullen** Village on the **Moray Firth**, 10km (6mi) east of **Buckie**.

The 13th-century church is all that remains of medieval Cullen. The existing planned village was laid out in the 1820s by the Earl of Seafield. Cullen was a successful fishing port and the fisherfolk lived in Seatown of Cullen, by the shore. The town is dominated by the viaduct of the former Moray Coast line of the Great North of Scotland Railway, opened in 1886 and closed in the 1960s.

**Cullen, William** (1710-90) Medical professor, b. Hamilton. Professor of Chemistry at **Glasgow** and of Medicine at **Edinburgh University**, he was an outstanding lecturer who emphasised the role of the nervous system in disease, and coined the term 'neurosis'.

**Cullen skink** A thick soup, originating in **Cullen**, on the north-east coast, made with smoked haddock, potatoes, onion and milk. Nowadays it appears as a traditional Scots dish on many menus.

**Culloden, Battle of** 16 April 1746. The **Jacobite** forces of Charles Edward **Stewart**, having retreated from Derby, made an abortive attempt to surprise the **Hanoverians**. Though his troops were hungry, wearied and dispirited, Charles insisted on fighting a battle on the inappropriate site of Drummossie Moor. This boggy and uneven site hampered the Jacobite charge, whilst enabling superior Hanoverian firepower to inflict horrendous casualties at very short range. The battle and the vicious reprisals which followed saw the end of the 1745–6 Rising and the destruction of much of the Highland way of life. This was the last battle on British soil. See also **Cumberland, Duke of**, **Jacobite Risings**. The **National Trust for Scotland** has a visitor centre at the battle site. Culloden House was the home of Duncan **Forbes** of Culloden; the present house dates from 1780 and is now a hotel. In recent decades a commuter village for **Inverness** has developed in the area.

**Culross** Village in west **Fife**, on the Firth of **Forth**, with many 17th- and 18th-century buildings restored by the **National Trust for Scotland**. The Palace, built in 1597 for mine-owner George Bruce of Culross (later of Carnock; d.1625), and the Tolbooth, dating originally from 1626, are two reminders of Culross's prosperous trading days. Culross Abbey was founded for Cistercian monks in 1215, but a religious community existed here many centuries earlier. Part of the abbey church serves as the parish church, and contains a remarkable monument to George Bruce of Carnock.

**Cults** Village southwest of **Aberdeen**, on the **River Dee**, now a popular commuter suburb.

**Culzean Castle** Near **Maybole**, Ayrshire. Elaborate castellated mansion with neo-classical interiors, designed by Robert **Adam** in the late 18th century for the Earl of Cassilis. It has a dramatic clifftop setting on the **Ayrshire** coast, and incorporates a 16th-century tower house. The **National Trust for Scotland** has owned the property since 1945, and a flat within it was reserved for the use of President Eisenhower to honour his wartime achievements. The landscaped park with terraced gardens and an Adam viaduct became a country park in 1969. The home farm, also by Adam, is the visitor centre.

**Cumberland, William Augustus, Duke of** (1721–65) Prince and British general, b. London. The second surviving son of George II, he fought gallantly but lost against the French at the Battle of Fontenoy in 1745. His troops defeated the **Jacobites** at the Battle of **Culloden** in 1746. He ordered the slaughter of the wounded on the battlefield and led vicious reprisals throughout the **Highlands**, becoming known as 'Butcher Cumberland'.

**Cumbernauld** (pop. 49,664) Town 21km (13mi) northeast of **Glasgow**. Originally a small industrial village which had thrived on handloom weaving and a landscaped park with a mansion by William **Adam**, it was designated a New Town in 1955. New housing and amenities were built to accommodate a new population, largely relocated from Glasgow. Business parks around the town offer employment in electronics, manufacturing and other industries.

**Cumbernauld and Kilsyth District** see **Strathclyde Region**

**Cumbraes** Two small islands in the Firth of **Clyde**. Great Cumbrae can be reached by ferry from **Largs**. The only town is Millport; its most interesting feature is the Scottish Episcopal Cathedral of the Isles and its cloistered college, built by the 6th Earl of Glasgow to designs by William Butterfield, 1849–51, reputedly the smallest in Europe. The island attracts many visitors, particularly from **Glasgow**. Little Cumbrae, which is privately owned, was the site of a castle used by **Robert II**. The surviving tower house is 14th and 15th century. There is also an early **lighthouse** on the island, and a more modern one.

**Cumming, Alan** (1965– ) Actor, b. Perthshire. After studying in Glasgow he became a regular on stage and TV in Britain, then graduated to film with appearances in *Prague* (1992) and *Goldeneye* (1995). His reputation in the USA grew significantly in 1998 when he took on the role of the MC in the stage version of *Cabaret*, and he has since enhanced that standing with commercially successful movies such as *Spy Kids* (2002).

**Cumnock** (pop. 9358) Town east of **Ayr**, which was heavily dependent on coal mining, but has also been known for the manufacture of snuff boxes. There were strong **Covenanting** sympathies in the area, and Alexander **Peden** is buried here. The village of New Cumnock, created in the 17th century, lies 10km (6mi) to the southeast.

**Cumnock and Doone Valley District** see **Strathclyde Region**

**Cunard Shipping Line** Samuel Cunard, a shipowner from Nova Scotia, went into partnership with Robert **Napier** and George **Burns** to build steamships to cross the Atlantic. Their first ship, the *Britannia*, was built on the **Clyde** and launched in 1840. Their British and North American Royal Mail Steam Packet later became the Cunard Line, today known for its luxury cruise liners, particularly the flagship *QE2* and *Queen Mary 2*.

**Cunningham, Phil** (1960– ) Musician, b. Edinburgh. A composer and performer and musical director of Scottish traditional music, he played accordion in the band Silly Wizard 1976–83, before concentrating on a solo career. Since 1988 he has formed a highly successful partnership with Aly **Bain**.

**Cunninghame** Area in **Ayrshire**, covering the northern part, which was held from the 12th century by the De Morevilles. From 1975 to 1996 it was a district of **Strathclyde Region**.

**Cunninghame Graham, Robert Bontine** see **Graham, Robert Bontine Cunninghame**

**Cupar** (pop. 8506) Town in northeast **Fife**, a royal **burgh** from 1328. A market town, it was the county town of Fife until 1975, and has many buildings which date from the 18th and 19th centuries, including Scotland's finest surviving early railway station (1847). The first performance of Sir David **Lyndsay**'s play *Ane Satyre of the Thrie Estatis* took place here in 1535.

**curling** Sport in which polished granite stones are slid across ice to a 'house'. It may have originated in Scotland, and the rules recorded at Duddingston Curling Club in 1804 were largely adopted as an international standard. It is known as 'the roaring game' because of the sound the stones make as they cross the ice. In 2002 the Scottish Women's Curling Team sparked great interest and celebrations by winning a gold medal at the Winter Olympics. A major outdoor curling match, the Bonspiel, which traditionally takes place on the Lake of **Menteith**, can only be held in the most severe winters.

**Currie** Village southwest of **Edinburgh**, which is now a suburb of the city. A paper mill operated on the **Water of Leith** in the 18th and 19th centuries. Lennox Tower, which dates from the 15th century and is now ruined, belonged to the Earls of Lennox and later to George **Heriot**. The campus of **Heriot-Watt University** is nearby.

**Currie, James** (1756–1805) Doctor and biographer, b. Kirkpatrick-Fleming, Dumfriesshire. After some years in America, he became an influential doctor and practised in Liverpool, before returning to his native Dumfriesshire. He is remembered as the first biographer and editor of Robert **Burns**; while his edition of the poems was successful and raised money for Burns's family, the biography portrayed him as an alcoholic womanizer.

**Currie, Ken** (1960– ) Artist, b. North Shields. After study at **Glasgow School of Art**, Currie became known in the mid 1980s for his large-scale works depicting moments in Scottish labour history; among the most notable is his series of 8 paintings for the People's Palace in Glasgow. More recently his works have avoided specific incidents, concentrating instead on depicting individuals whose hollow expressions reflect universal inhumanity and suffering.

**Cursiter, Stanley** (1887–1976) Artist, b. Orkney. In the early 1910s he produced a remarkable series of paintings influenced by the avant-garde Italian Futurists, but thereafter painted more conventional still lifes, interior scenes and landscapes. From 1930 he was Director of the **National Galleries of Scotland**, during which time he campaigned vigorously for a separate gallery of modern art.

**Cuthbert, St** (c.635–87) Monk and missionary, b. Lauderdale. He entered the monastery at Old **Melrose**, becoming prior there in 661 and was later bishop of Hexham and Lindisfarne. He was an active preacher and missionary and had spells living as a hermit. Under the pressure of Viking attack his remains were moved to various locations until they were finally settled at Durham in 999. Devotion to Cuthbert straddled the political divide between England and Scotland throughout the Middle Ages.

**Cutherbertson, Sir David** (1900–89) Doctor and biochemist, b. Kilmarnock. As a clinical biochemist at **Glasgow** Royal Infirmary, he did ground-breaking research on negative nitrogen balance as a consequence of traumatic injury. During World War II he was involved in significant research on the treatment of burns. From 1945 to 1965 he was Director of the **Rowett Research Institute**, Aberdeen, where he oversaw a major

expansion and a re-focussing of its research work onto improved animal nutrition to meet the needs of humankind. The Nutrition Society awards an annual Sir David Cutherbertson Medal, named in his honour.

**Cutler, Ivor** (1923– ) Writer and musician, b. Glasgow. The creator of such deadpan drollery as the *Life In A Scotch Sitting Room* series of recitals, he has been a regular performer on radio since the late 1950s. Though long resident in London, he has continued to find humour, by turns absurd and poignant, in the stereotypical misery of his homeland. His published work includes *A Flat Man* (1977), *Gruts* (1986) and *Glasgow Dreamer* (1990).

**Cutty Sark** Clipper ship built at **Dumbarton** in 1869, used initially for the tea trade with China and then for the Australian wool trade. Her name is that of the young witch in **Robert Burns**'s poem *Tam O' Shanter*. The ship has been restored and placed in a dry dock at Greenwich, and since 1957 has been open to the public.

*The Cutty Sark, Greenwich.*

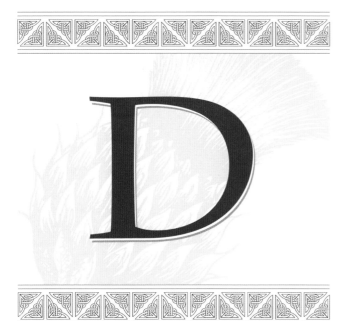

**Daiches, David** (1912– ) Scholar and literary critic, b. Sunderland. Son of a rabbi, he was brought up and educated in **Edinburgh** and Oxford. After a few years teaching in Chicago University, he worked in the British Embassy in Washington DC during World War II. He taught in Cornell and Cambridge Universities, and was the first Professor of English at the University of Sussex (1961–77) before retiring to Edinburgh. His many works of literary criticism and biography include *Robert Burns The Poet* (1950) and books on Sir Walter **Scott**, and R L **Stevenson**. Other works include *Two Worlds* (1956), an account of his Edinburgh upbringing, *Scotch Whisky: Its Past and Present* (1969) and *God and the Poets* (Gifford Lectures) (1983).

**Dailuaine** Distillery near **Aberlour**, founded 1851, one of the largest on **Speyside**. It had its own branch line from the Strathspey Railway.

**Daily Record** see **Newspapers**, p.288

**Dairsie** Village in Fife, 5km (3mi) northeast of **Cupar**, a late 18th-century weaving village, also called Osnaburgh, from the coarse linen woven there, similar to that of Osnabrück in Germany. To the south is the now closed parish church, Gothic survival with plate tracery built by Archbishop Spottiswoode in 1621. Nearby is the rib-arched bridge built by Archbishop James **Beaton** c.1530 and the later 16th century castle of the Learmonths, recently rebuilt from ruins.

**Dalbeattie** (pop. 4289) Small town 20km (13mi) southwest of **Dumfries**, of grey granite houses, with a tall-spired church by **Peddie & Kinnear** (1878–80). Also called Birch Holm, it was built at the head of tidal water on the River Urr. Granite has been quarried here since the mid 19th century, and for a time large quantities went to the building of docks, bridges etc throughout Britain.

**Dalcross** see Inverness

**Dale, David** (1739–1806) Industrialist, philanthropist and lay preacher, b. Stewarton, Ayrshire. Trained in the linen trade, he spotted the opportunities in cotton. In 1785, with Richard Arkwright, the English inventor of the spinning mule, he set up cotton mills in **New Lanark**, where, in advance of his son-in-law, Robert **Owen**, he pioneered new methods of employee welfare and education. He also invested in mills in **Catrine** and **Stanley**. He was the Glasgow agent for the **Royal Bank of Scotland**. In 1768 he co-founded a religious sect, the Old Scotch Independents, that preached practical Christianity.

*David Dale, by Peter Mackenzie, from his book Glasgow Characters, 1857.*

**Dalgarven Mill and Country Life Museum** see **Kilwinning**

**Dalgety Bay** (pop. 10,011) Fife town on a bay of the same name on the Firth of **Forth**, mainly a dormitory town for **Edinburgh**, developed in the 1960s on the Donibristle estate. It has some light industry. On the shore of the bay are the ruins of the 13th-century St Bridget's Church, in the care of **Historic Scotland**.

**Dalglish, Kenny** (Kenneth Mathieson) (1951– ) Footballer and football manager, b. Glasgow. He started his highly successful playing career with **Celtic** in 1967 and was transferred to Liverpool in 1977 for what at that time was a record fee. He played for Scotland 102 times. He was manager of Liverpool (1985–91) and Blackburn Rovers (1991–5) and then director of football until 1996.

**Dalhousie, Fox Maule, 2nd Baron Panmure and 11th Earl of** (1801–74) Soldier and politician, b. Brechin Castle. After 12 years in the army he became Liberal MP for Perthshire (1835–7), **Elgin** (1838–41) and **Perth** (1841–52) and was Secretary for War (1845–52). He was one of the few Scottish noblemen who supported the **Free Church** at the **Disruption** of 1843. He succeeded his father as Baron Panmure in 1852 and entered the House of Lords. He was again Secretary for War (1855–8) and oversaw the end of the Crimean War. He succeeded his cousin, the 10th Earl, in 1860.

**Dalhousie, J(ames) A(ndrew) Broun-Ramsay, 10th Earl and Marquis of** (1812–60) Politician, b. Dalhousie Castle. In 1837 he became MP for Haddingtonshire and the following year, on the death of his father, he took his seat in the House of Lords as Earl of Dalhousie. He became President of the Board of Trade (1845–7). He was Viceroy of India (1847–56), the youngest ever appointed. Influenced by the Utilitarian ideas of Jeremy Bentham and James **Mill**, he oversaw improvement of the administration and the development of the telegraph and railway systems. His dogmatic insensitivity to Hindu and Muslim culture and his annexation of Indian princely states when there was a lapse in the succession were resented. This did much to prepare the way for the great Mutiny of the Bengal sepoy army and the accompanying civil revolts in 1857.

**Dalhousie, John William Ramsay, 13th Earl of** (1847–87) Sailor and politician. After a career in the Royal Navy, he became MP for Liverpool in 1880 but in the same year, on the death of his father, Admiral George Ramsay, the 12th Earl, he was called to the House of Lords. In 1883 he was one of a royal commission enquiring into the state of Ireland, which led him to support Gladstone's home rule policy. In 1886 he was Secretary for Scotland.

**Dalhousie Castle** Curtain-walled castle in Midlothian, 2km (1mi) west of Newtongrange on the River South **Esk**. It dates from the mid 15th century, with main tower house, gate house and angle tower, remodelled internally by William **Burn** 1825. It is now a hotel.

*Kenny Dalglish, Scotland vs Holland, in the 1978 World Cup.*

**Dalkeith** (pop. 11,567) Market town in Midlothian, 10km (6mi) southeast of Edinburgh. It is now the administrative centre of **Midlothian** Council. An agricultural and later a mining centre, it now has a number of light industries. St Nicholas Church is a 15th-century collegiate church, its nave restored by David **Bryce** (1852). To the north is Dalkeith Palace, strictly Dalkeith House, former residence of the Dukes of Buccleuch, which was rebuilt as a great baroque palace by James **Smith** (1702–11) for Anna, Duchess of Monmouth and Buccleuch: its main front, probably deliberately, was a grander version of **William II and III**'s Het Loo in The Netherlands. It is now used as a base for students from the University of Wisconsin. Its grounds, an 18th-century planned landscape, form Dalkeith Country Park, through which the Rivers North and South **Esk** flow. It has nature trails, farm animals and the magnificent Montagu Bridge by Robert **Adam** (1792). **Newbattle Abbey** is nearby.

**Dallas** Village on the River Lossie, 10km (6mi) southeast of **Forres**. Its 16th-century 3m (12ft) high market cross dedicated to St Michael was said to mark the centre of the former county of **Moray**. The parish church was built in the 1790s on the site of earlier ones. Nearby Dallas Lodge was built as stables and steadings for Sir Robert Gordon of Gordonstoun in 1688; the planned mansion was never built. To the north is Dallas Dhu Distillery, founded in 1899, now a **whisky** museum in the care of **Historic Scotland**.

**Dalmahoy** Midlothian estate of the Earls of Morton, 3km (2mi) southeast of **Ratho**, famous for its trees. It is now a prestigious **golf** club and country club, with the mansionhouse as hotel; it was built by William **Adam** in 1725 and enlarged in 1830. Dalmahoy Hill to the southwest has the remains of Iron-Age and post-Roman/Dark-Age forts.

**Dalmally** (Gaelic **Dail-Mhàilidh**) Village in **Argyll** on the River **Orchy** near where it flows into **Loch Awe**. To the north is the octagonal Glenorchy Church, built 1810–11 on the site of an earlier church. To the southwest at a viewpoint is a monument to **Donnchadh Bàn Mac an t-Saoir**.

**Dalmellington** (pop. 1407) Small town 21km (13mi) southeast of **Ayr**, a former **burgh**, at the edge of the moors associated with the **Covenanters**. It had coal-mines in the 19th and 20th centuries. There was a priory here in the 13th century. The town is also Scotland's second book town (see **Wigtown**). See also **Dunaskin**.

**Dalmeny** Village 2km (1mi) east of **South Queensferry**. The 12th-century parish church of St Cuthbert, restored in the 20th century, is the best-preserved Norman church in Scotland. Dalmeny House, 3km (2mi) to the northeast, the home of the Earls of Rosebery, was the first Tudor revival house in Scotland, built in 1814–17. It has important collections of paintings, furniture, tapestries and porcelain and Napoleonic relics and memorabilia, some of it from the Rothschilds' Mentmore. The estate includes Dalmeny Woods (through which it is possible to walk from **Queensferry** to **Cramond**). The family's former home, Barnbougle Castle, close to the shore, is a 16th-century tower house restored as a library by Maitland **Wardrop** (1881) for the 5th Earl of **Rosebery**. The Eagle Rock, near the shore, has a carved figure attributed to the Romans (in the care of **Historic Scotland**).

**Dalmore** Large Victorian malt-**whisky** distillery at **Alness** on the north shore of the **Cromarty Firth** founded 1839. During World War I it was used as a base by American forces maintaining the submarine minefields in the North Sea.

**Dalnaspidal** Settlement south of **Drumochter**; its railway station, the highest in Scotland, was closed in 1962. A road built by General **Wade** in 1728–29, above the present road, is marked by the Wade Stone, 3km (2mi) to the east.

**Dalquharran** Massive 15th-century tower house of the Kennedys, on the Water of Girvan 10km (6mi) southwest of **Maybole**, Ayrshire, with a new house of 1679 attached, now roofless; above is the surprisingly sited new castle built by Robert **Adam** for his niece and her husband Thomas Kennedy in 1785, now also roofless. Nearby is a coal mine which caught fire in 1849 and burned for half a century.

**Dalradian** Major belt of varied metamorphic rocks occupying the southern part of the **Grampians**.

**Dal Riata** or **Dalriada** Kingdom whose twin centres were Antrim and **Argyll**, the latter settled by Irish colonists by the 6th century. With an important centre at **Dunadd**, Dal Riata was prominent in the political, religious and cultural life of North Britain. The kingdom of Scotland was founded on the fusion of Dal Riata and neighbouring Pictland, a process underway long before the unification of the kingdoms attributed to **Kenneth mac Alpin (Cináed mac Alpin)** in 843.

**Dalry** (pop. 5,398) Town on the River Garnock, 5km (3mi) north of Kilwinning, its central square, the Cross, dominated by the tall-spired St Margaret's Church designed by David Thomson (1874). One of the 18th-century **Ayrshire** weaving towns, it later became a centre for ironworks and mining, now gone. Nearby is Blair House, built (1617 and 1638) around a 15th-century keep, home of the Blair family for 700 years.

**Dalrymple, Alexander** (1737–1808) Pioneer hydrographer and father of the Admiralty chart, b. New Hailes, Midlothian. A younger brother of Sir David Dalrymple, Lord **Hailes**, he went out to Madras in the service of the East India Company in 1752 and rose rapidly through the patronage of Governor Lord Pigot. He cruised extensively in Eastern waters, reaching Canton in 1764 and returning to London in 1765. He would have commanded the Pacific expedition of 1768 sponsored by the government and the Royal Society to observe the transit of Venus in 1769, but his insistence on being granted a commission as a captain in the Royal Navy was unacceptable to the Admiralty and he was superseded by Captain James Cook. He then poured his energies into geographical and cartographic work, publishing extensively and becoming Hydrographer to the East India Company in 1779. With the establishment of a hydrographic office in the Admiralty in 1795 he became the Royal Navy's first official Hydrographer. In a contentious career ending in dismissal shortly before his death, he laid down the basis for the creation of global coverage by a series of Admiralty charts. Modified versions of some of his own charts were still in use in the 1960s. He even laid down precedents for the 19th-century policy of making these charts available to all other countries.

**Dalrymple, Sir David** see Hailes, Lord

**Dalrymple, James** see Stair, 1st Viscount

**Dalrymple, John** see Stair, 1st Earl of

**Dalrymple, John** see Stair, 2nd Earl of

**Dalrymple, Sir John, 4th Baronet of Cranston** (1726–1810) Lawyer, historian and improver. He championed John **Home**, the clerical playwright, in 1756. In 1757 he published an important study of feudal property, but after searching Continental archives, he proved in his 3-volume *Memoirs of Great Britain* (1771, 1790) that Whig politicians had accepted subsidies from Louis XIV and the exiled Stewarts.

**Dalrymple, William** (1967– ) Writer of travel books and history, b. Edinburgh. He now lives in London and Delhi. His travel books about the Middle East and India have won many awards; they include *In Xanadu* (1989), *City of Djinns* (1993), and *From the Holy Mountain* (1997). His historical work, *White Mughals* (2003), was judged Scottish Book of the Year.

**Dalswinton** Small village 10km (6mi) north of **Dumfries**. On a small loch in the grounds of Dalswinton House the first steamboat in Britain was tried out by Patrick **Miller** and William **Symington** in 1788. Beside the River **Nith** is the site of a large Roman fort.

**Dalwhinnie** (Gaelic **Dail-chuinnidh**) Village on the River Truim, north of **Drumochter** near the head of **Loch Ericht**, a centre for anglers and climbers. Dalwhinnie Distillery, founded in 1897, is the highest distillery in Scotland and has a visitor centre.

**Dalyell, Tam (General Sir Thomas Dalyell)** (c.1599–1685) Soldier, b. The Binns, West Lothian. Descended from a landed family, he served in the Royalist cause in Ireland 1642–50 and was at the Battle of Worcester in 1651. He was captured and imprisoned in the Tower of London from which he escaped in 1652. He went into exile but returned to Scotland in 1654 where he helped the Royalist side in **Glencairn**'s Rising. Wanted dead or alive, he fled again to the Continent where he joined the Russian army and campaigned against the Poles, Tartars and Turks. After returning to Scotland, in 1666 he was made Commander-in-Chief in Scotland to curb the **Covenanters**; he dispersed them at **Rullion Green** and was

*General Sir Thomas Dalyell.*

responsible for their further suppression. From 1678 until his death he was MP for **Linlithgow**. In 1681 he raised the **Royal Scots Greys**.

**Dalyell, Tam** (1932– ) Politician, b. The Binns, West Lothian, a descendant of the above. After an education at Eton and Cambridge he trained as a teacher and taught in **Bo'ness**. He became Labour MP for **West Lothian** (1962–83) and then **Linlithgow** (1983– ). Not a party hack, he opposed **devolution**, and raised what became known as the 'West Lothian question' on the problem of Scottish Westminster MPs being able to vote on English matters, when Scottish matters would be dealt with by the **Scottish Parliament**. Active in Parliament, he had strong views on issues such as the Falklands war, the **Lockerbie** disaster, the environmental fallout of the 1991 Gulf War, and the war against Iraq. In 2001 he became the Father of the House (oldest serving MP).

*King David I (pictured left, with his grandson, Malcolm IV) on a charter, published after his death, granting lands and other rights to the monks of Kelso Abbey.*

**D**

**Dalziel** Locality on the north bank of the River **Clyde**, between **Motherwell** and **Wishaw**. Dalzell House is a large courtyard castle of the Dalzells, who built the 15th-century tower house which is the nucleus of the present house, much enlarged after being bought by the Hamiltons of Dalzell in 1647. Remodelled by Robert William Billings (1857-9), who elaborated the splendid terraced gardens beneath it. The surrounding estate, open to the public, contains an early 19th-century arboretum and Japanese gardens created in the 1920s.

**Damian, John** (*fl.* 1504-13) Alchemist at the court of **James IV**, b. France or Italy. He was briefly Abbot of Tongland (1504-9). He is said to have attempted to fly from **Stirling Castle** with home-made wings attached to his arms (described in a poem by William **Dunbar**.)

**Darien Scheme** The term for a colonial venture that exploited the 1695 Act empowering the Company of Scotland Trading to Africa and the Indies to establish overseas trading establishments as a parallel to the English East India Company. The founder of the scheme was William **Paterson**, who identified the Darien peninsula in Panama as suitable for the first Scottish colonial emporium. The first of 3 expeditions, with Paterson on board, embarked in 1698, but when the Scots reached Darien, they were faced by the violent hostility of the Spanish government, which did not control the area but was determined to exclude other Europeans. For diplomatic reasons King William forbade English West Indies merchants to deal with the Scots. The climate engendered disease. As a trading site Darien was an idiotic choice and a sitting target for Spanish attacks from nearby Cartagena, so the scheme ended in disaster and was one of the factors that brought about the **Union** of 1707.

**Darling, Sir Frank Fraser** (1903-79) Naturalist and ecologist, b. Edinburgh. He became Chief Officer of the Imperial Bureau of Animal Genetics (1930) before turning to field research into red deer, thereafter studying and writing about a range of animals and other aspects of country life. He became an important figure in the conservation movement and was an adviser to the Nature Conservancy Council in setting up the red deer project on **Rum**. His works include *Island Years* (1940) and *Island Farm* (1943), accounts of his life spent on islands such as the **Summer Isles** and **North Rona**, and *The Natural History of the Highlands and Islands* (1947).

**Darnaway Castle** Large symmetrical castellated mansion to the southwest of **Forres**, by Alexander Laing (1802) for the 9th Earl of Moray, aggrandised by later terraced layout of the gardens. Behind it is Earl Randolph's Hall, built in the 1450s, still with its original roof; it contains the painting of the 'Bonnie Earl' (see James Stewart, Earl of **Moray**).

**Darnley, Henry Stewart, Lord** (1546-67) King consort, second husband of **Mary, Queen of Scots**, b. Temple Newsam, Yorkshire. Eldest surviving son of the 4th Earl of Lennox and Margaret Douglas, daughter of **Margaret Tudor** and the 6th Earl of **Angus**, he was next in succession to the throne of England after Mary, his cousin. His mother was ambitious for his marriage to Mary and her intrigues were watched closely by Queen Elizabeth, who in November 1561 summoned mother and son to London where they were kept in confinement for over a year. In 1565 Darnley married Mary at Holyrood and was created Earl of Ross and Duke of Albany; he was referred to as king, but denied real authority by his rapidly disillusioned wife. Dissatisfied with his position, he took part in the murder of David **Rizzio**, Mary's Italian secretary. He was charmed by Mary into betraying his associates, who set out to kill him. In 1567 there was an explosion in the house of Kirk o' Field, to the southeast of **Edinburgh**, where Darnley was convalescing from syphilis, and his body was found strangled in the garden.

**Darvel** (pop. 3361) Town on the River Irvine, a former **burgh**, 14km (9mi) east of **Kilmarnock**. A textile town, it specialised in machine-lacemaking from the late 19th century. Sir Alexander **Fleming** was born near Darvel.

**dauch** see **davach**

**davach** or **davoch** A land measure used for tax assessment etc, probably based originally on produce rather than area, varying from area to area. Used mainly in the **Highlands**, the word comes from Gaelic *dabhach* with similar meaning, literally a vat, large tub. Also found in the form *dauch*, especially in placenames.

**David I** (c.1080–1153) King of Scots (1124–53). The youngest son of **Malcolm III** and St **Margaret**, following the death of his parents in 1093 he was sent with his siblings to England for safekeeping. In 1100 his sister Matilda married Henry I of England, opening up opportunities for patronage such as the grant of his marriage to Matilda, widow of the Earl of Northampton, in 1114. After the accession of his brother **Alexander I** in 1107 David exercised rule in southern Scotland as Prince of Cumbria. In 1124 he succeeded his brother and introduced initiatives already tested in the south, featuring English and continental landholders (secular and ecclesiastic) and methods of government. Among the innovations were the establishment of **sheriffdoms** and **burghs** and the development of an indigenous coinage. He was interested in ecclesiastical reform also and was responsible for a number of new monastic foundations. (Because of this, his descendant **James I** is said to have described him as 'ane sair sanct for the croune', quoted by an early 16th century historian. With greater power and resources than any previous Scottish king, he intervened in the civil war in England between Stephen and Matilda from 1136. Although defeated at the Battle of the **Standard** (1138), territorial expansion was achieved and David died at Carlisle, master of a 'Scoto-Northumbrian' realm. He was succeeded by his grandson, **Malcolm IV**.

**David II** (1324–71) King of Scots (1329–71) b. Dunfermline. At the age of 4 he was married to Joanna, sister of Edward III of England and within a year succeeded his father, **Robert I**. Edward **Balliol**'s invasion and victory at **Dupplin Moor** in 1332 was followed by direct English intervention and another defeat for David's supporters at **Halidon Hill** in 1333. David and Joanna were sent to France for safekeeping, only returning in 1341 when the Bruce party again held sway in most of Scotland. The king now mounted attacks on England culminating in his

defeat and capture at **Neville's Cross** in 1346. Eventually released in 1357, the rest of the reign was dominated by attempts to pay the heavy English ransom and political discord between David and his nephew and heir, the future **Robert II**. The king outfaced magnate opposition and did oversee developments in Scottish governance before his sudden death aged just 46.

**David, Earl of Huntingdon** (1152–1219) Grandson of **David I** and younger brother of **Malcolm IV** and **William I**. An important magnate in both Scotland and England, he attained the earldom of Huntingdon in 1185 and helped spread Anglo-French influences in Scotland. On the death of William, he did not make a claim for the throne, supporting the succession of William's son, **Alexander II**. His son John 'the Scot' inherited his earldom, and his three daughters married Alan of Galloway, Robert Bruce and John Hastings and produced three descendants who in 1291 claimed the throne.

**Davidson, John** (1857–1909) Writer and poet, b. Barrhead, near Paisley. The son of a minister, he was educated at **Edinburgh University** and taught in various schools before moving to London in 1889. He worked as a journalist but, although he wrote plays and two novels, he became best known for his poetry, which looked at the modern world in an uncompromising, realistic manner. His poem, 'Thirty Bob a Week', was much admired by T S Eliot and Hugh **MacDiarmid**. His convinced atheism was expressed in a number of long philosophical poems, his 'Testaments'. After moving to Penzance, he committed suicide, oppressed by poverty and fear of illness.

**Davidson, Randall Thomas, Baron Davidson of Lambeth** (1848–1930) Anglican clergyman, b. Edinburgh. He was Bishop of Rochester and of Winchester, and then Archbishop of Canterbury (1923–8), during which time he worked hard to improve the role of the Anglican church and its relations with other churches.

**Davie, Alan** (1920– ) Artist, b. Grangemouth. In the 1950s, after seeing American Abstract Expressionist painting, he began to produce his own highly distinctive abstract works and quickly developed an international reputation. From the 1960s and '70s onwards his imagery – he has a great interest in non-Western cultures – has become more identifiable but his process of painting freely and intuitively (influenced by Zen Buddhism and his own ability as a jazz musician) has remained fundamental to his style.

**Davie, Elspeth** (1919-95) Novelist and short-story writer, b. Kilmarnock. Educated at **Edinburgh University** and **Edinburgh College of Art**, she taught art in various parts of Scotland before settling in Edinburgh. She married the philosopher George Elder **Davie**. Her first novel, *Providings*, was published in 1965. She won the Katherine Mansfield Award for her short stories; her collections include *The Night of the Funny Hats* (1980), *A Traveller's Room* (1985) and *Death of a Doctor* (1992).

**Davie, George Elder** (1912- ) Philosopher, b. Dundee. He spent most of his working life teaching philosophy in **Edinburgh University**. A scholar of the **Scottish Enlightenment**, he is best known for *The Democratic Intellect: Scotland and her Universities in the Nineteenth Century* (1961), an account of the generalist tradition in Scottish university education and its erosion, which he deplores. *The Crisis of the Democratic Intellect* (1986) looks at later developments.

**Daviot** Aberdeenshire see **Loanhead of Daviot**

**Daviot** Small village 8km (5mi) southeast of **Inverness**. Its early 19th-century church is a notable landmark. Daviot House is just to the northeast. The ruins of Daviot Castle are on the site of a prehistoric fort.

**Davies, Sir Peter Maxwell** see **Hoy, Kirkwall**

**Davis, Margaret Thomson** (1926- ) Popular novelist, who lives in Glasgow. The author of more than 20 novels, many set in **Glasgow**, especially the *Breadmakers* saga in 3 volumes (1972-3), the *Tobacco Lords* trilogy (1976-7) and the *Clydesiders* trilogy (2003). She has also written many short stories. In 2001, she won the Lord Provost's Award for Literature, for 'bringing Glasgow's history to vibrant life.'

**Davis, Peter Harland** (1918-92) Botanist and plant collector, b. Somerset. He travelled widely in the eastern Mediterranean and especially Turkey from which he introduced a great many new species while collecting over 50,000 plants. He was Reader in Plant Taxonomy at **Edinburgh University** and had a long association with the **Royal Botanic Garden Edinburgh**. His life work, *The Flora of Turkey*, in 10 volumes, greatly enhanced the reputation of the Garden but also changed the emphasis of research from southeast Asia to southwest Asia.

**davoch** see **davach**

**Dawyck House** Scots Jacobean house by William **Burn** (1832, extended 1898), in the River **Tweed** valley, 10km (6mi) southwest of **Peebles**. Its park and gardens are now Dawyck Botanic Garden, a specialist garden of the **Royal Botanic Garden**, in Edinburgh, with conifers, cotoneasters, berberis and Scottish native plants. It has a pinetum and an arboretum, planted from 1868 onwards, with landscaped walks, and the trees include the unique Dawyck Beech.

**Deacon Blue** Rock group formed in **Glasgow** in 1985 by singer and songwriter Ricky Ross (1957- ). The other members of the group are James Prime (1960- ), keyboard-player, Graeme Kelling (1957-2004), guitarist, Douglas Vipond (1966- ), drummer, and Ewan Vernal (1964- ), bass guitarist. Their other singer is Lorraine McIntosh (1964- ) who married Ross. Their debut album, in 1987, was *Raintown*, which was a UK chart success.

**Deacon Brodie** see **Brodie, William**

**Dean Castle** see **Kilmarnock**

**Dean Gallery** see **Scottish National Gallery of Modern Art**

**Dean of Guild** Originally the head of a guild in a royal **burgh**; latterly (until 1975) a member of the town council who presided over the Dean of Guild Court, which had jurisdiction over the buildings of a **burgh**. In earlier times it also dealt with **weights and measures**.

**Deans, Jeanie** A fictional character created by Sir Walter **Scott** in his novel *Heart of Midlothian* (1818). He based his morally strong and constant character on the real-life Helen Walker of Irongray (d.1791), who walked to London to plead to Queen Caroline the case for her sister who had been condemned to death for infanticide.

**Deas, Francis William** (1862-1951) Architect and gardener, b. Hasler, Hampshire. Closely associated with Robert **Lorimer**, he built outstanding Arts and Crafts houses at Braehead (St Boswells) (1905), Fyndynate (1909) and The Murrell, **Aberdour** (1908), built for himself, with a remarkable terraced garden inspired by Gertrude Jekyll.

**Debatable Land** Area in the western **Borders** between the Rivers **Esk** and Sark claimed both by Scotland and England. At times only grazing of cattle was tolerated in the disputed zone, only finally partitioned between the realms in 1552. The Scots' Dyke, cutting through the Debatable Land, still marks the boundary between England and Scotland.

**Declaration of Arbroath** see **Arbroath**

**decree,** earlier also **decrete, decreet** A (final) decision of a court. Decrees of the **Court of Session** are recorded in the Register of Acts and Decrees of Court of Session, which was started in 1542.

**Dee** Fifth-longest river in Scotland and the most rapidly flowing, it rises in the Wells of Dee in the **Cairngorms** and runs some

145km (90mi) south and then east to the North Sea at **Aberdeen**. Its lower valley, known as Deeside, is a popular tourist destination, with aristocratic estates alongside, such as **Balmoral**, **Invercauld** and Abergeldie.

**Dee** River that flows south from Loch Ken in Kirkcudbrightshire through Tongland Loch and into Kirkcudbright Bay. It is part of the Galloway Hydroelectric Scheme.

**Deep Sea World** see **North Queensferry**

**Deer, Book of** see **Book of Deer**

**Deeside** see **Dee, River**

**defamation** In Scots law, the injuring of a person's reputation either in writing or by speech, equivalent to English libel or slander.

**defender** In Scots law, a defendant in a civil case.

**Defoe, Daniel** (1660–1731) English writer, b. London. A Dissenter and supporter of **William II and III** and Mary, he was imprisoned (1703–4) for his ironic pamphlet advocating the suppression of Dissenters. After his release he was employed as a secret agent by the government. He undertook several journeys to Scotland (1706–8, 1712), acting as a political agent for the English government and as their leading pro-**Union** propagandist in 1706–7. Later he reported on **Jacobite** activities. His *Tour through Great Britain* was published 1724–6. His best-known work, *Robinson Crusoe* (1719–20), is based on the life of Alexander **Selkirk**.

**Delgatie Castle** see **Turriff**

**Demarco, Richard** (1930– ) Artist, b. Edinburgh. After studying at **Edinburgh College of Art**, in the 1960s he became an enthusiastic advocate of modern arts, promoting the work of both foreign and Scottish artists, including the German artist Joseph Beuys and the Polish artist and theatre director Tadeusz Kantor. He co-founded the **Traverse Theatre** in **Edinburgh** in 1963, and has been Director of the Richard Demarco Gallery since 1966. During the Edinburgh International Festival each year he organises programmes of dance, music and theatre as well as art.

**de Medina, Sir John** see **Medina, Sir John de**

**Denholm** Village 8km (5mi) northeast of **Hawick**. Formerly a stocking-weaving centre, it has a village green with an obelisk commemorating John **Leyden**, who was born here. It was also the birthplace of the botanist John **Scott** and the lexicographer Sir James **Murray**.

**Denness, Mike** (1940– ) Cricketer, b. Bellshill. Captain first of

*The River Dee at Braemar.*

Kent and then of England, he was acknowledged as one of the most astute post-war skippers. His first-class career included 4 Test centuries and over 25,000 runs.

**Denny, William, and Brothers Ltd** Shipbuilding company founded in **Dumbarton** in 1818 as William Denny and Son. The firm of Denny Brothers was formed in 1844, and as William Denny and Brothers settled in the Leven Shipyard in 1867. There were several other businesses owned by the family, including an engine works. The Leven Shipyard built the first ocean-going steel steamship in 1879, and at the same time constructed the world's first commercial ship-model experiment tank, which the company used to develop hulls for high-speed vessels. In 1901 they built the world's first steam-turbine driven commercial vessel, and developed a successful business in turbine-driven cross-Channel vessels. The firm closed in 1963, owing to the contraction of its traditional markets. The ship-model experiment tank has been preserved in Dumbarton.

*The Devil's Beef Tub.*

**Denny and Dunipace** Two small towns that formed one **burgh** and parish. **Denny** (pop. 9797) is an industrial town on the River Carron, 8km (5mi) west of **Falkirk**; it had iron-founding, coal-mining and paper mills and the latter survive. **Dunipace** (pop. 2441) adjoins Denny to the northwest, across the River Carron.

**Denny Ship-Model Experiment Tank** see **Denny, William** and **Dumbarton**

**Dere Street** The Roman road that ran from Yorkshire to the Firth of **Forth**. The modern A68 road follows its course in parts. Begun by **Agricola**, it ran through Corbridge (beside Hadrian's Wall) over the Cheviot Hills to **Cramond** via **Newstead**, **Lauderdale** and **Inveresk**. A stretch of it can be seen beside **Soutra** Aisle in **Midlothian** (in the care of **Historic Scotland**).

**Dervaig** Planned village on the Isle of **Mull**, 8km (5mi) south-west of **Tobermory**, founded by Alexander MacLean of Coll (1799). Kilmore Parish Church designed by MacGregor **Chalmers** (1904–5) is a prominent landmark with an Irish-type round tower. Nearby are 3 groups of standing stones dating from the 2nd millennium BC. The Mull Little Theatre was founded here in 1965–6.

**Deskford Church** Roofless medieval church in the small Northeast village of Kirktown of Deskford, 5km (3mi) south of **Cullen**, with a magnificently sculptured sacrament house of 1551, associated with the demolished castle of the Ogilvies; in the care of **Historic Scotland**.

**Dessary** see **Glen Dessary**

**Deuchar, Jimmy** (1930–93) Jazz musician, b. Dundee. A trumpeter, his first big breaks came in the late 1940s and early 1950s when he was part of the London scene. He later worked with the big band led by Kenny Clarke and Francy Boland.

**Deveron, River** Northeast river that flows for just under 99km (62mi) north and then east to **Huntly** and then in a northeasterly direction via **Turriff** to the North Sea near **Banff**. Over the years it has featured in several ballads.

**Devil's Beef Tub** A deep semicircular hollow in the hills at the head of **Annandale**, 8km (5mi) north of **Moffat**. The source of the River Annan, it was used by 16th-century **reivers** to hide cattle stolen in their raids. A Roman road runs along one of its flanks and a Roman jewel dating from 304–6 was found here in the 1780s.

**Devil's Elbow** Formerly a series of steep and tortuous turns on the A93 from **Braemar** to **Glenshee**, just to the south of Cairnwell Pass. It roughly followed an 18th-century military road but was re-aligned in the 1960s. It leads to one of Scotland's main ski centres, **Glenshee**, at the Cairnwell Pass.

**Devil's Point** (in Gaelic **Bod an Deamhain** the demon's penis). Mountain (1004m/3303ft) in the **Cairngorms**, a **Munro**, next to **Cairntoul**.

**Devil's Staircase** An old **drove road** that runs from near the head of **Glencoe** over Stob Mhic Mhartain to **Kinlochleven**. It was also used as a military road and is now part of the **West Highland Way**.

**Devine, Tom** (1946– ) Historian, b. Motherwell. After a long career in **Strathclyde University**, in 1998 he became director of the Research Institute of Irish and Scottish Studies, **Aberdeen University**. His publications, largely on economic and social aspects of Scottish history, began with *The Tobacco Lords* (1975) and include *The Great Highland Famine* (1988), *Scottish Emigration and Scottish Society* (1992), *The Scottish Nation, 1700–2000* (1999) and *Scotland's Empire 1600–1815* (2003).

**devolution** The movement in Scotland in the late 20th century towards more self-government, ending successfully in the opening of the new **Scottish Parliament** in 1999. See also **Campaign for a Scottish Assembly, Claim of Right, Scottish Constitutional Convention**.

**Devon** River that rises in the **Ochil Hills** and flows east through Glen Devon to the village of Glendevon and then southeast to Crook of Devon. From there it flows west to Menstrie and then south to join the River **Forth** just west of **Alloa**.

**Devorguilla** (c.1209–90) Daughter of Alan, Lord of Galloway and granddaughter of **David, Earl of Huntingdon**. In 1233 she married John Balliol of Barnard Castle and their son John **Balliol** became King of Scots in 1292. She was responsible, with her husband, for the foundation of Balliol College, Oxford, financed the first stone bridge in **Dumfries** and founded **Sweetheart Abbey**, where she is buried.

**Dewar, Donald (Campbell)** (1937–2000) Politician, b. Glasgow. Trained as a solicitor, he was the first Labour MP for Aberdeen South (1966–70). When he lost his seat he worked as a children's reporter in Lanarkshire before returning to parliament in 1978 as MP for Glasgow Garscadden (later Anniesland). A strong believer in **devolution**, he was Shadow Secretary of State for Scotland (1983–97), Secretary of State for Scotland (1997–9) and the first First Minister of the **Scottish Parliament** from 1999 until his premature death in 2000. As Secretary of State he initiated the construction of the new **Scottish Parliament** building at Holyrood.

**Dewar, John A, John Alexander Dewar, Lord Forteviot** (1856–1929) Distiller, b. Perth. With his brother Thomas he built his father's small wine and spirit merchant's business into a major **whisky** distilling business, which after mergers became part of the **Distillers' Company Ltd** in 1925. He was Liberal MP for **Inverness-shire** from 1900 until 1916 when he was ennobled, becoming the first 'whisky baron'.

**de Wet/de Witt, Jacob** see **Wet, Jacob de**

**Dick bequest** Significant endowment for schools in the Northeast, established in 1833 by James Dick, a wealthy merchant from **Forres**. The better salaries and accommodation this afforded accounted for the impressive quality of parish education in that area.

**Dick Veterinary College** see **Edinburgh University**

**Dickson, Barbara** (1947– ) Singer, songwriter and actress, b. Dunfermline. She first started singing in folk clubs and when her talent was recognised moved to a wider stage, appearing in 1973 in the musical by Willy Russell, *John, Paul, George, Ringo and Bert*. Her first success in the pop charts was 'Answer Me' (1976) followed by 'Another Suitcase, Another Hall' (1977). Her albums include *The Barbara Dickson Songbook* (1985).

**Dickson, Maggie** (*fl.* 1728) Fishwife who was hanged in the Grassmarket, **Edinburgh**, in 1728 for not revealing the death of her illegitimate child. The rattling of the cart carrying her body to Musselburgh jolted her back to life. She was allowed to go free because it was considered impossible to hang a person who had been officially pronounced dead. She was known as 'Half-Hangit Maggie'.

**dictionaries** see p.108

**Dighty Water** River which rises in the **Sidlaw** Hills and flows eastwards, through the northern suburbs of **Dundee**, to enter the **Firth of Tay** between **Broughty Ferry** and **Monifieth**. It was an important source of industrial water power for mealmills and linen manufacture, the only one in the area, and was used until surprisingly late; the Balouniefield bleachfield in Dundee used its water power until after World War II.

**Dillon, Des** (1961– ) Writer, b. Coatbridge. His novels include *Me and Ma Gal* (1995) and *Itchycooblue* (1998). His main plays are *Six Black Candles* (2001; published as a novel in 2004) and *Lockerbie 103* (2003). He has also written poetry, short stories and scripts for television.

**Dingwall** (Gaelic **Inbhir-pheofharain**) (pop. 5026) Market town at the head of the **Cromarty Firth**, 18km (11mi) northwest of **Inverness**, a former royal **burgh** and county town of **Ross and Cromarty**; from 1975 to 1996 it was the administrative centre of Ross and Cromarty District. It once had a royal castle and was a stronghold of the Earls of Ross until their downfall. It has an award-winning museum, and a tower on the hill to the south commemorates Sir Hector **MacDonald** ('Fighting Mac').

**dirk** A short dagger worn in the belt by Highlanders, now as part of **Highland dress**. See also **sgian dubh**.

**Dirleton** Village in East Lothian, 4km (2mi) west of **North Berwick**. It has a large green with 17th-, 18th- and 19th-century houses on 3 sides. On the 4th is the substantial ruin of Dirleton Castle, dating from the 13th century with 14th-, 15th- and 16th-century additions; the surrounding gardens include a restored Victorian garden and an early 20th-century Arts and Crafts garden; all in the care of **Historic Scotland**. The Open Arms Hotel is popular.

Scotland has a distinguished tradition in lexicography, not only in dictionaries of the Scots and Gaelic languages, but also in contributions by Scots to dictionaries of English.

The earliest known dictionaries in Scots are two small Latin-Scots vocabularies published in the 1590s. In the 18th century two very different trends produced word lists. As part of the attempt to anglicise language, lists of so-called Scotticisms were produced to help people to avoid them; see James **Beattie**. On the other hand many people saw the value of the Scots language and its literary traditions, and older texts were published with notes and glossaries; see Thomas **Ruddiman**. Robert **Burns** added a word list to his own poems in 1786 and 1787.

John **Jamieson**'s *Etymological Dictionary of the Scottish Language* is a remarkable work, well ahead of its time; it was first published in 2 volumes in 1808, with a so-called supplement of equal length in 1825, and it continued to be used, in its various later editions, well into the 20th century, overtaken only by the considerable Scottish content of the *Oxford English Dictionary* (OED, completed in 1928). The Scottish material is probably due in no small measure to the fact that two of its four main editors were Scots, including its main architect, Sir James **Murray**. Sir William Craigie (1867-1957) not only made a large contribution to the OED, but also edited the *Dictionary of American English* (1938-44) and became the first editor of the *Dictionary of the Older Scottish Tongue* (12 volumes 1931-2002), which covers Scots from its earliest medieval records and up to 1700. He was succeeded in the 1950s by A J Aitken (1921-98), who was a pioneer in the use of computers in lexicography.

In the early years of the 20th century a project of word collection was begun by William Grant (1863-1946) which eventually developed into the 10-volume *Scottish National Dictionary* (1931-76). Grant was succeeded by David Murison (1913-98) who brought the work to completion. Since then the *Concise Scots Dictionary* (1985) and other shorter works have brought these riches to a wider public, and the two major dictionaries are now available on the Internet in an electronic version produced in **Dundee University**, known as the *Dictionary of the Scots Language*. The work is being carried forward by Scottish Language Dictionaries.

Gaelic dictionaries have a less voluminous history but some interesting people have been involved in them. The first printed word list (1702) was by the Revd Robert **Kirk**. Alasdair **Mac Mhaighstir Alasdair** compiled *Leabhar a Theagasc*

*Ainminnin* (*Galick and English Vocabulary*, 1741) for the **SSPCK.** The first formal Gaelic dictionary was the *Galic and English Dictionary* (1780) by the Revd William Shaw (1749-1831). Nineteenth-century dictionaries included that of the Highland Society of Scotland completed in 1828, and the *Dictionary of the Gaelic Language* by Dr Norman **Macleod** (Caraid nan Gàidheal) and Dr Daniel Dewar.

In the early 20th century a remarkable work was produced by an Englishman, Edward Dwelly (1864-1939), the *Illustrated Gaelic to English Dictionary*, first published in parts (1903–11). Dwelly used Macleod and Dewar as a base and spent long years collecting data from all kinds of sources; the book remains a prime souce of information on Gaelic a century later. Many smaller dictionaries have been published, including the more specialised *Etymological Dictionary of the Gaelic Language* (1896) by Alexander MacBain and H C Dieckhoff's *Pronouncing Dictionary of Scottish Gaelic (based on the Glengarry Dialect...)* (1932), and more recently dictionaries compiled by Gaelic learners, such as Angus Watson's *Essential Gaelic-English Dictionary* (2001). A historical dictionary that was begun in **Glasgow University** in the 1960s ran into problems, but a new project is now being planned.

Scottish contributions to the lexicography of English have not been confined to the OED. The *Imperial Dictionary*, first published by **Blackie** & Son (1847-50), edited by John Ogilvie, revised by Charles Annandale (1882-3), became one of the most popular dictionaries of its time, not least because of its excellent illustrations and generous inclusion of technical terms and encyclopedic information. It later became a main source for the American *Century Dictionary* (1889-91, 6 volumes), which in its turn had considerable influence on 20th-century dictionaries of English.

The firm of W & R **Chambers** began publishing dictionaries in 1864 and, though now a subsidiary of a large French company, continue to produce important English, as well as bilingual, dictionaries under their new name of Chambers-Harrap. From 1911 till the 1990s they also published the 1-volume *Chambers Scots Dictionary*. William **Collins**, now HarperCollins, have long been publishers of dictionaries, from the little Collins Gems to the *Collins Dictionary of the English Language* (1979), and including the highly innovative dictionary for learners, *Collins Cobuild English Language Dictionary* (1987) edited by John M Sinclair. See also **language**.

Signing the Act of Separation and Deed of Demission *by David Octavius Hill, showing the signing of the document that signalled the formal break with the Church of Scotland, or the Disruption.*

**Discipline, Books of** see **Books of Discipline**

**Disruption** The term for the division in the **Church of Scotland** in 1843 when over a third of the ministers attending the **General Assembly** walked out over the issue of patronage of the church – whether landlords or members of parishes chose ministers. The dissenting ministers, led by Thomas **Chalmers**, formed the **Free Church of Scotland**.

**district** (1975–96) see **local government**

**district court** This court replaced the former JP and **burgh** courts, and is usually staffed by **justices of the peace** but in cities sometimes by stipendiary magistrates (paid and legally qualified). They deal with about 40% of lesser criminal cases.

**Distillers Co, The** Formed in 1877 by the amalgamation of 6 firms making grain **whisky**. In 1925 it amalgamated with the 'big four' whisky blenders and between the wars bought up many malt-whisky distilleries. The firm was taken over in the 1970s by Guinness and its assets are now part of the Diageo group.

**Divach Falls** see **Drumnadrochit**

**Dochart** River that runs northeast from **Loch Dochart** down Glen Dochart to the head of **Loch Tay**, with the picturesque Falls of Dochart at **Killin**.

**Docherty, Glen** see **Glen Docherty**

**Docherty, Tommy** (**Thomas Henderson**) (1928– ) Football player and manager, b. Glasgow. He was capped for Scotland 25 times and in 1971 became Scotland's team manager for just over a year. A flamboyant character, he managed various clubs, including Manchester United.

**Dods, Meg** see **Johnstone, Christian Isobel**

**Dolan, Chris** (1957– ) Writer, b. Glasgow. He travelled widely and lived abroad for spells, before returning to **Glasgow**. He has written short stories, including the collection *Poor Angels* (1995), as well as plays and documentaries for film and television. His writing has won several awards.

**Dollar** (pop. 2877) Small town, a former **burgh**, at the foot of the **Ochil Hills**, 10km (6mi) northeast of **Alloa**. Dollar Academy was set up in 1818, funded by John McNab, a Dollar boy who made his fortune as a sea captain; the original building was designed by William Henry **Playfair**. The town had textile mills in the late 18th and early 19th centuries and some coal-mining in the 20th. It is now a popular residential area and has an award-winning museum. To the north is lush, narrow Dollar Glen with bridges, paths and ravines leading up to 15th-century **Castle Campbell** at its head.

**Dolly the sheep** see **Roslin Institute**

**Don, River** Scotland's sixth-longest river, rising 11km (7mi) to the south of **Tomintoul** and flowing 128km (80mi) northeast and then east by **Strathdon**, **Alford** and **Inverurie** and then southeast to the North Sea at **Bridge of Don**, just north of Old **Aberdeen**.

**D**

**Donald** Name given to hills in the **Lowlands** of 2000ft (610m) or over; so named after Percy Donald who listed them. See also **Corbett** and **Munro**.

**Donald I** (**Domnall mac Alpín**) (d.862) King of Scots and Picts (Alba) (858–62). He succeeded his brother, **Kenneth mac Alpin** (Cináed mac Alpín), consolidated Scottish rule over the Picts and introduced the law of **Dal Riata**. He was succeeded by his nephew **Constantine I** (Castantín I), son of Kenneth (Cináed).

**Donald II** (**Domnall mac Castantín**) (d.900) King of Alba (889–900). Son of **Constantine I** (Castantín), he succeeded after deposing **Giric**, the previous king. He died at Forres, perhaps campaigning against a challenge to his own rule. His son eventually ruled as **Malcolm I** (Máel Coluim I).

**Donald III** (**Domnall mac Donnchada**) (or **Donald Bane** 'Donald the Fair') (c.1031–1100) King of Scots (1094–7). The younger son of **Duncan I** (Donnchad mac Crinain) brother of **Malcolm III** (Máel Coluim mac Donnchada), he profited from a native backlash against Anglo-Saxon influences after Máel Coluim's death and claimed the throne. He was briefly ousted by **Duncan II** (Donnchad mac Máel Coluim) in 1094 and was finally overthrown in 1097 by **Edgar**, both sons of Máel Coluim who enjoyed English support. Blinded and imprisoned, he died in captivity.

**Donald, Ian** (1910–87) Obstetrician, b. Paisley. Professor of Midwifery in **Glasgow University**, he was the inventor of the first successful diagnostic ultrasound machine and originator of the pregnancy scan.

**Donald Bane** see **Donald III**

**Donald Dubh** ('Black Donald') (c.1480–1545) Grandson of John, 4th and last **Lord of the Isles**. Kept prisoner by the Campbells of Argyll for much of his life, he escaped or was released in 1543 and attempted, with English help, to gain the lordship. He collected a force in Ireland, but the enterprise aborted after his sudden death.

**Donaldson, Sir David** (1916–96) Artist, b. Chryston, near Glasgow. He studied at **Glasgow School of Art**, where he subsequently taught, combining this with his career as one of Scotland's most recognised portrait painters of the 20th century. A portrait of Her Majesty the Queen (1966) led to Donaldson's appointment in 1977 as Painter and Limner to Her Majesty the Queen in Scotland.

**Donaldson, Gordon** (1913–93) Historian, b. Edinburgh, of Shetland extraction. He was Professor of Scottish History in Edinburgh University from 1963 until his retiral in 1979, when he was appointed Historiographer Royal in Scotland. His work was influenced by both his long service in the Scottish Record Office and his strong episcopalian religious views. He edited texts, produced important works of references and wrote engagingly for a wider readership, particularly on **Mary, Queen of Scots**.

**Donaldson, Margaret** (1926– ) Psychologist, b. Paisley. Educated at the Universities of **Edinburgh**, Geneva and Harvard, she was Professor of Developmental Psychology at Edinburgh from 1980 to 1982. Her publications on children's intellectual, linguistic and social skills, *A Study of Children's Thinking* (1963) and *Children's Minds* (1978), have been widely influential in developmental psychology and education.

**Donaldson Line** Shipping company, founded 1858. It traded from **Glasgow** primarily with Canada. In the early 20th century it became linked with the **Anchor Line**. The Anchor-Donaldson ship *Athenia* was the first British merchant ship sunk in World War II.

**Donegan, Lonnie** (1931–2002) Musician, b. Glasgow. One of the biggest British stars of the 1950s, he was the central figure in the skiffle boom which took off after his 1956 single 'Rock Island Line'. His later hits included 'Cumberland Gap' and the novelty recording 'Does Your Chewing Gum Lose Its Flavour On The Bedpost Overnight?'

**Donibristle** see **Dalgety Bay**

**Donnchadh Bàn Mac an t-Saoir** (**Duncan Bàn MacIntyre**) (1724–1812) Poet, b. Glen Orchy, Argyll. A gamekeeper, forester and later a member of the Edinburgh **town guard**, he composed some of the finest and most detailed nature poetry in the **Gaelic** language, though unable to write. His works include 'Òran Coire a' Cheathaich' (Song of the misty corrie), 'Moladh Beinn Dòbhrain' (The praise of Ben Doran) and a lament for Colin Campbell of Glenure.

**Donovan** (**Donovan Leitch**) (1946– ) Musician, b. Glasgow. A whimsical singer-songwriter of the hippie era, his first hits were 'Catch The Wind' and 'Colours' in 1965. Those simple ditties were followed by more self-consciously psychedelic offerings, such as 'Mellow Yellow' and 'Hurdy Gurdy Man'.

**Donovan, Anne** (1956– ) Novelist and short-story writer, b. Coatbridge, lives in **Glasgow**. She has worked as a teacher of English, and uses her awareness of the local dialect to enrich her fiction. Her short-story collection, *Hieroglyphics and Other Stories* (2001), was followed by the novel, *Buddha Da*

(2003), which was shortlisted for the Orange Prize for Fiction.

**doocot** Scots word for a dovecote, a building with compartments in the walls where pigeons would roost. Historically, pigeons were used in winter as a source of meat and eggs and their droppings were used as manure. They were hardly popular with the tenants on whose corn the birds fed. Doocots were allowed by law only to high-status individuals or corporate bodies (including priories and monasteries). Most are connected with **lairds'** houses, and many are of architectural interest.

**Doon** River that rises in **Loch Doon** and flows northwest to the Firth of **Clyde**, to the south of **Ayr**, passing through Bogton Loch, Patna and Dalrymple. Celebrated by Robert **Burns**, as in the song 'Ye Banks and Braes o Bonnie Doon'.

**Doonhamers** see **Dumfries**

**Doonhill Homestead** see **Dunbar**

**doonies** see **handba**

**Dornie** (Gaelic **An Dòirnidh**) Village 12km (8mi) east of **Kyle of Lochalsh** at the entrance to **Loch Long** near where it meets **Loch Duich**. A bridge was built across Loch Long in 1939 and replaced in the 1980s. To the south is **Eilean Donan Castle**.

**Dornoch** (pop. 1206) Town on the northeast coast just to the north of the **Dornoch Firth**. A former royal **burgh** and county town of **Sutherland**, it was once the seat of the bishops of **Caithness**. Dornoch Cathedral was founded in 1224. Partly destroyed by fire in 1570 it was restored in 1835–7 and 1924. The bishop's castle, built in the 13th century and restored in the 16th, is now the Dornoch Castle Hotel. Dornoch was probably the scene of the last execution of a witch in Scotland in 1727. **Golf** has been played on the links from early times and a distinguished new course was laid out in 1886 by Tom **Morris**.

**Dornoch Firth** Inlet of the North Sea stretching from **Bonar Bridge** in the west to Tarbat Ness in the east.

**Douai** see **Scots Colleges**

**Douglas** Village 13km (8mi) south of **Lanark**, with an industrial estate. A former **burgh**, it was once a place of considerable

*The Dornoch Firth.*

importance associated with the ruined Douglas Castle and the Georgian Douglas Castle of 1757–61, now demolished. The 14th-century choir of St Bride's Church survives, the Gothic tombs of the Earls of Douglas being the finest of their date in Scotland; in the care of **Historic Scotland**.

**Douglas, Archibald** see **Angus, Earls of**

**Douglas, Sir Archibald** (c.1296–1333) Youngest son of Sir William of Douglas, 'the Hardy', and brother of Sir James **Douglas** 'the Good'; he was one of the Scottish leaders during the minority of **David II**. He surprised and defeated Edward **Balliol** at **Annan** in 1332. Appointed **Guardian** of Scotland in 1333, he was defeated and killed at **Halidon Hill** later that year.

**Douglas, Archibald, 4th Earl of** (c.1372–1424) Succeeding to the earldom in 1400, his tenure marked the apex of **Black Douglas** power, featuring unprecedented dominance in southern Scotland and importance on the international stage. He was influential in the political triumph of the Duke of **Albany** over the Duke of **Rothesay** in 1401–2 and in the war policies pursued against England at the time. Douglas's military record was one of striking failure, leading a Scottish invasion to heavy defeat in England at **Humbleton Hill** in 1402 and being defeated again in the company of English rebels against Henry IV at Shrewsbury in 1403. His final defeat and death came when he led the Douglas affinity in France against the English at Verneuil in 1424.

D

**Douglas, Archibald, 5th Earl of** (c.1390–1439) Son of the 4th Earl, he was a leader of Scottish forces opposing the English in France and was at the Franco-Scottish victory at Baugé in 1421. After his return in 1423 he was passive in the face of **James I**'s policy of limiting **Black Douglas** power. After the king's assassination (1437) he was made lieutenant of the realm, but died of plague in 1439. His two sons were murdered at the 'Black Dinner' in 1440 and were succeeded by their great-uncle, James 'the Gross' (d.1443).

**Douglas, Archibald, 3rd Marquis, 1st Duke of** (1694–1761) Last marquis and only duke, he inherited at the age of 6. At the close of the **Scottish Parliament** in 1707 he carried the crown from Parliament House to **Edinburgh** Castle where the regalia were deposited. In 1715 he raised a regiment in support of the Government and maintained his loyalty in 1745 although his castle was occupied by Highlanders on their return from England. In 1725 in a fit of jealousy he killed his cousin, who was his guest, and was obliged to conceal himself in Holland for a time. Childless, he refused to acknowledge his sister's child as his heir, leading after his death to the **Douglas Cause**.

**Douglas, Bill** (1934–91) Actor, writer and film director, b. Newcraighall, Edinburgh. The illegitimate son of a miner, he used his poor childhood as the basis of his stark but poetic trilogy of films, *My Childhood* (1972), *My Ain Folk* (1973) and *My Way Home* (1977). His only other feature film was *Comrades* (1986), an account of the Tolpuddle Martyrs.

**Douglas, David** (1798–1834) Botanist and traveller, b. Scone. Son of a stonemason, he trained as a gardener before studying at the Botanical Garden, **Glasgow**. He undertook 3 journeys (1823, 1824–5, 1829–34) to North America as a collector for the Royal Horticultural Society. He introduced into Britain 50 trees and shrubs, including the conifer now known as the Douglas fir, and 100 herbaceous plants. In the Sandwich Islands he fell into a pit and was gored to death by a wild bull. The David Douglas Memorial stands in the grounds of the old church at Scone.

**Douglas, Gavin** or **Gawin** (c.1474–1522) Poet and bishop, b. Tantallon Castle. Third son of the 5th Earl of Angus, he was probably educated at **St Andrews University** and possibly in Paris. He had various benefices and became provost of St Giles in **Edinburgh** in 1501. After his nephew, the 6th Earl of Angus, married **Margaret Tudor**, widow of **James IV**, he became Bishop of **Dunkeld** in 1515. He was involved in the quarrels of the nobles that followed the death of James and was imprisoned for nearly a

year by the Duke of Albany, the regent. When the power struggle moved even more in Albany's favour, he fled to England where he died of the plague. His main works are the allegorical dream poem *Palice of Honour* (c.1501) and *Eneados* (completed in 1513); the first complete translation of Virgil's *Aeneid* in any form of English, it is a landmark in the development of the Scots language as a literary medium; see **language**.

**Douglas, Glen** see **Glen Douglas**

**Douglas, Sir James** (c.1286–1330), the 'Good', Lord of Douglas. Son of William Douglas, 'the Hardy', who supported **Wallace** and died in English captivity around 1299. James was an early supporter of **Robert I** and became one of his foremost military leaders. Present at **Bannockburn**, Douglas was also brutally effective in launching raids into northern England. Future **Black Douglas** (a sobriquet earned by Sir James) power was based on the extensive lands in southern Scotland with which he was rewarded. After Bruce's death, Douglas set out to take his heart to the Holy Land but was killed in battle in Spain.

**Douglas, James, 9th Earl of** (1426–91) Second son of James, the 'Gross', 7th Earl of Douglas, and brother of William, 8th Earl, whom he succeeded in 1452 when William was murdered by **James II**. Although the new Earl burned **Stirling** in response, a temporary accord was patched up with the king. In 1455 James II launched another anti-Douglas offensive, and the Earl fled to England, leaving his three brothers to fight for the Douglas cause at **Arkinholm**, where they were defeated, completing the downfall of the **Black Douglas** family. Long an exile in England, the Earl plotted to regain his lands but the Treaty of Westminster-**Ardtornish** came to nothing and he was captured at **Lochmaben** on a raid into Scotland in 1484 and died in confinement at the Abbey of **Lindores**.

**Douglas, (George) Norman** (1868–1952) Writer, b. Thüringen, Vorarlberg, Austria, where his father ran cotton mills in an effort to maintain the family estate of Tilquhillie, near **Banchory**. Educated in England and Germany, he joined the Foreign Office in 1894 and served in Russia before settling on the Italian island of Capri. His most famous novel, *South Wind* (1917), features the cosmopolitan and hedonistic expatriate inhabitants of Capri. He also wrote well-informed travel books, such as *Old Calabria* (1915), and an idiosyncratic autobiography, *Looking Back* (1933).

**Douglas, William, 8th Earl of** (c.1425–52) Son of James, 'the Gross', 7th Earl, whom he succeeded in 1443. In 1444, a papal dispensation allowed him to marry his cousin, the Fair Maid of Galloway, thus uniting the two principal estates of the family. As a youth he was a great friend of the young King **James II** but his great power and an alliance he made with the **Lord of the Isles** and the Earl of Crawford alienated the king. He was summoned to **Stirling** where James murdered him.

**Douglas Cause** Law case brought before the **Court of Session** in 1762 by the Duke of Hamilton challenging the right of succession to the Douglas estates by Archibald James Edward Douglas (formerly Stewart) (1748–1827), son of Lady

*Drove Roads: a 19th-century daguerrotype of a painting entitled* Cattle Droving, *showing a collie dog rounding up Highland cattle on their way to market.*

Jane Douglas, sister of the 1st Duke of **Douglas**, on the grounds that he was a French child, bought and substituted for a child of Lady Jane's that survived birth only briefly. The case caused widespread public excitement. In 1767, by the casting vote of Lord President **Dundas**, it found against Douglas. On appeal to the House of Lords, the verdict was reversed in 1769, though Douglas was granted only the estates, not the title. Douglas was created Lord Douglas of Douglas in 1790. None of his sons had issue and his estates descended through one of his daughters to the Earls of Home.

**Douglas Larder** Term for the conflagration of bodies and provisions when Sir James **Douglas**, having captured Douglas Castle from the English in 1308, burned all that lay within.

**Doune** Village 13km (8mi) northwest of **Stirling**, famous in the 17th century for the manufacture of pistols. It later became a cotton-manufacturing town, with mills across the river **Teith** at Deanston, and is now a commuter village for Stirling. To the south is Doune Castle, the well-preserved courtyard castle built in the 14th century beside the River Teith by the Duke of **Albany**. It was a royal castle from 1425 until the last years of the 16th century, when it came into the possession of the Earls of Moray, who restored it in the 1880s; now in the care of **Historic Scotland**.

**Dounreay** Experimental nuclear power station established in 1955 on a former airfield 15km (8mi) west of **Thurso**, halfway between London and the Arctic Circle, which contained the world's first fast-breeder reactor (1962–77) for generating power. A prototype fast-breeder operated from 1974 until 1994

and a nuclear fuel reprocessing plant was established. It was decommissioned in the late 1990s and work is now concentrated on acquiring decommissioning expertise, waste management and environmental reclamation. An explosion in a waste storage shaft in the late 1970s released radioactive particles into the environment and some washed ashore on nearby beaches.

**Dowding, Hugh Caswell Tremenheere, Lord** (1882–1970) Soldier and Air Force chief, b. Moffat. He joined the Royal Artillery in 1900, transferring to the fledgling Royal Flying Corps in 1914. Scientifically minded, he encouraged the development of radar. He alienated Churchill by resisting pressure to commit the bulk of his command to support a collapsing France in 1940. In the Battle of Britain later that year he showed outstanding grasp of the need to conserve trained pilots' lives. Despite his achievements he was soon abruptly dismissed by Churchill.

**Doyle, Sir Arthur Conan** see **Conan Doyle**

**Driesh** Mountain, a **Munro** (947m/3106ft), in **Angus**, 6km (4mi) west of **Glen Clova**. Along with the nearby Mayar (928m/3047ft), it makes a pleasant walk from **Glen Doll**.

**Drochil** Ruin of a massive double-pile Z-plan castle 11km (7mi) northwest of **Peebles**, built by the Regent **Morton**, who was executed while it was under construction in 1581.

**dropped scone** see **pancake**

**drove roads** The system of paths and tracks used to drive cattle or sheep to markets, especially from the 17th to the mid 19th century. **Crieff** and later **Falkirk** were important centres and the former now has the Highland Drovers Visitor Centre.

**Druchtag Motte** A 12th-century motte near Mochrum, Galloway. A circular earthen mound surrounded by a deep ditch from which the soil was dug to build it. The flat top of the mound once bore a wooden castle. In the care of **Historic Scotland**.

**Drum, Castle of** Castle, 16km (10mi) southwest of **Aberdeen**. It consists of the late-13th-century Tower of Drum, one of the first medieval Scottish tower houses, adjoining a Renaissance house built in 1619. The tower was a royal keep given by **Robert I** to his armour-bearer, William de Irwin, in 1323 and the Irvines lived there until 1976 when it was bequeathed to the **National Trust for Scotland**. It has notable portraits including works by **Raeburn** and Reynolds and fine 18th-century furniture. In the grounds is a historic rose garden, a 16th-century chapel and the Old Wood of Drum with ancient oaks and pines.

**Drum, House of** Richly detailed baroque villa at Gilmerton, to the east of **Edinburgh**, designed by William **Adam** for Lord Somerville 1726–34. The interior has remarkable plaster work by Samuel Calderwood and Thomas Clayton.

**Drumalban** (Gaelic **Druim-Albainn**, meaning 'the spine of Scotland') Old name for the ranges of mountains forming a watershed across northern Scotland.

**Drumchapel** Suburb of **Glasgow**, 8km (5mi) northwest of the city centre. It was built by Glasgow Corporation after World War II to house people displaced from the city centre by slum clearance. The original village is now known as Old Drumchapel.

**Drumclog** Village in South Lanarkshire, 8km (5mi) northeast of **Darvel**. An obelisk 2km (1mi) to the northwest commemorates a battle on 1 June 1679 in which Life Guards under Viscount **Dundee** were defeated by **Covenanters**, leading to the Battle of **Bothwell** Brig 3 weeks later. On the first Sunday of June each year there is a special service in Drumclog Memorial Kirk, built in 1912.

**Druminnor** L-plan palace block to the northeast of **Rhynie**, Aberdeenshire, built in 1577, originally attached to a tower house of 1440 which has disappeared; the seat of the Lords Forbes until Castle Forbes was built in 1815.

**Drumlanrig Castle** Ornate quadrangular palace in **Nithsdale**, 5km (3mi) northwest of Thornhill, built to designs by Robert **Mylne** and James **Smith** (1675–97) for the 1st Duke of Queensberry on the site of an earlier 14th-century castle of the Douglases. Now a seat of the Duke of **Buccleuch**,

it is surrounded by a notable designed landscape and is open to the public.

**Drummond, George** (1687–1766) Politician, placeman and speculator, b. Perthshire. A supporter of the **Union of Parliaments** of 1707, he was rewarded with the post of accountant-general of excise. He fought against the **Jacobites** at **Sheriffmuir** in 1715. By 1717 he was a member of **Edinburgh** town council and treasurer of the city. He acted as a government informer against suspected **Jacobites** after the 1745 Rising. Reliably subservient, especially to the Argyll interest, he was Lord Provost of Edinburgh 6 times between 1725 and 1764. He was a leading champion of and profited much by the development of the New Town of Edinburgh.

**Drummond, William, of Hawthornden** (1585–1649) Poet and author, b. Hawthornden, near Roslin, Midlothian. The son of Sir John Drummond, first laird of Hawthornden and gentleman usher to **James VI**, he studied law in **Edinburgh** and France but when he inherited his father's estate in 1610 he retired from public life and devoted his time to reading, poetry and mechanical experiments. He signed the **National Covenant** in 1638, but as a staunch royalist, he objected to the Covenanters' subsequent coercion of **Charles I**. His main works include *Teares on the Death of Moeliades* (on the death of Henry, James VI's eldest son, 1613) and *A Cypress Grove* (1630), a meditation on death. Ben Jonson visited him in 1518–19.

**Drummond Castle** Castle to the northwest of **Muthill**, Perthshire. The medieval castle was almost destroyed in 1745 by the **Jacobite** Duchess of Perth to prevent its use by government troops; it was partially rebuilt in the 1820s. The gardens were laid out about 1630 by John Drummond, the 2nd Earl of Perth, and contain the magnificent 17th-century parterre based on the saltire with its famous sundial at its centre. Some scenes from the film *Rob Roy* (1995) were shot here.

**Drummore** Village on the east coast of the **Rhinns of Galloway**, 7km (4mi) north of the Mull of **Galloway**.

**Drummossie Moor** see **Culloden**

**Drumnadrochit** (Gaelic **Druim na drochaid**) Village on the west side of **Loch Ness**, at the mouth of Glen Urquhart. It is a popular centre for outdoor sports and for spotting the Loch Ness monster. **Urquhart Castle** is nearby. Above the village are the Divach Falls, a 30.5m (100ft) waterfall on the River Enrick, overlooked by Divach Lodge where J M **Barrie** once stayed.

**Drumochter, Pass of** (Gaelic **Druim Uachdair**) Mountain pass, 9km (6mi) south of **Dalwhinnie**, between Glen Truim and **Glen Garry**. It carries the road and the railway line between **Perth** and **Inverness**. The road, following the line of the military road of General **Wade**, reaches a height of 458m (1504ft), and the railway, at 452m (1484ft), is the highest point of the British railway system.

**Dryburgh** Small **Borders** village, 8km (5mi) southeast of **Melrose**. In a beautiful setting on a horseshoe bend of the River **Tweed** are the ruins of **Dryburgh** Abbey, founded as a monastery for monks from Alnwick in Northumberland about 1152. The surviving ruins date mainly from the 12th and 13th centuries. Its proximity to the Border made it vulnerable during the Anglo-Scottish wars and it was attacked in 1322, 1385 and 1545. Sir Walter **Scott** and Field Marshal Earl **Haig** are buried here. In the care of **Historic Scotland**.

**Drymen** (pronounced **drim**in) Village 11km (7mi) northeast of **Balloch** and within 5km (3mi) of **Loch Lomond**. To the west is the site of Buchanan Castle, seat of the Grahams of Montrose from 1640 until the 1930s, now a **golf** course.

**Duart Castle** Castle on the east coast of the Isle of **Mull**, dating from the 13th century with later additions, built on a rocky and commanding cliff at the entrance to the Sound of Mull and opposite the south end of **Lismore**. It has a large keep, built in 1360, and was the home of the chiefs of the Macleans of Duart. Due to their massive indebtedness, it fell to their main creditor the Duke of Argyll in the 1670s. Though ruinous by the time of the 1745 **Jacobite Rising**, it was used as a government garrison to contain the ardent Jacobitism of the Macleans. In 1911 it was bought by the Maclean chief, who restored it, to designs by Sir John **Burnet** (1911–16); open to the public.

**Dubh Artach Lighhouse** Lighthouse on a very remote rock, 26km (16mi) southwest of the Isle of **Mull**.

**Duddingston** Suburb of **Edinburgh**, 5km (3mi) east of the city centre. Historically, in the 12th century it was a parish given by **David I** to the Abbot of **Kelso**, who leased it to Dodin, a Norman knight after whom it was named. Duddingston Kirk is mainly

*Duart Castle, Isle of Mull.*

12th-century. The Duddingston Curling Club, whose members played on Duddingston Loch, formulated the rules adopted for the game in 1804; the loch is now a bird sanctuary. Duddingston House, a neoclassical villa with a Corinthian portico, was built for the Duke of Abercorn by Sir William **Chambers** in the 1760s; it is now offices. A house in the village has associations with Prince Charles Edward **Stewart**, whose army camped at Duddingston after the Battle of **Prestonpans** in 1745.

**Duff House** Towered baroque mansion at **Banff** built in the 1730s by William **Adam** for the 1st Earl of Fife, who never lived in it. It later became a hotel, a sanatorium and in World War II a prisoner-of-war camp. It is now a country house gallery of the **National Galleries of Scotland** with a fine collection of paintings, furniture, tapestries etc.

**Dufftown** (pop. 1454) Small town 26km (16mi) southeast of **Elgin**, planned in 1817. It is known as a centre of the **whisky** industry – at one time it had 7 distilleries – and includes the **Glenfiddich**, **Balvenie** and **Mortlach** distilleries. Dufftown Museum is in Dufftown clock tower in the centre of the town. To the south is the 13th-century Mortlach parish church, which includes some Pictish stones. **Balvenie Castle** is in the village, and on a hilltop to the southeast are the ruins of the 15th-century **Auchindoun** Castle. Both are in the care of **Historic Scotland**.

115

**Duffus** Village near the Moray Firth, 8km (5mi) northwest of Elgin. Just to the east are the ruins of the medieval Church of St Peter with a 14th-century parish cross, over 5m (14ft) high, in the churchyard. To the southeast are the massive ruins of Duffus Castle, a Norman motte-and-bailey castle, once a stronghold of the Moray family. All in the care of **Historic Scotland**. Gordonstoun School is nearby.

**Duffy, Carol Ann** (1955- ) Poet and playwright, b. Glasgow. She now lives in Manchester, where she lectures in poetry at the Metropolitan University. She has published several poetry collections, including *Standing Female Nude* (1985), *Mean Time* (1993) and *The World's Wife* (1999), for which she has won several awards. She has also had her plays performed both in Liverpool and London. In 1999 she became a Fellow of the Royal Society of Literature.

**Dull** Village in Perthshire, 5km (3mi) west of **Aberfeldy**. It is the traditional site of a Celtic monastery founded by **Adamnan**, commemorated by a surviving cross. Nearby are the remains of many prehistoric monuments.

**Dumbarton** (pop. 20,527) Town 22km (14mi) northwest of **Glasgow**, at the confluence of the Rivers **Clyde** and **Leven**. A former royal **burgh** and county town of **Dunbartonshire**, it is now the administrative centre of **West Dunbartonshire** Council. It was the ancient capital of the kingdom of **Strathclyde**, and is dominated to the south by Dumbarton Rock, a 73m (240ft) high basalt volcanic plug, that has at the top the vestigial remains of an ancient royal castle, built on the site of a stronghold of the kingdom of the Britons from the 5th-10th centuries. At the foot of the rock is an 18th-century artillery fortification. Just east of the town centre is the Denny Ship Model Experiment Tank, the first commercial ship-model testing tank in the world, maintained by the **Scottish Maritime Museum**, a reminder of the shipbuilding industry that was important in the town from the 18th to the 20th centuries; ships built here include the *Cutty Sark* (1869). William **Denny** & Bros were world leaders in building small fast passenger ships until the firm closed in 1962. In 1938 Hiram Walker & Sons (Scotland) Ltd built a massive distillery on the site of another yard; it is now closed and threatened with demolition. There is still **whisky** warehousing and a large bottling plant on the edges of the town.

**Dumbarton District** see **Strathclyde Region**

**Dumfries** (pop. 32,146) Town on the River **Nith** 10km (6mi) north of the **Solway Firth**. A former royal **burgh**, it was the county town of **Dumfriesshire** and is now the administrative centre of **Dumfries and Galloway** Council. It played a prominent part in the wars against England and in **Border** warfare. In the 18th century it became an important port and a cotton-spinning and weaving town. Robert **Burns** lived here, working as an exciseman, from 1791 until his death in 1796; his house is now a museum. Dumfries Museum has a camera obscura, installed in 1836, and Heathhall Industrial Estate on the edge of the town has an aviation museum. The High Street is dominated by the magnificent Mid Steeple built 1705-8 and the pedimented Trades Hall (1804-6) in Queensberry Square. In the churchyard of the tall-spired St Michael's Church (1742-9) is the Burns Mausoleum by the English architect T F Hunt (1815). The Nith is crossed by the Old Bridge or **Devorguilla**'s Bridge, built 1430-32 and much rebuilt 1620, the longest of Scottish medieval bridges; it is now a footbridge. The town was an important centre for tweed manufacture and for a time in the 20th century it had the Arrol-Johnston motor car factory (by Henry Ford's architect Albert Kahn) at Heathhall; it is now a rubber works. Large parts of the much reduced Crichton Royal mental hospital were recently converted to form the Crichton University Campus, alongside the Crichton Business Park. It has campuses for the Universities of **Glasgow** and **Paisley**, the Dumfries and Galloway College and other colleges. Its 19th-century buildings have been retained, including the Crichton Memorial Chapel (1890-97) by Arthur George Sydney **Mitchell**. A nickname for the town, Queen of the South, has been adopted by the local football team. It is also used for the main female participant in the annual local festival which takes place in June, known as the Guid Nychburris Festival, originating from a court held in medieval times to resolve disagreements between neighbours. It incorporates many of the elements of Border festivals, including an inspection of the boundaries of the **burgh**. Natives of Dumfries are known as Doonhamers.

**Dumfries and Galloway Council** Local authority in southwest Scotland created in 1996 from the former **Dumfries and Galloway Region**. It stretches from the border with England at **Gretna** in the east to the **Rhinns of Galloway** peninsula in the west. See maps on pp.394-5 and **local government**. The main towns are **Dumfries** (the administrative centre),

Stranraer, Annan, Dalbeattie, Lockerbie, Castle Douglas, Newton Stewart and **Kirkcudbright**. There is forestry in the north and agriculture in the north and south.

## Dumfries and Galloway Region

One of the 9 regions forming the upper tier of local government from 1975 to 1996, formed from the former counties of **Dumfriesshire**, **Kirkcudbrightshire** and **Wigtownshire**. It consisted of the districts of Annandale and Eskdale, Nithsdale, Stewartry, and Wigtown. See maps on pp.394-5 and **local government**.

**Dumfries House** Large Palladian house to the west of **Cumnock**, Ayrshire, originally known as Leifnorris, in severe classical style with splendid rococo interiors, by John and Robert **Adam** (1754-8) for the Earl of Dumfries. It was later a seat of the Marquesses of **Bute**.

**Dumfriesshire** Former county in southwest Scotland. **Dumfries** was the county town. In 1975 most of it became the Annandale and Eskdale and Nithsdale Districts of **Dumfries and Galloway Region**. See maps on pp.394-5 and **local government**.

**Dumgoyne** Settlement on the edge of the **Campsie Fells**, 6km (4mi) northwest of **Strathblane**. It is also the name of a prominent hill above, formed by an old volcanic neck, popular with walkers. The Glengoyne distillery produces a single malt **whisky** and has a visitor centre.

**Dumyat** Hill in the **Ochils** (418m/1373ft), 5km (3mi) northeast of **Stirling**, with a prehistoric fort on its southwest shoulder.

**dun** Archaeological term, from Gaelic *dun*, a fort, referring to a small stonewalled defensive homestead of the Iron Age, often situated on an isolated site. It is a common place-name element, sometimes in the form dum-.

**Dun** Settlement in **Angus**, 5km (3mi) northwest of **Montrose**. The House of Dun, a baroque villa, was built in 1730 by William **Adam** for the Erskine family, associated with the area since the 14th century. It has superb plasterwork by Joseph Enzer. It was the home of Violet **Jacob**. In the care of the **National Trust for Scotland**.

*The ancient hillfort of Dunadd, Kilmartin Glen, Argyll.*

**Dunadd** (Gaelic **Dùn Athad**) Rocky outcrop in Kilmartin Glen in Argyll, 6km (4mi) north of **Lochgilphead**, with the remnants of an important early medieval hill fort. It was a stronghold of the kingdom of **Dal Riata** and rock markings indicate that it may have been the site of the inauguration of Dal Riata kings. In the care of **Historic Scotland**.

**Dunaskin Open Air Museum** Museum in Ayrshire between Patna and **Dalmellington**, established in the 1980s on the site of the former Dalmellington Iron Works, founded in 1847. It incorporates the remains of the works and of a brickworks built on the site in the 1930s.

**Dunbar** (pop. 6354) Town and resort on the coast of **East Lothian**, 43km (27mi) east of **Edinburgh**, a former royal **burgh** and Anglian stronghold of the 7th to 9th centuries. It has a well-preserved High Street with a spired 16th-century Tolbooth, the view northward closed by Robert **Adam**'s Lauderdale House (1790). The birthplace of John **Muir** is now a museum. On a headland above the small harbour are the fragments of a castle that was an important stronghold of the Earls of Dunbar and was defended by **Black Agnes** in a siege by English troops in 1338. Nearby are the sites of 2 battles: 3km (2mi) to the south Edward I defeated the Scots in 1296, and 3km (2mi) to the southeast Scots royalist forces commanded by David **Leslie** were defeated by Cromwell in 1650. In a naval battle offshore, Sir Andrew Wood defeated the English in 1489. To the south is Doonhill Homestead, the site of a 7th-century Anglian chief's hall, a rare record of Anglian occupation in southeast Scotland. In the care of **Historic Scotland**. Nearby is Belhaven Brewery, Scotland's last operating historic brewery. The town was an important centre of the grain and malt trades.

**Dunbar, Countess of** see 'Black Agnes'

**Dunbar, William** (c.1460–c.1514) Poet, probably from the Lothians. He may have studied at **St Andrews University**. He served at the court of **James IV** possibly as a scribe or secretary. One of the great poets of the golden age of Scots poetry, his works include: 'The Thrissill and the Rois', to celebrate the marriage of **James IV** and **Margaret Tudor** in 1503; 'The Flyting of Dumbar and Kennedie', his **flyting** with Walter Kennedy, from **Ayrshire** (still Gaelic-speaking at the time, and thus a contest between Lowlander and Highlander); 'Lament for the Makaris' mentioning recently dead fellow poets; and 'The Tretis of the Tua Mariit Wemen and the Wedo', 3 women talking entertainingly about their sex lives.

**Dunbartonshire** Former county on the north coast of the Firth of **Clyde**. **Dumbarton** was the county town. In 1975 most of it became the Dumbarton district of **Strathclyde** Region. See maps on pp.394-5 and **local government**, and see also **East Dunbartonshire, West Dunbartonshire, Lennox**.

**Dun Beag** Iron-Age **broch** at Bracadale, **Skye**, with a well-preserved entrance, cells and a stair within its 4m (13ft)-thick wall. In the care of **Historic Scotland**.

**Dunbeath** Village at the mouth of Dunbeath Water, on the east coast of **Caithness**, 29km (18mi) southwest of **Wick**. On the cliffs 2km (1mi) to the south is 15th-century Dunbeath Castle with 17th-century additions. Neil **Gunn** was born here and is commemorated in the Dunbeath Heritage Centre.

**Dunblane** (pop. 7911) Ancient cathedral city and former **burgh** on the Allan Water 8km (5mi) north of **Stirling**. The present Dunblane Cathedral, dedicated to St Blane, dates from the 13th century, with restorations in the 19th and 20th, its nave re-roofed by Rowand **Anderson** (1889–93); the furnishing of the choir by Robert **Lorimer** (1912–14). Beside the Cathedral are Dunblane Museum in a 17th-century building, the **Leighton Library** and Scottish Churches House, an interdenominational conference centre. In 1996 a tragedy occurred in the local primary school when 16 small children and their teacher were shot dead by Thomas Hamilton, a madman who then shot

himself. The incident led to a ban on handguns in the UK. On the outskirts is the Queen Victoria School and Memorial Chapel, the Scottish memorial to the Boer War.

**Dùn Caan** see **Raasay**

**Duncan I** (**Donnchad mac Crinain**) (c.1010–40) King of Scots (1034–40). Son of Bethoc, daughter of **Malcolm II**, and Crinan, abbot of **Dunkeld**. Already ruler of **Strathclyde**, he succeeded his grandfather Malcolm, and united Strathclyde with Scotia. He was defeated invading Northumbria in 1039 and domestic opposition to his rule culminated in his defeat and death at the hands of **Macbeth** (Macbethad mac Findlaech).

**Duncan II** (**Donnchad mac Máel Coluim**) (c.1060–94) King of Scots (1094). The eldest son of **Malcolm III** (Máel Coluim mac Donnchada), he was given in 1072 by his father as hostage to William I of England. When his uncle, **Donald III** (Domnall mac Donnchada), succeeded to the throne of Scotland in 1093, William II of England helped Duncan to defeat Donald, but he ruled for only 6 months before being killed by Donald, who resumed the throne.

**Duncan, Andrew** (1744–1828) Physician, b. Pinkerton, near **St Andrews**. He became Professor of Medicine at **Edinburgh** in 1790 where he campaigned for better public health and for improved treatment for the mentally ill.

**Duncan, Revd Henry** (1774–1846) Minister, b. Lochrutton, near **Dumfries**. As minister of **Ruthwell**, he made efforts to help his poorer parishioners and in 1810 set up a savings bank, which developed into the savings-bank movement; see **Trustee Savings Bank**. He restored the 7th-century **Ruthwell** Cross, now in the church.

**Duncan, John** (1866–1945) Artist, b. Dundee. He studied there and in Dusseldorf and taught in Chicago before settling in **Edinburgh**, where he was a close friend of Sir Patrick **Geddes** (painting murals for Geddes's home). Duncan was one of the most prominent artists of the Celtic Revival (which flourished in Edinburgh and **Dundee** around 1900), producing Symbolist paintings depicting subjects from Celtic mythology.

**Duncan, Rev J B** see **Greig, Gavin**

**Duncansby Head** The northeast point of mainland Scotland, almost 3km (2mi) east of **John o' Groats**. It consists of sandstone cliffs penetrated by deep geos (gashes), one of which is bridged by a natural arch. It has a lighthouse with fine views of **Orkney** and the Pentland Skerries. To the south are the Duncansby Stacks, 3 huge stone needles in the sea.

**Dun Carloway** see **Carloway**

**Dunchraigaig** see **Kilmartin**

**Dundas, Henry 1st Viscount Melville** (1742–1811) Politician, b. Dalkeith. Lord Advocate in 1777, he became Secretary of State for the Home Department in 1791, and also Governor of the **Bank of Scotland**. As the closest friend and colleague of Pitt the Younger, and the electoral manager of Scotland, he built up an enormous range of patronage. He was the first President of the Board of Control for India, principal manager of the war effort against France after 1792, and Secretary for the Navy. A patriotic Scot in his way, he was known as 'the Uncrowned king of Scotland', or 'Harry the Ninth'.

**Dundas, Robert Saunders, 2nd Viscount Melville** (1771–1851) Politician and administrator. Son of Henry **Dundas**, **Viscount Melville**, he inherited his role as manager of Scotland, finishing like his father as Governor of the **Bank of Scotland**, and Chancellor of **St Andrews University**, and also serving as First Lord of the Admiralty. He resigned office in 1829 and left politics gracefully after the Whig triumph of 1832.

**Dundas Castle** Giant L-Plan tower house of the **Dundas** family, to the south of **South Queensferry**, built in the 15th century, with a magnificent tiered Renaissance fountain and sundial, built in 1623. The Gothic new castle was built in 1818 by William **Burn** and is now used for corporate and social entertaining.

**Dundee** see p.120

**Dundee, John Graham of Claverhouse, 1st Viscount** (c.1649–1689) Soldier, b. near Dundee. After studying at **St Andrews University**, he went to the Continent to study the art of war, serving in the French and Dutch armies. In 1678 he joined the Government troops being raised to suppress the **Covenanters** in southwest Scotland. In 1679 he was defeated by the Covenanters at **Drumclog** but won a victory at **Bothwell Bridge**, earning the nickname 'Bloody Clavers' for his sometimes harsh treatment. He was made a viscount in 1688, leading to a second nickname, 'Bonnie Dundee'. In 1689 he led a rising on behalf of **James VII** in the Highlands. As commander of the cavalry of the small professional Scottish army, he refused to accept the Revolutionary settlement of 1688 and the succession of William and Mary. He won a victory at **Killiecrankie** but was mortally wounded in the battle.

**Dundee cake** A kind of fruit cake with the top covered in blanched almonds.

**Dundee Courier** see **Courier**

**Dundee District** see **Tayside Region**

**Dundee Football Club** Founded in 1893, their home ground is at Dens Park. Their first, and for a long time only, trophy was the Scottish Cup of 1910, but they at last established a consistently successful side in the 1950s. After becoming league champions in 1962 they went on to reach the semi-finals of the European Cup. See also **football**.

**Dundee Jazz Festival** Founded in 1983, the Festival takes place annually in May/early June and presents around 25 concerts featuring Scottish and international artists.

**Dundee United Football Club** Founded 1909, their home ground is at Tannadice. Originally named Dundee Hibernian to reflect their founders' Irish roots, they adopted their present name in 1923. Long the junior club in the city, they became a major force in the game from the late 1970s under Jim **McLean**. They won the league title in 1983, and were runners-up in the UEFA Cup in 1987. See also **football**.

**Dundee University** Founded in 1883 as University College, Dundee, by Mary Anne Baxter of Balgavies, a member of a wealthy linen dynasty, it was integrated with **St Andrews University** in 1890, and in 1954 was renamed the Queen's College of the University of St Andrews. It became an independent university in 1967. It has a Botanic Garden established in 1971, with a good collection of native plant communities, mountain to coastal habitats. It has an international reputation for medical research, especially cancer research and keyhole surgery. Duncan of Jordanstone College of Art and the Dundee campus of the former Northern College of Education are now both integrated into the University, which has 10,000 students.

**Dunderave Castle** (Gaelic **Dùn-dà-ràmh**) 16th-century tower house of the MacNaughtons near Dunderave Point on the northwest shore of **Loch Fyne**, 5km (3mi) northeast of **Inveraray**. It was restored by Sir Robert **Lorimer** as a private house in 1911.

**Dundonald** Village in Ayrshire, 8km (5mi) west of **Kilmarnock**. It has the imposing ruins of 14th-century Dundonald Castle, where **Robert II** died; in the care of **Historic Scotland**. It was added to in the 15th and 16th centuries before passing out of royal ownership and being used by the new owner, Sir William Cochrane, as a source of stone for nearby Auchans Castle, which he built in 1644. The very large Hillhouse quarry has produced hard stone since about 1900.

**Dundee** (pop. 154,674) Scotland's fourth-largest city, on the north side of the Firth of **Tay**, 29km (18mi) east of **Perth**, a former royal **burgh**, it became a county of city in 1929. In 1975 the City of Dundee became a district of **Tayside Region**, and also its headquarters. Since 1996 Dundee City has been a unitary authority; see **local government**.

Dundee grew into a major port and commercial and industrial centre, and became known for the three Js: **jute**, jam and journalism, only the last of which is still a major employer. In the 18th century the linen industry developed rapidly, specialising in coarse linen and sailcloth. From the 1830s jute was imported from India and after 1850 became a major industry, with 90% of the UK capacity, until the mid 20th century. Cox's Stack by James Maclaren (1865), in the western suburb of Lochee, is the finest factory chimney ever built in Scotland, a relic of the Camperdown Works, once the largest jute factory in the world. Shipbuilding was also important, and Captain Scott's polar research ship *Discovery*, which was built here, is now back in the city at the old ferry terminal, with the Discovery Point Visitor Centre. Docked a short distance away is the *Unicorn*, a Royal Navy frigate built in 1824. The town was a major centre of the whaling industry, the oil being used in the 'batching' (softening) of jute to prepare for spinning, but the trade failed to survive the transition to factory ships and catchers in the 20th century. **Keillers** of Dundee pioneered the manufacture of marmalade here, but during the 19th century moved the bulk of their operations to London, keeping only a nominal capacity to make marmalade and jam in Dundee. D C **Thomson** continues to be a major producer of newspapers and popular magazines, including the *Sunday Post* and the long-lasting comics, the *Beano* and the *Dandy*. Its headquarters is a magnificent Edwardian building by Niven & Wigglesworth, with sculpture by Albert Hodge.

Much of the town centre was replanned by William **Burn** in 1824 and again in the 1870s by William Mackison, inspired by Baron Haussmann's work in Paris. St Paul's Episcopal Cathedral by Sir George Gilbert Scott (1853-5), with its 64m (210ft) tall spire, is on the site where the castle once stood. The 15th-century St Mary's steeple is all that remains of a very large medieval burghal church.

Dundee was recovered from English control by **Robert I** in 1312. One of the 3 most important medieval royal **burghs**, it suffered a setback in the 1540s, when a major English garrison held **Broughty Ferry** Castle and raided Tayside. It took even longer to recover from the storming, massacre and sack of 1651 at the hands of the English General Monck. It was strongly

**Jacobite** in the 1715 Rising, much less so in the 1745. The jute industry was low-wage and woman-dominated, making Dundee a unique town with a poor female proletariat and high male unemployment. Restructuring after 1945 was necessarily traumatic, but new light industries and extensive slum clearance have dramatically improved it. Winston Churchill was Liberal MP for Dundee from 1908–22.

The city has several museums and an art gallery, the McManus Galleries, formerly the Albert Institute, a memorial to Prince Albert by Sir George Gilbert Scott (1865). The Mills Observatory on Balgay Hill is Britain's only full-time public observatory. The Dundee Rep Theatre, established in 1939, is home to Scotland's only full-time theatre company, and now an excellent theatre by Nicoll Russell (1982); associated with it is the Scottish Dance Theatre. Dundee Contemporary Arts has galleries, cinemas and other cultural and educational provisions in a large modern building by Richard Murphy in the Nethergate. The Verdant Works is a restored 19th-century jute works.

At 174m (571ft) the highest point in the city is Dundee Law, the remains of a volcanic plug and the site of an Iron Age vitrified fort. At its top is the city's war memorial with a beacon that is lit 4 times a year. Camperdown, now a well-equipped public park, was once the estate of the Earls of Camperdown. Admiral Adam Duncan, 1st Viscount Camperdown, defeated the Dutch fleet at the Battle of Camperdown off the Dutch coast on 11 October 1797. His son built the neo-Greek Camperdown House, designed by William Burn, in 1824-8; it is now used as a function venue, golf club and café. Other parks include the centrally situated Dudhope Park, the grounds of the 16th-17th-century Dudhope Castle, and Sir Joseph Paxton's Baxter Park (1863), to the east of the city. See also **Abertay University**, **Dundee University**, **Tay Bridges**.

*Dundee and the Firth of Tay.*

*Engraving of Dunfermline by John Slezer, from his book* Theatrum Scotiae, *1693.*

**Dundonald, Archibald, 9th Earl of** see **Cochrane, Archibald**

**Dundonald, Thomas Cochrane, 10th Earl of** see **Cochrane, Thomas**

**Dundonnell** Settlement at the head of Little Loch Broom, below An **Teallach** mountain, and therefore popular with climbers. To the southeast on the Dundonnell River is the 18th-century Dundonnell House, the garden of which, with a 2000-year-old yew tree, is open to the public.

**Dun Dornaigil** Iron-Age **broch**, also known as Dun Dornadilla, about 6km (4mi) south of **Loch Hope**. The front of the broch is imposing, with a great triangular lintel over the entrance. In the care of **Historic Scotland**.

**Dundrennan** Village 7km (5mi) southeast of **Kirkcudbright**, the ruins of the Cistercian Dundrennan Abbey, founded in 1142 by **David I**. **Mary, Queen of Scots** spent her last night in Scotland here in May 1568 before leaving for England. In the care of **Historic Scotland**. After the **Reformation** part of the abbey was used as a parish church until 1742.

**Dunecht** Large house, 19km (12mi) west of **Aberdeen**. The original part was built in 1820 by John **Smith** for William Forbes; in 1845 it was bought by the 7th Earl of Balcarres for his bibliophile son Lord Lindsay, who enlarged it as an Italianate house to designs by William Smith (1859), and then in 1867–80 built the enormous Romanesque library and chapel to designs by George Edmund Street. It was bought (1912) by Lord Cowdray who built the huge Tower Lodges and boathouse to Alexander Marshall Mackenzie's design, begun 1922.

**Dunfallandy Stone** Well-preserved Pictish cross-slab just off the main road to the south of **Pitlochry**; in the care of **Historic Scotland**.

**Dunfermline** (pop. 39,229) Town in southwest Fife, a former royal **burgh**; it was a royal residence from the 11th to the 17th century. Dunfermline Abbey was founded in the 11th century as a Benedictine religious house by Queen (St) **Margaret** on the site of an earlier church and made an abbey by **David I** in 1128. Many royal persons were buried there, including Queen Margaret, David I and **Robert I**, and the abbey guest house was used as royal residence until the **Reformation**, when it suffered damage, with other parts of the abbey. It was rebuilt as a palace in 1593, as the jointure for **James VI**'s queen, **Anne of Denmark**, and **Charles I** was born here in 1600. After the Reformation, the Romanesque nave continued in use as a parish church, but the abbey buildings suffered further damage over the centuries, and in 1818 a new parish church was built on the site of the choir and transepts. The nave and the remaining ruins are now in the care of **Historic Scotland** and the 16th-century Abbots House is now a museum. The town was an important centre of the linen industry, especially of damask table linen, from the 18th to the 20th centuries, its prosperity at that time expressed in the magnificent French late Gothic City Chambers, designed by James Campbell Walker (1875-9). Coal mining in the area (begun by monks in the 12th century) was also important, especially in the 19th century. Other industries have been introduced, including silk and artificial silk weaving and, in more recent times, electronics. The building of the **Forth Bridges** made the Dunfermline area convenient for commuting to **Edinburgh**. Nearby **Rosyth** is now part of the town. Andrew **Carnegie** was born in Dunfermline and was a generous benefactor to the town; his birthplace is a museum. Here he financed the first of the Carnegie libraries and in 1902 he bought Pittencrieff House and the surrounding parkland, just to the west of the town centre, and presented it to the town; it is now a public park and the mansion (1635), restored by Robert **Lorimer** (1908-11), is a museum.

### Dunfermline Athletic Football Club Founded in 1885.

One of Scotland's less noted teams for most of the last century, Dunfermline came into their own in the 1960s, inspired by the leadership of Jock **Stein**. With him as manager they won the Scottish Cup in 1961 and, after his departure, took the trophy again in 1968. See also **football**.

### Dunfermline District see Fife

### Dunglass Extensive courtyard castle on a low rocky cliff above

the Firth of **Clyde** to the southeast of **Dumbarton**, in the 15th and 16th centuries the chief stronghold of the Colquhouns; part of the 16th-century house remains but the remainder was reduced from 1735 when it was used as a quarry. To the southeast is the tall obelisk erected in 1835 to the memory of steamship pioneer Henry **Bell**.

### Dunglass Collegiate Church Near the coast, to the north-

west of **Cockburnspath**, a cruciform collegiate church founded by Sir Alexander Home in 1443, still with its stone slab roofs; in the care of **Historic Scotland**. It is in the grounds of the now demolished Dunglass House. Nearby is the magnificent railway viaduct by Grainger and Miller (1840), similar to the more famous one at Ballochmyle.

### Dunipace see Denny

### Dunkeld (Gaelic Dùn Chaillin, meaning 'fort of the

Caledonians') Ancient cathedral city and former royal **burgh** in an attractive setting on the River **Tay**, 24km (15mi) north of **Perth**. In the 9th century relics of St **Columba** were brought here from **Iona** for safekeeping and it became an important Pictish religious site. The Gothic Dunkeld Cathedral dates from the 12th century but is mainly 15th century and the choir is used as the parish church. The roofless but otherwise fairly complete nave is in the care of **Historic Scotland**. In 1689, after the Battle of **Killiecrankie**, **Jacobites** besieged Dunkeld, which was held by **Covenanters**, but they were repulsed and much of the town was burned. The houses rebuilt after the siege have been restored by the **National Trust for Scotland**, which also looks after Stanley Hill, a wooded hill to the west. Dunkeld Bridge is a 7-arched bridge and tollhouse built in 1809 by Thomas **Telford**. A riverside path from here leads to **Birnam** Oak, the last remnant of **Macbeth's** Birnam Wood. **Dunkeld** House, former seat of the Dukes of **Atholl**, is now an opulent hotel; its grounds have a splendid 18th-century arboretum and grottoes along the river bank.

### Dunlop Village in Ayrshire, 4km (2mi) north of Stewarton.

The process for making the area's famous Dunlop cheese was brought back to Ayrshire from Ireland by Barbara Gilmour, wife of a Covenanting farmer who had taken refuge in Ireland. In its churchyard is the notable 17th-century Clandeboye School, still intact and used as a church hall.

### Dunlop, John Boyd (1840-1921) Veterinary surgeon and

inventor, b. Dreghorn, Ayrshire. Trained in Belfast, he worked in **Edinburgh** and Belfast where in 1887 he devised an inflated rubber tyre for his son's tricycle and patented it in 1888. He sold the patent in 1890.

### Dunlop cheese see Dunlop

### Dunn, Douglas Eaglesham (1942- ) Poet, b. Inchinnan,

Renfrewshire. He trained as a librarian and worked in Hull University with Philip Larkin, who became his mentor. He has been Professor of English at **St Andrews** University since 1991. His first collection of poems, the bleak but humorous *Terry Street* (1969), established him as an important new poetic voice. Later collections include *Barbarians* (1979), *St Kilda's Parliament* (1981), *Elegies* (1985) and *Dante's Drum Kit* (1993). He has won many literary awards.

**D**

**Dunnet** Village on Dunnet Bay on the north coast of **Caithness**, 11km (7mi) east of **Thurso**. The parish church is a largely pre-**Reformation** building and one of its incumbents was Timothy **Pont**. Dunnet Head, 1.5km (1mi) to the north, is the northernmost point of the Scottish mainland. A bold sandstone promontory 127m (417ft) high, it has a **lighthouse** and views across the Pentland Firth to **Orkney** and along the north coast as far as **Ben Loyal** and **Ben Hope**.

**Dunnet Head** see **Dunnet**

**Dunnett, Alastair MacTavish** (1908–98) Journalist and business-man, b. Kilmacolm. Educated in **Glasgow**, he left a job in banking to start a boys' magazine. This failed but he became chief press officer to the Secretary of State for Scotland (1940–6) then Editor of the *Daily Record* (1946–55) before becoming Editor of *The Scotsman* (1956–72). He was Chairman of Thomson Scottish Petroleum. His wife was the novelist Dorothy **Dunnett**.

**Dunnett, Dorothy** (née **Halliday**) (1923–2001) Artist and novelist, b. Dunfermline. Educated in **Edinburgh**, she began her career in the Civil Service. She married the journalist Alastair **Dunnett** in 1946. She was a member of the Scottish Society of Women Artists and exhibited at the Royal Academy. Under her maiden name, she wrote several detective novels but she is best known for her two series of historical romances: the first features the fictional Scottish mercenary Francis Crawford of Lymond and the second the Burgundian-Scottish Niccolo.

**Dunnichen** Village in **Angus**, 6km (4mi) east of **Forfar**. To the east is the site of the battle of **Nechtansmere**, or Dunnichen, in 685.

**Dunnottar Castle** Ruined, partly restored castle on a rocky promontory 49m (160ft) above the sea on the east coast of **Aberdeenshire**, 4km (3mi) south of **Stonehaven**. Built on a fortified site first mentioned in the 7th century, it dates in part from the late 13th century. It was built by Sir William Keith and

*Dunnottar Castle, Aberdeenshire.*

became an impregnable fortress of the Earls Marischal of Scotland for 4 centuries. Its chapel was consecrated in 1276; the giant tower house was licensed 1346 but is 15th century in its present form. The Scottish regalia were brought here in 1651 for safekeeping and were heroically smuggled out and concealed nearby when it became clear that the castle could not resist the artillery of Cromwellian besiegers. In 1685 it was used as a prison for supporters of the rebellion led by the 9th Earl of **Argyll**. It is open to the public.

**Dunollie Castle** Ruined ancient stronghold of the MacDougalls, Lords of Lorne, just north of **Oban**, dating from the 12th century. Before then, it was probably one of the strongholds of the kings of **Dal Riata**. The present seat of the MacDougalls is the nearby Dunollie House (17th century and 1746).

**Dunoon** (pop. 9038) Town and resort in Argyll, 7km (4mi) from **Gourock** across the Firth of **Clyde**. It has the remains of a medieval Stewart castle of which the Campbells became hereditary keepers. It was destroyed in 1685 when the 9th Earl of **Argyll** was executed for treason. The town began to grow in the 19th century with holidaymakers from **Glasgow** travelling 'doon the watter' in the summer and was a focal point of the extensive Clyde-steamer services that developed during the later 19th century. From 1961 until 1992 it flourished owing to the nearby US military base at **Holy Loch**. There is a regular car ferry to Gourock.

D

*Dunstaffnage Castle, Argyll.*

**Dunrobin Castle** Large castle on the east coast of **Sutherland**, 2km (1mi) north of **Golspie**, the seat of the Countess of Sutherland. Originally built c.1275 as a square keep by Robert, Earl of Sutherland (after whom it was named Dun Robin), it was transformed into a great Scots Jacobean palace by the 2nd Duke of Sutherland with Sir Charles Barry and William Leslie as architects (1845–51); its main interiors are by Robert **Lorimer** (1915–21), after a fire. It is set in a great park with magnificent formal gardens and is open to the public.

**Duns** (pop. 2444) Market town in the **Borders** 21km (13mi) west of **Berwick-upon-Tweed**, former county town of **Berwickshire**. It began as a settlement on top of a 216m (710ft) high **dun**. Destroyed by English forces in the middle of the 16th century, it was rebuilt at the foot of the dun. It is said to be the birthplace of **Duns Scotus**, a statue of whom stands in the town. To the northwest is Duns Castle, a picturesque Gothic pile by Gillespie **Graham** (1818–22), built around the 14th-century tower of Randolph, Earl of Moray. **Manderston** House is nearby.

**Dunskey Castle** Large L-plan ruin of the castle of the Adairs of Kinhilt, in Galloway, to the southeast of **Portpatrick**. The present house is a simple but handsome Scots 17th-century style by James Kennedy Hunter and James Carrick (1901–4) for Charles and Lady Augusta Orr Ewing. The grounds include a walled garden and woodland walks.

**Duns Scotus, John** (Joannes Scotus **Duns** or **John of Duns**) (c.1265–1308) Philosopher. Little is documented of his life, but he was probably born in **Duns**. He entered the Franciscan order and may have studied in Oxford and then Paris and Cologne. Very widely read and known as Doctor Subtilis ('subtle doctor'), he wrote works of originality on grammar, logic, metaphysics and theology. Other philosophers disagreed with his concepts, so the term 'dunce' became derived from his name.

**Dunstaffnage** (Gaelic **Dun-stafhinis**) Dunstaffnage Castle is the well-preserved ruin of the 13th-century curtain-walled stronghold of the Macdougalls, Lords of **Lorne**. It stands on the shores of **Loch Etive** 5km (3.5mi) north of **Oban** on a commanding site overlooking the Firth of Lorn that may have been a seat of Pictish and **Dal Riata** kings. It was captured by **Robert I** in 1309 and passed to the Campbells (with a branch of which the captaincy remains). It was used by Government forces in the **Jacobite Risings** and was briefly a prison for Flora **MacDonald**. Next to it are the ruins of a fine 13th-century chapel. In the care of **Historic Scotland**. Nearby is the Dunstaffnage Marine Laboratory, a research station of the Scottish Association for Marine Science.

**Duntreath Castle** Large tower house 3km (2mi) northwest of **Strathblane**, built by the Edmonstone family in the late 15th century, restored 1857 and aggrandised by Sydney Mitchell (1889–93), most of whose work was removed in 1958.

**Duntrune Castle** Pentagonal 15th-century curtain-walled castle on the north shore of Loch Crinan in **Argyll**, containing a 17th-century L-plan house. Originally a Campbell house, it was acquired by the Malcolms in 1796.

**Dunure** Former fishing village on the Firth of **Clyde**, 8km (5mi) northwest of **Maybole**, with an early 19th-century harbour. The ruined Dunure Castle stands on a rocky cliff to the west. It was begun in the 13th century and added to in the 15th century. It was a Kennedy stronghold. In 1570, Gilbert Kennedy, 4th Earl of Cassillis, tortured the commendator of **Crossraguel Abbey** in the castle's vaulted basement in order to obtain the abbey's lands.

**Dunvegan** (Gaelic **Dun-bheagan**) Village on the west coast of the Isle of **Skye**, near the head of Loch Dunvegan. To the north is Dunvegan Castle, ancient stronghold of the Macleods of Skye. Home of the chiefs of Macleod for more than 800 years, its 14th-century keep and 16th-century Fairy Tower were connected in the 17th by Rory Mor (Roderick Macleod). The castle was given its present crenellated profile in 1790 and 1811–14, with further additions in 1840–50. It is open to the public and has many objects on display including the Fairy Flag, a Saracen flag captured on a crusade, and items connected with Prince Charles Edward **Stewart**.

**Dupplin** Locality on Dupplin Moor southwest of **Perth** where in 1332 a Scottish army commanded by the regent, Donald, Earl of **Mar**, was defeated by Edward **Balliol** and his English supporters in pursuit of the throne of **David II**. Mar was killed and Balliol was crowned Edward I of Scotland at **Scone** shortly afterwards.

**Dupplin Cross** Magnificent 9th-century stone cross, sculpted with panels of interlace decoration, animals, harpist, foot soldiers and a mounted horseman. Formerly it stood on the hillside above the River **Earn**, overlooking the site of the royal palace of **Forteviot**, but it is now in the care of **Historic Scotland** within St Serf's Church at Dunning. Traces of an inscription in Latin refer to **Constantine** (d.820).

**Dura Den** Gorge 4km (3mi) east of **Cupar**, Fife, the former site of 7 water-powered mills. An Old Red Sandstone quarry, which yielded a prolific fossil fish population, was sealed up after final excavations in 1912.

**Durham, Treaties of** Two treaties between King Stephen of England and **David I** as the latter sought to establish his control in northern England. By the terms of the first, drawn up in 1136, David allowed his son, Henry, Earl of Huntingdon, to do homage in return for territorial concessions. After further Anglo-Scottish warfare in 1138 the second treaty, sealed in 1139, conceded further land to the Scots as far south as the River Tees with the exception of Newcastle and Bamburgh.

**Durisdeer** Hamlet in Dumfriesshire, 10km (6mi) north of **Thornhill**. The parish church was built by the Dukes of Queensberry and contains elaborate monuments to the 2nd Duke of **Queensberry** and his wife.

**Durness** (Gaelic **Duirnis**) Village on the north coast of **Sutherland**, 15km (9mi) east of **Cape Wrath**. The minister here from 1726 until his death was the Revd Murdo MacDonald (1696–1763) who kept a diary, much of which is now lost,

and who inspired what is considered to be the finest elegy by **Rob Donn**. To the northwest is Balnakil, where Rob Donn is buried, and Balnakil House, the owner of which, Lord Reay, also features in Rob Donn's work. Nearby to the east are the **Smoo Caves**. It is a ferry point for excursions to **Cape Wrath**. Durness limestone is a thick rock unit extending from Durness to **Skye**, providing lime for grassland improvement and excellent pasture land.

**Duror** Settlement on the north bank of the River Duror in **Appin**. It is associated with the **Appin Murder**. James Stewart, hanged for the murder, lived at Acharn and is buried near the ruined church of Keil, 2km (1mi) to the south.

**Dutchman's Cap** see **Treshnish Islands**

**Duthac, St** see **Tain**

**Dwarfie Stane** see **Hoy**

**Dwelly, Edward** see **dictionaries**

**Dyce** (pop. 6359) Town on the south bank of the River **Don** 9km (5mi) northwest of **Aberdeen**, now contained within the city's conurbation. An airport established to the west of the town in the 1930s is now Aberdeen Airport. North Sea oil greatly increased its traffic, especially of helicopters. The ruined Dyce Old Kirk has the Dyce Symbol Stones, 2 fine examples of incised Pictish stones, in the care of **Historic Scotland**.

**Dyce, William** (1806–64) Artist, b. Aberdeen. Dyce was a polymath who combined his many interests (including theology, music, philosophy, science, architecture and art education) with his career as an artist. In his painting he was inspired by the early Renaissance, he himself producing large-scale frescos (notably for the Queen's Robing Room at the Palace of Westminster), although his finest works are the small oils he produced towards the end of his life.

**Dysart** Former royal **burgh** in Fife, now part of **Kirkcaldy**. There was salt-making in early times and it developed as a port, trading greatly with Holland, and was one of the first coal-mining towns, dating back to the 14th century when coal was used in the production of sea salt. Dysart Main coal seam, over 7.5m (25ft) thick, was subject to spontaneous combustion. Later Dysart also had textiles, shipbuilding and ironsmelting. The ruined St Serf's (former parish) Church dates from the 16th century, as do the Tolbooth and a considerable number of houses, restored by the **National Trust for Scotland**, alongside modern housing development by Wheeler and Sproson (1964–76), which attracted nation-wide attention.

E

**Eaglesham** A-plan Georgian village 7km (4mi) southwest of **East Kilbride**, dating from the Middle Ages, but rebuilt from 1769 by the 10th Earl of Eglinton to provide for workers at a nearby cotton factory. The centre is a conservation area. In 1941 the Nazi Rudolf Hess made a parachute landing near Eaglesham House.

**Eardley, Joan** (1921–63) Painter, b. Sussex. She studied at **Glasgow School of Art** and soon afterwards settled in **Glasgow**, where she concentrated on depicting the street-life of children from the city's tenements. From 1956 she was based at **Catterline**, on the Aberdeenshire coast, making highly expressive and original paintings (often executed in the open air) of the surrounding land- and sea-scape.

**Earlsferry** see **Elie**

**Earlshall Castle** Restored tower house near **Leuchars**, Fife. The original castle, built from 1546 onwards, was later abandoned and became a ruin. In the late 19th century it was carefully and lavishly restored by Sir Robert **Lorimer** for the owner, R W R Mackenzie, and the formal gardens were replanted. The castle is privately owned.

**Earlston** Village on the Leader Water, 6km (4mi) northeast of **Melrose**. Previously known as Ercildoune, it was the home of **Thomas the Rhymer**, and a small ruined 15th-century towerhouse is traditionally associated with him. In recent times it has had textile mills.

**Earn, River** Flows from **Loch Earn** at **St Fillans** for a distance of 51km (32mi) through **Strathearn**, past **Bridge of Earn** to the Firth of **Tay**.

**Earraid** see **Erraid**

**Eas-Coul-Aulin** Britain's highest waterfall, dropping 200m (656ft) at the head of Loch Glencoul in **Assynt**. Its remote location means it is most easily seen by boat from the loch.

**Easdale** (Gaelic *Éisdeal*) (pop. 58) Island in the Firth of **Lorn**, off **Seil** Island. Slate quarrying took place here from the 16th century, reaching its peak in the mid 19th century and ceasing in 1914; see also **Luing**. Today it has a small population and a number of holiday homes. The Easdale Island Folk Museum is housed in former quarriers' cottages. It is also the name of a small village on the shore opposite.

**East Ayrshire Council** Local authority in southwest Scotland created in 1996 by the amalgamation of the former **Strathclyde Region** districts of Kilmarnock and Loudon, and Cumnock and Doon Valley; see maps on pp.394–5 and **local government**; see also **Ayrshire**, **North Ayrshire**, **South Ayrshire**. The administrative centre is **Kilmarnock** and other towns include **Stewarton** and **Cumnock**. Agriculture is the main industry but tourism is also important as the area has associations with Robert **Burns** and Keir **Hardie**.

**East Calder** Village on the River **Almond**, 17km (12mi) southeast of **Edinburgh**, just to the east of **Midcalder**. The roofless ruin of St Cuthbert's Church stands in the village. Almondell and Calderwood Country Park incorporates two former estates, Almondell to the northeast and Calderwood to the southwest, as well as Oakbank, a **shale** bing landscaped in the 1980s.

**East Dunbartonshire** Local authority formed in 1996 from the Bearsden and Milngavie District and part of Strathkelvin District of **Strathclyde Region**; see maps on pp.394–5 and **local government**. The administrative centre is **Kirkintilloch** and other towns include **Bearsden**, **Milngavie** and **Bishopbriggs**.

**Easterhouse** Housing estate on the eastern edge of **Glasgow**, which was erected 1953–9 to house 25,000 people. It has suffered from high unemployment and related crime and poverty rates. The Greater Easterhouse Development Company was set up in the 1990s to assist regeneration.

**East Fortune** Aerodrome in **East Lothian**, 3km (2mi) west of **East Linton**. It was built in 1915 as a base for defence airships and some fighter aircraft. Although used again by the RAF in World War II, during peace time it was partially converted into a tuberculosis hospital. Since 1975 the Museum of Flight, part of the **National Museums of Scotland**, has been based here, and a Concorde is now on display. The annual Festival of Flight attracts many visitors.

**East Kilbride** (pop. 73,796) Town south of **Glasgow** which was Scotland's first **New Town**. The original village had thrived on farming, weaving and other industries, but the surrounding land was massively developed from 1947 onwards as part of an attempt to solve Glasgow's overcrowding problems. Employment is provided in a number of factories and industrial parks. To the northeast is Wester Kittochside Farm, now part of the **Museum of Scottish Country Life**.

**East Kilbride District** see **Strathclyde Region**

**East Linton** Village on the River Tyne, **East Lothian**, adjacent to the A1 road. There are a number of houses dating from the 18th century. The parish church of Prestonkirk, built in 1770, incorporates an impressive 13th-century chancel. Preston Mill and Phantassie Doocot, nearby, are owned by the **National Trust for Scotland**.

**East Lothian** Former county (formerly Haddingtonshire) stretching from the east of **Edinburgh** to the edge of the **Borders** at Cockburnspath. In 1975, with slightly altered boundaries, it became a district of **Lothian Region**, and since 1996, as East Lothian Council, it has been a unitary local authority; see maps on pp.394–5 and **local government**. The administrative centre is **Haddington** and other towns include **Dunbar**, **North Berwick** and **Tranent**. With much fertile land, farming remains important, but the former key industries of **fishing** and **coal** mining have declined. The area now has an increasing number of commuters to Edinburgh. Tourist attractions include castles, beaches and the championship **golf** course at **Muirfield**.

**East Lothian District** see **East Lothian** and **Lothian Region**

**East Neuk of Fife** The southeastern edge of **Fife**, comprising a string of coastal villages which were once prosperous centres of **fishing**, salt production and European trade. Though some fishing survives, they are now promoted as picturesque holiday destinations. See also **Anstruther**, **Crail**, **Elie**, **Pittenweem**, **St Monans**.

**East Renfrewshire Council** Local authority to the southwest of Glasgow, formed in 1996 from the Eastwood District of **Strathclyde Region**, slightly enlarged. See maps on pp.394–5 and **local government** and

see also **Renfrewshire**. The administrative centre is **Giffnock** and other towns include **Newton Mearns**, **Barrhead**, **Neilston** and **Eaglesham**.

**Eastwood District** see **Strathclyde Region**

**Ecclefechan** Village 8km (5mi) north of **Annan**. Thomas **Carlyle** was born here, in a house known as the Arched House. It is now a museum dedicated to his memory, run by the **National Trust for Scotland**. He is buried in the kirkyard.

**Ecclesiamagirdle** Remarkable group of unspoiled T-plan mansions of 1648 in Glenearn, **Perthshire**, built by the Carmichael family. There is a **doocot**, and small roofless pre-**Reformation** chapel picturesquely sited by a large fish pond.

**Eday** Island in the northern part of **Orkney**. Neolithic chambered cairns, notably at Vinquoy and on the Calf of Eday, and the Stone of Setter, a 4.5m (15ft) high standing stone.

**Eddleston** Village 6km (4mi) north of **Peebles**. Known for the Horseshoe Inn, which is housed in various old converted buildings, including the former blacksmith's workshop. Just to the west is Black Barony, formerly Darnhall, a 16th-century tower house of the Murrays, reconstructed about 1700 as a symmetrical 3-storey mansion with tall ogee-roofed towers. Now a hotel.

**Eden, River** Crosses the **Howe of Fife**, rising at Burnside, near **Strathmiglo**, and flowing eastwards for 48km (30mi) to **Guardbridge**. Here it opens into the Eden Estuary Nature Reserve, an important bird reserve, and flows into the North Sea 3km (2mi) north of **St Andrews**.

E

*The wreckage of Rudolf Hess's aeroplane, near Eaglesham, 1941.*

**Edgar** (c.1074–1107) King of Scots 1097–1107. Fourth son of **Malcolm III** and **Margaret**, he seized the throne with English help and continued to look towards England politically and culturally, for instance in his grant of **Coldingham** to the church of Durham in 1098. He died childless after a peaceful reign and is buried in **Dunfermline**.

**Edinample Castle** Z-plan castle picturesquely sited by **Loch Earn**, **Perthshire**, built in 1584 by Sir Duncan Campbell and remarkable for the complex geometry of its staircases; modified in the late 18th century but extensively restored in recent years. Privately owned.

**Edinburgh** see pp.130-3

**Edinburgh Castle** see p.130

**Edinburgh College of Art** Founded in 1906, the College was run by Edinburgh Corporation until 1960 when its management was transferred to a board of governors. It has links with **Edinburgh University**, with which it has a joint course in Fine Art, and **Heriot-Watt University**, with which it shares a School of Landscape Architecture and a faculty of Art and Design.

**Edinburgh Courant** Newspaper first published 14 February 1705. It was both edited and printed by James Watson (d.1722), who had produced the *Edinburgh Gazette* 5 years earlier.

**Edinburgh District** see **Edinburgh**, p.130

**Edinburgh Evening News** see **Scotsman**

**Edinburgh Festival Fringe** Begun as a few 'fringe' events in the early days of the **Edinburgh International Festival**, it has grown over the years until today it is one of the largest theatrical and arts events in the world. With its policy of including all comers in its programme, but letting them fend for themselves in all kinds of venues through the city, it has provided a starting point for many successful performers.

**Edinburgh International Book Festival** Founded in 1983, at first held every 2 years but more recently annually in August, it holds numerous literary events, some for children, and featuring world-class authors, in tents in the gardens of Charlotte Square in **Edinburgh**'s New Town.

**Edinburgh International Festival** World festival of music, drama and art founded in 1947, in a culture-starved postwar world, and continuing annually for 3 weeks in August/September ever since. Its largest crowd-puller is the **Edinburgh Military Tattoo**, and it is now accompanied by other festivals, notably the **Edinburgh Festival Fringe** and the **Edinburgh International Film Festival**.

**Edinburgh International Film Festival** Has been running since 1947 in August/September alongside the **Edinburgh International Festival**, growing from a documentary festival in the early days to become one of the world's most important film festivals.

**Edinburgh International Jazz and Blues Festival** Founded in 1978, the Festival takes place annually in late July/early August and presents about 100 concerts featuring Scottish and international artists.

**Edinburgh International Science Festival** Takes place every April with a wide range of exhibits and activities, many of them aimed at schools.

**Edinburgh Military Tattoo** Since 1950, the most popular event during the period of the **Edinburgh International Festival** in August, the Tattoo takes place nightly on the Esplanade of **Edinburgh** Castle, displaying military bands, including massed pipe bands and bands from overseas, to a large seated audience.

**Edinburgh rock** Stick-shaped pastel-coloured sweet, of friable texture, made of sugar, cream of tartar and water, in various delicate flavours. The recipe was created accidentally in 19th-century Edinburgh.

**Edinburghshire** see **Midlothian**

*The Cleveland San Jose Ballet Company, performing 'The Overcoat' at the Edinburgh International Festival.*

**Edinburgh University** Founded in 1582 with a charter from the City of **Edinburgh**, it was the first university in Britain with a non-ecclesiastical origin, and it was known as the Tounis College. Its main building, now known as the Old College, was designed by Robert **Adam** in 1789 and completed by William **Playfair** in 1818–34. The main arts campus is in nearby George Square, and most of the science buildings are at King's Buildings, 3km (2mi) to the south. The medical departments, world famous since the 18th century, have recently moved to the new Royal Infirmary on the outskirts of the city. The Dick Veterinary College, founded by William Dick (1793–1866), has been integrated into the University, now the Royal (Dick) School of Veterinary Studies. More recently Moray House College of Education has been incorporated, with its campus on the Royal Mile, including Moray House, built in 1625, and named after Margaret, Countess of Moray. The University has an internationally important collection of historic musical instruments. There are over 20,000 students. See also **New College**.

**Edinshall Broch** Prehistoric settlement near **Duns**. A large broch was added to an earlier fort, and later stone-built houses overlie the fort defences. In the care of **Historic Scotland**.

**Edmund** King of Scots 1094–7. Second son of **Malcolm III** and **Margaret**, he ruled with his uncle **Donald III**, before being defeated and deposed by **Edgar**. He ended his life in a monastery.

**Edradour** Scotland's smallest distillery, 3km (2mi) east of **Pitlochry**. It was established in 1825, and uses traditional methods and equipment.

**Education (Scotland) Act 1918** Fundamental Act for Scottish school education to the present day. The product of post-war idealism, its main architects were Robert Munro, Liberal Scottish Secretary, and John Struthers, Secretary of the Scottish Education Department. It had 4 main provisions: it allowed for the reorganisation of post-elementary schooling so that a proper secondary sector could emerge for the first time; it allowed for the transfer to public control of all the voluntary schools, notably those under the control of the Roman Catholic or Episcopal Churches; it transferred the local administration of public schools from over 900 parishes to 38 elected education authorities; and it established an Advisory Council which began to diversify influences on education policy.

**Educational Institute of Scotland** (EIS) The main teaching union in Scotland, founded in 1847. It now has over 52,000 members, around 80% of the Scottish teaching workforce.

**Edward, Alexander** (1651–1708) Architect and gardener,

*The Edinburgh Military Tattoo.*

b. Murroes, Angus. Dispossessed Episcopalian clergyman turned architect, formal gardener and **Jacobite** courier, closely associated with Sir William **Bruce**. His principal architectural work was **Brechin** Castle, remodelled 1696–1708, but his importance lies more in his study tour of France and the Low Countries and its influence on Scottish gardening, beginning with his own work at **Hopetoun** and Hamilton Palace.

**Edzell** Village 9.5km (6mi) north of **Brechin**. A planned village built in the 1840s to replace older housing. A memorial arch was erected in 1888 to commemorate the 13th Earl and Countess of **Dalhousie**, who died within 24 hours of each other. Edzell Castle, an extended 16th-century tower house which is now ruined, was built for the Lindsay Earls of Crawford. In the care of **Historic Scotland**, its gardens have the oldest complete and unaltered parterre layout in Scotland, dating from 1604. The walls contain chequered panels representing the Lindsay family crest and sculptured symbolic panels. Nearby is RAF Edzell, a military base used by the US Navy from 1960 until its closure in 1997.

**Egilsay** (pop. 37) Island in **Orkney**, east of **Rousay**. Its most prominent feature is the 12th-century church with distinctive round tower. It is dedicated to St **Magnus**, who was murdered here in 1117. A monument nearby marks the site of his death.

*Edinburgh Castle and the city from Salisbury Crags.*

**Edinburgh** (pop. 430,082) Scotland's capital city is a centre of government, **law**, commerce, culture and tourism. Situated near the south shore of the Firth of **Forth**, its skyline is dominated by Arthur's Seat, and by Edinburgh Castle. It had become a royal **burgh** by the early 12th century and was formerly part of the county of **Midlothian**. It became a county of city in 1929, and in 1975 a district of **Lothian Region** and also its administrative centre; since 1996 the City of Edinburgh has been a unitary local authority; see **local government**. Its trading port is **Leith**. Throughout the centuries the city was at the centre of political, religious and cultural events in Scotland. In the 18th century it was given the name 'Athens of the North', reflecting the astonishing cultural achievements of Edinburgh residents in Enlightenment society. Another less flattering nickname was 'Auld Reekie', which referred to the smoke produced by Edinburgh's many chimneys. The city centre has two parts, the Old Town and the New Town, now linked as a World Heritage Site.

Edinburgh was an important industrial town, with the largest concentration of breweries and printing works in Scotland, and an internationally important paper-machine-making industry. Today Edinburgh is home to the **Scottish Parliament** and civil service and to the national museums, galleries and library, and has a thriving financial sector. It attracts many tourists, not least to the **Edinburgh International Festival** and other festivals, and in winter to its Hogmanay street parties.

## THE OLD TOWN

Medieval Edinburgh clustered along a steep ridge, the result of a glacial feature known as crag and tail: the crag being the Castle Rock, the remains of an old volcano, and the tail the ridge descending to Holyrood Abbey at the foot. The street along the ridge has been known since the 16th century as the Royal Mile, as it runs between the two main residences of the medieval kings of Scots, the Castle and the Abbey (and later Palace) of Holyroodhouse.

**Edinburgh Castle** has been occupied since prehistoric times and has been recorded as a royal residence since the 11th century. The Palace, on the highest part of the Castle rock, dates from the 15th century and later, and contains the regalia of Scotland: crown, sceptre and sword of state, and now also the **Stone of Destiny**. The oldest building is St **Margaret's** Chapel, a small Romanesque building, restored many times. The Castle also contains the **National War Museum of Scotland** and the Scottish National War Memorial (1927, designed by Robert **Lorimer**). The Esplanade was built as a parade ground in the early 19th century and is now the scene of the annual **Edinburgh Military Tattoo**. The 15th-century cannon, known as Mons Meg and probably manufactured in Flanders, is the Castle's most famous piece of artillery.

Conspicuous on the Old Town skyline is the white dome of the Outlook Tower; it contains the Camera Obscura, installed in the 1850s to give a panoramic view of the city by means of revolving lenses and mirrors; see Patrick **Geddes**. Gladstone's Land is a well-preserved 17th-century house, renovated in the style of the period by the **National Trust for Scotland**.

The present structure of St Giles' Cathedral, more correctly the High Kirk of Edinburgh, dates mainly from the 14th and 15th centuries, though of the outer masonry only the crown tower dates from that period, the rest from very necessary renovations by William **Burn** (1829–33). Behind it in Parliament Square is **Parliament House**, a Renaissance building built for the old Scottish Parliament by Sir James Murray (1632–40), now incorporated within the law courts and library complex designed by Robert Reid in 1803–9. Also within this complex is the Signet Library, a magnificent colonnaded room by William Stark (1812–13). To the southwest the library of the Solicitors to the Supreme Court was added in 1888–92. **Parliament Hall**, with its great hammerbeam roof, is still used by lawyers and their clients. The new Scottish Parliament found a temporary home in the Assembly Hall erected on the Mound (see below) in 1858–9 to house meetings of the General Assembly of the **Free Church of Scotland**. From 1929 it has been the venue for the General Assembly of the Church of Scotland. The twin towers of the adjoining New College by W H **Playfair** (1844–6) form an impressive silhouette from below, along with the single spire of the former Tolbooth St John's Church (1842–4, James Gillespie **Graham**), now The Hub, headquarters of the **Edinburgh International Festival**.

The City Chambers was originally built as the Royal Exchange in 1753–61 by John Fergus, based on a design by John **Adam**; it was adapted for Council use in 1811. The Tron Kirk (1636–47) by John Mylne was reconstructed in the 18th century and a new tower was added in 1829, after the disastrous fire of 1824, which destroyed many Old Town buildings. Its fine Renaissance roof survives, and it is now an information centre. The John **Knox** House projects into the street; it is not certain whether Knox ever lived in it, but it certainly dates from the later 16th century. It now forms part of the Netherbow Arts Centre, near the site of an old city gate, demolished in 1764 to improve traffic flow.

Parallel to the High Street is the Cowgate, once an upper-class suburb, but a deplorable slum by the 19th century and now a rather undistinguished thoroughfare, not helped by a

major fire in December 2002. The Magdalen Chapel, built in the 1540s as the chapel of the Incorporation of Hammermen, contains the only pre-**Reformation** stained glass in Scotland still in its original site; it is now the headquarters of the Scottish Reformation Society and is open to the public. St Cecilia's Hall (1753) by Robert Mylne is modelled on the opera house at Parma in Italy. It belongs to **Edinburgh University** and is still used as a concert hall and houses an important collection of early keyboard instruments.

At the foot of the Royal Mile is the Palace of Holyroodhouse. Alongside is the ruin of the Augustinian abbey founded by **David I** in 1128, and rebuilt on a much grander scale 1195–1230, unroofed in the 18th century. It had been a medieval royal residence and a new palace was built in 1501, greatly added to in 1528–36. After damage in the Cromwellian period, complete reconstruction took place in 1671–9 to designs by Sir William **Bruce**, with another tower to the south balancing the 16th-century one, and joining and extending them into an impressive quadrangle.

A new focus has been given to the Holyrood area by the decision to site the new parliament building there; see **Scottish Parliament**, and there are further developments, including offices and hotels and a new home for the **Scotsman** newspaper. Our Dynamic Earth is a spectacular tent-like

*The Royal Mile.*

structure by Sir Michael Hopkins in which the story of the earth is dramatically told using the latest technology. Holyrood is on the edge of the Royal Park; with Arthur's Seat (251m/823ft), the Salisbury Crags and two lochs; it is a remarkable piece of open country close to the city centre.

The lowest part of the Royal Mile is the Canongate, formerly a **burgh** separate from Edinburgh, with Holyrood Abbey as its parish church. When **James VII** had the nave converted as the chapel of the new Order of the **Thistle**, the Canongate Kirk was built (1691) to designs by James **Smith**; its kirkyard has the graves of many famous Scots, including Robert **Fergusson** and Adam **Smith**. Canongate Tolbooth (1591) is now a museum, as is Huntly House, built in stages in the 16th and 17th centuries. Queensberry House, an impressive late 17th-century house which has seen many changes of use, has been restored as part of the Scottish Parliament complex.

To the south of the Old Town is Edinburgh's earliest Georgian development, George Square (1760s–70s), almost destroyed by 1960s **Edinburgh University** planning. Nearby are the buildings of the former Royal Infirmary of Edinburgh (Scots **baronial** by David **Bryce**, with advice from Florence Nightingale, 1870-9) George Heriot's School (see George **Heriot**), and Greyfriars Kirk (1620), which was the first church to be built in Edinburgh after the **Reformation**; in 1638 it was the scene of the signing of the **National Covenant**. The kirkyard has the tombs of many famous people in Scottish history. A statue of a small dog near the entrance commemorates a terrier, known as **Greyfriars' Bobby**, who remained at his master's grave for 14 years after the latter's death in 1858.

## THE NEW TOWN

By the mid 18th century the cramped conditions of the old Edinburgh had become a major problem and plans were made

*The Scott Monument.*

for expansion to the north. The Nor Loch below the Castle Rock was drained and the North Bridge was built to link to the new developments. The first phase of the New Town, Princes Street, George Street and Queen Street, with adjoining streets in a grid pattern, was built to a plan by a young architect, James **Craig,** in the 1770s, with Charlotte Square to the east and St Andrew Square to the west (now the site of Edinburgh bus station). St George's Church in Charlotte Square, now West Register House, was completed in 1814, to a design by Robert **Adam**, greatly altered by Robert Reid. Much of the south side of the square is occupied by the **National Trust for Scotland**, which also has the Georgian House on the north side, furnished in the style of the period. Bute House, formerly owned by the Marquess of Bute, is now the official residence of the First Minister of the Scottish Parliament.

St Andrew's Church (1785-7), now St Andrew's and St George's, was built at the eastern end of George Street, since the appropriate site in nearby St Andrew Square had been occupied by the town house of Sir Laurence Dundas (1771) by Sir William Chambers, now the **Royal Bank of Scotland**, with a domed banking hall added at the rear (1857) by John Dick

*Moray Place and Ainslie Place, the New Town.*

Peddie. Also in George Street are the **Assembly Rooms**, built in 1787 by the Rome-trained John Henderson to house social events such as dances. It is now a prominent venue for the Edinburgh Festival Fringe and other events. The Music Hall was added by William **Burn** in 1843. At the east end of Princes Street is Register House, begun in 1774 by Robert Adam, headquarters of the **National Archives of Scotland**.

Further New Town areas were built in the early 19th century, to the north, the northwest, and to the northeast below the Calton Hill, where the Nelson Monument (1807, Robert Burn), some 30m (100ft) high, provides an excellent viewpoint on a clear day; the unfinished National Monument, to the dead of the Napoleonic Wars, aimed to be a replica of the Parthenon in Athens. At the foot of the Calton Hill is the former Royal High School (1825-9) by Thomas **Hamilton**, and Thomas Tait's 'sculpturesque' classical modern St Andrew's House (1933-9); see **Scottish Office**.

Access to the Old Town was improved by a causeway known as the Mound. Overlooking it is the domed **Bank of Scotland** headquarters, originally built by Richard Crichton and Robert **Reid** (1803-6) and remodelled as a neo-baroque pile by David **Bryce** (1865-70). At its foot are the two classical buildings of the **National Gallery of Scotland** (1845, W H **Playfair**) and the **Royal Scottish Academy** (completed 1836, W H Playfair, originally housing other bodies). A little to the east, the Sir Walter **Scott** Monument (1844) by George Meikle Kemp, a soaring Victorian Gothic pile of fantastic intricacy, dominates the skyline. On the north side of Princes Street is Jenners department store; established in 1838, it is the world's oldest independent department store. The current building (1895) by William Hamilton Beattie is remarkable for its spacious toplit galleried saloon, still virtually unaltered.

Princes Street Gardens provide a green oasis, in spite of the railway running below the Castle Rock to Edinburgh's main terminus at Waverley Station. At the west end of Princes Street is St John's Episcopal Church (William **Burn** 1815-18), a splendid example of early Gothic Revival. St Cuthbert's Church (1892-5), below in the Gardens, is on the site of earlier churches dating back to the Middle Ages; it retains the tower of its 18th-century predecessor. Its entrance is in Lothian Road, formerly known mainly for Edinburgh's main concert hall, the Usher Hall (1910-14) by Stockdale Harrison, and the Royal Lyceum Theatre (1883) by the London theatre specialist C J Phipps. The area has seen major commercial developments in recent years, with many new office blocks, and the Sheraton Hotel (1982). Saltire Court (1991) houses the **Traverse**

*Looking west above Princes Street and Princes Street Gardens.*

**Theatre**, as well as offices. The Edinburgh International Conference Centre is nearby (1995).

## WEST END

In the late 19th century Victorian terraces spread comfortable living to the west of the city centre. The skyline of the area is dominated by the 3 towers of St Mary's Episcopal Cathedral (Sir George Gilbert Scott 1874-1917). The **Water of Leith** runs through the area and, nestling on its banks below the majestic span of the Dean Bridge (Thomas **Telford**, 1829-31), is the Dean Village. It grew round the flour mills which had used the river's water power for centuries, and is now a popular residential area with renovated old buildings as well as new. Nearby is the **Scottish National Gallery of Modern Art**, and opposite it the **Dean Gallery**. Donaldson's College for the Deaf is a huge quadrangular building in Elizabethan style by W H **Playfair** (1842-50). Two other impressive school buildings in the area are Daniel Stewart's and Melville College, also Elizabethan (David Rhind, 1848), and the great late-Gothic chateau of Fettes College (David Bryce, 1863-70).

Edinburgh Airport, at Turnhouse to the west of the city, has grown in recent years as an international airport. On its edge is Castle Gogar, a stepped L-plan mansion of 1625, with fine Renaissance detail, built by John Cowper.

See also **Craiglockhart, Craigmillar, Cramond, Duddingston, Edinburgh University, Edinburgh College of Art, Edinburgh International Festival, Edinburgh Festival Fringe, Edinburgh International Book Festival, Edinburgh International Film Festival, Edinburgh International Jazz and Blues Festival, Edinburgh International Science Festival, Edinburgh Military Tattoo, Granton, Heriot-Watt University, Ingliston, Lauriston Castle, Leith, Morningside, Murrayfield, Napier University, Newhaven, Prestonfield House, Royal Botanic Garden.**

E

*Eilean Donan Castle.*

**Eigg** (Gaelic **Eige**) (pop. 67) Island in the Inner **Hebrides**, of the **Small Isles**, 6km (4mi) southeast of **Rum**, reached by ferry from **Mallaig**. The skyline is dominated by An Sgurr, 393m (1289ft). There are prehistoric forts, a Pictish cemetery and an Early Christian monastery at Kildonnan. In 1997 the islanders succeeded in purchasing the island. The Heritage Trust which now runs Eigg is a partnership of residents, Highland Council and the Scottish Wildlife Trust.

**eightsome reel** Popular **reel** danced by 4 couples, with most of the movements in a circle, often danced at weddings and other social occasions.

**Eilach an Naoimh** see **Garvellachs**

**Eildons** Three hills dominating the town of **Melrose** from the south, the highest point is 422m (1385ft). The remains of a Roman and of an earlier British fort can be found on the north summit. Legends surround them, linking their origin with Michael **Scott** and suggesting that King Arthur and his knights lie sleeping beneath them.

**Eilean Donan Castle** Built on an island in **Loch Duich**, 13km (8mi) east of **Kyle of Lochalsh**. Much photographed because of its dramatic setting, it consists of a 14th-century tower house surrounded by a 13th-century wall. It belonged to the Mackenzies, later Earls of Seaforth, and was held for them by the MacRaes. Badly damaged during the **Jacobite** Rising of 1719, the castle was rebuilt 1912–32. It has featured in a number of films, including *Highlander* (1986). It is privately owned and open to the public.

**Eilt, Loch** see **Loch Eilt**

**EIS** see **Educational Institute of Scotland**

**Elcho Castle** Large multi-towered castle, picturesquely sited on the south bank of the River **Tay**, near **Perth**, built by the Wemyss family about 1600 and still very complete. In the care of **Historic Scotland**.

**elder** Each **Church of Scotland** congregation is run by a group of elders, known as the Kirk Session, of whom the minister is the 'teaching elder'. The office has existed since the **Reformation**. Since 1966 women as well as men have been ordained to the eldership. The position is held for life, and involves pastoral care of the congregation and authority in spiritual and disciplinary matters.

**Elder, John** (1824–69) Marine engineer and shipbuilder, b. Glasgow, son of David Elder, Robert **Napier**'s works manager at Lancefield. He developed, and patented in 1853, the compound marine engine, going into partnership with Charles Randolph to build these engines, whose economy extended the useful range of steamships. When Randolph retired in 1868 Elder formed the company of John Elder and Co, and built the Fairfield Shipyard in Govan. He died at the height of his powers in the following year.

**Elderslie** Village near Paisley, best known for its claim to be the birthplace of William **Wallace**. Industries in the 19th century included textiles and a distillery, and in the 20th century carpets.

**Elgin** (pop. 20,829) Town in **Moray**, 42km (26mi) east of **Inverness**, a former royal **burgh**, which is dominated by the ruins of the cathedral, consecrated in 1224. In 1390 both town and cathedral were burnt by Alexander **Stewart**, the Wolf of Badenoch, who had been excommunicated by the Bishop of Moray. The cathedral ruin is in the care of **Historic Scotland**, and the town is remarkable for its outstanding classical public buildings, notably Dr Gray's Hospital (1815–18) by Gillespie **Graham**, the Parish Church (1825–8) and Anderson's Institution (1830–3) by Archibald **Simpson** and the Museum by Thomas **Mackenzie**. The town expanded in the 19th century with the coming of the railway, and is now the administrative centre of Moray Council. To the southeast is the 17th-century Coxton Tower.

**Elgin, James Bruce, 8th Earl of, and 12th Earl of Kincardine** (1811–63) Politician and diplomat, b. London.

His influential political career saw him serve on several continents, including as Governor-General of Canada (1847-54), Envoy to China (1857) and Viceroy of India (1861). Several communities in Ontario, Canada are named after him.

**Elgin, Thomas Bruce, 7th Earl of, and 11th Earl of Kincardine** (1766-1841) Diplomat and antiquarian. As Ambassador to the Ottoman Empire (1799-1803), he brought the Parthenon Frieze – also known as the Elgin Marbles – from Athens to England, claiming that he was saving it from destruction, which he probably was. His actions, controversial at the time, contributed to his own bankruptcy and have led to ethical disputes ever since. The sculptures were eventually sold at a heavy loss to the British government, and are housed in the British Museum.

**Elgin, Victor A Bruce, 9th Earl of, and 13th Earl of Kincardine** (1849-1917) Politician, b. Montreal. He became chairman of the Scottish Liberal Association in the 1880s. As Viceroy of India (1894-7), he had to cope with nationalism, border unrest, serious famine and bubonic plague. He proved a competent and moderate proconsul. On his return he chaired a committee on British failures in the Boer War, whose sensible conclusions were largely ignored. A friend of **Campbell-Bannerman**, he was Colonial Secretary (1905-8) but could not control his egotistical and disloyal subordinate, Winston Churchill. He was dumped by Asquith in 1908.

**Elginshire** see **Moray**

**Elgol** Village on **Skye**, at the tip of the Strathaird Peninsula. It provides spectacular views of the **Cuillins**, and is the starting-point for trips to **Loch Coruisk**. One cave nearby was a hiding place for Prince Charles Edward **Stewart** in 1746, and another, the Spar Cave, is referred to by Sir Walter **Scott** in 'The Lord of the Isles'.

**Elie** Coastal village on the Firth of **Forth**, part of the **East Neuk of Fife**, popular with tourists. A former **burgh**, in 1929 it joined the adjacent royal burgh of Earlsferry. Elie House dates from the late 17th century with 18th- and 19th-century additions.

**Elizabeth of Bohemia** (1596-1662) Princess and queen, b. Falkland Palace. The daughter of **James VI** and **Anne of Denmark**, she married Frederick V, Elector Palatine, in 1613, and lived in Heidelberg. During the Thirty Years' War her husband was chosen as King of Bohemia (1619), but their reign lasted only one winter, earning Elizabeth the title 'The Winter Queen'. After her death Elizabeth would provide the link between the **Stewart** and Hanoverian dynasties, as her daughter Sophia was the mother of **George I**. She was also known as the 'Queen of Hearts'.

**ell** see **weights and measures**, pp.382-4

**Ellen's Isle** see **Loch Katrine**

**Elliot, Archibald** (1760-1823) and **James** (1771-1810) Architects, b. Ancrum, Roxburghshire, practising in London and **Edinburgh**, notable Greek revivalists who designed Waterloo Place and Rutland Square in Edinburgh in 1819, and built the great Gothic **Taymouth** Castle for the Earl of **Breadalbane**, 1806-10.

**Elliot, Jane** (1727-1805) Poet, b. Minto House, near Hawick. The daughter of Gilbert Elliot, 2nd Lord Minto, she is remembered for writing a version of the words of 'The **Flowers of the Forest**'.

**Elliot, Walter** (1888-1958) Politician, b. Lanark. Conservative MP for **Lanark** (1918-23) and for Kelvingrove (1924-45), he became Secretary of State for Scotland in 1936. As Minister of Health (1938-40), he introduced free milk for schoolchildren and organised the evacuation of children from London. Winston Churchill denied him office because of his association with Neville Chamberlain and appeasement.

**Ellisland** Farm north of **Dumfries** which was rented by Robert **Burns** from 1788 to 1791. The poems he wrote while living here include *Tam O' Shanter*, but his attempts at farming were unsuccessful and he moved to Dumfries. The farm is now a museum.

**Ellon** (pop. 8754) Town 27km (17mi) northeast of **Aberdeen**, built around a ford on the River **Ythan**. Little remains of medieval Ellon Castle, which was replaced by an 18th-century building which has itself been demolished, but the great terraced garden remains. Agriculture has provided the main employment, but since the 1970s many oil workers have lived in the town.

**Elphinstone, George Keith** (1746-1823) Admiral, b. Elphinstone Tower, Stirling. He fought in the War of the American Revolution and in the French Revolutionary and Napoleonic Wars. As commanding officer, he secured the surrender of Cape Town and Ceylon (now Sri Lanka) in 1795 and 1796, captured Malta and Genoa in 1800. An amphibious warfare expert, he landed Sir Ralph **Abercromby**'s army in Egypt in 1801. Unusually, he achieved greatness without winning a major fleet engagement.

**Elphinstone, Mountstuart** (1775-1859) Colonial administrator, b. Cumbernauld. East India Company employee in Bengal from 1795, he was the first British envoy to Kabul in1808. As Resident in Poona he was involved in the last Mahratta war. He was Governor-General of Bombay 1819-27. Deeply influenced by **Scottish Enlightenment** ideas, he massively reformed south India's land revenue system before retiring to write history.

E

# EDUCATION

Scottish education has an emblematic status for the nation's culture, having often in the last couple of centuries been taken to signify the essence of the country's identity. At no time has this been more true than in the last 40 years, when the concept (or slogan) of the 'democratic intellect' has seemed to sum up the aspiration towards a new kind of civic democracy that could be inaugurated by political self-government.

Like all social myths, that of Scotland's alleged democratic intellectualism does not admit of any simple interpretation. Nevertheless, its very complexity may help to explain its durability and its broad appeal. Two dominant strands may be discerned, inter-related but independent of each other, and pointing to paradoxes in the country's culture as well as in its system of instruction. The first is the principle that education is a public good, in the sense that the whole of society benefits from the better education of each individual. A neat starting point for this may be found in an Act of **James IV** in 1496 which sought to require that the eldest sons of substantial landowners should have a good education in order that 'justice may reigne universalie throw all the realme'. Of more lasting effect, however, were the educational principles of the **Reformation**, embodied in the First **Book of Discipline** of 1560. This ordained that there should be a school in every parish, a high school in every town, and universities in each province, notably those in **Aberdeen, St Andrews, Glasgow** and **Edinburgh**. Although this utopian scheme took many decades to be realised, it was largely in place by the early part of the 18th century, and helps to explain the relatively high levels of basic literacy when Scotland started to industrialise. That legacy created a nation in which there were enough well-educated people to provide the students for the expanding university system of the 18th and 19th centuries and an audience for the writings of the professors.

The **Scottish Enlightenment** was unusual in being university-based and also in being concerned with the practical work of social improvement. Its most lasting legacies were in science and technology, and belief that a well-governed commonwealth requires to be educated. Philosophy was at the core of the university curriculum because it alone could refine the common sense of the community, especially if students were educated in all the broad aspects of human culture. That philosophical principle had its most notable political influence in the new American constitution, but it also pervaded Scottish civic life in the 19th century. Thus Scottish liberalism was never merely individualistic, depending also on a certain kind of civic virtue. Education might offer individual opportunity, but that was to a social purpose.

The great liberal Education Acts of 1872 and 1918 (laying the basis for universal elementary and secondary education) carried this principle forward into the 20th century. It was taken up by the nascent labour movement, drawing into the same current also a strong belief by Catholics that education was the means to their community's emancipation (a belief now shared by Scotland's more recent immigrant cultures). Reinterpreted by social democratic politicians as the principle of equal opportunities through comprehensive schooling, and more recently through a system of mass higher education, the legacy from the Reformation thus remains a guiding though modified motif of Scottish education today. But the other side to all this is a competitive individualism that is as firmly a legacy of presbyterianism as the idea of a civic community.

The term 'democratic intellectualism' was coined by the Conservative politician Walter **Elliot**, who characterised Scottish culture as one 'wherein intellect, speech and, above all, argument are the passports to the highest eminence in the land'. If philosophy was at the centre of this, it was as a training in ruthless debate, not as a guide to social harmony. The classic icon of Scottish education in the 19th century is the **lad o pairts**, a lad on the make, using his intellect to escape his potentially parochial community. Far from serving the community through his education, he – in many thousands of cases – would then travel all over the globe (or at least the Empire), sometimes but not always doing good in a paternalistic kind of way, but with the driving force of individual advancement as his inspiration. It is doubtful whether any of this competitive individualism was diminished at all when girls and women were admitted to it from the late 19th century. The story of the 20th century may then partly be a matter of political radicals agitating for the enlightenment of the community. But it is at least as much about competition – equality as the opportunity to compete equally, rather than as the basis of a well-educated, whole community.

A dominant criticism of Scottish education at the beginning of the new century is that, in the name of equal opportunities, the whole education system has come to be driven by examinations to the exclusion of real learning. So the significance of Scottish education for the national identity is ambiguous. The price that has been paid for offering opportunity to almost everyone is that everyone has to be sifted and ranked. Insistent testing has been the answer to the accusation that mass systems are incapable of maintaining high academic standards. It is because the resulting style of education may be described as both a national success and as a national dilemma that education remains inescapably at the heart of national concern.

E

**Elphinstone, William** (1431-1514) Bishop of Aberdeen, b. Glasgow. A leading political and religious figure, he was appointed Bishop of **Aberdeen** in 1483 and was also Chancellor of Scotland (1488) and Keeper of the Privy Seal from 1492. His greatest legacy was King's College, which he founded in Aberdeen in 1495. He was also responsible for the *Aberdeen Breviary* (1509-10), a Scottish service book which was designed to be used in place of English versions in churches across the country.

**Elshieshields Tower** Picturesque turreted L-plan house to the northwest of **Lochmaben**, near **Dumfries**; built in 1567 by the Johnstones, incorporating an older 15th-century tower, extended in the 18th century. From the mid 1960s it was the home of the Byzantine scholar Sir Steven **Runciman**.

**Encyclopedia Britannica** Founded in **Edinburgh** by Andrew Bell, an engraver, and Colin Macfarquhar, a printer. The first edition was published between 1768 and 1771, with William **Smellie** as editor. Another edition followed between 1777 and 1784, edited by James Tytler. Later editions continued to be published in Edinburgh over the next century. Still a successful publication, the *Encyclopedia Britannica* has been published in America since 1921.

**Engagement** An agreement between a group of more moderate **Covenanters** and **Charles I**, signed December 1647. The Scots promised military aid to Charles, who was a prisoner of Cromwell's Parliamentarians, in return for a promise to introduce a 3-year trial of Presbyterianism in England. The Engagers were defeated at Preston in August 1648.

**English** see **language**

**Episcopal Church** see **Scottish Episcopal Church**

**Enlightenment** see **Scottish Enlightenment**

**Equivalent** Compensation (£400,000 and further payments) paid to Scotland as part of the Treaty of Union in return for accepting a share of England's National Debt.

**Ercildoune** see **Earlston**

**Eriskay** (Gaelic **Eiriosgaigh**) (pop. 133) Island in the Outer **Hebrides**, lying south of **South Uist**, to which it has been joined by a causeway since 2001. In 1745 Prince Charles Edward **Stewart** made his first landing on Scottish soil here, at the start of his campaign to regain the throne for the Stewarts. The SS *Politician* ran aground here carrying a load of **whisky** in 1941, an incident which inspired Compton **MacKenzie**'s novel *Whisky Galore*, later a successful film. Today fishing provides the main source of employment. St Michael's Church was built by the local community in 1903 and has an altar made from the bow of a lifeboat. The Gaelic song known in English as the 'Eriskay Love Lilt' was one of those collected by Marjory **Kennedy-Fraser**.

**Erraid** or **Earraid** Small tidal island off the southwest tip of **Mull**. Robert Louis **Stevenson** stayed here while accompanying his father on visits to **lighthouses**, and the island appears in his novel *Kidnapped*. Erraid is privately owned, but is cared for by the **Findhorn** Foundation. Their community here is centred round organic gardening, and they run courses and retreats on the island.

**Erse** Old name for **Gaelic**.

**Erskine** (pop. 15,347) Town on the River **Clyde**, 8km (5mi) north of **Paisley**. Nearby the Erskine Bridge, opened in 1971, crosses the river to Old Kirkpatrick on the north side. Erskine House, a great Tudor house with impressive interiors designed by Sir Robert

*Eriskay, Outer Hebrides, looking north towards the village with South Uist in the distance.*

*Ensign Ewart capturing a French standard at the Battle of Waterloo (1815), by Christopher Clark (1875–1942).*

Smirke for Lord Blantyre in 1828, is a hospital for ex-servicemen and women, which opened in 1916 as The Princess Louise Scottish Hospital for Limbless Soldiers and Sailors. A new complex of buildings was completed in 2002.

**Erskine, Ebene(e)zer** (1680–1754) Minister, b. Dryburgh. An **evangelical**, he was minister in Portmoak, Kinross-shire from 1703 and in **Stirling** from 1731. In 1733 he was suspended for preaching against the Patronage Act, which gave patrons rather than congregations the right to choose their minister. He was among the founders of the Associate Presbytery or **Secession Church**, and was its first moderator. His younger brother Ralph, minister in **Dunfermline**, joined the seceders in 1737. See also **Presbyterian churches**.

**Erskine, John** (1695–1768) Lawyer. An advocate from 1719, he became Professor of Scots Law at the University of **Edinburgh** in 1737. He wrote *Principles of the Law of Scotland* (1754), and his *Institutes of the Law of Scotland* (1773) became a standard work, still in use today.

**Erskine, Ralph** see **Erskine, Ebene(e)zer**

**Esk, River, Black and White** (Dumfriesshire). River formed when the Black and White Esks unite at **Eskdalemuir**. It flows for 35km (22mi) through Eskdale and crosses the border with England to enter the Solway Firth south of **Gretna**.

**Esk, River, North and South** (Angus) The North Esk travels southeastwards through Glen Esk for a distance of 47km (29mi), entering the sea to the north of **Montrose**. The South Esk also flows southeast for 79km (49mi) through Glen Clova and into the Montrose Basin. The Earls of Northesk and Southesk are members of the **Carnegie** family.

**Esk, River, North and South** (Midlothian) The River Esk, which flows into the Firth of **Forth** at **Musselburgh**, is formed when the Rivers North and South Esk unite near **Dalkeith**. Both rivers flow in a northeasterly direction through **Midlothian**, the North Esk rising at **West Linton** and the South Esk at **Temple**.

**Eskdalemuir** Village in **Dumfries and Galloway**, 22km (14mi) northwest of **Langholm**. The Samye Ling monastery and Tibetan Centre was established here in 1967. The grounds and temple are open to the public. There is also a meteorological observatory at Eskdalemuir.

**Established Church** see **Church of Scotland**

**Ethernan, St** (d.669) Irish or Pictish monk who played a significant role in converting the **Picts**. He is associated with the Isle of **May**, where excavation has uncovered an early Christian cemetery close to the later Benedictine monastery.

**Ethie** Large mainly 17th-century castle, near the **Angus** coast to the northeast of **Arbroath**, latterly the seat of the Earls of Northesk but in the earlier 16th century the home of Cardinal **Beaton** as Abbot of Arbroath.

**Etive** see **Glen Etive, Loch Etive**

**Ettrick** River which rises near **Moffat** and flows 53km (33mi) northeastwards into the River **Tweed** near Melrose.

**Ettrick and Lauderdale** see **Borders Region**

**Ettrick Forest** The name once given to much of **Selkirkshire**, which was a popular medieval royal hunting ground, and belonged at times to the Douglases and to the Scotts of Buccleuch. The ancient **Caledonian forests** are long since gone, and the Ettrick Forest now consists largely of sheep pasture, but partly reafforested in the 1980s.

**Ettrick Shepherd** see **Hogg, James**

**Evangelicals** Evangelicalism can be used to describe a religious culture which stresses the need to pass on the gospel message and emphasises the direct relationship between the believer and Christ. As a party label in the **Church of Scotland** it originated in the Scottish response to 'the Great Awakening', the series of enthusiastic religious revivals of the 1740s in the North Atlantic world. After the English Methodist George Whitefield had preached in Scotland in 1741, a succession of Scottish revivals began with the Cambuslang Wark in 1742. Because of their stress on individual assurance of salvation, these revivals tended to be highly emotional and to stress the rights of congregations. The **Moderate** party, which identified enthusiasm with fanaticism and which was unenthusiastic about missionary work either at home or abroad, was alienated. Increasingly opponents of the Moderates in the **General Assembly** became known as Evangelicals. They were theologically conservative, with a great zeal for preaching and conversion. Their greatest leader, Thomas **Chalmers**, had an emotional conversion experience as a parish minister in Fife, but still hoped to forge a dynamic Christian alliance with the State. Disillusioned in his hopes and hostile to lay patronage, he reluctantly headed the 1843 **Disruption**, which led to the formation of the **Free Church**. Other, smaller, churches (**Baptist**, **Congregational** etc) were also regarded as evangelical in their theological tenets.

**Evening Express** see **Press and Journal**

**Evening News** see **Scotsman**

**Evening Telegraph** see **Courier**

**Evening Times** see **Herald**

**Ewart, Charles** (1769-1846) Soldier. A sergeant in the **Royal Scots Greys**, he is famed for his capture of the Imperial eagle and standard of the French 45th Regiment at the Battle of Waterloo, for which he was promoted ensign. He is commemorated by a statue on the Esplanade at **Edinburgh** Castle and in the Ensign Ewart public house in Edinburgh's Lawnmarket.

**Ewart, Gavin Buchanan** (1916-96) Poet, b. and brought up in England, of Scottish parents. One of the foremost writers of verse in the 20th century, he commented outspokenly on many aspects of social life and manners from the 1930s onwards, using a wide variety of poetic forms and styles. His apparently light humorous tone and disregard for propriety masked a fundamental seriousness and social concern, and may have been the reason for the consistent undervaluing of his poetry by critics.

**Ewe, Loch, River, Isle of** see **Loch Ewe**

**Ewing, Winifred (Winnie)** (1929- ) Politician and solicitor, b. Glasgow. A prominent campaigner for Scottish independence, she was Nationalist MP for Hamilton (1967-70) and for Moray and Nairn (1974-9). She became a member of the European Parliament in 1975, and Member of the **Scottish Parliament** for Highlands and Islands in 1999. As the oldest MSP, she took the Presiding Officer's chair at the first session of the new Scottish Parliament in 1999.

**Eyemouth** (pop. 3383) Town on the east coast, 13km (8mi) north of the English Border at **Berwick-upon-Tweed**. It is still a thriving **fishing** community, with a busy harbour. In 1881 disaster struck the town, when a storm sank around 23 fishing boats, with the loss of 129 Eyemouth men. The event is commemorated by a monument in the park and in the Eyemouth Museum. Across the Eye Water is Gunsgreen house by James **Adam** (1775), a classical villa presiding over a semi-circular gun battery.

**Eynhallow** Small island in the Eynhallow Sound which runs between mainland **Orkney** and **Rousay**. Now a nature reserve, it has been uninhabited since 1851. On the Island there are ruins of a 12th-century church, which may have been a Benedictine monastery.

E

*Gunsgreen House and the Harbour, Eyemouth, in the late 19th century.*

**Faa, Johnnie** King of the Gypsies in the 16th century. According to legend he abducted the Countess of Cassilis and was hanged by the Earl of Cassilis. The events are recounted in the ballad 'Johnnie Faa, the Gipsie Laddie' and the Faa family also feature in S R **Crockett**'s best-known novel, *The Raiders*.

**Fada, Lochan** see **Lochan Fada**

**Faed, John** (1819–1902) and **Thomas** (1826–1900) Artists, b. Gatehouse-of-Fleet, near Kirkcudbright. Two of the most prominent Scottish artists of the Victorian period, the brothers John and Thomas Faed established their careers in **Edinburgh** before settling in London. Their subject matter was typical of the age, encompassing the historical, literary and the landscape, but they were at their most successful with genre scenes of Scottish life. Thomas's *Last of the Clan* (Glasgow Art Gallery) is one of the finest 19th-century works of this type. Their siblings, James and Susan, were also accomplished artists.

**Fairbairn, Sir William** (1789–1874) Mechanical and structural engineer, b. Kelso. He spent his working life in Manchester, where his firm was much involved in large water-power installations, and in the design and construction of large malleable-iron railway bridges, including Robert Stephenson's Menai and Conwy tubular girder bridges in north Wales, and Joseph **Mitchell**'s bridges on what became The Highland Railway. Fairbairn was a pioneer in the study of the design of structural ironwork. His firm is credited with the invention of the north-light weaving shed, a building type of enormous importance. The firm also built railway locomotives, machine tools, and other machinery.

**Fairburn** Fairburn Tower is a very tall, slim 5-storey tower house, 6km (4mi) northwest of **Muir of Ord**, built by Murdoch Mackenzie in the 1540s, remodelled as an L-plan in the early 17th century. Fairburn House, to the north, is a late 19th-century house built for the Stirlings of Fairburn; it is now a care home and activity centre.

**Fairfield Shipbuilding and Engineering Co Ltd** Leading shipyard and engine works at **Govan**, begun in 1864 by Randolph & Elder. The firm made great advances in shipbuilding, including the compound marine engine, which made steamships much more efficient and competitive on longer routes. They built some of the largest and finest passenger liners and many warships. The **Lithgow** Group acquired the yard in 1933. Since the 1960s the yard has undergone a number of changes in ownership and management. From 1988–99 the Norwegian group Kvaerner owned the yard, and it is now operated by BAE Systems Marine.

**Fair Isle** (pop. 69) Island in Shetland, which lies between the **Orkney** and **Shetland** islands. The island is home to many bird colonies, and a bird observatory was set up in 1948. The community is known for its crafts, and particularly for producing a distinctive pattern of knitting. Many ships have been wrecked here, including the *El Gran Grifon* of the Spanish Armada, which stranded 300 Spanish seamen on the island for 2 months in 1588. Two **lighthouses** were erected in 1892, and the South Lighthouse became the last manned lighthouse in the country. The island has belonged to the **National Trust for Scotland** since 1954.

*Fair Isle: looking across South Harbour towards Springfield, Vaasetter and Sheep Rock.*

**Fairlie** Village 5km (3mi) south of **Largs**, on the **Ayrshire** coast. The parish church (1883), by J J **Stevenson**, has glass by Morris & Co. From the late 18th century until 1985 William Fife and his descendants ran a boatyard which became renowned for its high-quality yachts. See also **Kelburn Castle**.

**Fairlie, Andrew** (1963– ) Chef, b. Perth. He did much of his training in France and after some years in England, he returned to Scotland as chef at One Devonshire Gardens in **Glasgow**. In 2001 he set up his own award-winning restaurant in **Gleneagles** Hotel. He was Scottish Chef of the Year in 2002.

**Fairweather, Al** (1927–93) Jazz musician, b. Edinburgh. A trumpeter, he had a recording career which spanned nearly 40 years. He worked with Kenny Ball and George Chisholm among others, and later led a number of bands, including the Fairweather-Brown All Stars.

**Falaise, Treaty of** 8 December 1174. Treaty between **William I**, who had been taken prisoner at Alnwick, and Henry II, recognising the English king as overlord of Scotland and giving him possession of Scottish castles.

**Falkirk** (pop. 32,379) Town in a historically significant position between **Edinburgh**, **Stirling** and **Glasgow**. It is now the administrative centre of Falkirk Council. The High Street has good 19th- and early 20th-century buildings, dominated by the classical Town Steeple by David **Hamilton** (1812–14). The massive parish church by James Gillespie **Graham** (1810–11) retains William **Adam**'s tower of 1738. There are important Roman remains, including sections of the **Antonine Wall**. William **Wallace** was defeated at the Battle of Falkirk in 1298, and in 1746 the retreating **Jacobite** army won a victory here. Industrial development was dominated by the **Carron Ironworks** and by other large iron foundries. In the 18th century the Falkirk Tryst became the most important cattle market in Scotland, at which cattle from across the **Highlands** were sold. The Falkirk Wheel, which opened in 2002, is the world's only rotating boatlift. It was built to transfer boats between the **Forth and Clyde** and **Union Canals** as part of the **Millennium Link**, a project to allow coast-to-coast travel by canal for the first time in 70 years. See also **Callendar House**.

*The Falkirk Wheel, the world's only rotating boatlift, which opened in 2002.*

**Falkirk Council** Local-authority area on the Firth of **Forth**. From 1975–96 the area was a district of **Central Region**; see maps on pp.394-5 and **local government**. The administrative centre is **Falkirk** and other towns include **Grangemouth** and **Larbert**.

**Falkirk Wheel** see **Falkirk**

**Falkland** Village in Fife, a royal **burgh** from 1458, 13km (8mi) north of **Glenrothes**, below the **Lomond Hills**. The lands were a favourite hunting ground of the early Stewart kings, and Falkland Palace was built in the early 16th century on the site of an earlier castle. It is now in the care of the **National Trust for Scotland**, and includes many early Renaissance features and a restored 'real' tennis court, and a fine garden. The Percy Cane design of shrub borders and the long herbaceous border make for interest throughout the year. There is a spired town house and a great number of 17th- and 18th-century houses in the village, which thrived on **linen** weaving. In the 20th century it had linoleum manufacture; it is now principally a tourist centre. Nearby is Falkland House, a splendid neo-Jacobean house by William **Burn** (1839–42). The landscape park is currently being restored by Falkland Heritage Trust.

**Falloch, Glen, River** and **Falls of** (Gaelic **Falach**) The River Falloch rises near the foot of Beinn a' Chroin and flows northeast and then southwest through Glen Falloch, from **Crianlarich** to the north end of **Loch Lomond**. The Falls of Falloch lie 7km (4mi) southwest of Crianlarich. The A82 road and the West Highland Railway line run through the Glen.

F

*The half-yearly feeing market in Arbroath High Street photographed in the 1890s.*

**Fannich(s)** Loch Fannich in **Ross and Cromarty** lies 24km (15mi) northwest of **Strathpeffer** and is encircled by mountains. The range of mountains (**Munros**) to the north is known as the Fannichs; the highest is Sgurr Mor, 1110m (3642ft). Part of a major hydroelectric scheme, a dam has raised the water level in the loch.

**Fare, Hill of** Hill above **Banchory**, 470m (1545ft). It was the site of the Battle of Corrichie (28 October 1562), in which the Gordons of **Huntly** were defeated by James Stewart, Earl of **Moray**.

**farm servant** Old-fashioned expression for a farm worker. The farm servant was largely the creation of the Agricultural Revolution, where people sought employment rather than land on which to raise crops or stock.

**Farnell** Small village to the southeast of **Brechin**. Farnell Castle is a late medieval tower house of the Bishops of Brechin with large crowsteps and a prominent garderobe shaft, extended after the lands of the bishopric were secularised in 1566. The parish church was designed by James **Playfair** in 1789. Its plaster-vaulted interior is an important pioneer example of the revival of Gothic for church architecture in Scotland.

**Farquharson, Anne** see **Macintosh, Anne**

**Faskally, Loch** see **Loch Faskally**

**Faslane** Emergency port built during World War II on the east side of the **Gare Loch**, used subsequently for shipbreaking, and later converted into the base for the Royal Navy's Polaris and later Trident nuclear submarines. A peace camp beside the base opened in 1982.

**Fast Castle** Ruined castle near **St Abbs**. It belonged to the Dunbars, the Homes and then the Logans of Restalrig, who forfeited it because of involvement in the **Gowrie Conspiracy** in 1600. There are rumours of treasure buried here, and the castle featured as 'Wolf's Crag' in Sir Walter **Scott**'s *Bride of Lammermoor*.

**Fastern's E'en** Festival held on the last Tuesday before Lent, Shrove Tuesday. In some towns ball games were held; see **handba**.

**Fearn** Village 8km (5mi) southeast of **Tain**. A Premonstratensian abbey was founded here in the 13th century. Part of it was incorporated into the parish church and is still in use. In 1742 the roof collapsed, killing many of the congregation. There was a military airfield nearby during World War II.

**feeing market** Place where farmers and farm workers sought to make either a 6- or 12-month contract of employment for the May or September **terms** or periods, also known as fairs, such as Bell's Fair at **Dundee**.

**Fenton** Tall and long L-plan house, to the southwest of **North Berwick**, built by Sir John Carmichael, Warden of the Middle Marches, in 1577, and a prominent landmark; long roofless, it has recently been carefully restored and reoccupied.

**Fenwick Moor** Area to the northeast of **Kilmarnock**, traversed by the A77 **Glasgow-Stranraer** road. It has recently been partly afforested and is the proposed site of a wind farm.

**Fergus MacErc** (*fl. c.*500) Also known as Fergus Mor. He is traditionally believed to have established the kingdom of **Dal Riata** in Scotland, but more probably shifted the power centre of an existing kingdom from Antrim to **Argyll**.

**Ferguson, Sir Alex** (1941– ) Football manager, b. Glasgow. After a career as a professional footballer, he became a highly successful manager. Under his leadership **Aberdeen** won the Scottish Championship and Cup and the European Cup. He became manager of Manchester United, where his greatest success was to win the 'treble' of English Premiership, FA Cup and Champions League in 1999.

**Ferguson, Patrick** (1744–80) Soldier, b. Edinburgh. He invented the breech-loading rifle, which could be loaded and fired more quickly. In spite of earlier injuries, he fought bravely in the War of the American Revolution and was killed at the Battle of King's Mountain.

**Fergusson, Adam** (1723–1816) Philosopher, b. Logierait, Perthshire. A Gaelic speaker. At **Edinburgh University** he was Professor of Natural Philosophy (1759) and of Moral Philosophy from 1764 to 1785. His *Essay in the History of Civil Society* (1767) laid the foundations of sociology.

**Fergusson, Sir Bernard, 1st Lord Ballantrae** (1911–80)
Soldier and military historian, b. London, but a Fergusson of
Kilkerran, **Ayrshire**. Commissioned in the **Black Watch** in 1931,
he fought in Burma in World War II. Having served after 1945 as
Inspector-General of Palestine Police, he became a brigadier in
1956. He was Governor-General of New Zealand (1962–7).
His books include *The Black Watch and the King's Enemies* (1950)
and the autobiographic *The Trumpet in the Hall* (1970). He also
published excellent light verse.

**Fergusson, Sir James** (1832–1907) Diplomat, b. Edinburgh.
Chief of the Clan Ferguson from 1849, and MP for **Ayr** 1854–7,
1859–68. He served as Governor of South Australia from 1868 to
1872, of New Zealand from 1872 to 1874, and of Bombay from
1880 to 1885. He was killed in an earthquake in Jamaica.

**Fergusson, J(ohn) D(uncan)** (1874–1961) Artist, b. Leith.
Largely self-taught, he spent much of his career in Paris and
London, but from 1939 he settled permanently in **Glasgow** with
Margaret **Morris**. His openness to avant-garde developments led to his adoption of the bold colouring and
design associated with the Fauve artists, and he
became recognised in Scotland and internationally as
one of the most progressive British artists of the time.
Along with **Peploe**, **Cadell** and **Hunter** he is known as
one of the **Scottish Colourists**. There is a gallery
devoted to his work in the former **Perth** waterworks.

**Fergusson, Robert** (1750–74) Poet, b. Edinburgh.
Working as a clerk in **Edinburgh**, he published verses
in Ruddiman's *Weekly Magazine* from 1771. He wrote in
English and Scots and is possibly best known for 'Auld
Reekie' (1773). He died in the Edinburgh Bedlam.
Robert **Burns** said he owed much to Fergusson and
erected a monument to him in Canongate kirkyard,
Edinburgh, in 1789.

**Ferintosh** Scattered community on the **Black Isle**,
near Conon Bridge, whose name is associated with
**whisky**. The distillery there was owned by Duncan
Forbes of **Culloden**, and from 1689 he was exempt
from payment of duty on his whisky as a reward for
his loyalty to King William. This lasted until 1786, and
during the 18th century so much whisky was distilled
here that whisky was sometimes known as 'Ferintosh'.

**ferm toun** Literally *farm town*, it has two meanings.
First, the historical township, or centre of a collective

joint-tenancy pre-improvement farm. Second, the buildings or
centre of a farm, still current north of the River **Tay**.

**Ferniehirst Castle** Long Z-plan house south of **Jedburgh**.
The original castle was built for the Kerrs around 1470, but was
destroyed and rebuilt in the 1590s, and later extended. It still
belongs to the Kerrs, now Marquesses of Lothian. From 1934 to
1984 it was used by the Scottish Youth Hostels Association, but
it was restored in 1988 and has limited public opening.

**Ferrier, Susan** (1782-1854) Novelist, b. Edinburgh. A friend of
Sir Walter **Scott**, she published 3 novels, *Marriage* (1818), *The
Inheritance* (1824) and *Destiny* (1831). She later gave up writing
fiction through religious conversion, on joining the **Free Church**.

**ferries** Now reduced almost entirely to sea-going services on the
**Clyde**, and between mainland Scotland and the islands, they
were, however, historically very widespread, with rivers like the
**Clyde**, **Tay** and **Spey** crossed at many points before bridges were
built. Until the 1950s and 60s the ferries across the Clyde at

*The dome of the Kibble Palace glass house in Glasgow's
Botanic Gardens, painted by J D Fergusson in 1953.*

F

*Fasque House, near Fettercairn, childhood home of W E Gladstone, Prime Minister during the reign of Queen Victoria.*

Erskine and **Renfrew**, across the **Forth** at **Queensferry**, and across the Tay from **Newport** to **Dundee** were vital components of the main road network. There were also important ferries in the **Highlands**, across the **Beauly Firth** at Kessock, and at **Ballachulish**, **Kyle of Lochalsh** and **Kylesku**. The construction of bridges and causeways has eliminated most such ferries, the **Corran** ferry across **Loch Linnhe** being the last short mainland-to-mainland route in operation.

**Ferryden** see Montrose

**Feshie** see **Glen Feshie**

**Fetlar** One of the **Shetland** Islands to the east of **Yell**, known as The 'Garden of Shetland'. It is divided into two by a prehistoric boundary dyke known as the Funzie Girt. A ring of low stones at Haltadans, traditionally a group of petrified trolls, is probably a Bronze Age burial monument.

**Fettercairn** Village in southern Aberdeenshire, the starting point for the **Cairn o' Mount** road. An archway commemorates the visit in 1861 of Queen Victoria and Prince Albert. To the north lie Fettercairn House, built in 1666 by the 1st Earl of Middleton, remodelled in 1826 by William **Burn** for Sir John Forbes of Sir William **Forbes**'s bank, and Fasque House, which was built in 1809. It was the childhood home of W E Gladstone, and is still owned by the family and open to the public. Balbegno Castle is a 16th-century tower house, remarkable for its rib-vaulted hall with heraldic paintings; privately owned but not occupied. Fettercairn Distillery was founded in 1824 and includes a visitor centre.

**feu** A form of tenure of property. An annual payment in money or kind, known as 'feu duty', was fixed in perpetuity and gave the owner (sometimes referred to as the feuar) security. This system has been gradually phased out over the past few decades.

**Feugh** River which flows northwards from Birse, 32km (20mi) to **Banchory**, where it joins the River **Dee**. The Falls of Feugh lie just to the west of Banchory, and are known for their salmon leap.

**fiars** Prices of grain, set annually in each county by the **sheriff** and a local jury. These prices were used to determine the level of rents and ministers' stipends, which were based on the value of crops.

**Fiddes** Late 16th-century turreted L-plan house, 6km (4mi) south-west of **Stonehaven**, with elaborate corbelling, built by the Arbuthnot family in the late 16th century.

**fiddle** The fiddle has been a popular instrument in Scotland since at least the 17th century. Elements which characterise the Scottish style of fiddle-playing include the 'up-driven bow' which employs a jerk of the wrist on the upstroke of the bow, and a performance sequence of march, **strathspey** and **reel** tunes. Notable Scottish exponents of the 18th century include Niel **Gow** and William **Marshall**. More recent well-known fiddlers are James Scott **Skinner**, Tom **Anderson**, Alastair Hardie, Aly **Bain** and Alasdair Fraser.

**fiery cross** (Gaelic **crann-tàra** or **crois-tàra**) In the **Highlands** in former times, a piece of wood, burnt at one end and dipped in blood at the other, carried from place to place by a succession of runners to summon the fighting men of the district to arms.

**Fife** Known as 'the Kingdom of Fife', this local-authority area lies between the Firths of **Forth** and **Tay**, with the North Sea to the east. It is the only part of Scotland to retain its boundaries through 2 major local-government reforms: as a county till 1975, as a **region** (consisting of **Dunfermline**, **Kirkcaldy** and North-East Fife districts) till 1996 and now as Fife Council, a unitary local authority; see maps on pp.394-5 and **local government**. Its importance in the medieval period is demonstrated in the historic towns of **St Andrews** and Dunfermline and the royal

F

palace of **Falkland**. Farming, **fishing** and textiles, especially **linen**, have all been important industries, and **coal** mining dominated many West Fife communities until the closure of the pits brought massive unemployment. Kirkcaldy was a major centre of linoleum manufacture. Agriculture and some fishing continue today, along with business and hi-tech industries in towns like **Glenrothes**, now the administrative centre, Kirkcaldy and Dunfermline. Tourism is important, with visitors particularly attracted to the 'home of **golf**' at St Andrews and to the **East Neuk**.

**Fife Adventurers** A group of 12 merchants from **Fife** who settled on **Lewis** in 1598, as part of **James VI**'s policy of planting Lowlanders in the **Highlands** to control the local people. The venture was unsuccessful – they were imprisoned by members of the local population, and returned home.

**Fife Ness** The most easterly point in Fife, this headland lies at the end of the **East Neuk of Fife**. A small mesolithic site has been excavated here. A wildlife reserve attracts migrating birds, and the small **lighthouse** was established in 1975.

**Fifteen, The** see **Jacobite Risings**

**fillabeg** see **kilt**

**Fillan, St** (d. c.777) Missionary, b. Ireland. He preached in the Glendochart area of Perthshire, where he built a church, but also travelled widely in Scotland. A crosier and a bell associated with him were preserved for centuries at **Strathfillan** Priory, and are now in the **Museum of Scotland**.

**Findhorn** Village and former port on the **Moray Firth**, at the entrance to Findhorn Bay. It is best known for the Findhorn Foundation, an international community devoted to an alternative lifestyle, founded in 1962.

**Findhorn** River which flows northeast for a distance of 99km (62mi) from the **Monadhliath** Mountains into Findhorn Bay on the **Moray** coast.

**Findlay, John Ritchie** (1824-98) Journalist, b. Arbroath. In 1842 he joined *The Scotsman*, and owned it from 1870. Secretary of the **Society of Antiquaries** for 6 years, he financed the building of the **National Museum of Antiquities of Scotland** and the **Scottish National Portrait Gallery** and the rebuilding of the Dean Village (see **Edinburgh**).

**Findon** see **Finnan haddie**

**Fingal** Legendary hero, also known as Fionn mac Cumhaill. A warrior, and leader of the Irish Fianna, his mythical deeds feature in ballads and folklore throughout Gaelic Scotland and Ireland. See also **Ossian**.

**Fingal's Cave** see **Staffa**

**Finlaggan** Location on **Islay** which was the headquarters of the **Lords of the Isles** from around the 12th to 15th centuries. Two artificial islands in the loch were once linked by causeways. The smaller island, Eilean na Comhairle, held the council chamber of the Lords of the Isles, and buildings on Eilean Mor included a chapel and the Great Hall. Other buildings stood on the shores of the loch. The complex may have been destroyed when the Lords of the Isles were forfeited. The site has recently been excavated, and a visitor centre opened.

**Finlarig Castle** (Gaelic **Fionnlairig**) Near **Killin**, a ruined late 16th-century Z-plan tower house. It was built for Sir Duncan **Campbell** of Glenorchy. A beheading-pit is said to be in the grounds. The family later became Earls of **Breadalbane**, and their ruined mausoleum is nearby.

**Finlay, Ian Hamilton** (1925- ) Poet and artist, b. Nassau, Bahamas, coming to Scotland with his parents while a child. Finlay began his career as a writer and poet and started to introduce visual imagery into his texts in the 1960s. He is celebrated for his challenging fusion of poetry, graphic art, sculpture and landscape gardening, most potently expressed in the remarkable garden he has created at his home, Little Sparta, in the Pentland Hills, to the south of **Edinburgh**.

**Finlay, Kirkman** (1773-1842) Merchant and politician, b. Glasgow. A leading cotton manufacturer, he founded a shipping line which brought the first consignment of tea from India to Glasgow. He was MP for **Glasgow** (1812-18) and Lord Provost from 1812, and was in favour of the harsh treatment of the **Radicals**. The firm he founded, James Finlay & Co, was for many years a major tea grower and cotton manufacturer.

**Finlaystone House** Large Georgian mansion to the west of **Langbank**, Renfrewshire, built c.1760 by John Douglas for the earls of **Glencairn**. The 14th Earl was an important patron of Robert **Burns**. Sumptuously remodelled by Sir John **Burnet** for the ship-owner G J Kidston (1898-1900), it is now the home of the Macmillans and open to the public.

**Finnan, Glen** see **Glenfinnan**

**Finnan haddie** A haddock split, lightly cured in brine and smoked. It takes its name from the fishing village of Findon, 14km (8mi) south of **Aberdeen**.

**Finnart** Oil-tanker terminal on **Loch Long**, 4km (2 1/2mi) north of **Garelochhead**, with a pipeline connecting it to **Grangemouth**.

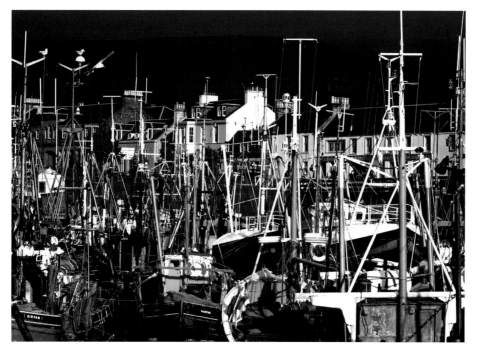

*Commercial fishing fleet at Girvan, Ayrshire.*

**Firth of Forth** see **Forth, River** and **Firth of**

**Firth of Lorn** see **Lorn, Firth of**

**fiscal** see **procurator fiscal**

**Fisher, Gregor** (1953– ) Actor, b. Glasgow. A versatile performer on the stage and on television, he is best known for his portrayal of the titular buffoon in the TV comedy series *Rab C Nesbitt* (1989). He has also appeared in the TV remake of *The Tales of Para Handy* (1994), and in films such as *White Mischief* (1987) and *Love Actually* (2003).

**Fisher, James** (1697-1775) Minister, b. Barr, Ayrshire. One of the founders of the **Secession** Church, he was the son-in-law of Ebenezer Erskine. He was minister of Kinclaven, Perthshire, later in **Glasgow**. He prepared an edition of the Shorter Catechism which became widely used. See also **Presbyterian churches**.

**Fisher family** Folk singers, influential in the Scottish Folk Song Revival of the 1960s–80s. All b. Glasgow. Archie (1939– ) and Ray (1940– ) appeared as a duo on television, then had very successful solo careers, Archie as a broadcaster, guitar stylist and performer. Younger sisters Joyce, Cindy and Audrey also performed in various groupings. Cilla (1952– ) formed a duo with Artie Trezise (1947–) and became highly successful as the Singing Kettle children's show.

**fishing** see p.147

**Fitt, Matthew** (1968– ) Poet and novelist, b. Dundee. Most of his writing is in **Scots**, including the ground-breaking novel *But N Ben A-Go-Go* (2000), a science-fiction story using the language in a new and innovative way. He is one of the editors of the Itchy Coo project to produce Scots texts aimed especially at schools.

**Five Articles of Perth** Religious reforms introduced but not enforced by **James VI** in 1618, and passed by the **General Assembly** at **Perth**. The festivals of the Christian year were to be observed, private baptism and communion were to be accepted, bishops were to confirm children and most controversially, kneeling was to be introduced at communion. These reforms provoked fears among Scottish Presbyterians that Episcopalian or Catholic worship would be imposed.

**Fintry** Village on the Endrick Water, to the north of the **Campsie Fells** and to the southwest of the Fintry Hills. The village was largely built to provide housing for workers at a cotton mill founded in the 1790s by Alexander Spiers, a prosperous **Glasgow** merchant, who owned Culcreuch Castle, just to the northeast. An early 16th-century tower house, it was greatly extended by Spiers; it is now a hotel. The Endrick Water drops 29m (94ft) at Fintry in a waterfall known as the Loup of Fintry.

**Fionn Loch** Large loch in **Wester Ross**, 10km (6mi) east of **Poolewe**.

**Fionnphort** Village at the southeastern tip of **Mull**, the location for the ferry crossing to **Iona**. The St **Columba** Centre is a visitor centre giving information on Iona and Columba.

**Firbush Point** Field centre offering outdoor activities, run by **Edinburgh University**. It lies on **Loch Tay** 3km (2mi) east of **Killin**, Perthshire.

**fire and sword, letters of** Commissions issued by the government giving those who held local power the right to use unlimited force against people under their authority.

**fire-raising** In Scots law, the crime of deliberately setting fire to a property, equivalent to English arson.

**firlot** see **weights and measures**, pp.382-4

**first-footing** see **Hogmanay**

**First Minister** see **Scottish Parliament**

**Firth of Clyde** see **Clyde, River** and **Firth of**

# THE FISHING INDUSTRY

Fishing is probably the oldest remaining occupation in Scotland, with origins going back to the Mesolithic hunter-gatherers. Basic fish-catching devices evolved over the millennia – spears, traps, hook and line, inshore nets – but commercial fishing, with specialised communities of fisherfolk, did not emerge fully until the second half of the last millennium.

Even up to the latter half of the 20th century, tens of thousands of ordinary folk, outwith the fishing community proper, maintained a keen interest in fish-catching. With hand-lines and rod and line they fished from favoured rocks or from small open boats, catching mainly coalfish, pollack, codling, haddock and whiting. With long-shafted spears they harvested flounder and plaice from the shallows, 'tramping' the fish with their bare feet or scanning the sandy seabed from rowing-boats.

Fish were eaten fresh or salted and hung or spread to dry for winter provision. Fish-livers were rendered into oil for household use, particularly as fuel for lamps. On the west coast of Scotland, the huge basking shark was hunted with harpoons for its oil-rich liver, weighing up to a tonne.

By the 12th century, Scotland had a well-established internal trade in fish, but with government encouragement of herring-fishing in the mid 18th century, that industry entered a period of unprecedented expansion. Annual exports of cured herring to Continental markets increased from an average of 224,655 barrels in 1851-5 to 1,143,207 barrels in 1881-5. These markets, however, never recovered from the catastrophic disruption of World War I.

Herring were caught by drift-net – strings of net panels generally set at dusk and allowed to drift, attached to the boat, throughout the night, enmeshing fish by the gills. Huge fleets of drift-net boats followed the migratory shoals south along the Scottish east coast as far as East Anglia. These fleets were, in turn, followed by teams of associated workers – curers, their female gutters and packers, and coopers and labourers.

The fleets of herring-boats – scaffies, fifies, baldies and zulus on the East Coast alone – were sail-powered, but in 1898 the steam-drifter arrived in Scotland and, within a decade, low-powered paraffin engines began to be installed widely in smaller boats, developments which were to change the entire character of fishing.

On the west coast, smaller herring-fisheries flourished, such as that in the Firth of **Clyde**, where an active method of fishing, known as ring-netting, evolved. Shoals were located by natural means – seeing, hearing and smelling – and surrounded in a two-boat operation. Ring-netting, which principally supplied fresh markets, expanded in the early 20th century, but on the east coast was largely confined to the **Moray Firth** and Firth of **Forth**.

In the 1960s, two deadlier methods of herring-fishing were adopted, mid-water trawling and purse-seining. These eventually displaced both the drift-net and ring-net and were widely blamed for the general collapse of herring stocks on the Scottish coasts in the 1980s.

Traditionally, demersal or white fish were caught commercially with long lines – thousands of baited hooks laid on the seabed – and either sold fresh or salted and dried. Trawling – the towing of a bag-net across the sea-bottom – did not come into its own until the advent of steam. Steam-trawling began in 1882-3 in **Aberdeen**, which became the main trawling port in Scotland, its fleets, later diesel-powered, ranging as far as Iceland, Skagerrak and Lofoten as more accessible grounds were depleted of cod, haddock, plaice, sole and the other main species.

In the 1920s, another method of white-fishing was adopted by Scottish fishermen. This was the seine-net, which operated by encircling bottom-dwelling fish by ropes. From the Moray Firth – chiefly **Lossiemouth** – it extended gradually around the entire Scottish coast and in 1950, for the first time, the seine-net fleet outfished the trawl fleet: 1,604,490 hundredweights against 1,469,793 hundredweights.

A wide range of shellfish and crustaceans is taken off the Scottish coasts. A commercial fishery for lobsters began in the mid 18th century using baited traps or 'creels'. Oyster-dredging, established for centuries, was followed in the 1930s by scallop-dredging, and, after World War II, a lucrative trawl-fishery on the hitherto ignored Norway lobster, or 'prawn', commenced. Markets now exist for several species hitherto despised – the small green shore crab, the velvet swimming crab and the whelk, or 'buckie', among them.

Fishing is now a highly mechanised industry, largely reliant on high-powered engines and a battery of electronic wheelhouse instruments to locate fish, chart fishing grounds and regulate net performance. The current trend appears to favour large multi-million pound, high-performance ocean-going craft, but over-regulation of the industry and diminishing fish-stocks are driving many boat-owners into early retirement and the future is, to say the least, uncertain.

F

*Alexander Fleming pictured in his laboratory in 1943.*

**Five Sisters of Kintail** Mountains above Glen Shiel, 4 of which are **Munros**. They form part of the Kintail and Morvich estate, owned by the **National Trust for Scotland**.

**Flanders Moss** A large area of peat bog lying west of **Stirling**, much of which was drained for cultivation from the late 18th century and now forms the **Carse of Stirling**. The remaining area of bog is now protected as a Site of Special Scientific Interest and is a National Nature Reserve. Part of it is owned by the Scottish Wildlife Trust.

**Flannan Isles** Uninhabited islands in the Outer **Hebrides**, north-west of **Lewis**. The **lighthouse** on Eilean Mor is associated with the mysterious disappearance in 1900 of the 3 keepers, an event commemorated in Wilfred Wilson Gibson's poem 'Flannan Isle'.

**Fleet, River** Flows from **Lairg** for 27km (17mi) southeastwards, entering the sea at Loch Fleet, 4km (2.5mi) southwest of **Golspie**. It is crossed by the **Mound**.

**Fleet, Water of** The Big Water of Fleet and Little Water of Fleet come together 10km (6mi) north of **Gatehouse of Fleet**, and flow as the Water of Fleet into Fleet Bay, opening into the **Solway Firth**. The Islands of Fleet lie at the mouth of the bay.

**Fleming, Sir Alexander** (1881–1955) Discoverer of penicillin, b. near Darvel, Ayrshire. A surgeon, he was on the staff at St Mary's Hospital, Paddington, London. He discovered the natural anti-bacterial substance penicillin in 1928, but its potential was not fully developed until the 1940s by Howard Florey and Ernst Chain. The 3 men shared the Nobel Prize for Medicine in 1945.

**Fleming, Mary** see 'four Marys'

**Fleming, Robert** (1845–1933) Father of the investment trust/mutual fund, b. Dundee. He worked as a confidential clerk for the Baxter family of textile barons and learned about the oportunities for profitable investment in the USA during its post-Civil War boom. Aged 28 he established the Scottish American Investment Trust in 1873, creating a large capital from many modest investors and investing it in America's westward expansion, especially in undervalued railway stock. Many other investment trusts were later established in Scotland. He moved to London and died head of the biggest investment trust in the City. He was the grandfather of Ian Fleming, novelist and creator of 'James Bond'.

**Fleming, Tom** (1927– ) Commentator, actor and director, b. Edinburgh. His career has included many classic theatre and film roles. He was Director of the Scottish Theatre Company 1982–7, during which time he produced *The Thrie Estaites*. He was well known as a television commentator on royal and state occasions.

**Fletcher, Andrew, of Saltoun** (1653–1716) Politician and landowner, b. Saltoun, East Lothian. He was MP for Haddingtonshire from 1678. In 1681 he went into exile in England, returning at the Revolution in 1689. He was a passionate leader of the opposition to the **Union of the Parliaments**, and in 1707 left the parliament and concentrated on the agricultural improvements on his estates. These included the introduction from Holland of a mill to produce pot barley, known at the time as Saltoun barley.

**Flint, Sir William Russell** (1880–1970) Painter, b. Edinburgh. Worked in London from 1900 as an illustrator, and in the 1910s began painting in watercolour and producing etchings. Worked abroad extensively from 1920 onwards, becoming widely known for his prodigious output of female semi-nudes posed in exotic, foreign settings.

**Flodden, Battle of** Battle fought on 9 September 1513 at Flodden, Northumberland, between the Scots under **James IV**

and an English army under the Earl of Surrey. James was seeking to support the French king against Henry VIII of England, but the result was a disastrous defeat for the Scots, with James and much of his nobility killed. This contributed to a fundamental shift in the Scottish approach to relations with England.

**Floors Castle** Mansion near **Kelso**, built for the 1st Duke of Roxburghe 1718–25 by William **Adam**, perhaps with advice from Sir John Vanbrugh. Reconstructed by William **Playfair** 1838–49 as a great neo-Jacobean palace, it is still occupied by the Duke and Duchess of Roxburghe. It is open to the public in summer.

**Flotta** (pop. 81) Island in **Orkney**, east of **Hoy**. Since 1974 it has been dominated by an oil terminal which is linked by a 230km (142mi) pipeline to 2 North Sea oilfields.

**'Flowers o(f) the Forest, The'** Song traditionally said to be a lament for the men of the **Ettrick Forest** who were killed in the Battle of **Flodden**. The air is in the 1620 Skene manuscript; the well-known verses are mid 18th century by Jane **Elliot**, who drew on an ancient fragment and on earlier 18th-century verses by Alison **Cockburn**.

**flyting** Scots word for quarrelling, scolding, specifically a verse contest between poets in mutual abuse; see William **Dunbar**.

**Fochabers** Village on the River **Spey**, 13km (8mi) east of **Elgin**, Moray. It was built to a plan by John Baxter for the 4th Duke of Gordon in 1776, replacing the original village which had grown up nearby. The fine spired parish church (1795-7) is also by Baxter. Gordon Castle, privately owned, was built in the 15th century but was rebuilt 1769–82 and has been largely demolished. Just outside Fochabers is the **Baxters** food factory.

**Foinaven** or **Fionne Bheinn** Mountain ridge, 908m (2980ft) high, near the west coast of **Sutherland**, in the **Reay** forest.

**football** see p.151

**Forbes, Alexander** see **Pitsligo, Alexander Forbes, 4th Lord**

**Forbes, Duncan, of Culloden** (1685-1747) Advocate, b. Bunchrew, near Inverness. He was **Sheriff** of Midlothian from 1709, and became Lord Advocate in 1725 and Lord President of the **Court of Session** in 1737. In 1736 he attempted to reduce the punishment imposed on the city of **Edinburgh** after the **Porteous** riots. As Laird of **Culloden** he persuaded many northeast **Jacobites** not to join the 1745 Rising.

**Forbes, Sir William, of Pitsligo** (1739-1806) Banker, b. Edinburgh. He was a partner in the banking firm Coutts & Co. (see John **Coutts**), which later became Forbes, Hunter & Co. He carried out agricultural improvement on his **Aberdeenshire**

estates, and was involved in cultural and benevolent enterprises in **Edinburgh**.

**Ford** Small village to the southeast of **Dalkeith**, Midlothian. Ford House is a perfect small L-plan house built in 1680 by Colonel Fraser, one of the Frasers of **Lovat**.

**Ford** Small Argyll village at the south end of **Loch Awe**, to the northeast of **Kilmartin**.

**Fordell** Town house of the Hendersons of Fordell, near **Inverkeithing**, Fife, built in 1567, burnt and rebuilt in a taller Z-plan form in 1580. In the later 20th century it was the home of Sir Nicholas Fairbairn. Nearby is the chapel built in 1650 with fine Renaissance and Gothic survival detail.

**Fordun, John of** (c.1320–c.84) Chronicler, who was probably a priest in Aberdeen. In the 1380s he wrote *Chronica Gentis Scotorum*, a patriotic history of the Scots from their mythical beginnings to 1153. A continuation to the 1380s seems not to have been the work of Fordun himself. Walter **Bower** used all this material as a source for his *Scotichronicon*.

*Duncan Forbes of Culloden. The painting is attributed to Jeremiah Davison (1695-1745).*

F

*Scotland's Jim Baxter in action against England at Wembley, 1967.*

**Fordyce** **Burgh** of Barony established by Bishop Elphinstone in 1499, to the southeast of **Cullen**. A wonderfully picturesque village centred on the turreted tower house built in 1592 by Thomas Menzies of Durn, Provost of **Aberdeen**, and the ruins of the medieval church of St Talorgan or Tarquin.

**Forfar** (pop. 13,206) Town in Angus, 22.5km (14mi) northeast of **Dundee**, its town centre little changed since the mid 19th century, with a county hall and former courthouses at the Cross. A 12th-century royal **burgh**, it became the county town of **Angus** (formerly Forfarshire) and is now the administrative centre of Angus Council. In the 19th century industry was dominated by the **jute** and **linen** mills, and textiles are still produced here. Restenneth Priory, long ruined, was built in the 13th century on the site of the earlier church erected by King **Nechtan**; see also **Nechtansmere**.

**Forfar bridie** A kind of pie made with a circle of pastry folded over with a filling of meat, onion etc, orginally made in **Forfar**.

**Forfarshire** see **Angus**

**forfeited estates** The estates of many **Jacobite** lairds were forfeited after the Risings of 1715 and 1745. Some were sold while others were administered by a Board of Annexed Estates, until they were returned to their owners in 1784.

**Forman, Sir Denis** (1917– ) Film director, b. near Dumfries. He was Chairman of Granada Television from 1974 to 1987, and Deputy Chairman of the Granada Group from 1984 to 1990. He is particularly associated with the successful series *The Jewel in the Crown* (1984). His publications include his 2-volume autobiography.

**forpit** see **weights and measures** pp.382-4

**Forres** (pop. 8967) Town in **Moray**, a royal **burgh** from the 12th century, with a fine **tolbooth**, rebuilt in 1838, reproducing its 17th-century form. The Falconer Museum, designed by Alexander Reid in 1868, contains a collection of fossils and local antiquities. Forres features in Shakespeare's *Macbeth*, as the location for Duncan's castle, with the witches' 'blasted heath' nearby. On the eastern edge of the town is Sueno's Stone, a Pictish stone carved with a battlescene and a cross, now in a protective case to prevent erosion; in the care of **Historic Scotland**. The Benromach Distillery is next to the site of a former fertiliser factory. The Dallas Dhu distillery to the south is now a whisky museum.

**Forrest, George** (1873–1932) Plant collector, b. Falkirk. Between 1904 and 1932 he conducted 7 major expeditions to southwest China for the **Royal Botanic Garden** in **Edinburgh** and private sponsors. He spent 17 years in the wild and, with the help of trained local tribesman, collected over 31,000 herbarium accessions accompanied by seeds. The resulting rhododendrons (over 300 new species), conifers, trees, shrubs, herbs and alpines have transformed our gardens. The specific name *forrestii* commemorates this able, doughty and adventuresome collector whose collections have helped to make the Garden the specialist institution for Sino-Himalayan research. He died of a heart attack at Tengyueh, after he had completed his packing, on what was to have been his last expedition.

**Forsyth, Bill** (1946– ) Film director, b. Glasgow. His greatest fame came as writer and director of *Gregory's Girl* (1981) and *Local Hero* (1983).

**Forsyth, Michael, Lord Forsyth of Drumlean** (1954– ) Politician, b. Montrose. A right-wing Conservative, he was MP for **Stirling** from 1983 to 1997, when he lost his seat. After holding a succession of ministerial positions he was a beleaguered Secretary of State for Scotland from 1995 to 1997 and as an unsuccessful gesture of appeasement to nationalist sentiment, he had the **Stone of Destiny** returned to Scotland in 1996.

# FOOTBALL

An informal street sport for centuries, football in Scotland became more organised in the third quarter of the 19th century. The foundation of the Queen's Park football club (9 July 1867) is the accepted starting point for the game as we know it today, and pre-dated the **Scottish Football Association**, the national governing body, by 6 years.

By the time the SFA was established, the first international in the history of the sport had already been played. The Scotland team, composed entirely of Queen's Park players, drew 0–0 with England at the Hamilton Crescent cricket ground in Glasgow in November 1872. Matches between the 2 countries became an annual event, and fixtures against Wales and Ireland soon followed.

Unsurprisingly, given their seniority, Queen's Park were the dominant club in Scotland for some time. They won the Scottish Cup for the first 3 seasons (1874–76) of that competition, but their strict adherence to amateurism as the game slowly went professional ensured they would be left behind. The decline of Queen's Park left the field clear for 2 other Glasgow clubs, the so-called Old Firm of **Rangers** and **Celtic**, to establish a duopoly. Rangers were joint champions in the first season (1890–1) of the Scottish League, Celtic took the title 2 years later, and since then their supremacy has been challenged only occasionally. While those 2 clubs have thrived on their rivalry, they have also often been the focus for sectarian rivalry between the Protestant and Roman Catholic communities of the west of Scotland.

The Scottish national team, by contrast, has been a unifying force for much of the nation, and at times a repository of improbable hopes. Victories over England are particularly celebrated: among those most fondly recalled are the 1928 5–1 win in London by the side which came to be known as the Wembley Wizards; the 3–2 triumph at the same venue in 1967, when England were world champions; and the 2–1 result in 1977, although that match is remembered more for its aftermath, in which Scots supporters tore down the goalposts and ripped up the turf, than for the actual football.

Scotland's introduction to the World Cup, in the 1954 finals, was a traumatic one, and showed how far the game had left it behind. They lost 1–0 to Austria and 7–0 to Uruguay, thus starting a long and ignoble tradition of failing to reach the latter stages of the competition. Qualifying again in 1958, they showed a modest improvement by drawing a match, but then went 16 years without reaching the finals. In 1974, however, they did perform with distinction and, although they failed to progress past the opening phase, they ended up as the only unbeaten side in the tournament.

Four years later, under the management of Ally **Macleod**, the team which reached the 1978 finals seemed capable of great things, and a wave of romantic self-delusion swept the nation. But that team, too, was knocked out at the first stage of the competition, and Macleod's successors have all taken a more modest, cautious approach.

In contrast to the national team's record, 3 clubs have made their mark at European level. In 1967 Celtic, managed by Jock **Stein**, became the first British team to win the European Cup, overcoming the sterile tactics of Inter Milan with a 2–1 victory in the final. Rangers won the European Cup Winners' Cup 5 years later, and Aberdeen also lifted the latter trophy in 1983.

Scots have helped to spread the game around the world: in 1953 when Hungary beat England 6–3 in London, at the final whistle, the Hungarians ran over to where Jimmy Hogan, now over 70, was sitting in the crowd and thanked him for what he had done for Hungarian football.

The past 20 years have seen a relative decline of Scottish football at all levels. The national team has found it more difficult to qualify for major international competitions; leading clubs have made less impact in Europe; and fewer players graduate from the domestic scene to the English league.

Any number of anguished inquiries have been made into the state of the sport, with blame being apportioned to, among other supposed culprits, computer games and lack of teachers. As both these phenomena exist in other countries, where skilful players are still regularly produced, the real responsibility for Scottish failings surely rests elsewhere.

Yet, despite any stylistic shortcomings, football remains a national sport, and interest in it is probably higher than ever. That interest may not be shown in attendance at matches, which is far lower in today's all-seat stadiums than it was from the 1930s to the 1950s, but it does find expression in a vastly expanded media coverage of the sport. For many of its followers, no matter how badly our teams may fare, football remains one of the key components of Scottish national identity.

F

*Fort George on the Moray Firth, east of Inverness.*

**Fort Augustus** Village at the southwest end of **Loch Ness**. It was formerly known as Cill Chuimein or Kilchumin, and barracks were built here in 1715. In 1730 General **Wade** built a new fort and barracks, creating Fort Augustus, which he named after the young son of George II. In 1867 it was bought by Lord Lovat who gave it to Benedictine monks in 1876; they rebuilt it as a great Gothic pile (1876–80) designed by Joseph Aloysius Hansom (of hansom cab fame). Until 1993 the monastery housed a boys' school and the monastery closed in 1998. In 2003 the building was sold for conversion to flats. The **Caledonian Canal** passes through the village.

**Forter Castle** Late 16th-century tower house of the Ogilvies, in Glen Isla, strategically placed to command the passes to **Glenshee** and **Braemar**; 'the bonnie house of Airlie', burned by the Earl of Argyll in July 1640, was rerooofed and reoccupied in the early 1990s.

**Forteviot** Village 9km (6mi) southwest of **Perth**. It has historic importance as a royal centre of the **Pictish** kings of Fortriu and **Kenneth mac Alpin** may have died in the palace here.

The 9th-century **Dupplin** cross, now in St Serf's Church at Dunning (in the care of **Historic Scotland**), stood nearby. The village was rebuilt on formal English Arts and Crafts lines between 1925 and 1927 by Lord Forteviot, the Chairman of Dewar's distillery, to designs by James Miller.

**Fort George** Originally sited on the hill now crowned by the 19th-century **Inverness** Castle, it proved vulnerable in the 1745 **Jacobite Rising**, and was replaced by a huge state-of-the-art artillery fort and barracks, built between 1748 and 1769 as part of the Hanoverian government's preparations to quell the next **Jacobite** rebellion in the **Highlands**. The finest complete 18th-century artillery fortress in Europe, the complex covers 6 hectares (16 acres) to the east of Inverness, jutting out into the **Moray Firth**. It was designed by William Skinner and the building contract went to William **Adam**, being carried out by his sons after his death in 1748. Politically it was already irrelevant by the time of its completion and was never used for defensive purposes. It was refurbished as an army base in the 1960s and is in the care of **Historic Scotland**; much of it is open to the public and it contains the Regimental Museum of the **Queen's Own Highlanders**.

**Forth, River** and **Firth of** The River Forth is formed by two streams, the Duchray Water and the Avondhu, coming together near **Aberfoyle**. It flows southeastwards to **Stirling**, where it becomes tidal and begins to widen into what becomes, east of **Kincardine**, the Firth of Forth, which runs eastwards to enter the North Sea between **Dunbar** and **Fife Ness**. The Firth is crossed by three bridges, the **Kincardine** Bridge, and the two **Forth Bridges**. There are a number of small islands in the Firth, including **Inchcolm** and the Isle of **May**. The Forth has been a vital channel for trade and industrial development for centuries. Much of its major shipping today is directed to **Rosyth** and **Grangemouth**, although **Leith** remains an important port. Hound Point oil terminal near **South Queensferry** and the Braefoot Brae gas terminal, to the west of **Dalgety Bay**, are also important.

**Forth and Clyde Canal** Opened in stages between 1775 and 1790 to allow ships to cross the Lowlands between **Grangemouth** on the **Forth** and Bowling near **Dumbarton** on the **Clyde**. It has 40 locks along its 56km (35mi) length, and was Scotland's busiest canal. It was closed in 1962, but reopened in 2001, after the major Millennium Link redevelopment project. See also **Falkirk**.

**Forth Bridges** The world-famous cantilever railway bridge which crosses the Firth of **Forth** between **North** and **South Queensferry** was opened in 1890. Ferries had crossed the river at this point, and the decision to erect a railway bridge was made in 1873. It was designed by John Fowler and Benjamin Baker and constructed by William Arrol. Its main span of 521m (1709ft) was the longest in the world for about 30 years after it was built. Ferries continued to cross the Forth here until 1964, when the Forth Road Bridge, a suspension bridge with a main span of 1005m (3297ft), was completed.

**Fortingall** Village 13km (8mi) west of **Aberfeldy**. According to an unlikely legend the father of Pontius Pilate was a Roman officer on a mission here, and so this became the birthplace of his famous son. There is a very ancient yew tree in the churchyard. The village was rebuilt from 1889 in English arts and crafts style, designed by James Marjoribanks MacLaren for Sir Donald Currie of the Union Castle shipping line.

**Fortrenn, Fortriu** A kingdom of Pictland. Centred on **Strathearn** and **Menteith**, Fortriu was the most powerful Pictish kingdom and its rulers were often able to establish overlordships over other Pictish kings.

**Fortrose** (pop. 1174) Town on the **Black Isle** near Rosemarkie, now a holiday and dormitory town and a popular site for spotting dolphins in the **Moray Firth**. Although comparatively little remains of the great cathedral which was built between the 13th and 15th centuries, the ruins (in the care of **Historic Scotland**) dominate the town. A cairn on Chanonry Point to the east of the town marks the supposed site at which the **Brahan Seer** was burnt.

**Fortune, Robert** (1812–80) Plant collector, b. Blackadder, Berwickshire. A gardener at the **Royal Botanic Garden, Edinburgh** and later at Chiswick, the garden of the Horticultural Society of London (later to become the Royal Horticultural Society). He was chosen by the latter to collect plants from China following the settlement of the Opium Wars in 1842 and in 4 major expeditions collected in east China and Japan until 1861. His introductions such as winter jasmine, tree peonies, camellias, chrysanthemums and the hardy Chusan palm which bears his name, *Trachycarpus fortunei,* caused a sensation. But he is also remembered for his introduction of improved forms of China tea into Assam (Arunachal Pradesh) and Ceylon (Sri Lanka) under the auspices of the British East India company.

**Fort William** (pop. 9908) Town at the head of **Loch Linnhe**. A fort was built here by General **Monck**, then rebuilt in 1690 and named Fort William. Today the town is a tourist centre, overlooked by **Ben Nevis**, Britain's highest mountain. It lies at the start of both the **Caledonian Canal** and the 'road to the isles', which runs past **Glenfinnan** to **Mallaig**. In the 1920s the Lochaber Aluminium Smelter was built near the town, and still operates. There were 3 distilleries, only one of which, Ben Nevis, still operates. Employment was increased for a few years by a pulp mill at **Corpach** nearby.

F

*The Forth Bridge from South Queensferry.*

**Forty-five, The** see **Jacobite Risings**

**Foula** (pop. 31) Island in **Shetland**, 45km (27mi) west of **Scalloway**. With dramatic cliffs, one of them the highest in the British Isles, it is one of the most isolated inhabited islands in Britain, and is often cut off in bad weather. It was the last place in which **Norn** was spoken (see **language**). The small community centres round crofting and fishing. The bird population, particularly the large colony of great skuas, has led to the island's designation as a Special Protection Area.

**Foulis, Robert** (1707–76) Printer and bookseller, b. Glasgow. With his brother Andrew he set up business in **Glasgow**, and produced highly regarded editions of classics. They were appointed official printers to **Glasgow University** in 1741, and founded an Academy of Fine Arts in Glasgow in the 1750s.

**Foulis Castle** Castle to the southwest of **Evanton**, Ross and Cromarty, seat of the chief of Clan Munro, an impressive Georgian mansion partly formed from the ruin of the old castle, burnt in 1750.

**Fountainhall** Small mansion to the southwest of **Pencaitland**, East Lothian, surviving complete and unaltered in a form dating from 1638. It was the home of Sir John Lauder, Lord Fountainhall (1646–1722), author of *Fountainhall's Decisions.*

**four cities** Name given to Scotland's 4 largest towns: **Aberdeen, Dundee, Edinburgh, Glasgow**, which were all made 'counties of city' in 1929; see **local government**.

**'four Marys'** Four girls of noble birth who were companions to **Mary, Queen of Scots**, and accompanied her to France when she went there for safety in 1548: Mary Beaton, Mary Fleming, Mary Livingston and Mary Seton. The song 'Yestreen the Queen had Four Maries' appears to draw on 2 instances of execution for infanticide, one of a French woman servant of Mary, in Edinburgh, the second of a Mary Hamilton, maid of honour at the court of Peter the Great in Russia.

**Fowler, William** (c.1560–1610) Scholar and poet, b. Edinburgh. A poet in the court of **James VI**, a member of the **Castalian band**, he was secretary to **Anne of Denmark**.

**Fowlis Easter** Village in the **Sidlaw** Hills 10km (6mi) northwest of **Dundee**, best known for its well-preserved 15th-century church. It contains a rare example of a pre-Reformation painted wooden rood screen, originally used to separate the choir area from the nave, but relegated to the walls by a disastrous Victorian 'restoration'.

**Fowlis Wester** Village 6km (4mi) northeast of **Crieff** which once thrived on weaving and agriculture. The 13th-century church of St Bean, rebuilt in neo-medieval form by J Jeffrey Waddell in 1927, has 2 9th-century Pictish cross-slabs, one of which shows Jonah being swallowed by the whale. A replica of a taller slab stands in the village. There are standing stones to the north of the village.

**Foyers** Village on the east side of **Loch Ness**. The waterfall, although still impressive, is used to provide power to the Foyers hydroelectric power station, which also operates as a pumped-storage station. A modest earlier scheme in the 1890s, providing power for an aluminium works, was the first use in Britain of hydroelectric power for industrial purposes.

**Frame, Ronald** (1953– ) Writer, b. Glasgow. He has written many novels, including *Winter Journey* (1984), *Penelope's Hat* (1989), *Bluette* (1990) and *The Lantern Bearers* (1999). He has won the Betty Trask Prize for Fiction, and has also written for television, radio and the theatre.

**Fraser, Castle** see **Castle Fraser**

**Fraser, Sir Alexander** see **Fraserburgh**

**Fraser, Hugh, Lord Allander** (1903–66) Businessman, b. Glasgow. During his management the family business expanded massively from a successful draper's store in Glasgow to the major House of Fraser firm, of which he became Chairman and Managing Director in 1941. He acquired a number of other firms, including Harrods, and his department stores dominated retailing in many Scottish and northern English towns.

**Fraser, Marjory Kennedy** see **Kennedy-Fraser, Marjory**

**Fraser, Simon** see **Lovat, Simon Fraser, Lord**

**Fraser, Captain Simon, of Knockie** (1773–1852) Fiddler and collector of Highland folk melodies, b. Abertarff, Inverness-shire. His book, *The Airs and Melodies Peculiar to the Highlands of Scotland and the Isles* (1816), contains 230 tunes of Gaelic song airs and instrumental tunes, including apparent examples of the ancient harp music of Scotland. His illegitimate son Angus Fraser (c.1800–70) continued his collecting and editing work.

**Fraserburgh** (pop. 12,454) Fishing town on the northeast corner of the Aberdeenshire coast, known locally as 'the Broch'. It was founded in the 16th century by the Frasers of Philorth. A university was founded here in 1592 by Sir Alexander Fraser but only lasted about 10 years. The town expanded rapidly in the 19th century with the success of herring **fishing**, and remains

F

an important fishing port with a fish-processing factory. Kinnaird Head Lighthouse, built in 1787 on top of the Fraser tower house of c.1570, was the first to be built by the Commissioners of the Northern Lighthouses. Now in the care of **Historic Scotland**, it houses the Museum of Scottish **Lighthouses**. To the southwest is the very large Bronze Age Memsie Cairn, enlarged during field clearance in more recent centuries.

**Fraser's Highlanders** Regiment (of the British army) raised in the 1750s by Simon Fraser of **Lovat** (who had fought on the **Jacobite** side in the 1745 Rising and narrowly escaped execution). It fought with distinction in the battle of the Plains of Abraham, outside Quebec, in 1759, climbing the cliff and enabling General Wolfe to win the battle and secure Canada from the French. They also fought in the War of the American Revolution.

**Frazer, Sir James G** (1854–1941) Anthropologist, b. Glasgow. His detailed examination of religious beliefs, *The Golden Bough* (1890–1915), was ground-breaking and highly influential at its time. He was a Fellow of Trinity College, Cambridge from 1879, and the first Professor of Social Anthropology at the University of Liverpool from 1907 to 1922.

**Free Church of Scotland** A Presbyterian, Evangelical denomination which was founded in 1843 by those ministers and elders who left the **Church of Scotland** at the **Disruption**. Its first Moderator was Thomas **Chalmers**. It flourished until 1900, when the majority of the church united with the United Presbyterian Church to form the United Free Church; it reunited with the Church of Scotland in 1929. A small number of congregations, especially in the Highlands and Islands, remained out of the union of 1900 and now form the **Free Church of Scotland**, sometimes known as the 'Wee Frees'. See also **Presbyterian churches**.

**Free Church of Scotland (Continuing)** Founded in 2000 when a small group of ministers and adherents left the **Free**

*Fraserburgh Harbour at the height of the herring fishing season in the 19th century.*

**Church of Scotland** following a period of acrimonious disputes, focussed on alleged liberalising of the theological position.

**freemasonry** Freemasonry emerged originally from the lodges of Scottish medieval working stonemasons, which cultivated fellowship and mutual charity. From the early 17th century in Scotland, men from the upper classes joined masons' lodges, bringing new ideas derived from Renaissance humanism and religious idealism. These leaders tended to be from conservative Catholic families, such as the dynasties of royal architects and masons, or the Sinclairs of **Roslin**. This persisted into the 18th century when **Jacobites** like the Chevalier Ramsay founded Jacobite lodges on the Continent to encourage Protestant support for the exiled Catholic Stewarts. However, freemasonry's stress on the undesirablity of sectarian division had given it wide appeal and Covenanting generals could also be found in its ranks. Scottish Speculative or Free Masonry originally seems to have had only two degrees: Entered Apprentice and Fellow Craft. If the 17th century was the Scottish century of freemasonry, the 18th was the English and Irish, as the movement spread to the other two kingdoms, and to America and Europe. Scots adopted the third degree of Master Mason in the mid 18th century for the sake of conformity with England, and established a national Grand Lodge only in 1736, after England (1718) and Ireland (1725). Masonic lodges became the social club of 18th-century elites and standard-bearers of **Scottish Enlightenment** values, which explains why men like Robert **Burns** and Henry **Dundas** were freemasons. In the 19th century there was an explosion of masonic orders and rites. Scottish, like other Anglophone Masonry, never made the leap to admission of women, which began on the Continent in the late 18th century. Most of the so-called 'Scottish rites' are in fact of French origin, apart from the Royal Arch, the only masonic order with its headquarters in Scotland. Masonry flourished in 19th-century Scotland, but has had difficulty recruiting younger members in the 20th and 21st centuries. It has always had problems with the churches due to its secrecy and blending of religious traditions.

**Free Presbyterian Church of Scotland** A denomination which was formed in 1893 by a group who seceded from the **Free Church of Scotland**, hence its popular name, the **Seceders**. It is conservative in theology and is particularly known for its commitment to observing the Sabbath. Like the Free Church it is sometimes known as the 'Wee Frees'. See also **Associated Presbyterian Churches** and **Presbyterian churches**.

**Freiceadan Dubh** see **Black Watch**

**Freuchie** Village in the **Howe of Fife**, near **Falkland**, noted for the success of its village cricket team over many years.

**Friel, George** (1910–75) Author, b. Glasgow. He is best remembered for his 3 novels *The Boy Who Wanted Peace* (1964), *Grace and Miss Partridge* (1969) and *Mr Alfred M.A.* (1964). Depicting life in the **Glasgow** streets and tenements of the 1950s and 60s, they have been republished as *A Glasgow Trilogy*.

**Friends, Religious Society of** (nicknamed **Quakers**) Originally an English group disillusioned with clerical leadership and relying on the inner light of Christ. It spread to Scotland with the Cromwellian armies and the visit of the Quaker leader George Fox in 1657. Early converts included lairds such as David Barclay of Urie, a provost of **Aberdeen**, Alexander Jaffray, and George Keith, who later emigrated to Pennsylvania. Increasingly introspective in its piety, Scottish Quakersim survives into the 21st century with about 20 organised meetings of Friends.

**Fruin** see **Glen Fruin**

**Fulton, Rikki** (1924–2004) Actor, b. Glasgow. His career included theatre and films, but he is best known for his television comedy sketches in *Scotch and Wry* (1978), which was later

*Rikki Fulton in Molière's* The Miser *at the Lyceum Theatre, Edinburgh, May 1973.*

traditionally broadcast in Scotland at **Hogmanay** for many years, and for his ironic character, the Revd I M Jolly.

**Furnace** Village on the west shore of **Loch Fyne**, 11km (7mi) southwest of **Inveraray**. The Argyll Furnace, a charcoal-fuelled iron-smelting furnace, worked from 1755 to 1812. There is a large granite quarry on the outskirts of the village and there was formerly a gunpowder works.

**Fyffe, Will** (1885–1947) Comedian, b. Dundee. He performed in music halls and in films, and is particularly remembered for his song 'I Belong to Glasgow'.

**Fyne** see **Loch Fyne**

**Fyvie** Aberdeenshire village, 11km (7mi) southeast of **Turriff**. To the north of the village lies Fyvie Castle, originally built as a quadrangular royal fortress by **Alexander III**, and reconstructed as a great symmetrically fronted pile in 1599 by Alexander Seton, Earl of Dunfermline and Chancellor of Scotland. It contains art and antiquities acquired by Alexander Forbes-Leith, who had made his fortune in American steel. It now belongs to the **National Trust for Scotland** and contains an important collection of 18th- and 19th-century Scottish portraits. The parish church of St Peter has an important window by the American artist Comfort Tiffany.

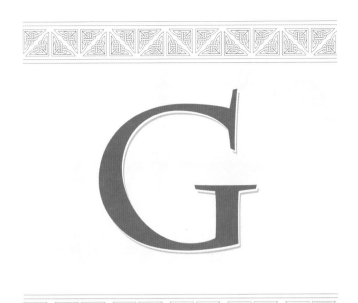

**Gaelic** The Celtic language of the **Highlands** and Islands. See **language**, p.220

**Gairloch** (Gaelic **Geàrr-Loch**) Holiday resort and former **fishing** village on the Gair Loch in **Wester Ross**, between **Loch Ewe** and **Loch Torridon**. The Gairloch Heritage Museum has displays on the history of the area. Flowerdale House, to the southeast of the village, home of the Mackenzies of Gairloch, dates from the early 18th century with early 20th-century addition.

**Gairm** Quarterly **Gaelic** magazine, founded in 1952 by Derick **Thomson**, who edited it until its closure in 2002.

**Galashiels** (pop. 14,361) Town on the Gala Water, 10km (6mi) north of **Selkirk**. It has had a woollen industry since the 16th century, greatly flourishing in the 19th and early 20th, mainly making **tweed**, though now much reduced. It has the Scottish Borders Campus of **Heriot-Watt University**, formerly the Scottish College of Textiles. As in other **Border** towns Gala rugby team has an important role, and has produced many internationalists in past decades. The Braw Lads' Gathering takes place in June, in part commemorating an incident in 1337 when local men were killed in a field of wild plums; hence the town's motto 'soor plooms', also used as a nickname for the inhabitants; see also **Soor Ploom**.

**Galcacus** see **Calgacus**

**Gallacher, Bernard** (1949– ) Golfer, b. Bathgate. He won 21 world-class titles during his career. He was the youngest member of the European Ryder Cup Team in 1969, played regularly in subsequent teams, and captained the team from 1991 to 1995.

**Gallacher, Willie** (1881–1965) Politician and trade unionist, b. **Paisley**. An engineering worker, he was a leading unionist involved in the struggles of **Red Clydeside**. He was a founding member of the Communist Party in Britain, and was Communist MP for West Fife from 1935 to 1950.

**Gallery** Symmetrical house on the River North **Esk**, 8km (5mi) northwest of **Montrose**, built in 1677–80 by Thomas Wilkie for Sir John Falconer of Balmakellie; a fine walled garden adjoins the property.

**Galloway** Area of southwestern Scotland, formerly consisting of the counties of **Kirkcudbrightshire** and **Wigtownshire**, now part of **Dumfries and Galloway**. The Solway Firth lies off the southern coast, and the Irish Sea lies to the west. The Mull of Galloway is the westernmost headland. Ranges of hills separate it from the Central Lowlands and the eastern Borders. **Whithorn** was the base for St **Ninian**, in popular belief the first to bring Christianity to Scotland. Galloway was part of the shipping-based Irish Sea economy, and was a region where the Scottish crown faced difficulties exercising authority into the 14th century. Ferries cross from **Stranraer** and **Cairnryan** to Ireland. The Galloway Forest Park covers a wide area of Dumfries and Galloway and South Ayrshire. Its main forests are the Forests of Ae, Mabie, Dalbeattie, Clatteringshaws, Carrick, **Glentrool** and Kirroughtree. As well as timber production, the forests provide many amenities, including routes for walkers and cyclists, and there are visitor centres at Kirroughtree, Clatteringshaws and Glentrool. The Galloway hydroelectric scheme, developed in the early 1930s, was Scotland's first large-scale scheme. It includes 6 power stations: Carsfad, Drumjohn, Earlstoun, Glenlee, Kendoun and **Tongland**. See also **Rhinns of Galloway**.

**Galloway, George** (1954– ) Politician, b. Dundee. Labour MP for **Glasgow** Hillhead since 1987.

**Galloway, Janice** (1956– ) Author, b. Saltcoats. She has worked as a journalist but is best known for her fiction. Her first novel, *The Trick is to Keep Breathing*, was published in 1989. Later work has included *Foreign Parts* (1994), which won the McVitie's Prize, and *Clara* (2002), based on the life of Clara Schumann, which won the Saltire Prize.

**Galloway, Jim** (1936– ) Jazz musician, b. Glasgow. A clarinettist and saxophonist, his career took off when he moved to Canada in 1965. He toured to Europe regularly from the mid 1970s, and led his own quartet, sextet and big band in his adopted homeland.

G

*A Belted Galloway cow*

**Galloway, Mull of** see **Galloway**

**Galloway, Rhinns of** see **Rhinns of (Galloway)**

**Galloway cattle** This native breed is either all-black, or identified by a white band round their middle, and known as Belted Galloways or Belties. Hardy hill beasts, they are the hornless cousins of **Highland cattle**.

**Galloway House** Massive Palladian house near Garlieston, to the southeast of **Wigtown**, built by John Baxter from designs by John Douglas and Sir John **Clerk** for Lord Garlies from 1740 onwards. The interior was grandly remodelled by Sir Robert **Lorimer** in 1909.

**Galoshans** A play or entertainment formerly performed by boys in some areas at **Hogmanay** and other winter festivals.

**Galston** (pop. 5000) **Ayrshire** town, 8km (5mi) east of **Irvine**. It expanded rapidly from the late 18th century with the development of **textile** and **coal** mining industries. The spired parish church of 1808 occupies a site used for Christian worship from the 13th century, and the elaborate Roman Catholic church was designed by Robert Rowand **Anderson**, 1885-6, for the Marquess of **Bute**, and is based on Hagia Sophia in Istanbul. Within the town is Barr Castle, the 15th-century tower house of the Lockharts. Loudoun Castle, now ruined, was a 19th-century mansion incorporating a 15th-century tower house. It was gutted by fire in 1941, and the ruin now forms part of the Loudoun Castle Theme Park, Scotland's largest leisure theme park. It has a variety of rides, including the country's highest roller-coaster. There is also a 200 hectare (500 acre) park with large areas of woodland.

**Galt, John** (1779-1839) Author and businessman, b. Irvine. He is best known for his novels dealing with Scottish life and society, his 'theoretical histories' including *Annals of the Parish* (1821), *The Entail* (1823) and *Ringan Gilhaize* (1823). Galt was unusual in using **Scots** words and expressions in the text of his novels, as well as in the dialogue. A prolific writer, his other work includes short stories, biography and an autobiography published in 1833. As an agent for the Canada Company, he visited Upper Canada to promote emigration and founded the town of Guelph, Ontario.

**Gantocks** A dangerous group of rocks in the Firth of **Clyde**, near **Dunoon**.

**Garbh Chioch Mhor** see **Glen Dessary**

**Garde Ecossaise du Corps du Roi** Scottish bodyguard of the French kings from the 15th century until the French Revolution.

**Garden, Mary** (1874-1967) Opera singer, b. Aberdeen. She made her debut in 1900 at the Opéra-Comique in Paris, and was the leading soprano at the Chicago Opera House for 20 years. The role of Mélisande in the opera *Pelléas et Mélisande* was created for her by Claude Debussy. Gardenia perfume is named after her.

**Gardenstown** Village above Gamrie Bay on the **Banff** coast. Partly built on the clifftop, it winds steeply down to the original fishing port at the foot of the cliffs. Gardenstown-owned boats are now operated from larger harbours.

**Gardyne Castle** Tower house of the Gardynes of Leys, 10km (6mi) to the northwest of **Arbroath**, built in 1568, remarkable for its very original detailing, inside and out, the crenellated angle turrets having stone spiralets with lucarnes.

**Gare Loch** Sea loch running from **Garelochhead** to **Helensburgh**, where it opens into the Firth of **Clyde**. During World War II an emergency port was opened at **Faslane** which was subsequently converted into a nuclear submarine base.

**Garelochhead** Village at the head of the **Gare Loch**, 11km (7mi) from **Helensburgh**. The **Faslane** nuclear submarine base is nearby.

**Garioch** (pronounced 'geery') District to the northwest of **Aberdeen**. It consists mainly of fertile farming country, and the main town is **Inverurie**.

**Garioch, Robert** (pen name of **Robert Garioch Sutherland**) (1909–81) Poet, b. Edinburgh. He wrote mainly in **Scots**, and many of his poems were satirical observations of **Edinburgh** life. He also translated other works from French, Latin and Roman dialect into Scots. His *Complete Poetical Works* was published in 1983.

**garron** Working pony or small horse. Most garrons are descended from an outcross of **Highland** ponies with a dash of **Clydesdale horse**, and are compact and powerful workhorses.

**Garry, River** (Gaelic **Garadh**) (Inverness-shire) Flows from **Loch Quoich** through **Glen Garry**, opening out to form Loch Garry and then on to enter **Loch Oich** at **Invergarry**. The loch and river both form part of the Garry-Moriston hydroelectric scheme.

**Garry, Loch** and **River** (Gaelic **Garadh**) (Perthshire) Loch Garry lies south of the Pass of **Drumochter**, 397m (1303ft) above sea level. The River Garry flows from the loch for a distance of 35km (22mi) through Glen Garry and joins the River **Tummel** near **Pitlochry**. It drops nearly 300m (1000ft) on its journey. It is part of the very large Tummel Garry hydroelectric power scheme.

**Gartcosh** Village in **Lanarkshire**, near **Coatbridge**. The Gartcosh Ironworks were founded in 1865, and later developed to make steel sheets. The works were acquired by the Colville Group and completely rebuilt as a cold strip mill, operating in connection with the **Ravenscraig** works, but they were closed by British Steel by 1986. See also David **Colville**.

**Garten** see **Boat of Garten, Loch Garten**

**Gartocharn** Village near **Drymen**, south of **Loch Lomond**. On the shore of the loch nearby lies Ross Priory, a mansion dating from 1693, remodelled in 1812 by James Gillespie **Graham** as a picturesque Gothic mansion; it now belongs to **Strathclyde University** as a staff club. Sir Walter **Scott** wrote some of *Rob Roy* here.

**Garve** (Gaelic **Gairbh**) Village in **Ross-shire**, northwest of **Strathpeffer** and near Loch Garve, where the roads from **Inverness** to **Ullapool** and **Kyle of Lochalsh** meet.

**Garvellachs** (Gaelic **Garbh Eilach**) A group of uninhabited islands in the Firth of **Lorn**, west of **Luing**. The largest island is Garbh Eilach. A ruined 13th-century castle on Dun Chonuill was probably built by the MacDougalls, and on Eilach an Naoimh there are remains of an early Christian monastery, with 'beehive' cells, unique in Scotland.

**gas** see **oil and gas**, p.293

**Gatehouse of Fleet** (pop. 892) Small planned town 10km (6mi) northwest of **Kirkcudbright**, near where the Water of **Fleet** flows into Fleet Bay. It grew up around the cotton industry in the second half of the 18th century, the story of which is now told in the Mill of Fleet Visitor Centre. Cardoness Castle, nearby, is a ruined 15th-century keep, which is in the care of **Historic Scotland** and is open to the public.

**Gaughan, Dick** (1948– ) Musician, b. Glasgow. He grew up in **Leith**, and recorded his first solo album in 1971. A guitarist, songwriter and record producer, he has worked principally in Celtic folk music.

**Geddes, Andrew** (1783–1844) Artist, b. Edinburgh. Studied at the Royal Academy Schools, London, then settled in **Edinburgh** where he established himself as a portrait painter. Best known for his stylish portrait of artist Sir David **Wilkie** (1816, **Scottish National Portrait Gallery**), he is also recognised for his important work as a print-maker.

**Geddes, Jennie** According to tradition, an **Edinburgh** woman who threw her stool at the pulpit in St Giles' on 23 July 1637, in protest at the reading of the New Book of Common Prayer, thus sparking a riot.

**Geddes, John Maxwell** (1941– ) Composer, b. Glasgow. He has written both orchestral and solo instrument works, including *Symphony No. 1* (1975), *Voyager* (1985) and *Second Symphony* (1993). His music has been performed at many international festivals.

**Geddes, Sir Patrick** (1854–1932) Town planner and botanist, b. Ballater. He began his career teaching botany and was Professor of Botany at **Dundee** (1889–1914). Motivated by a desire to improve social conditions for those living in Edinburgh's slums, he became involved in town planning and embarked on an extensive programme of redevelopment and refurbishment in the Old Town. In the 1890s he bought the Outlook Tower

**G**

on Castlehill (see **Edinburgh**) for use as 'the world's first sociological laboratory'. He also replanned towns overseas, notably in India and Jerusalem.

**Geikie, Archibald** (1835–1924) Geologist, b. Edinburgh. A leading geologist of his generation, he joined the Geological Survey of Scotland, and became its first Scottish director in 1867. He was Professor of Geology at **Edinburgh University** (1871–81), and from 1882 to 1901 was Director-General of the Geological Survey of Great Britain.

**Geikie, Walter** (1795–1837) Artist, b. Edinburgh. Deaf and dumb from childhood, he is known for his *Etchings Illustrative of Scottish Character and Scenery*, a collection of sketches of everyday life.

**Geilston Garden** Garden in **Cardross**, near **Dumbarton**, in the care of the **National Trust for Scotland**, centred on a small 16th- or 17th-century house, extended in the 18th.

**genealogy** see **Scottish Genealogy Society**

**General Assembly** The **Church of Scotland**'s highest court and governing body, set up at the **Reformation**. In its present form it meets annually each May in the Assembly Hall, **Edinburgh**. It consists of around 850 ministers and **elders** representing each presbytery, and is presided over by the **Moderator**, who holds office for a year. It takes decisions about the running of the Church, hears reports from different committees, and is the final court for certain cases and appeals. The monarch is represented by a Lord High Commissioner.

**George Heriot's School** see **Heriot, George**

**Gibbon, Lewis Grassic** (pen name of **James Leslie Mitchell**) (1901–35) Writer, b. Auchterless, Aberdeenshire. He worked as a journalist and served in the army and the RAF, before concentrating on writing fiction. His best-known work is the highly acclaimed *A Scots Quair*, a trilogy of novels – *Sunset Song* (1932), *Cloud Howe* (1933) and *Grey Granite* (1934) – which moves between rural and industrial Scotland before and during World War I and the Depression and follows the life of the heroine, Chris Guthrie. Other works include *The Thirteenth Disciple* (1931) and *Spartacus* (1933). There is a Lewis Grassic Gibbon Centre at **Arbuthnott**, where he grew up.

**Gibbs, James** (1683–1754) Architect, b. Aberdeen. He was educated for the priesthood at the **Scots College** in Rome, but changed to architecture and trained under the papal architect Carlo Fontana, who combined a subdued baroque style with classical elements. Patronised by the Harley family and the Tory party, he designed important London churches such as St Mary-le-Strand and St Martin-in-the-Fields as well as country houses, and the Radcliffe Camera for Oxford University and the Library for Cambridge. In retirement he supplied plans for the reconstruction of West St Nicholas Kirk in **Aberdeen**.

**Gibson, Sir Alexander** (1926–95) Conductor, b. Motherwell. He was the first Scottish director of the **Scottish National Orchestra**, pioneering the performance of avant-garde music. He played a key role in establishing **Scottish Opera**.

**Giffnock** (pop. 16,178) Town to the south of **Glasgow**, a suburb of the city, now the administrative centre of **East Renfrewshire** Council.

**Gifford** Village in East Lothian, 6km (4mi) south of **Haddington**. The parish church dates from 1710, and has a 17th-century pulpit and a 15th-century bell. A memorial on a wall nearby is to John **Witherspoon**, who was born here. Yester House was designed by James **Smith** for the Marquis of Tweeddale, and built in 1700–15. It was partly remodelled by William and Robert **Adam** in 1730 and 1788. It belongs to the Italian composer Gian Carlo Menotti. The ruined 13th-century Gifford castle which lies in the grounds includes an underground chamber, the 'Goblin Ha', which appears in Sir Walter **Scott**'s *Marmion*.

**Gigha, Isle of** (Gaelic **Giogha**) (pop.110) Island in the Inner **Hebrides**, 5km (3mi) west of the **Kintyre** peninsula. Just 10km (6mi) long by 2km (1mi) wide, it is reached by ferry from Tayinloan. Ardminish is the only village. The island is fertile, with a moderate climate, and visitors are attracted to the subtropical, woodland gardens of Achamore House, established by Sir James Horlick. In 2002 the islanders purchased the island, and it is owned and managed by the Isle of Gigha Trust.

**Gight Castle** Ruined 16th-century tower house near **Fyvie** which belonged to the Gordons of Gight. The castle was inherited by Catherine Gordon, mother of Lord **Byron**, but it was sold in 1787 to clear her husband Jack Byron's gambling debts.

**gigot** (pronounced **jig**it) **Scots** word for a leg of lamb, from French.

**Gilchrist, Dr Marion** (1864–1952) Doctor, b. Bothwell, Lanarkshire. She began by working on her father's farm, but managed to get a university education, eventually in medicine in 1894, becoming the first woman medical graduate of **Glasgow University**. She went into general practice, developing an interest in diseases of the eye. Financially and professionally independent, she became openly politically active; during 1903 she joined the Glasgow and West of Scotland Association for Women's Suffrage. She became a surgeon for diseases of the eye at the Victoria Infirmary and later at Redlands Hospital for Women. She was a prominent member of the British Medical Association and the first woman chairman of the Glasgow division.

**Gille Chaluim** see **Highland dancing**

**Gillespie, James** (1726–97) Snuff manufacturer and merchant, b. Roslin, near Edinburgh. A successful businessman, he built Spylaw House in **Edinburgh** for himself (1773), and left money to establish a hospital in Edinburgh, which became James Gillespie's High School. It was taken over in 1908 by Edinburgh School Board and became a girls' secondary school. Since 1973 it has been a co-educational comprehensive.

**Gillespie, Thomas** see **Relief Church**

**Gillespie Graham, James** see **Graham, James Gillespie**

**Gillies, Anne Lorne** (1944– ) Gaelic singer. She began as a traditional Gaelic singer, then undertook classical training in Edinburgh, Italy and London. Has since performed throughout the world her eclectic repertoire of song in **Gaelic**, **Scots** and English, employing a rich soprano voice and strong interpretive skills. She has collaborated with the **Royal Scottish National Orchestra**, **Scottish Opera**, and the **Whistlebinkies**.

**Gillies, John MacDougall** (1855–1925) Piper, b. Aberdeen. He won many awards and as Pipe Major of the **Highland Light Infantry** (TA) he won the first World Pipe Band Championship 1906 and won it 5 times in total. He taught many other pipers.

**Gillies, Sir William George** (1898–1973) Artist, b. Haddington. Studied at **Edinburgh** College of Art, where he subsequently taught from 1925, eventually becoming Principal in 1960, and consequently influencing several generations of Scottish artists. Restricting his subject matter to still life and landscape, Gillies is best known for the numerous distinctive watercolours and drawings he produced of the landscape of Scotland (a country which he rarely left), which he painted freely and directly from nature.

**Gilmorehill** see **Glasgow University**

**Gilmour, Barbara** see **Dunlop**

*Dr Marion Gilchrist, 1894,
first female medical graduate of Glasgow University.*

**Gilnockie** (or **Hollows**) **Tower** Mid 15th-century **Borders** tower house of the Armstrongs, to the south of **Langholm**, successor to that which had belonged to Johnnie **Armstrong**; it is remarkable for the signalling beacon lantern on its south gable. Reroofed and reoccupied, 1979–80.

**girdle** An iron plate used for baking, traditionally circular with a hooped handle for holding it over a fire. Used especially for **oatcakes**, **scones** (girdle scones), and **pancakes**.

**Giric** (d. 889) King of **Alba** from 878 to 889, reigning at the same time as Eochaid, who may have been a client-king in **Strathclyde**. Characteristically for the era, Giric gained the throne through violence and was toppled in his turn by **Donald II**.

**Girvan** (pop. 6992) Coastal town in **Ayrshire** which has long been a popular holiday and day-trip resort for people from the **Glasgow** area. It was also an important fishing port, and in the 19th century it was used for shipping coal. Boats run to **Ailsa Craig**, 16km (10mi) offshore, which dominates the views from Girvan.

**Gladsmuir** see **Prestonpans**

**Gladstone's Land** see **Edinburgh**

G

*Glasgow Cathedral.*

**Glasgow** (pop. 629,501) Scotland's largest city, on the River **Clyde**. It became a **burgh** in 1175 and was granted the right to hold a fair every July; see **Glasgow Fair**. Formerly part of Lanarkshire, it became a county of city in 1929. In 1975 the City of Glasgow became a district of **Strathclyde Region**, and also its headquarters, and in 1996 Glasgow City became one of the new unitary local authorities; see **local government**.

Glasgow's origins are said to lie with the arrival of St **Kentigern** (Mungo) in the 6th century. His church was established on the site of the present Glasgow Cathedral, a Gothic building dating largely from the 13th century, though the ornately carved stone quire screen is from the 15th century. The vaulted Lower Church has a shrine to St Mungo. Most of the stained glass is of recent Scottish origin, installed since World War II. The city's ecclesiastical significance was increased by the founding of **Glasgow University** in 1451. In most other respects it remained relatively unimportant until the late 17th century, when its prosperity increased, especially after the **Union of the Parliaments** in 1707. It was ideally placed to exploit the new trade opportunities opening up with North America and the West Indies. One of the chief imports was **sugar** and Glasgow became a centre of the sugar industry. But the most spectacular development was the import of tobacco from Virginia; see **Tobacco Lords**. Deepening of the River Clyde in the late 18th century allowed it to become a deep-water port and helped it to survive when its trade was threatened by the War of the American Revolution.

Manufacturing developed too, as new markets were available for export. By the late 18th century **cotton** had replaced tobacco as the principal import, and cotton mills, calico-printing works and bleachfields developed in and around Glasgow. Progress in **coal** mining and **iron** manufacture saw Glasgow in the 19th century take its place as a leading centre of heavy industry, and particularly of shipbuilding, marine engineering, locomotive building and sugar-machinery manufacture. It became one of the finest of Victorian cities, with an enviable range of municipal services. Concern, however, also grew over social problems of overcrowding, crime and disease as the population expanded to meet the demand for labour, with many immigrants from Ireland and from the **Highlands**. The population also grew with other immigrant groups, notably Italians (mainly in the catering trade) and Jewish refugees from eastern Europe. As the heavy industries declined in the 20th century, the social problems increased. In certain areas of Glasgow deprivation and health problems continue, but the city has latterly reinvented itself as a cultural centre, a development which in part arose out of its designation as European City of Culture in 1990.

Medieval Glasgow clustered closely round the Cathedral, and one of the few survivors of the period is Provand's Lordship, opposite the Cathedral, a late 15th-century house, rescued from demolition in the early 20th and now a museum. Close by is the St Mungo Museum of Religious Life and Art, opened 1993, the first museum in the world dedicated solely to the study of religion. The High Street descends to Glasgow Cross, near the river. Of the 7-storey Tolbooth or Town House (1626), all that survives is the Tolbooth Steeple with its crown tower. The nearby Mercat Cross is a 20th-century replacement of one long since demolished. Another survivor is the Tron Steeple in the Trongate (completed 1636), the remains of the Tron Church which was burnt down in 1793; the church was

*The High Street.*

*The Gallery of Modern Art.*

rebuilt nearby and now houses the Tron Theatre, founded as a theatre club in 1979, but public since 1989. From the Cross the Saltmarket leads to Glasgow Green, for centuries a focal point of city life, both for recreation and for meetings of various kinds. The People's Palace was built in 1893–8 as a recreation centre for the east end; it is now a museum of Glasgow's social history. Nearby is the Barras, Glasgow's famous weekend bargain market, next to the Barrowland Ballroom, with concerts and other events.

The 18th-century merchant city expanded west along the river. The Trades House in Glassford Street, designed by Robert **Adam**, was opened in 1794 as the headquarters of the Trades House of Glasgow. Nearby in Ingram Street is Hutcheson's Hospital Hall (1802–5, David **Hamilton**), now in the care of the **National Trust for Scotland**; its elegant classical façade contains two 17th-century statues of the brothers George and Thomas Hutcheson, who founded a hospital for aged men and later orphan boys; their trust also set up Hutcheson's Grammar Schools. In Queen Street a mansion house of 1778–80 was converted into the Royal Exchange in 1827–32 by David Hamilton. In 1954 the

building became Stirling's Library and it is now the Gallery of Modern Art. Parts of the merchant city, especially those closer to the river, had fallen into disrepair, but late 20th-century renewal has produced a pleasant city-centre residential area. On the river is St Andrew's Roman Catholic Cathedral (1816) by James Gillespie **Graham**, one of the earliest Gothic Revival buildings in Glasgow. To the west is the Broomielaw area, which grew round the 'Bremmylaw Quay', built in the later 17th century as Glasgow's first quay. It was once an embarkation point for transatlantic and Irish shipping, now for Clyde boat trips. The area is being developed as an international centre for financial services.

To the north of the city centre is Port Dundas, established in 1790 around a basin where the **Forth and Clyde** and **Monkland Canals** met, helping to create a flourishing industrial area. The canal office (1812) and the impressive warehouses have been restored in recent years.

Middle-class residential expansion began in the early 19th century, first to the south in the **Gorbals**, which enjoyed a brief spell of prosperity. There were later developments towards the west, notably around the Botanic Gardens, laid out in 1842. In 1873, the spectacular glass-domed Kibble Palace (originally a conservatory built by John Kibble, a Glasgow businessman, for his home on the Clyde coast) was re-erected here as a hothouse and social venue. It has a collection of temperate plants including the National Collection of *Dicksonia* tree ferns. In adjacent glass houses there are national collections of *Begonia* species and dendrobiums.

The area became known as **Kelvinside** and increased in popularity when the University moved here in 1870. The River **Kelvin** flows through the west end of the city and near its confluence with the River Clyde is Kelvingrove Park, which

*The Kibble Palace in the Botanic Gardens.*

G

*The City Chambers and George Square.*

contains the city's Art Gallery and Museum (1891–1901, J W Simpson and E J Milner Allen). It has one of the finest municipal art collections in Britain, especially strong in 17th-century Dutch paintings, including *The Man in Armour* by Rembrandt, and 19th-century French paintings; the **Glasgow Boys** are well represented.

Glasgow is above all a Victorian city, evident in the massive City Chambers in George Square (1883–88, William Young); the marble-clad interior, especially the staircase, is a worthy monument to the opulence of 19th-century Glasgow. The area to the west developed on a grid pattern; now the commercial and retail centre of the city, with Sauchiehall Street to the north and Argyle Street to the south, it originally had elegant residential streets, such as Blythswood Square (1823–9, John Brash). Impressive commerical buildings include Stock Exchange House in Buchanan Street (1875–77, John Burnet senior, with addition by J J **Burnet**), and the Lion Chambers (1905, J Salmond and J Gaff Gillespie). Buildings in central Glasgow by Alexander 'Greek' **Thomson** include the former St Vincent Street Church (1859), the Grosvenor Building (1859–61), the Grecian Buildings (1865) and the Egyptian Halls (1873).

The turn of the 20th century saw developments in the modern style, including much Art Nouveau, most spectacularly in the work of Charles Rennie **Mackintosh**; see also Kate **Cranston**. The Mitchell Library, to the west of the city centre, is the largest civic-owned reference library in Europe, founded in 1877 with a bequest from Stephen Mitchell, a tobacco merchant. The current imposing building was designed by W B Whitie and completed in 1911.

While the shipyards and docks of the Clyde have dwindled, their riverside sites have been put to good use. On the north bank, the Scottish Exhibition and Conference Centre (SECC) was opened in 1985. In 1988 the Glasgow Garden Festival occupied the site of the Princes Dock on the south side of the river and the area is now being developed with offices etc as Pacific Quay. A new headquarters for BBC Scotland is also planned there.

On the south side of the city is the very large Pollok Country Park, with **Pollok House** and the **Burrell** Collection. To the north of it is Bellahouston Park, scene of the Empire Exhibition of 1938 and the visit of Pope John Paul II in 1982. The House for an Art Lover has been recently constructed there from designs by Charles Rennie Mackintosh. Further east is **Hampden Park**. Glasgow Airport, at Abbotsinch south of the Clyde, is now a major international airport.

Glasgow today is having to face a post-industrial economy and reduced population, largely due to the movement of many people to towns outside the city in the 1950s and 60s. Older immigrant groups have been joined by large numbers of Asians, mainly from Pakistan. See also **Bearsden, Citizens' Theatre, Glasgow Fair, Glasgow Caledonian University, Glasgow School of Art, Glasgow University, Gorbals, Govan, Ibrox, Red Clydeside, Rouken Glen, Strathclyde University**.

*Glasgow School of Art, designed by Charles Rennie Mackintosh.*

**Glamis** Village in **Angus**, near **Forfar**. The Glamis Folk Museum, run by the **National Trust for Scotland**, gives an insight into the social history of this former weaving and agricultural community. A Pictish cross-slab stands in the grounds of the Manse. Glamis Castle was recast as a near-symmetrical baroque mansion by the 3rd Earl of Strathmore between 1669 and 1683, centred on the Great Tower, built in the early 15th century and remodelled in its present turreted form in 1606–26. The hall has splendid plasterwork of 1621. It still belongs to the Earls of Strathmore, and is open to the public. It was the childhood home of Queen Elizabeth, the Queen Mother and the birthplace of Princess Margaret.

**Glas, John** (1695–1775) Religious leader, b. Auchtermuchty, Fife. Minister at Tealing near **Dundee**, he criticised the **Church of Scotland** and was deposed in 1726. He founded a sect known as the Glas(s)ites which interpreted scripture literally and modelled itself on the New Testament church. It was continued and extended by his son-in-law Robert Sandeman (see **Sandemanians**). The last congregation, in **Edinburgh**, disbanded in the 1990s, and their meeting house is now owned by a trust.

**Glasgow** see pp.162–4

**Glasgow, Port** see **Port Glasgow**

**Glasgow Boys** The collective name given to a number of Scottish artists (including James **Guthrie**, E A **Hornel**, George **Henry**, and E A **Walton**) who in the late 19th century reacted against the sentimental and historical themes which had come to dominate Victorian painting, in favour of an art based on the observation of realist subject matter. In this they were influenced by contemporary French and Dutch realist artists, and followed their example in establishing artist colonies in rural areas, such as at Brig o' Turk in the **Trossachs** and at **Cockburnspath**. Many of their most progressive works were exhibited at the Royal Glasgow Institute, and although not all were from **Glasgow**, they became associated with the city.

**Glasgow Caledonian University** Founded as a university in 1993 by a merger of the Glasgow Polytechnic and Queen's College, it has a modern campus in the centre of **Glasgow**, with over 14,000 students.

**Glasgow District** see **Glasgow**

**Glasgow Fair** In the 12th century **Glasgow** was granted the right to hold a fair every July. The Glasgow Fair continues to this day as a public holiday in the middle of July and

*Glasgow University Tower, Kelvingrove.*

the following 2 weeks, known as 'Fair Fortnight' are, or were until very recently, the annual holiday of many factories and works.

**Glasgow Herald** see **Herald**

**Glasgow Orpheus Choir** Formed in Glasgow in 1901 as 'a sideline of Toynbee Men's Social Club', it became Orpheus Choir in 1905 in Glasgow, and achieved international fame under the conductorship of Sir Hugh Roberton, who also arranged Scottish songs for the choir. Recorded Scottish secular songs and psalm tunes, and choral pieces, including most of Elgar's unaccompanied choral works, until 1951.

**Glasgow School of Art** Founded in 1845 as a Government School of Design, it moved in 1899 into the world-famous building designed by Charles Rennie **Mackintosh**, still the core of its city-centre campus, and now known as the Mackintosh Building. An independent institution, centrally funded by the **Scottish Executive**, it awards **Glasgow University** degrees. It has 1400 students.

**Glasgow University** Established in 1451 by Bishop William Turnbull, it is the second oldest of the Scottish universities. Its early 17th-century buildings erected in the High Street were demolished in the 1870s and 80s to make way for a railway goods yard. They were replaced by Sir Gilbert Scott's Gothic-revival new university buildings at Gilmorehill, above Kelvingrove Park in the city's west end. The Glasgow Veterinary School was incorporated in 1949, and St Andrew's College of Education has recently been incorporated and a new building has been opened near the main campus. Today the university has approximately 20,000 students. The Hunterian Museum was begun with the collections of William **Hunter**; opened in 1807,

**G**

*Glencoe.*

it was Scotland's first public museum. As well as an important collection of paintings left by Hunter, its collections include anatomy, zoology, geology, Roman history and an important coin collection. The Hunterian Art Gallery, opened in 1980, includes a reconstruction of Charles Rennie **Mackintosh**'s Glasgow home and an extensive collection of works by him, and also paintings by James McNeill Whistler, the **Glasgow Boys**, and the **Scottish Colourists**.

**Glasites** see John **Glas**

**Glas Maol** Mountain, a **Munro**, north of Glen Shee, 1068m (3504ft) high, close to the **Glenshee** skiing area.

**Glass, John, Glassites** see **Glas, John**

**gleann** see **glen**

**glebe** A piece of land belonging to the church, held by a minister as part of his remuneration. Today many glebes have been sold and built over.

**glen** Scots word for a valley, especially a narrow, steep-sided one, from Gaelic *gleann*. Common in place-names; see below, and see also **strath**.

**Glen Affric** (Gaelic **Gleann Afraig**) The forested valley of the River Affric which flows northeast through **Loch Affric** to join the River Glass near **Cannich**. The glen is surrounded by **Munros**, making it popular with walkers and climbers. Glenaffric Forest also offers walks and wildlife.

**Glenarn** Garden in **Rhu**, near Helensburgh. One of finest original specimens (1849) of Joseph Hooker's *Rhododendron*

*falconeri* grows here among a superb collection of rhododendrons and exotic trees and shrubs.

**Glen Artney** Valley of the Water of Ruchill which flows northeast and then north to join the River **Earn** near **Comrie**. It appears in Sir Walter **Scott**'s 'The Lady of the Lake'.

**Glen Brittle** Valley of the River Brittle which flows from the **Cuillins** in **Skye**, west and then south to enter Loch Brittle. The village of Glenbrittle lies on the coast at the end of the glen.

**Glenbuchat Castle** Roofless Z-plan tower house in **Strathdon**, Aberdeenshire, of the Gordons of Glenbuchat (the last of whom was a noted **Jacobite**). It was disused by 1738 and is now in the care of **Historic Scotland**.

**Glencairn, William Cunningham, 9th Earl of** (c.1610–64) Politician and soldier. Active in the **Covenanting** revolution, he joined the bulk of the aristocracy in reconciling himself with the Stewart dynasty and led Glencairn's Rising in the Highlands against General **Monck**'s Cromwellian forces in 1653. Though defeated the Rising made the Cromwellians anxious to appease the Scottish nobility.

**Glencalvie** Valley in **Sutherland** of the Water of Glencalvie which flows north to join the River Carron, now a large sporting estate; Glencalvie Lodge has self-catering accommodation. The name has become a poignant memorial to the **Clearances**. In 1845 the people of Glencalvie were evicted from their homes by the Duke of **Sutherland** and took shelter in nearby Croick Church, one of the **Parliamentary** churches, built in overcrowded parts of the **Highlands** in the 1820s. The words they scratched on windows can still be seen today – 'Glen Calvie people was in the churchyard May 24th 1845', and 'Glen Calvie people the wicked generation'.

**Glen Clova** One of the **Angus** glens, to the north of **Kirriemuir**, through which the River South **Esk** runs. The 16th-century Clova Castle, a home of the Ogilvies, is a ruin.

**Glencoe** (Gaelic **Gleann Comhann**) Dramatic mountainous valley lying between **Rannoch** Moor to the southeast and Loch **Leven** to the north. The village of Glencoe is near **Loch Leven**. The main A82 road from **Fort William** to **Glasgow** runs through

G

the glen, which is popular with tourists, offering walking, climbing and skiing. Most of the area has belonged to the **National Trust for Scotland** since the 1930s. It is forever associated with the events of February 1692, known as the Massacre of Glencoe. As part of an agreement with the **Jacobite** chiefs loyal to the exiled **James**, King **William** required an oath of allegiance. Alasdair MacIan, chief of the MacDonalds of Glencoe, was prevented by bad weather and misunderstanding from taking the oath within the set time. This failure was used as an excuse for retargetting a savage primitive strike originally aimed at MacDonell of Glengarry: The MacDonalds (or Maclains) of Glencoe became the new victims. Troops quartered in local homes for 12 days, enjoying their hospitality, turned one morning and murdered 38 of the clan, including the chief and some of his family. John Dalrymple, Master of Stair, Secretary of State for Scotland (later 1st Earl of **Stair**), was believed to be responsible, but the reputation of King William in Scotland was also damaged. These events are explored along with other aspects of the history and environment of the area in the Glencoe Visitor Centre.

**Glencorse** Village in Midlothian, 3km (2mi) north of **Penicuik**. The Barracks here were the headquarters of the **Royal Scots** for 100 years, and more recently of the Army Training Regiment.

**Glen Derry** (Gaelic **Gleann Doire**) Valley in the **Cairngorms** of the Derry Burn which flows south to join the Lui Water at Derry Lodge.

**Glen Dessary** Valley of the River Dessary which flows southeast from Garbh Chioch Mhor (a **Munro**, 1013m/3323ft), to join the River Pean just to the west of the head of **Loch Arkaig**. The village of **Glendessary** is near the foot of the Glen.

**Glendevon** Valley of the River **Devon** running east through the Ochil Hills to the village of Glendevon. It has 3 water-supply reservoirs for **Fife**. The 15th-century Glendevon Castle belonged to William **Douglas**, 8th Earl of Douglas. It was extensively rebuilt in later centuries, and is now privately owned.

**Glen Docherty** Valley that runs from a point 8km (5mi) west of **Achnasheen** northwest to **Kinlochewe**. There are excellent views of **Loch Maree** and the mountains surrounding it.

**Glendoick** House 9km (6mi) east of **Perth**, a tall mid Georgian villa, built in 1740. The Cox family have developed a fine collection of southeast Asian plants, rhododendrons particularly, over a period of 80 years and are continually adding to them from their expeditions and their breeding of garden-worthy rhododendrons.

**Glen Doll** One of the **Angus** glens, a valley of the White Water which flows southeast to join the South **Esk** at the head of **Glen Clova**. Surrounded by mountains, it is a popular glen for walkers.

**Glen Douglas** Valley of the Douglas Water which flows eastwards to enter **Loch Lomond** at Inverbeg. It has major military installations.

**Gleneagles** Valley running through the **Ochil** Hills. The lands belonged for many centuries to the Haldane family. Their medieval castle, now ruined, was abandoned in favour of Gleneagles House, built in 1720; its main block was never constructed. A 12th-century chapel, rebuilt in the 16th century, which gave the glen its name (from Gaelic *eaglais* meaning church) was restored in 1925 as a family war memorial. The name Gleneagles is now synonymous with the internationally renowned 5-star hotel near **Auchterarder**, planned by the Caledonian Railway in 1909 and built 1913–25 to designs by James Miller and Matthew Adams. It has 2 championship **golf** courses and 2 others, and a prize-winning restaurant (see Andrew **Fairlie**).

**Glen Einich** see **Loch Einich**

**Glenelg** (Gaelic **Gleann Eilg**) Village in a remote Highland peninsula, lying across the **Sound of Sleat** from **Skye**. A ferry crosses to Kylerhea, following a route once popular with cattle drovers. Two well-preserved **brochs** are nearby, in the care of **Historic Scotland**. The area featured in Gavin Maxwell's novel *Ring of Bright Water* and a cairn marks the site of his cottage; see also **Kyleakin**.

**Glen Esk** The most easterly of the **Angus** glens, the valley of the River North **Esk**, which flows east from the **Grampian** mountains and then southeast. The Glen Esk Folk Museum, housed in a former shooting lodge, is at Tarfside, 14km (9mi) northwest of **Edzell**.

**Glen Etive** (Gaelic **Gleann Éite**) Mountainous valley of the River Etive, running southwest from **Glen Coe** to **Loch Etive**.

**Glen Falloch** see **Falloch, Glen, River** and **Falls of**

**Glenfarclas** Distillery at **Ballindalloch**, established in 1836, which produces a well-known malt **whisky**. It still belongs to the Grant family, who acquired it in 1865. It has a visitor centre.

**Glen Feshie** (Gaelic **Gleann Feisidh**) The valley, to the west of the **Cairngorms**, of the River Feshie which flows northwards to join the River **Spey** at **Kincraig**. The River contains the best example in the UK of a braided reach, where the river flows in several shallow interconnected channels. Glenfeshie Forest lies to the east.

*Glenfiddich whisky label.*

**Glenfiddich** Distillery on **Speyside**, near **Dufftown**. One of the best-known malt **whisky** distilleries, it was one of the first to popularise the drinking of single malts in the 1960s. It was founded in 1887 by William **Grant**, and is still owned by the company. It has a visitor centre.

**Glenfinnan** (Gaelic **Gleann Fhionain**) Village at the mouth of Glen Finnan and at the head of **Loch Shiel**, on the 'Road to the Isles' from **Fort William** to **Mallaig**. It was here that Prince Charles Edward **Stewart** gathered his supporters and raised his standard at the start of the 1745 **Jacobite Rising**. A column topped with a statue of a clansman stands as a memorial on the lochside, erected by Alexander Macdonald of Glenaladale in 1815; the **National Trust for Scotland** runs a visitor centre nearby. Glenfinnan is also known as one of the most spectacular points on the West Highland Railway line, with an impressive 21-arch concrete viaduct, built by Sir Robert **MacAlpine**.

**Glen Fruin** (Gaelic **Gleann Freòin**) Valley, near **Helensburgh**, of the Fruin Water which flows southeast to **Loch Lomond**. In 1603 a battle here between the Colquhouns and the MacGregors led to the proscription of the MacGregors.

**Glen Garry** (Inverness-shire) Valley of the River **Garry** which flows east from Loch Quoich to Loch Garry. It belonged to the MacDonnells of Glengarry. Their chief raised a regiment, the Glengarry Fencibles, in 1774. Between 1802 and 1804 many of the Glengarry Fencibles emigrated to Glengarry County, Ontario, where the regiment was re-formed and fought against the American invaders in the war of 1812.

**Glen Garry** (Perthshire) see **Garry, Loch** and **River**

**Glengoyne** see **Dumgoyne**

**Glen Isla** The most westerly of the **Angus** glens, valley of the River Isla which flows south from **Glenshee**, eventually joining the River **Tay** to the east of **Coupar Angus**. When snow conditions permit, it is popular for Nordic skiing.

**Glenkinchie** Distillery near **Pencaitland**, East Lothian, established in 1837. One of the few remaining Lowland distilleries to produce single malt **whisky**. It has a visitor centre with a Museum of Malt Whisky Production.

**Glenkindie** Small northeast village near the confluence of the River **Don** and the Kindie Burn. To the west is Glenkindie House, a 16th- and 17th-century U-plan house, Georgianised in 1741; the main block was largely rebuilt in asymmetrical form by Sydney **Mitchell** in 1900. It has splendid 17th- and 18th-century walled gardens with topiary work.

**Glenlivet** Isolated village, 16km (10mi) north of **Tomintoul**, with a famous distillery which was founded by George Smith in 1824. It is now owned by Pernod Ricard, and includes a visitor centre. At the Battle of Glenlivet, fought in 1594 to the northeast of the glen, government forces under the Earl of Argyll were defeated by the 6th Earl of Huntly.

**Glen Lochay** (Gaelic **Gleann Lòchaidh**) Valley of the River Lochay which flows east to **Loch Tay** at **Killin**.

**Glen Lochy** (Gaelic **Gleann Lòchaidh**) Valley, in **Argyll**, of the River Lochy which flows southwest to join the River **Orchy** near **Dalmally**.

**Glen Lyon** (Gaelic **Gleann Lìobhunn**) Perthshire valley of the River **Lyon** which flows eastwards from Loch Lyon to join the **Tay** between **Aberfeldy** and **Kenmore**. The 17th-century Glenlyon House was remodelled for Sir Donald Currie in 1891 by Dunn and Watson from sketches by James Marjoribanks MacLaren, who designed the remarkable Arts and Crafts steading and farmhouse adjoining it. See also **Meggernie Castle**.

**Glenmorangie** Distillery on the **Dornoch Firth**, to the northwest of **Tain**, established in 1843, it produces one of the most popular malt whiskies. It has a visitor centre.

**Glenmore** Area just to the north of the **Cairngorms**. Glenmore Forest Park is managed by the Forestry Commission; it includes a remnant of the ancient Caledonian pinewoods. The area offers many outdoor activities, including watersports on Loch **Morlich**. Glenmore Lodge is an outdoor training centre.

**Glenmore** see **Great Glen**

**G**

**Glen Nevis** (Gaelic **Gleann Nibheis**) Valley of the River Nevis, running west and then northwest below the slopes of **Ben Nevis**, with the main starting point for its climbers at the entrance to the glen. It was used for filming scenes from Mel Gibson's **Braveheart**. A visitor centre provides information on the history and wildlife of the area.

**Glennie, Evelyn** (1965– ) Musician, b. Aberdeen. An internationally renowned composer and percussionist, she has been deaf since childhood. She has performed with some of the world's finest orchestras and has released many solo recordings. Many percussion works have been written specially for her.

**Glenochil** see **Tullibody**

**Glen Ogle** (Gaelic **Gleann Oguil**) Leads 11km (7mi) northwestwards from **Lochearnhead**, following the course of the River Ogle. The main A85 road passes through the glen, and the former **Callendar** and **Oban** Railway through the glen is now a cycleway.

**Glen Orchy** (Gaelic **Gleann Urchaidh**) Valley which carries the River **Orchy** from **Bridge of Orchy** to the head of **Loch Awe**. The Campbells of Glenorchy later became Earls of **Breadalbane**.

**Glen Prosen** One of the **Angus** glens, carrying the Prosen Water to join the South **Esk** at the foot of **Glen Clova**.

**Glenrothes** (pop. 38,679) Town in Fife, 8km (5mi) from **Kirkcaldy**. It was founded as Scotland's second New Town in 1949 (largely on the basis of a new coalmine which soon failed), and is now the administrative centre of **Fife** Council. Much of the housing was built in the 1950s and 1960s, and a number of industrial estates provide employment around the town, especially in electronics, giving the area the nickname of 'Silicon Glen'.

**Glen Roy** (Gaelic **Gleann Ruaidh**) Valley of the River Roy which flows south to join the River **Spean** at **Roy Bridge**. At the end of the Ice Age the valley contained a loch, and its receding levels are marked by the 'Parallel Roads', 3 terraces on the slopes on either side.

**Glen Sannox** (Gaelic **Gleann Shanaig**) Valley on the island of **Arran**, leading down from the mountain Cir Mhor to Sannox Bay on the northeast coast of the island. Barytes was fomerly mined there.

**Glenshee** (Gaelic **Gleann Sith**) Dramatic valley reaching northwards from **Blairgowrie** into the **Grampian** mountains, containing one of Scotland's leading ski centres, based largely on the **Cairnwell** and **Meall Odhar**. The A93 runs through the glen and over the **Cairnwell** Pass to the north.

**Glen Shiel** (Gaelic **Gleann Seile**) Valley running southeastwards from **Loch Duich** to Loch Cluanie, between the **Five Sisters of Kintail** and the **Saddle**, making it a popular area for hillwalking and climbing. A battle took place here in 1719; see **Jacobite Risings**.

**Glen Shira** (Gaelic **Gleann Siora**) Valley of the River Shira which flows southwestwards into **Loch Fyne** north of **Inveraray**. At the top are reservoirs forming part of a large hydroelectric scheme. Lower down is the ruin of a house where **Rob Roy** lived in exile for several years.

**Glentanar** (Gaelic **Gleann Tanar**) Forested valley, running southwest from **Aboyne**, Aberdeenshire. The Glentanar estate offers walking and fishing to tourists, and includes the Braeloine Visitor Centre.

**Glen Tilt** (Gaelic **Gleann Teilt**) Valley of the River **Tilt**, eroded along a major geological fault; it flows in a southwesterly direction from the **Cairngorms** to join the River **Garry** at **Blair Atholl**, also eroded along a major geological fault.

**Glentrool** Valley of the Water of Trool which flows from Loch Trool southwest to join the River **Cree** 15km (9mi) north of **Newton Stewart**. The Glen Trool Forest Park forms part of the extensive **Galloway** Forest Park. The village of Glentrool is at the western end. The **Southern Upland Way** passes through the Glen. The Battle of Glentrool took place in April 1307, when **Robert I** defeated an English force. It was also the site of the killing of 6 **Covenanters** in January 1685.

**Glenuig** Small village on Glenuig Bay to the south of the Sound of **Arisaig**, very isolated until the building of a road from **Kinlochmoidart** to **Lochailort** in the 1960s.

*Glenmorangie whisky label.*

**G**

Although other countries, especially the Netherlands, also make claims to its obscure origins, the game of golf is inextricably linked with Scotland. The word golf, in Scotland also known as gowf, and in times past as goff, goif, and gouff etc, almost certainly comes from a medieval Dutch word, *kolf*, meaning a stick used in some kind of similar ball game. How the modern game developed is the subject of international dispute. Its popularity in Scotland from early times was helped on the east coast by the links, ie stretches of undulating sandy ground which provided ideal terrain for the game, and many of the best golf courses are to be found there to this day.

Golf was played at all levels of society. The expenditure of King **James IV** on a visit to **Falkland** included the purchase of 'golf clubbes and balles ....that he playit with', and subsequent monarchs, among them **Mary, Queen of Scots**, were also keen players. An Act of Parliament of 1457 tried to prevent ordinary people from playing golf and football, in favour of archery practice. Later prohibitions were of Sunday golf, with the stricter observance of the Sabbath after the **Reformation**.

In the 18th century the game became more structured. The Honourable Company of Edinburgh Golfers, originally just the Gentlemen Golfers, founded in 1744, is widely accepted as the world's first golf club; it is now based at **Muirfield**, East Lothian. Ten years later, the **Royal and Ancient** Golf Club began as the Society of **St Andrews** Golfers. For the following century and more, different clubs played by different rules. Even by 1860, when the Open Championship was first held, golf had not become the standard 18-hole contest of today, but gradually the authority of the Royal and Ancient Golf Club was accepted. The R&A, as it is known, is one of the 2 governing bodies of the sport, along with the United States Golf Association.

Before 1848 the ball was a leather case stuffed tightly with feathers: it was fragile and expensive. Then a ball of gutta percha (a kind of rubber from the East Indies) was introduced. It was much cheaper and enabled the game to grow rapidly. In 1885 there were 161 clubs in Britain; 20 years later there were 1939.

The first Open, held at **Prestwick**, was won by Willie Park, but subsequent playings were dominated by a father and son. Tom **Morris** senior, or Old Tom, won the 2nd, 3rd, 5th and 8th Opens; Young Tom won the trophy in 1868, 1869 and 1870, thereby winning the Championship Belt outright. Without a trophy, the Open was not held the following year, but in 1872 it returned with a new prize, the claret jug, which is still competed for. Young Tom won it that year too. The names of those early champions are still revered, and the Open enjoys a

secure place as the greatest tournament in the golfing world. Yet, although Scotland continued to produce great players, and participation in the sport continued among men and women alike, there was a gradual decline before and during World War I. The recession of the 1930s and the period of austerity during and after World War II also had a depressive effect.

After the introduction of the rubber-cored ball, invented in the US in 1902, the game became increasingly popular in America and after World War I the best Americans were the world's leading players, but only a few were able to travel to Britain. In the 1950s, improved economic conditions, particularly the boom in transatlantic air travel, led to the transformation of golf into the global game it is today. The St Andrews Open of 1955 was the first to be televised, and 5 years later at the same venue the American Arnold Palmer attracted a great following. The Open Championship is held annually on one of a number of British courses, of which the Scottish venues are St Andrews, Muirfield, **Carnoustie**, **Troon** and **Turnberry**. The Old Course at St Andrews is recognised as golf's spiritual home, and the Open departs from its usual rotation to return there for special anniversaries. It is not the most intriguing or complex of courses, but its setting and its historic significance ensure it continues to attract sporting tourists from as far afield as Japan.

Just as their courses do, so Scottish golfers also maintain a prominent position in the game. Bernard Gallacher, 8 times a competitor in the Ryder Cup, a biennial competition between Europe and the US, was also a successful team captain. Sam **Torrance**, European captain in 2002, will long be remembered for the putt which won Europe the Cup in 1985. Sandy Lyle, the Anglo-Scot, also enjoyed a halcyon period in the 1980s, winning the Open in 1985 and the US Masters in 1988. The most consistently successful Scots golfer of recent decades has been Colin **Montgomerie**. Although yet to win one of the 4 majors, he was the leading player on the European Tour for 7 consecutive years.

Such players are now richly rewarded for their talents, and their lifestyles have more in common with professionals from other countries than they do with their less gifted compatriots. But, while golf elsewhere has at times had an élitist image, and been an expensive pastime, in Scotland it has also remained a sport of the people. There are clubs and courses which can only be accessed by the well connected, but public courses abound. With rugby only retaining a narrow social base, and Scotland's football team having seen its fortunes dip dramatically, there is a good case to be made for golf being the country's real national sport.

**G**

**Glen Urquhart** (Gaelic **Gleann Urchardain**) Valley of the River Enrick which flows southeast and then east through Loch Meikle to **Loch Ness** at **Drumnadrochit**.

**Glenwhan** Garden near Dunragit, to the east of **Stranraer**, one of the most recent gardens, developed from wild moorland. By providing shelter the garden now contains a remarkable collection of rare trees, shrubs and herbaceous plants around 4 ponds. Viewpoints on the hillocks give amazing views of the garden and beyond.

**Gloag, Ann** see **Stagecoach**

**Glomach, Falls of** (Gaelic **Eas na Glòmaich**) Remote spectacular water-

*The Royal and Ancient Clubhouse and the Swilcan Bridge, Old Course, St Andrews.*

fall in **Kintail**, dropping 113m (370ft). The Falls are on the Kintail and Morvich estate, which now belongs to the **National Trust for Scotland**. Although access is comparatively difficult, the National Trust for Scotland Visitor Centre at Kintail gives suggested routes.

**Goatfell** (Gaelic **Gaoda-bheinn**) The highest peak on **Arran**, (874m/2866ft), lying to the north of **Brodick**. It is part of an area which belongs to the **National Trust for Scotland**.

**Goblin Ha** see **Gifford**

**Gododdin** Kingdom of the people in southeast Scotland and northeast England, known to the Romans as the 'Votadini', probably centred on **Edinburgh**. The original of an early poem, *The Gododdin* of **Aneirin**, in the Brythonic language of the south of Scotland, is believed to have been composed in or near **Edinburgh** in the 6th century, recording failed efforts to oppose the expansive Anglian kingdom of **Bernicia**; it survives in a Welsh manuscript.

**Godred Crovan** (Gaelic **Goraidh Crobhan**) (d.1095) King of Man and the Isles, b. Islay. He conquered the Isle of Man in 1079, and brought together an extensive western sea-based kingdom. Also known as 'King Orry'.

**gold** Gold has been extracted in Scotland since at least the 15th century, especially in the area around **Leadhills** and **Wanlockhead** in Lanarkshire, which provided the gold not only for the Scottish crown but also for the mace for the new **Scottish Parliament** in 1999. The Wanlockhead Mining Museum

is situated here, and gold panning can still be learned and practised in the area. Another area associated with gold is Kildonan in **Sutherland**, where a 'gold rush' took place in 1868–9 following the discovery of gold in the Kildonan Burn, a tributary of the River **Helmsdale**. Gold has more recently been mined in the hills above **Tyndrum** in Argyll.

**golf** see p.170

**Golspie** Village on the northeast coast, 16km (10mi) north of **Dornoch**. St Andrew's Church, built 1736–7 and enlarged 1750–1, includes the original canopied pulpit with a sounding board, wood panelling and carving. Behind Golspie is Ben Bhraggie, on which stands a massive statue of the 1st Duke of **Sutherland** by Sir Francis Chantrey, erected 1836–8. **Dunrobin** Castle is nearby.

**Gorbals** Area in central **Glasgow**, south of the **Clyde**, originally a separate village. It had a brief spell as an expensive suburb in the early 19th century, but the wealthy soon moved further out and it became known for the great density of population housed in its tenements, and after World War II for poverty and deprivation, when many tenements were subdivided in an attempt to solve the postwar housing crisis. In the 1960s high-rise flats were built, some by Sir Basil **Spence**, which have since been demolished. The area has also been known for its strong sense of community, and regeneration is currently underway. Current landmarks include the **Citizens' Theatre**.

**G**

**Gordon, Alexander, of Auchintoul** (1669–1751) Soldier, b. Banffshire. He rose to the rank of General in the Russian army and served as military tutor to Peter the Great, of whom he wrote a biography. He returned to Scotland in 1711 and fought on the Jacobite side in the 1715 **Jacobite Rising**.

**Gordon, Douglas** (1966– ) Artist, b. Glasgow. Internationally recognised for his work using text and film, with which he explores and highlights personal and psychological conditions. He has become widely known for his use of classic movies, which he has shown in slow-motion (such as his *24 Hour Psycho*) or otherwise manipulated to draw attention to human fears and neuroses. He won the Turner Prize in 1996.

**Gordon, George** see **Huntly, 4th Earl of**

**Gordon, George** see **Huntly, 1st Marquis of**

**Gordon, Hannah** (1941– ) Actress, b. Edinburgh. She has acted for theatre, radio, film and television, and her credits include the TV series *Upstairs, Downstairs* (1971) and the films *Spring and Port Wine* (1970) and *The Elephant Man* (1980). She often narrates television and radio programmes.

**Gordon, Harry** (1893–1954) Entertainer, b. Aberdeen. He performed as 'The Laird o' Inversnecky', starring at the **Aberdeen** Beach Pavilion from 1924 to 1940. In pantomime he had a very successful partnership with Will **Fyffe**, notably at the Alhambra Theatre in **Glasgow**.

**Gordon, Sir John Watson** (1788–1864) Artist, b. Edinburgh. He studied at Edinburgh's Trustees' Academy, and after the death of Henry **Raeburn**, became Scotland's pre-eminent portrait painter, whose sitters included Sir Walter **Scott** and James **Hogg**. In 1850 he was appointed President of the **Royal Scottish Academy** and The Queen's Limner in Scotland.

**Gordon, Robert** see **Robert Gordon University**

**Gordon, Robert, of Straloch** (1580–1661) Cartographer, b. near Inverurie. He revised and completed Timothy **Pont**'s maps of Scotland, preparing them for publication in **Blaeu's Atlas**.

**Gordon, Thomas** (d.1741) Naval commander. After an early career in the Scottish and British navies, he took service under Peter the Great in Russia from 1717, rising to the rank of Admiral and becoming Governor of Kronstadt.

**Gordon District** see **Grampian Region**

**Gordon Highlanders** Regiment of the British army raised in 1794 by the 4th Duke of Gordon (with the help of the Duchess who is said to have offered to kiss new recruits). The regiment served in Europe, including at Waterloo, and throughout the British Empire. In 1881 it merged with the 75th Regiment. They fought in both world wars and have been involved in peace-keeping and anti-terrorist operations. In 1994 they joined with the **Queen's Own Highlanders (Seaforth and Camerons)** to form the **Highlanders**. Traditionally the regiment drew its recruits from the Northeast, and the Gordon Highlanders Museum is in **Aberdeen**.

**Gosford House** Seat of the Earls of Wemyss and March, to the north of **Longniddry**, East Lothian, designed by Robert **Adam** 1790, but not built until 1800 and not completed. New wings with magnificent double-height entrance hall in marble and alabaster by William Young were completed in 1891. It has a remarkable park with artificial lakes and islands, and a pyramidal mausoleum of c.1800. The towered west lodge is by the historian architect Robert William Billings (1854). Open to the public in summer.

**Gospatrick** see **Cospatric**

**Gourock** Town south of the **Clyde**, to the west of **Greenock**. It has attracted visitors travelling 'doon the watter' from **Glasgow** since the 19th century. A new railway pier, opened in 1890, made it a focal point for Clyde steamer services. The **Caledonian MacBrayne** ferry company is based here. Ferries run from Gourock to **Dunoon**, **Hunters Quay**, **Helensburgh** and **Kilcreggan**. Cloch **Lighthouse** was built in 1797 on **Cloch Point** to the southwest.

**Govan** Area of **Glasgow** south of the River **Clyde**, once a separate village, and later a **burgh**, with an impressive French Beaux Arts town hall designed by Thomas Sandilands (1897–1901). It is believed to be the site of a 6th-century Celtic monastery. The present Old Parish Church, designed by Robert Rowand **Anderson**, dates from 1883–8, but has an outstanding collection of early Christian stones, moved from the churchyard to the church in 1926; they include a richly carved sarcophagus which traditionally held relics of **Constantine I**. Govan expanded with the deepening of the Clyde, and by the later 19th century was a centre of shipbuilding and engineering. As the industry declined in the later 20th century, the area suffered unemployment and depression, but the former Fairfield yard is still building ships.

**Gow, Nathaniel** (1766–1831) Musician, b. Inver, near Dunkeld. Son of Niel **Gow**, he was a fiddler, composer and teacher, and published his own and his father's works.

**Gow, Niel** (1727–1807) Musician, b. Inver, near Dunkeld. A fiddler and composer of **strathspey** and **reel** tunes, he flourished under the patronage of the Duke of Atholl, becoming celebrated in **Edinburgh** and London society. He produced a musical family, the most famous of whom was Nathaniel **Gow**.

**Gowrie, William Ruthven, 1st Earl of** (c.1541–84) The leader of the **Ruthven** Raid of 1582, and therefore briefly leader of the government. Following **James VI**'s escape from captivity he was executed for treason. His father had been a key figure in the murder of David **Rizzio**.

**Gowrie Conspiracy** On 5 August 1600 **James VI** went to Gowrie Castle, apparently on the invitation of Alexander, Master of Ruthven. What happened next remains unclear, and rests on the testimony of the king, who claimed that the Master and his supporters threatened to assassinate him. The king's supporters came to the rescue, and the Master of Ruthven and his brother, the Earl of Gowrie, were killed. The true circumstances of their deaths have provoked debate ever since.

**Graham, James** see **Montrose, 1st Marquis of**

**Graham, James Gillespie** (1776–1855) Architect, b. **Dunblane**. He designed the Moray estate in **Edinburgh**, and was also known for his Gothic-style churches, notably St Andrew's Roman Catholic Cathedral, **Glasgow**, and his castellated mansions, such as Duns Castle and Duninadd. In his later years he collaborated with A W N Pugin, notably on the interiors of **Taymouth** Castle and the Victoria Hall in Edinburgh (later Tolbooth St John's Church, now The Hub).

**Graham, John, of Claverhouse** see **Dundee, John Graham of Claverhouse, 1st Viscount**

**Graham, Robert Bontine Cunninghame** (1852–1936) Politician and writer, b. London. He was Liberal MP for Northwest Lanarkshire 1886–92, and was first President of both the **Scottish Labour Party** (1888) and the **National Party of Scotland** (1928). Also known as 'Don Roberto', he spent some years in South America, and published books and articles about his travels there and in North Africa. His other works included history, biography, short stories, and *Notes on the District of Menteith* (1895).

**Graham, Thomas, Lord Lynedoch of Balgowan** (1748–1843) Military commander, b. near Methven, Perthshire. He raised the 90th Regiment of Foot, the Perthshire Volunteers, in 1793, and served with it in a number of campaigns, including Malta, Ireland and Spain. In the Peninsular War he won the Battle of Barossa and was second-in-command to Wellington. He was created Lord Lynedoch of Balgowan in 1814.

*Niel Gow, by Sir Henry Raeburn, 1787.*

**Grahame, Kenneth** (1859–1932) Author, b. Edinburgh. Best known for his children's book *The Wind in the Willows*, (1908), he also published collections of essays. He was Secretary of the Bank of England from 1898 to 1908.

**Graham's Dyke** see **Antonine Wall**

**Grainger, Thomas** (1795–1852) Civil engineer, b. Ratho, near Edinburgh. He formed with John **Miller** the firm of Grainger and Miller, the most prolific of Scotland's pioneering railway engineering firms. They designed, among other lines, the **Edinburgh** and **Glasgow** and North British **railways**, and the lines that became the Glasgow and South Western Railway in 1850. The quality of their design is still evident in bridges, viaducts, tunnels, and cuttings on these routes.

**Grampian Region** One of the 9 regions forming the upper tier of local government from 1975 to 1996, formed from the former counties of **Aberdeenshire**, **Banffshire**, **Kincardineshire**, parts of **Moray** and the City of **Aberdeen**. It consisted of the districts of Aberdeen, Banff and Buchan, Gordon, Kincardine and Deeside, and Moray. See maps on pp.394–5 and **local government**.

**Grampians** Mountain area in north-central Scotland, between the **Highlands** and the **Lowlands**, formed of **Dalradian** metamorphic rocks and granites. It includes the **Cairngorms**.

**G**

*Grangemouth Refinery.*

**Grampian Television** see **Scottish Television**

**Grandtully** (pronounced 'grantly') Village on the River **Tay**, near **Aberfeldy**, a favourite spot for white-water canoeing. Grandtully Castle, 2km (1mi) to the southwest, is a 16th-century tower house to which a large mansion was added in 1893. The nearby 16th-century St Mary's church, built in 1533, in the care of **Historic Scotland**, has a biblical and heraldic painted ceiling of 1636.

**Grange, Lady, Rachel Erskine** (née **Chiesly**) (d.1743) Wife of James Erskine, Lord Grange (1679–1754) lawyer and politician, Lord Justice Clerk from 1710, who imprisoned her on Heisker and **St Kilda** for 7 years, to keep her from revealing his **Jacobite** sympathies.

**Grangemouth** (pop. 17,771) Town on the River **Forth**, at the eastern end of the **Forth and Clyde Canal**, which it was created to serve. Set in industrial Central Scotland, it has long been an important port, and was the main port for the **Carron** Ironworks. Today massive industrial expansion has taken place, and a BP **oil** refinery, now processing North Sea oil, and associated chemical plant dominate the landscape for miles around. The story of the development of the town is told in the Grangemouth Museum.

**Grant, Anne** (Mrs Grant of Laggan, née **MacVicar**) (1755–1838) Writer, b. Glasgow. Daughter of an army officer, she spent part of her childhood in America. She married James Grant, minister of **Laggan**, and after he died in 1801, leaving her with 8 children, she published a book of poems (1802), *Letters from the Mountains* (1806), *Memoirs of an American Lady* (1808) and *Essays on the*

*Superstitions of the Highlands* (1811). She lived in **Edinburgh** from 1810.

**Grant, Archibald, of Monymusk** (1696–1778) Agricultural improver. He was MP for **Aberdeenshire**, until expelled from the house for corruption. Latterly he divided his time between trying to marry wealthy elderly women and innovative and successful developments on his estate, including enclosure, drainage, crop rotation and new crops.

**Grant, Elizabeth, of Rothiemurchus** (1797–1885) Writer, b. Edinburgh. She is remembered for her diaries, published posthumously as *Memoirs of a Highland Lady*, *A Highland Lady in France* and *A Highland Lady in Ireland*. These vividly describe her life as the daughter of a **Speyside** landed family, the family's financial troubles, and her later life married to Colonel Henry Smith in Ireland.

**Grant, Sir Francis** (1803–1878) Artist, b. Edinburgh. Son of Francis Grant, Laird of Kilgraston, Grant's social position contributed to his success as a portrait painter. By the late 1830s he had become established in London, in demand particularly for his equestrian portraits. In the 1840s two portraits of Queen Victoria compounded his success. In 1866 he was elected President of the Royal Academy.

**Grant, William** (1839–1923) Distiller, b. **Dufftown**. He worked at Mortlach Distillery for 20 years before establishing the **Glenfiddich** distillery, which opened in 1887. The company William Grant & Sons has remained an independent family firm, and is still successful today.

**Granton** Area of **Edinburgh**, on the **Forth** between **Newhaven** and **Cramond**, originally an estate belonging to the Duke of Buccleuch, who built the impressive harbour to serve his coal interests and to provide a ferry to **Burntisland**, built by Robert Stevenson (1834–6) and Burgess & Walker of London (1837–44). It became the terminal of the world's first train ferry, which operated between Granton and Burntisland from 1847 until the opening of the **Forth** Railway **Bridge**. Granton Square, by William **Burn** (1838), provided the grand hotel required for carriage trade traffic. Thanks to the Buccleuch position at court, it welcomed Queen Victoria and Prince Albert in 1842. Granton was for many years a base for

**G**

a fleet of deep-sea trawlers. Today it is dominated by industrial premises including the gas holders of Granton Gas Works, but it is central to plans for the regeneration of Edinburgh's waterfront. Next to the gas works is Caroline Park, an imposing quadrangular mansion, built in the 1690s by Sir George Mackenzie of Tarbat (later Earl of **Cromartie**), on the basis of an earlier house. Known as Royston, it was renamed in honour of his daughter by the 2nd Duke of **Argyll**, who bought it in 1739. After many tears as a workplace, it is once more a private house.

**Grantown-on-Spey** (pop. 2166) Town in **Speyside**, formerly Castletoun of Freuchie. A planned town, it was laid out by Sir Ludovic Grant of Grant in 1765. Since Victorian times it has been a holiday town, with many hotels and guest houses. The Grantown Museum and Heritage Centre tells its history. **Castle Grant** lies on the edge of the town.

**Gray, Alasdair** (1934– ) Writer and artist, b. Glasgow. As an artist he has painted portraits and murals, but is best known for his work as an author He has published a number of novels, novellas and short-story collections, many of which he also illustrated. His works include the highly regarded *Lanark* (1982), *1982, Janine* (1984), *Poor Things* (1992) and *The Ends of Our Tethers* (short stories 2003). His writing has a strong element of social and political criticism. He was Professor of Creative Writing at **Glasgow University** from 2001 till 2003.

**Gray, Cardinal Gordon Joseph** (1910–93) Roman Catholic clergyman, b. Edinburgh. Ordained as a priest in 1935, he became Archbishop of **St Andrews** and **Edinburgh** in 1951 and a cardinal in 1969.

**Gray, John** see **Greyfriars' Bobby**

**Gray, Muriel** (1959– ) Journalist and television and radio presenter, b. East Kilbride. She has presented a wide range of television and radio shows, including Channel 4's *The Tube* (1982) and *The Munro Show* (1991), produced for Scottish TV by her own television production company, Gallus Besom. She was the first female rector of **Edinburgh University** (1988–91). She has also published horror fiction. With her husband, Hamish Barbour, she runs a production company; formerly Ideal World, it has now joined with **Wark**-Clements to form IWC Media.

**Gray's School of Art** see **Robert Gordon University**

**Great Cause** Legal process to determine the rightful ruler of Scotland after the death of **Alexander III**'s last direct heir, **Margaret, Maid of Norway**, in 1290. There were 2 main claimants to the vacant throne, Robert Bruce, lord of Annandale

(grandfather of **Robert I**) and John **Balliol**. The English king, Edward I, eventually adjudicated in favour of the latter, who became King John in November 1292. During the legal process Edward had ensured that his status as overlord of Scotland was recognised. Scottish rejection of this relationship with the English king led to the **Wars of Independence** from 1296.

**Great Cumbrae** see **Cumbrae**

**Great Glen** A geological faultline extending for 96km (60mi) from **Inverness** on the east coast to **Fort William** on the west, effectively divides the **Highlands** in two, creating this beautiful glen, also known as Glenmore. Since the 1820s the major lochs – **Ness, Oich** and **Lochy** – have been linked by the **Caledonian Canal** which runs the length of the glen. The Great Glen Way offers a relatively flat means of crossing the Highlands on foot (some of it on roads), a journey of around 5 days.

**Great Michael, the** At the time one of the biggest and most powerful ships in Christendom, the *Great Michael* was built at **Newhaven**, near **Edinburgh**, on the orders of **James IV**. Completed in 1511, it took 6 years to build the 73m (240ft) long fighting ship, which reputedly used up the forests of Fife in its construction. It had little impact, however, on the course of the Anglo-Scottish war in 1513 and was later sold to France.

**Great North of Scotland Railway** see **railways**, p.312

**'Greek' Thomson** see **Thomson, Alexander**

**Greenbank Garden** Garden in the care of the **National Trust for Scotland**, at Clarkston, to the south of **Glasgow**. It is centred on a villa in the style of James **Gibbs** built by a Glasgow merchant c.1765–70.

**Greenknowe Tower** Classic L-plan tower house in the **Borders**, near Gordon, to the northeast of **Earlston**, built 1581 for the Setons of Touch. Roofless but otherwise complete; in the care of **Historic Scotland**.

**Greenock** (pop. 45,467) Town on the **Clyde**, 37km (23mi) north-west of **Glasgow**. A port which expanded rapidly from the mid 18th century, it was a frequent departure and arrival point for migrants between Scotland, Ireland and America. In the 1840s it had the worst slums in Europe. Major industries were **shipbuilding**, marine engineering and **sugar**, all of which suffered subsequent decline. It was badly blitzed in 1941. More recently the computer and electronics industries have been the main employers. It is now the administrative centre of **Inverclyde** Council. Greenock Morton is the local football club. The engineer James **Watt** was born here in 1736.

G

**Gregory family** Distinguished family of medical and scientific professors who flourished in the 17th and 18th centuries. David Gregory of Kinnairdie (1627–1720) was an Aberdeenshire laird and doctor. His brother James (1638–75) was a professor of mathematics who invented the reflecting telescope in 1661 and went on to be Professor of Mathematics in **St Andrews** (1668) and **Edinburgh** (1674). His nephew David Gregory, son of Kinnairdie, was Professor of Mathematics at Edinburgh (1683), and when deprived of his chair there at the Revolution of 1688 became Savilian Professor of Astronomy in the University of Oxford and an important populariser of the work of Sir Isaac Newton. James Gregory's grandson John Gregory (1724–73) became Professor of Medicine in Edinburgh in 1766, and a major figure in the **Scottish Enlightenment** due to his friendship with David **Hume** and Lord **Monboddo**. His publications are important sources for the status of women in Scotland as well as for the role of the physician in contemporary society.

**Gregory, William** (1803–58) Professor of Medicine and Chemistry, b. Edinburgh. A descendant of the remarkable **Gregory family**, he became Professor of Chemistry at **Glasgow**, **Aberdeen** and **Edinburgh** Universities.

**Greig, Gavin** (1856–1914) Folksong collector, b. Parkhill, Aberdeenshire. Along with Revd J B Duncan (1848–1917) he compiled an outstanding collection of folksongs. He was also a poet, writing in the Northeast folksong style. *The Greig-Duncan Folk Song Collection* was published in 8 volumes between 1981 and 2002. A 1-volume Performance Edition of the work is forthcoming.

**Greig, John** (1942– ) Football player and manager, b. Edinburgh. He joined **Rangers** in 1960, and devoted his career to the **Glasgow** club. The Scottish Player of the Year in 1966 and 1976, he was captain when Rangers won the European Cup Winners' Cup in 1972. He retired as a player in 1978, immediately becoming the club's manager, a position he held for 5 years. He won 44 Scotland caps.

**Greig, Samuel** (1735–88) Admiral, b. **Inverkeithing**, Fife. He played a significant role in modernising the Russian Navy, which he had joined in 1764, and recruited many officers from Scotland. His victories included the defeat of the Turks in the Battle of Chesme (1770) and he was made Admiral in 1782.

**Gretna** and **Gretna Green** The village of Gretna, near the English border, was built during World War I near the older

*Greyfriars' Bobby statue, Edinburgh.*

village of Gretna Green, to house workers in an enormous military explosives factory, which was demolished after the war. Gretna Green has a reputation as a refuge for eloping couples which began in 1754 when irregular marriages – before witnesses without a minister – were outlawed south of the border. In the 20th century the differing age of parental consent in Scotland and England, which continued until 1969, perpetuated Gretna Green's role. Nowadays the Old Blacksmith Shop, where the weddings traditionally took place, has been developed into a tourist attraction. The village is also associated with the worst railway disaster in Britain, which took place nearby at Quintinshill in May 1915. A troop train carrying two companies of **Royal Scots** crashed into a stationary train, and was in turn hit by another train; the wreckage caught fire, causing the deaths of 215 soldiers and the serious injury of many more.

**Greyfriars' Bobby** Famous 19th-century **Edinburgh** terrier. When his master, John Gray, was buried in Greyfriars Churchyard in 1858, the dog Bobby refused to leave his graveside. He was fed by Edinburgh residents, and awarded the Freedom of the City. He died in 1872. A statue of the dog stands near the entrance to the churchyard and he has been the subject of numerous books and films, including a proposed new film.

**Grey Mare's Tail** Waterfall 16km (10mi) northeast of **Moffat**, which drops 61m (200ft) from Loch Skeen into Moffat Water. The surrounding area is cared for by the **National Trust for Scotland**; with many rare plants the Moffat Hills is now a Special Area of Conservation.

**Greywalls** see **Gullane**

**Grierson, John** (1898–1972) Film producer, b. near **Doune**. A pioneer of documentary film-making in Britain and in Canada, his work included *The Drifters* (1929), an innovative film looking at North Sea herring fishing. He presented *This Wonderful World*, a series featuring different documentaries for Scottish Television. He also established the National Film Board of Canada, and became Head of Film with UNESCO in 1946.

**Grieve, Christopher Murray** see **MacDiarmid, Hugh**

**Grieve, John** (1924–2003) Actor, b. Glasgow. A variety performer with Stanley **Baxter** and Jimmy **Logan**, he also had bit parts in some films. He is best remembered as the lugubrious, accident-prone engineer, MacPhail, in the 1960s TV series *The Vital Spark*.

**Grimond, Jo** (1913–93) Politician, b. St Andrews. He was Liberal MP for **Orkney** and **Shetland** from 1950 to 1983. As leader of the Liberals from 1956 to 1967 he led the modernisation of the party and saw an improvement in their fortunes.

**Gruinard Bay** Sandy bay with beautiful views in the northwest, about 18km (11mi) north of **Poolewe**. The south side of the bay has the oldest rocks in Scotland. Gruinard Island, in the bay, was used by the Ministry of Defence in 1942 as a site for anthrax testing. Signs were erected forbidding the public to land. The island was decontaminated in 1987 and officially declared safe in 1990. Gruinard House garden has an excellent collection of plants primarily laid out for their foliage and texture effect.

**Guardbridge** Village in Fife, 5km (3mi) from **St Andrews**, on the estuary of the River **Eden**; the original bridge which gave the village its name was built by Bishop **Wardlaw** of St Andrews in the early 15th century. It was the site of an important grain **whisky** distillery, converted to a paper mill in the late 19th century, which still operates.

**Guardian** Term used in the 13th and 14th centuries to refer to the regent or governor of the kingdom. Six Guardians were appointed following the death of **Alexander III**, and the title was in use again after the abdication of John **Balliol** in 1296. William **Wallace** was appointed one of the Guardians in 1297.

**guga** Gaelic word for the young of the solan goose (gannet), eaten as a delicacy on the island of **Lewis**; see **Sula Sgeir**.

**Guid Nychburris Festival** see **Dumfries**

**Guise, Mary of** (1515-60) Queen and Queen Regent, b. France. The daughter of Claude de Lorraine, Duke of Guise, she married **James V**. She was sometimes also known as Mary of Lorraine. The mother of **Mary, Queen of Scots**, she became Regent in 1554, during her daughter's minority, and supported the French and Catholic cause against the English and Protestant party.

**guiser, guising** see **Halloween, Up Helly Aa**

**Gullane** (pop. 2172) Coastal town in **East Lothian**, near **North Berwick**, now a residential area. With extensive sandy beaches, it attracts many visitors. It is famed for its proximity to **Muirfield** Golf Course, and also offers 3 additional 18-hole golf courses. The ruins of the 12th-century church remain. Greywalls, a mansion and garden designed in 1901 by Edwin Lutyens and Gertrude Jekyll, is now a hotel.

**Gunn, Neil M** (1891–1973) Writer, b. Dunbeath, Caithness. His novels were influenced by his passion for Highland history and society, and include *Butcher's Broom* (1934), on the Highland **Clearances**, *Highland River* (1937) and *The Silver Darlings* (1941). *The Green Isle of the Great Deep* (1944) is an anti-totalitarian fable. The autobiographical *The Atom of Delight* (1956) reflects his spiritual journey, including his interest in Zen Buddhism. A friend of Hugh **MacDiarmid**, he became part of the 20th-century Scottish literary renaissance.

**Guthrie, Sir James** (1859–1930) Artist, b. Greenock. Along with his fellow **Glasgow Boys**, in the 1880s Guthrie introduced into Scottish art a new naturalism in painting, which rejected the sentimentality that had come to characterise much Victorian art. His most progressive work was produced at the rural artists' colonies of Brig o' Turk in the **Trossachs** and at **Cockburnspath**; later in life he worked predominantly as a portraitist.

**Guthrie, Thomas** (1803–73) Minister, b. Brechin. At the **Disruption** he joined the **Free Church**, and became the first minister of Free St John's, Castlehill, **Edinburgh**. His main concern was for destitute children, and he was a founder of the Ragged Schools in 1847, which offered free education to poor children.

**Gylen Castle** see **Kerrera**

G

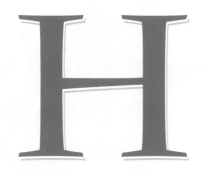

**Hadden Rig, Battle of** An English force led by Sir Robert Bowes was surprised and defeated near **Kelso** on 24 August 1542 by a Scottish army led by the 4th Earl of **Huntly**. The Scots were victorious and took 600 prisoners. Conflict in the **Borders** was to continue until **Solway Moss** later in the year.

**Haddington** (pop. 8851) Town in **East Lothian** on the River Tyne, 26km (16mi) east of **Edinburgh**. Former royal **burgh** and county town, it is now the administrative centre of East Lothian Council. It suffered repeatedly from English attack during the 13th and 14th centuries, and in 1548 it was besieged by an English army. By the Treaty of Haddington between the Scots and the French, it was agreed to send the young **Mary, Queen of Scots** to France for safety. St Mary's Church, which dates from the 15th century, was largely roofless for 400 years until the transepts and choir were restored 1971–3. It is sometimes known as 'the Lamp of Lothian', though the name probably originally designated the Franciscan friars' church, destroyed by the English in 1356; Holy Trinity episcopal church now stands on its site. The Lamp of Lothian Collegiate Centre provides venues for cultural events in Haddington. The town centre has changed little since the mid 19th century and contains architecturally interesting buildings, including the town house, designed by William **Adam** in 1742 but largely rebuilt in 1788, with a steeple by James Gillespie **Graham** (1831). The childhood home of Jane Welsh **Carlyle** is now a museum, restored in the style of her time. Haddington was the focal point of the East Lothian grain trade, and had breweries and distilleries. One mill

still makes malt flour for baking. In recent years an increasing number of commuters to **Edinburgh** have come to live in Haddington. **Lennoxlove** House is nearby.

**Haddington, Thomas Hamilton, 1st Earl and Lord of the Regality of** (1563–1637) Advocate and politician. Also known as 'Tam o' the Cowgate', referring to his **Edinburgh** home. He became Lord Advocate in 1596. Highly regarded by **James VI**, he was appointed Secretary of State for Scotland in 1612, and from 1616 he was President of the **Court of Session**.

**Haddingtonshire** see East Lothian

**Haddo House** Mansion in Aberdeenshire, near **Ellon**, with extensive and well laid out gardens. It was built by William **Adam** in the 1730s for the 2nd Earl of Aberdeen, and refurbished with neo-Adam interiors by Wright and Mansfield (1879–81) and a Gothic chapel by G E Street (1876–81). It was acquired by the **National Trust for Scotland** from the 4th Marquess of Aberdeen and Temair, and is open to the public. The Haddo House Choral Society holds concerts in a theatre beside the house. See 1st Marquis of **Aberdeen** and Ishbel-Maria **Marjoribanks**.

**Haddow, Sir Alexander** (1907–76) Experimental pathologist, b. Broxburn, West Lothian. He was Director of the Chester Beatty Research Institute, and a pioneer in the chemical treatment of cancer. He also worked on the transmission of yellow fever from monkeys to man.

**Hadrian's Wall** see Antonine Wall

**haggis** A traditional dish of sheep's heart, liver and lungs chopped and mixed with oatmeal, suet, onion, salt and spices, and cooked in a bag made from the sheep's stomach. It is particularly associated with **Burns'** Suppers and **St Andrew**'s Night meals, served with 'neeps and tatties' (turnip and potato). Robert Burns's poem 'Address to a Haggis' has contributed to the international fame of this dish, and indeed to its association with Scotland; at least until the 18th century, it was widely eaten in England. Nowadays a vegetarian version is also made with beans and lentils.

**Haggs Castle** Tower house in Pollokshaws, **Glasgow**, with rich sculptured detail, built in 1585–7 and subsequently altered. It belonged to the Maxwells of Pollok, and during the 17th century was used for **conventicles**. The castle was abandoned in 1763 but restored by 1860. Glasgow Corporation bought it in 1972, and used it as a museum. It has been privately owned since 1998.

H

**Haig, Douglas, 1st Earl Haig of Bemersyde** (1861–1928) Military commander, b. Edinburgh, a member of the Haig family of distillers. He served in the Boer War and in India. He displaced his fellow cavalryman, Sir John French, to become commander-in-chief of the British Expeditionary Force in France during World War I, becoming Field Marshal in 1917. Admired at the time, he was later criticised for the human cost of his campaigns. More recently his generalship has been strongly defended, and his 1918 offensives were undoubtedly decisive victories. In later years he was concerned for those who had been wounded and bereaved, and founded the Earl Haig Poppy Fund, which provides for disabled ex-servicemen.

**Hailes, Sir David Dalrymple, Lord** (1726–92) Judge and historian, b. Edinburgh. A barrister in England and then an **advocate** in Scotland, he became a Judge of the **Court of Session** in 1766, and is best remembered for his *Annals of Scotland from the Accession of Malcolm Canmore to the Accession of the House of Stuart* (1776).

**Hailes Castle** Ruined castle on the River Tyne, near **East Linton**. The curtain wall dates from the 13th century, while the keep is 14th century with later additions. It belonged to the Hepburn family, and James **Hepburn**, Earl of Bothwell, brought **Mary, Queen of Scots** here on their flight in 1567. By the early 18th century it was owned by the Dalrymples, who abandoned it for their mansion of **Newhailes**. It is now in the care of **Historic Scotland**.

**Haldane, James Alexander** (1768–1851) Preacher, b. Dundee. He travelled through Scotland and England preaching as an evangelist from 1797. He and his brother Robert founded the Society for Propagating the Gospel at Home, leading to the establishment of the Congregational Church. They also erected a Tabernacle or church in **Edinburgh** in 1801, where he preached. Their followers were known as Haldanites.

**Haldane, Richard Burdon, 1st Viscount** (1856–1928) Lawyer and politician, b. Edinburgh. He studied philosophy.at the University of Göttingen and then law, becoming a barrister in 1879 and a Queen's Counsel in 1890. From 1885 he was Liberal MP for **East Lothian**, and was Secretary of State for War from 1905 to 1912. In this post he was influential in reorganising the armed forces, and created the Territorial Army. He was Lord Chancellor in 1912 and, having moved to the Labour Party, was again Lord Chancellor in 1924.

**Haldane, Robert** see **Haldane, James Alexander**

**Haldanite** see **Haldane, James Alexander**

**Halidon Hill** Battle on 19 July 1333 when a Scottish army led by Sir Archibald Douglas was heavily defeated attempting to relieve the siege of **Berwick** by Edward III and Edward **Balliol**. Many prominent supporters of **David II** were killed and a period of Balliol and English ascendancy in Scotland ensued.

**Halkirk** Village in **Caithness**, 9km (6mi) south of **Thurso**, re-planned around 1800. Nearby are the ruins of Braal Castle, which dates from the 13th and 14th centuries and belonged to the Earls of Caithness. In 1222 the murder of Bishop Adam took place at an episcopal residence here.

**Hallbar Tower** Slim 5-storey rectangular tower house at Braidwood, to the south of **Carluke**, Lanarkshire, with a stone-slabbed cap-house built in 1581 by Harie Stewart of Gogar, with what has been a timber **doocot** cantilevered out from the north gable to provide food in the event of siege. Since about 1662 it has been the property of the Lockharts of Lee.

**Halloween** 31 October, the eve of All Saints' Day, the last day of the year in the old Celtic calendar, associated with witches and the powers of darkness, and celebrated with bonfires, divination rites etc; now mainly a children's festival when they go around guising, ie going from door to door in disguise offering entertainment in return for gifts or money. Another custom is 'dooking for apples', trying to get a bite from an apple floating in a basin of water. Halloween festivals in one form or other became very popular in North America and some of their customs, such as 'trick or treat', have been re-imported back across the Atlantic in recent years.

**hamesucken** In Scots law, the crime of assault on someone in their own home.

**Hamilton** (pop. 48,546) Town 18km (11mi) southeast of **Glasgow**. It was originally known as Cadzow, and Cadzow Castle, ruined since the 16th century, lies nearby. It has a ducal parish church by William **Adam** (1731–34) and impressive neo-baroque municipal buildings by the Hamilton firm of Cullen, Lochhead and Brown (1906–14). The major local landowners were the Dukes of Hamilton, who have featured prominently in centuries of Scottish history, and had their palace here until the 1920s, when it was demolished. An avenue of trees linked the palace with their hunting lodge of **Chatelherault** to the south of the town. **Linen** weaving was an important industry and from the late 18th century this area was at the centre of the Lanarkshire **coal** field, one of Scotland's largest. Hamilton is now the administrative centre of **South Lanarkshire** Council, mainly a commercial centre.

H

*A game of handba' on Fastern's E'en, Jedburgh, 1955.*

**Hamilton, Anne, Duchess of** (1632–1716) The daughter of the 1st Duke of Hamilton, she became Duchess in her own right. She is remembered for her strength of character and her management of the family estates during years of political instability. She was responsible for the construction of Hamilton Palace, which was demolished in 1920. She married William Douglas, 1st Earl of Selkirk, and from that time onwards the family were known as Douglas-Hamilton.

**Hamilton, David** (1768–1843) Architect, b. Glasgow. He began his career as a late 18th-century neo-classicist, as at Hutcheson's Hospital, **Glasgow**, but became a neo-Greek and neo-Roman notably at Hamilton Palace and the Royal Exchange (now the Gallery of Modern Art) and the former Western Club in Glasgow.

**Hamilton, Douglas Douglas-Hamilton, 14th Duke of and 11th Duke of Brandon** (1903–73) Politician and pilot, b. London. He was Conservative MP for East Renfrewshire from 1930 to 1940. In 1933 he and David McIntyre were the first men to fly an aeroplane over Mount Everest. He had met Hitler's close associate Rudolf Hess, and Hess landed at **Eaglesham** in 1941 on his way to the Hamilton shooting lodge at Dungavel in an unsuccessful bid to negotiate peace between the UK and Germany.

**Hamilton, Gavin** (1723–98) Artist, b. Lanark. Educated at **Glasgow** University and in painting in Rome, he worked as a portraitist in London before returning to Rome where he spent most of his career and where he immersed himself in the classics and antiquity. He excelled as a history painter, producing large-scale paintings in particular on Homeric subjects, which were much admired in their day and important in the development of Neoclassicism.

**Hamilton, James, 1st Lord** (d.1479) He was created Lord Hamilton in 1445. He married Mary Stewart, daughter of **James II** c.1474, and their son became the 1st Earl of Arran. This association with the royal house meant that a Hamilton was often close to the royal succession during the next century.

**Hamilton, James, 1st Duke of** (1606–49) Politician and soldier, b. England. He became a Privy Councillor in 1628, and from 1631 to 1633 he fought in the Thirty Years' War (1618–48). **Charles I** gave him his dukedom in 1643 to reward his loyalty, but he was later imprisoned as a result of the allegations of his rival the Marquis of **Montrose**. He was the commander of the Royalist army which was defeated at **Preston** in 1648, and was subsequently executed.

**Hamilton, James Douglas, 4th Duke of** (1658–1712) Known for his extravagance, he flirted with **Jacobitism**, but was bribed to betray the anti-Union alliance he led in the Scottish parliament in 1706-7. He was killed in a duel with homicidal Lord Mohun.

**Hamilton, Patrick** (1504–28) Scholar and martyr, b. near Glasgow. He was influenced by Lutheran theology when studying in Paris and Louvain. On returning to **St Andrews** he was burned as a heretic by Archbishop **Beaton** outside St Salvator's Chapel. His martyrdom was a significant element in the spread of the **Reformation** in Scotland.

**Hamilton, Thomas** see **Haddington, 1st Earl of**

**Hamilton, Thomas** (1784–1858) Architect, b. Edinburgh. Based mainly in **Edinburgh**, he worked mainly in Greek Revival, and was influential in the planning of the city from 1827, designing the George IV Bridge and Victoria Street. He is best known for the Royal High School on Calton Hill (1829), the **Royal College of Physicians** (1846) and the Dean Orphanage (1831-3), now the Dean Gallery.

H

**Hamilton, Sir William** (1730–1803) Ambassador. He was British ambassador in Naples from 1764 to 1800 and was a keen collector and archaeologist, taking part in excavations of Herculaneum and Pompeii. His wife Emma was the mistress of Lord Nelson.

**Hamilton, Sir William** (1788–1856) Philosopher and educational reformer, b. Glasgow. He made his name by writings in the *Edinburgh Review* criticising the state of English education. Professor of Logic and Metaphysics in Edinburgh 1838–56, where he edited the works of Thomas **Reid** and popularised the approach of the Scottish **Common Sense Philosophy**.

**Hamilton District** see **Strathclyde Region**

**Hamilton House** see **Preston**

**Hammer of the Scots** Nickname applied to Edward I of England (reigned 1272–1307), who claimed to be overlord of Scotland. He attempted firstly to rule through John **Balliol** and then to conquer Scotland by force.

**Hampden Park** Scotland's national **football** stadium, in **Glasgow**. The home ground of Queen's Park football club, the only amateur team to play in Scottish league football. The pitch has been used for major national and international matches since the early 20th century. It also houses the Scottish Football Museum.

**Handa** Island off the northwest coast, opposite **Scourie**. Uninhabited since the potato famine of the mid 19th century, it is privately owned but is managed by the **Scottish Wildlife Trust**. The island is surrounded by sheer cliffs and is home to a great range of sea birds. Passenger boats sail from Tarbet on the adjacent mainland.

**handba(ll)** Game, also known as 'the Ba', played with a small ball thrown with the hands, between 2 teams which might consist of men from opposite ends of the town (uppies and doonies), or unmarried men against husbands. Often played as part of an annual festival, for example at New Year in **Orkney**, or on **Fastern's E'en** (Shrove Tuesday) in various places in the **Borders**; it is still played on that day in **Jedburgh**.

**handfasting** Ceremony of betrothal, or of trial marriage lasting a year and a day, after which the couple were free to separate.

**Hardie, Andrew** (c.1791–1820) Weaver, b. Glasgow. One of the 'radical martyrs'. During a period of industrial unrest he joined John **Baird** in an attempt to seize **Carron Ironworks**.

Government troops overcame the rebels at Bonnymuir, near **Falkirk**, and Hardie was among those arrested and executed for treason.

**Hardie, James Keir** (1856–1915) Politician, b. near Holytown, Lanarkshire. A **coal** miner, he was dismissed for campaigning for better working conditions, but continued to be involved in setting up miners' working organisations. He became a journalist. In 1888, having been rejected as a Liberal parliamentary candidate, he founded the **Scottish Labour Party**, the first party in Britain set up to represent the working classes. In 1892 he became the first Labour MP, and represented first West Ham and then Merthyr Tydfil in parliament.

**Hare, William** see **Burke, William**

**Harlaw, Battle of** Donald **Lord of the Isles** led a **Highland** force eastwards during the period when **James I** was a prisoner in England. He was met at Harlaw, near **Inverurie**, on 24 July 1411 by Alexander Stewart, Earl of Mar, with an army consisting of **Aberdeen** burgesses and other northeastern men. The battle itself was fierce, and brought an end to the attempt of the Lord of the Isles to expand eastwards. A memorial was erected at the battle site in 1911, and the battle is the subject of a famous ballad.

**harp** see **clarsach**

**Harray** Area in mainland **Orkney**, with the **Loch of Harray** to the west. Many of the outstanding archaeological sites are in this area, including **Maes Howe**, the Ring of **Brodgar** and the Stones of **Stenness**. A picture of 19th-century life is presented by the Corrigall Farm Museum.

*J Keir Hardie addresses a peace rally in Trafalgar Square, London, c.1914.*

**H**

181

**Harris, Isle of** (Gaelic **Na h-Earradh**) (pop. Lewis and Harris, 19,918) Island in the Outer **Hebrides**, lying north of **North Uist**. It is part of the same island as **Lewis**, to the north, from which it is divided by Loch Seaforth in the east and Loch Resort in the west. Together Lewis and Harris are known as 'the **Long Island**'. Harris combines mountainous terrain with outstanding west coast beaches. **Tarbert**, the main town, can be reached by ferry from **Uig** (Skye) or **Lochmaddy**. There is also a ferry from **Leverburgh** in the south to **Berneray**. The island is known for the manufacture of **Harris Tweed**, where it remains a cottage industry. There was a long-running controversy over the proposal to create a superquarry in the south of the island; plans were abandoned in 2004. Tourism, fishing and crofting also provide employment. See also Lord **Leverhulme**, **Scalpay**, **Taransay**.

**Harris Tweed** Registered trademark name, along with the orb symbol, for **tweed** woven in their own homes by islanders in **Lewis**, **Harris**, **North Uist**, **Benbecula**, **South Uist** and **Barra**. The cloth is finished in a mill in Lewis and marketed worldwide. The finishing was formerly also carried out in the home; see **waulking** songs.

*The Harris Tweed logo.*

**'Harry the Ninth'** see **Dundas, Henry**

**Harthill** Village near the M8, 3km (2mi) west of **Whitburn**. Formerly a mining and quarrying community, it now has the Harthill Motorway Service Station midway between **Glasgow** and **Edinburgh**.

**Harthill** see **Oyne**

**Harvey, Alex** (1935–82) Rock musician, b. Glasgow. As the leader of the Sensational Alex Harvey Band, he became famous in the mid 1970s for his uncompromising tough-guy image and his spectacular stage shows. The band's hits included 'The Boston Tea Party' and 'Delilah'. He died of a heart attack at the end of a tour.

**Harvey, Sir George** (1806–76) Artist, b. St Ninians, Perthshire. Harvey was known during his lifetime for his paintings of scenes from Scottish history, in particular on the **Covenanters**. His paintings of more commonplace subjects (such as *The Curlers*, 1835 **National Gallery of Scotland**) and studies of individual figures have a simplicity and dignity which have made them more enduring.

**Hastings, A Gavin** (1962– ) Rugby player, b. Edinburgh. Former captain of Scotland and of the British Lions (1993, New Zealand tour). His Scotland debut came in 1986 alongside his brother Scott. He played at fullback and was often goal kicker. He scored over 700 points in test matches during a career which included 61 Scotland caps, 20 as captain of his country.

**Haston, Dougal** (1940–77) Mountaineer, b. Currie, Midlothian. His achievements included being the first Briton to climb the north face of the Eiger in 1966, and being part of the first ascent of the southwest face of Mount Everest in 1975. He was killed in an avalanche while skiing in Switzerland.

**Hatton Castle** Large Z-plan house near Newtyle, to the northeast of **Dundee**, built by the 4th Lord Oliphant c.1580–90, originally for the Master of Oliphant, exiled in 1584 for his involvement in the **Ruthven Raid**.

**Hatton Castle** Symmetrical castellated house 5km (3mi) southeast of **Turriff**, built in 1814, incorporating the castle of Balquholly, a seat of the Mowats and later of the Duffs.

**Havergal, Giles** see **Citizens' Theatre**

**Hawick** (pop. 14,573) Town on the River **Teviot**, 19km (12mi) south of **Selkirk**. It flourished in the 19th and 20th centuries due to the expansion of the fine **tweed** and hosiery industries. In the later 20th century it became internationally known for cashmere woollens. It has an architecturally impressive High Street, with fine former bank buildings, dominated by a Scottish **baronial** town hall, designed by James Campbell Walker (1885). Hawick's **Common Riding** festival in June commemorates the victory in 1514 of a group of Hawick youths or 'callants' over some English soldiers. The main participant is known as the Cornet.

**Hawthornden** Castle on a cliff just outside **Roslin**, Midlothian. In 1638 the poet William **Drummond** added a mansion house onto the ruined 15th-century tower house. Below the castle

H

are man-made caves and passages, said to have been used by **Robert I**. Ben Jonson visited Drummond here in 1618. The castle, which has once more been restored, belonged to the Drummonds until the 1970s, when the poet's possessions were unfortunately dispersed. It is now a privately owned retreat for writers.

**Hay, George Campbell** (**Deorsa Maclain Deorsa**) (1915–84) Poet, b. Elderslie, Renfrewshire, the son of John MacDougall **Hay**. Though he was not a native **Gaelic** speaker, most of his work is in Gaelic. His first collection of Gaelic poems, *Fuaran Slèibh*, was published in 1947. His works drew on his childhood in **Argyll**, his war years in the Middle East and his nationalist sympathies. He also worked in **Scots** and English, and translated literature from many other languages.

**Hay, Ian** (pen name of **John Hay Beith**) (1876–1952) Author, b. Manchester, with a Scottish background. He wrote humorous novels and plays, of which the best known was *The First Hundred Thousand* (1915), based on his experiences in World War I.

**Hay, John MacDougall** (1881–1919) Writer and minister, b. Tarbert, Argyll. Minister of **Govan** and **Elderslie**, he is particularly remembered for his acclaimed novel *Gillespie* (1914), a grimly realistic work on 19th-century **Tarbert**.

**Healabhal Mhòr, Healabhal Beag** see **Macleod's Tables**

**Heart of Midlothian Football Club** Edinburgh club founded in 1874, with its home ground at Tynecastle, to the west of the city centre. One of the country's most successful sides in the 1890s and 1900s, they then endured a long barren spell until the mid 1950s. In the decade that followed they won all three major domestic trophies. A lengthy decline followed, but in recent years they have enjoyed better fortunes, and in 1998 they won the Scottish Cup. Their traditional rivals are **Hibernian**. Known informally as Hearts and by the rhyming slang nickname of Jam Tarts. See also **football**.

**Hearts** see **Heart of Midlothian**

**heather ale** A drink brewed from heather flowers etc, according to legend originally made from a long-lost **Pictish** recipe. A modern recipe contains heather, hops, barm, syrup, ginger and water. It is now produced commercially as Fraoch (Gaelic for heather), containing heather, malted barley and herbs.

**Hebrides** Group of islands off the northwest coast. The name comes from the Norse *Havbredey*, 'isles at the edge of the sea'. They are divided into the Outer Hebrides (see **Western Isles**), which stretch from the Butt of **Lewis** in the north to Berneray in the south, and the Inner Hebrides, which include **Skye**, **Mull**, **Islay** and many smaller islands. During the medieval period the islands formed part of a vast sea kingdom, coming at times under Norse and Manx control. In the 14th and 15th centuries **Islay** was the centre of the **Lordship of the Isles**. The later history of the islands has been one of the survival of a distinctive culture, and includes the poverty, famine and **clearance** of the mid 19th century. Declining population and lack of jobs have remained concerns, but tourism, **fishing**, distilling and crofting continue to provide employment.

**Helensburgh** (pop. 14,626) Town on the Firth of **Clyde**, 12km (8mi) northwest of **Dumbarton**. Founded in 1777 by Sir James Colquhoun of Luss and named after his wife, it was laid out on a grid pattern as a resort and residential community, with great numbers of very grand late Victorian and Edwardian houses set in finely wooded gardens. It remains a commuter town and is also popular with tourists. **Glen Fruin** is nearby. See also The **Hill House**.

*The Curlers, 1835, by Sir George Harvey.*

**Hell's Glen** Steep-sided valley leading down to Loch **Fyne**, with a road running from **Lochgoilhead**.

**Helmsdale** Village on the northeast coast, 20km (15mi) northeast of **Golspie**, at the mouth of the River Helmsdale, which is renowned for its fly-fishing. The harbour was built and the town established in the 19th century to provide employment in herring **fishing** for crofting families evicted from the Strath of **Kildonan**. The Timespan Heritage Centre tells the story of the area.

**Henderson, Alexander** (1583–1646) Minister, b. Creich, Fife. Minister of **Leuchars**, he was one of the authors of both the **National Covenant** and the **Solemn League and Covenant**, and was **Moderator** of the revolutionary **General Assembly** of 1638 which abolished episcopacy, and made war with **Charles I** inevitable.

**Henderson, Hamish** (1919–2002) Poet, songwriter, folksong collector, b. Blairgowrie. His war experiences led him to become a peace campaigner, and also inspired his collection of poetry, *Elegies for the Dead in Cyrenaica* (1948). He wrote in **Scots** and also collected many Scots traditional songs and tales. As one of the founders of the School of Scottish Studies in **Edinburgh University**, he was a key figure in the creation of a collection of recorded folk material there, and in the recognition of traditional singers, such as Jeannie **Robertson**. His song 'Freedom Come All Ye' has been suggested as a Scottish national anthem.

**Hendry, Stephen** (1969– ) Snooker player, b. Edinburgh. At 15, he was the youngest player to win the Scottish Amateur Championship, then turned professional and became the youngest World Champion in 1990. He has been World Champion 7 times, and has won 72 world titles throughout his career.

**Henry, Prince of Wales** (1594–1612) Heir to the throne, b. Stirling. The elder son of **James VI** and **Anne of Denmark**, he was heir to the Scottish and English thrones, and is believed to have shown much promise as an able future monarch. His death from typhoid led to the succession of his younger brother as **Charles I**.

**Henry, George** (1858–1943) Artist, b. Irvine. Henry worked closely with fellow artist E A **Hornel**, producing works with a greater decorative and symbolic quality than his fellow **Glasgow Boys**, and occasionally collaborating with Hornel on single paintings (*The Druids: Bringing Home the Mistletoe*,

1890 Glasgow Art Gallery). Henry and Hornel travelled to Japan together in 1893 (although many of Henry's works were ruined on the return journey). Henry moved to London in 1906 where he worked mostly as a portraitist.

**Henry Benedict, Cardinal, Duke of York** see **Stewart, Henry Benedict**

**Henrysoun, Robert** (c.1420–c.1500) Poet. Although not much is known about his life, he appears to have been a schoolmaster in **Dunfermline**. One of the greatest of the medieval Scots poets, his best-known works were *The Testament of Cresseid* and his *Morall Fabillis of Esope*. He was dead by 1505, when he is mentioned in a poem by William **Dunbar**.

**Henry the Minstrel** see **Blind Harry**

**Hepburn, James** see **Bothwell, Earl of**

**Hepburn, John** (c.1598–1636) Mercenary soldier, b. Athelstaneford, East Lothian. He campaigned for the Elector Palatine in Bohemia (1620–23) and thereafter until 1633 he served Gustavus Adolphus of Sweden, commanding from 1632 the famous Green Brigade of 4 Scottish mercenary regiments. He entered French service in 1633, where his regiment eventually incorporated what was left of the Royal Scottish Archer Guard. After his death his unit eventually became the **Royal Scots**.

**Her Majesty's Inspectorate** (HMI) Government agency, established in 1840, with the power to regulate standards in schools and with significant influence in the development of educational policy.

**Herald, The** Glasgow-based broadsheet newspaper. Formerly the *Glasgow Herald*, it was first published in 1783. It was renamed *The Herald* in 1992, and is now owned by Newsquest Media Group. It has sister papers, the *Evening Times* and the *Sunday Herald*. See also **newspapers**.

**Herd, David** (1732–1810) Editor and collector of songs, b. St Cyrus, near Montrose. A writer's clerk in **Edinburgh**, he was interested in Scottish literature and antiquities. His collection of songs and ballads was published in part in 1769 and 1776 as *Ancient and Modern Scots Songs*, and was drawn on by Sir Walter **Scott**.

**Heriot, George** (1563–1624) Goldsmith, b. Edinburgh. He was jeweller and moneylender to **James VI** and his queen, **Anne of Denmark**, and lived mainly in London from 1603. His wealth, made in part from moneylending, was bequeathed to found Heriot's Hospital in **Edinburgh**, now George Heriot's

H

School, built (1628–60) in the style of a Renaissance palace. It is still in use as a school, formerly for boys, now for both sexes. He appears as a character in Sir Walter **Scott**'s *The Fortunes of Nigel,* with the nickname 'Jinglin' Geordie'.

**Heriot–Watt University** Established in **Edinburgh** in 1821 as a 'School of Arts', it became a college of science and technology and has been a university since 1966. Its original intention was to offer mathematics, science and drawing classes, and known now for its engineering, science and business management departments. Since the 1970s it has been based on a campus at Riccarton on the edge of Edinburgh.

*George Heriot's School, Edinburgh.*

Its name commemorates inventor James **Watt**, and also George **Heriot**, whose trust provided some funds for the institution. There is also a campus at **Galashiels**. It has 6800 students.

**heritable jurisdictions** Ancient rights, often hereditary, held by landowners, entitling them to administer civil and criminal justice in local courts; abolished in 1748. See also **sheriff, barony, regality.**

**heritors** Group of local landowners in a parish, who were responsible for maintaining, among other things, the church, **manse** and **glebe** until 1925 and the school until 1872.

**Hermitage Castle** Impressive castle 8km (5mi) from Newcastleton, near the English border. The original 14th-century keep of the Dacres was absorbed into a massive tower house built by the Earl of Angus from 1398 onwards. In 1492 it passed to the Hepburns of Bothwell, the Douglases exchanging it for Bothwell Castle. **Mary, Queen of Scots** visited the injured Earl of **Bothwell** here in 1566. Abandoned in the mid 17th century, it was partly restored in the 19th, and is in the care of **Historic Scotland.**

**het pint** A hot drink made from ale and **whisky** with nutmeg, sugar and eggs, drunk at celebrations such as New Year, weddings, childbirth. It was traditionally carried round the streets in copper kettles.

**Hibernian** Football club founded in 1875, and based in Easter Road, **Edinburgh.** The club is usually known as 'Hibs' or 'Hibees'.

Their most successful period was the early 1950s, when their forwards were known as the 'Famous Five'. Their traditional rivals are **Heart of Midlothian.** See also **football,** p.151

**High Bridge** Ruined bridge over the River Spean, west of **Spean Bridge.** It was built in 1736 by General **Wade** to cross a deep gorge. Although ruined since its partial collapse in 1913, it is still spectacular. It was the site of a skirmish at the outset of the 1745 **Jacobite Rising,** in which 2 companies of government troops were surprised and captured by about 10 Highlanders.

**High Court of Justiciary** Supreme criminal court in Scotland, which tries the most serious crimes, and hears appeals from all criminal courts. It consists of the Justice General, **Justice Clerk,** and Commissioners of Justiciary, and sits in **Edinburgh** and on circuit in larger towns and cities of Scotland. Known informally as the High Court. See also **law,** p.223.

**Highers** Courses which are taken by pupils in their 5th and 6th years, and are widely used to qualify for further education and employment. They originated in the Higher **Leaving Certificate,** introduced in 1888. In the 1990s Higher Grade examinations underwent extensive reform and a new system known as 'Higher Still' was introduced, bringing together vocational qualifications, Highers and the **Certificate for Sixth Year Studies.** Grades are awarded for a combination of course work and examinations in the subjects studied.

**Highland** see **Highland Council, Highland Region, Highlands**

**H**

**Highland Boundary Fault** Major geological feature running from the southwest at **Helensburgh** on the Firth of **Clyde** to the northeast at **Stonehaven**. It marks the northern margin of the Midland Valley of Scotland. See **Southern Uplands Fault**.

**Highland Council** (Gaelic **Comhairle na Gaidhealtachd**) The largest local-authority area in Scotland, formed in 1996 from **Highland Region**; see maps on pp.394-5 and **local government**. **Inverness** is the administrative centre, and tourism is a principal industry in this sparsely populated landscape of mountains, lochs and coastlines.

**Highland dancing** Dances based on traditional Highland figures, mainly military in origin, usually performed solo. Highland dancing is frequently performed in competitions, especially at **Highland Games**, and has been regulated by the Scottish Official Board of Highland Dancing since 1953; based in **Edinburgh**, it coordinates and regulates the various examining bodies, to maintain standards worldwide. The dances include: the Highland fling, involving the 'flinging' of the free foot into the air; the sword dance (in Gaelic, *Gille Chaluim*), performed over 2 crossed swords; and the *sean triubhas* (Gaelic, meaning 'old trousers'), an intricate slow dance, said to reflect efforts of Highlanders to shake off the trousers imposed on them when the **kilt** was banned after the 1745 **Jacobite Rising**.

**Highland dress** The costume of Highlanders as developed in modern times, now worn throughout Scotland, especially on ceremonial occasions. The **kilt** is worn with different upper garments, for example: by Scottish regiments as part of dress uniform; by pipers, in pipe bands often accompanied by a **plaid**; by Scottish country dancers, usually with a white shirt; at formal balls, weddings etc, with black jacket, white shirt, black bow tie and fur **sporran**; on less formal occasions with tweed jacket and plainer leather sporran; by football fans etc supporting their team abroad, with T-shirt. There is no real female equivalent, but for dancing women sometimes wear a white dress with a tartan sash over the shoulder. See also **balmoral, dirk, kilt, plaid, sgian dubh, sporran, tartan, trews**.

**Highlanders** (**Seaforths, Gordons and Camerons**) Regiment formed in 1994 by amalgamation of the **Queen's Own Highlanders** (Seaforth and Camerons) and the **Gordon Highlanders**. They recruit from the Northeast, the Highlands and Islands and Glasgow.

**Highland fling** see **Highland dancing**

**Highland Folk Museum** see **Newtonmore**

**Highland Games** Also known as Highland gatherings, these events are held annually in the summer months throughout the **Highlands** and elsewhere, and include competitions in piping, **Highland dancing**, tossing the caber (a large pole), throwing the hammer and other feats of strength and agility. They derive from traditional athletic competitions in the Highlands and became more formalised from about the 1820s, probably encouraged by the stage-managed visit of King George IV to Scotland in 1822. In the 20th century they became more professional and their rules are now governed by the Scottish Games Association. The **Braemar** Gathering became famous through association with the royal family, beginning with the visit of Queen Victoria in 1848. Other popular events include the **Argyllshire Gathering**, with important piping competitions, the **Cowal** Highland Games, held at **Dunoon**, and the **Aboyne** Highland Games. In North America, Australia and elsewhere, descendants of Scots emigrants celebrate their heritage at Highland games. One of the best-known overseas events is the Grandfather Mountain Highland Games and Gathering of Clans in North Carolina.

**Highland Land League** A political organisation formed in 1882 to agitate for land reform for crofters. It was at its most effective in the 1880s, with 4 candidates returned to Parliament in the 1885 elections. Less active after the **Crofters' Act**, the League eventually merged with the **Scottish National Party**.

**Highland Light Infantry** In 1881 the 71st Highland Light Infantry, dating back to 1777, merged with the 74th Highlanders, originally raised in 1787, to form the Highland Light Infantry, renamed Highland Light Infantry (City of Glasgow Regiment) in 1923. In 1959 they amalgamated with the **Royal Scots Fusiliers** to form the **Royal Highland Fusiliers**.

**Highland line** A line dividing the **Lowlands** from the **Highlands**, generally regarded as running southwest-northeast from **Dumbarton** on the River **Clyde** to **Ballater** on the **Dee** and then northwest to **Nairn**.

**Highland regiments** see **regiments**

**Highland Region** The largest (in area) of the 9 regions forming the upper tier of local government from 1975 to 1996, formed from the former counties of **Caithness, Sutherland, Nairn** and parts of **Ross and Cromarty** and **Inverness-shire**. It consisted of the districts of Badenoch and Strathspey, **Caithness, Inverness, Lochaber, Nairn, Ross and Cromarty**, Skye and Lochalsh, and **Sutherland**. See maps on pp.394-5 and **local government**.

H

**Highland Roads and Bridges** see **Commission for**

**Highlands** (Gaelic **A' Ghaidhealtachd**) The northern part of Scotland, generally defined as north of the **Highland Boundary Fault** and west of **Aberdeenshire**. Historically the Scottish monarchy found it hard to exert authority in the Highlands, where the **clan** system remained strong for centuries, the **Gaelic** language was prevalent and customs, culture, terrain and lifestyle differed sharply from the **Lowlands**. This isolated way of life was badly weakened in the 18th and 19th centuries, not least by harsh government reprisals in the aftermath of the Battle of **Culloden**, but also by improvements in roads (see General **Wade**, Major **Caulfeild** and **Commission for Highland Roads and Bridges**). In the 19th century there was a romanticised revival of interest in Highland culture, but at the same time economic hardship, due to integration into a competitive capitalist economy, and the **Clearances** saw great depopulation of the area. Today the Highland economy depends greatly on tourists attracted to the stunning scenery, outdoor pursuits, history and heritage of the area. Recent decades have also seen an influx of longer-term residents from the Lowlands, England and abroad, attracted by a more relaxed lifestyle, which many more people can enjoy in the electronic age. See also **Highland Council**.

**Highlands and Islands Development Board** see **Highlands and Islands Enterprise**

**Highlands and Islands Enterprise** Government-funded organisation which aims to encourage economic diversification and development in communities throughout the Highland area, providing support and services. It replaced the Highlands and Islands Development Board, set up in 1965.

**Highland Show** see **Royal Highland Show**

**high school** With **academy**, the most common name for a school providing secondary education.

**Hill, David Octavius** (1802–70) Artist and photographer, b. Perth. He was already a recognised painter when, in partnership with Robert **Adamson** (1821–48), he carried out pioneering photographic work. His best known painting is 'Signing the Act

*Lamp and wall stencils in the drawing room, The Hill House, Helensburgh.*

of Separation and Deed of Demission', 1843–67, a vast work depicting the founders of the **Free Church**, for which each individual was photographed, then painted (see p.107). He produced many photographic portraits with Adamson in their studio at Rock House on Calton Hill, **Edinburgh**, including famous images of the fisherfolk of **Newhaven**.

**Hillend** On the southeast edge of **Edinburgh**, this is the location for the Midlothian Ski Centre, the biggest artificial ski run in Europe on the northern slopes of the **Pentland Hills**. It includes 2 main slopes and nursery slopes, and equipment and instruction can be hired.

**Hill House, The** Mansion house in **Helensburgh**, designed by Charles Rennie **Mackintosh** in 1902–4. It was commissioned by **Glasgow** publisher Walter **Blackie**. Mackintosh designed not only the house but many of the furnishings, and his wife Margaret **Macdonald** supplied fabric designs and the gesso overmantel. The house was saved for the nation by the **Royal Incorporation of Architects in Scotland** and is now in the care of the **National Trust for Scotland**.

**Hill of Tarvit** Mansion house 3 km (2mi) south of **Cupar**. It was built in 1696, possibly by William **Bruce**, and known formerly as Wemyss Hall. In 1906 it was remodelled by Robert **Lorimer**, to house the rich collection of artistic treasures of its new owner, Mr F B Sharp. The house and collection are now in the care of the **National Trust for Scotland**. See also **Scotstarvit**.

**Hills, Joan** see **Boyle family**

**Hills Tower** Kirkcudbright. Rectangular tower house near Lochfoot, to the west of **Dumfries**, built by Edward Maxwell after 1528 with a 2-storey wing of 1721; very unusually the gatehouse to its court has survived.

**Hillslap Tower** Originally Calfhill, a tall L-plan tower house near **Melrose** built by the Cairncross family in 1585, 'Glendearg' in Sir Walter **Scott**'s novel *The Monastery*. Long roofless, it was carefully restored and reroofed by the architect Philip Mercer in the 1980s.

**hillwalking** see **mountaineering and hillwalking**, p.278

**Hilton of Cadboll** Village on the coast of the **Moray Firth**. An important 9th-century Pictish stone which stood here is now displayed in the **Museum of Scotland**. A replacement has been erected near the site of the original. Cadboll Castle, now ruined, was built by a Bishop of Ross, and from 1592 by the Sinclairs. It was replaced by a new house built by Aeneas Macleod, Town Clerk of Edinburgh, who bought the estate c.1680.

**Hislop, Joseph** (1887–1977) Opera singer, b. Edinburgh. A leading tenor, he performed across the world and was particularly successful in Argentina and the United States. From 1936 he retired to be a tutor to many future leading opera singers, both in Britain and in Sweden, where he himself had trained.

**Historic Scotland** Government agency established in 1991 to care for Scotland's built heritage. It is part of the **Scottish Executive**'s Education Department, and was previously known as Historic Buildings and Monuments. Historic Scotland lists buildings and schedules monuments to bring them under protective legislation. On behalf of the state it cares for more than 300 properties, and provides advice and financial assistance to private owners of important properties.

**HMI** see **Her Majesty's Inspectorate**

**Hoddom Castle** Impressive tower house 6.5km (4mi) southwest of **Ecclefechan**, built in 1565–68 by John Maxwell, 4th Lord Herries. It was later extended, but parts have been demolished. It is privately owned, and is surrounded by a caravan park.

**Hogg, James** (1770–1835) Writer, b. Ettrick in the Borders, popularly known as the Ettrick Shepherd. He gave up his life as a shepherd to participate in the literary life of **Edinburgh**, where he was a close friend of Sir Walter **Scott** and contributed regularly to *Blackwood's Magazine*. He collected and wrote songs and ballads, and wrote many short stories and four novels, the best known of which is the masterpiece, *The Private Memoirs and Confessions of a Justified Sinner* (1824). After many years of

neglect, he is now recognised as one of the major Scottish writers of the later **Scottish Enlightenment**.

**Hogmanay** The name given to 31 December in Scotland. Until fairly recently New Year's Day and not Christmas was a holiday in Scotland, and so Hogmanay was the greater of the 2 festivals. Many traditions continue, such as 'first-footing', or visiting the homes of neighbours and friends soon after midnight. To bring good luck, traditionally the first foot should be male, dark, and should carry a piece of peat or coal. '**Auld Lang Syne**' is sung soon after midnight at events across the world. Many towns throughout Scotland have their own Hogmanay fire festivals, including **Biggar**, **Burghead**, **Comrie** and **Stonehaven**. **Edinburgh** and **Glasgow** both host large-scale street parties.

**Holloway, Most Revd Richard** (1933– ) Clergyman, b. Glasgow. He was Bishop of **Edinburgh** from 1986 and Primus of the **Scottish Episcopal Church** from 1992 until his retirement in 2000. An outspoken figure, his controversial theological views have often brought him media attention. He has written many books, contributed to newspapers and has presented his own television series.

**Hollows Tower** see **Gilnockie**

**Holmes, Arthur** (1890–1965) Geologist, b. Newcastle-upon-Tyne. After several posts abroad and in London, he was Professor of Geology in Durham University (1925–43) and in **Edinburgh University** (1943–56). His book, *Principles of Physical Geology* (1944), was a cornerstone in the libraries of students into the 1990s.

**Holmwood** see **Cathcart**

**Holy Island** Small island just off the southeast coast of **Arran**, reached by ferry from **Lamlash**. It is associated with St Molaise. The island now belongs to Buddhists from the Samye Ling Tibetan Centre at **Eskdalemuir**, who use it as a retreat.

**Holy Loch** Sea loch on the **Cowal** Peninsula, opening out into the **Firth of Clyde** north of Dunoon. Until 1992 this was the site of a US nuclear submarine base. The mausoleum of the Dukes of Argyll is at **Kilmun**, on the northern shore of the loch.

**Holyrood** see **Edinburgh**

**Home, Alexander Douglas, Lord Home of the Hirsel** (1903–95) Politician, b. London. The 14th Earl of Home, he renounced his title to become Prime Minister in 1963. After a long political career he was Foreign Secretary under Harold Macmillan from 1960, before succeeding Macmillan as Prime Minister. His period of office was short, lasting only until he lost the General Election of 1964, albeit by a very narrow margin. He was once more Foreign Secretary from 1970 to 1974, and then was made a life peer as Baron Home of the Hirsel.

**Home, John** (1722–1808) Playwright, b. Leith. A minister, he is remembered for his acclaimed play *Douglas*, produced in **Edinburgh** in 1756. He was suspended by the presbytery over his playwriting, and later resigned from the ministry. He became private secretary to the Earl of **Bute** and had further literary success in London.

**Homildon Hill** see **Humbleton Hill**

**Honeyman, John** (1831–1914) Scholar-architect, b. Glasgow, equally adept in Greek Renaissance and Gothic architectural styles. He trained with William **Burn** in London. He designed the tall-spired churches of Park, **Helensburgh** (1862), Lansdowne, **Glasgow** (1862) and St Matthew's, **Perth** among many others. The **Coats** Library, Museum and Observatory at **Paisley** (1866 and 1881–3) show his skill as a classicist while the façade of the Ca' d' Oro building in Gordon Street, Glasgow, shows originality in the use of cast-iron technology. In his later years he was assisted by his partner John Keppie and by Charles Rennie **Mackintosh**. During those years he restored the cathedral at **Brechin** and commenced the abbey of **Iona**.

**Honeyman, Tom** (1891–1970) Gallery director, b. Glasgow. Began his career as a doctor, then worked as an art dealer before becoming the dynamic Director of **Glasgow** Art Gallery and Museum from 1939 to 1954, which coincided with the gift of **Burrell**'s collection to the city. In addition to his important acquisitions of modern French painting (by Matisse, Bonnard and others) Honeyman is best known for his purchase, controversial at the time, of Salvador Dali's 'Christ of St John of the Cross'.

**Honours of Scotland** Scotland's coronation regalia, the oldest in the British Isles. The silver-gilt sceptre was said to have been given to **James IV** in 1494 by Pope Alexander VI, and was remodelled in the mid 16th century. The sword of state was also a papal gift to James IV, this time from Julius II. The crown was remade for **James V** in 1540 from an earlier version. The Honours were used in the coronations of subsequent monarchs, and were symbolically present at sittings of the **Scottish Parliament**. After the **Union** of 1707

they were locked away, and were brought back into public view by Walter **Scott**, so that they could be presented to King George IV on his visit to **Edinburgh** in 1822. Nowadays they are on display in Edinburgh Castle, together with the **Stone of Destiny**.

**Hope** see **Ben Hope, Loch Hope**

**Hopeman** Fishing village on the **Moray** coast, near **Burghead**. It was founded in 1805 by William Young of Inverugie, and the harbour added in the 1880s, during the herring-**fishing** boom of that period. Sandstone quarrying has also been an important local industry.

**Hopetoun House** Mansion house near **South Queensferry**, originally built in 1698–1701 to designs by William **Bruce** for the Hope family who became Earls of Hopetoun. Reconstruction on a palatial scale was begun in 1721 and carried out in phases by William, John and Robert **Adam**. It is still the home of the descendants of the Hope family, presently the Marquess of **Linlithgow**, but belongs to a heritage trust set up by the family. It is open to the public.

**Hopetoun, Earl of** see **Linlithgow, 1st Marquess of**

**Hornel, E(dward) A(tkinson)** (1864–1933) Artist, b. Australia. Moved to Scotland as a child. In 1885 he met fellow artist George **Henry**, and with him became associated with the **Glasgow Boys**, sharing with the group an interest in natural, rural subjects, although Hornel's work (like Henry's) is more

*The Honours of Scotland.*

*The Old Man of Hoy, Orkney.*

overtly symbolic. In the decades after 1900 he produced numerous paintings showing children at play in an outdoor setting, which tend towards the repetitive. His home in **Kirkcudbright**, Broughton House, and its beautiful Japanese-inspired garden, is now in the care of the **National Trust for Scotland**.

**Horner, Francis** (1778–1817) Politician and advocate, b. Edinburgh. He was interested in political economy, and was an MP in Cornwall. He was also one of the founders of the *Edinburgh Review* in 1802.

**horning** Being put to the horn was a process by which a debtor could be declared an outlaw – by 3 blasts of a horn – and his goods confiscated by the Crown to be passed on to his creditors. Letters of horning were issued in the name of the monarch and under the signet seal.

**horseman** A ploughman, in the pre-tractor era, usually referring to an unmarried man. It was a badge of pride, implying a skill and familiarity with heavy horses, and the ability to plough a good *fur* or furrow. The horseman's word was the secret formula to be whispered in a horse's ear that would ensure mastery and obedience. This might be imparted to novice ploughmen in a mock-Masonic ceremony, ranging from harmless fun to something worse.

**Hourn** see **Loch Hourn**

**House of Fraser** see **Fraser, Hugh, Lord Allander**

**House of Pitmuies** 18th-century house 11 km (7mi) to the east of **Forfar**. The extensive gardens, open to the public, include a

walled garden with herbaceous borders, old-fashioned roses and delphiniums, and a riverside walk with abundant spring bulbs.

**Houston** Village 9km (6mi) northwest of **Paisley**. In the 1780s the ancient village and castle were largely demolished and a new enlarged village built nearby, on a regular plan, in connection with the cotton industry. The mansion of Houston House was built in the 17th century, but the present house is mainly of 1872 and 1893–5; it is privately owned and is divided into flats.

**Houston House** House at **Uphall**, West Lothian, built for the advocate Sir Thomas Shairp in 1600, enlarged 1780 with good interiors of that date. It is now a hotel.

**Howe of Fife** The fertile valley of the River **Eden** in central **Fife**, between the **Lomond** and the North Fife Hills. Mainly agricultural, it includes the towns of **Cupar** and **Ladybank** and many small, attractive villages such as **Ceres**, **Kingskettle** and **Balmullo**.

**Howe of the Mearns** Area at the northeastern end of the valley of **Strathmore**, and south of **Stonehaven**. **Laurencekirk** is the main town in this fertile, agricultural area, made famous in the novels of Lewis Grassic **Gibbon**. See also **Kincardineshire**.

**Howson, Peter** (1958– ) Artist, b. London. He studied at **Glasgow School of Art**, and has become well known for his large-scale figurative paintings, which take as their subject aspects of contemporary life, frequently at its most overtly masculine and aggressive. In 1993 he travelled to Bosnia as Britain's Official War Artist.

**Hoy** The second-largest island in **Orkney**, southwest of Mainland. The northern part of Hoy is hilly: Ward Hill (479m/150ft) is the highest point in Orkney, and most of the population lives in the more fertile south. The island's best-known feature is probably the sea stack known as the Old Man of Hoy (137m/450ft), which stands out from sandstone cliffs on the northwest. The small village of Rackwick was formerly the home of the composer Sir Peter Maxwell Davies. The Dwarfie Stane is a Neolithic chambered cairn cut from a single block of sandstone. The village of Lyness on the southeast coast had an oil service base. It was the World War II base for the fleet in **Scapa Flow** and it now has the Scapa Flow Visitor Centre, in the former oil-pumping station, with information on Orkney's involvement in World Wars I and II, and the sinking of the *Royal Oak*. The village of Longhope at the south end of the island was the base of the Longhope lifeboat, whose 8 crewmen died in 1969 while attempting to rescue the tanker *Irene*. There are 2 martello towers, dating from the Napoleonic Wars, at Crockness and Hackness, the latter in the care of **Historic Scotland**. The charming 18th-century house of Melsetter was renovated in Arts and Crafts style by W R Lethaby in 1898. The nearby chapel of St Colm and St Margaret (1900) is also by Lethaby.

**Hughes, Edith Mary Wardlaw** (née **Burnet**) (1888–1971) Pioneer woman architect and teacher of architecture, b. Edinburgh, niece of Sir John **Burnet**. She studied art and architecture in Paris, Dresden, and Florence (1909–12) and graduated as an architect from Gray's School of Art, Aberdeen in 1914. She taught architecture and design there until her marriage with her head of school, Thomas Harold **Hughes**. In 1920 they moved to **Glasgow**, where her practice was mainly domestic and church furnishing, but she designed Glasgow's replacement Mercat Cross (1927–30). After World War II she practised in **Edinburgh**.

**Hughes, Thomas Harold** (1888–1949) Architect, b. Staffordshire. He studied at the Royal College of Art and was head of the school of architecture at Gray's School of Art, Aberdeen (1910–14). He married Edith Burnet (see above) and was a partner in the firm of her uncle, Sir John **Burnet** from 1919 until 1922, when he became Professor of Architecture in the Royal College in **Glasgow**. By inclination a classicist, he designed some remarkable modern buildings for **Glasgow University**: the Sports Pavilion (1936), the Institute of Chemistry (1936–9) and the circular Reading Room (1939–40). He also had an extensive practice in Oxford.

**humanity** Name given to Latin in Scottish universities.

**Humbleton Hill** (**Homildon Hill**), **Battle of** On 14 September 1402 an invading Scottish army under the 4th Earl of **Douglas** was defeated attempting to return to Scotland, by the English under Henry Percy ('Hotspur') and the renegade 10th Earl of March, near Wooler in Northumberland. Massive Scottish losses destabilised domestic politics and discouraged invasions on this scale for a century.

**Hume, David, of Godscroft** (c.1560–1630) Historian, b. Dunbar. He wrote a *History of the House of Douglas and Angus*, and a *History of the Humes of Wedderburn*. He was Secretary to the 8th Earl of **Angus**, thus gaining access to family papers.

**Hume, David** (1711–76) Philosopher, b. Edinburgh. With Adam **Smith**, widely regarded as representing the highest intellectual achievement of the **Scottish Enlightenment**, and a hero of the 18th-century Age of Reason. His innovative philosophical works included a *Treatise on Human Nature* (1738–40). Though influential with 20th-century logical positivist philosophers because of his deconstruction of cause and effect arguments and his general scepticism, he was better known in his lifetime as a political essayist and historian. He wrote *Essays Moral and Political* (1741), and a celebrated *History of England* in 5 volumes (1754–62), from the 'philosophic Whig' point of view. He spent time in France but lived mainly in **Edinburgh**, where his application for the chair of moral philosophy failed through well-justified claims of heresy and atheism. He was Keeper of the Advocates' Library from 1752 to 1757; see **National Library of Scotland**.

**Hume, David** (1757–1838) Judge, b. Ninewells, Berwickshire, nephew of David **Hume** (above). He was sheriff of **Berwick-upon-Tweed** from 1783 and of **Linlithgow** (1793–1811), and Baron of the Scottish Court of Exchequer (1822–34). His main work on the criminal law of Scotland is regarded as institutional. As Professor of Scots Law in **Edinburgh University** (1786–1822), he also lectured on civil law.

*The philosopher David Hume by Allan Ramsay, 1766.*

*William Hunter lecturing on the muscles of the back at the Royal Academy of Arts, by Johann Zoffany c.1775.*

**Hume, Joseph** (1777–1855) Radical politician, b. Montrose. He became an East India Company surgeon, but transferred to civil service, making a fortune in the Mahratta War of 1802–7. He returned to sit in parliament for Scottish constituencies. A vocal exponent of the Benthamite creed of James **Mill**, he was a passionate spokesman for severe economy, minimal government, free trade (especially for India), Catholic emancipation, and many other radical Whig causes.

**Hume, Sir Patrick, of Polwarth** (1641–1724) Covenanter. Imprisoned in 1674 and 1678, he spent a month hidden in the family vault in Polwarth Church in Berwickshire, during which he was looked after by his daughter Lady Grizel **Baillie**. He escaped to Holland where he was an adviser to **William of Orange**. Under William and Mary he became Lord Chancellor of Scotland (1696), and he was made 1st Earl of Marchmont in 1697.

**Hunter, George Leslie** (1879–1931) Artist, b. Rothesay, Bute. Emigrated to California with his family while young and first worked as an illustrator before returning to Scotland c.1906. The paintings he produced up to c.1918, invariably still lifes and dark in tone, are quite different from the exuberantly executed and boldly coloured works he produced thereafter and which led to his grouping with the other **Scottish Colourists**. During the 1920s he spent extended periods painting in the south of France, but also in **Fife** and at **Loch Lomond**, where he produced some of his finest works.

**Hunter, John** (1728–93) Surgeon, b. near East Kilbride. He was a surgeon in the army, writing about the treatment of gunshot wounds. He was also based at London hospitals and in 1776 was surgeon extraordinary to the king. He created an extensive collection of human and animal specimens, which now belongs to the Royal College of Surgeons. Brother of William **Hunter**.

**Hunter, Russell** (1925–2004) Actor, b. Glasgow. A shipyard worker before taking to the stage, he made his professional debut in 1947 and later worked with the Royal Shakespeare Company. His most acclaimed roles included the 2 one-man plays *Cocky* (1969) and *Jock* (1972) and the part of Lonely in the 1970s television series *Callan*.

H

**Hunter, William** (1718–83) Surgeon, b. near East Kilbride. He specialised in obstetrics and like his brother **John** was based in London. He was Physician to Queen Charlotte, and carried out pioneering research into gynaecology. His anatomical and other collections were gifted to **Glasgow University**, forming the beginnings of the Hunterian Museum.

**Hunterian Museum** See **Glasgow University**

**Hunter's Quay** Village to the north of **Dunoon**, on the **Firth of Clyde**, at the entrance to the **Holy Loch**, which developed as a holiday resort. Its name dates from 1828, when the local landowner James Hunter built a pier here. It was formerly the headquarters of the Royal Clyde Yacht club whose magnificent clubhouse, designed by Thomas Lennox Watson in 1889, is now the Marine Hotel. A ferry, operated by Western Ferries, runs to **Gourock**.

**Hunterston** Site of 2 nuclear power stations, 8km (5mi) south of **Largs**. Hunterston 'A' which opened in 1964 has been closed since 1990 and is currently being decommissioned. Hunterston 'B' opened in 1976 and is still operational, with a visitor centre. It was also the site of an iron-ore terminal opened in 1978, now used for importing coal. The power stations are close to Hunterston Castle, a 15th-century tower house which was restored by Sir Robert **Lorimer**, and is now the Clan Hunter Association Centre.

**Huntingtower Castle** Tower house which lies 5km (3mi) northwest of **Perth** and was originally known as Ruthven Castle. It consists of 2 separate towers, dating from the 15th and 16th centuries, joined by a later structure; it has important painted decoration of the 15th and 16th centuries. It belonged to the Ruthven family, and the **Ruthven Raid** took place here. The family were proscribed following the **Gowrie Conspiracy**, and the name of the castle was changed. It is now in the care of **Historic Scotland**. It is also the name of a nearby village.

**Huntly** Town in Aberdeenshire, 53km (33mi) northwest of **Aberdeen**, near where the Rivers **Deveron** and Bogie meet. In 1776 the town was laid out on a grid pattern with a central square by the Duke of Gordon. It has some impressive buildings, including the Brander Library (1883–5) by John **Rhind**, the neo-Jacobean Gordon's School by Archibald **Simpson** (1839–41) and the neo-Gothic Scotts Hospital by A Marshall Mackenzie (1901). The octagonal Roman Catholic Church of St Margaret, financed by the Spanish sherry merchant, John Gordon of Wardhouse, has a Spanish baroque tower and Spanish paintings.

The ruins of Huntly Castle, which was attacked and restored several times, include outstanding early 17th-century decorative stonework. A stronghold of the powerful Earls of Huntly, it is in the care of **Historic Scotland**.

**Huntly Castle** see **Huntly**; see also **Castle Huntly**

**Huntly, George Gordon, 4th Earl of** (1514–62) A powerful magnate in the north, he was the victorious commander at the Battle of **Hadden Rig**. He was Chancellor in 1546, and joined the **Lords of the Congregation** in 1560. He rebelled against **Mary, Queen of Scots**, and was defeated by a royal army under the Earl of Moray in 1562. He died shortly after being captured.

**Huntly, George Gordon, 6th Earl and 1st Marquis of** (1562–1636) Of Catholic sympathies, his religious allegiance was nevertheless sufficiently ambiguous for him to be close to **James VI**. He killed the Earl of **Moray** ('the bonnie Earl' of the ballad) in 1592, after Moray had recklessly provoked him by challenging his supremacy in the Northeast. Later he was implicated in Catholic conspiracy, leading to his exile. Despite this he remained a favourite of **James VI**. He returned in 1596, and was created Marquis in 1599.

**hunt the gowk** or **huntygowk** Term used to refer to 1 April, April Fool's Day; a fool's errand on this day or the person on whom the trick is played. 'Gowk' is **Scots** for 'cuckoo' and also means 'fool'.

**Hutcheson, Francis** (1694–1746) Philosopher, b. County Armagh, Ireland. Professor of Moral Philosophy at **Glasgow University** from 1729, his pioneering ideas influenced the leading figures of the **Scottish Enlightenment**, including Adam **Smith** and David **Hume**. His *System of Moral Philosophy* was published after his death.

**Hutton, James** (1726–97) Geologist, b. Edinburgh. He studied medicine and chemistry, but developed a passion for geological research. His *Theory of the Earth* (1788) proposed a radical new understanding of how rocks were formed and, in recognising that processes active on the earth's surface today were similarly active in the geological past, laid the foundations of modern geology. He used unconformity in the rocks at Siccar Point, near **Dunbar**, on the East Lothian coast as a main example to show that the earth must be very much older than held by religious belief. He later demonstrated the intrusive nature of granite from sites in **Glen Tilt** and **Arran**. Much of his work was illustrated by John Clerk of Eldin (1778–1812).

H

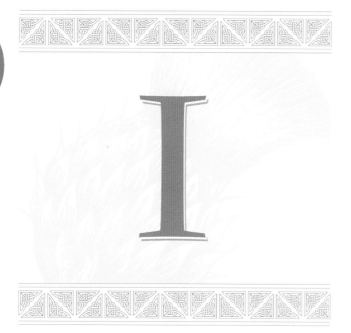

**Iain Lom** (**John MacDonald**) (c.1624–1710). Gaelic poet, from the family of Keppoch MacDonalds. His poetry deals with political events from the **Montrose** campaigns to the **Union of Parliaments**, as well as with the activities of his clan. Tobar nan Ceann, the **Well of the Seven Heads**, beside **Loch Oich**, is a monument to his bloody vengeance on the murderers of his chief.

**Ibrox** District of Glasgow which has Ibrox Stadium, home ground of **Rangers** football club. It was the scene of 2 major sporting disasters: in April 1902, when 25 people died following the collapse of a section of terracing at a Scotland-England match, and in January 1971, when barriers on a stairway collapsed, killing 66 spectators at an **Old Firm** match.

**ICI** see **Imperial Chemical Industries**

**Imlach, Hamish** (1940–96) Musical entertainer, b. Calcutta. The most popular performer of the 1960s Scottish folksong revival, he appeared on some 40 LP recordings and performed around the world. A guitar stylist who taught John **Martyn**, a raconteur who influenced Billy **Connolly**, his most popular song was 'Cod Liver Oil And The Orange Juice'.

**immigration** see p.195

**Imperial Chemical Industries Ltd (ICI)** Company founded in 1925, on the lines of the German chemical giant I G Farben, on the initiative of Sir Harry McGowan, the Scots chairman of Nobel's Explosives Ltd. It brought together the largest chemical companies in Britain. In Scotland its largest works were at **Ardeer**, St Rollox (Glasgow) and **Grangemouth**. It secured a dominant position in fertiliser manufacture in Scotland in the 1930s, which it ran through its subsidiary Scottish Agricultural Industries Ltd. The parent company was disaggregated in the late 20th century. The Grangemouth dyestuffs plant, now owned by Zeneca plc, is the largest surviving part of ICI's Scottish empire.

**Improvers** 18th-century agricultural innovators. See **Cockburn, John, of Ormiston**; **Grant, Archibald, of Monymusk**; **Kames, Lord**

**Inaccessible Pinnacle** see **Sgurr Dearg**

**Inchaffray** Site near **Crieff** on which the Earl of Strathearn founded an Augustinian Abbey in 1220.

**Inchcailloch** see **Loch Lomond**

**Inchcolm** Island in the Firth of **Forth** opposite **Aberdour**. The Augustinian abbey, a well-preserved ruin in the care of **Historic Scotland**, was founded c.1153 and it was probably here that the *Inchcolm Antiphoner*, a remarkable collection of the plainchant sung by early monks, was written down; Walter **Bower** was abbot here when he wrote the *Scotichronicon*. The island can be reached by boat from **South Queensferry**. Military defences built during the 2 World Wars remain.

**Inchinnan** Village to the north of **Paisley**, once a **Knights Templar** site, now industrial; its major surviving monuments are the neoclassical bridges over the White **Cart** and the Black Cart Rivers, designed by the engineer Robertson Buchanan (1809–12).

**Inchkeith** Island in the Firth of **Forth** opposite **Kinghorn**. Fortified in the 16th and 19th centuries, it has been used as a prison and an isolation hospital. Plague sufferers were transported there from Edinburgh in 1497. **James IV** is said to have left 2 babies and a dumb nurse on the island as a linguistic experiment. The **lighthouse**, designed by Robert Stevenson, was built in 1803.

**Inchmahome** Island on the Lake of **Menteith**, site of a ruined Augustinian priory founded in 1238. **Mary, Queen of Scots** spent some weeks here as a child. It is the burial place of Robert Bontine Cunninghame **Graham**. The priory is in the care of **Historic Scotland**.

**Inchmurrin** see **Loch Lomond**

**Independent Companies** Autonomous units raised by the issue of royal commissions to local landlords and chiefs in the **Highlands**. They were used for scouting and police duties, and not required to serve furth of Scotland. The government of **William II and III** and Mary raised such units after 1689. Latterly they consisted of a few officers and non-commissioned officers and 50 'sentinels', plus a piper. After 1725 a series of independent companies was raised to 'watch' or patrol in the central **Highlands**, mainly to suppress robbery and cattle theft.

# IMMIGRATION

At the end of the Roman period in the 4th century, the land that became Scotland was inhabited by Celtic tribes, in the south by Britons, related to the population further south, and in the north by the Picts. By the 5th century the Scots from Ireland had established the kingdom of Dal Riata on the west coast, and in the 7th century the Angles had moved north as far as the Firth of Forth (see Bernicia). From the 9th to the 13th century, there were Norse incursions on the Northern and Western Isles and on the adjoining mainland. Although these were often temporary warring attacks, many Norsemen settled in these areas and left their mark on the population. In the 11th and 12th centuries Anglo-Norman landowners and monasteries arrived from northeast England, accompanied by much larger numbers of English servants, craftsmen and traders (see language). Throughout the rest of the Middle Ages, smaller numbers of Dutch, Flemish and French people arrived, often with skills then lacking in Scotland.

Immigration on a large scale began again in the 19th century when, seeking work in Scotland, and escape from near-starvation, substantial numbers of Irish families began to arrive. Many of them found employment around the Clyde, but a significant percentage travelled further east. By the mid 19th century, according to the 1851 Census, over 18% of the population of both Dundee and Glasgow were Irish-born, with a marginally higher proportion in the former.

A far smaller influx of Jewish people, many of them fleeing persecution, began around the same time. Edinburgh had a synagogue (1816) before Glasgow (1823), but the population in the latter city soon outgrew that in the capital. In the early 20th century larger numbers of Jews arrived, especially from Russia and Lithuania, to escape poverty and political oppression in the Russian empire, sometimes as a staging post to further emigration to North America. Other Lithuanians arrived and settled mainly in Lanarkshire; they are now mostly assimilated, but there is still a Lithuanian presence, especially in Bellshill.

From 1880 to World War I, the biggest group of immigrants were the Italians, many of whom established a niche for themselves in the catering business, with ice-cream cafés, fish-and-chip shops and delicatessen, many of which survive to this day. World War II saw the arrival of a Polish community. Begun as a mixture of civilian refugees and servicemen, it became more permanent when, following the Soviet occupation of Poland, many chose not to return to their homeland.

The most numerous arrivals in the second half of the last century came from the Indian subcontinent: Pakistanis and Indians, and in Dundee the Bangladeshis who arrived when it was a centre of the **jute** industry. The Chinese community, mostly Cantonese speakers from Hong Kong, is also now firmly established. Unlike much of England and Wales, however, there has as yet been little Afro-Caribbean immigration into Scotland.

Scotland has greater ethnic diversity now than at any time in its history. The country benefits directly from the many skills and ideas of its immigrant people, and has been enriched culturally by the wider influences brought here from around the world.

---

The financial honesty and political reliability of company commanders such as Simon Fraser, Lord **Lovat**, were rightly questioned and in 1739 the Independent Companies were regimented as the 43rd Regiment of Foot, later renumbered the 42nd – the 'forty twa', from 1740 known as the **Black Watch**.

**infield** Before agricultural improvements, the best part of the cultivated ground of a farm, nearest the farm buildings, heavily manured and kept under crop. See also **outfield**.

**Inglis, Elsie Maud** (1864–1917) Surgeon, b. India. She opened a maternity hospital for the poor in **Edinburgh**, and founded the Scottish Women's Suffragette Federation in 1906. During World War I, after being rejected by the Royal Army Medical Corps and the Red Cross, she set up her own women's ambulance units in France, Serbia and Russia. Her name was commemorated in the Elsie Inglis Memorial Maternity Hospital in Edinburgh (1925–88).

**Ingliston** West of Edinburgh, this is the location for the Royal Highland Centre, an exhibition centre belonging to the Royal Highland Agricultural Society of Scotland. It is the venue for the annual **Royal Highland Show**. There is also a motor racing track, and a regular Sunday market.

**Innellan** Village near **Dunoon**. In 1881–2 the blind local minister, George Matheson, wrote the hymn 'O Love that wilt not let me go'. The ruins of 16th-century Knockamillie Castle are nearby.

**Inner Hebrides** see **Hebrides**

**Inner House** see **Court of Session**

**Innerleithen** (pop. 2586) Town near Peebles, which had a thriving textile industry and was also known as a spa town in the 19th century. It was brought to prominence in the early 19th century as the scene of Sir Walter Scott's novel *St Ronan's Well*. Robert Smail's Printing Works, founded in 1837, is run by the **National Trust for Scotland**, and gives a working example of Victorian technology.

**Innerpeffray** Small village to the southeast of **Crieff**. The Collegiate Church of the Blessed Virgin was built in 1508. Attached to it is Scotland's oldest public library. It was established around 1680 by the 3rd Lord Madderty in the now-ruined Innerpeffray Castle. The current library, an attractive Palladian building designed by Charles Freebairn, dates from 1758–62. The collection contains many early and rare books, mostly religious or classical.

**Inner Sound** Stretch of water separating the island of **Raasay** from **Wester Ross**.

**Innes** Tall towered L-plan house in **Moray**, to the northeast of **Elgin**, with details similar to Heriot's Hospital, **Edinburgh**, built for the senior branch of the Innes family between 1640 and 1653 by the same master mason, William Aytoun: a landmark in the transition from tower house to classical house design.

**Innes, Calum** (1962– ) Artist, b. Edinburgh, recognised internationally for his abstract paintings, which are produced using a technique of applying paint and then removing or erasing certain areas. He was short-listed for the Turner Prize in 1995 and awarded the Nat West Art Prize in 1998.

**Innes, Cosmo** (1798–1874) Advocate and historian, b. Durris, Aberdeenshire. He was Professor of History at **Edinburgh University**, and edited many important Scottish historical texts.

**Innes, Michael** see **Stewart, J I M**

**Innes, Thomas** (1672–1744) Catholic priest, Jacobite and historian, b. Drumgask, Aberdeenshire. Associated with the **Scots College** in Paris where his brother Lewis was principal and archivist to the exiled Stewarts. He debunked the mythological history of early Scottish kings invented by George **Buchanan** to support the right of subjects to resist a tyrannical monarch. Although Innes did this to sustain the **Jacobite** theory of divine-right monarchy, his *Critical Essay on the Ancient Inhabitants of Scotland* (1729) helped lay the foundations of a critical approach to sources in Scottish historiography.

**Innis Chonnel Castle** Ruined early medieval castle on an island in **Loch Awe**, the main stronghold of the Campbells until **Inveraray** Castle was built.

**Insch** Village northwest of **Inverurie**. Above are the ruins of the 13th-century Dunnideer Castle, built on the site of much earlier forts.

**interdict** Scots legal term for a court order prohibiting some action complained of as illegal or wrongful; corresponding to English injunction.

**intromission** see **vicious intromission**

**Inveralligin** Hamlet on the north shore of Loch Torridon. A ferry crossed the loch from Inveralligin to **Shieldaig** until the present road was built.

**Inverallochy** Coastal village southeast of **Fraserburgh**, with original fisher cottages still standing, so close to Cairnbulg that only natives know where the boundary runs. One of these cottages, 'Maggie's Hoosie', can be visited. The ruins of 16th-century Inverallochy Castle are nearby.

**Inveraray** (Gaelic **Inbhir Aora**) Small town on **Loch Fyne** which became **Argyll**'s first royal **burgh** in 1648. The original village was demolished in 1758 by the Duke of Argyll to form the landscaped park around Inveraray Castle, the first major neo-Gothic castle built in the UK, designed by Roger Morris for the 3rd Duke of Argyll, 1745–1761 with splendid classical interiors by Robert **Mylne** of the 1780s. The new town was planned by John **Adam** in 1750 and has a remarkable double church by Robert Mylne 1795–1802 for English and Gaelic congregations. The courthouse by Gillespie **Graham** (1813) and the jail (1820) are now tourist attractions.

**Inverawe** (Gaelic **Inbhir Atha**) Estate near **Taynuilt**, with a working salmon smokehouse and fisheries, which distributes smoked salmon and other gourmet foods across Britain and overseas.

**Inverbervie** (also **Bervie**) (pop. 2094) Small town north of **Montrose**. **David II** landed here on his return from exile in France in 1341, and he granted it royal **burgh** status. In 1788 Scotland's first flax mill was established here, and textile production remained important for over 200 years. The old bridge (1799) is remarkable for its 31m (103ft) span with cellars for coal and lime (and reputedly prisoners) in the abutments. Now principally a commuter town.

**Invercauld** Invercauld Castle, east of **Braemar**, is a Victorian mansion house by J T Wimperis (1875) incorporating a 16th-century tower house. It was used by the Earl of **Mar** during the 1715 **Jacobite Rising**. It is owned by the Farquharson family and is now available for holiday letting and functions.

**Inverclyde Council** Local-authority area formed in 1996 from the Inverclyde **District** of **Strathclyde Region**; see maps on pp.394–5 and **local government**. The administrative centre is **Greenock** and other towns include **Gourock**, **Port Glasgow** and **Kilmacolm**.

**Inveresk** Village on the southern edge of **Musselburgh** which

*The River Ness and Inverness, looking towards the castle.*

was the site of a Roman fort. Many of the 18th-century houses were built for wealthy Edinburgh residents. Alexander **Carlyle** was minister here for 57 years. The gardens of Inveresk Lodge are run by the **National Trust for Scotland**, and the tall-spired classical church by Robert Nisbet (1875) had a separate upper gallery for the fisherfolk.

**Inverewe** (Gaelic **Inbhir-iù**) The gardens at Inverewe were begun in 1862 by Osgood Mackenzie, son of the laird of **Gairloch**. He transformed an estate at the head of **Loch Ewe** into an exotic garden of 20 hectares (50 acres) which now contains around 2500 species from across the world. It was gifted to the **National Trust for Scotland** in 1962.

**Invergarry** (Gaelic **Inbhir-gharadh**) Village southwest of **Fort Augustus** which was the stronghold of the MacDonnells of Glengarry. Invergarry Castle had a turbulent history and was finally reduced to ruin in 1746 by the Duke of Cumberland. An early iron-smelting works operated here from 1727–36.

**Invergordon** (pop. 3890) Town on the **Cromarty Firth** which was established by the Gordon family in the 18th century. The deep-water harbour was the site of a naval base until 1956, and is now used for the maintenance of oil rigs. Cruise liners also berth at Invergordon.

**Invergowrie** Village to the west of **Dundee**, dominated by the central spire of All Souls Episcopal Church by Hippolyte Jean Blanc (1891). An important Pictish stone, the Bullion stone, was discovered here in 1934, and the ruins of Dargie Church lie on an early Christian site. The Scottish Crop Research Institute is based at Invergowrie.

**Inverie** (Gaelic **Inbhir Eigh**) On the north shore of **Loch Nevis**, the only village in **Knoydart** is reached by boat. The Old Forge pub is listed in the *Guinness Book of Records* as the most remote pub in mainland Britain.

**Inverkeithing** (pop. 5412) Town on the **Fife** coast of the Firth of **Forth**, a former royal **burgh**, with the remains of a priory. Shipbreaking is still an important industry here, and engineering and papermaking continue. The parish church (1826–7) by Gillespie **Graham** retains the 14th-century tower of the old church. The Greyfriars monastery founded c.1350 was remodelled in 1559 and is now a museum. The baroque town house of 1754 survives, together with several notable 17th-century houses.

**Inverkip** Lying southwest of **Gourock** on the River **Clyde**, this village has a popular marina. Inverkip Power Station, Scotland's only oil-fired power station, is south of the village; it was opened in 1976, but was mothballed in 1987 because of rising oil prices and the opening of **Torness**.

**Inverlochy Castle** (Gaelic **Inbhir Lòchaidh**) Near **Fort William**, it dates from the 13th century and was a **Comyn** stronghold. Scene of the Battle of Inverlochy in 1645, in which the Marquis of **Montrose** defeated a Covenanting army led by the Earl of **Argyll**. The quadrangular castle is now ruined. A nearby mansion house, also known as Inverlochy Castle, dates from 1863 and is now a luxury hotel.

**Invermoriston** Village northeast of Fort Augustus, on the shore of **Loch Ness**. The ruined **Telford** bridge over the River Moriston can still be crossed on foot.

**Inverness** (Gaelic **Inbhir Nis**) (pop. 40,949) Known as 'the capital of the Highlands', Inverness is the administrative centre of **Highland Council** and was designated a city in 2000. The River

Ness flows through the centre. Historically Inverness was important in the Cromwellian and Hanoverian governments' attempts to control the **Highlands**. The castle, which dominated the town, was destroyed in the 1745 **Jacobite Rising** and eventually replaced by William **Burn**'s castellated Sheriff Court, 1833–5. The town acquired an impressive architectural character in late Georgian and Victorian times, notably Thomas Mackenzie's **Bank of Scotland** (1847) and Alexander Ross's twin-towered Episcopal Cathedral of St Andrew (1866). The city is now a fast-growing business and tourist centre, with good road and rail connections and an airport at Dalcross, 13km (8mi) to the northeast.

**Inverness District** see **Highland Region**

**Inverness-shire** Former county, Scotland's largest in area, until 1975 when part of it became the Inverness District of **Highland Region**; see maps on pp.394–5 and **local government**. It stretched from the **Moray Firth** in the east to **Fort William** in the west, and included **Skye** and the Outer **Hebrides** south of **Lewis**. The county town was **Inverness**.

**Inverpolly** This area to the northeast of **Ullapool** is a National Nature Reserve. The dramatic landscape of lochs and mountains includes **Stac Pollaidh** and **Suilven**.

**Inverquharity** (pronounced 'inver**whar**ity') L-plan tower house near **Kirriemuir** built by Alexander, Lord Ogilvy, 1444. The tower was reoccupied and the damaged jamb rebuilt, 1970.

**Inversnaid** Village on the east shore of **Loch Lomond**. The spectacular Falls of Inversnaid were celebrated in the poetry of William Wordsworth and Gerard Manley Hopkins. Inversnaid Barracks, now ruined, were erected in 1719 to house troops to check the depredations of the MacGregors. The area has close associations with **Rob Roy**.

**Inveruglas** Site on the west side of **Loch Lomond** of a power station from the **Loch Sloy** hydroelectric scheme, and the largest hydroelectric station in Scotland. A visitor centre was opened at the viewpoint here in 2001.

**Inverurie** (pop. 10,882) Small town 22km (14mi) northwest of **Aberdeen**, on the confluence of the Rivers **Don** and Urie, established as a **burgh** in the late 12th century by **David, Earl of Huntingdon**. The Bass, on the edge of the town, was the site of his motte and bailey castle. There are many significant Pictish stones

*Iona Abbey and St Martin's Cross; St John's Cross stands beside the West Range, rebuilt in 1965.*

in the area. Inverurie was an important railway engineering town for most of the 20th century, and papermaking is now the principal industry. Just to the south was the end of the **Aberdeen Canal**.

**Iona** Small island, just off the southwest coast of **Mull**, with enormous spiritual significance. It was the location of St **Columba**'s monastery, founded in 563. It became a destination for pilgrims from Scotland and beyond, and a burial place for many of the kings of Scots. In 1994, the late leader of the Labour Party, John Smith, was also buried here. The medieval Benedictine abbey church was restored between 1875 and 1910, and the monastic buildings in 1938–59. There is also a partially restored Augustinian nunnery, founded c.1200. It is accessible by a regular ferry service from **Fionnphort** on the adjacent coast.

**Iona Community** An ecumenical Christian community based in Iona Abbey and associated buildings, with headquarters in **Glasgow**. It was founded in 1938 by Revd George **Macleod**. The Community places emphasis on social and political issues and on developing new, inclusive worship. It has members and associate members across Britain and overseas.

**Ireland, John** (c.1440–95) Theologian. He became Rector of the Sorbonne and was sent on diplomatic missions by Louis XI before returning to Scotland. In 1484 he was **James III**'s ambassador to France. He was private chaplain to James III and **James IV**, and wrote *The Meroure of Wisdome*, the earliest known original work of Scots prose.

**Irn Bru** see **Barr, A G and Co**

**ironfounding** For much of the 19th and 20th centuries one of Scotland's most significant industries. Iron castings were essential components of most machines, of many buildings, and were used in almost all industries and in public utilities, notably in water and gas supply. The rails on British railways were supported on cast-iron 'chairs', and early railways had cast-iron rails. The rise of the **Lanarkshire** and **Ayrshire** iron-smelting industries after the invention of the hot-blast process by James Beaumont **Neilson** in 1828, was a powerful stimulus to the industry. Glasgow was renowned for heavy castings for engineering, and for the water and gas industries, and for ornamental architectural castings. The leading firms in the latter business, Walter Macfarlane & Co of the Saracen Foundry and George Smith and Co of the Sun Foundry, led the world. The **Falkirk**, **Larbert** and Bonnybridge areas were noted for light castings, including heating and cooking stoves, rainwater goods and cooking pots, Carron Company being the pioneering firm. The industry shrank dramatically beween the 1960s and 1990s, and is now a very minor one.

**iron industry** There was a dispersed charcoal-fuelled iron industry in the 17th- and 18th-century **Highlands** (see **Bonawe Furnace, Furnace, Invergarry**). Large-scale production using coal began in Scotland with the establishment of the **Carron Ironworks** in 1759. In 1828 James Beaumont Neilson invented the hot-blast system of iron production, increasing efficiency and turning Scotland into a world leader in the production of iron for heavy industry, especially in **Lanarkshire** and **Ayrshire**. The industry declined in the 20th century and is now extinct. See also **steel, Ravenscraig**.

**Irvine** (pop. 33,090) Town on the River Irvine on the Ayrshire coast, a former royal **burgh** and once an important trading port, although overshadowed by **Port Glasgow** from the 18th century. It became an important industrial town in the 19th century. In the late 1960s Irvine was selected to be a 'New Town', and modern buildings and extensive leisure facilities were built around its historic centre. It now has Scotland's largest paper mill. It is the administrative centre of **North Ayrshire** Council. The Scottish Maritime Museum is at Irvine Harbour, its main building being the giant Victorian engineering shop originally built at Stephens' shipyard, Linthouse, **Glasgow**.

**Irvine, Andy** (1951– ) International rugby player, b. Edinburgh. He is remembered for his pace and attacking skills. He won 51 caps for Scotland, captaining the team 15 times, and took part in 3 Lions Tours: of South Africa (1974), New Zealand (1977), and again South Africa (1980).

**Irvine, Sir James Colquhoun** (1877–1952) Organic chemist and university administrator, b. Glasgow. He was laboratory assistant to Professor Thomas **Purdie** in **St Andrews** from 1895 and later studied organic chemistry in Leipzig. He pioneered the modern chemistry of sugars, succeeded Purdie, and in 1920 became Principal of **St Andrews University**. Helped by American endowments, he did much to restore the residential and international character of the university.

**Irving, Edward** see **Catholic Apostolic Church**

**Isaacs, Sir Jeremy** (1932– ) Television producer and filmmaker, b. Glasgow. He was the first Chief Executive of Channel 4 Television, and is known for series such as 'The World at War' (1975) and 'Cold War' (1998). He was Director General of the Royal Opera House in London 1988–96.

**Isla, Glen** see **Glen Isla**

**Islay** (Gaelic Ìle) Island in the Inner **Hebrides**, with ferry links to Kennacraig on the mainland and to **Jura**. Many important standing stones and medieval remains can be seen, including Finlaggan, the centre of power of the **Lords of the Isles**, and the elaborately carved Kiloran cross, with links to **Iona**. The principal villages are Port Ellen and Bowmore. With its 7 distilleries Islay is renowned for its malt whiskies, and agriculture and tourism are also important.

**Islay, Earl of** see **Argyll, Archibald Campbell, 3rd Duke of**

**Isle of Harris** see **Harris, Isle of**

**Isle of Lewis** see **Lewis, Isle of**

**Isle of May** see **May, Isle of**

**Isle of Skye** see **Skye**

**Isle of Whithorn** Fishing village 5km (3mi) south of **Whithorn**, once an island but now linked to the mainland by a causeway. The ruined 13th-century St Ninian's chapel may have been used by pilgrims travelling to Whithorn. (In the care of **Historic Scotland**.) The *Solway Harvester* trawler was tragically lost from here in 2000.

**Isleornsay** Village in the south of the Isle of **Skye**, on the estate of Sir Iain Noble, who has done much to revive **Gaelic** culture; see **Sabahl Mor Ostaig**. It takes its name from the Isle of Ornsay (Eilean Iarmain), just offshore, on which are a **lighthouse** and ruined chapel.

**Isles, Lords of the** see **Lords of the Isles**

**Italian Chapel** see **Orkney**

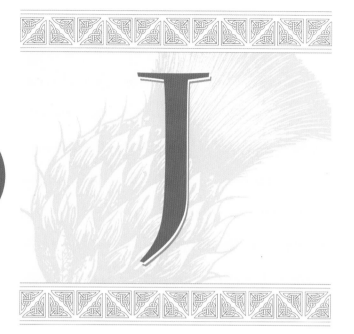

**Jackson, Gordon** (1923–90) Actor, b. Glasgow. He was well known for his television roles in *Upstairs, Downstairs* (1970-5) and *The Professionals* (1977-81). He also starred in many films including *Whisky Galore* (1949), *The Prime of Miss Jean Brodie* (1969) and *A Town Called Alice* (1980).

**Jacob, Violet** (née **Kennedy-Erskine**) (1863–1949) Poet and author, b. Dun, near Montrose. Daughter of the 18th Laird of Dun, she wrote in the Scots of her Angus home, as well as in English. Her work includes novels, short stories and travel diaries, especially of India, illustrated by her own watercolours, but she is principally remembered for her poetry, including 'Tam i' the Kirk'.

**Jacobites** Supporters of the exiled **James VII** and his descendants, James Francis Edward **Stewart** and Charles Edward **Stewart**, who held court in France and Italy. The Jacobites attempted to regain the throne on several occasions, most notably 1715 and 1745. See **Jacobite Risings**, p.201.

**Jags** see **Partick Thistle**

**James I** (1394–1437) King of Scots 1406-37, b. Dunfermline. He was a prisoner at the English court for 18 years, and married Joan **Beaufort**, a cousin of Henry V of England. A poet, he (almost certainly) wrote *The Kingis Quair*. In 1424 he returned to Scotland and ruled capably and ruthlessly. He was assassinated by a disaffected noble faction in **Perth**.

**James II** (1430–60) King of Scots 1437-60, b. Edinburgh. After a turbulent minority he strengthened the authority of the monarchy and destroyed the powerful **Black Douglas** family. In 1449 he married **Mary of Gueldres**. He was killed by an exploding cannon attempting to recover **Roxburgh** Castle from English control.

**James III** (1452–88) King of Scots 1460-88. He gained **Orkney** and **Shetland** for Scotland as part of his marriage treaty with Margaret of Denmark. He was unpopular, partly because of attempts to make peace with England. He was killed at **Sauchieburn** in battle against rebellious magnates nominally led by his son, the future **James IV**.

**James IV** (1473–1513) King of Scots 1488-1513. An able king and patron of the arts, he faced little domestic opposition to his rule, although the suppression of the Lordship of the Isles caused lasting local turbulence. He married **Margaret Tudor**, daughter of Henry VII of England, but died in battle against the English at **Flodden**.

**James V** (1512–42) King of Scots 1513-42, b. Linlithgow. A capable and ruthless king, his artistic leanings were expressed in patronage of architecture. He strengthened Scotland's links with France and its stance of Catholic orthodoxy by marrying first Madeleine, the daughter of Francis I, and then **Mary of Guise**. He built new palaces at **Stirling** and **Falkland**, and extended that of Holyroodhouse, **Edinburgh**. He died soon after his army's defeat by the English at **Solway Moss**, and was succeeded by his days-old daughter **Mary**.

**James VI** (1566–1625) King of Scots 1567-1625, King James I of England and Ireland 1603-25, b. Edinburgh. He did much to extend the authority of the monarchy in both the **Borders** and the **Highlands**. In 1589 he married **Anne of Denmark**, and in 1603 he succeeded to the English throne and moved to London, only returning once in 1617 to visit Scotland. After 1603 he was able to revitalise the never-abolished episcopal order in the Church, but his attempts to introduce liturgical change to bring the churches of England, Ireland and Scotland closer together met with widespread resistance.

**James VII** (1633–1701) King of Scots and King James II of England and Ireland 1685-9, b. London. A Roman Catholic, his attempts to introduce religious toleration were met with suspicion, and he was replaced on the throne by his daughter **Mary II** and her husband **William III**. He was defeated by William at the Battle of the Boyne, and died in exile in France.

**Jameson, Sir Leander Starr** (1853–1917) Statesman, b. Edinburgh. As a close friend of Cecil Rhodes he was involved in the settlement of Rhodesia (now Zambia and Zimbabwe). In 1895 he was the leader of the ill-fated Jameson raid, leading to his brief imprisonment. From 1904-8 he was Premier of the Cape Colony, and in 1913 he became President of the British South Africa Company.

# JACOBITE RISINGS

The term 'Jacobite' comes from *Jacobus*, the Latin form of the name James, as these struggles aimed to restore King James **VII** and **II** to the thrones of England, Scotland and Ireland and later to enthrone his son, Prince James Francis Edward **Stewart** (known as the Old Pretender) as James VIII and III. The main episodes were:

**1688** James VII and II fled from England to France and was replaced on the English and Scottish thrones by his daughter **Mary** and her husband **William** of Orange. James then went to Ireland to assert his rights there with French assistance. In the spring of 1689 John Graham of Claverhouse, Viscount **Dundee**, gathered an army in the **Highlands** in support of James. He fought a successful battle at the Pass of **Killiecrankie** against government troops under Major-General Hugh **Mackay** of Scourie, but the victory was marred by Dundee's death in the battle. His army was defeated at **Dunkeld** by the **Cameronian** regiment, commanded by William **Cleland**, and was finally routed at the Haughs of **Cromdale** in Moray in May 1690.

**1708** This is the least-known of the Jacobite risings, largely because of efforts to cover up facts about it by the British and French governments. It is held to have had more chance of success than any other, and might have broken the recent union between Scotland and England. The arrival of the young Prince James with the French fleet was fatally delayed by his illness, by stormy weather, and by incompetent navigation by the French admiral. In the face of a Royal Navy squadron off the Fife coast, the French chose to flee with James and return to France.

**1715** ('The Fifteen') In September the Jacobite standard was raised by the Earl of **Mar** on the Braes of Mar. There was great support for the rebellion, especially in the Highlands and in the Episcopalian Northeast but it failed, largely owing to military ineptitude, in spite of further support from small risings in the Scottish **Borders** and the northeast of England, where the Jacobite army was defeated at Preston in December. At the same time, Mar failed to defeat a much smaller government army under the Duke of Argyll at **Sheriffmuir** near **Stirling**. Thus by the time James finally arrived from France, at **Peterhead**, in December, the chances of success were virtually gone.

**1719** Spain, quarrelling with the British government over European issues, planned to invade England under the Jacobite banner. It sent forces to the Highlands under George **Keith**, Earl Marischal, as a diversionary measure. After delays by storms, they landed first in **Lewis** and then on **Loch Alsh**, which should have given them a route to Inverness through **Kintail**, Glen Moriston and **Loch Ness**. Further support however was limited and poor security alerted the Hanoverian command. Royal Navy warships destroyed the Jacobite base with its ammunition at **Eilean Donan** Castle and on 10 June troops under General Wightman defeated the Highland and Spanish army at Shiel Bridge.

**1745–6** ('The Forty-Five') In August 1745 James's son Prince Charles Edward **Stewart** landed at **Loch nan Uamh** on the west coast of Scotland. His standard was raised at **Glenfinnan** and he was joined by some of the Highland clans, but not the hoped-for strength. A growing army had some initial success at the battles of **Falkirk** and **Prestonpans** and the Prince held court in Edinburgh. A subsequent march into England had to be abandoned at Derby, largely due to lack of support in England. Promised French help failed to materialise and on 16 April 1746, Charles faced the Hanoverian army under the Duke of Cumberland on an inappropriate site at **Culloden** near Inverness, selected by the Prince and his Irish adviser, Thomas O'Sullivan, and was catastrophically defeated. After some months on the run he escaped to France, leaving his Highland supporters to ruthless persecution by Cumberland.

It is often said that Culloden ended the Gaelic way of life in the Highlands and Islands. In fact it was already in sharp decline, but this was certainly hastened by measures to prevent another rising. As well as forfeiture of estates and the abolition of the main structures of clanship, such as the tenure of land by military service and private jurisdiction, these included prohibitions on the holding of arms and the wearing of **Highland dress**, which continued until the 1780s. (See **heritable jurisdictions**.)

*The Battle of Culloden, 16 April 1746. An 18th-century engraving.*

**J**

**Jamesone, George** (1589/90–1644) Artist, b. Aberdeen. The first major figure in the history of Scottish art, Jamesone trained in **Edinburgh**, but established himself as a portrait painter in his native city. His reputation spread and he was soon patronised all over Scotland, to the virtual exclusion of any other artist practising there. He painted the ceremonial decorations for the arrival of **Charles I** in Scotland in 1633.

**Jamie, Kathleen** (1962- ) Poet, b. Renfrewshire. She now lives in Fife where she lectures in Creative Writing at **St Andrews University**. Her travels in Central Asia and the Middle East have fuelled some of her poetry. She has published several poetry collections, including *Black Spiders* (1982), *The Autonomous Region* (1993), *The Queen of Sheba* (1994) and *Jizzen* (1999). Her *Selected Poems* appeared in 2002.

**Jamieson, John** (1759–1838) Lexicographer and literary editor, b. Glasgow, he was a **Secessionist** minister. He compiled the *Etymological Dictionary of the Scottish Language* (1808–9), the earliest British dictionary to support its definitions with dated quotations. It went into many more editions, long after his death. He also published sermons and edited **Barbour** and **Blind Harry**.

**Jam Tarts** see **Heart of Midlothian**

**Jardine, Quintin** Crime writer, b. in the west of Scotland. He worked as a journalist and for the Government Information Service before becoming a freelance writer and public relations consultant. He has written a long series of crime novels featuring Skinner, an Edinburgh police detective, including *Skinner's Rules* (1993), *Skinner's Ghosts* (1998) and *Fallen Gods* (2003). He has also written under the pseudonym of Matthew Reid.

**Jardine Matheson and Company** Trading company established by Dr William Jardine and James **Matheson** in 1828–9. Initially they exported opium from India to China to fund the purchase of tea at Canton for the British market. They opened a warehouse in Hong Kong and dealt in a wide range of imports. The trading network has diversified and expanded to become a major conglomerate, based in Asia and other markets.

**Jarlshof** Archaeological site on **Shetland**, near **Sumburgh** Airport. Excavations have revealed occupation by Stone Age, Bronze Age, Iron Age, Pictish, Viking and medieval peoples, including a **broch**, wheel-houses and a Viking longhouse. A 16th-century mansion house was named 'Jarlshof' by Sir Walter **Scott**, and the name was later given to the entire site.

*Jarlshof, Shetland.*

**Jedburgh** (also **Jeddart**, **Jethart**) (pop. 4090) Border town on the Jed Water, a tributary of the River **Teviot**. It was frequently caught up in warfare between Scotland and England. Despite repeated attack, the church of the Augustinian abbey, built between 1150 and 1225, remains fairly complete and very impressive. The late 16th-century house used by **Mary, Queen of Scots** in 1566, is now a museum. Jedburgh was the county town of **Roxburghshire**, and had an important woollen industry. The local rugby team, Jedforest, has produced a number of international players. The game of Fastern's E'en **handba**, played on Shrove Tuesday, supposedly originated when local men played with the heads of their defeated English enemies. The Jedburgh Callant's Festival is held every June. The phrase **Jeddart** or **Jethart Justice** refers to hanging a man first and trying him later. On the site of the former castle and gallows, Archibald Elliot designed an impressive prison in the form of a castle, now a museum.

**Jeddart snail** A kind of sweet of dark brown toffee, with a mild peppermint flavour, made in **Jedburgh**. The recipe is said to have been given to a local baker by a French prisoner-of-war in his employment.

**Jeffrey, Francis** (1773–1850) Judge, literary critic and Whig politician, b. Edinburgh. Co-founder and first editor of the *Edinburgh Review*. He became Lord Advocate in 1830 and shared the drafting of the Scottish Reform Bill (1832). He was a Judge of the **Court of Session** from 1834.

**Jenkins, Robin** (1912- ) Author, b. Cambuslang. One of Scotland's leading 20th-century novelists, his works include *the Thistle and the Grail* (1954), *The Cone Gatherers* (1955), *Guests of War* (1956), *Fergus Lamont* (1979), and *Matthew and Sheila*

(1998). He taught English both in Scotland and abroad and some of his novels are set in other countries: Afghanistan in *Some Kind of Grace* (1960) and *Dust on the Paw* (1961); Borneo in *A Figure of Fun* (1974) and *Leila* (1995).

**Jesus and Mary Chain, The** Rock group from East Kilbride, founded in the mid 1980s by the brothers Jim and William Reid. After achieving notoriety for the brevity and cacophony of their early performances, they had a number of hit singles and albums with their trademark sound of fetching melodies and screeching feedback. Their debut album was *Psychocandy*.

**Jethart** see **Jedburgh**

**Jocelin** (d.1199) Bishop of Glasgow from 1175. He began the rebuilding of **Glasgow** Cathedral following a fire, and dedicated it in 1197. He obtained **burgh** status for Glasgow and the right to hold the **Glasgow Fair**.

**Jock Tamson's bairns** Scottish expression for the human race, common humanity.

**John, King of Scots** see **Balliol, John**

**John Barleycorn** Nickname for **whisky**, popularised by Robert **Burns**, especially in his poem *Tam O' Shanter*: 'Inspiring bold John Barleycorn,/ What dangers thou canst make us scorn!'

**John Muir Trust** see **Muir, John**

**Johnnie Walker** Whisky blend possibly established by John Walker (1805–59), a **Kilmarnock** grocer, but certainly developed by his son Alexander. Formerly known as 'Walker's Kilmarnock whisky', the blend was exported worldwide. Red and Black Label brands are still blended and bottled in Kilmarnock.

**John o' Groats** Village in **Caithness** which attracts tourists because it is traditionally but inaccurately believed to be the most northerly settlement in Britain. It was named after a Dutchman, Jan de Grot, who settled here and established a ferry link to Orkney in the late 15th century. A summer-only passenger ferry to Burwick on **South Ronaldsay** still operates.

**Johnson, James** (c.1772–1811) Music publisher and engraver, b. Ettrick Valley. Initiator in 1787 of the song book *The Scots Musical Museum* (6 volumes, 1787–1803) for which Robert **Burns** collected and rewrote many songs.

**Johnston, Archibald of Warriston** (1611–63) Advocate, b. Edinburgh. Deeply religious, he played a key part in drafting the **National Covenant**. His diaries give an insight into his character and beliefs. He opposed **Charles I** and **Charles II**, and after the Restoration was captured and executed.

**Johnston, Calum** (1891–1973) and **Annie** (d.1963) Gaelic

singers, b. Barra. Brother and sister whose rich knowledge of **Gaelic** song and heritage made them important informants for collectors such as Marjory **Kennedy-Fraser** and John Lorne **Campbell**. Calum was also a knowledgeable piper.

**Johnston, Sir Reginald Fleming** (1874–1938) Colonial administrator and traveller, b. Edinburgh. During his years in the colonial service in Hong Kong and Weihaiwei, he travelled widely in China and surrounding countries and wrote scholarly works on life and religion there, especially on Confucianism. In 1919 he became tutor to the 13-year-old Puyi, the last Emperor of China. He described his 6 years in Beijing in *Twilight in the Forbidden City* (1934). In 1925, after the young emperor had been seized in a coup, he returned to colonial service; he later became Professor of Chinese in the School of Oriental Studies, University of London. In 1934, he bought the island of Eilean Righ, in **Loch Craignish**, Argyll.

**Johnston, Thomas** (1881–1965) Politician, b. Kirkintilloch. One of the few exciting figures in the succession of pre-devolution Secretaries of State for Scotland. Editor for 25 years of the socialist periodical *Forward*, he became a Labour MP in 1922. As Secretary of State for Scotland 1941–5, he enjoyed unusual latitude due to Churchill's concentration on the war. In 1942 he set up an influential advisory Scottish Council (Development and Industry). He also established the **North of Scotland Hydro-Electric Board** (of which he was later chairman), and prefigured many of the achievements of the post-1945 Labour government. Realising that there was no place for him in the highly centralised UK Labour government, he left politics and went on to serve on such bodies as the Forestry Commission in Scotland and the Hydro-Electric Board.

**Johnstone** (pop. 16,468) Town near **Paisley** which was built to a grid plan in the late 18th century and prospered principally through textiles, coal and machine-tool manufacture. The spired octagonal parish church dates from 1792 (now housing Scotland's only shoelace factory), and Johnstone mill, one of the earliest cotton mills to survive, from 1782.

**Johnstone, Christian Isobel** (1781–1857) Novelist and journalist, b. Fife. With her husband, John Johnstone, an editor and printer, she made considerable contributions in the early years of the *Inverness Courier* and, after moving to **Edinburgh**, to various periodicals, notably *Tait's Magazine*. As well as short stories, she wrote novels: *Clan-Albin: A National tale* (1815), a romantic tale set in the **Highlands** and Ireland, and *Elizabeth* *de Bruce* (1827). But she is probably best remembered for *A Cook and Housewife's Manual*, first published in 1826, under the name Meg Dods (a character in Walter **Scott's** *St Ronan's Well*).

**Johnstone, Jimmy** (1944– ) Footballer, b. Viewpark, Lanarkshire. Played for **Celtic** 1961–75 and was a member of the 'Lisbon Lions' team who won the European Cup in 1967. A talented winger, he was known as 'Jinky'.

**Johnstone, William** (1897–1981) Artist, b. Denholm, Roxburghshire. With his cousin F G **Scott** and C M Grieve (Hugh **MacDiarmid**), Johnstone was, from the 1920s onwards, active in promoting a renaissance in the Scottish arts. His openness to continental developments in art (in particular Surrealism) influenced his own painting, which is amongst the most individual produced in Scotland in the mid 20th century, and he was also a highly respected teacher of art.

**Jones, John Paul** (1747–92) Naval officer, b. Kirkbean, Dumfriesshire. Originally John Paul, he changed his name to Paul Jones when he settled in Virginia to escape criminal charges. A supporter of the American Revolution, he carried out daring raids around the coast of Britain. He became known as 'the father of the American Navy', but also served in the French and Russian navies.

**Jordanhill** Area of northwest **Glasgow**, best known as the home of Jordanhill College of Education, built 1913–22. Situated in the former Jordanhill estate, the college is now part of **Strathclyde University**.

**jougs** Iron collar, attached to a wall, which was fastened round the neck of an offender. Jougs were often found at the mercat cross or the church gates. **Kirk Sessions** and civil authorities ordered their use for offences including blasphemy, slander and Sabbath breaking.

**Judd, J(ohn) W(esley)** (1840–1916) Geologist, b. Portsmouth. An outstanding igneous petrologist, he worked extensively on **Mull**, and demonstrated former volcanic centres there and at **St Kilda**, **Ardnamurchan**, **Rum** and **Skye**. He eventually became a professor at the Royal College of Science in London.

**Junor, Sir John** (1919–97) Journalist, b.

Black Isle. Editor of the *Sunday Express* 1954–86, he was known for his extreme right-wing views.

**Jura** (Gaelic **Diùra**) (pop. 188) Island in the Inner **Hebrides**, northeast of **Islay**. Most of the sparsely populated island is accessible only on foot, and the southern part is dominated by the hills known as the 'Paps of Jura'. The island consists largely of sporting estates which offer deer-stalking. There is a distillery, producing Isle of Jura malt **whisky**, in Craighouse, the only village. George Orwell spent several summers at the north end of the island at the end of his life. See also **Corrievreckan**.

**Justice Clerk** see **Lord Justice Clerk**

**Justice General** see **Lord Justice General**

**Justice of the Peace** (JP) Lay magistrate, appointed from 1609 originally on the English model, with increased powers after 1707 in both judicial and administrative matters. From the Local Government (Scotland) Act of 1889, the administrative powers have been reduced to a minimum, now vested in the local authorities. JPs are the judges in the **district courts**.

**Justiciary, High Court of** see **High Court of Justiciary**

**jute industry** After some earlier experiments, jute fibre imported from Bengal was successfully processed in eastern Scotland from the 1830s. The material was woven into a cheap fabric used for sacking, wool-packs and later linoleum and carpet backing. **Dundee** became a leader in European jute production, and was known as 'juteopolis'. The industry declined in the 20th century because of competition from India and the production of cheap synthetic materials.

*Tay Jute Works, Dundee, in the 19th century.*

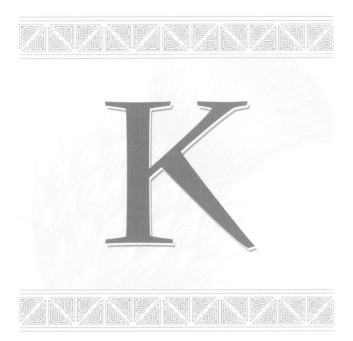

**kail** Also spelt **kale**. Vegetable of the cabbage family, especially a curly variety (curly kail), in the past the most widely used vegetable in Lowland Scotland, so that the word is used in several wider senses. It can refer to a soup or other dish of which kail is the main ingredient, or indeed a soup made with other vegetables, and it has also been used as the name of the main meal. The kailyard was the kitchen garden and the term 'kailyard' was coined by J H Millar in 1895 to denigrate the oversentimental style employed by writers such as J M **Barrie**, S R **Crockett** and Ian Maclaren in their idealised tales of rural and village life, popular in the late 19th and early 20th centuries.

**kailyard** see **kail**

**Kailzie Garden** Garden near **Peebles**. The 7 hectares (17 acres) comprise woodland walks with spring bulbs, informal herbaceous plantings and one of the oldest larch trees in Scotland. In the walled garden there is a series of rose gardens and brightly planted shrub and herbaceous borders.

**kale** see **kail**

**Kames** 16th-century 5-storey tower house of the Bannantynes of Kames; on Kames Bay on the east side of the island of **Bute**; it and its steading are now holiday houses. Nearby is Wester Kames, a tall tower house rebuilt from ruins by Robert Weir Schultz 1897–1900 for the 3rd Marquess of Bute.

**Kames, Henry Home, Lord** (1696–1782) Philosopher, judge and agricultural improver, b. Kames, Berwickshire. He used **Scots** in court and elsewhere. As well as law and legal history, he wrote on philosophy (*Essays on the Principles of Morality and Natural Religion* 1751), aesthetics (*Elements of Criticism* 1762) and farming (*The Gentleman Farmer* 1776). His wide range of interests typify the **Scottish Enlightenment** in action.

**Kay, Jackie** (1961– ) Poet, playwright and novelist, b. Edinburgh. Her poetry collections include *The Adoption Papers* (1990) and *Other Loves* (1993); her plays are *Chiaroscuro* (1986) and *Twice Over* (1988). Her novel, *Trumpet* (1998), won the Guardian Fiction Award, and her collection of short Stories, *Why Don't You Stop Talking?* (2002), was listed for the Saltire Book of the Year Award.

**Kay, John** (1742–1826) Artist, b. near Dalkeith. A barber before setting up a shop selling his own etchings, he is most famous for his *Series of Original Portraits And Caricature Etchings with Biographical Sketches and Anecdotes* (1837), entertaining caricatures of people in **Edinburgh**, giving a vivid picture of life at the time.

**Keeper of the Records** The official in charge of the **National Archives of Scotland**, controlling public records regarded as worthy of preservation, and a large collection of private and business records.

**Keiller, James and Janet** In the early 18th century Seville oranges were landed at **Dundee** and were difficult to sell. A load was bought by John Keiller, and his wife Janet, a confectioner and baker, made them into marmalade. The business was developed by their son James; its success grew and later the family set up a marmalade factory. Quite early the firm moved its main activity first to the Channel Islands and then to Silvertown in the London docks, keeping only a nominal capacity to make marmalade and jam in Dundee.

**Keiss** Village on the east coast of **Caithness** 11km (7mi) north of **Wick**. Keiss Castle is a tall Z-plan castle of the Earls of Caithness built on the cliff edge in the early 17th century; the new castle by David **Bryce** (1859) stands farther back from the sea.

**Keith** (pop. 4491) Small northeast town on the River Isla, 16km (10mi) northwest of **Huntly**, developed around the now ruined Milton Tower of the Ogilivies, built 1480. A 'new town' was added, centred on spacious Reidhaven Square, by the Earls of Seafield in 1750. There is a Gothic Parish church by Gillespie **Graham** 1816–18, and a neo-classical St Thomas RC Church by Revd Walter Lovi and William Robertson. Textiles and distilleries prospered and the latter survive. In 1785 the ancient Milton brewery became one of Scotland's earliest legal distilleries, now Strathisla; it has a visitor centre. The Glenkeith distillery was founded in 1958, the first in Scotland since 1900.

**Keith, George** (c.1639–1716) Missionary, b. Aberdeen. Reared a Quaker, he later joined the Church of England and became one of the first missionaries of the Society for the Propagation of the Gospel in America in 1702–4. He spent some years in Pennsylvania (1688–94)

**Keith, George, 10th Earl Marischal** (c.1693–1778) With his brother James he joined the **Jacobites** in the 1715 Rising; as a result their titles were attainted and estates forfeited. He participated in the disastrous Spanish and Jacobite invasion of the northwest Highlands in 1719, but afterwards escaped to the Continent. He became a favourite of Frederick the Great of Prussia. He disapproved of the 1745 Rising and after taking the oath to George III in 1763, he was allowed to buy back most of the Keith family estates. He ended his life as Governor of the detached Prussian possession of Neufchâtel.

**Keith, James** (1696–1758) Soldier, b. Inverugie, near Peterhead, brother of George **Keith**, 10th Earl Marischal, joined the **Jacobite Rising** in 1715 and was twice forced to escape to the Continent. After 9 years in the Spanish army he became a major-general in the Russian forces, but in 1747 left to be a field-marshal in the army of Frederick the Great of Prussia, who relied greatly on his military talents. He was killed at the battle of Hochkirch.

**Keithhall** Originally Caskieben, a 16th-century Z-plan house to the southeast of **Inverurie**, to which a symmetrical front with an impressive armorial was added in the later 17th century for Sir John Keith, created Earl of Kintore in 1677; now houses and flats.

**Kelburn Castle** Z-plan tower house of 1581, near **Fairlie** on the Ayrshire coast, now the northwest wing of a symmetrical late Stewart house completed in 1722. It was built for the Boyle family, now Earls of Glasgow, who still live there. Within the grounds there is a pyramidal monument by Robert **Adam** (1775). The Kelburn Country Centre is open to the public, using the mid 18th-century stables as a visitor centre.

**Kellie, Thomas Erskine, Earl of** (1732–1781) Composer, b. **Kellie Castle**, Fife. Scotland's greatest composer of symphonies during the 'classical period', in 1756 he brought to Britain the avant-garde orchestral writing style of Mannheim in southwest Germany.

**Kellie Castle** Near **St Monans**, Fife, the castle is mainly 16th–17th century, with parts from the 14th, built by the Lords Oliphant and later a seat of the earls of Mar and Kellie. Restored in 1878 for Professor James Lorimer, father of the architect Robert **Lorimer** and painter John Lorimer and renowned for its plasterwork and its walled garden, managed on organic principles with mixed fruit, shrub and herbaceous borders but also a Lorimer catmint border feature. A small gallery of the works of the sculptor Hew **Lorimer** has been formed in his studio. (In the care of the **National Trust for Scotland**.)

**Kello, John** (d.1570) Minister who murdered his wife in the manse at Spott, near Dunbar, hoping it would be believed a suicide, then went into church to preach a sermon. Suspicions were raised by his plans to remarry, and he was hanged after confessing his crime.

**Kelly, Dr William** (1861–1944) Architect-historian. He inherited the Smith of **Aberdeen** practice; his finest new buildings were the Savings Bank and St Ninian's Church in Aberdeen, but he was also responsible for much sensitive restoration work notably at King's College Chapel, Old Aberdeen and on the Cowdray estates.

**Kelly Castle** Tall tower house to the southwest of **Arbroath**, built by the Elliots in the late 16th century, its courtyard buildings very completely preserved.

**Kelman, James** (1946– ) Novelist, b. Glasgow. Kelman's early novels of working-class life, including *The Busconductor Hines* (1984), and *A Disaffection* (1989), were highly regarded, and *How Late It Was, How Late* won the Booker Prize in 1994, though it was criticised for its brutal realism. He has also published *Translated Accounts* (2001) and the short story collection *The Good Times* (1998). He was Professor of Creative Writing at **Glasgow University** from 2001 till 2003.

**kelp** Varieties of large brown seaweeds that grow in shallow water on rocky coasts. It is used as a fertiliser, and its ashes provided chemicals especially for soap- and glassmaking and bleaching. Gathering kelp provided employment, especially in the **Western Isles**, in the 18th and early 19th centuries, but hardship was caused by decline in demand, due to renewed availability of cheaper substitutes from the Mediterranean after the Napoleonic Wars. There is still a small trade using kelp stems to make alginates for adding to ketchup, ice cream, beer, etc.

**Kelso** (pop. 5116) Pretty market town in the **Borders**, opposite the confluence of the Rivers **Tweed** and **Teviot**, developed around a ford (later a bridge) over the Tweed, notable for the ruins of once massive Kelso Abbey, transferred to this site from **Selkirk** by **David I** in c.1127 (in the care of **Historic Scotland**). Predominantly a mid to late Georgian town, centred on a spacious central square with an Edwardianised town hall built in 1816, its skyline is dominated by the tall-spired North Church built by Frederick Pilkington for the hymn-writer, Horatius Bonar, in 1866. Also in Roxburgh Street is Walton Hall, the home of Sir Walter **Scott**'s publisher John Ballantyne. Behind the square is the octagonal Parish Church (1771–3); and crossing the Tweed is the first major bridge by John **Rennie**, prototype of his Waterloo Bridge in London. Nearby is **Floors Castle**.

**Kelty** (pop. 5628) Small town in Fife 3km (2mi) northwest of Cowdenbeath. Mining was important from the 18th century to the 1960s and opencast mining was begun, since closed due to flooding.

**Kelvin** River which rises near **Kilsyth**, and runs west and then southwest through **Glasgow**; the **Forth and Clyde Canal** runs parallel to it for some distance. In its last stretch it formerly powered several cornmills and a flint mill, before entering the River **Clyde** at **Partick**.

**Kelvin, William Thomson, 1st Baron** (1824–1907) Inventor and physicist, b. Belfast. He moved to **Glasgow** at the age of 8, going to Glasgow University aged 10. At 16 he went to Cambridge University, where he was second Wrangler (second-highest-scoring maths student). He became Professor of Mathematics and **Natural Philosophy** (1846–99) at **Glasgow University**. He created the Kelvin temperature scale (1848), and solved problems in electrostatics, thermodynamics and hydrodynamics, also inventing electrical and telegraphic devices, often produced by his company Kelvin & White. He was the chief consulting engineer for the first transatlantic cable (1857–8). Lord Kelvin was buried in Westminster Abbey next to Isaac Newton.

**Kelvinside** Area of the west end of **Glasgow** alongside the River **Kelvin**, including the parkland of the Botanic Gardens, developed in the mid 19th century for housing the mercantile classes. It has given its name to a rather over-refined middle-class accent, now virtually extinct. It features some impressive terrace blocks by architects such as Alexander **Thomson**, Charles Wilson and John Thomson Roch.

**Kemnay** Village on the River **Don** northwest of **Aberdeen**, developed for the granite industry (and mostly of granite), supplying material and masons to Britain and overseas. Its quarry supplied stone for many important structures, most recently the new **Scottish Parliament** building. A by-product which originated at Kemnay is the reconstituted stone Fyfestone. Nearby is Kemnay House, built by Sir Thomas Crombie in the 17th century and from the 1780s a seat of the Burnetts. **Castle Fraser** is also nearby.

**Kemp, Lindsay** (1939– ) Mime artist, dancer and director, b. Isle

*William Thomson, Lord Kelvin, giving his last lecture to students at Glasgow University in 1899.*

of **Lewis**. After training with Ballet Rambert he developed his colourful style with his own company, creating several ballets, teaching mime (notably to David Bowie) and appearing in films by Derek Jarman and Ken Russell.

**Kemp, Robert** (1908–67) Dramatist and journalist, b. Hoy, Orkney. A producer for BBC radio, he encouraged the broadcast of **Scots** dramas, and later created his own, most famously adapting David **Lyndsay**'s *Satyre of the Thrie Estatis* for the stage (1948), and also translating Molière into Scots. He was a founder of the Edinburgh Gateway Theatre and a regular contributor to The **Herald** newspaper.

**Ken** see **Loch Ken**

**Kenmore** (Gaelic **A' Cheann' Mhor** ) Model village at the foot of **Loch Tay**, near **Aberfeldy**, built by the Earls of Breadalbane in the mid 18th century and made picturesque with bargeboarded gables in the mid 19th century. It has a splendid bridge over the River **Tay** by John Baxter (1774). The Scottish Crannog Centre is nearby; see **crannog**. To the northeast is **Taymouth Castle** and beyond it Croft Moraig, a large circle of standing stones.

**Kennaway, James** (1928–68) Novelist, b. Auchterarder, Perthshire. His first and best-known novel, *Tunes of Glory* (1956), about class and personality conflict in a Highland regiment, became a major film (scripted by himself) starring Alec Guinness and John Mills. Other novels include *Household Ghosts* (1961), also filmed, and he wrote a number of film scripts, especially for *The Battle of Britain*. He was killed in a car crash.

**Kennedy, A(lison) L(ouise)** (1965– ) Writer and reviewer, b. Dundee. Renowned for elegant but pointed and realistic work including the short story collections *Night Geometry and the*

*Deborah Kerr.*

*Garscadden Trains* (1991) and *Indelible Acts* (2002) and the novels *So I Am Glad* (1995) and *Everything You Need* (2000). She has also written TV and radio plays.

**Kennedy, Charles** (1959– ) Politician, b. Inverness. A journalist and broadcaster, he became Social Democratic Party MP for Ross, Skye and Inverness West in 1983, the youngest MP at the time, and was the first SDP MP to back a merger with the Liberals after the 1987 election. Leader of the Liberal Democrats since 1999.

**Kennedy, Helena, Baroness Kennedy of the Shaws, QC** (1950– ) Barrister, b. Glasgow. Frequently appearing for victims of miscarriages of justice (Guildford Four), she is also a broadcaster and writer on human rights and particularly women's rights, publishing *Eve was Framed* (1992).

**Kennedy, James** (c.1408–65) Prelate, grandson of **Robert III** and nephew of **James I**. Bishop of **St Andrews** from 1440, he was an influential advisor to **James II** and a prominent figure during the minority of **James III**. He founded St Salvator's College at St Andrews.

**Kennedy, Kate** A fictitious 'niece' of James **Kennedy**, a Victorian invention, now a central figure in the annual April procession (revived in 1926) commemorating the historic figures of **St Andrews**, always played by a male first-year student.

**Kennedy, Ludovic** (1919– ) Writer and broadcaster, b. Edinburgh. After a varied career in television, including *Panorama*, he has concentrated on examining miscarriages of justice in writing: *10 Rillington Place* (1961); *A Presumption of Innocence* (1974), *The Trial of Stephen Ward* (1989), *The Airman and the Carpenter* (1986) about the Lindbergh case, *In Bed with an Elephant* (1995) on Scotland's relationship with England, *36 Murders and 2 Immoral Earnings* (2002); and on television: *Your Verdict*, *A Life With Crime*. He is married to the ballet dancer and actor Moira Shearer.

**Kennedy, Walter** see **Dunbar, William**

**Kennedy Castle** see **Castle Kennedy**

**Kennedy-Fraser, Marjory** (1857–1930) Musician. With Kenneth **Macleod**, she collected, modernised and anthologised **Gaelic** songs, published in *Songs of the Hebrides* (1909). She also made recordings of this music.

**Kenneth mac Alpin (Kenneth I, Cináed mac Alpín)** (d.858) King of Picts. Little is known about Kenneth, but he is not now thought to have brought about a unified Pictish and Scottish Dál Riatic kingdom. His significance lies instead in the lasting dynasty which he founded, his descendants successively monopolising power in the kingdom of Alba (much of mainland Scotland north of the **Forth**) and the kingdom of Scotland. After a war-torn reign he died at **Forteviot** and is buried on **Iona**.

**Kenneth II (Cináed mac Máel Coluim)** (d.995) King of Scots, son of **Malcolm I** (Máel Coluim mac Domnaill), he succeeded Culen in 971. After raids on England early in his reign, Kenneth's authority in Cumberland and **Lothian** was recognised by the English king Edgar at Chester in 973. Domestically, dynastic struggles culminated in Kenneth's murder near **Fettercairn**. He was buried on **Iona**.

**Kenneth III (Cináed mac Duib)** (d.1005) King of Scots, son of Dubh and grandson of **Malcolm I** (Máel Coluim mac Domnaill), succeeded **Constantine III** (Castantin mac Culen) in 997. The future **Malcolm II** (Máel Coluim mac Cináeda) son of **Kenneth II** (Cináed mac Máel Coluim) defeated and killed Kenneth at the Battle of Monzievaird after a reign marked by dynastic struggles.

**Kentigern, St** (d. c.612) According to legend, son of a **Lothian** princess Thenew, and brought up in a monastery at **Culross** by St Serf (who in fact lived a century later). He is often known as Mungo ('dear friend'); having spread Christianity in Cumbria, Wales and **Glasgow**, he was buried in the Glasgow cathedral that took this name.

**Ken, Water of** see **Loch Ken**

**Kerr, Deborah** (Originally **Jane Kerr-Trimmer**) (1921– ) Actor, b. Helensburgh. A trained dancer, she appeared in wartime British films including *The Life and Death of Colonel Blimp* (1943), but *Black Narcissus* (1947) led to a distinguished Hollywood career, which included the films *From Here to Eternity* (1953) and *The King and I* (1957). After retiring from films she made many stage and television appearances.

**Kerr, Jim** see **Simple Minds**

**Kerrera** (Gaelic **Cearrara**) Island in the Firth of **Lorn** opposite **Oban**, protecting the harbour. **Alexander II** died here in 1249, and Haakon of Norway gathered his troops here on the way to the Battle of **Largs**. Gylen House is a tall slim L-plan tower house with richly sculptured detail, built in 1582 by Duncan MacDougall of MacDougall. It stands on a rocky promontory at the south end of the island.

**Kerry, River** (Gaelic **Abhainn Chearraidh**) A salmon river near **Gairloch** in **Wester Ross**, supporting a population of freshwater mussels. In the 1940s the Kerry Falls hydroelectric scheme caused controversy over its environmental impact but brought electricity to the area.

**Kessock Bridge** Road bridge, built in 1980, linking **Inverness** to the promontory of the **Black Isle**.

**Kesson, Jessie** (originally **Jessie Grant McDonald**) (1916–94) Novelist and dramatist, b. Inverness, in the workhouse. Her early life, much of it homeless or in a children's home, formed the basis of *The White Bird Passes* (1958). She was encouraged by Neil **Gunn** and Nan **Shepherd** in her realistic and often humorous writings about the struggles of the poor. *Another Time, Another Place* (1983) is about Italian prisoners of war.

**Kidd, Carol** (1945– ) Jazz singer, b. Glasgow. A singer with a trad jazz band from the age of 15, she only turned professional in the early 1990s after Frank Sinatra invited her to sing with him at Ibrox. She has since enjoyed considerable acclaim, and was voted Best Vocalist at the Cannes Jazz Awards.

**Kidd, Dame Margaret Henderson** (1900–88) Lawyer, b. Linlithgow. In 1923 she was the first woman to be called to the Bar in Scotland and in 1948 the first woman QC in Scotland. She was also the first woman **sheriff** of a county, part-time in **Dumfries** (1960–6) and in **Perth** (1966–74). She was Keeper of the Advocates' Library (1956–69). See **National Library of Scotland**.

**Kidd, William (Captain Kidd)** (c.1645–1701) Privateer, b. Greenock. A sea trader out of New York, he was rewarded for piratical actions protecting Anglo-American trade in the West Indies, and in 1695 was entrusted with an English expedition against pirates in the Indian Ocean. However, his victims included merchant ships, and he was tricked into surrendering in Boston, shipped to London and hanged.

**Kilbarchan** Small town to the west of **Paisley**, built in 1723, prominent in the weaving industry in the 18th century. Its main landmarks are the Steeple at the Cross, built 1755 and 1782 to house the school and market, the old parish church, built in 1724, and a restored weaver's cottage built in 1723, now in the care of the **National Trust for Scotland**.

**Kilberry Castle** Small picturesque T-plan castle, in a fine setting on the shore of Loch Caolisport, on the Argyll coast, 26km (16mi) southeast of **Tarbert**. It was built on the site of the 1595 one by the antiquary John Campbell to designs by Thomas Brown (1844), and enlarged by Charles Kinnear in 1873.

**Kilbirnie** Town on River Garnock, north of **Irvine**, formerly a textile centre, making **linen** thread and **fishing** and other nets. The nearby Glengarnock steelworks closed in 1979. The parish church, built from 1470 onwards, contains the magnificent baroque Crawford loft of 1705, the finest laird's loft surviving in Scotland.

**Kilbrandon Report** The Report of the Committee on Children and Young Persons chaired by Lord Kilbrandon, published in 1964, recognised the needs of children as being the overriding consideration in criminal proceedings, and established the system of referral of offenders under 16 to a **Children's Hearing**.

**Kilbrandon Report** see **Scottish Parliament**, p.340

**Kilbrannan Sound** Stretch of water between **Arran** and **Kintyre**.

**Kilchoan** (Gaelic **Cill Chomhghan**) Village on the south shore of the **Ardnamurchan** peninsula, furthest west in the British mainland. It is the base for the ferry to **Tobermory**. Ardnamurchan **lighthouse** is nearby.

**Kilchurn Castle** (Gaelic **Caol 'a Chùirn**) On a spectacular site at the north of **Loch Awe**, near Dalmally, a splendid ruined 16th-century keep built by Sir Colin Campbell of Glenorchy, extended in 1693 with the first purpose-built barracks in Scotland. It was occupied by Hanoverian troops after the 1745 **Jacobite** Rising. In the care of **Historic Scotland**.

**Kilcreggan** Small resort on the Rosneath peninsula opposite **Greenock**, developed from the mid 19th century, and from the 1840s with picturesque marine villas, several of them by Alexander **Thomson**.

K

*Kildrummy Castle, Aberdeenshire.*

**Kildalton Cross** Superb 8th-century cross in the churchyard of an early 13th-century ruined church on **Islay**, 11km (7mi) north-east of **Port Ellen**. The ringed cross stands 2.65m (8ft 8in) high and is elaborately carved in high relief with snake-and-boss ornament, lions and the Virgin and Child.

**Kildonan** One of Scotland's finest Edwardian houses, at Bowhill, Ayrshire, a huge English manorial pile in the Lutyens manner built for Captain Euan Wallace by James Miller in 1914–15.

**Kildonan** see **gold**

**Kildrummy Castle** About 15km (10mi) west of **Alford** in Aberdeenshire, the spectacular ruins of Kildrummy Castle are a fine example of a 13th-century defensive structure, with much of the internal layout remaining. A stronghold of the earldom of Mar, it was a refuge for **Robert I**'s family in 1306, only falling to English besiegers when a fire broke out in the great hall. The castle became the seat of the Erskines of Mar until forfeited after the 1715 **Jacobite** Rising. A garden in the nearby quarry has bright spring and summer flowers and autumn colours from maples. In the care of **Historic Scotland**.

**Killearn** Commuting village 26km (16mi) northwest of **Glasgow**, on the edge of the **Campsie Fells**. A monument, designed by James **Craig** (1788), commemorates George **Buchanan** who was born nearby. The impressive neo-Jacobean mansion and terraced gardens built in 1897–1900 for the Ogstons is now a hotel. The finest of the Victorian and Edwardian mansions around the village is Auchenibert, designed by Charles Rennie **Mackintosh** (1904–7).

**Killiecrankie** The Pass of Killiecrankie, a tree-hung gorge on the

River **Garry** near **Pitlochry**, is a famous beauty spot and site of the 1689 battle between supporters of **James VII** under Viscount **Dundee** and the army of **William III** under Major General Hugh **Mackay**. Dundee was killed; although the **Jacobites** were victorious, their bid to break out in the **Lowlands** was blocked by defeat at **Dunkeld**, and they were finally routed at the Haughs of **Cromdale**. The Soldier's Leap marks the spot where one of Mackay's troops leapt across the gorge to escape his pursuers.

**Killin** (Gaelic **Cill Fhinn**) Village at the west end of Loch **Tay**, at the mouths of the Rivers **Dochart** and Lochay. The Falls of Dochart are a tourist attraction and the **Ben Lawers** and Ptarmigan hills make it popular with walkers. Its octagonal 18th-century church contains an ancient 7-sided font. Nearby are the ruins of **Finlarig Castle**. Until the 1960s there was a branch line of the **Glasgow-Oban** railway which it joined at Killin Junction.

**Killing Time** The persecution of the **Covenanters** under **James VII** in the 1680s after the Battle of **Bothwell** Brig, during which a number were killed and some transported.

**Killochan** Very tall stepped L-plan tower house to the northeast of **Girvan**, Ayrshire, built by John Cathcart in 1585, adjoined by a handsomely symmetrical mid 18th-century service court.

**Kilmacolm** Popular commuting village for **Glasgow**, **Paisley** and **Greenock**, 10km (6mi) southeast of Greenock; nearby is the ruined church of St Fillan and a holy well. It is memorable for its late Victorian and Edwardian houses, notably the **Salmons'** own Rowantreehill (1898) and Charles Rennie **Mackintosh**'s Windyhill (1899–1900) and St Columba's Church by William **Leiper** (1901–3).

**Kilmarnock** (pop. 43,558) Town on Kilmarnock Water and the River Irvine, north of **Ayr**, perhaps founded by the missionary Mernoc in the 7th century. It is now the administrative centre of **East Ayrshire** Council. The town's involvement in the textile industry dates from the medieval period; the Kilmarnock bonnet is a flat cap of blue, red or black woollen cloth, widely worn in the past by Scotsmen. In the 19th century the town became a centre for carpet weaving and locomotive engineering; see Andrew **Barclay** and **BMK**. There was also coalmining in the surrounding area. Other industries include distilleries and footwear. The most memorable buildings are the towered plain Georgian High (1732) and Laigh (1802) Kirks, and the fine mid to late Victorian buildings on John Finnie Street. The Dick Institute Museum and Art Gallery, belated new-classicism by Robert Ingram (1897–1901); as well as art collections, it has local and industrial history, and science, including geology. On the outskirts of the town is Dean Castle, now also a museum, built by the Boyds. It comprises a massive tower house of 1400, a palace block of 1460 and a gatehouse, rebuilt from ruins by Lord Howard de Walden from 1905.

**Kilmarnock and Loudon District** see **Strathclyde Region**

**Kilmarnock Football Club** Founded in 1869, their home ground is Rugby Park. Twice winners of the Scottish Cup in the 1920s, and again in 1997, they have also been league champions once, in 1965. See also **football**.

**Kilmartin** (Gaelic **Cill Mhàrtainn**) Village to the north of **Lochgilphead**; the area is rich in prehistoric and early historic monuments, including Temple Wood stone circles, Nether Largie chambered cairns, both dating from the 2nd or 3rd millennium BC; a group of Bronze Age cairns, including Dunchraigaig, and many cup and ring marks. The last include the Kilmichael Glassary Rock Carvings, two rock outcrops bearing many carved hollow cups, grooves and cup-and-ring markings, and the Achnabreck Cup and Ring Marks, decorated rock outcrops, from around 2000 BC, carved with small hollows (cups) surrounded by multiple grooved rings (up to 7), together with a few spirals. A number of early gravestones and crosses are preserved in Kilmartin churchyard. Kilmartin House Museum provides interpretation and displays artefacts from the sites. Kilmartin Castle is a round-towered Z-plan house built about 1580 for Neil Campbell, Bishop of Argyll. Nearby Carnasserie Castle is another good example of a 16th-century tower house, built by John **Carswell**.

**Kilmaurs** Village near **Kilmarnock** with a well-preserved tolbooth, known as 'The **jougs**', with an ashlar spire and a notable T-plan house of 1620, the Place of Kilmaurs. The parish church was handsomely rebuilt by Robert Ingram in 1888, but retains the 1600 Glencairn Aisle with a remarkable monument to the 8th Earl and Countess of Glencairn, surrounded by their weeping family.

**Kilmelfort** (Gaelic **Cill mhealaird**) Small village at the head of Loch Melfort, 20 km (12mi) south of **Oban**, with a popular yacht anchorage nearby. It had a gunpowder works 1838–67; the buildings survive and now form a holiday village.

**Kilmichael Glassary Rock Carvings** see **Kilmartin**

**Kilmun** (Gaelic **Cille Mhunna**) Village on **Holy Loch**, near **Dunoon**, with a substantial arboretum of exotic tree species which thrive in this humid environment. The tower of the medieval church

survives beside the present church by Thomas **Burns** (1841). Attached to it is the half-classical, half-Gothic domed mausoleum of the Dukes of Argyll, built in 1794. Kilmun Pier was built by David **Napier** for his pioneering steamboat services.

**Kilpatrick Hills** Hills northeast of **Dumbarton**. Duncolm is the highest point.

**Kilravock Castle** Impressively sited medieval tower house of the Roses of Kilravock, on the River Nairn, 11km (7mi) southwest of **Nairn**. A very tall new house was added (1665–7) and it has been little altered since early Georgian times.

**Kilrimont** Former name for a promontory into the North Sea to the east of **St Andrews**. In the medieval period it was a distinct ecclesiastical jurisdiction covering a collection of churches and shrines, of a kind not uncommon in Gaelic Scotland and Ireland. The name is from Gaelic, meaning 'head of the king's hill', the first element later altered to 'cill', meaning 'church'. The modern Gaelic for St Andrews, *Cill Rimhinn*, is derived from this. See **St Andrews**.

**Kilsyth** (pop. 9816) Town northeast of **Glasgow**. Heavy industry led to badly overcrowded housing until measures were taken to improve conditions in the 1920s and 30s. St Patrick's RC Church (1964) is one of the finest works of the renowned practice of Gillespie Kidd & **Coia**. Kilsyth was the site in 1645 of a virtual massacre of a Covenanting army by **Montrose**.

**kilt** A part of modern male **Highland dress**, a knee length 'skirt' of **tartan** cloth, thickly pleated at the back, probably descended from the woollen **plaid** worn by the Highlanders from early times, in **Gaelic** *féileadh-mór*; the modern kilt is known as the *féileadh-beag*, giving the **Scots** term 'fillabeg' or 'philabeg'.

**Kilwinning** (pop. 15,908) Town 7km (5mi) east of **Ardrossan**, with a ruined Abbey, founded in the 1160s. It is the home of the Ancient Society of Kilwinning Archers, who hold an annual contest. Nearby is Dalgarven Mill, in a 17th-century building but dating from medieval times, in process of restoration; in the 5-storey grain store is a Country Life Museum.

**Kincardine** see **Kincardine on Forth**, **Kincardineshire**

**Kincardine and Deeside District** see **Grampian Region**

**Kincardine Bridge** Built in 1936 at **Kincardine on Forth**, the only vehicle crossing of the Forth between **Stirling** and the ferry of **Queensferry** until the completion of the **Forth** Road **Bridge** in 1964. Construction of a new bridge is due to start in 2005, for completion in 2008.

**Kincardine Castle** Pretty Gothic house to the south of **Auchterarder**, Perthshire, by James Gillespie **Graham** (1805) on a dramatic site in Kincardine Glen, once occupied by the castle of the Duke of Montrose.

**Kincardine Castle** see **Kincardineshire**

**Kincardine O'Neil** Village on the River **Dee** 11km (6mi) west of **Banchory**, with the roofless ruin of 14th-century church. The magnificent baronial Kincardine House by the London firm of Niven and Wigglesworth (1897) stands high above the village.

**Kincardine on Forth** Small town and former port on the River **Forth** 7km (4mi) southeast of **Alloa**, at the north end of the **Kincardine Bridge**, once an important salt-boiling centre. It was the site of a large mid 20th-century power station. See also **Tulliallan**.

**Kincardineshire** Former county, also known as the Mearns, on the northeast coast of Scotland, subsumed into **Kincardine** and **Deeside** District of **Grampian Region** in 1975 and now part of Aberdeenshire local authority; see maps on pp.394–5 and **local government**. Its former county town, Kincardine, was replaced by **Stonehaven** in 1607, and now survives only in the ruined Kincardine Castle, near **Fettercairn**, a royal castle since at least 995 when it was allegedly the scene of **Kenneth II**'s death. The scant remains are of a great 13th-century curtain walled castle with 2 round towers. See also **Howe of the Mearns**.

**Kinclaven, Perthshire** Ruin of the early 13th-century square-plan curtain-walled castle, in Perthshire opposite the confluence of the Rivers **Tay** and **Isla**, probably built by **Alexander II**. William **Wallace** is said to have captured the castle from an English garrison, in the much later source, **Blind Harry**'s *Wallace*.

**Kincraig** (Gaelic **Ceann na creige**) A village near the **Cairngorms**, on Loch Insh, 9km (6mi) northeast of **Kingussie**, popular with tourists. Insh church, early 18th century, restored 1963, is said to be on a site used for Christian worship since the 6th century.

**kindly tenant** A person with a tenancy on a hereditary basis at low or no rent, surviving in the King's Kindly Tenants of Lochmaben, near **Dumfries**, until the recent ending of the feudal system of land tenure in Scotland.

**Kinfauns Castle** Impressively sited Gothic castle of the Lords Grey, 5km (3mi) east of **Perth**, set on a bastioned terrace, designed by Sir Robert Smirke (1820–26), now a hotel.

**King, Jessie Marion** (1875–1949) Artist, b. New Kilpatrick (now Bearsden), Dunbartonshire. Recognised as one of the most talented artists who studied at the flourishing **Glasgow School of Art** in the years around 1900 under **Newbery**, King is best known for her book illustrations as well as for her designs for

*And To The Christening, an illustration from Sleeping Beauty by Jessie M King.*

jewellery, pottery and textiles. She was married to the artist Ernest Archibald Taylor (1874–1951) and eventually settled in the artists' colony of **Kirkcudbright**.

**Kingdom of Fife** see **Fife**

**Kinghorn** Former royal **burgh**, and **linen**-manufacturing and shipbuilding centre, now a commuting and resort town on the Firth of **Forth** in Fife. Nearby is the site of **Alexander III**'s death after falling from his horse.

**Kingis Quair** *The Kingis Quair* or *King's Quair* (King's Book) is a long poem by **James I**, probably written after his return from imprisonment in England in 1424, during which he married Lady Joan **Beaufort**. The poem combines the story of their romance in allegorical terms with reflections on the Consolations of Boethius, a popular philosophical theme of the period.

**King's College** see **Aberdeen University**

**King's House** Hotel in **Glencoe**, popular with walkers on the **West Highland Way** and skiers on the nearby Meall a' Bhuiridh. One of Scotland's oldest inns, it was built after the 1745 **Jacobite Rising** as part of the government scheme for the new 'king's highways'; see **military roads**. The term 'King's house' was applied to the government-funded inns on the system. The name also survives in an inn near **Balquhidder**.

**Kingskettle** Village in the **Howe of Fife**, 10km (6mi) west of **Cupar**, once a watering hole of a royal hunting forest. A former **linen** mill centre, it is now a commuter village for Cupar and **Glenrothes**. It is the home of the 'Singing Kettle' group of children's entertainers; see **Fisher family**.

**King's Own Scottish Borderers** (KOSB) Regiment of the army raised in 1689 by the Earl of Leven as the Edinburgh Regiment (he allegedly recruited 800 men in 2 hours). Their first battle was Killiecrankie. They became the 25th Regiment of Foot and were named the King's Own Borderers in 1805, the Scottish was added in 1887 to recognise their origins. They are based in **Berwick-upon-Tweed** and recruit from the south of Scotland.

**King's Quair** see **Kingis Quair**

**Kingussie** (Gaelic **Cinn a' Ghiuthsaich**) (pop. 1410) Town on the River **Spey**, 67km (42mi) south of **Inverness**, popular for winter sports, climbing, golf and angling. On the opposite bank of the river stand the remains of Ruthven Barracks, built after the **Jacobite** rising of 1715, and destroyed by Jacobites in 1746. The Highland Folk Museum contains reconstructed buildings, from all over the **Highlands**, including a **black house**; now in the care of **Historic Scotland**.

**Kinloch, William** (*fl.* 1582) Musician, b. probably Dundee. A brilliant player and composer of keyboard music. In 1582 he was a secret emissary to **Mary, Queen of Scots** in her English incarceration. His most extensive work was the *Battel of Pave*, a keyboard piece commemorating the earlier conflict of 1525 in northern Italy between papal forces and the French, for whom the Duke of Albany, Regent of Scotland, was a commander.

**Kinlochaline** 15th-century tower house of the MacLeans of Duart, remodelled 1600 and reoccupied 1890. On a rock ridge at the head of Loch Aline, it is a prominent landmark.

**Kinlochbervie** (Gaelic **Ceann Loch Biorbhaidh**) Northwest village on Loch Inchard, 12km (7mi) south of **Cape Wrath**, developed since the 1940s as a fishing port.

**Kinlochewe** Village at the head of **Loch Maree**, near **Torridon**, a centre for angling and climbing.

**Kinlochleven** A village at the head of **Loch Leven**, near **Glencoe**, centred on an aluminium works established 1905–9 and the hydroelectric scheme constructed to supply it with electricity. The aluminium works closed about 2000 but the power now contributes to the National Grid. See also **Blackwater Dam**.

**Kinlochmoidart** Village at the head of Loch Moidart. Kinlochmoidart House is one of the finest **baronial** mansions in Scotland with stunning unaltered interiors by William **Leiper** for the distiller Robert Stewart (1885).

**Kinlochrannoch** Village at the east end of **Loch Rannoch**, on the River Tummel, popular with holidaymakers as the centre of a particularly scenic area. It has a fine bridge of 1764. The Black Wood of Rannoch, part of the ancient **Caledonian Forest**, is a conservation area.

**Kinloss** Village on the estuary of the River **Findhorn**, 4km (3mi) northeast of **Forres**, with remains of a Cistercian abbey founded by **David I**. Nearby is an RAF base, centre of the UK air-sea rescue service.

**Kinmont Willie** (**William Armstrong**) (c.1530–c.1600) Border reiver who thieved cattle from both English and Scots, subject of an eponymous ballad which tells how he was imprisoned in Carlisle and rescued by Walter Scott of Buccleuch.

**Kinnaird** Near symmetrical Franco-Scottish chateau of the Earls of Southesk, in Angus, to the southeast of **Brechin**, by David **Bryce** (1854–9), partly recasing a much earlier house, set in a magnificent park with splendid formal gardens.

**Kinnaird** Picturesque Perthshire village in the **Carse of Gowrie**, with a church of 1815. Nearby is Kinnaird Castle, a tall rectangular tower of the 15th century with a detached kitchen wing of 1510.

**Kinnaird, Alison** (1949– ) Visual artist and musician, b. Edinburgh. Her distinctive style of glass engraving has won her many commissions and awards. Her playing, teaching, recordings and writing have helped revive and develop the repertoire of the **clarsach**, the Scottish small harp.

**Kinnaird Head** see **Fraserburgh**

**Kinnaird House** Birthplace of the Abyssinian traveller James **Bruce**, to the north of **Falkirk**. His house has gone, replaced by a massive neo-Jacobean pile by James Thomson of Glasgow (1895).

**Kinnear, Charles George Hood** see **Peddie & Kinnear**

**Kinneil House** see **Bo'ness**

**Kinninmonth, Sir William** (1904–88) Architect, b. Edinburgh. He worked for Sir Edwin Lutyens and joined Basil **Spence** as partner 1933 with the much older Arthur Balfour Paul. He designed a notable modernist house for himself in Dick Place (1933), the neo-**Adam** Adam House in Chambers Street (1954), Pollock Halls (1959) and the Scottish Provident Institution in St Andrew Square (1961), all in **Edinburgh**. He was President of the **Royal Scottish Academy** 1969–73.

**Kinnordy** Impressive neo-Jacobean house by Maitland **Wardrop** (1879–81) in Angus, near **Kirriemuir**, looking out over a small

*Kirkcaldy Harbour in the mid 19th century.*

**K**

loch. The predecessor house was the home of Sir Charles **Lyell**, geologist, whose museum stands in the grounds.

**Kinnoull Hill** see **Perth**

**Kinross** (pop. 4681) Former county town of Kinross-shire, near the west shore of **Loch Leven**, with some interesting 17th-, 18th- and early 19th-century buildings, notably the Salutation Hotel of 1721, the Old Kirk spire of 1751 now that of the town hall, the old County Building by Robert **Adam** (1771) and the handsome neo-classical new County Buildings of 1826-7 by Thomas Brown. Nearby is **Lochleven Castle**. To the east is Kinross House, designed by Sir William **Bruce** for himself (1679-93), set in a great formal garden on the axis of Lochleven Castle, all restored in 1902-8.

**Kinross-shire** Small former county of central Scotland, absorbed into Perth and Kinross District of **Tayside Region** in 1975, and since 1996 part of **Perth and Kinross** local authority; see maps on pp.394-5 and **local government**. See also **Perthshire**.

**Kinross, John** (1855-1931) Scholarly architect, b. Edinburgh. He was a pupil of Maitland **Wardrop** and the author of an important volume of Italian Renaissance studies. He designed **Manderston**, Duns, in the **Adam** manner and The Peel, Clovenfords, in the **baronial**; and the outstandingly fine St Peter's Episcopal Church at **Fraserburgh** and Our Lady RC Church at **Glenlivet**.

**Kintail** (Gaelic **Cinntàile**) Scenic area at the head of Loch Duich, now in the care of the National Trust for Scotland, dominated by the **Five Sisters of Kintail**. See also **Glenshiel, Jacobite Risings**.

**Kintore** Small town northwest of **Aberdeen**, former royal **burgh** with a fine town house, built 1740; nearby are the remains of once massive Hallforest Castle, and the late turreted manor of Balbithan Castle. Nearby is the site of a Roman camp.

**Kintyre** (Gaelic **Cinntire**) Long peninsula between the Firth of **Clyde** and the Atlantic, stretching from a narrow isthmus at **Tarbert** in the north to the **Mull of Kintyre** at its southern end. **Campbeltown** is near its southern end.

**Kippen** Village 14km (9mi) west of **Stirling**, once famed for a magnificent and productive grape vine. The church by William Stirling (1823-7) has a remarkable collection of earlier 20th-century art works as a result of the interest of the painter Sir D Y **Cameron**. Nearby is Gribloch, the finest of Basil **Spence**'s early houses, built for the steel magnate John Colville.

**kirk** Scots word for a church, common in place-names; see below. 'The Kirk' often refers informally to the **Church of Scotland**.

**Kirk, Alexander Carnegie** (1830-92) Shipbuilder and marine engineer, b. Barry, Angus. He took over the management of Robert **Napier** and Sons' business after Napier's death in 1876. In 1883 he installed a high-pressure boiler and triple-expansions in the SS *Aberdeen*, achieving such economy in coal consumption that similarly-conceived vessels rapidly came to dominate world trade

**Kirk, Robert** (c.1641-92) Minister and author, b. Aberfoyle. Minister at **Balquhidder**, then at **Aberfoyle**, he translated the Psalms into **Gaelic** and worked on the Gaelic Bible. An Episcopalian and passive **Jacobite**, he was so respected that he was left in peace after 1688, to write his remarkable work on the fairy kingdom, *The Secret Commonwealth of Elves, Faunes and Fairies*. His tomb can be seen in Aberfoyle kirkyard, but his spirit was believed to have entered the nearby Fairy Knowe.

**Kirkcaldy** (pop. 46,912) Town on the north shore of the Firth of **Forth** in Fife, known as the Lang Toun from the length of its main street. It has an impressive series of early 19th-century banks, Victorian commercial buildings and some older buildings, notably the Sailors Walk. Birthplace of Adam **Smith** and Robert **Adam**. Textile and carpet industries led to large-scale linoleum manufacture, from the late 19th century to the 1960s. It was a centre of engineering and linen manufacture and there are still flour mills and distillery maltings. The ruined 15th-century Ravenscraig Castle, an important early artillery fortification built by **Mary of Gueldres** in 1460, stands on a promontory on the seafront. It has an excellent Museum and Art Gallery. Its football team is Raith Rovers.

**Kirkcaldy, William, of Grange** (c.1520–73) Politician. Imprisoned in France for his part in the murder of Cardinal **Beaton**, he was committed to the **Reformation** but became a minister and devoted supporter of **Mary, Queen of Scots**. He was finally hanged by Regent **Morton** for protracting the destructive civil war between the King's Men (who supported **James VI**) and the Queen's Men, by an intransigent but hopeless defence of **Edinburgh Castle** (1571–3) on behalf of the exiled Mary.

**Kirkcaldy District** see **Fife**

**Kirkconnel Hall** Tower house of 1448, to the east of **Ecclefechan**, Dumfriesshire, heightened in the early 16th century, to which a substantial house was added 1755–60; belonged to the Maxwells, whose adherence to the Catholic faith is expressed in the large brick-built chapel of 1815.

**Kirkcudbright** (pop. 3447) Town on the mouth of the River **Dee**, on Kincardine Bay, former royal **burgh**, county town of **Kirkcudbrightshire** and busy port. It has many 17th- and 18th-century buildings, including a spired tolbooth, and the massive ruin of MacLellan's Castle (1581). The Stewartry Museum has local collections. The town and surrounding area were popular with artists in the early 20th century; Broughton House was the home of E A **Hornel**.

**Kirkcudbrightshire** Former county in southwest Scotland, also known as the Stewartry (of Kirkcudbright). In 1975 most of it was divided between the Stewartry and Nithsdale Districts of Dumfries and Galloway Region, and it is now part of the large local authority of **Dumfries and Galloway**.

**Kirkdale** Superb granite-built classical house to the southeast of Creetown, Kirkcudbrightshire, by Robert **Adam** (1787–8) for Sir Samuel Hannay, the interior of the main block unfortunately replaced after a fire in 1893.

**Kirkhope Tower** Square plan tower house of the Scotts of Harden, to the southwest of **Ettrickbridge**, burnt 1543 by the Armstrongs and rebuilt; reroofed 1994.

**Kirkintilloch** (pop. 20,281) Town just north of **Glasgow**, former **burgh**, it is on the site of one of the stations of the **Antonine Wall**. It lies on the **Forth and Clyde Canal** and had yards for building **puffers**. It was a notable centre for ironfounding. It is the administrative centre of **East Dunbartonshire** Council. The Auld Kirk of 1644 is now a museum.

**Kirkliston** Village on the River **Almond** to the west of **Edinburgh**.

Its church has a saddleback tower and interesting 12th-century features. It has an extract-of-malt factory on the site of a large 19th-century distillery. Nearby is Newliston House, a tall neoclassical house by Robert **Adam** (1789), set in a great formal garden designed by William **Adam** for Field Marshall the 2nd Earl of **Stair** c.1730; of his intended palace only the stables were built.

**Kirk o' Field** see **Darnley, Henry Stewart, Lord**

**Kirk o' Shotts** East of **Airdrie**, a church by James Gillespie **Graham** (1819), a prominent landmark halfway between **Edinburgh** and **Glasgow**, site of the preaching of a sermon by John **Knox**. The Watch House in the churchyard did not prevent raids by resurrectionists **Burke and Hare**. Above the church is a mast for BBC television and radio transmission, set up in 1952.

**Kirkoswald** Village 15km (9mi) southwest of **Ayr**, famous as the home of John Davidson, the original of Souter Johnnie, the story-telling cobbler in **Burns**'s poem *Tam O' Shanter*. His cottage is now a Burns museum (**National Trust for Scotland**). The Parish Church of 1777 has particularly fine Palladian detailing befitting the Earls of Cassilis's church.

**Kirkpatrick-Durham** Planned village in the southwest, 8km (5mi) northeast of **Castle Douglas**, laid out by the local minister 1783, still with its original houses.

**Kirkpatrick-Fleming** Long narrow village in the southwest, 10km (6mi) southeast of **Ecclefechan**, with a church of 1775.

**kirk session** In the Presbyterian churches, the lowest church court, consisting of the minister and other **elders** of the congregation.

**kirkton, kirktoun, kirktown** Scots word for a town or village round a parish church, common in place-names, as in Kirkton of Auchterhouse, near **Dundee**, Kirkton Manor, near **Peebles**; equivalent to Gaelic **clachan**.

**Kirkwall** (pop. 6206) Main town of **Orkney** on the east side of Mainland, with a fine harbour, and inhabited since prehistoric times, it was the main seat of the Norse rulers of the northern islands; they built the fine Romanesque cathedral of St Magnus in the 12th century, which survives to this day; it was repaired in 1847–50 and again in 1913–30 when the spire was added. The 16th-century Bishop's Palace is built on the foundations of an earlier building, where King Haakon died in 1263. Close by is the ruin of Earl Patrick **Stewart**'s magnificent palace, built in 1606, which has survived remarkably complete. Tankerness House Museum provides a history of Orkney in an elegant merchant-laird's house, mainly of 1722. The St Magnus Festival is held in

June, with music and other performances of international standing; the composer Peter Maxwell Davies was director from 1977–86. Kirkwall is now the administrative centre of Orkney Islands Council, and a port for ferry services and for the local shellfish industry. Its airport is at Grimsetter to the southeast.

**Kirkwood, David** (1872–1955) Trade unionist and politician, b. Glasgow. His opposition to World War I and fight for workers' rights, including the 40-hour week, made him unpopular with the authorities; he was imprisoned for treason in **Edinburgh** Castle. But in 1922, along with a number of other militant socialists, he was elected as Independent Labour MP (for Dumbarton Burghs), and he joined the Labour Party in 1933, and became Baron Kirkwood in 1951.

**Kirk Yetholm** Small village on Bowmont Water, twin of Town Yetholm, it was once known as a base of Scottish gypsies and is the north end of the Pennine Way.

**kirn** Scots word for a churn; the same word, though from a different origin, is used in central and southern Scotland for a harvest celebration, and also for the last harvest sheaf.

**Kirriemuir** (pop. 5963) Former **linen** and **jute** town to the northwest of **Forfar**, the birthplace of J M **Barrie**, which he disguises as 'Thrums' in his stories; the **National Trust for Scotland** have created a museum in his home. There is a particularly fine church by Ninian Comper, St Mary's Episcopal, 1903, and a camera obscura on Kirriemuir hill, gifted to the town by Barrie. Airlie Castle is a little to the west.

**Kishorn** (Gaelic **Ciseorn**) Short inlet of **Loch Carron**, Wester Ross. An oil-patform construction yard was sited here in the 1970s and 80s.

**Kisimul Castle** Castle of the Macneils of Barra, built on a rock in Castle Bay, **Barra**. Probably dating from the 15th century, it consists of a tower house and a curtain wall enclosing other buildings. It was abandoned in the 18th century, badly damaged by fire in the 1790s and in the 19th century by fishermen who used it as a quarry for ballast. It was bought back and restored in the 20th by the clan chief, American Robert Macneil. Now in the care of **Historic Scotland.**

**kist** Scots word for a chest, applied especially to one for the storage of meal or linen. It also means a coffin and is used as an archaeological term for an ancient square or rectangular slab-lined coffin. In this usage it is nomally spelt 'cist', possibly with influence from the **Gaelic** borrowing *ciste*, with similar meanings.

**Kittochside** The Museum of Scottish Country Life, jointly run by the **National Trust for Scotland** and the **National Museums of Scotland**, is based on a farm at Wester Kittochside, near **East Kilbride**.

**klondyker** An exporter to Europe orginally of fresh herring by fast ships, more recently (1980s–90s) of mackerel to factory ships for processing on board; the word also refers to these ships when anchored in Scottish sea lochs, notably **Loch Broom**. So called (after the Alaskan gold rush) because of the substantial profit margin in the trade.

**Knapdale** The area in **Argyll** between **Lochgilphead** and **Tarbert**, bounded on the north by the **Crinan Canal** and on the south by West and East Loch Tarbert. On the west side on the shore of Loch Caolisport is the cave (reputedly) of St **Columba**, which was used by early Christians, and in the southwest are the Kilberry stones, a collection of medieval gravestones.

**Knights Templars** (Knights of the Temple of Solomon) A military religious order established in Jerusalem in the early 12th century to protect the Holy Sepulchre and routes of pilgrimage. The village of **Temple** in Midlothian was their Scottish base and they drew revenues from real estate and from churches and chapels, including Dalry, Maryculter, Drem and Inchinnan. Accused of heresy and other crimes by Philip IV of France, they were suppressed in 1312, when many of their properties were given to the Knights of St John.

**Knockan** (Gaelic **Cnocan**) Hamlet north of **Ullapool** in the northwest **Highlands**. Knockan Cliff is a geological feature crossed by the **Moine Thrust**. The succession of Cambrian layered rocks has been broken by a fault so that the older metamorphic rocks are on top of the younger.

**Knockando** A village on Speyside, overlooked by the peak of Ben Rinnes. Knockando distillery, founded in 1898, produces a single-malt **whisky**, as well as contributing to blends; it has a visitor centre. Nearby is Tamdhu distillery, founded in 1897; it also produces a malt and contributes to blends, including the Famous Grouse. There is a small woollen mill, the last of its kind in Scotland.

**Knock Castle** Roofless square-plan early 17th-century tower house of the Gordons at the entrance to Glenmuick, near **Ballater**, memorable for the feud between the Gordons and the Forbeses of Strathgirnock; Alexander Forbes murdered a Gordon suitor for his daughter and all 7 of his brothers to avoid reprisals; in this he was not successful, being hanged by another branch of the Gordons.

**Knockfarril** Vitrified fort high above the village of **Strathpeffer**, Ross-shire. Dating to around 1100 BC, the fort had

*John Knox, 16th-century Protestant Reformer.*

a stone wall with an internal timber framework. It was set on fire, with the result that the stone fused together in vitrified masses.

**Knox, John** (c.1513–72) Protestant reformer, b. in or near Haddington, East Lothian. A priest who converted to Protestantism, he joined the murderers of Cardinal **Beaton** in **St Andrews** Castle and after its fall spent some time as a prisoner on the French galleys. After release he went to England and became a chaplain to Edward VI, though he declined the offer of a bishopric. He fled to Geneva to avoid the persecution of Protestants under Mary I, and came under the influence of Calvin. In 1558 he wrote the *First Blast of the Trumpet against the Monstrous Regiment of Women*, directed against the rule of women (specifically Mary of England). In 1559 he returned to Scotland and obtained the help of England to overthrow the control of regent **Mary of Guise**, establishing Protestantism as Scotland's religion in 1560. Knox was firmly opposed to **Mary, Queen of Scots**, and allied himself with Moray, regent for **James VI**. The political turbulence of his later years led to him spending some time in retirement in St Andrews, where he wrote the *History of the Reformation in Scotland*, which reveals his humour and predictably exaggerates his role in the **Reformation** crisis.

**Knox, John** (1778–1845) Artist, b. Paisley. After an early career as a portrait painter, he specialised in refined, panoramic landscapes, depicting scenes across Scotland and the Lake District. A number of Scottish artists were pupils in his Glasgow studio (including Horatio **McCulloch**) and he is credited as having contributed to the establishment of Glasgow as a centre of art.

**Knox, Robert** (1791–1862) Anatomist, b. Edinburgh. Conservator of the Royal College of Surgeons from 1824, he ran a successful anatomy school, but gained opprobrium by obtaining some of his dissection subjects from **Burke** and Hare. He is the subject of James **Bridie**'s play, *The Anatomist*.

**Knoydart** A remote and wild peninsula in the west Highlands, only accessible on foot or by boat from **Mallaig**. Its village is **Inverie**. Part of the area is now owned by the **John Muir Trust**.

**KOSB** see **King's Own Scottish Borderers**

**Krankies, The** A husband and wife entertainment act, the wife playing a young schoolboy, 'Wee Jimmy'. They began as a stage act which later found success on television in the 1980s. They had a hit single in 1981 based on their catch phrase 'Fandabidozi', and they also appeared in pantomime and on tours abroad.

**Kyle Akin** (Gaelic **Caol Acain**) Strait that separates the northeastern point of **Skye** from the mainland at **Kyle of Lochalsh**, now crossed by the Skye Bridge.

**Kyleakin** (Gaelic **Caol Acain**) Village on the east coast of **Skye**, close to the Skye Bridge and formerly the Skye terminal of the ferry from **Kyle of Lochalsh**. Ruins of the medieval Castle Maol (Gaelic *Caisteal Maol*) stand on a rocky promontory. The Ring of Bright Water visitor centre is named in memory of the author Gavin **Maxwell**, who lived for a time in the **lighthouse** on Eilean Bàn, the island now under the Bridge, which is a wildlife centre owned by the local communities.

**Kyle and Carrick District** see **Strathclyde Region**

**Kyle of Lochalsh** (Gaelic **An Caol**) Village in **Wester Ross**, at the end of the railway from **Inverness**. Before the building of the nearby **Skye Bridge** it was the ferry terminal to **Skye**, and earlier had a ferry service to **Lewis**.

**Kylerhea** Village on **Skye**, linked by ferry to **Glenelg**.

**Kylesku** Narrows on the west coast of **Sutherland**, where Loch a' Chàirn Bhàin, Loch Glendhu and Loch Glencoul meet. A ferry linked the road to the north coast here until the Kylesku bridge was built in 1984.

**Kyles of Bute** The narrow stretches of water separating the north end of the Isle of **Bute** from the mainland.

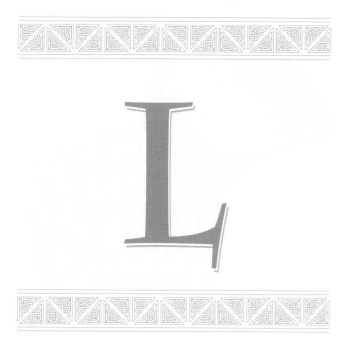

**Lacasdal** see **Laxdale**

**Ladhar Bheinn** A mountain, a **Munro** (1020m/3345ft) in **Knoydart**, **Lochaber**.

**lad o pairts** A **Scots** expression describing a talented young man, especially one from a poor or humble background. Also **lass o pairts**.

**Ladybank** (pop. 1373) Small town, a former **burgh**, in the fertile **Howe of Fife**, northeast of the **Lomond Hills**. It expanded in the 19th century with the **linen** industry and from 1848 when it became a junction of the railway lines from **Edinburgh** to **Dundee** and **Perth**.

**Lagavulin** (Gaelic **Lag a' Mhuilinn**) Village on the south coast of **Islay**. Its distillery, built in the 19th century on the site of an illicit still, makes one of the Islay malt whiskies.

**Laggan** (Gaelic **An Lagan**) Hamlet on the River **Spey**, 16km (10mi) southwest of **Kingussie**.

**Laggan** (Gaelic **An Lagan**) Hamlet at the northeast end of **Loch Lochy**, near Invergarry. Laggan Swing Bridge, to the north, carries the main road across the **Caledonian Canal** at the southwest end of **Loch Oich**.

**Laggan, Loch** see **Loch Laggan**

**Laggangarn** Site of 2 prominent standing stones in Galloway, 9km (5mi) northeast of New Luce, on the **Southern Uplands Way**. They possibly date from the 2nd millennium BC, but have early Christian incised crosses, probably of 7th-9th century date.

**Laidon, Loch** see **Loch Laidon**

**Laing, David** (1793-1878) Antiquarian and author, b. Edinburgh. The son of a bookseller, whom he joined in partnership, he became librarian of the Signet Library in 1837. He bequeathed his valuable personal library, including many rare manuscripts, to **Edinburgh University**.

**Laing, R(onald) D(avid)** (1927-89) Psychiatrist, b. Glasgow. His controversial views on mental illness, especially schizophrenia, regarding it as a potentially positive experience, first appeared in *The Divided Self* (1960). Other books include *Self and Others* (1961), *The Politics of Experience* (1967) and *The Voice of Experience* (1982).

**laird** Scots word for a landowner.

**laird's loft** Special gallery in a church used by the local **laird** and his family.

**Lairg** (Gaelic **Luirg**) Village in Sutherland at the southeast end of **Loch Shin**. It is a junction for 5 roads and the railway from **Inverness** to **Wick**. It is an important centre for sheep sales. A hydroelectric scheme was built nearby in the 1950s. The River **Shin**, with its Falls, flows south from the village.

**Lairig Ghru** Mountain pass running through the **Cairngorms** from **Speyside** to **Deeside**, and between **Ben Macdui** to the east and **Braeriach** and **Cairn Toul** to the west. It is 30km (19mi) long and is popular with hillwalkers.

**Lake of Menteith** see **Menteith**

**Lallans** Term for the **Scots** language (see **language**), used since the time of Robert **Burns**. It now usually refers to a literary variety of the language, and especially to the works of the writers of the **Scottish Renaissance** of the mid 20th century. Lallan is a variant form of Lowland, Lawland.

**Lamington** Village on the left bank of the River **Clyde**, 11km (7mi) southwest of **Biggar**. The area is associated with William **Wallace** whose supposed wife, Marion Bradfute, was said to be the heiress of Lamington. The 18th-century Lamington Church has a Romanesque arch and a bell dating from 1647.

**Lamington** Small village in Easter Ross, to the southwest of **Tain**.

**Lamlash** (pop. 900) Small port on the east coast of **Arran**, on Lamlash Bay, 6km (4mi) south of **Brodick**, where the Highland scenery of the north of the island gives way to the Lowland landscape of the south. It has some distinctive architecture from the era of the Dukes of Hamilton, notably Hamilton Terrace by Sir John **Burnet** (1895). It is a sailing and sea-angling centre, Lamlash Bay being protected by Holy Island. In 1263 King Haakon moored his fleet here *en route* to the

Battle of **Largs**. It was used as a naval base during both World Wars. See also **Holy Island**.

**Lammas** 1 August, one of the Scottish **term days**, originally a harvest festival for the consecration of the new bread. A Lammas Fair is still held in **St Andrews** and **Inverkeithing**.

**Lammermuir Hills** Range of moorland hills in southeast Scotland that form a natural barrier between **Lothian** and the **Border** country. The highest hill is Meikle Says Law (535m/1755ft). The area features as the setting for Sir Walter **Scott**'s novel *The Bride of Lammermoor*.

**Lamond, Frederic** (1868–1948) Pianist and composer, b. Glasgow. He studied under Liszt, and made his début as a pianist in 1885 in Berlin and specialised in playing Beethoven. His compositions include an overture, symphony and piano works.

**Lamp of Lothian** see **Haddington**

**Lanark** (pop. 8253) Market town above the east bank of the River **Clyde**, southeast of **Motherwell**, a former **burgh** and county town of **Lanarkshire**. It grew up around a castle built by **David I**, which was important in the **Wars of Independence** but has now totally disappeared. A bell from the 12th-century Church of **Kentigern** (now a ruin) is still in use in the Town Steeple and is the oldest bell in Britain. Another bell, a silver one made in 1590, was the prize for an annual race at Lanark Race Course from 1628 until the 20th century. The festival of Lanimer Day, Lanark's **riding of the marches**, takes place in early June. **New Lanark** World Heritage Village is 2km (1mi) to the south.

**Lanarkshire** Former county of south central Scotland. Between 1975 and 1996, the area was divided into Clydesdale and other districts of **Strathclyde Region**. These are now divided between the local authorities of **North Lanarkshire** and **South Lanarkshire**. See maps on pp.394–5 and **local government**.

**Land o Cakes** Name occasionally used to refer to Scotland, the cakes being **oatcakes**, long an important part of the Scottish diet.

**Land o the Leal** Heaven, literally land of the faithful, i.e. those who have kept the faith, as in the song by Lady **Nairne**: 'Now fare-ye-weel, my ain John. ... We'll meet and we'll be fain, In the land o' the leal.'

**Lang, Andrew** (1844–1912) Scholar, essayist and poet, b. Selkirk. His wide range of writing includes historical works (notably a 3-volume *History of Scotland*), volumes on anthropology, e.g. *Myth, Ritual and Religion* (1887), and fairy stories for children, e.g. *The Blue Fairy Book* (1889).

**Lang, (William) Cosmo Gordon** (Baron Lang of Lambeth)

(1864–1945) Anglican clergyman, b. Fyvie, Aberdeenshire. He became Bishop of Stepney in 1901, Archbishop of York in 1908 and was Archbishop of Canterbury (1928–42) during the abdication crisis of 1936.

**Langbank** Village in **Renfrewshire**, on the south bank of the River **Clyde** opposite **Dumbarton**, that grew up with the development of the railway from **Glasgow** to **Greenock**. It is named after the Lang Bank, a submergible wall defining the navigable channel of the River Clyde. Nearby is **Finlaystone House**.

**Langholm** (pop. 2311) Small town on the River **Esk**, east of **Lockerbie** and about 13km (8mi) from the border with England. It was the birthplace of Hugh **MacDiarmid** (Christopher M Grieve) and there is a memorial to him above the town. A tall obelisk at the top of Whita Hill just outside the town is a memorial to 'the Knights of Eskdale', the 4 sons of an 18th-century minister of the town who were all awarded knighthoods for services to the state; one of them, Sir Pultney Malcolm, was Governor of St Helena while Napoleon was a prisoner there. The town is also associated with the 16th-century sheep rustler Johnnie **Armstrong**. It has long had woollen mills and in the 19th century also had distilleries.

**Langside** Southern suburb of Glasgow, where the Battle of Langside took place in 1568 between the forces of Regent **Moray** and **Mary, Queen of Scots**, following Mary's escape from **Lochleven Castle**. Moray was the victor.

**Lang Toun** see **Kirkcaldy**

**language** see p.220

**Lanimer Day** see **Lanark**

**Laoghal, Beinn** see **Ben Loyal**

**Laoigh, Beinn** see **Ben Lui**

*Lagavulin Distillery, Port Ellen, Islay.*

Scotland at the present time has three main languages:

**ENGLISH**, the international language now the medium of administration and of most formal writing and speech.

**SCOTS**, descended from a northern variety of Old English, which reached southeast Scotland in the 7th century. In the medieval period, it diverged from the more southerly dialects which eventually became standard English, but from the 16th century political events have drawn it closer to English. Today it is a continuum from Scottish Standard English to demotic urban speech and rural dialects of considerable diversity.

**GAELIC**, the Celtic language of the **Highlands** and Islands, closely related to Irish, now enjoying a revival with more support from the public and from government, especially in education.

At the time of the Roman invasions of Britain, most people in what is now southern Scotland spoke a Celtic language related to modern Welsh, variously known as Cumbric, Britonnic, Brythonic, British. (Welsh and Gaelic are examples of the two divisions of the Celtic family of languages: P-Celtic and Q-Celtic, from the different initial sounds in certain words, as in the word for 'head' in Welsh *pen*, in Gaelic *ceann*.) The **Picts**, north of the **Forth-Clyde** valley, have left little trace of their language, but from the meagre evidence available, modern scholarship suggests that it too was a P-Celtic language, but containing other elements from a pre-Celtic people. During the Norse occupations of the medieval period, a Norse language, Norn, was spoken in **Shetland**, **Orkney** and parts of **Caithness**. It survived in places till at least the 18th century and has left a strong legacy in the Scots dialect of these areas.

As in most European countries, Latin was the formal written language in medieval times; indeed the earliest sources for both Scots and Gaelic are notes and glosses in Latin documents. The Acts of the **Scottish Parliament** were written in Latin until the early 15th century, thereafter in Scots. It has also had a strong literary tradition (see George **Buchanan**), enabling Scots to participate in European culture, and this continued into the 18th century, especially in conservative **Jacobite** circles (see Thomas **Ruddiman**).

Roughly from the 5th to the 11th century the Scots gained power over what is now mainland Scotland and their Gaelic language flourished. In the 11th century, Anglo-Norman settlers brought with them large numbers of followers from northeast England and their Scandinavian-influenced northern English became the language of trade and later of administration. This language was enriched by other influences, notably French, especially at the time of the **Auld Alliance**, and Dutch, through the strong trading links with the Low Countries. By the beginning of the 16th century, now known as Scots, it was well

on the way to becoming the national language of Stewart Scotland, just as the East Midland dialect of English was becoming the standard language of Tudor England.

Events told against it however: the Scottish **Reformation** in 1560: in particular there was no translation of the Bible into Scots available and an English one was used in Scottish churches; the **Union of the Crowns** in 1603, when **James VI** moved his court, and thus the centre of culture, from **Edinburgh** to London. The King James Bible of 1611 was a further powerful influence on the speech and writing of educated Scots; the **Union of the Parliaments** in 1707, by which time English had become the medium of most formal communication.

Thus English effectively became the official language of Scotland, and as a product of education and social ambitions it spread throughout society over the next three centuries. Both Gaelic and Scots have survived with increasing difficulty in the face of the supremacy of a combined British, American and international usage of English. It has for a long time been the language of choice for all media, administrative, commercial and scientific speech and writing, and for most literary purposes.

Scots has nevertheless survived vigorously in poetry and song, and in the speech of ordinary folk; today it is gaining respect, with strong literary revival in the 20th and 21st centuries, and the realisation that variety of language is a valuable element in human culture. While the oppositional attitudes of the past have been much reduced, official support for Scots in education is minimal, but efforts are being made to raise awareness of its value, for example in a new imprint, Itchycoo, set up by James **Robertson** and Matthew **Fitt**, to produce material for all ages of children, and by the schools publications of **Scottish Language Dictionaries**, notably the Sculwab, its website for schools.

Gaelic is also gaining from more enlightened attitudes but it has suffered even more loss than Scots. From the 11th century it was pushed further and further towards the northwest and the **Western Isles**. During the medieval period it maintained a vigorous, largely oral culture along with the closely related Irish across the sea; up to the 17th century a common cultural and linguistic heritage was maintained. This had already broken down by the time the **Jacobite risings** of the 18th century had further damaged the Gaelic way of life, already weakened by massive emigration. But Gaelic has survived, like Scots greatly aided by its songs and poetry. The 20th century saw an amazing revival in literature, with recognition in the education system, and to some extent in public life.

Other languages have reached Scotland in the modern period, including Chinese, Arabic, Urdu, Punjabi and Bengali.

**Laphroaig** Village on the south coast of **Islay**, near Port Ellen. Its distillery, founded in 1815, makes one of the Islay malt whiskies.

**Lapworth, Charles** (1842–1920) Geologist, b. Faringdon, Berkshire. He began as a schoolteacher in **Galashiels** and **St Andrews**, but became interested in geology through observation of the landscape, and was later Professor of Geology in Birmingham. As a geological surveyor, he was the first to unravel the complexity of northwest Highland structures and later made major contributions to the geology of the **Southern Uplands**. He detailed palaeontological successions and established sequences retained today. He proposed the Ordovician period between the Cambrian and the Silurian.

**Larbert** (pop. Larbert and Stenhousemuir 10,070) A former iron-founding town and railway junction, northwest of **Falkirk**. In the 19th and 20th centuries it had several mental hospitals, including the Royal Scottish National Hospital.

**Largo** see **Lower Largo, Upper Largo**

**Largs** (pop. 11,241) Town on Largs Bay on the Firth of **Clyde**, a former **burgh**, its harbour sheltered by the island of Great **Cumbrae**. Now a resort and yachting centre, it has a Viking Centre commemorating the Scots victory over the Norsemen under King Haakon at the Battle of Largs in 1263. In the town centre is the 17th-century mausoleum, Skelmorlie Aisle, and 6km (4mi) to the south are the Hunterston nuclear power station and an ore and coal terminal.

**Larkhall** (pop. 15,549) Industrial town 6km (4mi) southeast of **Hamilton**. In the 19th century its industries included mining and brickworks, as well as textiles. These have been replaced by lighter industries.

**lass o pairts** see **lad o pairts**

**Lasswade** Midlothian village on the steep slope of the North **Esk** river valley, adjoining Bonnyrigg, 3km (2mi) southwest of **Dalkeith**. William **Drummond** of Hawthornden and Henry **Dundas**, 1st Viscount Melville, are buried in the old churchyard. Walter **Scott** spent the first 6 years of his married life in Lasswade, where he was visited by James **Hogg** and the Wordsworths, and the English poet Thomas De Quincey (1785–1859) spent his last years in the neighbouring village of Polton. Both Lasswade and Polton were noted for papermaking.

**Latheron** Village on the east side of **Caithness** that consists of 2 parts, Latheron and Latheronwheel (formerly Janetstown), which has a sheltered natural harbour on the coast. The parish church (1725–38) is now the Clan Gunn Centre. The **Achavanich Standing Stones** are nearby.

*Sir Harry Lauder.*

**Latin** see **language** p.220

**Lauder** (pop. 1081) **Borders** town, a former royal **burgh**, on the Leader Water, 14km (9mi) north of **Melrose**. It has a **tolbooth** and a parish church in the shape of a Greek cross, with an octagonal steeple, designed by Sir William **Bruce** (1673). To the northeast is **Thirlestane Castle**, and to the southwest Lauder Common, an open space of moorland.

**Lauder, Sir Harry** (1870–1950) Comedian, b. Portobello. A miner in his youth, he began entertaining in amateur concerts, but soon became professional. Coming from a long tradition of Scottish music hall, he brought Scottish comedy into a wider international world. His kilted figure, leaning on a crooked stick, became a caricature image of a Scotsman.

221

**Lauder, Robert Scott** (1803–69) Painter, b. Edinburgh. A painter of historical subjects, Lauder's greatest success was as Master of the Trustees Academy (the most important art school in Scotland at the time) from 1852. There he inspired a notable generation of Scottish artists, including George Paul Chalmers, William Quiller **Orchardson**, John McWhirter and William **McTaggart**, instilling in them an appreciation of colour and painterly technique, values which remained important for several succeeding generations of Scottish artists.

**Lauder, Sir Thomas Dick** (1784–1848) Writer, b. Fountainhall, Midlothian. He married a Morayshire heiress. His works include the romances *Lochindhu* (1825) and *The Wolf of Badenoch* (1827) and the non-fictional *Account of the Great Morayshire Floods* (1830) and *Scottish Rivers* (1847–9) as well as compilations of Highland legends. As secretary of the Board of Trustees for Manufacturers and Fisheries (1839–48) he travelled widely and advocated the setting up of art and technical schools.

**Lauder, William** (c.1680–1771) Literary forger who between 1747 and 1750 attempted to show that John Milton had plagiarised 17th-century poets to produce *Paradise Lost*. Following his exposure by Bishop John Douglas in 1751, he emigrated and died in poverty.

**Lauderdale** Valley in the **Borders** of the **Leader Water** which flows southeast through **Lauder** and Earlston to join the River **Tweed**. Important in the Middle Ages as the main route between Lothian and the eastern Borders.

**Lauderdale, James Maitland, 8th Earl of** (1759–1839) Lawyer, economist and politician, b. Ratho, near Edinburgh. He began his political career as a Whig but later supported the Tory cause and opposed parliamentary reform. His writings in economics were influential and are important for their criticisms of Adam **Smith**; they include *An Inquiry into the nature and origin of Public Wealth* (1804).

**Lauderdale, John Maitland, Duke of** (1616–82) Politician, b. Lethington (now **Lennoxlove**), East Lothian. He succeeded his father as Earl of Lauderdale. Originally a **Covenanter** and imprisoned under Cromwell for supporting the **Engagement**, he was created duke in 1672 due to his strong support for the Restoration regime of Charles II. He was Scottish Secretary of State (1666–80), and dominated policy making, but his mixture of conciliation and repression failed to pacify Scotland, leading to his dismissal in 1680. His dukedom died with him.

**Laud's Liturgy** A misleading name given to the Scottish Prayer Book, which was published in 1637 by order of **Charles I**. Archbishop Laud in England had advocated that the Scots adopt the English Prayer Book, but the Scottish bishops secured extensive modifications.

**Laurencekirk** Planned village in the **Howe of the Mearns**, northeast of **Brechin**, that was developed in the 18th century by Lord Gardenstone, who established the manufacture of snuff-boxes and weaving, both of which trades have died out. The inn used by Dr Johnson remains but the library he admired has gone. To the east, the Hills of Garvock separate the Howe of Mearns from the coastal plain. Johnston Tower, at the highest point of the Hills of Garvock (279m/914ft), overlooks the town.

**Laurie, John** (1897–1980) Actor, b. Dumfries. A stage actor throughout the 1920s, he made his film debut in 1930 and went on to play a memorable supporting role in *The 39 Steps* (1935). He is best remembered for his role as Frazer, the undertaker whose catchphrase was 'We're doomed', in the TV sitcom *Dad's Army* (1968–77).

**Laurie, Simon Somerville** (1829–1909) Educationalist and philosopher, b. Edinburgh. As the first Professor of Education at **Edinburgh University** (1876–1903), he was a key figure in the improvement of secondary education, and advocated a more liberal, child-centred primary education. He was also secretary of the **Church of Scotland** Education Committee. He published works on wide-ranging aspects of educational theory and practice. He also wrote on philosophy, sometimes under the pseudonym of 'Scotus Novanticus'.

**Lauriston Castle** Mansion house on the northwest outskirts of **Edinburgh**, by William **Burn** (1827) for the banker Thomas Allen, incorporating a 16th-century tower built by Sir Archibald Napier of Merchiston. It was altered by several family owners, the last of whom gave it to the city of Edinburgh in 1926. It is open to the public.

**Lavery, Sir John** (1856–1941) Artist, b. Belfast. He moved to **Glasgow** in 1873, then studied in Paris. The 'en plein-air' paintings he produced at the artists' colony of Grez in France and in Scotland in the 1880s, including *The Tennis Party* (**Aberdeen Art Gallery**), are among the finest and most innovative paintings of the Glasgow School, of which he was a leading member. From the 1890s he was much in demand as a society portrait painter and latterly was based in London, where he found considerable success and recognition.

**law** see p.223

# LAW

Scots law is based on a different system from that of England and was one of the 3 areas (along with the church and education) left separate by the Treaty of Union in 1707. It had a greater input of Roman law than English law. This Roman influence came partly from the canon law of the medieval church, which provided most professional lawyers, and partly from the education of Scots lawyers in European countries with a Roman-law system; even after the Union of 1707, many were trained in universities such as Leiden.

Scots law has many more terms of Latin origin than English law (whose terms derive more from Norman-French). Examples include avizandum (for consideration), culpable homicide (corresponding to English manslaughter).

In the 1570s legal writers such as Sir James **Balfour** drew together all the existing parts of Scots law and, a century later, Viscount **Stair** gave the law a systematic and philosophical treatment in his *Institutions of the Law of Scotland* (1681). He was followed by others whose writings were relied upon in the courts, such as George **Mackenzie,** Andrew Macdowall, Lord Bankton, John **Erskine**, David **Hume** (1757–1838), George Joseph Bell.

From the 19th century Scots law has been increasingly influenced by English law, and more recently also by European law. It still however maintains its own spirit and many distinctive features. See also **Court of Session, District Court, High Court of Justiciary, Justice of the Peace, sheriff.**

The chart below of appeals in the Scottish courts gives some idea of how the court system works:

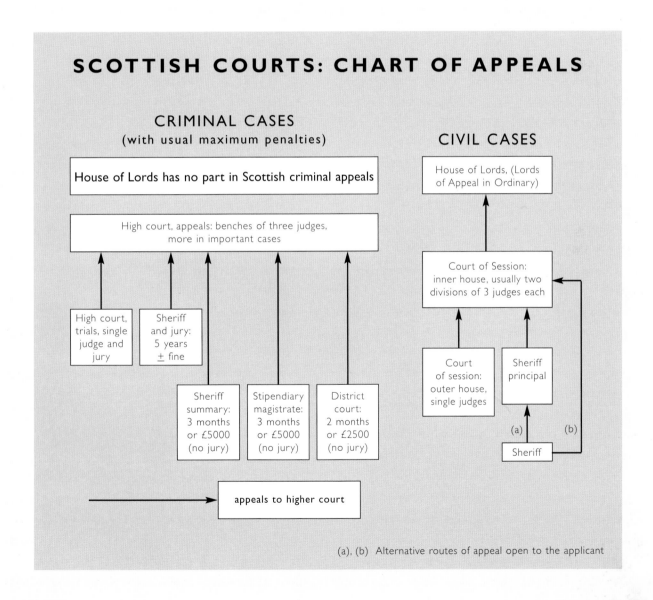

## SCOTTISH COURTS: CHART OF APPEALS

### CRIMINAL CASES
(with usual maximum penalties)

### CIVIL CASES

House of Lords has no part in Scottish criminal appeals

House of Lords, (Lords of Appeal in Ordinary)

High court, appeals: benches of three judges, more in important cases

Court of Session: inner house, usually two divisions of 3 judges each

High court, trials, single judge and jury

Sheriff and jury: 5 years ± fine

Court of session: outer house, single judges

Sheriff principal

Sheriff summary: 3 months or £5000 (no jury)

Stipendiary magistrate: 3 months or £5000 (no jury)

District court: 2 months or £2500 (no jury)

(a)

(b)

Sheriff

appeals to higher court

(a), (b) Alternative routes of appeal open to the applicant

L

223

**Law** Tall 16th-century rectangular tower near **West Kilbride**, with corbelled parapet and massive stacks framing the cap house, interesting wall-chambered plan, built for the Boyd family; recently re-roofed and re-occupied.

**Law, Andrew Bonar** (1858–1923) Politician, b. New Brunswick, Canada, of an Ulster father and Scottish mother, brought up in Glasgow. He entered British politics in 1900 as a Unionist MP and was Chancellor of the Exchequer 1916–18, cooperating in the coalition of Prime Minister David Lloyd George. Reluctantly but decisively he broke the coalition, becoming Tory Prime Minister 1922–3.

**Law, Denis** (1940– ) Footballer, b. Aberdeen. He made his international début aged 18 and spent most of his playing career with Manchester United.

**Law, John** (1671–1729) Financier, political economist, gambler, b. Edinburgh. He was imprisoned for killing a man in a duel in London, but escaped to the Continent. He returned to Scotland and tried unsuccessfully to persuade the **Scottish Parliament** to boost the economy by state credit creation (through the issue of paper currency). Later in France, he won the ear of the Regent Orléans and briefly dominated French economic policy, taking control of state debts and forming a monopolistic overseas trading company as the basis for a credit-inspired boom. This was eventually destroyed by hyperinflation, and Law was forced to leave France. He ended his life in Venice as a professional gambler.

**Lawers** (Gaelic **Labhar**) Village on north side of **Loch Tay** 11km (7mi) southwest of **Kenmore**, just below **Ben Lawers**.

**Lawers** House to the north-east of **Comrie**, Perthshire (c.1725) of General James Campbell, who fought at Dettingen at the age of 75 and was killed in battle in 1745 at Fontenoy at the age of 78. The house was much enlarged with a portico and long colonnaded wings by Richard Crichton (1815–17).

**Lawrie, William** (1881–1916) Piper, b. Ballachulish. A pupil of John **MacColl**, he won many awards and was a highly acclaimed composer of pipe music. He was Pipe Major in the **Argyll and Sutherland Highlanders** in 1914.

**Laxdale** (Gaelic **Lacasdal**) Village at the head of the estuary of the River Laxdale, just to the north of Stornoway on **Lewis**.

**Laxford** (Gaelic **Camus-bhradan**) River in Sutherland that rises in Loch Stack and flows northwest into the sea at Loch Laxford 2km (1mi) beyond **Laxford Bridge**.

**Laxford Bridge** Village on the northwest coast, at the head of Loch Laxford, where the west-coast road from **Durness** crosses the River Laxford; it is also the junction of the road from **Lairg**, 60km (37mi) to the southeast.

**lazy bed** A method of horticulture formerly widely used in rocky crofting areas, based on strips of soil covered with manure and sods from adjacent trenches, which provided drainage. Used especially for growing potatoes and oats.

**lead** Lead was mined in the **Lowther Hills**, particularly around **Leadhills** and **Wanlockhead**. There is a museum of the lead-mining industry at **Wanlockhead**. Lead was also mined at **Tyndrum**, on **Islay**, in **Kirkcudbrightshire** and in **Glenesk**.

**Leader Water** River that rises in the **Lammermuir Hills** and flows southeast and south through Lauderdale to join the River **Tweed** at Leaderfoot, east of **Melrose**.

**Leadhills** Village in the **Lowther Hills** southwest of Abington, just to the northeast of **Wanlockhead**, at 411m (1350ft) above sea level, one of the highest villages in Scotland. Lead was mined here from the 13th to the early 20th century, and gold from the mines was used in the crown of Scotland and in a brooch given to Queen Elizabeth in 1951. The remarkable Lead Miners' Library was set up in 1741 by the miners themselves and in 1756 a building for it was gifted by the poet Allan **Ramsay**, who was born here in 1686.

**Leaving Certificate** Examination introduced to secondary schools in 1888, largely under the direction of Henry **Craik**. Its introduction was a significant step forward in bringing common standards into Scotland's schools. See also **Highers**, **Lowers**.

**Lecht** Mountain pass in Moray on the road from **Grantown-on-Spey** to Bridge of Gairn near **Ballater**. It is the second-highest road pass in the country, beginning at Cock Bridge at 410m (1344ft) and rising rapidly to 644m (2114ft) before descending gradually towards Conglass Water and **Tomintoul**. It was developed in the 1970s as a skiing area, especially for beginners, and now has several ski lifts, and all-year-round activities.

**Ledi, Ben** see **Ben Ledi**

**Lee, Ben** see **Ben Lee**

**Lee, Jennie** (Baroness Lee of Ashridge) (1904–88) Labour politician, b. Lochgelly, Fife. The daughter of a miner, she became MP for North **Lanark** at the age of 24, the youngest MP of her time. She married Aneurin Bevan in 1934. She became the first woman Arts Minister in 1964 and was instrumental in the founding of the Open University.

**Leighton Library** Library in **Dunblane** founded by Robert Leighton, Bishop of Dunblane, in the 1680s. The small building, on the site of the medieval bishop's palace, still houses Leighton's books.

**Leiper, William** (1839–1916) Architect, b. Glasgow. He worked for J L Pearson in London and became interested in the Anglo-Japanese movement in interior decoration. He returned to **Glasgow** in 1864, building the tall-spired churches at Dowanhill and Camphill, the Venetian Gothic **Templeton** carpet factory and many large country and suburban houses in both the Scots **baronial** and Norman Shaw-inspired 'Old English' manners.

**Leith** Seaport for **Edinburgh** and a separate burgh until 1920. It is 3km (2mi) north of the city centre and is situated where the Water of Leith enters the Firth of Forth. Lamb's House, where **Mary, Queen of Scots** stayed on her return to Scotland in 1561, a merchant's house renovated in the 18th century, is the oldest house. Trinity House, an elegant Georgian building in the midst of the 1960s Kirkgate Shopping Centre, is the headquarters of the Incorporation of Masters and Mariners of Leith, now in the care of **Historic Scotland**, and open to the public, including the vaults of an earlier, probably 16th-century building. The central area is remarkably rich in major Georgian public buildings: the former Leith Bank by John Paterson (1806); the Greek Doric Custom House by Robert **Reid** (1812); Exchange Buildings by Thomas Brown (1816); and the Town Hall by R R Dickson (1928). To the east are Leith Links, where **golf** was played until the late 19th century and which has the remains of artillery mounds built by Scots and English troops who were besieging French troops at the Siege of Leith in 1560. The town was sacked by English troops in 1544 and 1547. By the Treaty of Leith in 1560 between England and France the French withdrew their forces from Scotland and recognised Elizabeth Tudor as Queen of England (though the treaty was not ratified by Mary, Queen of Scots). Important industries included corn- and flour-milling, distilling and **whisky** blending, glassmaking, engineering and shipbuilding. The first ship to cross the Atlantic under continuous steam power, the *Sirius*, was built in Leith.

*Leith Harbour, painted around the early 18th century.*

After a period of undistinguished development in the 1960s, Leith has recently seen major improvements in housing and in the renovation of its predominantly Georgian buildings. The headquarters of the **Scottish Executive** is now situated at Victoria Quay. The royal yacht *Britannia* has become a major tourist attraction in Leith docks; nearby is the Ocean Terminal shopping and leisure centre.

**Leith, Water of** see **Water of Leith**

**Leith Hall** Turreted 17th- and 18th-century house, near Kennethmount on the road from Insch to **Huntly**, home of the Leith and Leith-Hay family until 1945, when it was gifted to the **National Trust for Scotland**.

**Lendalfoot** Village on the Ayrshire coast, 10km (6mi) southwest of **Girvan**, where the Lendal Water reaches the sea. Once a haunt of smugglers, it became a fishing village and now is a resort. Inland are the striking ruins of Carleton Castle, the home of the Cathcart family.

**Lennox** An ancient Celtic earldom of **Strathclyde** of British origin, covering roughly what later became the county of **Dunbartonshire**. It was the power base of the earls, and later dukes of Lennox.

**Lennox, Annie** (1954– ) Popular singer, b. Aberdeen. She formed The Tourists group and then The Eurythmics with Dave Stewart. She stopped performing with The Eurythmics in 1990 and embarked on a solo career in 1992. In 2004 she won an Oscar for her song, 'Into the West', from the film *Lord of the Rings: The Return of the King*.

**Lennox, Earls of** After the older Celtic holders of the title were eliminated, it was used by the Crown from 1473 for junior branches of their own Stewart house. The 4th Stewart Earl married the daughter of the Earl of Angus and **Margaret Tudor**, sister of Henry VIII, and their son, Henry Stewart, Lord **Darnley**, became the second husband of **Mary Queen of Scots**. The dukedom of Lennox was created in 1581 by **James VI** for his cousin, Esmé Stewart. When the 6th duke died without an heir, the title reverted to **Charles II**, who allocated it in 1675 to one of his illegitimate sons, the Duke of Richmond. The 6th Duke of Richmond and Lennox was made Duke of Gordon in 1876.

**Lennoxlove** Historic house to the south of **Haddington**, East Lothian, with 15th-century tower and later additions. Under the name of Lethington, it was the home of the Maitland family from the 14th to the 17th century, and its Politician's Walk of lime trees is named after William **Maitland** (1528–73), secretary to **Mary, Queen of Scots**. In 1682 the estate was bought by Frances, Duchess of Lennox and Richmond, a mistress of **Charles II**, and the name was changed to Lennoxlove in 1704. Now owned by the Duke of Hamilton, it is open to the public.

**Lennoxtown** (pop. 4524) Small town 13km (8mi) north of **Glasgow**, at the foot of the **Campsie Fells**, set up in the 1780s with the introduction of calico-printing works and bleachfields (the former lasting until 1930). It also had alum works, coal-mining and nail-making. Just to the west is the vast neo-Norman Lennox Castle, built (1837–41) by David **Hamilton**; it was used as a mental hospital from the 1920s to the 1990s. Behind the town the scenic Crow Road leads steeply, through Campsie Glen, to **Fintry**.

**Leny** Short river that rises in **Loch Lubnaig** and flows south into the River Teith near **Callander**, through the narrow Pass of Leny with the picturesque Falls of Leny. The river is popular for white-water canoeing. At the north end of the pass is the ruin of the ancient Chapel of St Bride, which was described by Sir Walter **Scott** in his *Legend of Montrose*. The chapel was restored in the early 19th century as a memorial to Scott. Near where the rivers meet, to the north of the hamlet of Kilmahog, is Leny House, now a hotel, which consists of a small **baronial** house by David **Bryce** (1845), built round a 16th-century tower house.

**Lenzie** (pop. 8873) Town 10km (6mi) northeast of **Glasgow**. Expanded from a village in the 19th century by inducements from a railway company, it remains a popular commuter suburb.

**Leonard, Tom** (1944– ) Poet, b. Glasgow. His first collection, *Six Glasgow Poems* (1969), was written in a colloquial Glasgow Scots, using phonetic spelling, and with an unsentimental approach, subversive of authority, to which he has adhered in his later works, notably in *Intimate Voices* (1984). He has also edited *Radical Renfrew: Poets from the French Revolution to the First World War* (1990) and *Places of the Mind* (1993) is a study of the 19th-century poet, James **Thomson**. He became Creative Writing Tutor in 2000 and then Professor of Creative Writing in 2001 at **Glasgow University**.

**Lerwick** (pop. 6830) Town on the east coast of Mainland **Shetland**, situated on Bressay Sound. Former county town of Shetland and now the administrative centre of Shetland Islands Council (see **local government**), it is the northernmost town in the British Isles. It is also a fishing port and a service base for North Sea **oil** fields as well as the terminus of ferry services from **Aberdeen**. Fort Charlotte, a 5-sided artillery fort built by John **Mylne** (1665–6) and modernised in the 1780s, and the nearby Iron Age **broch** of Clickimin are both in the care of **Historic Scotland**. The annual festival of **Up-Helly-Aa** (held in January) reflects Shetland's Viking heritage.

**Leslie** Village 5km (3mi) southwest of **Insch**, Aberdeenshire. Leslie Castle, is a 3-storey L-plan tower house built 1661, on the site of an earlier castle, rebuilt in the 1970s.

**Leslie** (pop. 2998) Small town 3km (2mi) northwest of **Glenrothes**, Fife, a former **burgh**. The main industrial activities are papermaking, especially paper recycling. To the east are the remains of Leslie House, once the home of the earls of Rothes. It was built by John and Robert **Mylne** (1667–72) around a quadrangle, but after a fire in 1763, only the west range was reconstructed. It was a home for the elderly until 2003.

**Leslie, Alexander, 1st Earl of Leven** (c.1580–1661) Soldier who was born as the illegitimate son of the Captain of **Blair Atholl** Castle. He served in the Swedish army, becoming a field marshal, before returning to Scotland to command the Covenanting army against **Charles I**. He fought at the Battle of Marston Moor (1644) and accepted Charles I's surrender at Newark (1646) but supported agreement with **Charles II** in 1650 and fought Cromwell in Scotland 1650–1. He was captured and imprisoned but released on parole in 1654.

**Leslie, David, Lord Newark** (1601–82) Soldier, who served in the Swedish army before joining the Covenanting army under Alexander **Leslie** in 1643. He fought at the Battle of Marston Moor (1644) and defeated **Montrose** at **Philiphaugh** (1645). He was defeated by Cromwell at **Dunbar** (1650) and taken prisoner at Worcester, spending 9 years in the Tower of London until the Restoration of **Charles II** in 1660.

**Leslie, John** (c.1527–96) Ecclesiastical judge and bishop, b. Kingussie. He trained in Scotland and France. A strong supporter of **Mary, Queen of Scots**, he was imprisoned for plotting against Elizabeth and on his release returned to France. His writings include *History of Scotland* (1578).

**Leslie, Sir John** (1766–1832) Physicist, b. Largo, Fife. He became Professor of Mathematics at **Edinburgh University** (1805) and later of **Natural Philosophy** (1819). He invented several types of meter and in 1810 he succeeded in producing ice artificially, the first recorded instance of this.

**Lesmahagow** (pop. 3685) Former mining town on the west bank of the River Nethan, 8km (5mi) southwest of **Lanark**. The ruined Lesmahagow Priory was founded in 1144 by **David I**, and the monks became pioneers of fruit-growing in the **Clyde** valley.

**Lessels, John** (1808–83) Architect, b. Kirkcaldy. He planned much of **Edinburgh**'s West End for the Walker Trust, and with David **Cousin**, replanned and rebuilt much of the Old Town of Edinburgh for the City Improvement Trust. His son of the same name (b.1833 at Dawyck) was responsible for the entrance front of Hampton Court as it now exists.

**Lethington** see **Lennoxlove**

**Letterewe** Estate on the northeast shore of **Loch Maree** in **Wester Ross**, 10km (6mi) northwest of the head of the loch. The first iron-smelting works in Scotland was established here in the 17th century by Sir George Hay. In 1993 the Dutch owner, Paul van Vlissingen, along with user groups, published the Letterewe Accord, an access agreement between landowners, climbers and hillwalkers. See also **Loch Ewe**.

**Letterfourie** Tall cubical house to the southeast of **Buckie**, by Robert **Adam** for James Gordon (1773). Within the grounds is a remarkable bridge composed of superimposed arches, which may be at least partly an Adam essay in the picturesque.

**Leuchars** Village in northeast **Fife**, with an RAF base at the mouth of the River **Eden**. The parish church retains its Romanesque choir and apse, with a tower added by John Douglas in 1774. Leuchars Station, some distance to the east, serves **St Andrews** as well as the surrounding area.

**Leven** (pop. 8051) Fife industrial town, a former **burgh**, on Largo Bay. In former times textiles and coalmining were important, and more recently engineering and sawmilling.

**Leven** River in the central **Highlands** that runs west from the Blackwater Reservoir to the head of **Loch Leven** at **Kinlochleven**.

**Leven** River that rises in **Loch Leven** in Fife and flows east to Largo Bay, entering the sea between Leven and Methil. Outflow from the Loch is controlled by the paper industry on the banks of the river.

**Leven** River that runs from **Loch Lomond**, through the **Vale of Leven** and into the Firth of **Clyde** at **Dumbarton**.

**Leven, Loch** see **Loch Leven**

**Leverburgh** (Gaelic **An t-Òb**) Village on the southwest coast of South **Harris**, at the head of Loch Obbe, to the northwest of **Rodel**. Formerly called Obbe, it was renamed when Lord **Leverhulme** expanded the village in his unsuccessful attempt to revolutionise the island's **fishing** industry between 1919 and 1923. It has a car ferry to **Berneray**.

**Leverhulme, William Hesketh Lever, 1st Lord** (1851–1925) English industrialist, b. Lancashire. After amassing a fortune in soap manufacture, he bought **Lewis** in 1917 and **Harris** in 1919, with the intention of developing the land and revitalising the **fishing** industry. He roused opposition to his methods in Lewis, failed, and gave up in 1923, gifting the parish of **Stornoway** to the people, to be administered by the elected Stornoway Trust.

**Lewis, Isle of** (Gaelic **Eilean Leodhais**) The northern part of the largest and most northerly island of the Outer **Hebrides**, the southern part forming **Harris**. Lewis has a largely peaty and treeless upland landscape with many small lochs and streams. There is still some crofting and fishing and **Harris tweed** is made in the island. **Gaelic** is spoken in most areas. **Stornoway**, the main town, is the administrative centre of the **Western Isles** local authority. Many prehistoric sites include the standing stones at **Calanais**, chambered cairns and a **broch** at **Carloway**. The Butt of Lewis is the most northerly point of The Outer **Hebrides**. There is a **lighthouse** here that was first lit in 1862. See also **Arnol, Leverhulme**.

**Lewisian** Metamorphic and igneous rocks stretching from the Outer Isles to the west coast, which are the oldest rocks in the British Isles, dating back to 3300 million years ago.

**lexicography** see **dictionaries**

**Leyden, John** (1775–1811) Antiquarian, poet, physician and orientalist, b. Denholm, Roxburghshire. He helped Walter **Scott** with his *Minstrelsy of the Scottish Border* (1802–3) before travelling to work as a doctor in India. He journeyed in the Far East where he learned many oriental languages, translating the gospels into several of them. He died in Java of a fever (caught in an unventilated library), leaving behind a collection of ballads, poems and articles on language.

*Eric Liddell winning the 400-metre final at the Olympic Games, Paris, 1924.*

**Lhuyd, Edward** (1660–1709) Welsh Celtic scholar, b. near Oswestry. His tour of Celtic countries (1697–1701) included visits to parts of **Argyll**, including **Mull** and **Iona**, and he made records of many aspects of culture, including archaeology, botany and **Gaelic** dialects; he collected many Gaelic manuscripts.

**Liathach** Mountain ridge in **Torridon**, Wester Ross, with 2 **Munro** peaks, Spidean a' Choire Leith (1054m/3458ft) and Mullach an Rathain (1023m/3356ft).

**Liberton** Suburb of **Edinburgh**, 5km (3mi) southeast of the city centre. Liberton Tower is an early 16th-century 4-storey tower house and Liberton House, also early 16th century, was built for William Little, whose son Clement was founder of **Edinburgh University**. Both have been restored in recent years.

**Lickleyhead** Fine L-plan house, to the south of **Insch**, Aberdeenshire, built for Sir William **Forbes**, reputedly in 1629; the details are very similar to those of **Craigievar**. A further wing was added in the 18th century. It is now available for holiday letting and functions.

**Liddel Water** River in the **Borders** that rises in the Cheviot Hills, 13km (8mi) southwest of **Carter Bar**, and runs southwest through **Liddesdale** to the English border at Kershopefoot. It continues southwest along the border to join the River **Esk** 3km (2mi) south of Canonbie.

**Liddell, Eric Henry** (1902–45) Athlete and missionary, b. China to Scottish parents. He won bronze and gold medals at the 1924 Olympic Games in Paris, an achievement that is celebrated in the film *Chariots of Fire* (1981). He later became a missionary in China and died while in Japanese internment.

**Liddesdale** Valley in the **Borders**, notorious until the 17th century for the criminality of its inhabitants, that carries the **Liddel Water** southwest from Saughtree through the village of Newcastleton to Caulside.

**Liddesdale** Small settlement on the south shore of Loch Sunart, 4km (3mi) southwest of Strontian.

**Life and Work** The monthly publication of the Church of Scotland. It was first published in 1879 and it has had a **Gaelic** Supplement since 1880.

**lighthouses** see p.229

**Limekilns** Fife village on the north bank of the Firth of **Forth**, 5km (3mi) west of **Inverkeithing**, taking its name from the lime industry in the area, developed especially in the 18th century by the Earls of Elgin.

**Lincluden Abbey** Ruined 15th-century choir and transept of an abbey to the north of **Dumfries**, founded as a Benedictine convent in the 12th century and later a collegiate church.

**Lind, James** (1716–94) Physician and health researcher, b. Edinburgh. While serving in the Royal Navy as a surgeon he discovered the anti-scurvy properties of fresh fruit, especially lemon juice, and published *A Treatise of the Scurvy* in 1753. His findings were not implemented until after his death.

**Lindores Abbey** Ruins of a Tironensian abbey just to the east of **Newburgh**, Fife, founded c.1178 by **David, Earl of Huntingdon**, of great importance until the **Reformation**. The village of Lindores and Lindores Loch are a short distance to the southeast.

**Lindsay, Alexander Dunlop** (**Lord Lindsay of Birker**) (1879–1952) Philosopher and educationalist, b. Glasgow. He was Professor of Moral Philosophy at **Glasgow University** (1922–4) and a pioneer of the Workers' Education Association before becoming Master of Balliol College, Oxford, and later Vice Chancellor of Oxford University and then founder and first principal of Keele University. His works include *The Modern Democratic State* (1943).

# LIGHTHOUSES

Lights were used to guide ships into harbour or away from dangerous rocks from early times, but the first recorded lighthouse in Scotland, a simple coal fire on a masonry floor on top of a tower, was in 1635 on the Isle of **May**. As shipping and dangers to shipping increased, the need for an organised system of lights was recognised, and the Commission for Northern Lights was established by Parliament in 1786. Its first lights were on Barra Head and **Kinnaird** Head, on the Mull of **Kintyre**, and on **North Ronaldsay**, and were equipped with parabolic reflectors and whale-oil burners, an invention of Thomas Smith, the Commission's engineer.

Developing technology went hand-in-hand with the lighthouse designs of the Stevenson family, beginning with Smith's son-in-law, Robert Stevenson (1772-1850), who followed Smith as Engineer to the Board, and began the dynasty of the 'Lighthouse Stevensons'. Robert Stevenson invented intermittent and flashing lights, and designed and supervised the construction of 15 lighthouses in Scotland and others on the Isle of Man and overseas, most famously the **Bell Rock**, lit in 1811, also providing a new lighthouse for the Isle of May in 1816.

Robert's son, Alan (1807-65) built **Skerryvore**, the tallest, and some think the finest, of Scottish lighthouses, while Alan's brothers David (1815-86) and Thomas (1818-87), father of

*Neist Point, Isle of Skye.*

Robert Louis **Stevenson**, built lighthouses on the Scottish islands, such as those at **Kyleakin** and **Bressay**, as well as St Abb's Head and **Inchcolm**. Between them they built 80 in Scotland. David also designed earthquake-proof lighthouses for Japan.

David A Stevenson (1854-1938) and his brother Charles (1855-1950), sons of David Stevenson, also lit up the islands, with lighthouses at **Fair Isle**, **Dunvegan** and **Flannan Isles** among others, and also the **Bass Rock**. Charles improved optic and foghorn design, and explored the use of radio communications. The first automated light in Scotland was on Oxcars in the Firth of **Forth** in 1894.

By 1914 the coasts of Scotland and the Isle of Man had been thoroughly lit by the Commission, with 90 major and many minor lights; few new lights have since been lit. Lighthouse keepers kept the lights and fog signals in working order; on the remoter lights they worked 4 weeks on and 4 weeks off. The solitary nature of their life was brought home by the disappearance in 1900 of all 3 keepers on the Flannan Isles, a mystery that has never been solved. In the 1980s and 90s a massive programme of automation was undertaken, and the Commission now has no manned lights; the last manned light, Fair Isle South, was converted in 1998. Some, including the Bell Rock, are now being converted to solar-electric power.

*Muckle Flugga.*

*Mull of Galloway.*

*Spinning flax for linen cloth, Aberdeenshire, in the 1890s.*

**Lindsay, Sir David** see **Lyndsay, Sir David**

**Lindsay, David** (1879–1945) Novelist, b. London of a Scottish father and English mother. After World War I, in which he served, he left his City career to become a full-time novelist. His first novel, *A Voyage to Arcturus* (1920), is regarded as a classic of imaginative fiction.

**Lindsay, Frederic** (1933– ) Novelist and crime writer, b. Glasgow. After a career in teaching and lecturing, he made a literary mark with his powerful novel, *Brond* (1983), followed up with *Jill Rips* (1987) and *A Charm against Drowning* (1988). He has been one of the pioneers of the new realistic school of Scottish crime fiction. He currently writes a series of novels featuring the Edinburgh police detective, Jim Meldrum, including *Kissing Judas* (1997) and *Death Knock* (2000).

**Lindsay, Ian Gordon** (1906–66) Architect and author, b. Edinburgh. He restored **Iona** Abbey, the villages of **Inveraray**, **Cramond** and **Culross** and became the leading conservation architect of his generation.

**Lindsay, (John) Maurice** (1918– ) Critic, poet and editor, b. Glasgow. He trained as a musician and was music and drama critic for *The Bulletin* (1946–60) before working for Border Television. In 1967 he became Director of the Scottish Civic Trust and in 1983 Honorary Secretary General of Europa Nostra. He has published many volumes of poetry and a wide range of prose works, including books on Robert **Burns** and a *History of Scottish Literature* (1977).

**Lindsay, Robert, of Pitscottie** (c.1500–c.1565) Historian, b. Pitscottie, near Cupar, Fife. Little is known of his life except that he wrote *Historie and Cronicles of Scotland*, which draws on various sources, notably the history of Hector **Boece**, to cover the period of Scottish history from 1436 to 1575. Pitscottie excels as a teller of tales, but the reliability of his chronicle is often questionable.

**linen** Linen production began in medieval times in Scotland as a domestic activity but by the end of the 17th century linen products were being exported. With the collapse of Scottish woollen exports due to English competition after 1707, linen became the main industrial growth point in the Scottish economy and was state-sponsored through the **Board of Trustees for Manufactures and Fisheries**. Heavy imports of flax from the Baltic and increasing exploitation of water-powered sites by flax spinners created conditions that allowed spectacular growth after 1750. The industry became particularly strong in **Aberdeenshire**, **Angus** and **Fife** but by 1820 was in decline in **Glasgow** and the west of Scotland where the next wave of textile manufacture in the shape of the cotton industry was taking over. In the 19th century linen became regionally specialised on a UK basis. **Dunfermline** in Fife specialised in the finest types of linen. Dundee and Angus continued to make coarser cloths such as sailcloth, but substituted **jute** for much of the coarsest end of the trade. Belfast in Ulster dominated the domestic linen market and Leeds in England increasingly specialised in the production of the necessary machinery. By the end of the 20th century the Scottish linen industry was extinct, even in Dunfermline.

**Linga Sound** A stretch of water that separates the island of West Linga from the west coast of the island of **Whalsay**, Shetland.

**Lingard, Joan** (1933– ) Novelist, b. Edinburgh. Brought up in Northern Ireland, her novels, for both children and adults, feature the complexities and secrecies of family relationships, the effects of social change and the divisions of Northern Ireland, especially in the Kevin and Sadie series. She has also written for television, including a series in the 1980s, *Maggie*, based on her quartet of books for teenagers, focussed on the Scottish **Highlands**. Her books have been widely translated and their themes range across Europe. Her recent adult novels include *After Colette* (1993) and *The Kiss* (2002).

**Linklater, Eric Robert** (1899–1975) Novelist, b. Penarth in Wales of an Orcadian father and a Scottish mother. He regarded himself as an Orkneyman and chose to live much of his life in **Orkney**. He served in World War I before attending **Aberdeen University**. His postgraduate study in the USA provided inspiration for his satirical novel *Juan in America* (1931), which brought him instant fame as a writer. He wrote many other novels, of which the best known are *The Men of Ness* (1932), the semi-autobiographical *Magnus Merriman* (1934) and *Private Angelo* (1946).

**links** Scots word for undulating sandy ground near the shore where traditionally **golf** began to be played in medieval times. Most Scottish coastal golf courses are laid out on such terrain.

**Linlithgow** (pop. 13,370) Ancient town in **West Lothian**, 26km (16mi) west of **Edinburgh**. Former royal **burgh** and county town of West Lothian. It was once an important manufacturing and trading town with its port first at Blackness and after 1680 at **Bo'ness**. At the Cross is a splendid town house, built by John Smith (1668–70). Behind it is St Michael's Church, founded in 1242 and rebuilt 1424–1532, a fine example of Scots Gothic, its tower now topped by a wood and aluminium spire replacing its lost crown. To the north, on a knoll above the south side of Linlithgow Loch, are the substantial ruins of Linlithgow Palace, built between 1424 and 1541, the birthplace of **James V** (1512) and **Mary, Queen of Scots** (1542); burnt in 1746, it is now in the care of **Historic Scotland** and undergoing considerable restoration. The 18th-century Annet House has Linlithgow Story Museum. The **Union Canal** runs through the south of the town and to the southwest is the 12-arched Avon Aqueduct carrying it over the River **Avon**. To the south in the **Bathgate** hills is Beecraigs Country Park, with a deer farm, sawmill and recreational activities, including fishing.

**Linlithgow, John Adrian Louis Hope, 7th Earl of Hopetoun, 1st Marquess of** (1860–1908) Politician, b. Hopetoun House, near South Queensferry. He was the first Governor General of Australia from 1900 to 1902, when he was created Marquess of Linlithgow. He was Secretary for Scotland in 1905.

**Linlithgowshire** see **West Lothian**

**Linnhe, Loch** see **Loch Linnhe**

**Linnhouse** Superb, little-altered house near **Mid Calder**, West Lothian, the original part stepped L-plan of 1589, the remainder built by the Muirheads who acquired the estate in 1631. A small loch with an island was formed within its park in 1975.

**linoleum** Invented by Frederick Walton in Staines, Middlesex, in 1863, but its manufacture became particularly associated with the town of **Kirkcaldy**, where in 1876 it was grafted onto a well-established industry making floorcloth by applying layers of paint to a canvas backing, started in 1847 by Michael Nairn. In linoleum a mixture of cork and linseed oil was applied to a canvas backing. The floorcloth factories took up the new product, and several new plants were built in the town which could for many years be identified by the smell of linseed oil from drying linoleum. There were also works in **Falkland**, and in **Newburgh**, also in Fife. The development of vinyl floorcoverings, and the fashion for fitted carpets, led to a rapid decline in the industry in the late 1950s and early 1960s. Only one company, Forbo-Nairn, still makes the material.

**Linwood** (pop. 9058) A large residential development in Renfrewshire, just to the northeast of **Johnstone**, that began as an industrial village around a large cotton mill built in 1792 and was expanded in the 1960s around a steel works and car factory that are now defunct; see **Rootes Ltd**.

*The linoleum works, Kirkcaldy, 1918.*

*David Livingstone, c.1855.*

**Lion Rampant** Heraldic personal symbol of the Scottish monarch, the image of a red lion on a yellow ground, standing on its hind legs, the right foreleg raised above the left. It may have been adopted by **William I**, 'the Lion', as his standard and by 1286 it appeared on the Great Seal of Scotland. It has become one of the most popular symbols of Scotland itself.

**Lipton, Sir Thomas Johnstone** (1850–1931) Grocer and entrepreneur, b. Glasgow. He revolutionised the grocery trade by ensuring continuity of supply and developing marketing techniques in his chain of grocery stores. A keen yachtsman, he challenged 5 times for the Americas Cup but always unsuccessfully. He also helped start the World Cup in football (1910).

**Lismore** (Gaelic **Lios Mór**) Long, narrow, fertile island in **Argyll**, at the mouth of **Loch Linnhe**. It is about 10km (15mi) long and 2km (1mi) wide. It was Christianised by St Moluag in the 6th century and by the 13th century had become an important ecclesiastical centre, with the cathedral of the diocese of Argyll. After the **Reformation**, the cathedral became ruinous, but the choir was rebuilt in 1749 as the parish church; the nave and the tower at its west end are only just visible. There are medieval graveslabs in the church and in the graveyard. There is

a harbour at Port Ramsay from which a ferry runs to Port Appin on the mainland.

**Liston, Robert** (1794–1847) Surgeon, b. Linlithgow. Trained in **Edinburgh** and London, he lectured in surgery and anatomy in Edinburgh before becoming Professor of Clinical Surgery at University College London. He devised the Liston splint and in 1846 was the first to use a general anaesthetic. His writings include *Elements of Surgery* (1831).

**Lithgow, William** (c.1582–1650) Traveller and author, b. Lanark. In 1614 he published an account of his travels on foot in Europe and the Middle East during which his ears were cut off by the Spanish Inquisition.

**Lithgows Ltd** Company founded in 1918 by William and Henry Lithgow, when they took over the **Port Glasgow** shipbuilding business of Russell and Co, run by their father, W T Lithgow, since 1891. Russell and Co had established itself as the builder of the largest annual tonnage of ships on the **Clyde**, specialising in bulk-cargo sailing ships – windjammers – and moderately sized tramp steamers. Lithgows Ltd continued to build tramp steamers, of increasing size. In 1969 the company became part of Lower Clyde Shipbuilders, a Government initiative to rationalise the shipbuilding industry, and the company's yards were re-equipped to build very large crude carriers (in halves, joined together after launching) and large bulk dry-cargo vessels. The largest yard, the Glen Yard, then built large oil-industry structures until it closed in the 1980s. The berths have now been demolished.

**Livingston** (pop. 50,826) New town in **West Lothian**, to the west of **Edinburgh**, 2km (1mi) northeast of Livingston village, established in 1962 and planned by Peter Daniel, now the administrative centre of West Lothian Council and home to various technological industries. It has the Almond Valley Heritage Centre, based on Livingston Mill Farm. Of the old village the parish church of 1732 and the main street remain. Livingston Football Club, which began as a Ferranti works team, is now in the Scottish Premierleague.

**Livingston Football Club** Founded in 1974 as Meadowbank Thistle. Based at the Commonwealth stadium in Edinburgh, Meadowbank had grown out of the works team Ferranti Thistle. When the support failed to grow to match the improving fortunes of the club, its owners moved it to the new town in 1995. Since moving Livingston have been promoted to the Scottish Premierleague. See also **football**.

**Livingston, Mary** see **'four Marys'**

# LOCAL GOVERNMENT

From medieval times, some local-government power was vested in the **sheriffs** and **regalities**, in the Church, and from the 17th century in **justices of the peace** and in the Commissioners of Supply (a group of local landowners).

Massive reforms have taken place from the early 19th century on, beginning with Acts in 1833 giving wider powers to elected **burgh** councils.

The parish had civil as well as ecclesiastical functions from the 17th century. In particular the church had shared with the heritors (landowners) responsibility for poor relief until an Act of 1845 transferred it to a representative, partially elected board. In 1894 parochial boards were replaced by elected parish councils with increased powers.

Another important milestone was the Scottish Education Act of 1872 by which the running of burgh and parish schools was transferred to elected school boards.

The Local Government (Scotland) Act of 1889 set up county councils with wide local power, taking over most of the administrative powers of the Commissioners of Supply, the justices of the peace and other agencies. The Education (Scotland) Act of 1918 transferred responsibility for schools to elected education authorities that covered the same territory as the counties, but which were elected separately from them by a system of proportional representation.

A further Act of 1929 vested full local powers (including over education) in county and town councils and in district councils (formed from district committees and consisting of the relevant county councillors along with elected members). The burghs were classified as 'county of city' (**Aberdeen**, Dundee, Edinburgh, Glasgow**), 'large burgh' (20,000 or more inhabitants), and 'small burgh' (with lesser powers).

The last quarter of the 20th century saw great upheavals in the Scottish local-government system. For centuries up to 1975 the main unit was the county, with some towns having independent status as **burghs**. Alterations to boundaries were made over the years, often in response to changes in population. See map on p.395 for the counties as they were in 1975.

In 1975 a two-tier system was set up with 9 regional and 53 district councils, and with **Shetland**, **Orkney** and the **Western Isles** forming 3 unitary island authorities. See **Wheatley Report** and map on p.395. On the whole the regions took over the wider functions, including education, social work, roads, strategic planning and industrial development, while the districts dealt with more local matters such as housing, cleansing, recreation and leisure, and local planning.

In 1996 further drastic changes took place when the 2-tier system was reversed and 33 unitary authorities were created in their place, mainly formed from districts or joinings of districts. Four regions, Borders, Dumfries and Galloway, Fife, and Highland, became unitary authorities and the 3 island authorities continue. See maps on pp.394-5.

See also **baillie**, **burgh**, **Convention of Royal Burghs**, **Convention of Scottish Local Authorities**, **Justice of the Peace**, **provost**, **sheriff**.

There are plans to change the election system for councillors from 'first past the post' to a form of proportional representation.

---

**Livingstone, David** (1813-73) Weaver who became a medical missionary and explorer, b. Blantyre, Lanarkshire. He travelled the length of Lake Tanganyika, and was the first European to discover the Victoria Falls. He wrote with passion against the evils of the slave trade in Africa. He published several journals of his travels and died while attempting to discover the source of the River Nile.

**Livingstone, William** see **MacDhunléibhe, Uilleam**

**Livingston Mill Farm** Alternative name for Almond Valley Heritage Centre. See **Livingston**.

**Loanhead** (pop. 6384) A former mining town in **Midlothian**, 9km (6mi) south of **Edinburgh**, based on a colliery at Bilston Glen, to the southwest. It is in an area of great geological interest.

**Loanhead of Daviot** Recumbent stone circle in **Aberdeenshire** to the north of Daviot, 7km (5mi) northwest of Inverurie. It dates from the 3rd/2nd millennia BC and encloses a ring cairn. Nearby is a small Bronze Age cremation cemetery.

**local government** see above

**loch** Scots word for a lake, from Gaelic *loch*, applied to all natural lakes in Scotland, except the Lake of **Menteith**. A sea loch is an arm of the sea, especially a fjord-shaped one, of which there are many on the west coast. Most of the lochs, both freshwater and sea lochs, are long and narrow, excavated deeply during the Ice Age by valley glaciers. Often found in place-names; see over.

**Loch, James** (1780-1855) Lawyer, politician and agricultural improver. As estate manager for the Duke of Sutherland he planned the clearance of the **Sutherland** estates carried out by Patrick **Sellar** and others. He was MP for **Wick** from 1830 until 1852.

**Lochaber** (Gaelic **Lochabar**) Mountainous moorland district that stretches from **Knoydart** and **Morar** in the west to the **Monadhliath** Mountains and Glen Spean in the east. In 1975 it became the Lochaber District of **Highland Region** with its administrative centre at **Fort William** and it is now part of **Highland** local authority; see maps on pp.394-5 and **local government**.

**Lochaber axe** A long-shafted weapon that had a long axe blade on one side and a hook on the other. The hook was used to pull mounted soldiers from their horses. It was a traditional weapon of the **town guard** of **Edinburgh**.

**Lochaber District** see **Lochaber** and **Highland Region**

**Loch Achray** Small loch in Achray Forest in the Queen Elizabeth Forest Park, 11km (7mi) west of **Callander**. The Pass of Achray is a part of a narrow, steep-sided glen that carries Achray Water east from **Loch Katrine** to Loch Achray.

**Loch Affric** (Gaelic **Loch Afraig**) Loch in Glen Affric that is formed in the course of the River Affric, 19km (12mi) southwest of Cannich.

**Loch Ailort** Sea loch bounded on the north by the peninsula of Ardnish and on the south by **Moidart**. At its head, in a scenic setting, is the hamlet of Lochailort, on the 'Road to the Isles'.

**Lochaline** Village on the west side of the entrance to Loch Aline in **Lochaber**. Its churchyard has a 16th-century stone with one of the earliest known depictions of a kilted figure. Nearby are turreted Lochaline House and the 14th-century ruins of **Ardtornish** Castle, stronghold of the **Lords of the Isles**. The main feature of the village is a mine which produces the highest quality silica sand in the UK used for optical glass and other purposes. This is the only location in the UK where silica sand is mined rather than extracted by opencast methods.

**Loch Alsh** The area of sea bounded to the west by **Kyle Akin**, and stretching inland to **Eilean Donan**, where **Loch Long** runs into it from the northeast and **Loch Duich** from the southeast.

**Lochalsh** (Gaelic **Lochaillse**) Area in **Wester Ross** around **Loch Alsh**. See also **Kyle of Lochalsh, Skye and Lochalsh**.

**Lochalsh Woodland Garden** see **Balmacara**

**Loch an Eilein** Small loch in **Badenoch**, 5km (3mi) south of **Aviemore**. It is noted for its triple echo, and there are ruins of a medieval castle, enlarged as a stronghold of the Wolf of **Badenoch**, on a small island in the loch.

**Lochan Fada** Loch in **Wester Ross**, northeast of **Poolewe**. It lies 305m (1000ft) above sea level. A stream carries the waters down through Gleann Bianasdail to **Loch Maree**.

*Loch Affric in the Highlands.*

**Loch Ard** Loch in the **Trossachs**, 5km (3mi) west of **Aberfoyle**. The Loch Ard Forest is part of the **Queen Elizabeth Forest Park**.

**Loch Arkaig** (Gaelic **Loch Airceig**) Loch connected to **Loch Lochy** in the **Great Glen** by the short River Arkaig. The name is also applied to the district near Achnacarry that was strongly **Jacobite** in 1745. See also **Loch nan Uamh**.

**Loch Assynt** (Gaelic **Loch Asainn**) Loch in **Assynt**, Sutherland, 7km (5mi) east of **Lochinver**, with the village of Inchnadamph at its head. It is over 10km (6mi) long and its maximum depth is 86m (282ft).

**Loch Awe** (Gaelic **Loch Obha**) Long, narrow, deep loch in **Argyll**, 39km (24mi) long, extending northeast from Ford to **Kilchurn Castle** near **Dalmally**. The loch, noted for salmon and trout fishing, has several islands, including Inishail, which has a ruined convent and chapel, and **Innis Chonell**, which has a ruined castle of the Campbells. In the heyday of the Campbell Clan, Loch Awe acted as a kind of natural moat for their protection. At the northwest end of the loch is the Cruachan hydroelectric pumped-storage scheme, deep in the bowels of Ben **Cruachan**, on the Pass of **Brander**.

**Lochawe** Village in Argyll on the northwest bank of **Loch Awe**, 5km (3mi) west of Dalmally. St Conan's Kirk, built by the Campbells of Blythswood between 1881 and 1930, exhibits eccentrically mixed styles and incorporates ancient fragments gathered from other sites. To the west is the **Cruachan** Power Station and to the east **Kilchurn Castle**.

**Lochay** see **Glen Lochay**

**Loch Ba** Loch on the Moor of **Rannoch**, close to the main road to **Glencoe**. It is drained by the River Ba, which flows the short distance to **Loch Laidon**.

**Lochboisdale** (Gaelic **Loch Baghasdail**) Village and port in **South Uist**, on the north shore of Loch Baghasdail. Ferries run from here to **Oban**, **Barra** and **Tiree**.

**Loch Broom** (Gaelic **Loch Bhraoin**) Long sea loch on the northwest coast, running southeast-northwest. **Ullapool** is near the end of its narrower southerly section, and where it widens into the **Minch** are the **Summer Isles**. See **klondyker**.

**Lochbroom** Name for the area round **Loch Broom**, and specifically an extensive parish, one of the largest in Scotland.

**Lochbuie** Settlement and estate on the south coast of the isle of **Mull**, on the isthmus between Loch Buie and Loch Uisg. There are 3 former homes of the Maclaines of Lochbuie: the ruined 15th-century keep of Moy Castle (which featured in the film *I Know Where I'm Going*); Old Lochbuie House, built in 1752, where Dr Johnson and James **Boswell** stayed in 1773 (described by Boswell as 'a poor house, though of two storeys indeed'), now part of the outbuildings of the present Lochbuie House, which dates from 1793. Prehistoric monuments in the area include an ancient stone circle to the north, one of the few in the west of Scotland.

**Loch Carron** (Gaelic **Loch Carrunn**) Sea loch in **Wester Ross** running northeast-southwest to the narrows at **Stromeferry**. Since 1973 the road from **Inverness** to **Kyle of Lochalsh** has followed its eastern shore, alongside the railway, avoiding the need for a ferry crossing at Strome. At the head of the Loch is Glen Carron, which includes Achnashellach Forest, one of the first forests set up by the Forestry Commission and the scene of research into the reclamation of bog land.

**Lochcarron** Village near the head of **Loch Carron**, formerly known as Jeantown, noted for its locally woven tartans and as a centre for exploring the area, especially the hills of **Torridon**, **Applecross** and around Achnashellach.

**Loch Cluanie** Long narrow loch running west-east from the head of **Glen Shiel**, one of the upper reservoirs of the Garry-Moriston hydroelectric scheme. Cluanie Inn, near the head of the Loch, is a favourite haunt of weary climbers and walkers.

**Loch Coruisk** (Gaelic **Loch Coir' uisge**) In a spectacular location on the Isle of **Skye**, surrounded by the **Cuillin** mountains, this long, narrow loch has no road access, only footpaths, one of which crosses a tricky part known as the Bad Step.

**Loch Craignish** (Gaelic **Loch Creaginnis**) Opening out into the Sound of **Jura**, this loch and its shores are a popular destination for tourists, particularly with pleasure boats. A road runs along the shore to Craignish Point. The privately owned 19th-century Craignish Castle is built on the site of an earlier tower house which belonged to the Campbells. At the head of the loch is the village of Ardfern, a popular yachting centre.

**Loch Creran** Sea loch in **Argyll**, opening out into **Loch Linnhe**. **Barcaldine Castle** overlooks the loch from **Benderloch**, and the Scottish Sea Life Sanctuary is on the shore.

**Loch Dochart** Small loch to the east of **Crianlarich**. On an islet in the middle of the loch are the ruins of a castle.

**Loch Doon** Large loch and reservoir in hilly country in **Ayrshire** at the head of the River **Doon**, 8km (5mi) south of **Dalmellington**. Water from the loch travels through a tunnel into the River Ken watershed, forming part of the hydroelectric scheme. When the level of the loch was raised in the 1930s for the scheme, the remains of the early 14th-century Loch Doon Castle, which formerly stood on an island in the loch, were moved to the lochside; in the care of **Historic Scotland**.

**Loch Duich** (Gaelic **Loch Dubhthaich**) Sea loch, 8km (5mi) long, that runs northwest from **Glen Shiel** into **Loch Alsh** at **Eilean Donan**.

**Loch Dunvegan** see **Dunvegan**

**Loch Earn** (Gaelic **Loch Éire**) Long narrow loch 17km (11mi) west of **Crieff**, drained by the River **Earn**, near **St Fillans** at the eastern end.

**Lochearnhead** Village at the west end of **Loch Earn** and at the mouth of Glen Ogle. It owes its existence to the meeting of roads and railways going north with the road from the east, along **Loch Earn**, and is now a centre for sailing and water-skiing on the loch and for climbing in the surrounding hills, including Ben Vorlich. To the southeast and on the shores of the loch is **Edinample Castle**, built in 1584 for Sir Duncan Campbell, and east of Edinample is Ardvorlich House, from 1580 the home of the

L

*Loch Garten, Abernethy Forest Reserve, Cairngorms National Park.*

L

Stewarts of Ardvorlich, rebuilt 1790: a stone at the gate records the internment of 7 MacDonalds of Glencoe, killed when attempting to harry Ardvorlich, *Anno Domini 1620*.

**Loch Eck** (Gaelic **Loch Aic**) Narrow loch on the **Cowal** peninsula, with the Younger Botanic Gardens at **Benmore** on its southern shore.

**Loch Eil** (Gaelic **Loch Iall**) Sea loch which runs 11km (7mi) eastwards and opens into **Loch Linnhe** at **Fort William**. The Chiefs of the Clan Cameron have taken the name 'Lochiel'.

**Loch Eilt** Loch near the west coast to the east of **Loch Ailort**, the West Highland Railway runs along its southern side. The River Ailort leads from the loch into Loch Ailort.

**Loch Einich** Loch which is completely surrounded by mountains, at the head of Glen Einich, a deep glacial valley running through the **Cairngorms** to the west of **Braeriach**.

**Loch Eriboll** Long sea loch in **Sutherland**, running southwest-northeast into the sea on the north coast.

**Loch Ericht** (Gaelic **Loch Eireachd**) A long narrow loch running 24km (15mi) south-south-west from Dalwhinnie, on the boundary between **Perth and Kinross** and **Highland** Council areas. It is overlooked by **Ben Alder** at its southern end. The River Ericht flows from the south of the loch into **Loch Rannoch**.

**Loch Etchachan** Small high-level loch in the **Cairngorms**, to the northeast of **Ben Macdui**.

**Loch Etive** (Gaelic **Loch Éite**) Long narrow sea loch in Argyll, running southwest from **Glen Etive**, and then west to open out into the Firth of **Lorn**. There is no road access to the shores of the loch in its upper parts, except near the head. The narrows near its mouth are spanned by **Connel** Bridge and **Dunstaffnage Castle** stands on a promontory to the west.

**Loch Ewe** (Gaelic **Loch Iù**) The River Ewe rushes for 5km (3mi) from **Loch Maree** into Loch Ewe, a sea loch 16km (10mi) long on the west coast. **Poolewe** is at the head of the loch, near the exotic **Inverewe Gardens**. In the 17th century, the Ewe powered the Red Smiddy blast furnace at Poolewe, the second such in Scotland; see also **Letterewe**. At the village of Aultbea, on the east shore, there were anchorages for the Home Fleet in World Wars I and II. During World War II Arctic convoys assembled here *en route* for Russia. There is now a NATO refuelling depot nearby. The small Isle of Ewe, in the middle of the loch, made it easier to construct an anti-submarine boom in World War II.

**Loch Fannich** see **Fannich(s)**

**Loch Faskally** Man-made reservoir 2.5km (1.5mi) from **Pitlochry**, formed when the Tummel valley was dammed as part of a hydroelectric scheme in 1947–50. A salmon ladder built into the dam at Pitlochry attracts many visitors.

**Loch Fyne** (Gaelic **Loch Fine**) Sea loch in Argyll, stretching firstly southwest and then southeast, to open into the Sound of **Bute**. It is well known for fishing and oysters, and the Loch Fyne Oyster Bar at the head of the loch is a renowned outlet for these. It had an important herring-fishing industry, practised from distinctive Loch Fyne skiffs. The **Crinan Canal** enters the loch at **Ardrishaig**.

**Loch Garry** see **Garry, Loch and River**

**Loch Garten** (Gaelic **Loch Ghartain**) Near **Boat of Garten**, this small loch forms part of a nature reserve. The Abernethy Forest Reserve of the Royal Society for the Protection of Birds on the shores of the loch is home to nesting **ospreys**, and was crucial in encouraging the re-establishment of these rare birds in Scotland.

**Lochgelly** (pop. 6749) Former **burgh** and market town in **Fife**, 11km (7mi) southwest of **Glenrothes** that became, from the middle of the 19th century until the 1980s, the centre of the eastern part of the Fife coalfields. It also had a large iron-smelting works. Another former industry was the manufacture of the leather 'tawse' used by many generations of teachers to punish unruly pupils until corporal punishment in schools was abolished.

**Lochgilphead** (Gaelic **Ceann Loch Gilp**) (pop. 2326) Small town in **Argyll**, at the head of Loch Gilp. In the late 18th century it was laid out as a planned town after the building of a road from **Inveraray** to **Campbeltown**. It expanded further as a result of the opening of the **Crinan Canal** in 1801. The road from **Oban**, and steamers to **Glasgow** from nearby **Ardrishaig**, added to its importance as a route centre. It is the administrative centre of **Argyll and Bute** Council, as well as a tourist and shopping centre.

**Lochgoilhead** (Gaelic **Ceann Loch Goibhle**) Victorian village and small resort in **Argyll**, at the head of Loch Goil, an arm of **Loch Long**. The parish church is 18th-century T-plan in form, but medieval in origin; restored 1957. The village has fine views to the south of **Argyll's Bowling Green**, hills in the Argyll Forest Park. To the northwest is **Hell's Glen** Pass (summit 219m/719ft) leading to **Loch Fyne** and to the northeast the **Rest and be Thankful** pass.

**Lochhead, Liz** (1947– ) Poet and dramatist, b. Motherwell. She studied at **Glasgow School of Art** and taught for 9 years before becoming a full-time writer. She has developed an ironic style as a poet, illustrated in collections such as *True Confessions and New Clichés* (1985). Several of her plays, e.g. *Mary Queen of Scots Got Her Head Chopped Off* (1987), are inspired by historical subjects. She uses a vigorous **Scots** language, not least in her translations of plays: *Tartuffe* (from Molière; 1990), *Medea* (2000).

**Loch Hope** Long narrow loch in the north of **Sutherland**, joined by the short River Hope to **Loch Eriboll** at its northern end.

**Loch Hourn** (Gaelic **Loch Shuirn**) Long sea loch on the west coast, to the north of **Knoydart**, opening into the Sound of **Sleat**.

**Lochhouse Tower** Tall square 16th-century tower house of the Johnstones of that Ilk, re-roofed in 1973 and a prominent landmark near **Beattock**.

**Lochiel** *see* **Cameron, Donald; Loch Eil**

**Lochindorb Castle** Ruined 13th-century castle on an island in a loch of the same name on Dava Moor between the Rivers **Spey** and **Findhorn**, 10km (7mi) northwest of **Grantown-on-Spey**. Once a hunting seat of the Comyn family, it became better known as one of the strongholds of the Wolf of **Badenoch**. It came into the hands of Archibald Douglas, Earl of **Moray** but he was defeated and killed in rebellion against **James II** in 1455 and the castle was destroyed and left as a ruin.

**Lochinvar** The young hero in the fifth canto of Sir Walter **Scott**'s ballad *Marmion*, who, when his 'fair Ellen' is on the point of being married to 'a laggard in love and dastard in war', gatecrashes the bridal feast and demands a dance with her. As the couple reach the hall door, he swings her out and onto his horse and they ride off.

**Lochinver** (Gaelic **Loch an Inbhir**) Fishing village and resort at the head of Loch Inver on the west coast of **Sutherland**. Glencanisp Forest, 7km (4mi) southeast, has the mountain **Suilven**, which towers impressively behind the village.

**Loch Katrine** (Gaelic **Loch Ceiteirein**) Large loch in the **Trossachs**, 13km (8mi) west of **Callander**. Since 1859 it has been the major source of water for **Glasgow**. It features in Sir Walter **Scott**'s poem 'The Lady of the Lake', with Ellen's Isle at its eastern end. The steamship *Sir Walter Scott* operates on the loch in summer.

**Loch Ken** Long narrow loch running southeast from **New Galloway**, fed by the Water of Ken. The level of the loch was raised in the 1930s to form part of the Galloway hydroelectric scheme. The lower part of the loch is also known as the River Dee, which flows from its southern end.

**Loch Kishorn** see **Kishorn**

**Loch Laggan** Long narrow loch to the southwest of **Newtonmore**; the Laggan Dam was built in 1926 to supply hydroelectric power to the aluminium works at **Fort William**. The area has been used by the BBC for the filming of the TV series *Monarch of the Glen*.

**Loch Laidon** Long narrow loch on the **Rannoch Moor**, running southwest-northeast to near Rannoch Station on the **West Highland Railway**.

**Loch Laxford** see **Laxford Bridge**

**Loch Leven** Loch that runs 17km (11mi) west from **Kinlochleven**

*Loch Lomond, Scotland's largest loch.*

to Loch **Linnhe**. A bridge now carries the road over the narrows near its mouth, replacing the **Ballachulish** ferry.

**Loch Leven** Loch on the east side of **Kinross**, noted for its brown trout. It is a nature reserve. It has 7 islands; the medieval ruins of Lochleven Priory are on the largest island, St Serf's; the ruined 15th-century Lochleven Castle is on Castle Island. **Mary, Queen of Scots** was imprisoned here in 1567 but escaped in 1568 with the help of William Douglas. The level of the loch was raised in the 19th century to provide water power for the industries of the Leven Valley.

**Loch Linnhe** Long sea loch that runs 35km (22mi) southwest from **Fort William** to **Mull**. The southern end of the **Caledonian Canal** is at the head of the loch.

**Loch Lochy** Loch in the Great Glen, in **Lochaber**, that runs 16km (10mi) southwest from **Laggan** to Gairlochy. It forms part of the **Caledonian Canal**.

**Loch Lomond** (Gaelic **Loch Laomainn**) Scotland's largest loch, situated northwest of **Glasgow**, in the **Loch Lomond and the Trossachs National Park**, it is also the largest area of inland water in Britain. It extends 39km (24mi) north from **Balloch** to Ardlui. At its wider southern end there are some 30 wooded islands, many of which were inhabited in the 5th century by Irish missionaries. On Inchmurrin, the largest, St Mirren is believed to have founded a monastery in the 6th century and there are ruins of the 14th-century castle of the earls of Lennox. Inchcailloch, owned by **Scottish Natural Heritage**, means 'island of the old women', leading to the belief that there was a nunnery there, though no

trace has been found. It is the burial place of the MacGregors and the Macfarlanes. Several of the islands lie along the **Highland Boundary Fault**. There are cruising and boating facilities and the southeast corner is a nature reserve. The **West Highland Way** long-distance path runs along the east bank. The Loch Lomond Golf Club, on the **Rossdhu** estate, is a championship course and is currently used for the annual Scottish Open.

**Loch Lomond and the Trossachs National Park** (Gaelic **Parc Naiseanta Loch Laomainn is nan Troiseachean**) Scotland's first national park, set up, after much controversy, in 2002, and the third-largest national park (at 1865 sq km/720 sq mi) in the UK after the **Cairngorms** and the Lake District. Situated northwest of **Glasgow**, it comprises the former Loch Lomond Regional Park, the Argyll Forest Park, and the **Trossachs**, including the Queen Elizabeth Forest Park. There are visitor centres around **Loch Lomond**, at Loch Lomond Shores in **Balloch**, **Balmaha**, **Luss**, **Inveruglas** and **Tarbet**, and also at **Aberfoyle** and **Callander** in the Trossachs, at **Tyndrum** and at Ardgarten on **Loch Long**.

**Loch Long** Long, narrow, deep inlet of the Firth of **Clyde** that extends 27km (16mi) northeast from **Kilcreggan** at the southern end of the Rosneath peninsula to Arrochar. At Arrochar it is only 2.8km (1.75mi) from **Loch Lomond**, and it was across this strip of land that the Vikings pulled their boats to raid central Scotland before the Battle of **Largs**. On its eastern side there is a large oil terminal at Finnart and a naval base at **Coulport**.

**Loch Long** Narrow loch in **Wester Ross** that runs into **Loch Alsh** at Dornie.

**Loch Loyal** (Gaelic **Loch Laghail**) Large loch in **Caithness**, 7km (4mi) south of **Tongue**. **Ben Loyal** rises above its west side.

**Loch Lubnaig** Narrow loch between **Callander** and Strathyre that is popular with anglers. It is drained by the River **Leny**, and Ben **Ledi** towers above its western bank.

**Loch Luichart** (Gaelic **Loch Luicheart**) Loch 10km (6mi) west of **Strathpeffer**, Ross and Cromarty. In the 1950s the level of the loch was raised by a 20m (65ft) dam as part of an extensive hydroelectric scheme in the area. The village of Lochluichart, its station and a stretch of railway had to be relocated at a higher level.

L

**Loch Lyon** (Gaelic **Loch Liobhunn**) Isolated large loch at the head of **Glen Lyon** that is also a reservoir, part of a hydroelectric scheme.

**Lochmaben** (pop. 1953) Small town and ancient royal **burgh** in Dumfries and Galloway 6km (4mi) west of **Lockerbie**, surrounded by several small lochs. A handsome, spired tolbooth of 1723 and 1741 dominates the long triangular market place which forms the High Street. On the south shore of one of the lochs, Castle Loch, is ruined 13th-century Lochmaben Castle, now in the care of **Historic Scotland**, which is said to have been the birthplace of **Robert the Bruce**. This was the focal point of English control in southwest Scotland in the 14th century.

**Lochmaddy** (Gaelic **Loch na Madadh**) Port and chief village of **North Uist**, on the west shore of Loch na Madadh. It is the terminal for the vehicle and passenger ferry to Uig on **Skye**.

**Loch Maree** (Gaelic **Loch Ma-ruibh**) Large loch near **Gairloch**, Wester Ross. Slopes contain the **Beinn Eighe** National Nature Reserve and a fragment of the **Caledonian forest**. It has several islands, one of which, Isle Maree, held a cell of St **Maelrubha**. See also **Letterewe**.

**Loch Melfort** (or **Melford**) Sea loch on the Argyll coast, opposite **Luing**, 18km (11mi) south of **Oban**, with **Kilmelfort** near its head, where there is good yacht anchorage.

**Loch Moidart** see **Moidart**

**Loch Monar** Remote loch to the east of Glen Carron in the northern **Highlands**. Now dammed to form a reservoir for a hydroelectric scheme, it is surrounded by mountains, many of which are **Munros**.

**Loch Morar** see **Morar**

**Loch Morlich** Loch to the north of the **Cairngorm** mountains, to the east of **Aviemore**, it has a sandy beach at a height of over 300m (985ft), and is very popular for watersports and walking.

**Loch Muick** (pronounced 'mick') Loch at the foot of **Lochnagar**, near **Ballater**, part of the Loch Muick and Lochnagar Wildlife Reserve, established by the royal **Balmoral** Estate.

**Loch Mullardoch** A large, very remote loch, to the north of **Glen Affric**, surrounded by mountains many of which are **Munros**; it is now dammed as part of a hydroelectric scheme.

**Lochnagar** (Gaelic **Loch na gàire**) Mountain ridge on the royal **Balmoral** Estate, southeast of **Braemar**, the grandeur of which is noted in a poem by Lord Byron with the line 'The steep frowning glories of dark Lochnagar'. The main **Munro** summit is Cac Carn Beag (3786ft/1155m) and there are several subsidiary summits, including Cuidhe Cròm (3552ft/1083m) and Meikle Pap (3214ft/980m).

**Loch na Keal** Sea loch on the west coast of **Mull**, which at its east end is less than 5km (3mi) from Salen, a village on the Sound of **Mull**.

**Loch nan Uamh** Sea loch and offshoot of the Sound of Arisaig between **Arisaig** and the peninsula of Ardnish, on the **Lochaber** coast. Prince Charles Edward **Stewart** landed here in August 1745 at the beginning of his attempt to retrieve the British crowns, and it was from here that he left Scotland for ever in September 1746; the Prince's Cairn, on the north coast of the Loch, marks the spot. In 1746 there was a naval battle in the loch when two French ships with supplies for the **Jacobites** were intercepted by Royal Navy frigates. The French escaped and gold they were carrying is said to have been carried inland to **Loch Arkaig** where it still lies hidden.

**Lochnaw** 16th-century rectangular tower house, 7km (5mi) west of **Stranraer**, with a long 2-storey and attic wing, formerly the seat of the Agnew family.

**Loch Ness** (Gaelic **Loch Nis**) Long, very deep loch running south-west-northeast from **Fort Augustus** to the outskirts of **Inverness**. It forms part of the **Caledonian Canal**. There have been reported sightings in the loch, especially since the 1930s, of a very large creature, known as the Loch Ness Monster (or Nessie); in spite of many investigations, no explanation has been found. See also **Urquhart Castle**.

**Loch Nevis** (Gaelic **Loch Nibheis**) Large sea loch between **Knoydart** and **Morar**, leading into the Sound of **Sleat**. On its north shore is the remote village of **Inverie**.

**Loch of Harray** Large loch to the south of Dounby on Mainland **Orkney**. At its southern end it is separated from **Loch of Stenness** by a narrow tongue of land, on which stands the Ring of **Brodgar** and a causeway.

**Loch of Lowes** Small loch just to the northeast of **Dunkeld**. Ospreys nest there and can be viewed from the Observation Hide at the Scottish Wildlife Trust's wildlife reserve.

**Loch of Stenness** Large loch on Mainland **Orkney**, to the northeast of **Stromness**. It is separated at its eastern end from the **Loch of Harray** by a narrow tongue of land.

**Loch of the Lowes** Small loch that runs into the head of **St Mary's Loch** in Ettrick Forest.

**Loch Oich** Narrow loch in the **Great Glen**, forming part of the **Caledonian Canal**, between the larger **Loch Lochy** and **Loch Ness**.

**Lochore** (pop. Lochore and Ballingry 5961) Former mining town near **Cowdenbeath**. Lochore Meadows Country Park, 1km (0.5mi) to the southwest, is a recreation area on the north side of Loch Ore, formed by landscaping an area of mining dereliction.

**Loch Ossian** Loch to the north of the Moor of **Rannoch**, close to **Corrour** station. Corrour Shooting Lodge is at its northeastern end, and there is a Youth Hostel at its southwestern end.

**Loch o' the Lowes** Small loch 2km (1mi) northwest of New Cumnock, **Ayrshire**.

**Loch Pattack** (Gaelic **Loch Patag**) Small loch 10km (7mi) southwest of **Dalwhinnie**, close to **Ben Alder**. It is drained by the River Pattack, which flows north and then west into **Loch Laggan**.

**Loch Quoich** (Gaelic **Loch Cuaich**) part of the Garry-Morriston hydroelectric scheme in Inverness-shire. Built in the 1950s, the Quoich Dam, with a maximum height of 38m (126ft), flooded many of the old settlements in the area, including Glen Quoich Lodge. A single-track road goes along the loch shore to Kinloch Hourn on the west coast.

**Loch Rannoch** (Gaelic **Loch Raineach**) Long narrow loch to the east of the Moor of **Rannoch**. At its western end on the River Gaur is a large power station, part of the **Tummel** hydroelectric power scheme.

**Lochranza** (Gaelic **Loch Raonasa**) Small village and resort at the north end of the Isle of **Arran** on Loch Ranza. 'Loch Ranza'

means 'loch of safe anchorage', and **Robert the Bruce** landed here from Ireland in 1306 at the beginning of his campaign for independence from England. Lochranza Castle dates from early medieval times, but was probably reconstructed in the 16th century; in the care of **Historic Scotland**.

**Loch Riddon** Sea loch leading into the **Kyles of Bute** from the north.

**Loch Roag** (Gaelic **Loch Ròg**) Large sea loch on the northwest coast of **Lewis**, with many islands. It is divided into East and West Loch Roag by the island of **Bernera**.

**Loch Scavaig** Large sea loch on the south coast of **Skye**, to the south of the **Cuillins**.

**Loch Scridain** Long sea loch on the west coast of **Mull**.

**Loch Seaforth** Long narrow sea loch on the southeast coast of **Lewis**, which for part of its length forms the boundary between Lewis and **Harris**, reaching a considerable distance inland.

**Loch Shiel** (Gaelic **Loch Seile**) Running from **Glenfinnan** to Acharacle, a narrow loch with splendid mountain scenery. On St Finan's Isle in the loch is a ruined chapel. Prince Charles Edward **Stewart** sailed up the loch in 1745 and raised his standard at Glenfinnan.

**Loch Shin** see **Shin** (River)

**Loch Sloy** (Gaelic **Loch Sloidh**) Near the north end of **Loch Lomond**, Loch Sloy has been greatly enlarged by one of the first

*Loch Shiel and the Glenfinnan Monument, Lochaber.*

hydroelectric schemes, taking advantage of one of the highest rainfalls in Scotland. See **Inveruglas**.

**Loch Snizort** Large sea loch on the northwest coast of **Skye**, between the Trotternish and Vaternish peninsulas.

**Loch Striven** Narrow, remote sea loch leading southwards to meet the east end of the **Kyles of Bute**. It has often been used as a harbour for ships when they are not in commission.

**Loch Sunart** (Gaelic **Loch Suaineart**) Long sea loch on the west coast between **Ardnamurchan** and **Morvern**. It has fine oak woods on its northern shore. See **Strontian**.

**Loch Sween** (Gaelic **Loch Suain**) Sea loch in **Argyll**, running parallel to the Sound of **Jura**, south of **Crinan**. Castle Sween on its eastern shore dates back to the 12th century; in the care of **Historic Scotland**, as are medieval chapels at Kilmory Knap and Keills, which contain outstanding West Highland sculptured grave slabs. The village of **Tayvallich** is near its northern end.

**Loch Tay** (Gaelic **Loch Tatha**) Long loch in the central **Highlands**, running southwest-northeast from **Killin** to **Kenmore**, and overlooked by **Ben Lawers**. Its irregular shape is due to displacement of the central part along the Loch Tay geological fault. There are the sites of at least 23 **crannogs** in the loch, and near Kenmore is the Scottish Crannog Centre.

**Loch Torridon** (Gaelic **Loch Toirbheartan**) Large sea loch in Wester Ross, between **Torridon** and **Applecross**. It is split into 3 parts; Upper Loch Torridon is furthest inland, separated by a narrow channel from Loch Shieldaig in the centre, with Loch Torridon proper extending to the open sea.

**Loch Treig** Long, narrow loch to the north of **Rannoch** Moor. It is the main reservoir for the hydroelectric scheme which powers the aluminium smelter at **Fort William**.

**Loch Trool** see **Glen Trool**

**Loch Tulla** Loch in **Argyll**, near Bridge of Orchy, close to the main road through **Glencoe**; drained by the River Orchy.

**Loch Tummel** (Gaelic **Loch Teimheil**) A long, narrow loch near **Pitlochry**; with the Clunie Dam at the east end, it forms part of the Tummel hydroelectric power scheme. On a high point near the east end is the Queen's View, where Queen Victoria admired the scenery in 1866.

**Loch Venachar** (Gaelic **Loch Bheannchair**) Loch in the **Trossachs**, near **Aberfoyle**, source of the River **Teith**, a renowned beauty spot, with a magnificent neo-classical sluice house by James Bateman (1856–9), part of Glasgow's **Loch Katrine** water supply scheme.

*Loch Voil, Perthshire.*

**Loch Voil** (Gaelic **Loch Bheothail**) Narrow loch in the Perthshire hills, to the west of **Balquhidder**.

**Lochwinnoch** (pop. 2570) Small town, 19km (12mi) southwest of Paisley, at the southwest end of Castle Semple Loch. Textile mills and bleachworks were set up in the late 18th century. Later industries included furniture-making and coopering. To the northwest of the Loch are the ruins of the Gothic Castle Semple Collegiate Church, in the care of **Historic Scotland**. The village is surrounded by the **Clyde Muirshiel Regional Park** and nearby is a reserve of the Royal Society for the Protection of Birds.

**Lochy** see **Glen Lochy**, **Loch Lochy**

**Lockerbie** (pop. 4009) Market town in Annandale 17km (11mi) east of **Dumfries**. It grew up round the 16th-century Johnstone Tower. In a battle here in 1593 between the feuding Johnstone and Maxwell families the victorious Johnstones mutilated many of their victims by a slash on the face, known in the area as a 'Lockerbie lick'. The town has a remarkably grand **baronial** town hall by the local architect F J C Carruthers (1887–91), probably drawing an earlier design by David **Bryce**. In December 1988, Lockerbie made international news when PanAm flight 103 to New York exploded above the town as a result of terrorist action, killing all its passengers and 11 of the town's residents; the disaster is commemorated by the Lockerbie Air Disaster Memorial in the town's cemetery.

**Lockhart, George, of Carnwath** (1673–1731) Politician and **Jacobite**. As a member of parliament from 1703 to 1715 he opposed the union with England but, probably due to confusion, was made one of the Commissioners to negotiate the Union Treaty of 1707. He supported the **Jacobite Rising** in 1715, for which he was arrested but subsequently freed. He was killed in a duel. His memoirs give a Jacobite account of the Union.

**Lockhart, John Gibson** (1794–1854) Lawyer, literary critic and author, b. Cambusnethan, near Wishaw. He became an assistant editor and one of the main contributors to *Blackwood's Magazine* and as such attacked several of the Romantic poets, e.g. Keats, but supported others, e.g. Wordsworth and Coleridge. He was editor of *The Quarterly Review* (1825–53) and published fictional works and translations. He is best remembered for his comprehensive and personal *Memoirs of the Life of Sir Walter Scott* (1837–8), who was his father-in-law.

**Logan, Jimmy** (**James Short**) (1928–2001) Comedian and actor, b. Glasgow into a showbusiness family. He and his siblings appeared on stage in the 1930s with their parents as The Logan Family. He appeared in pantomime for the first time in 1944 and on screen in 1949. As a radio comedian, he starred with Stanley **Baxter** in the 1950s show *It's All Yours*. He also established a reputation as a straight actor both on stage and screen.

**Loganair** Short-haul internal airline established in 1962 by William Logan, a public-works contractor based in **Muir of Ord**, who personally found the need for improved internal air routes. The company was associated with British Midland Airways for a period, but was the subject of a management buyout in 1997. It now operates internal services in **Orkney**, and other internal Scottish services on behalf of British Airways.

**Logan Botanic Garden** Subtropical garden in **Galloway**, on **Luce Bay**, just to the north of Port Logan, an outstation of the **Royal Botanic Garden** in **Edinburgh**. Its sheltered temperate frost-free position enabled a rare collection of shrubs and trees to be established out of doors in the 19th century. It now contains large collections of southern-hemisphere plants, particularly from Chile. The Botanic Garden section was split from Logan House and

now belongs to the Logan Gardens Trust. The house was built in 1702, subsequently enlarged but returned to its original size in 1952 for Olaf Hambro; previous to 1949 it was the home of the McDouall family for many centuries.

**Logan Water** River in Lanarkshire that rises on Spirebush Hill and runs east to the River Nethan, near **Lesmahagow**.

**Logierait** Village at the meeting point of the Rivers **Tay** and **Tummel**, 7km (4mi) southeast of **Pitlochry**. It may have been a hunting seat of King **Robert II** and was the site of the Regality Court of the Lords of Atholl and its prison (which included **Rob Roy** MacGregor among its inmates in 1717); neither of these survives.

**Lomond** see **Ben Lomond, Loch Lomond**

**Lomond Hills** A range of hills in **Fife**, northeast of Loch **Leven**, with 2 peaks, West Lomond (522m/1712ft) and East Lomond (424m/1391ft).

**Long, Loch** see **Loch Long**

**Longannet** Site of the last active coal mine in Scotland and of Scotland's largest coal-fired power station on the north shore of the Firth of **Forth** near **Kincardine**, built on what was formerly a War Department ammunition store. Stone from a quarry at Longannet was used in the 17th century to build what is now Amsterdam Town Hall.

**Longforgan** (pop. 668) Small town 10km (6mi) west of **Dundee** that grew up around **Castle Huntly**.

**Longformacus** Village in the valley of the Dye Water in the **Lammermuir Hills**, 10km (6mi) west of **Duns**. Some 7km (4mi) to the northwest is the Mutiny Stones, a long cairn dating from the 3rd millennium BC that appears to be part of a group of long cairns in southeast Scotland. The early 18th-century Longformacus House was remodelled later that century and again in the later 19th.

**Longhope** see **Hoy**

**Long Island** Name given to the **Outer Hebrides**, sometimes limited to **Lewis** and **Harris** only.

**Longman** A shingle point to the north of **Inverness** that extends into the **Moray Firth**, now largely occupied by an industrial estate.

**Longniddry** Village in **East Lothian** 19km (12mi) east of **Edinburgh**, a former weaving village, now mainly residential and a commuter town for Edinburgh. To the east is **Gosford House**.

**Lord Advocate** The senior Crown law officer in Scotland. All prosecutions are run in his name, and he represents many government departments. He is a member of the government but need not be a Member of the **Scottish Parliament**. See also **advocate**.

**Lord High Commissioner** The representative of the sovereign appointed annually to the **General Assembly** of the **Church of Scotland**.

**Lord Justice Clerk** Scotland's second-ranking judge. In criminal matters he is second to the **Lord Justice General** and in civil matters second to the **Lord President**. He presides over the second division of the Inner House, the appellate division of the **Court of Session**. R L Stevenson's unfinished novel *Weir of Hermiston* was originally to have been entitled *The Justice-Clerk* and the principal character is based on Lord **Braxfield**.

**Lord Justice General** Scotland's senior criminal judge. Apart from heading the Criminal Appeal Court, he also has heavy administrative responsibilities. He now also holds the office of **Lord President of the Court of Session** at the same time.

**Lord Lyon King of Arms** The chief herald of Scotland, who deals with heraldry and precedence. It is an ancient office derived from the Celtic **shenachie**. As a judge he presides over the Lyon Court, which sits on the ancient druidic feast days of Beltane and Samhain. It has all the powers of an ordinary court, such as to fine and imprison.

**Lord of the Isles** Title adopted in the 14th century by the MacDonalds of **Islay**, who held sway in a region previously dominated by Norse-Celtic warlords, notably **Somerled** in the 12th century. The lords enjoyed wide powers and presided over a flowering of Gaelic culture in their domains. Their often hostile relations with the Scottish crown culminated in the forfeiture of the lordship in 1493, which proved lasting despite numerous revolts against royal authority. Since then the title has been held by the heir to the throne.

**Lord President of the Court of Session** Scotland's senior civil judge. The Lord President chairs the first division of the Inner House, the appellate division of the Court of Session. He now also holds the office of **Lord Justice General**.

**lords of the articles** see **Scottish Parliament**

**Lorimer, Hew** (1907–1993) Artist, b. Edinburgh, the son of the architect, Sir Robert **Lorimer**. One of the most notable Scottish sculptors of the 20th century, he worked principally as a carver in stone on religious and secular commissions. His works include the massive *Lady of the Isles* on **South Uist** and the figures for the façade of the **National Library of Scotland**. His studio at **Kellie Castle**, Fife, is open to the public.

**Lorimer, Sir Robert Stodart** (1864–1929) Architect, b. Edinburgh. Influenced by the Arts and Crafts movement, he began independent practice in 1892, building or remodelling about 50 country houses, including Rowallan in Ayrshire and Marchmont in Berwickshire. His public works included the Thistle Chapel at St Giles, **Edinburgh**, Scottish National War Memorial in Edinburgh Castle, the restoration of **Paisley** Abbey and the furnishing of **Dunblane** Cathedral.

**Lorn, Firth of** The stretch of sea between the southeast coast of **Mull** and the mainland.

**Lorne** (Gaelic **Lathurna**) The coast and inland area of **Argyll** bounded by **Loch Awe**, **Loch Etive** and the Firth of **Lorn**. In ancient times the lordship of this district was held by the MacDougalls of Dunstaffnage until they were defeated by **Robert I** in 1309.

**Losgaintir** see **Luskentyre**

**Lossiemouth** (pop. 6803) Fishing port and resort at the mouth of the river Lossie near **Elgin**, with a large harbour now used as a marina. It was the birthplace of Ramsay **MacDonald**, first Labour Prime Minister of Britain. It has an RAF base, specialising in pilot training. Innes House, 6km (4mi) southeast, is a handsome 17th-century mansion built by William Aitoun for Sir Robert Innes of that Ilk between 1640 and 1653.

**Loth** Crofting township 9km (6mi) north of **Brora** at the mouth of the Loth Burn. At the foot of Glen Loth is a stone that commemorates the killing of the last wolf in Sutherland about 1700. The area is rich in **brochs**. About 3km (2mi) south is the ruin of Cinn Tolla broch, excavated to show an entrance passage 2m (7ft) high, 5m (18ft) long and 1m (3ft) wide with a cell. The interior of the broch is 9m (31ft) in diameter and 3m (11ft) high and has a well 2m (7ft) deep with steps leading to it.

**Lothian** Name originally applied to the district southward from **Edinburgh**, but by the 12th century extended to the region between the Firth of **Forth** and the Rivers **Tweed** and **Teviot**. Later it became restricted to the land from the River **Avon** west of **Linlithgow** to **Cockburnspath** south of **Dunbar**. The Lothians is a modern name referring to **West**, **Mid-** and **East Lothian**. See **Lothian Region**.

**Lothian Region** One of the 9 regions forming the upper tier of local government from 1975 to 1996, consisting of the districts of **East Lothian**, **Midlothian**, **West Lothian** and the City of **Edinburgh**. These were formed, with somewhat altered boundaries, from the former counties of the same names and they are now unitary authorities; see maps on pp.394-5 and **local government**.

L

*Simon Fraser, Lord Lovat, 1746.*

**Loudoun Castle Park** see **Galston**

**Loudon Hill, Battle of** Victory of **Robert I** over English forces near **Darvel** in Ayrshire in 1307 which was important in his transition from defeated refugee to genuine claimant for the Scottish crown.

**Lovat, Simon Fraser, 11th Lord** (c.1667–1747) Clan chief, b. Tomich, Ross-shire. In 1697 he was found guilty of rape for forcibly marrying a lady of the Atholl family. In 1702 he fled to France, returning to Scotland the following year as a **Jacobite** agent. He provided the plan for the abortive 1708 Jacobite invasion, though he was jailed in France to stop him betraying it. Returning for the 1715 Rising he changed to the government side, obtaining a full pardon and possession of his title and estates. In the 1745 Rising he feigned Hanoverian loyalism, but sent his son and clan to fight for Prince Charles Edward **Stewart**. After **Culloden** he was taken to London for trial and beheaded.

**Lovat Scouts** Regiment raised in 1900 by the 14th Lord Lovat mainly from gamekeepers and stalkers to match Boer marksmanship and scouting skills in the South African War. It also took part in World Wars I and II.

**Lower Largo** Former fishing village (and **burgh**) on Largo Bay on the south coast of Fife 18km (11mi) east of **Kirkcaldy**, now adjoining **Lundin Links**. It was the birthplace of Alexander **Selkirk** who returned to Lower Largo after his adventure, and there is a statue of Robinson Crusoe on his cottage. It had one of the earliest fishing-net factories in Scotland. See also **Upper Largo**.

**Lowers** Examinations which formed one level of the National Leaving Certificate, introduced in 1888. They were replaced in 1962 by **Ordinary Grades**.

**Lowes** see **Loch of Lowes, Loch of the Lowes, Loch o' the Lowes**

**Lowlands, the** The low, generally flat region of Scotland south and east of the **Highland Line**, and north and west of the **Southern Uplands**, often used in contrast to the **Highlands**. See also **Central Lowlands**.

**Lowther Hills** Range of hills forming part of the **Southern Uplands**, framed by **Nithsdale** to the west, Tweeddale and Annandale to the east. The range is traversed by Roman roads with notable Mennock and Dalveen Passes. It is a former centre of lead mining, especially to the north of the range around **Wanlockhead** and **Leadhills**. The **Southern Upland Way** lies along part of the range, including Lowther Hill, the second highest (725m/2378ft). Other notable peaks are Green Lowther, the highest at 732m (2401ft); East Mount Lowther (631m/2070ft), with its excellent viewpoint, and Ballencleuch Law (691m/2266ft).

**Loyal** see **Ben Loyal, Loch Loyal**

**Lubnaig, Loch** see **Loch Lubnaig**

**Luce Bay** Large bay on the southwest coast of Scotland between the **Rhinns of Galloway** to the east and the **Machars** to the west, with the village of Glenluce at its head and Port William and Drummore on its shores.

**luckenbooth brooch** A kind of brooch, usually of engraved silver in the shape of a heart, or 2 hearts entwined, originally used mainly as a love token or betrothal brooch. The name comes from the Luckenbooths, a row of small lockable shops near St Giles' Kirk in **Edinburgh** (demolished in 1817).

**Luffness House** A 16th-century tower house belonging to the Hope family, just to the northeast of **Aberlady**, East Lothian.

It was extended by William **Burn** in 1822 and remodelled by David **Bryce** (1846–9).

**Lugar Water** Ayrshire river, the main tributary of the River Ayr on which sits the former iron-smelting village of Lugar.

**Lui, Ben** see **Ben Lui**

**Luichart, Loch** see **Loch Luichart**

**Luing** Island off the Argyll coast, opposite **Loch Melfort**, between **Seil** and Scarba. With Seil and **Easdale**, it was one of the 3 slate-producing islands lying off the mainland. The first quarries were opened in about 1700, before **Ballachulish**, and much of Lowland Scotland's buildings were roofed with slates from these islands.

**Lulu** (**Marie Lawrie**) (1948– ) Singer and entertainer, b. Glasgow. Her first hit single, 'Shout' in 1964, was followed 2 years later by the theme tune from the film *To Sir With Love*, in which she also acted. In the 1970s she was the host of a variety show, which took precedence over her recording career for a while. She still performs and records regularly today.

**Lumphanan** Aberdeenshire village, 8km (5mi) northeast of **Aboyne**. Macbeth's Cairn, to the northwest, is said to mark the site where **Macbeth** was killed by **Malcolm III** in 1057. The Peel Ring of Lumphanan, to the southwest, is the site of a medieval castle; in the care of **Historic Scotland**. About 3km (2mi) southwest is the Loch of Auchlossan, which was drained to produce fertile land.

**Lumphinnans** Small former mining and ironworking community in Fife between **Cowdenbeath** and **Lochgelly**.

**Lumsden** Upland Aberdeenshire village 6km (4mi) south of **Rhynie** that was established in 1825 by a local landowner, Harry Leith Lumsden. The Scottish Sculpture Workshop was set up here in 1979 by Fred Bushe.

**Lunan Bay** Long sandy bay on the east coast between **Arbroath** and **Montrose**. At its mid point, where the Lunan Water runs into the bay, is **Red Castle**.

**Lunan Burn** A river that rises on Craig More, 4km (3mi) northeast of **Dunkeld**, and flows east through a series of small lochs, and then southeast to the River Isla, 4km (3mi) northeast of the confluence of the River Isla with the River Tay.

**Lunardi, Vincent** (1759–1806) Italian balloonist who ascended from London in an air balloon on 15 September 1784 and on 5 October 1785 performed the same feat from Heriot's Green, **Edinburgh**, landing near Pitscottie in east Fife. Robert **Burns** refers to a balloon-shaped bonnet as a Lunardi in his poem 'To a Louse'.

**Luncarty** (pop. 1265) Small town in Perth and Kinross, on the west bank of the River **Tay**, 7km (4mi) north of **Perth**. In the 19th and 20th centuries it had extensive linen bleaching fields. Denmarkfield, just to the north, is the traditional site of a battle of 990 in which the Danes were defeated by the Scots.

**Lundin Links** Village on Largo Bay, Fife, 18km (11mi) northeast of **Kirkcaldy**, next to **Lower Largo**. The **golf** course is an Open qualifier. Lundin Tower is all that remains of Lundin House, probably 16th century with late 18th-century additions. Nearby are 3 remaining tall standing stones, dating from the 2nd millennium BC.

**Lunga** Uninhabited island north of Scarba and west of **Luing** across the Sound of Luing.

**Lunga** see **Treshnish Isles**

**Luskentyre** (in Gaelic **Losgaintir**) Settlement on **Harris**, 8km (5mi) west of **Tarbert**. It has one of the finest beaches on the west coast, sheltered by the offshore island of **Taransay**.

**Luss** Picturesque early 19th-century village on the west shore of **Loch Lomond**, 12km (8mi) north of **Balloch**. It has views of the loch's wooded islands and of Ben **Lomond** across the loch. It has

*Lulu (Marie Lawrie).*

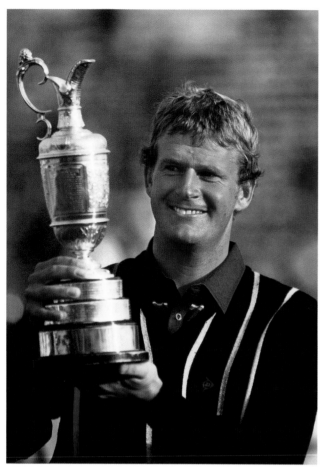

*Sandy Lyle, winner of the Open Golf Championship in 1985.*

a visitor centre for the **Loch Lomond and the Trossachs National Park**. To the south is **Rossdhu**, the former seat of the Colquhoun family, with the Loch Lomond Golf Club. The village was used as the setting for the TV soap opera *High Road*.

**lute** This instrument has been played in Scotland since medieval times. Most early collections of Scottish airs and instrumental music are preserved in manuscript lute books of the 1620s, the Rowallan, Skene and Straloch books. The sparse style of Scottish lute music suggests the influence of earlier **clarsach** music. The foremost current Scottish lutenist is Rob McKillop.

**Lybster** Small village on the north coast of **Caithness**, 9km (6mi) west of **Thurso**. Nearby on Crosskirk Bay is St Mary's Chapel, probably dating from the 12th century. Though roofless, its walls are almost complete.

**Lybster** (pop. 677) Small town on the east coast of Caithness, 20km (12mi) southwest of Wick. Laid out as a planned village in 1802, it prospered as a fishing village in the 19th century. Its harbour was begun in 1833 and enlarged later in the century. The countryside around is rich in prehistoric sites,

including the Grey Cairns of Camster and the Hill o' Many Stanes.

**Lyell, Sir Charles** (1797–1875) Geologist, b. Kinnordy, Angus. His *Principles of Geology* (1830–33) confirmed and developed the theory of continuity of geological processes first advanced by James **Hutton**. Lyell used mollusc and mammal evolution to subdivide the last 65 million years of geological time.

**Lyle, Abram** see **sugar**

**Lyle, Sandy** (1958– ) Golfer, b. Shrewsbury to Scottish parents. After a promising career as an amateur, he turned professional and played a significant part in restoring the international reputation of British **golf**. His first major was the Open Championship of 1985, a triumph followed 3 years later by victory in the US Masters.

**Lynch, Michael** (1946– ) Historian, b. Aberdeen. Sir William Fraser Professor of Scottish History at **Edinburgh University** since 1992, he specialises in the history of religion and politics in the 17th and 18th centuries. His publications include *Edinburgh and the Reformation* (1981), *The Early Modern Town in Scotland* (1986), *Scotland: a New History* (1991) and he was editor of *The Oxford Companion to Scottish History* (2001).

**Lyndsay, Sir David, of the Mount** (c.1486–1555) Poet, dramatist and courtier. One of a prominent Fife family (with land near **Cupar**), he served at the courts of **James IV** and **James V**, reaching the rank of **Lord Lyon King of Arms**, and he was tutor to the young **James V**. His masterpiece is his morality play, *Ane Pleasaunt Satyre of the Thrie Estaitis* (1540), in which the Three Estates (lords, commons and clergy) are punished for their malpractices on the people. It has been revived in recent years at the **Edinburgh International Festival**, and at Cupar where it was first performed.

**Lyne** Village 5km (3mi) west of **Peebles**, near where the Lyne Water joins the **Tweed**. Its very small 17th-century church has a period pulpit and canopied pews said to be of Dutch workmanship. West of the church is the site of a Roman fort and camp. Drochil Castle, a short distance upstream, now ruined, was built by Regent **Morton** in the late 16th century as a retirement home but he was executed soon after its completion.

**Lynedoch, Lord** see **Graham, Thomas**

**Lyness** see **Hoy**

**Lyon** River that runs east from **Loch Lyon** down **Glen Lyon** to join the River **Tay** 6km (4mi) west of **Aberfeldy**.

**Lyon Court, Lyon King of Arms, Lord** see **Lord Lyon King of Arms**

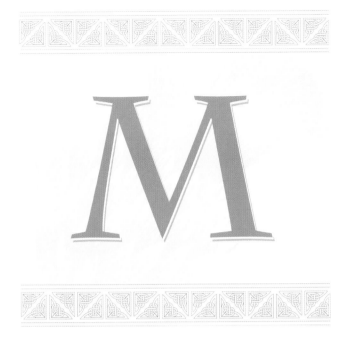

**MacAdam, John Loudon** (1756–1836) Inventor and engineer, b. Ayr. Though successful in business in New York, his loyalty to the losing side in the American Revolution led to the confiscation of his property and his return to Scotland in 1783. He was the inventor of the macadam road surface, made of pieces of crushed or broken stone of uniform small size. It was cheaper than earlier ways of metalling roads, and was widely adopted. The later addition of a tar binder to the stone resulted in tarmacadam.

**Macallan** Distillery near **Craigellachie** on **Speyside**, founded in 1824. Rebuilt in the 1950s, it now produces one of the most popular single malt whiskies.

**MacAlpine, Sir Robert** (1847–1934) Innovative builder, b. Newarthill, Lanarkshire. Known as 'Concrete Bob' because of his early promotion of the use of concrete in construction. He is particularly remembered for the viaducts on the West Highland Extension Railway, especially at **Glenfinnan** and Borrodale. He founded the eponymous company in 1869 – now one of the best-known building contractors in the world.

**MacBeath, Jimmy** (1894–1972) Scots singer, b. Portsoy, Banffshire. After many years of tramping the road, living in poverty and singing for pennies, MacBeath became celebrated in the 1950s as a major source of traditional Scottish and **bothy** ballads, and a remarkable gravel-voiced performer on recordings and in concert.

**Macbeth** (Mac Bethad mac Findlaech) (d.1057) King of Scots 1040–57. Ruler of **Moray**, he became king after killing **Duncan I**

in battle near **Elgin**. In 1050 he made a pilgrimage to Rome, a remarkable demonstration of the security of his rule. He was killed at Lumphanan, Aberdeenshire, by **Malcolm III** (Malcolm Canmore), Duncan's eldest son. The legend of Macbeth's life inspired Shakespeare's play.

**McBey, James** (1883–1959) Artist, b. Newburgh near Aberdeen. Taught himself etching while working for a bank in **Aberdeen**, which he wrote about in a remarkable autobiography, and gradually established himself as an artist, eventually finding great success. He is known in particular for his etchings and watercolours of Venice and Tangiers (where he settled); he also worked in Egypt and Palestine as an official artist in World War I.

**MacBrayne, David** (1815–1907) Shipowner, b. Glasgow. Formed a shipping firm in 1851 with David and Alexander Hutcheson, and in 1852 obtained a mail contract for the **Western Isles**. His company developed ferry routes throughout the Western Isles and on the west coast north of the **Clyde**. The firm he founded became part of **Caledonian MacBrayne** in 1973.

**MacBryde, Robert** see **Colquhoun, Robert**

**MacCaig, Norman** (1910–96) Poet, b. Edinburgh. Earlier a schoolteacher, he was Writer in Residence in **Edinburgh University** and later Reader in Poetry at **Stirling University**. His works include *Far Cry* (1943), *Riding Lights* (1955), *A Round of Applause* (1962), *The White Bird* (1973), *Voice-Over* (1988) *Collected Poems* (1985) and *New Collected Poems* (1990). He received many awards, including the Queen's Medal for Poetry (1986). Much of his poetry is based on his observations of **Edinburgh** and of his favourite part of Scotland, **Assynt** in Sutherland.

**McCance, William** (1894–1970) Artist, b. Cambuslang. Married to Agnes Miller Parker, the important British printmaker, McCance lived in London from 1920 working as an illustrator, lecturer and critic. In his painting he adopted a near abstract style based on machine imagery, exceptional among Scottish artists of the time. He later became controller of the Greynog Press in Wales, producing fine-edition books.

**McClelland, William** (1894–1970) Educationalist, b. Newton Stewart. As Professor of Education at **St Andrews University** (1925–41), he also ran the regional teacher training centre in **Dundee**. His most significant contribution to education in Scotland was his promotion of the use of tests to try to establish in a fair way which pupils should receive secondary education, as detailed in his publication *Selection for Secondary Education* (1942).

*Hugh MacDiarmid by Robert Heriot Westwater (1962).*

M

**MacCodrum, Iain** (**John MacCodrum**) (1693–1779) Gaelic poet, b. North Uist. Bard to Sir James Macdonald of **Sleat** from 1763, he was famous for his witty and original songs. Many were comic, but he also composed a poignant lament on the forced emigration of the Macdonalds from **North Uist**, *Òran do na Fògarraich* ('Song to the Exiles'). He was consulted by James **Macpherson** about Ossianic poetry.

**MacCoist, Ally** (1962– ) Footballer, television personality and commentator, b. Bellshill, Lanarkshire. He spent most of his footballing career with **Rangers**, becoming their most prolific goalscorer ever in 1997, and he also played for St Johnstone, Sunderland and **Kilmarnock**. He has 57 caps for Scotland.

**McColgan, Liz** (née **Lynch**) (1964– ) Middle- and long-distance runner, b. Dundee. Persevering with her running despite knee injuries, she won gold medals for the 10,000 metres at the 1986 and 1990 Commonwealth Games, silver for the same distance at the 1988 Olympics, and in 1996 won the London Marathon. Married to steeplechaser Peter McColgan, she works with young athletes in Dundee.

**MacColl, Ewan** (**Jimmie Miller**) (1915–89) Musician, dramatist and folklorist, b. Salford. Brought up in Perthshire, he was a pioneer of popular theatre, but later became involved in the revival of folk music, especially in exploring the use of folk styles in modern media. His most famous songs include 'Dirty Old Town' and 'The First Time Ever I Saw Your Face'. Much of his work was done in partnership with his third wife Peggy Seeger.

**MacColl, John** (1860–1943) Piper, b. Kentallen, Argyll. He won many awards and was a brilliant composer of pipe music, particularly pipe marches. He also excelled as a dancer, athlete and sportsman.

**MacColla, Alasdair** (**Alexander MacDonald**) (d.1647) Renowned Highland soldier. Also known by his father's sobriquet Colkitto (Gaelic *Coll Ciotach*, left-handed Coll). He pursued the clan rivalry with the Campbells and was **Montrose**'s lieutenant-general in the campaign for **Charles I** in 1644–5. He was the principal architect of victory and when he left to pursue his own agenda in **Argyll**, Montrose went down to defeat.

**McConnell, Jack Wilson** (1960– ) Politician, b. Irvine. A school teacher, he later held various local-government posts and was General Secretary of the Scottish Labour Party (1992–8). He became MSP for Motherwell and Wishaw in 1999 and held various government posts, becoming **First Minister** in 2002.

**MacCormick, John MacDonald** (1904–61) Solicitor and nationalist, b. Glasgow. Founder member of the **Scottish National Party** in 1934 and its first chairman. He later became Chairman of the Scottish Convention, and of the Scottish Assembly which organised the Scottish Convention in 1949 (attracting 2 million signatures). He was involved in the mystery disappearance of the **Stone of Destiny** from Westminster Abbey in 1950. He publicised the fact that the present Queen Elizabeth was the First and not the Second of Scotland.

**MacCrimmon family** Family of pipers who were hereditary pipers to the Chief of the Clan Macleod and leaders of the influential MacCrimmon School of Piping at Borereaig in **Skye**. **Donald Mór** (1570–1640) was the first of the MacCrimmons to be hereditary piper to the Chief of the Clan Macleod. He may have been the originator of the MacCrimmon school of piping in Skye. **Patrick Mór** (1595–1670) succeeded his father **Donald Mór** as head of the MacCrimmon school of piping. Considered to be one of the greatest composers of **piobaireachd**. His best known work is 'The lament for the children', said to have been written in memory of 7 of his 8 sons who died in one year. **Patrick Òg**

(1645–1730) succeeded his father **Patrick Mór** as head of the MacCrimmon school of piping. Tradition has it that he was the greatest of the MacCrimmon players and a master teacher.

**MacCrone, Guy** (1898–1977) Novelist, b. Birkenhead, moving to **Glasgow** (his parents' home) as a boy. A founder of the Glasgow **Citizens' Theatre**, with James **Bridie**, he was also its manager. He wrote several Glasgow novels, the best known being the *Wax Fruit* trilogy (1947).

**MacCulloch, Horatio** (1805–67) Painter, b. Glasgow. Began his career painting snuffbox lids, then moved to **Edinburgh**, swiftly becoming a popular and influential painter, especially of romantic **Highland** landscapes (contributing to the Victorian image of Scotland). He was a teacher and a regular exhibitor at the **Royal Scottish Academy**.

**MacCunn, Hamish** (1868–1916) Composer, conductor and teacher, b. Greenock, but spent most of his life in London. His music, much of it based on Scottish themes, was very popular, though now suffering from the unpopularity of Victorianism. His most famous pieces include 'The Land of the Mountain and the Flood', 'The Dowie Dens o' Yarrow', and the opera 'Jeanie Deans'.

**MacDiarmid, Hugh** (Christopher Murray Grieve) (1892–1978) Poet, b. Langholm. Worked as a schoolteacher in **Edinburgh** and as a journalist in **Montrose** and London, and served in the RAMC in World War I. He lived on a croft on Whalsay, **Shetland**, from 1933–41, and worked as an engineer on the River **Clyde** in World War II, later settling permanently in **Biggar**, Lanarkshire. A Scottish Nationalist and Communist, he wrote in English and **Scots** and was the key figure in the Scottish Renaissance of the mid 20th century. He made an important contribution to the development of literary Scots, not least in his early lyric poetry (*Sangshaw* 1925, *Penny Wheep* 1926). His major works include *A Drunk Man Looks at the Thistle* (1926), *To Circumjack Cencrastus* (1930), *A Kist of Whistles* (1947) and *In Memoriam James Joyce* (1955), and autobiography such as *Lucky Poet* (1943) and *The Company I've Kept* (1966).

**McDermid, Val** (1955– ) Crime novelist, brought up in Kirkcaldy. After working as a journalist in **Glasgow** and Manchester, she turned to writing and has produced novels featuring the private detectives Kate Brannigan and Lindsay Gordon. Her most recent work, including

*The Wire in the Blood* (1997) and *A Place of Execution* (1999), concerns the partnership of Dr Tony Hill, a crime profiler, and Detective-Inspector Carol Jordan, and has been televised.

**MacDonald Alexander** see **MacColla, Alasdair; Mac Mhaighstir Alasdair, Alasdair**

**MacDonald, Donald** (1749–1840) Piper, b. Glenhinisdale, Skye. He won the Prize Pipe at the **Edinburgh** competition in 1817. He was a pipe maker in Edinburgh and published *A Collection of the Ancient Martial Music of Caledonia* in 1822 and *A Collection of Quicksteps Strathspeys Reels and Jigs* in 1828.

**Macdonald, Flora** (1722–90) b. South Uist. After the **Jacobite** Rising of 1745 she led Charles Edward **Stewart**, disguised as her maid, to safety in **Skye**. As a result she was imprisoned in the Tower of London, but released in 1747. Married in 1750 to Alan Madonald of Kingsburgh, Skye, she emigrated to North Carolina in 1774, but returned to Scotland in 1779 after her husband was captured fighting on the Loyalist side in the American War of Independence. He joined her in 1781.

*Flora Macdonald by Richard Wilson (1747).*

M

**Macdonald, Frances** (1874–1921) Artist. See Charles Rennie **Mackintosh**

**Macdonald, George** (1824–1905) Novelist, b. Huntly, Aberdeenshire. He left his work as a Congregationalist minister in 1855, and became a journalist. He is best remembered for his stories for children, such as *At the Back of the North Wind* (1871) and *The Princess and the Goblin* (1872) and for his allegorical fantasies *Phantastes* (1858) and *Lilith* (1895), which inspired later fantasy writers, including C S Lewis.

**Macdonald, Sir George** (1862–1940) Archaeologist and numismatist, b. Elgin. Honorary Curator of the Hunter Coin Cabinet in **Glasgow University** for 47 years, he laid the foundations of Roman archaeology in Scotland and of Roman frontier studies in western Europe. His book, *The Roman Wall in Scotland*, was the first detailed study of the **Antonine Wall**.

**MacDonald, Gus** (1940– ) Politician, journalist, media executive, b. Glasgow. He worked as a marine engineer and active trade unionist in Govan, then in the media, for The **Scotsman**, Granada TV and Channel 4. In 1986 he became Director of Programmes for Scottish Television, and Chairman of the Scottish Media Group in 1997. He was made a life peer – Lord MacDonald of Tradeston – in 1998 and Minister for Transport in 1999. He was later Minister of State at the Cabinet Office and Chancellor of the Duchy of Lancaster; he resigned in the government reshuffle of 2003.

**MacDonald, Sir Hector Archibald** ('Fighting Mac') (1853–1903) Soldier, b. Black Isle. A crofter's son, he joined the British Army as a private and became a major-general, fighting in the Afghan War, both Boer Wars and saving British troops from certain death at Omdurman. He was knighted in 1901 and became Commander-in-Chief in Ceylon (now Sri Lanka) in 1902. His career ended in tragedy when he committed suicide in Paris rather than return to Ceylon to face charges of homosexuality. He left a widow and son and he is buried in the Dean Cemetery in **Edinburgh**.

**Macdonald, John** see **Iain Lom**

**MacDonald John** (1865–1953) Piper, b. Glentruim. A pupil of Malcolm (Calum Piobair) **MacPherson**, he won many awards. He was the first **Piobaireachd** Society instructor to the Army School, and Honorary Piper to the King. He taught many top pipers.

**MacDonald, Sir John Alexander** (1815–91) First Prime Minister of Canada, 1867–73 and 1878–91. He promoted links with Britain and helped to develop the Pacific railway.

**Macdonald Joseph** (1739–62) b. Durness, Sutherland. Author of *A Compleat Theory of the Scots Highland Bagpipe* written in 1760 and published in 1803, the first book on the subject. Brother of Patrick **Macdonald**.

**Macdonald, Margaret** (1863–1933) Artist. See Charles Rennie **Mackintosh**

**MacDonald, Margo** (1945– ) Politician, broadcaster, journalist, b. Hamilton. As a Scottish Nationalist she took Govan from Labour in 1973. She was Deputy Leader of the **Scottish National Party** (1974–9), but was ousted from the party in 1982, and became a radio and television presenter and columnist. In 1999 she was elected to the **Scottish Parliament** as an SNP member for the Lothians and again in 2003 as an independent, not having been reselected by the SNP. She is married to Jim **Sillars**.

**Macdonald, Revd Patrick** (1729–1824) Collector of music, b. Durness, Sutherland. He and his brother Joseph were pioneer collectors of **Gaelic** music. In 1784 Patrick published *A Collection of Highland Vocal Airs*, which he said included the 'most genuine remains of the ancient harp-music in the Highlands', music which had stopped being played 100 years before.

**MacDonald, (James) Ramsay** (1866–1937) British statesman. b. Lossiemouth, Moray. With little formal education, he worked as a clerk, but became an organiser of the Labour Party and an MP in 1906. He was leader of the Independent Labour Party 1911–14 and 1922–31, and Prime Minister of the first Labour Government in Britain in 1924. He was again Prime Minister 1924–35 and in 1931 he formed a (largely Conservative) National Government to combat the Depression. He was defeated by Emmanuel **Shinwell** in 1935, but returned to Parliament in 1936, slightly outrageously as a representative of the Scottish universities, which he had never attended.

**MacDonald, Rory** see **Runrig**

**MacDonald, Sharman** (1952– ) Playwright, b. Glasgow. She was an actor when her first play *When I was a Girl I used to Scream and Shout* was performed in 1984, and then became a full-time dramatist; her plays include *The Brave*, *When we were Women*, *The Winter Guest* and *After Juliet*.

**Macdonell, A(rthur) G(ordon)** (1895–1941) Novelist, b. Aberdeen. Famous for the gentle satire *England, their England* (1933), he wrote *My Scotland* (1937). He also wrote detective novels under the name of Neil Gordon.

**MacDonell, Sorley Boy** (in Gaelic **Somhairle Buidhe**, yellow-haired Sorley) (c.1505–80) b. Antrim. Leader of the MacDonalds who invaded Northern Ireland and established a regional ascendancy in northeast Antrim, in the area known as the Route. His descendants became the Marquises of Antrim after 1603.

**MacDougall, Carl** (1941– ) Novelist, b. Glasgow. He worked as a journalist in Glasgow before publishing short stories in *Elvis is Dead* (1986) and the novels, *Stone Over Water* (1989), *The Lights Below* (1993) and *The Casanova Papers* (1996). He has edited a major collection of Scottish short stories, *The Devil and the Giro* (1989), and has written social commentary in *Painting the Forth Bridge* (2001).

**McEwan, William** (1827–1913) Brewer. He established the Fountain Brewery in **Edinburgh** in 1856, and later became known for his good works and as MP for Edinburgh Central. McEwan's ales are still produced by Scottish and Newcastle.

**MacEwen, Sir William** (1848–1924) Surgeon, b. Rothesay, Bute. As a student in **Glasgow University**, he was inspired by Joseph Lister, then Regius Professor of Surgery, a chair he was later to hold himself. He became a pioneer in surgery, especially in brain and bone surgery and he extended Lister's antiseptic techniques.

**Macfarlane, Norman Somerville, Lord Macfarlane of Bearsden** (1926– ) Businessman. He established his reputation through his Clansman group of companies, integrated suppliers of office stationery, equipment and other consumables. After the merger of The Distillers' Co Ltd and Guinness in 1986, to form United Distillers, and the discrediting of Ernest Saunders, the first chairman, Lord Macfarlane, then Sir Norman, took over. His role in returning United Distillers to respectability was of the utmost importance for the reputation of Scottish business in general, and of the Scotch **whisky** industry in particular, as United Distillers were by far the largest firm in the industry. He retained the post until a further merger in 1997 created the Diageo Corporation.

**MacGeechan, Ian** (1946– ) Rugby union international, b. Leeds. Played for Scotland 1972–9, was coach to the national team and is now Director of Rugby.

**MacGibbon, David** (1831–1902) and **Ross, Thomas** (1839–1930) Architects, now more famous as historians and authors of *The Castellated and Domestic Architecture of Scotland* (1887–92) and *The Ecclesiastical Architecture of Scotland* (1896–7).

**McGibbon, William** (c.1695–1756) Violinist and composer, b. Edinburgh. Leading Scottish composer of his day, whose baroque-era sonatas for 2 or 3 instruments and folk-tune settings successfully combined Scottish airs and baroque idioms.

**MacGillivray, Alexander** (1759–93) Creek chief, American Loyalist and US general. Son of Lachlan MacGillivray, Scots Indian trader working out of Charleston, South Carolina, and Sehoy-Marchand, a half-French Creek woman of the Wind Clan. He was educated in Charleston by his kinsman, the Revd Farquhar MacGillivray, and he entered the Indian trade in Savannah, Georgia. He rose to be a leader of the Creek nation as well as an example of the culture of the **Scottish Enlightenment**. A staunch Loyalist in the War of the American Revolution, he tried to preserve his people from the imperialism of the new United States of America after 1783. For a decade he succeeded by a mixture of prevarication and reliance on the diplomatic support of Spain, and by supplies from the Scots firm of Panton and Leslie, of which he was a director. President Washington, whom he met, tried to flatter him with the honorary rank of US Brigadier General, but MacGillivray was too shrewd ever to trust him.

**MacGillivray, William** (1796–1852) Known as the 'father of British ornithology', b. Aberdeen. He studied medicine in **Aberdeen** and in 1823 became assistant to the Professor of Natural History in **Edinburgh** and keeper of the **Edinburgh University** Museum. In 1830 he was introduced to John James Audubon, greatest of American ornithologists, who between 1826 and 1839 paid 6 visits totalling more than two and a half years to Edinburgh where he was to publish the bulk of his magnificent *Birds of America*. The work was printed by the Edinburgh engraver William Lizars in large 'elephant' page size as collections of loose plates, not bound volumes (to avoid the legal obligation to send complete sets of this hugely expensive work to all the UK deposit libraries). MacGillivray provided so much of the scientific background for the work as to rank as almost a joint author, working from the **Royal College of Surgeons** Museum in Edinburgh, where he became Curator in 1831. In 1841 he was appointed to the Regius Chair of Natural History in **Aberdeen University**. Between 1837 and 1852 he laid the foundations of British ornithology with the 5 volumes of his *A History of British Birds*.

**McGinn, Matt** (1928–77) Songwriter, singer, b. Calton, Glasgow. He left school at 14, and at 31 left factory shift work to become a teacher, but was soon a full-time writer and performer of folk-style songs, full of trenchant social comment and hilarious absurdity. Songs include 'Red Yo-Yo', 'Coorie Doon', and 'Three Nights and a Sunday'.

M

*William McGonagall.*

**M**

**McGonagall, William** (c.1825–1902) Self-styled poet, b. Edinburgh. Son of an immigrant Irish family, spent part of his childhood in **Orkney** but later settled in **Dundee**. His interest in the theatre led him to become an amateur Shakespearean actor. His first collection of poems was published in 1878, and he subsequently earned his living by giving readings and selling printed poems. His audience was a mixture of supporters and hoaxers, mostly the latter, fascinated by his terrible rhyme and metre; this fascination continues to the present day. Particular favourites were his tragic poems, such as 'The Tragic Death of the Rev A H Mackonochie' and 'The Tay Bridge Disaster'. He took himself very seriously and finally left Dundee, on the grounds that it could not support a poet of Shakespearean stature like himself!

**MacGrath, John** (1935–2001) Playwright, television writer and director, b. Birkenhead, Cheshire. Established the 7:84 Theatre Company in Glasgow in the 1970s, writing powerful plays such as *The Cheviot, the Stag and the Black, Black Oil*. He made his name on television with *Z-Cars*, and he wrote more than 50 plays.

**McGregor, Ewan** (1971– ) Actor, b. Crieff. He left school at 16 to join the Perth Repertory Theatre, then studied drama in London, but left just before graduating after winning a role in the TV series *Lipstick On Your Collar* (1993). The following year he had a part in the critically acclaimed film *Shallow Grave*, but it was with *Trainspotting* (1996) that he became established as one of British film's biggest names. He has since become internationally renowned through his appearances in the Star Wars films.

**MacGregor, Jimmie** (1932– ) Musician, writer and broadcaster, b. Glasgow. Joined Robin Hall to form a popular folk duo of the 1960s and 70s. Later became a writer on Scottish and nature topics, and presenter of TV and radio programmes.

**MacGregor, Rob Roy** see **Rob Roy**

**MacGregor, William York** (1855–1923) Artist, b. Finnart, Dunbartonshire. The most senior of the radical young artists known as the **Glasgow Boys**, who flourished in Scotland and internationally from the 1880s onwards. MacGregor's Glasgow studio became a meeting place for the group, and he is frequently referred to as the Boys' father-figure. He is best known for his painting *The Vegetable Stall* (1884, **National Gallery of Scotland**).

**McGuire, Eddie** (1948– ) Composer, flautist and harper, b. Glasgow. His many classical compositions often draw on and rework elements of traditional Scottish music. At the same time he has performed for over 20 years with the traditional group the **Whistlebinkies**, and composed traditional-style music for them. Among his compositions are the *Peter Pan* score for **Scottish Ballet** (1989) and the opera *The Loving Of Etain* (1990).

**machair** Gaelic word for a stretch of low-lying land adjacent to the sand of the seashore, with short grass and numerous flowers in summer, found especially in the **Western Isles**.

**Machar, St** Alleged to have been a companion of St **Columba**, and to have founded a church in Old **Aberdeen**, where St Machar's Cathedral now stands.

**Machars** A level peninsula in **Galloway**, between **Luce Bay** and Wigtown Bay, rich in agriculture and history. Places of special interest are St Ninian's Priory at **Whithorn**, and **Wigtown**, the 'book town' of Scotland.

**Macherie** see **Cairnryan**

**Machrihanish** Near Campbeltown, Kintyre. A seaside village with a famous international **golf** course. **Coal** was mined here from the late 15th to the 19th century and again in the mid 20th. Between 1903 and 1936 a narrow-gauge railway linked it to **Campbeltown**. A small airfield (but with an unusually long runway) has had military uses at various times.

**McIlvanney, Hugh** (1933– ) Journalist, b. Kilmarnock, Ayrshire, brother of William **McIlvanney**. Many times Sports Writer of the Year, he is acknowledged as one of the finest writers on sport, particularly on boxing, football and horseracing.

**McIlvanney, William** (1936– ) Novelist and poet, b. Kilmarnock, Ayrshire, brother of Hugh **McIlvanney**. Left teaching in 1975 to write full time. His novels of working life in the west of Scotland, including *Docherty* (1975), *The Big* Man (1985) and *The Kiln* (1996), feature powerful characters; this trend continues with his move into the police genre with *Laidlaw* (1977) and succeeding novels. He also writes poetry, short stories and journalism.

**MacInnes, Hamish** (1930– ) Mountaineer, writer and photographer b. Gatehouse of Fleet, Kirkcudbrightshire. An experienced climber, he is now an authority on mountain safety and rescue.

**Macintosh, Anne, 'Colonel Anne', 'Anne Farquharson of Invercauld'** (1723–87) Married Aeneas, chief of Clan **Macintosh**, a supporter of the Hanoverians, in 1741. She herself supported the **Jacobite** cause and raised a regiment from the Clan Chattan to fight for it. She and her husband were both captured at different times and each released into the other's custody.

**Macintosh, Charles** (1766–1843) Chemist and inventor, b. Glasgow. He discovered dissolved india rubber in 1818, which led to the development of the mackintosh, a waterproof coat made of rubberised cotton. He founded a waterproofing company in **Glasgow** in 1834, later moved to Manchester, and (with Charles **Tennant**) he invented bleaching powder and processes to convert iron to steel and to produce quality cast iron. He also joined David **Dale** in making mordants for turkey-red dyeing.

**MacIntyre, Duncan Bàn** see **Donnchadh Bàn Mac an t-Saoir**

**MacKay, Angus** (1813–54) Piper, b. Raasay. Son and pupil of John **MacKay**, he won many awards. In 1843, he was appointed as the first Piper to Queen Victoria. He published a *Collection of Ancient Piobaireachd* in 1838, an instant success, and *The Piper's Assistant* in 1843. He was one of the originators of the competition march.

**Mackay, Fulton** (1927–87) Actor, b. Paisley. Working in theatre (especially **Glasgow's Citizens' Theatre**), TV and film, his most famous roles were in the film *Local Hero* (1983) and in the TV series *Porridge*, as the prison warder.

**MacKay, General Hugh, of Scourie** (c.1640–92) Soldier. Served with the Scots Brigade in Holland and made Commander-in-Chief in Scotland by **William II and III**, Prince of Orange, in 1689. He opposed Viscount **Dundee** at the Battle of **Killiecrankie**, losing the battle but, after Dundee's death, winning the campaign. He died at Steinkirk fighting for the Dutch against Louis XIV.

**MacKay, John** (1767–1848) Piper, b. Raasay. Pupil of the MacKays of Gairloch and the **MacCrimmons**, he won the Prize Pipe at the Edinburgh Competition in 1792. Music he left in manuscript was used by his son Angus in the production of his book. He taught many pupils and most present-day pipers can trace their tuition back to him.

**Mackay, Robert** see **Rob Donn**

**Mackay, Shena** (1944– ) Novelist and short-story writer, b. Edinburgh. She has written many novels, beginning with the short novel, *Dust Falls on Eugene Schlumburger* (1964), and including *Music Upstairs* (1965), *Dunedin* (1992), and *Heligoland* (2003).

**Mackendrick, Alexander** (1912–93) Film director, b. Boston, USA, to Scottish parents. Growing up in Scotland, he attended **Glasgow School of Art**. His first feature film, *Whisky Galore* (1948) for Ealing Studios, led to several more Ealing comedies, most darker in nature, like *The Man in the White Suit* (1951) and *The Ladykillers* (1955). He made *The Maggie*, about an old puffer, in 1953. His Hollywood film *Sweet Smell of Success*, though critically acclaimed, was not a box-office success.

**Mackenzie, Sir Alexander** (c.1755–1820) Fur trader and explorer, b. Stornoway, Isle of Lewis. The Canadian river whose course he mapped to the Arctic Ocean in 1789 was named after him (though he called it the River Disappointment). A party led by him was the first to cross the Rockies, reaching the Pacific in 1793.

**Mackenzie, Alexander** (1822–92) Politician, b. Logierait near Dunkeld. Emigrated to Canada in 1842 to follow his sweetheart, working as a stonemason, later a journalist. He became Liberal Party leader in 1873 and Canada's second Prime Minister in 1874. The party lost power in 1878, but he remained an MP till his death. He refused the offer of a knighthood 3 times.

**Mackenzie, Alexander** (1848–1933) see **Mackenzie family**

**Mackenzie, Sir Alexander Campbell** (1847–1935) Composer and conductor, b. Edinburgh. Principal of the Royal Academy of Music, he composed operas, chamber music and songs; his best-known work is the oratorio *The Rose of Sharon* (1884).

*Sir Compton Mackenzie by Robert Heriot Westwater (1962).*

**Mackenzie, Alexander George Robertson** see **Mackenzie family**

**Mackenzie, Sir (Edward Montague) Compton** (1883–1974) Writer and novelist, b. West Hartlepool, Cleveland. He added the family name of Mackenzie as a tribute to his Scottish heritage. In 1928 he settled on **Barra** in the Outer **Hebrides**. He helped found the **Scottish National Party**. His best-known works include *Sinister Street* (1913), *The Four Winds of Love* (1937–45), novels of Scottish life including *The Monarch of the Glen* (1941) and *Whisky Galore* (1947), as well as several volumes of autobiography. In his later years, he lived in **Edinburgh**.

**Mackenzie, Sir George, of Rosehaugh** (1636–91) Writer and advocate, b. Dundee. Despite acting as defence counsel in the Earl of **Argyll**'s treason trial, he had a glittering legal career in the Restoration period, becoming **Lord Advocate** in 1677, and earning, rather unjustly, the title 'Bluidy Mackenzie' for his part in prosecuting the **Covenanters**. He wrote widely on law, politics and history; he was author of the first Scottish novel, *Aretina*, (1660). His work on criminal law was important and his *Institution of the Law of Scotland* (1684) was a useful legal text. He oversaw the creation of the Advocates' Library, the germ of

the **National Library of Scotland**. His refusal to accept the Catholic faith of **James VII** led to his loss of power, and after 1688 he lived in retirement in Oxford.

**MacKenzie John Ban** (1796–1864) Piper, b. Achilty, Ross-shire. Pupil of John **MacKay**. Known as the 'King of Pipers', he won many awards. He was a pipe maker and was piper to the Marquess of Breadalbane 1832–60.

**Mackenzie, R(obert) F(raser)** (1910–87) Schoolteacher, b. Lethenty, Aberdeenshire. He was headmaster of Braehead School, Buckhaven from 1957 to 1968, and then of Summerhill, **Aberdeen**. His strong and progressive views, influenced by A S **Neill**, included opposition to corporal punishment and to examinations. His child-centred approach led him into conflict with the education authorities and with parents and staff, and he was suspended from Summerhill in 1974. He published a number of books, including *The Unbowed Head* (1977), his own account of events at Summerhill.

**Mackenzie, Thomas** and **William** see next

**Mackenzie family** Family of architects of whom the most important were **William Macdonald** (1797–1856), architect of the old infirmary at **Perth**, now the A K Bell Library; his brother **Thomas** (1815–54) of **Elgin**, architect of the Caledonian Bank (now Bank of Scotland) at **Inverness**, Milne's School at Fochabers and many castle restorations and remodellings; Thomas's son **Alexander Marshall** (1848–1933) of **Aberdeen**, architect of Crathie Church (1893) and the reconstruction of Marischal College, Aberdeen (1893–1906); and **Alexander George Robertson** (1879–1963) of London and Aberdeen, son of Alexander Marshall, architect of Australia House and the Waldorf Hotel in London, and of the modernist Northern Hotel in Kittybrewster, Aberdeen.

**Mackintosh, Charles Rennie** see p.255

**Mackintosh, Ewart Alan** (1893–1917) Poet, b. Brighton. His Highland parents encouraged his study of **Gaelic**. His early verse was derivative of the Celtic Twilight school, but his active service in World War I brought out a striking talent, cut short by his death in action. His poems were published in *A Highland Regiment* (1917), *War, the Liberator* (1918) and *Miserere* (1919).

**Mackintosh, William, of Borlum** (1658–1743) Soldier and agriculturalist, b. Inverness-shire. One of the leaders of the **Jacobite** Rising in 1715, Brigadier Mackintosh fought at **Sheriffmuir**. He also took part in the 1719 Rising, and was imprisoned after both. During his imprisonment, he wrote an early and intelligent treatise on agriculture (1729); he grasped the importance of cultivating fodder to sustain cattle through the winter.

**Mackintosh, Charles Rennie** (1868–1928) Architect, artist and designer, b. Glasgow. Celebrated internationally for his work, Mackintosh remains one of the most original artistic talents to emerge from Scotland. Apprenticed to an architect, he worked in the office during the day, and attended **Glasgow School of Art** in the evenings, where his talents came to the attention of the Director, Francis **Newbery**. On completing his apprenticeship he won the Alexander **Thomson** Travelling Studentship and went to France and Italy, producing numerous sketches and formulating his views on architecture. During the 1890s, through his continuing attendance at Glasgow School of Art, Mackintosh's interests expanded to include painting and design. He met the sisters Frances and Margaret Macdonald (the latter whom he married in 1900) and together with his friend Herbert McNair (his architectural colleague), the four, who called themselves 'the Immortals', developed a distinctly Scottish variant of the European Art Nouveau style and began to exhibit their work.

In 1897 Mackintosh won (through his firm Honeyman and

*Fritillaria, Walberswick, 1915.*

Keppie) the competition to design a new building for the Glasgow School of Art. In the following years Mackintosh worked on a number of domestic and commercial projects such as The **Hill House**, Helensburgh and Miss **Cranston**'s Glasgow Tea Rooms (including the Willow Tea Rooms, Sauchiehall Street), wherever possible conceiving all the furnishings and fittings. His startling, innovative designs and unified decorative schemes, and in particular his use of white, brought him attention from abroad (he exhibited with the Vienna Secessionists in 1901) and led to his being considered a pioneer of Modernist design. In his home country he found work increasingly difficult to come by and moved away, living in London from 1915 where, with the notable exception of a house at 78 Derngate, Northampton, few of the private commissions he worked on were realised. During this period he made textile designs and continued to paint. In 1923 he moved to the south of France (to the Roussillon) where he dedicated himself to painting, producing a series of watercolours of the surrounding area that are among his most impressive. In 1927 he returned to London and was diagnosed as having cancer. He died there in December 1928. The most concentrated collection of his work is now at the Hunterian Art Gallery, **Glasgow University**, which includes a remarkable reconstruction of the Mackintoshes' Glasgow home.

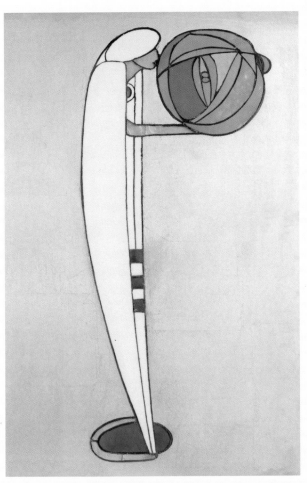

*Cabinet door (1902), silver painted wood inlaid with glass, at the Mackintosh House, Hunterian Art Gallery.*

**M**

*Sorley Maclean (1991).*

**Maclaurin, Colin** (1698–1746) Physician, mathematician and astronomer, b. Kilmodan, Argyll. Appointed to a chair at Marischal College, **Aberdeen**, at the age of 19, and later at **Edinburgh** (on the recommendation of Isaac Newton). A key figure in the **Scottish Enlightenment**, his *Treatise on Fluxions* (1742) gave a systematic account of Newton's approach to the calculus.

**McLaverty, Bernard** (1942– ) Novelist and short-story writer, born Belfast, but resident for many years in Scotland. He worked as a medical laboratory technician for 10 years before turning to writing. His novels include *Lamb* (1980), *Cal* (1983), *Grace Notes* (1997), which won the Saltire Book of the Year Award and was shortlisted for the Booker and Whitbread Prizes, and *The Anatomy School* (2001). He has also written plays for radio and television and screenplays for *Cal* and *Lamb*.

**Maclean, Alistair** (1922–87) Novelist, b. Glasgow to a Gaelic-speaking family. He spent his youth in the **Highlands** and joined the Royal Navy in 1941. In the 1960s and 70s he was one of the bestselling thriller writers in the world, using his wartime experiences as inspiration. Many of his books were filmed, including *The Guns of Navarone* (1957), *Fear is the Key* (1961), *Ice Station*

*Zebra* (1963), *Where Eagles Dare* (1967) and *Force 10 from Navarone* (1968). His other books include *The Dark Crusader* (1961) and *The Satan Bug* (1962), under the name of Ian Stuart. He was one of the founders of Radio Clyde.

**McLean, Bruce** (1944– ) Artist, b. Glasgow. During the 1960s and onwards McLean became prominent among a generation of artists making work in opposition to, and critical of, traditional forms of studio-based art. He has produced work in a wide variety of media (photography, painting, installation, slide projections, set design), characterised more by its subversive wit than by any formal style.

**MacLean, Dougie** (1954– ) Traditional and folk singer and composer, b. Dunblane, Perthshire. Involved in the Celtic music revival since the 1970s, he has played with the **Tannahill Weavers** and Silly Wizard.

**McLean, Duncan** (1964– ) Novelist and playwright, b. Aberdeenshire and living in Orkney. His works include *Bucket of Tongues* (1992), *Blackden* (1994) and *Bunker Man* (1997). He has also published a volume of his plays.

**Maclean, Sir Fitzroy** (1911–96) Diplomat, soldier and writer. Adventurous careers in the British Foreign Service and during World War II provided material for many of his books, including *Eastern Approaches* (1949) and *Back from Bokhara* (1959), though he also wrote on historical subjects. He was thought by some to be the inspiration for James Bond and for Alistair **Maclean**'s *The Guns of Navarone*. He latterly ran a hotel at his home in **Strachur**, Argyll.

**McLean, Jim** (1937– ) Football player and manager, b. Larkhall. A player with Kilmarnock and **Dundee**, he briefly became coach with the latter club before moving to their city rivals, **Dundee United**, as manager in 1971. Along with Sir Alex **Ferguson** at Aberdeen, McLean created the so-called New Firm to rival the Old Firm of **Rangers** and **Celtic**. His United side were champions in 1983, and reached the final of the UEFA Cup 4 years later. He stood down as manager in 1993 but remained as the presiding figure at the club for a further decade.

**Maclean, John** (1879–1923) Political worker and teacher, b. Glasgow. Member of the Marxist Social Democratic Federation (Social Democratic Party). His enthusiastic promotion of workers' education helped lead to the founding of the Scottish Labour College. Imprisonment several times between 1916 and 1922 for his anti-war and anti-capitalist activities contributed to his early death.

**Maclean, Sorley** (1911-99) Poet, b. Raasay. A major influence on recent Scottish Gaelic poetry, his early work, *Dàin do Eimhir agus Dàin Eile* (*Poems to Eimhir and Other Poems*, 1943), is composed of love poems and elegies, and several poems were inspired by the Spanish Civil War and by World War II and informed by his political commitment to Communism and Scottish Nationalism. Later concerns included family, tradition, Irish politics and the threats facing Gaelic Scotland and its culture. His poems were collected in *Reothairt is Contraigh* (*Spring Tide and Neap Tide* 1977) and *O Choille gu Bearradh* (*From Wood to Ridge* 1989). His work in translation has reached an international readership.

**MacLehose, Agnes** (1759-1841) b. Glasgow. 'Clarinda' to Robert **Burns**'s 'Sylvander' in a chaste but passionate relationship begun in **Edinburgh** in 1787, while her husband was abroad. She inspired the poem 'Ae fond kiss', published in 1792.

**MacLellan, Ian** (1937- ) Piper, b. Clydebank. As Pipe Major of the Strathclyde Police he won the World Pipe Band Championship 12 times, including 6 consecutive wins 1980-6.

**MacLellan, John** (1875-1949) Piper, b. Dunoon. Pipe Major Argyll and Sutherland Highlanders and a highly acclaimed composer of pipe music.

**MacLellan, John A** (1921-91) Piper, b. Dunfermline. Pupil of William **Ross** and John **MacDonald**. He won many awards. He was Pipe Major Seaforth Highlanders then Instructor and Director of Army School of Piping 1968-76. A commissioned Captain, he was the first piper to be commissioned in this post. He published *Music for the Highland Bagpipe* in 1961, *The Pipers' Handbook* in 1964, *Bagpipe Music for Dancing* in 1968, *More Music for the Highland Bagpipe* in 1968 and *Ceol Beag agus Ceol Mor* in 1971.

**MacLennan, George S** (1883-1929) Piper, b. Edinburgh. Pupil of his father and uncle and John MacDougall **Gillies**, he was Pipe Major Gordon Highlanders. He won many awards. He was a highly acclaimed composer of pipe music, a pipe maker and published *Highland Bagpipe Music* in 1929.

**Macleod, Ally** (1934-2004) Football player and manager, b. Glasgow. He was manager of the Scottish **football** team which qualified for the World Cup final stages in Argentina in 1978. The disappointment of inflated national and media expectations in these games led to an undue degree of blame being placed upon him.

**MacLeod, Donald** (1916-82) Piper, b. Stornoway. Pupil of John

MacDonald, he was Pipe Major in the Seaforth and Queen's Own Highlanders. He won many awards and was a highly acclaimed composer and arranger. He taught many pupils and from 1954 on he published *Pipe Major Donald MacLeod's Collection of Music for the Bagpipe* Books 1 to 6 and *Donald MacLeod's Collection of Piobaireachd.*

**Macleod, Fiona** see **Sharp, William**

**MacLeod, George (Lord Macleod of Fiunary)** (1895-1991) Clergyman, writer and broadcaster, b. Glasgow. After ministry in **Edinburgh** and **Govan** he founded the **Iona Community** in 1938, with support from Sir James Lithgow. Moderator of the **General Assembly** 1957-8, he became a life peer, Baron MacLeod of Fiunary, in 1967, though maintaining his left-wing commitments.

**Macleod, John James Rickard** (1876-1935) Physiologist, b. Dunkeld. Joint winner of the Nobel Prize in 1923 for his discovery of insulin and work on diabetes.

**Macleod, Ken** (1954- ) Science-fiction novelist, b. Stornoway, brought up in Greenock. He has published the *Fall Revolution* sequence comprising 4 novels beginning with *The Star Fraction* (1995), which won the Prometheus Award for Science Fiction in 1996, and a trilogy, *The Engines of Light*, beginning with *Cosmonaut Keep* (2000).

**Macleod, Revd Kenneth** (1871-1955) Minister, Gaelic writer and collector, b. Eigg. He was minister in **Colonsay** and **Gigha**. He wrote **Gaelic** prose and collected folklore and song, collaborating with Marjory **Kennedy-Fraser**. He wrote the words of the song 'The Road to the Isles'.

**Macleod, Mary** see **Màiri nighean Alasdair Ruaidh**

**Macleod, Norman** (1780-1866) Pioneer clergyman, b. Clachtol, Assynt, Sutherland. A man of stern Calvinist views, his disaffection with the **Church of Scotland** led to his emigration in 1817 to Pictou, Nova Scotia. Again disillusioned, he moved with his flock to Cape Breton, and thence to Australia in 1851. Dissatisfied with Australian ways he finally settled at Waipu, New Zealand, in 1854.

**MacLeod, Revd Dr Norman, 'Caraid nan Gaidheal'** ('friend of the Highlanders') (1783-1862) Minister and author. He helped to encourage education in the **Highlands**, and poor relief during the 1830s and 40s. He edited **Gaelic** magazines and encouraged new writing in Gaelic. His own publications include sermons and educational works and he was co-editor of a Gaelic dictionary; see **dictionaries**.

M

**Macleod, Norman** (1812–72) Minister and writer, b. Campbeltown, Argyll. In 1851 he became minister of the Barony, **Glasgow**, and in 1869 Moderator of the **General Assembly**. He was author of the well-known hymn 'Courage brother, do not stumble' and his books include *Reminiscences of a Highland Parish* (1867).

**MacLeod's Tables** Two basalt and lava hills, Healabhal Mhòr and Healabhal Bheag, to the southwest of **Dunvegan** in **Skye**. Legend tells that Alasdair Crotach MacLeod entertained **James V** (or another celebrity) to a banquet on his massive 'tables'.

**Mac Mhaighstir Alasdair, Alasdair** (**Alexander MacDonald**) (c.1695–c.1770) Poet, b. Moidart, son of an episcopal minister in western Inverness-shire. He may have been educated at **Glasgow University**. From 1729 he spent some years as a teacher with the **SSPCK**, who commissioned his *Leabhar a Theagasc Ainminnin* (*Galick and English Vocabulary*) (1741). He took part in the 1745 Rising as a captain in the **Jacobite** army. Foremost of the 18th-century Gaelic poets, his poems show many contrasts, contradictions and sources, including Latin poetry. The best-known of his nature poems, 'Allt an t-Siùcar' ('Sugar Burn'), describes the **Ardnamurchan** countryside. 'Birlinn Chlann Raghnaill' ('Clanranald's Galley') is a vivid and detailed evocation of a stormy voyage and its participants. A collection of his poems of 1751 was the first book of secular poetry published in **Gaelic**.

**MacMhuirich family** The chief family of Scottish Gaelic bards, descended from the 13th-century poet Muireadhach Albanach, the last of the line being Niall (c.1637–c.1726). The family served the MacDonalds of the Isles, and then the Clanranalds.

**Macmillan, Daniel** (1813–57) Bookseller and publisher, b. Arran. Beginning as a bookseller in Scotland, Cambridge and London, he and his brother Alexander set up in publishing, first in Cambridge and then in London, publishing educational books and also prominent authors of the day. The firm grew and prospered and remained in family hands until recently; it is now owned by a large German media company. Harold Macmillan took an active part, especially after he retired as Prime Minister.

**Macmillan, General Sir Gordon** (1897–1986) Soldier, b. Bangalore, Madras. Commissioned into the **Argyll and Sutherland Highlanders**. He fought in World War I and in World War II led the 51st Highland Division across the Rhine; as C-in-C Palestine he supervised British withdrawal from the Mandate.

He was chairman of **Cumbernauld** New Town Corporation after 1955, and in 1968 led the successful campaign against the disbandment of his old regiment.

**Macmillan, Hector** (1929– ) Playwright, b. Glasgow. Has written for theatre, television and radio. Plays include *The Rising* (1970), *The Sash* (1973) and *The Hypochondriac* (1986).

**Macmillan, James** (1959– ) Composer and conductor, b. Kilwinning, Ayrshire. One of the most successful living composers, he incorporates references to Scottish folk music as well as to his strong political and religious beliefs. His works include *Tryst* (1989), *The Confession of Isobel Gowdie* (1990), *Veni, Veni, Emmanuel* (1992, for Evelyn **Glennie**), and the opera *Ines de Castro* (1996). He became Affiliate Conductor of the **Scottish Chamber Orchestra** in 1990, Visiting Composer of the Philharmonia Orchestra in 1991, and composer/conductor of the BBC Philharmonic Orchestra in 2000.

**Macmillan, Sir Kenneth** (1929–92) Ballet dancer and choreographer, b. Dunfermline. He trained and later performed with the Sadler's Wells Theatre Ballet. Choreographer and director of the Royal Ballet, his ballets include 'Anastasia', 'Isadora', 'The Judas Tree' and 'Mayerling'.

**MacMillan, Kirkpatrick** (1812–78) Maker (and possibly inventor) of bicycles, b. Thornhill, Dumfriesshire. He followed his father as a blacksmith and may have been the first to develop a rear-wheel-driven safety bicycle. A plaque on his smiddy home says 'he builded better than he knew'.

**MacMillan, Roddy** (1923–79) Actor and dramatist, b. Glasgow. A member of the **Citizens' Theatre, Glasgow**, he appeared in many plays and also wrote *All is Good Fair* (1954) and *The Bevellers* (1973). Helped to revive interest in Neil Munro by his portrayal of Para Handy in the 1960s and 70s TV series *The Vital Spark*.

**Macmillan publishers** see **Macmillan, Daniel**

**McNair, Herbert** see **Mackintosh, Charles Rennie**

**MacNeil, Flora** (1928– ) Gaelic singer, b. Barra. At a time when **Gaelic** singers were expected to have trained voices, her pure voice, extensive repertoire, distinctive interpretations and assured technique revitalised interest in and assisted the revival of traditional Gaelic singing.

**MacNeill, F Marian** (1885–1973) Writer, b. Orkney. Best known for her substantial work on Scottish folklore, *The Silver Bough* (1957–68) and her books on food and drink, including *The Scots Kitchen* (1929) and *The Scots Cellar* (1956).

**MacNeill, Seumas** (1917–96) Piper, b. Glasgow. Joint founder with Thomas Pearston of the College of Piping in 1944. Published *The Seumas MacNeill Collection of Bagpipe Music Book 1* (1960) and *Book 2* (1985). Author of *Piobaireachd a BBC Publication* (1968), *4 Tutors for the Bagpipe* with Thomas Pearston, an *Acoustical Study of the Highland Bagpipe* with J Lenihan, *Piobaireachd and its Interpretation* with Gen. F Richardson (1987), Editor of the highly regarded piping magazine the *Piping Times* (1950–96).

**MacPherson, Donald** (1922– ) Piper, b. Glasgow. Pupil of his father who was a pupil of John MacDougall **Gillies**, considered to be the greatest prize-winning piper of the 20th century. He has taught many top pipers.

**MacPherson, Ewen, of Cluny** (d.1756) Chief of the MacPhersons and a reluctant supporter of Charles Edward **Stewart**, he brought his clansmen to join the **Jacobite** army after the Battle of **Prestonpans**, but they missed the Battle of **Culloden**. Meanwhile Cluny's home had been burned, and he took refuge in 'Cluny's cage', a cave on the side of **Ben Alder**, where he was joined by the Prince until the latter's escape to **Skye**. Never betrayed by his people, despite the offer of reward, Cluny finally escaped to France in 1755, but soon died there.

**Macpherson, James** (1736–96) Poet, b. Ruthven, Inverness-shire. A collector and translator of **Gaelic** oral poetry, he became famous with the publication of *Fragments of Ancient Poetry Collected in the Highlands of Scotland and Translated from the Gallic or Erse Language* (1760). This inspired hopes in the literati of Edinburgh that a large body of national poetry might survive, especially in the form of epics about the hero **Fingal** by his son **Ossian**. Macpherson did further research in the **Highlands**, resulting in *Fingal* (1762), *Temora* (1763) and *The Works of Ossian* (1765). The excitement at the discovery of this body of work was tempered by the gradual realisation that much of the poetry had been invented by Macpherson, though some original oral poetry was included.

**MacPherson, Malcolm** (1833–98) Piper, b. Uigshader, Skye, known as Calum Piobair. Taught by his father Angus, who was a

*The Sailing of the Emigrant Ship by William McTaggart (1895).*

pupil of the **MacCrimmons**. He and his father, his 5 sons and grandson, Malcolm R, made up the MacPherson School of Piping. He won many awards and was piper to MacPherson of Cluny.

**MacPherson, Mary** see **Màiri Mhòr nan Òran**

**MacQuarie, Lachlan** (1762–1824) Soldier and administrator, b. Ulva, off Mull. Joined British Army at the age of 14, and served in Nova Scotia, Jamaica, India and Egypt. In 1810 became Governor of New South Wales, Australia, still a penal colony. Against the wishes of the free settlers he encouraged released convicts to settle in Australia, and laid the ground for the Australia of today. He is regarded as the 'father of Australia'.

**MacQueen, Robert** see **Braxfield, Lord**

**McTaggart, William** (1835–1910) Artist, b. Aros, Kintyre. One of a generation of important 19th-century artists who studied in Edinburgh under Robert Scott **Lauder**, McTaggart's earliest works were anecdotal but without the stuffiness of much Victorian painting. From the 1860s onwards his interest turned predominantly to land- and seascape. Making particular use of dramatic lighting and atmospheric effects, he produced works that are boldly coloured and energetically painted with an unconventional loose finish which did not detract from their popularity during his lifetime. He is sometimes dubbed 'the Scottish Impressionist'.

Poppies against the Night Sky
by Sir William MacTaggart (c.1962).

**M**

**MacTaggart, Sir William** (1903–81) Artist, b. Loanhead, Midlothian. With William **Gillies** and Anne **Redpath**, MacTaggart (grandson of the 19th-century William **McTaggart**) is known as one of the Edinburgh School of artists, who flourished in the mid 20th century and whose painting was most often of the Scottish scene. He is known particularly for his series of still-life paintings of poppies, set against the night view from his **Edinburgh** studio window.

**Máel Coluim mac Cináeda** see **Malcolm II**

**Máel Coluim mac Domnall** see **Malcolm I**

**Máel Coluim mac Donnchada** see **Malcolm III**

**Maelrubha, St** (642–722) Abbot and martyr, b. County Derry. Made many missionary journeys in Argyll, and founded a mission centre at **Applecross**, Ross-shire. He became a very popular saint in the northwest. He had a cell on an island in **Loch Maree**. He died on 21 April, but his Scottish feast day is 27 August.

**Maes Howe** A magnificent stone chamber tomb in Mainland **Orkney**, covered by a circular cairn and with a ring ditch, built before 2700 BC. The burial chamber is square, with 3 rectangular cells opening from raised doorways. The long entrance passage was aligned upon the setting sun at the midwinter solstice. Norsemen broke into the mound in the 12th century and carved many runic inscriptions upon the walls of the chamber.

**Maggie's Centres** Centres set up to provide support and information for people suffering from cancer, inspired on the basis of her own experience by Maggie Keswick Jencks, who died of cancer in 1995. There are now Centres in **Edinburgh**, **Glasgow** and **Dundee**, and many more are planned, some furth of Scotland. She and her husband Charles created a spectacular garden at their home, Portrack House, on the River **Nith**, 8km (5mi) north of **Dumfries**; known as the Garden of Cosmic Speculation, it reflects modern views of the universe.

**Magnus, St** (d.c.1117) Earl of Orkney. A popular pacifist, he was joint earl with his cousin Haakon, who in jealousy had him killed and buried in **Birsay**. His nephew Rognvald built the cathedral at **Kirkwall** to commemorate him and the miracles associated with the place of his burial, and had him reburied there.

**Magnus 'Barelegs'** King of Norway. Leader of a major expedition to the Scottish Isles in 1098. The campaign was celebrated in a poem by Bjorn Cripplehand and ended in a treaty with **Edgar**, King of Scots, confirming Norwegian sovereignty over the **Western Isles**.

**Magnusson, Magnus** (1929– ) Broadcaster and writer, b. Reykjavik, Iceland. A journalist on Scottish newspapers before joining the BBC and working on *Chronicle* and, most famously, as presenter of the TV quiz programme *Mastermind* for 25 years (1972–97). He has also been involved in environmental issues, especially as chairman of **Scottish Natural Heritage**.

**maiden** A portable execution device resembling the later guillotine, used for beheading at public executions in **Edinburgh** from 1564–1710. It is now in the **Museum of Scotland**. Famous victims included the 4th Earl of **Morton** (who introduced it) in 1581, the Marquess of **Argyll** in 1661 and the 9th Earl of **Argyll** in 1685.

**Mains Castle** Tall 15th-century rectangular tower of the Lindsays of Durod, in **East Kilbride**, standing on a knoll and a prominent local landmark. Recently re-roofed and re-occupied.

**Mains Castle** Courtyard house in **Dundee**, built 1562, 1582 and later 17th century, with a tall stair tower heightened in 1630 as an outlook tower, built by the Grahams of Fintry. Re-roofed in recent years; open to public within surrounding Caird Park.

**Mair, John** see **Major, John**

**Màiri Mhòr nan Òran (Mary MacPherson)** (1821-98) Gaelic poet, b. Skye. Stung into composing verse by a personal injustice when living in **Inverness**, she championed the cause of the crofters during the Land Agitation of the 1870s and 1880s. Her songs about **Skye** have a particularly strong emotional appeal.

**Màiri nighean Alasdair Ruaidh (Mary Macleod)** (c.1615-1705) Gaelic poet, b. Rodel, Isle of Harris. Lived with the MacLeods of Dunvegan, Isle of **Skye**, and composed songs in their honour and to celebrate the generosity and splendour of other clan chiefs. Sixteen of her works still survive.

**Maitland, Sir Richard, of Lethington** (1496-1586) Lawyer and poet, b. East Lothian. He served **James V**, **Mary, Queen of Scots** and **James VI**. In his later years he devoted himself to writing poems and to collecting earlier poetry, preserved in the Maitland Folio Manuscript, which includes works by **Dunbar** and **Henrysoun**. His daughter Marie compiled a manuscript of later poetry, including verse by **James VI**. Both manuscripts are in Magdalene College, Cambridge.

**Maitland, William, of Lethington** (c.1525-73) Politician. The 'Michael Wylie' (Machiavelli) of Scottish politics, he was Secretary of State to **Mary of Guise**, and later to **Mary, Queen of Scots**. Originally a Protestant English sympathiser, like the Earl of Moray, and implicated in the murders of **Rizzio** and **Darnley**, he later supported Mary and defended **Edinburgh Castle** on her behalf. He probably committed suicide after its capture.

**Major, John (John Mair)** (1467-1550) Philosopher and historian, b. North Berwick. His *Historia Majoris Britanniae* (1521) covered Scotland and England and fostered the idea of union. He was critical of corruption in religious circles and less credulous of myth and legend than many earlier and contemporary historians. At **St Andrews University** he taught John **Knox** and George **Buchanan**.

**makar** Scots word for a poet, often referring to one of the poets of the late 15th and early 16th centuries, and to those of the **Scottish Renaissance** of the mid 20th century. The word is now being used as an honorary title; see Stewart **Conn**, Edwin **Morgan**.

**Malcolm I** (Máel Coluim mac Domnall) (d.954) King of Scots 943-54. Killed in **Moray** in a conflict possibly related to the succession within the royal kin-group.

**Malcolm II** (Máel Coluim mac Cináeda) (d.1034) King of Scots 1005-34. Widely regarded as one of the most formidable early medieval Scottish kings, he was ruthless in eliminating rivals to the throne and extended his power to the south. Victory over the Angles at **Carham** in 1018 ensured control over **Lothian**.

**Malcolm III** (Máel Coluim mac Donchada, known as **Malcolm Canmore**) (c.1031-93) King of Scots 1057-93. Son of **Duncan I**, he spent most of his early life in exile in England while his father's killer, **Macbeth**, was on the throne. After defeating Macbeth and gaining the crown in 1057, he stamped his authority on his kingdom and sought to extend his influence southwards. The last of many invasions of England ended in his death at Alnwick. He married first Ingibjorg, widow of **Thorfinn**, Earl of **Orkney**. His second wife, St **Margaret**, was an important conduit for new, southern influences in Scotland, and the 'MacMalcolm' dynasty, carried on by their offspring, was to endure until 1290.

**Malcolm IV** (nicknamed 'the Maiden') (1141-65) King of Scots 1153-65. Aged 12 at his accession, he faced immediate domestic challenges and was forced to surrender **David I**'s conquests in northern England to Henry II in 1157. Malcolm faced full-scale revolt after serving abroad on Henry's Toulouse campaign of 1159-60, but again outfaced his domestic opponents. He died unmarried, but the MacMalcolm dynasty endured in the person of his brother, **William I**.

**Mallaig** West-coast **fishing** port on the Sound of **Sleat**, with ferry to Armadale in Skye; the end of the Road to the Isles, created in connection with the West Highland Extension Railway, as the ferry port for services to the **Outer Isles**.

**Malleny Garden** Balerno, Edinburgh. Walled garden with old-fashioned roses, herbaceous borders and 16th-century yews. Open to the public, in the care of the **National Trust for Scotland**. Malleny House, dating from the 17th-18th centuries, with an 1820 addition, is open only occasionally.

*Maes Howe, Orkney.*

M

*Margaret, 'Maid of Norway', depicted in a 19th-century stained-glass window in Lerwick Town Hall, Shetland.*

**Malt Tax** Duties on malt imposed, but not implemented, in 1713, and revived by Sir Robert Walpole in 1725, resulted in protests in many towns, most seriously a brewers' strike in **Edinburgh** and a riot in **Glasgow**.

**Mamores** Popular name for the Mamore Forest, a mountainous area, near **Fort William**, between the head of **Loch Leven** and **Glen Nevis**. It has 11 **Munros**, including Binnein Mór, 1128m (3700ft), Na Gruagaichean, 1055m (3442ft) and Sgurr Eilde Mhór, 1008m (3279ft). The **West Highland Way** runs along its southwest edge and part of the 1995 film *Braveheart* was filmed here.

**Mam Sodhail** (**Mam Soul**) Mountain, a **Munro** (1181m/3875ft) to the northwest of **Loch Affric**. It and its neighbour Carn Eighe (1183m/3881ft) are the highest peaks north of the **Great Glen**.

**Man, Isle of** An important part of the early medieval Scandinavian domination of the Irish Sea zone, Man became a possession of the Norwegian crown. It was ceded by the King of Norway to Scotland in 1266, but was taken by Edward I in 1290. Despite repeated Scottish attempts to regain the island, and some periods in possession, English control was to prove lasting. In the 18th and early 19th centuries there was an extensive smuggling trade between Scotland and the island. Its language, Manx Gaelic, closely related to Irish and Scottish Gaelic, recently died out, but is now being revived.

**Manderston House** Magnificent neo-Georgian house to the east of **Duns**, Berwickshire, built in the 1790s and enlarged (1903–5) by John Kinross for Sir James Miller, Russia merchant. One of the finest Scottish Edwardian country houses, owned by Lord and Lady Palmer, it is open to the public. It is set in splendid formal gardens and Buxley, just to the north, was built c.1900 as model farm offices, with a vaulted marble dairy and a cloister.

**manse** House provided for the minister of a particular church. The term is also used for former professorial residences of **Aberdeen University** in Old Aberdeen.

**Manson, Sir Patrick** (1844–1922) 'Mosquito Manson', Parasitologist, b. Aberdeenshire. A pioneer worker in malaria research, with Sir Ronald Ross, he helped found the London School of Tropical Medicine.

**Manuel, Peter** (1927–58) Serial killer, b. USA. He moved to Scotland with his Scottish parents in 1932. First a petty criminal, he was convicted of the murders of 7 people in **Glasgow** and the Lowlands between 1954 and 1958, and confessed to several more. He was hanged at **Barlinnie**.

**Maoile Lunndaidh** Very remote mountain, a **Munro** (1007m/3304ft), to the north of Loch Monar, Ross and Cromarty.

**Maol Chean-dearg** Mountain, a **Munro** (933m/3061ft) to the northwest of Glen Carron, Ross and Cromarty.

**Mar, John Erskine, Earl of** (c.1510–72) As Lord Erskine he was keeper of **Edinburgh** and **Stirling** castles, which gave him the power to intervene in the struggles between **Mary of Guise** and the nobles. In 1565 **Mary, Queen of Scots** created (or restored) the earldom of Mar for him, and in 1567 he was given custody of the infant **James VI**. He later became Regent of Scotland.

**Mar, John Erskine, 11th Earl of** (1675–1732) b. Alloa. Known as 'Bobbing John' because of his frequent change of political allegiance. A strong advocate of the Union of 1707, he was allied to the English Tory party but hoped to survive in office when the accession of George I led to the dominance of the Whig party. When it became clear that George I would not give him office, he led the 1715 **Jacobite** Rising, apologising for his support for the Union and promising to rescind it. Despite widespread support for the Rising in Scotland, his uninspired leadership led to its collapse after the indecisive Battle of **Sheriffmuir**. He was an important innovator in the mining and glass industries around **Alloa**, where the Gartmore Dam is still a monument to his enterprise. He died in exile on the Continent.

**Marches** The border country between Scotland and England, scene of many battles, once divided into West, Middle and East, each section governed by a warden. See also **riding of the marches**.

**Maree, Loch** see **Loch Maree**

**Margaret, 'Maid of Norway'** (c.1283–90) Queen of Scots (1286–90). Daughter of Margaret (daughter of **Alexander III**) and Eric, King of Norway, she succeeded to the Scottish throne on the death of her grandfather. It was planned that she should marry Edward, eldest son of Edward I of England. Her death at **Kirkwall** in **Orkney**, on her way to Scotland, was followed by conflict over the succession and the 'Wars of Independence'; see **Great Cause**.

**Margaret, Queen of Norway** (1261–83) Daughter of **Alexander III**, married Eric, King of Norway in 1281. Died giving birth to **Margaret, 'Maid of Norway'**.

**Margaret, St** (c.1046–1093) Queen of Scots. Wife of **Malcolm III** and daughter of Edward of Wessex, she brought English influences to Scotland, especially to the Church. She died after hearing of Malcolm's death at the Battle of Alnwick, and was canonised in 1249, after a royal campaign to gain a saint for the MacMalcolm dynasty. The Queen's Ferry across the **Forth** was named after her.

**Margaret Tudor** (1489–1541) Queen of Scots. Daughter of Henry VII of England. She married **James IV**, binding Scotland and England in 'perpetual peace'. The peace did not last, but her great-grandson, **James VI** and I would unite the English and Scottish crowns in 1603. After the death of James, she married Archibald, 6th Earl of **Angus**. In 1526 she divorced him and married Henry Stewart, later Lord Methven.

**Marie de Coucy** Queen of Scots. Daughter of Enguerrand de Coucy, a French nobleman, she married **Alexander II** in 1239. Mother of **Alexander III**, she played little part in the politics of his minority after returning to France in 1250.

**Marischal College** see **Aberdeen University**

**Marjoribanks, Ishbel-Maria, Lady Aberdeen** (1857–1939) b. London. Married the 7th Earl of **Aberdeen** and had as main residence **Haddo House**. An activist for education, health, social work and the rights of working women, she assisted Gladstone in his work reforming prostitutes and helped relieve the conditions of the Irish peasantry.

**mark** see **merk**

**Markinch** Small town in Fife, to the northeast of **Glenrothes**, a former **burgh**, and once perhaps capital of Fife, has a parish church of 1786 with a fine Romanesque tower. Papermaking survives, notably in the now employee-owned Tullis-Russell papermill. It was for many years the headquarters of the Haig **whisky** business. The classical Balbirnie House, in its present form by Richard Crichton (1815–19), is now a hotel. In its grounds is a reconstructed stone circle with a central rectangular setting and burial cists. The circle originally stood some 125m (410ft) to the northwest.

**Mar Lodge Estate** A vital nature conservation and historic landscape to the north of the River **Dee**, near **Braemar**, covering part of the **Cairngorms**. Contains 4 of the highest mountains in Britain and remnants of the **Caledonian forest**. Open to the public, in the care of the **National Trust for Scotland**.

**Marsco** A peak (736m/2415ft) of the Red **Cuillin** mountains, **Skye**, overlooking Glen Sligachan.

**Marshall, William** (1749–1833) Musician, b. Fochabers. Famous for his fine fiddle playing and his compositions. Self-educated, he became butler and factor to the Duke of Gordon, a JP, a clockmaker and a surveyor. He composed 257 fiddle tunes,

*Mary, Queen of Scots.*

the slow **strathspey** being his favourite form. Robert **Burns** wrote the lyric 'Of a' the airts the wind can blaw' for Marshall's composition 'Miss Admiral Gordon's Strathspey'.

**Martin, Martin** (1660–1718) Author, b. Skye. Best known for his very detailed *A Description of the Western Islands of Scotland* (1703, but written c.1695), which was used by **Boswell** and Johnson on their tour to the **Hebrides** in 1783. He also wrote *A Late Voyage to St Kilda* (1697).

**Martinmas** 11 November, one of the Scottish term days, though the date for removals and employment was later changed to 28 November. It was used as the name for the autumn term in some of the Scottish universities. The feast day of St Martin of Tours, it is often associated with uncanny or supernatural events.

**Martin, Rhona** (1966– ) Curler, b. Irvine. The silver medallist in the 1998 European Championships, she found fame 4 years later when skipping the British women's team to gold in the Winter Olympics at Salt Lake City.

**Martyn, John** (1948– ) Singer/songwriter, b. Glasgow, as Ian McGeachy. Learned guitar technique from Hamish **Imlach**, then

developed his own highly influential idiosyncratic guitar style, melding blues, jazz and folk elements, and utilising electronic delay, echo and sustain effects, coupled with richly slurred vocals. His songs include 'May You Never' and 'I Couldn't Love You More' and albums include *Grace and Danger* (1980) and *Church with One Bell* (1998).

**Marwick Head** Headland near **Birsay**, Orkney. Striking cliffs, part of an RSPB nature reserve. The Kitchener Memorial commemorates Lord Kitchener's death in the sinking of HMS *Hampshire* there in 1916.

**Mary of Gueldres** (d.1463) Queen of Scots. Niece of the Duke of Burgundy, she married **James II** in 1449, in what was a prestigious match for the king. After her husband's death in 1460 she capably led the minority government of her son **James III**, negotiating the return of **Berwick-upon-Tweed** to the Scots for the last time in 1461.

**Mary of Guise** (1515–60) Queen of Scots. Daughter of the Duke of Guise, she married **James V** in 1538. Their 2 sons died in infancy, leaving a daughter, **Mary, Queen of Scots**, just one week old when her father died in 1542. Active in the politics of her daughter's minority, Mary of Guise became Regent in 1554, but was unable to stem the rebellion of 1559, which led to the rejection of French influence and the acceptance of the reformed church.

**Mary, Queen of Scots** (1542–87) Born in **Linlithgow** Palace just before the death of her father **James V**, she became queen when a few days old. Her early years were marred by struggles between Scotland and England and between her mother, **Mary of Guise**, and some of the Scottish nobles, and in 1548 she sailed for France, where she was betrothed to the Dauphin, son and heir of Henry II of France. They married in 1558 and in 1559, her husband became King Francois II. Their marriage might have led to a union of Scotland and France, but Francois died in 1559 and Mary returned to Scotland to rule in 1561. She took as her second husband her cousin, Henry Stewart, Lord **Darnley**, in 1565. Their relationship rapidly cooled and Darnley was implicated in a conspiracy to murder Mary's Italian secretary, David **Rizzio**. Their son, the future **James VI and I**, was born in 1566. Early in 1567 Darnley was murdered and some suspicion of involvement, never proved, was attached to Mary. One of the murderers was certainly James Hepburn, Earl of **Bothwell**, who became her third husband. Relations with the nobles thereby broke down and, after her surender at **Carberry**

**Hill**, she was imprisoned on an island on **Loch Leven**, and forced to abdicate in favour of her son. She escaped, but her army was soon defeated at the Battle of **Langside** and she fled to England to seek the protection of her cousin, Queen Elizabeth. A dangerous presence in England, Mary was a Catholic with a good claim to the throne. Imprisoned for 19 years, she was finally executed in 1587 after being linked to a plot against Elizabeth. See also '**four Marys**'.

**Massey-Harris Ltd** Agricultural implement makers, they built a large factory at Crosshouse, near **Kilmarnock**, immediately after World War II, to build tractors and combine harvesters, for which there was a rapidly expanding market. The company later amalgamated with Fergusons, another tractor-building company, and rationalised production as Massey-Ferguson Ltd. The Crosshouse factory closed in 1977.

**Massie, Allan** (1938– ) Novelist and critic, b. Singapore, brought up in Aberdeenshire. A major novelist whose works include a quartet from Roman history, *Augustus* (1989), *Tiberius* (1990), *Caesar* (1993), *Antony* (1997), and a biblical work, *King David* (1995). Among his best-known novels are *The Sins of the Father* (1991) and *A Question of Loyalties* (1989). *The Ragged Lion* (1994) is a study of Sir Walter **Scott**.

**Masson, Francis** (1741–1805). Plant collector, b. Aberdeen. A gardener at the Royal Botanic Garden, Kew, he was their first plant collector and was sent to South Africa where in 2 expeditions (1772–5 and 1785–95), he introduced to Kew over 500 new species. In 1778–80 he collected in Madeira, the Azores, the Canaries and Tenerife and the West Indies, followed by Spain and Portugal in 1783–85. His last expedition was to North America in 1797 where he died of hypothermia. His introductions include livingstone daisies, *Nerine sarniensis*, *Strelitzia reginae*, *Gladiola*, ixias, cape heaths and the king protea.

**Matheson, Sir James** (1796–1878) b. Lairg, Sutherland. He met William Jardine while working for the East India Company, and in 1832 with him created **Jardine Matheson**, Hong Kong's oldest firm, originally based on the opium trade. With his fortune he bought the Isle of **Lewis** and built Lews Castle (see **Stornoway**).

**Mauchline** Town in Ayrshire, a former **burgh**. Mauchline Castle, or Abbot Hunter's Tower, was the administrative centre of **Melrose** Abbey's Ayrshire estates. The Battle of Mauchline Moor was fought in 1648 between the **Covenanters** and the king's forces, and 5 Covenanters were hanged in the town in 1685. Robert **Burns** wrote poetry here between 1784–88, and lived briefly in the town. Jean **Armour**'s and Nanse Tinnock's houses were restored by the Burns Federation in the 1920s. To the south is the Ballochmyle Viaduct, the longest single span of any masonic viaduct in the UK.

**Mavisbank** Splendid classical mansion, in a precarious state, to the southeast of **Loanhead**, Midlothian, designed in the 1720s by Sir John **Clerk** of Penicuik and William **Adam**. In the 19th century it was extended and used as an asylum. In the 20th century it fell into disrepair and was gutted by a disastrous fire in 1973. The shell is now in the ownership of the Mavisbank Trust and in 2003 the house appeared on the BBC televison programme *Restoration*. Cost for restoration was estimated at £7 million.

**Mavor, O(sborne) H(enry)** (O H) see **Bridie, James**

**Maxton, James** (1885–1946) Politician, b. Glasgow. Became a Labour MP in 1922 and wrote *Lenin* (1932) and *If I were Dictator* (1935). Opposing the disaffiliation of the Scottish Independent Labour Party, he said 'if you cannot ride two horses you have no right in the circus', and, less charitably, in response to the last speech of Ramsay **MacDonald**, 'Sit down man. You're a bloody tragedy.'

**Maxwell, Gavin** (1914–69) Author, b. House of Elrig, Wigtownshire. After army service in World War II, he bought the island of **Soay** and briefly set up shark fishing there. His books include *Shaken by the Wind* (1958) on the Marsh Arabs of Iraq, but his fame rests on *A Ring of Bright Water* (1962), an account of his life in a cottage near **Glenelg**, and his pet otters. See also **Kyleakin**.

**Maxwell, James Clerk** (1831–79) Physicist, b. Edinburgh. His contributions to physics in the 19th century are considered to be as important as those of Newton in the 17th/18th century and Einstein in the 20th. His most famous work is the formulation of the Theory of Electromagnetism which showed that electomagnetic waves travel at the speed of light and established the theoretical foundation for the electromagnetic spectrum which includes X-rays, radio waves etc. Einstein stated that Maxwell's theory completely altered the scientific view of matter as propounded by Newton, and that his development of his Theory of Relativity would not have been possible without it. The theory underpins much of modern communication technology. Maxwell's work on gas dynamics is

M

also considered to represent the depth of his genius. In this he introduced the use of statistical methods in relation to the movement of gas molecules, which is one of the foundations of modern quantum mechanics. He also made important discoveries in control theory, theory of colour, astronomy and structural mechanics. He studied at **Edinburgh** and Cambridge Universities and was appointed to a chair of Natural Philosophy at King's College, **Aberdeen**, at the age of 25. He also held the chair of physics at King's College London. He was of independent means and spent 5 years at his estate in Galloway at which time he did important research towards the Theory of Electromagnetism and on gas dynamics. He combined his outstanding theoretical skills with excellent experimental work. His last appointment was as the first Cavendish Professor of Physics at Cambridge where he established the standard of excellence in research at the newly endowed Cavendish Laboratory which continues to this day. He died of cancer at the tragically early age of 48.

**Maxwell, John** (1905–62) Artist, b. Dalbeattie. His paintings have a poetic, dream-like quality, based on his own imaginative fantasies and influenced by the symbolism and style of the artist Marc Chagall. Highly self-critical, he frequently re-painted his works; as a result his paintings, and in particular his oils, are comparatively rare. He was a close friend of William **Gillies** and for a while taught alongside him at **Edinburgh College of Art**, where both had studied.

**May, Isle of** Largest island in the Firth of **Forth**, a National Nature Reserve noted for its bird (especially puffin) and seal colonies. The ruined 12th-century chapel of St Adrian (originally Ethernan) belonged to a Benedictine monastery founded on the site of a 9th-century church and cemetery. The first permanently manned **lighthouse** was built here in 1636 by Alexander Cunningham and a later light was designed by Robert **Stevenson** in 1815–16. Accessible to the public in spring and summer, by boat from **Anstruther**, Fife, and **North Berwick**.

**Mayar** see **Driesh**

**Maybole** A small town to the south of **Ayr**, a former **burgh**, once capital of the region of **Carrick**. It is dominated by Maybole Castle, a magnificent tower house built 1620 by the Earl of Cassilis. There also survive the ruins of a fine collegiate church of 1371 and the 17th-century town house of the Blairquhan estate, now the Town Hall. On the outskirts of the town is a second tower house, Kilhenzie, built by the Baird

family c.1600. In the 19th century Maybole was known for boot and shoe manufacture. Nearby are **Culzean Castle** and **Crossraguel Abbey**.

**meal** In Scotland, often refers to oatmeal. See **oats**.

**meal and ale** A harvest festival, especially in the Northeast, at which the main dish is made with oatmeal, ale and **whisky**, with the addition of sugar, cream etc.

**Meall Odhar** Name of several Scottish hills, notably the **Munro** in **Glenshee** (920m/3019ft), part of the Glenshee ski centre.

**Mearns, the** see **Howe o the Mearns, Kincardineshire**

**Mears, Sir Frank** (1880–1953) Architect, planner, b. Tynemouth, Northumberland. He was closely associated with his father-in-law Patrick **Geddes**, and particularly interested in bridge design. He founded the Association for the Preservation of Rural Scotland (1926), and Scotland's first town-planning course at **Edinburgh College of Art**.

**measures** see **weights and measures**

**Medina, Sir John Baptiste de** (1659–1710) Artist, b. Brussels, of Spanish parentage, he moved first to London, then in 1693/4 to **Edinburgh**, where he received numerous portrait commissions from the Scottish aristocracy, becoming the most successful portraitist in Scotland and remaining in the country until his death. The Scottish-born portraitist, William **Aikman**, studied under him.

**Meggat Water** River in Dumfriesshire, flowing south to join the **Esk**, 10km (6mi) northwest of **Langholm**.

**Meggernie Castle** Tower house with squat turrets, on the River Lyon, in **Glen Lyon**, built 1585 by Colin Campbell of Glenlyon, and extended in 1673 by Robert Campbell. It boasts the ghost of the murdered wife of a Menzies laird who, due to her gruesome end, materialises in two halves.

**Megget Water** River flowing into the west side of **St Mary's Loch**. Part of its course is now flooded as Megget Reservoir, one of the main sources of water for **Edinburgh**.

**Megginch** Large turreted house 11km (7mi) east of **Perth**, built 1585 for Peter Hay and enlarged by the Drummonds in 1790, perhaps by Robert and John **Adam**, again in 1820 by William Macdonald **Mackenzie**. It has a picturesque Gothic stable court 1707 and 1809.

**Meigle** Village between **Blairgowrie** and **Forfar**. The Meigle Sculptured Stone Museum features a collection of locally found Pictish stones (in the care of **Historic Scotland**). Nearby is a Roman fort, at Cardean, dating from the 1st century AD.

**Meikle, Andrew** (1719–1811) Agricultural engineer and inventor, b. Houston Mill near Dunbar, son of James Meikle, who helped Andrew **Fletcher** to introduce a pot-barley mill from Holland. A millworker at Phantassie, **East Lothian**, his inventions included improvements to windmill design and the first practical threshing machine. The principle of this machine is still embodied in the modern combine harvester. His son George invented a water-raising wheel, used in draining Kincardine Moss (1787).

**Meikle Ferry** Near **Dornoch**, on the **Dornoch Firth**. Once the only means of crossing the Firth. Meikle Ferry was the scene of a terrible disaster in 1809 when an overloaded ferry bringing people back from the **Lammas** Fair at **Tain** sank with the loss of 99 lives. A bridge was soon built at Bonar (1812) and a new road via Lairg. In 1991 a new road bridge was opened, a little to the east of the old ferry.

**Meikleour** Village 6km (4mi) south of **Blairgowrie**, Perthshire, famous for the magnificent beech hedge planted in 1746, now 26m (85ft) high and 0.5km (587yd) long. Meikleour House is mid 18th century, remodelled as a chateau by David **Bryce** (1869) for the Dowager Marchioness of Lansdowne, daughter of the Comte de Flahault.

**Melbost** see **Stornoway**

**Meldrum** see **Oldmeldrum**

**Melfort** see **Loch Melfort**

**Melgund Castle** Roofless tower house near **Aberlemno**, Forfar, Angus. Built by Cardinal David **Beaton** for his mistress Marion Ogilvy in 1543. Recently partly restored and reoccupied.

**Mellerstain House** Near **Kelso**, Borders. Wings built by William **Adam** for George and Grizel **Baillie** in 1725, the castellated main house by Robert **Adam** in 1770–9. It has some exquisite plasterwork by the latter, and a magnificent collection of paintings. Owned by a trust; open to the public.

**Mellon Udrigle** Hamlet near **Aultbea** with a superb white sand beach and views of the **Summer Isles** and **Gruinard**.

**Melrose** Small Borders town 6km (4mi) east of **Galashiels**. Near the centre are the ruins of Melrose Abbey, founded by **David I** in 1136 for the Cistercian order; the present church is mainly 15th century. It was a frequent casualty in Border raiding. **Alexander II** is buried here, as is the heart of **Robert I**. In the care of **Historic Scotland**, the Commendator's house is now the museum. Old Melrose, on a promontory formed by the River **Tweed**, was the site of a monastery founded in the 7th century by St **Aidan** in which St **Cuthbert** was trained. The early 19th-century Harmony Hall, in the care of the **National Trust for Scotland**, takes its name from the Jamaican plantation of its original owner; its splendid early 20th-century garden is open to the public, as is that of Priorwood, once the house of the publisher Adam **Black**.

**Melsetter** see **Hoy**

**Melville, Andrew** (1545–1622) Theologian, b. Baldovie, Angus. Seen as the founder of Scottish Presbyterianism, he developed the concept of the division between Church and State. Although he originally had royal support because of his anti-Catholic theories, he was later exiled. He was for a time Principal of **Glasgow University** and then of **St Andrews**.

**Melville, Arthur** (1855–1904) Artist, b. Loanhead-of-Guthrie, Angus. Outstandingly gifted as a painter in watercolour, Melville is best known for his paintings made on his expeditions to the Middle East and to Spain from the early 1880s onwards. He is also considered one of the **Glasgow Boys**, and frequently worked alongside James **Guthrie**, E A **Walton** and others of the school in Scotland and France.

**Melville, Henry Dundas, 1st Viscount** see **Dundas, Henry**

*Engraving of Melrose Abbey by John Slezer from* Theatrum Scotiae *(1693).*

**M**

**Melville, James** (1556–1614) Writer and reforming minister. Nephew of Andrew **Melville** and supporter of Presbyterianism. Exiled in England 1584–5, he was minister of **Anstruther** from 1586 until he was again exiled in 1606 by **James VI**. His writings include a lengthy autobiography and diary in **Scots** and *A Short Relation of the State of the Kirk of Scotland since the Reformation*. In 1588 when the king brought to Fife the crew of a Spanish Armada galleon wrecked on **Fair Isle**, he established a friendship with the captain.

**Melville, Robert Saunders Dundas, 2nd Viscount** see **Dundas, Robert Saunders**

**Melville Castle** Castle near **Dalkeith**. Designed by James **Playfair** in 1786–91 for Henry Dundas, later Viscount **Melville**, built on the site of an earlier castle. After World War II, it had various uses, including some years as a hotel, but it became derelict. It has now been restored and is once more a hotel.

**Melville House** Tall classical palace to the north of **Ladybank**, Fife, with formal forecourt built by James **Smith** for the 1st Earl of Melville (1697–1703). The severity of the exterior contrasts with the magnificent baroque woodwork within. Latterly a school, but now to be re-occupied as a house.

**Mennock** The Mennock Water flows down the Mennock Pass, on the road through the **Lowther Hills**, and then southwest to join the River **Nith** at the village of Mennock.

**Menstrie Castle** Approximately one half of a great quadrangular house in Menstrie, near **Alloa**, built by Sir William **Alexander**, 1st Earl of Stirling, restored 1961 as part of a housing estate; in the care of the **National Trust for Scotland**.

**Menteith** The district of Menteith lies between the rivers **Teith** and **Forth**. The Lake of Menteith is the only 'lake' in Scotland (the normal Scottish word being 'loch'); the name is probably due to confusion with the Scots word *laigh*, 'low ground'. The village of Port of Menteith is near the lake. See **Inchmahome** island; another smaller island is almost wholly occupied by the ruins of Talla Castle.

**Menteith, Sir John, Earl of Lennox** (fl. 1296–1320) In 1296 he was captured by the English, but was released in 1297 and served Edward I in local administration, acting as keeper of **Dumbarton**. He captured William **Wallace** in 1305, but fought for **Robert I** from 1307, and was a signatory to the Declaration of **Arbroath** in 1320.

**Menzies, Archibald** (1754–1842). Surgeon-naturalist, b. Weem near Aberfeldy. Starting as a gardener at the **Royal Botanic Garden, Edinburgh**, he studied medicine, eventually becoming surgeon in the Royal Navy. Sir Joseph Banks had him appointed surgeon with Captain Corbett to collect plants on his circumnavigation of the world (1786–9). So successful was this that the government appointed him as surgeon-naturalist with Captain George Vancouver. This voyage (1790–5) was especially to map the coastline of the Pacific in the northwest USA. His knowl-

*Silver thistle merk of James VI (1602).*

edge and skill prevented the loss of any crew from scurvy using spruce beer. He found many plants new to science which were later introduced by David **Douglas**. From this expedition he introduced the first monkey puzzle tree to cultivation. He is commemorated by the genus *Menziesia*, a relative of heather.

**Menzies, John** (1852–1935) Bookseller and newsagent, b. Edinburgh. Established a business in **Edinburgh** in 1833, which grew into a chain of bookstores and newsagents. Now Menzies Group, the company is involved in newspaper distribution and aviation ground handling services; the retail chain was sold to rival W H Smith in 1998.

**Menzies Castle** see **Castle Menzies**

**Merchiston Castle** 15th-century tower house in Edinburgh, the home of John **Napier**, restored in 1961 as part of Napier College, now **Napier University**. It was formerly a boys' school, which moved to the outskirts of Edinburgh in 1931. It contains an important painted ceiling of 1581 brought here from Prestongrange in 1964.

**merk** or **mark** Until the late 17th century a coin or monetary amount equal to two thirds of a pound Scots. It could also refer to English currency, and as the Scots pound became devalued it began to apply to a fixed amount of English pence.

**Merrick** Hill 19km (12mi) north of **Newton Stewart**, in the Galloway Forest Park. At 843m (2765ft) the highest hill in the **Southern Uplands**.

**M**

**Merse, the** The fertile lowlands of the Tweed valley south of the **Lammermuirs** and north of the River **Tweed**. Its name derives from Old English *mersc*, 'marsh', and its poor drainage was a hindrance to the armies and raiders who regularly passed through it. Once drained it became fine agricultural land.

**Mertoun** Pedimented classical mansion in the **Borders**, to the northeast of **Newtown St Boswells**, built by Sir William **Bruce** for the Scotts of Harden (1703); the previous house of 1677 stands nearby. Returned to its original form by Ian G **Lindsay** for the Duke of Sutherland (1953–6).

**Methil** Town in Fife, on the Firth of **Forth** to the southwest of **Leven**, once famous for its dockyards, established in the late 19th century principally for the export of **coal** from the collieries of the Wemyss family of **Wemyss Castle**. Mining was important. Methil joined with the former **fishing** village of Buckhaven to the southwest (which had strong historic links with the Netherlands). They formed a joint **burgh** from the early 20th century till 1975.

**Methlick** Estate village of Haddo, on the River **Ythan**, 11km (7mi) northwest of **Ellon**, Aberdeenshire. It has a fine parish church with saddleback tower by Maitland **Wardrop** (1865–7).

**Methodist Churches in Scotland** John Wesley made many visits to Scotland, but the initial success of Methodism was hampered by later controversy and it was difficult to maintain a sufficient number of itinerant preachers. Later 11 preachers were ordained which aided expansion to some extent. There was a modest increase in membership, especially in industrial areas, but Methodism had considerable success in **Shetland** from about 1819 and it became the second-largest denomination there, after the **Church of Scotland**.

**Methven** Village 10km (6mi) west of **Perth**. **Robert I** was defeated by the English here in 1306, soon after he was crowned king. The present church dates from 1781 with a spire of 1825, but the churchyard contains the 15th-century Methven Aisle from the previous church and also the remarkable neo-classical mausoleum by James **Playfair** (1792), built for the legendary beauty Mrs Graham, by her husband Thomas **Graham**, Lord Lynedoch. To the east is Methven Castle, a prominent landmark, a tall square house with circular angle towers built (1678–82) by Patrick Smythe, apparently designed by James **Smith**, its conservative form probably determined by the retention of earlier fabric.

**Mey, Castle of** see **Castle of Mey**

**Michael, the Great** see **Great Michael, the**

**Mid Calder** West Lothian village to the southeast of **Livingston**, just to the west of **East Calder**. It was once a stopping-point on the coaching route from **Glasgow** to **Edinburgh** and became prosperous in the 19th century with development of the shale-oil industry. The parish church was built in 1542 as the choir of a much larger church; the transepts were built by Brown and **Wardrop** in 1863. Calder House, to the west, has belonged to the Sandilands family since medieval times; the building dates from the 16th century with later additions. John **Knox** celebrated the reformed communion in the house in 1556, and Chopin was a guest in 1848. The huge stable court is now offices.

**Middelburg** see **staple**

**Middleton, John, 1st Earl of** (1608–74) Soldier and politician, b. Caldhame, near Forfar. After service in the French army, he returned to join the **Covenanters** and was second in command at **Philiphaugh**. Reconciled to the king by embracing the **Engagement**, he was captured at both **Preston** and Worcester, but escaped both times, latterly to France. In 1653 he was the military commander of the unsuccessful Royalist **Glencairn**'s Rising in the **Highlands**. As Earl of Middleton, C-in-C Scotland and royal commissioner after 1660, he fell from power in 1663 after confrontation with his arch-rival **Lauderdale**. He was sent to command a garrison in Tangier, where he died.

**Midhope** Tower house 6km (4mi) west of **South Queensferry**, built 1582 by Alexander Drummond, to which the Hope Earls of Linlithgow added a mansion in the later 17th century; it has a fine Renaissance gateway at the entrance to its forecourt.

**Midhowe Broch** see **Rousay**

**Midlothian** Former county of southeast central Scotland; formerly known as Edinburghshire, it included **Edinburgh** until 1929. From 1975–96 it was a district of **Lothian Region**, and, as Midlothian Council, it is now a unitary local authority; see maps on pp.394–5 and **local government**. Its administrative centre is **Dalkeith** and other towns include **Penicuik**, **Newtongrange** and **Bonnyrigg**. It was formerly noted for coal-mining and papermaking.

**Midlothian District** see **Midlothian** and **Lothian Region**

**Midmar Castle** Fine turreted castle, originally Ballogie, near **Echt**, Aberdeenshire, built in 1575 by George Bell for George Gordon, restored and reoccupied 1977–80. The roofless St Ninian's church nearby (1677) has a private door for the laird. George Bell was burnt in its churchyard in 1575.

**mile** see **weights and measures**, pp.382–4

M

**military roads** There were military roads in Scotland from Roman times, but they became important after the 1715 **Jacobite Rising**, when a network of roads was built by soldiers under the command of General George **Wade**, with bridges built by civilian contractors. These roads linked the **Lowlands** with a series of forts and barracks designed to deter a further rising. After the 1745 Rising the network was overhauled and much extended by Major William **Caulfeild**. The military roads were designed as strategic routes for marching troops to military objectives, but many of them formed the basis of civilian routes through the **Highlands**. After the Napoleonic Wars, roads for mainly military purposes were built from Carlisle to **Glasgow** and Portpatrick (for Ireland), and from east to west across Lanarkshire. The routes of some military roads are still in use, but in many instances the modern routes diverge from them, though their remains can still be traced.

**militia** A militia raised and commanded by the Scottish nobility became the main armed force at the disposal of the Crown in the Restoration era. Under **Charles II** it virtually replaced the standing army, apart from a few guards and garrisons. It was the militia that crushed the Earl of **Argyll**'s rising in 1685. Thereafter **James VII** deliberately dismantled the militia because he preferred to have a professional standing army to coerce his subjects if they resisted his Catholicising policies. This had the paradoxical effect of leaving his supporters disorganised at the time of the Revolution of 1688–9. Queen Anne formally vetoed a proposal for a restored Scots militia because she did not trust it to fight the French. Hanoverian governments refused to countenance a Scottish militia for fear it might turn **Jacobite**. Despite agitation in the 1760s (see **Poker Club**), it was not until the Militia Act of 1797 that a ballot system was established to call up Scots for compulsory paid military service anywhere within the UK in militia units; in contrast to the volunteer units who were unpaid and served only in their local area. By this time the legislation was resented and led to rioting. In 1854 the 1852 English Militia Act was applied to Scotland; this used a compulsory ballot to supplement voluntary enlistment.

**Mill, James** (1773–1836) Historian, philosopher and economist, b. Logie Pert, near Montrose. Employed by the Honourable East India Company in London, he published a history of British India (1817–18), notable for violent Whig bias. He was an ardent follower of the Utilitarian ideas of his friend Jeremy Bentham, with their stress on government action to secure the greatest

happiness for the greatest number. He also wrote on political economy and psychology and was the father of the rather more famous John Stuart Mill.

**Millennium Link** Project name for the reopening of the **Forth and Clyde** and **Union Canals**, undertaken by British Waterways between 1998 and 2001. It was the largest project in Scotland undertaken with grant assistance from the Millennium Commission, and was also assisted by the local authorities and enterprise companies on the route, and by the European Regional Development Fund. The canals had been severed in 1933 by the closure of the connecting locks and further split into sections by road- and house-building in the 1960s. Major works include restoration of the route through the Wester Hailes housing estate in **Edinburgh**, a new cut to the River Carron at **Grangemouth**, the world's first 'drop lock' at Dalmuir, and the spectacular 'Falkirk' Wheel', the world's first rotating boat lift, with its associated tunnel and new section of canal. The Wheel has become a major visitor attraction.

**Miller, Hugh** (1802–56) Geologist and writer, b. Cromarty. Largely self-taught, his early career as a stonemason developed his interest in geology. His most important work is *The Old Red Sandstone* (1841), but he also wrote poetry and many essays, most of which were collected after his death. He was involved in the controversy that led to the **Disruption** of the **Church of Scotland**, and started *The Witness*, newspaper of the evangelical side. It may have been overwork or the mental struggle between science and religion that led to his suicide in Portobello. His cottage in **Cromarty** is now a museum (in the care of the **National Trust for Scotland**).

**Miller, James** (1860–1947) Architect, b. Auchtergaven, Perthshire. His career began with the Caledonian Railway and he designed several important stations. He was the dominant architect in **Glasgow** in the earlier 20th century, designing the Royal Infirmary, the North British Locomotive Company Offices (now Springburn College) and the Union Bank. He also built the great hotels at **Turnberry** and **Peebles**, and planned that at **Gleneagles**.

**Miller, James** (1893–1987) Artist and teacher, b. Dennistoun, Glasgow. Travelled and painted widely in France, Italy and North Africa, and had a particular empathy with Spain. He also lived and painted on **Skye**. His strong watercolour style proved particularly effective in his paintings of the **Glasgow** Blitz.

**Miller, John** (1805–83) Civil engineer. He and Thomas **Grainger** were Scotland's leading railway engineers in the 1830s and 40s,

*Wee Willie Winkie, written by William Miller, illustration from Edward Hamilton Bell's* Nursery Numbers.

and as good as any in Britain at the time. Miller was probably the greatest designer of masonry railway viaducts of all time. His Ballochmyle Viaduct at **Mauchline** (1848) and his 40-arch Almond viaduct (1850), near **Ratho** on the **Edinburgh** and **Glasgow** Railway are outstanding.

**Miller, John** (1911–75) Artist and teacher, b. Glasgow. Particularly skilled in colour, he painted many scenes of the west coast and the **Clyde**, showing a marked French influence.

**Miller, Patrick** (1731–1815) Inventor. b. Glasgow. A pioneer of the steamboat, he launched one on the loch at **Dalswinton** (his own estate) in 1788, powered by an engine made by William **Symington**.

**Miller, William** (1810–72) Writer for children and furniture maker, b. Glasgow. Originally intending a medical career, he was forced into woodturning by ill-health. His works include *Wee Willie Winkie and other Songs* (published after his death).

**Millport** see **Cumbraes**

**Milnathort** Near the **Ochil Hills**, Perth and Kinross. Originally a small market town with ties to Burleigh Castle, it became a wool and spinning centre in the 19th century. Now largely a commuter town.

**Milne family** see **Mylne**

**Milngavie** (pronounced mill**guy**) (pop.12,795) Dormitory town 11km (7mi) northwest of **Glasgow**, it was once a mill town based on the River Allander. It expanded in the Industrial Revolution to encompass cotton and distilling, among other manufactures. It now has 2 reservoirs. Gavin's Mill, possibly the origin of the town's name, has been restored. To the north is the Mugdock Country Park, with the ruins of the 14th-century Mugdock Castle and the 19th-century mansion, Craigend Castle.

**Milroy, Jack (James Cruden)** (1915–2001) Comedian, b. Glasgow. Partner to Rikki **Fulton**, in their teddy-boy act 'Francie and Josie', he concentrated on live performance in the music-hall style.

**Milton of Campsie** Village on the Glazert Water, 3km (2mi) from **Kirkintilloch**, north of **Glasgow**. Once a 'mill town', hence its name, it is now a commuter village for Glasgow.

**Mina, Denise** (1966– ) Crime novelist, b. Glasgow. She trained in law and taught criminology and criminal law before turning to writing. She has written a trilogy comprising *Garnethill* (1998), *Exile* (2000) and *Resolution* (2002). In 2003 she published *Sanctum*.

**Minard** Small village on the west shore of **Loch Fyne**. To the south is Minard Castle, a giant Tudor Gothic house with lavish interiors built 1842–8 by John Thomas **Rochead**. It now has bed-and-breakfast and self-catering accommodation.

**mince and tatties** A traditional Scottish dish of minced beef cooked with onion, often also with carrot and turnip, and eaten with mashed or plain boiled potatoes.

**Minch, the** A channel separating the Outer **Hebrides** and the mainland of **Sutherland** and **Wester Ross**, rich in wildlife including dolphins, porpoises, whales and seals, and many rare birds. Allegedly home to a race of supernatural sea creatures, the Blue Men of the Minch, who lure sailors to their doom. The Minch is divided into two, the Minch, between the Isle of **Lewis** and the mainland, and the Little Minch, between the Isle of **Skye** and **Harris**.

**Minchmoor** Hill near **Traquair** (567m/1860ft). Site of a spring called the Cheese Well – so called as an offering (of cheese) should be left for the fairies to ensure a safe journey on the Minchmoor road, an ancient drove road renowned for banditry.

**Mingary Castle** A substantial ruin near the mouth of **Loch Sunart**. Fortifications date from the 13th century, were expanded in the late 16th and early 17th centuries, later refined into more comfortable accommodation. It was held at various times by the Maclans of **Ardnamurchan** and by the Campbells.

**Mingulay** Second most southerly island in the **Hebrides**, north of **Berneray**. With the third-highest cliffs in the UK it is a refuge for birds such as the guillemot and kittiwake. The last human inhabitant left in 1912.

**minor** In Scots law, a minor is a male over the age of 14 or a female over the age of 12, and under 18 (formerly 21); a pupil is a male under the age of 14 or a female under the age of 12. This system has been more or less superseded.

**Minto, Gilbert John Murray Kynynmound-Elliot, 4th Earl of** (1845-1914) Colonial administrator, b. London. A popular Governor-General of Canada (1898-1904), he was Viceroy of India (1905-10) and began India's move to self-rule, increasing native representation.

**Mitchell, (Arthur George) Sydney** (1856-1930) Architect, b. Larbert. He was the son of Sir Arthur Mitchell and pupil of Robert Rowand **Anderson**. He specialised in hospital buildings, notably the giant Craighouse, now **Napier University**, **Edinburgh**, and the Crichton Royal at **Dumfries** where he built the cathedral-like Crichton Memorial Church; at the end of his career in 1911 he built the United Free Church (now **Church of Scotland**) offices on Edinburgh's George Street.

**Mitchell, James Leslie** see **Gibbon, Lewis Grassic**

**Mitchell, Joseph** (1803-83) Engineer, b. Forres. Trained as an engineer by Thomas **Telford**, he followed his father as Chief Inspector to the **Commissioners for Highland Roads and Bridges**. He also contributed to the construction of railways and harbours, constructing much of the Highland Railway. His lively and controversial *Reminiscences of my Life in the Highlands* was published after his death.

**Mitchell, Sir Thomas Livingstone** (1792-1855) Explorer, b. Craigend, Stirlingshire. Surveyor-General of New South Wales from 1828, he made 4 major expeditions mapping eastern and tropical Australia.

**Mitchell Library** see **Glasgow**

**Mitchison, Naomi M** (née **Haldane**) (1897-1999) Writer, b. Edinburgh, daughter of J S Haldane. Married Gilbert Richard Mitchison, later a Labour MP, in 1916. During her long and eventful life she wrote a great deal of fiction, poetry and varied non-fiction. Her series of novels on Greece and Sparta were followed by *Corn King and Spring Queen* (1931), an evocation of Central Asia and the Eastern Mediterranean and *The Bull Calves* (1947), set in Scotland in the years following the 1745 **Jacobite Rising**. Her interest in travel and culture led to her becoming

Tribal Mother to the Bakgatla of Botswana. She was famed for her Socialist views and unorthodox lifestyle.

**Mither Tap** see **Bennachie**

**Mochrum, Old Place of** Two tower houses in Galloway, at the north end of Mochrum Loch, 5km (3mi) from the east shore of **Luce Bay**. Dating from the 15th and 16th centuries, they were linked together (1873) as an occasional residence for the 3rd Marquess of Bute, greatly enriched with formal garden by Robert Schultz Weir for the 4th Marquess (1903-8).

**Mod** The Royal National Mod, organised by An **Comunn Gaidhealach**, is Scotland's largest festival of Gaelic music and poetry. Held annually in a different venue each year, it was first held in 1892 in **Oban**. There are also a number of 'local' Mods held around Scotland and internationally.

**Moderate** After 1690, the **Church of Scotland** was Presbyterian but led by men like William **Carstares** who were deliberately moderate and conciliatory in their policies. With the forcible restoration of lay patronage in 1712 by the Westminster government, the Church of Scotland was afflicted with division by exponents of the rights of congregations to call ministers, and locked in endless conflict with the British government over the issue. From the 1750s a minority of able ministers, led by William **Robertson**, contrived to dominate the **General Assembly** with a programme of accepting and enforcing lay patronage, as a prelude to forging a more constructive and dignified relationship with the state. This Moderate Party was opposed by **Evangelicals** who parodied Moderates, often unfairly, as lacking pastoral and theological commitment. The Moderates finally lost control of the General Assembly in the late 18th century when a new spirit of missionary zeal and their failure to command respect from government made their conservatism obsolete.

**Moderator** The minister who acts as chair of the **General Assembly** of the **Church of Scotland**, an honorary 12-month post. Also, more generally, the minister, or nowadays sometimes elder, who presides over a Presbyterian church court.

**Moffat** Small town to the northeast of **Dumfries**. It became a centre for cattle theft, with the stolen beasts corralled in the **Devil's Beeftub**. Later it became a market town, and from the mid 17th century to the 1920s a spa resort based around two mineral wells. It is still a centre of tourism. Its exceptionally wide and spacious High Street is lined with 18th- and 19th-century hotels. Moffat House, now also a hotel, was designed by John **Adam** in 1762.

**Moffat, Robert** (1795–1883) Missionary, b. Ormiston, East Lothian. He began life as a gardener, before becoming a missionary in southern Africa with the London Missionary Society. He spent many years with the Tswana peoples in what is now Botswana. He translated the New Testament into Setswana and, with a colleague, also the Old Testament. Other publications include *Missionary Labours and Scenes in Southern Africa* (1842). He influenced David **Livingstone**, who married his daughter Mary.

**Moffat toffee** A kind of hard toffee, amber- and gold-striped with a sherbert layer, now made commercially by a **Moffat** family who have been making toffee for generations.

**Moidart** (Gaelic **Mùideart**) Area on the west coast, south of **Arisaig**, to the west of **Loch Shiel**. Loch Moidart is a sea loch north of the **Ardnamurchan** peninsula. 13th-century **Castle Tioram** stands on an islet off the south shore of the loch.

**Moine, the** A stretch of road across the **Sutherland** moors between Kyle of Tongue and Eriboll.

**Moine Thrust** A low-gradient geological fault extending along the northwest **Highlands** from **Loch Eriboll** to **Skye**, and along which metamorphic Moinian rocks moved northwestwards by 100km (63mi) over fossiliferous Low Palaeozoic sedmimentary rocks about 430 million years ago. It is best seen at **Knockan** Crags.

**Moir, David MacBeth** (1798–1851) Doctor and author, b. Musselburgh, East Lothian. Using the Greek delta sign as a pen name, he wrote poetry for *Blackwood's Magazine*, which he eventually came to edit, and the lively novel *The Life of Mansie Wauch, Tailor in Dalkeith* (1828).

**Molesworth, Mary Louisa** née **Stewart** (1839–1921) Writer, b. Rotterdam, she spent much of her childhood in Scotland. Best known as a writer of stories for children, such as *The Cuckoo Clock*, but also recognised for her ability in the supernatural field, her best collection being *Uncanny Tales*.

**Mollison, James Allan** (1905–59) Aviator, b. Glasgow. Made record-breaking flights both alone (Australia to England in under 9 days in 1931, England to South America in 1933) and with his wife Amy Johnson (first flight from England to USA 1933, from England to India, 1934).

**Monach Islands** Group of islands to the west of **North Uist**. Ceann Ear was inhabited until 1943.

**Monadhliath** A range of mountains between **Loch Ness** and the River **Spey**, featuring several **Munros**. Carn Dearg (945m/3100ft) is its highest point.

**Monar, Loch** see **Loch Monar**

**Monboddo, James Burnett, Lord** (1714–99) Judge and philosopher, b. Monboddo House, Kincardineshire. His eccentric work, *Origin and Progress of Language* (1773–92) postulated a relationship between humans and monkeys before Charles Darwin's *Origin of Species*. His views were more popular in London than in Scotland, and he made regular visits there, becoming a great friend of James **Boswell**.

**Monck** (or **Monk**), **General George, 1st Duke of Albemarle** (1608–70) English soldier. A favourite of Oliver Cromwell's, he was sent to pacify Scotland in 1650, and was largely successful, defeating the Scots at **Dunbar**. Returning to Scotland after Cromwell's death, he played a major part in the restoration of **Charles II**, seeing no future in the chaotic government of Richard Cromwell.

**Moness Falls** Spectacular waterfall on the Moness Burn, a tributary of the **River Tay**, at the top of the Birks of **Aberfeldy**.

**Monessie Gorge** Wild gorge channelled by the River Spean, a scenic feature of the West Highland Railway line between **Roybridge** and Tulloch.

**Moniack Castle** Castle 10km (6mi) to the east of **Inverness**, a 17th-century L-plan house, remodelled 1804–7. The Fraser family now run a winery there, some of the wines from local products such as elderflower and silver birch; they also produce liqueurs, fruit jellies etc.

**Moniack Mhor** A restored croft house in the hills to the south-west of **Inverness**, now run by the Moniack Trust (with support from the Avron Foundation) to provide courses for writers. It is also available for holiday letting.

**Monifieth** Small town on the **Angus** coast 9km (6mi) east of **Dundee**. Industries have included textile machinery, carpet weaving, ironfounding and quarrying.

**Monkland Canal** James **Watt** was commissioned to build this canal to bring coal from the Monkland fields; it joined the **Forth and Clyde Canal** at Port Dundas in the north of **Glasgow**. Work began in 1770, but funding proved difficult, and though taken over by Andrew Stirling it was not finished until 1794. It provided vital transport for the new iron industry from 1830, but was abandoned in the 1940s, and much of it was piped and built over in the 1960s for the M8 motorway.

**Monklands** Area to the east of **Glasgow**; from 1975 to 1996 a district of **Strathclyde Region**; see maps on pp.394–5 and **local government**.

M

**Monktonhall** Small village to the south of **Musselburgh**, now a suburb. Monktonhall Colliery was the last of the Lothian deep mines, opened in 1953, closed 1998. Monkton House is a Scottish Renaissance mansion of the 16th and 17th centuries, built by the Hays of Yester, partly rebuilt in the 18th century.

**Monreith** Small village in Galloway, on Monreith Bay 8km (5mi) west of **Whithorn**. To the north is the classical Monreith house by Alexander Stevens (1791) with Greek Doric porch by Robert Smirke (1821); the gardens were greatly developed by Sir Herbert Maxwell in the late 19th and early 20th centuries. The early 17th-century Old Place of Monreith was restored in 1985; within the park are the remains of Myreton Castle, a motte with a fragment of the 15th-century castle of the McCullochs.

**Monro, Alexander, 'Monro Primus', 'Monro Secundus', 'Monro Tertius'** Grandfather (1697–1767), father (1733–1817) and son (1773–1859), who followed one another as professors at **Edinburgh University**. Monro Primus was a distinguished anatomist, who helped found Edinburgh Royal Infirmary and wrote several works on anatomy and medicine.

**Monro, Alexander 'Secundus'** see above

**Monro, Alexander 'Tertius'** see above

**Monro, Donald** (c.1500–c.1575) Archdeacon of the Isles. His *Description of the Western Isles* (c.1548) is one of the earliest detailed accounts of the area.

**Mons Graupius, Battle of** The first documented battle in Scotland (recorded by Tacitus in *Agricola*) fought in AD 83 between the Romans and tribes led by Calgacus, allegedly resulting in terrible but not disabling losses on the side of the tribes. The site of the battle is much debated, but may have been near **Bennachie** in **Aberdeenshire**.

**Mons Meg** see **Edinburgh**

**Montgomerie, Alexander** (c.1545–c.1610) Poet, b. near Beith, Ayrshire, enjoying great but temporary influence at the court of **James VI**; he was a member of the **Castalian band**. His Catholicism and political associations led to his banishment as a traitor in 1597. His best-known works are 'The Cherrie and the Slae' (1597) and the sonnet 'To his Mistress'.

**Montgomerie, Colin** (1963– ) Golfer, b. Glasgow. Consistently the best golfer on the European Tour for much of the 1990s, he has never made the breakthrough to win a major. He lost a play-off in the 1994 US Open, and suffered the same fate the following year in the US PGA. In 1996 he was the World No.2 player, and at the 2002 Ryder Cup he was the epitome of self-control when his magnificent performance played a key role in the European victory.

**Montgomery, Catriona** (1947– ) Gaelic poet, b. Roag, Skye. Her verse, which employs both modern and traditional forms, includes personal reflections on her own life, her community and island, and satires. Her poetry has been published in magazines and anthologies and in the collection *Rè na h-Oidhche* (1994).

**Montgomery's Highlanders** During the Seven Years' War William Pitt the Elder, faced by a shortage of infantry, decided to recruit troops from the former **Jacobite** areas of the **Highlands**. A commission was given to the reliably Whig Archibald Montgomery, son of the Earl of Eglinton, who established in 1757 the 77th Regiment of Foot, also known as Montgomery's Highlanders. They fought against the French in America, after which they were invited to settle there. Many did, and fought in the War of the American Revolution on the side of the British.

**Montrose** A town in Angus at the mouth of the South **Esk** River, with a commercial port, leisure harbour and holiday beach. It was formerly a **linen** manufacturing and brewing centre. It has one of the widest High Streets in Britain, with an interesting series of 17th- and 18th-century mansions entered from its closes. The skyline is dominated by Gillespie **Graham**'s parish church spire (1832) and there is a particularly interesting series of public buildings, notably the Town House (1763), the Academy (1815) by the local architect David Logan and the Museum (1839) by John Henderson. Montrose Basin is a large tidal bay behind the town, with a Local Nature Reserve important for bird life. Its southern suburb is Ferryden, a former **fishing** village, which has been a North Sea oil-supply base since the 1970s. The House of **Dun** is nearby.

**Montrose, James Graham, 5th Earl and 1st Marquis of** (1612–50) Soldier. Originally a supporter of the **Covenant**, he led Scottish troops in the **Bishops' Wars**. Subsequently he quarrelled with his great rival the Earl of **Argyll**, insisting that the concessions already made by **Charles I** were sincere and sufficient. In brilliant campaigns in 1644, he defeated a succession of Covenanting armies, drawing heavily on support from Highland clans and on Ulster MacDonalds brought over by Alasdair **MacColla**. He aspired to be the King's principal subject in Scotland, but was routed by David **Leslie** at **Philiphaugh** and went into exile in Europe. Returning to Scotland in an attempt to avenge the execution of **Charles I**, he recruited heavily in **Orkney**, before invading the north of Scotland. He was routed by Covenanting cavalry at **Carbisdale** in 1650 and fled.

Captured by Macleod of Assynt, he was hanged in May 1650 in the High Street of **Edinburgh**. His remains were given proper burial in 1661 in St Giles'.

**Monymusk** Planned village near **Aberdeen**, laid out in 1716, with the 12th-century Augustinian church of St Mary, containing a Pictish symbol stone. Monymusk House is a fine 16th-century tower house, enlarged in 1716, after purchase by Sir Francis Grant. The Monymusk Reliquary, a tiny wood and metal casket, also known as the *Brec Bennoch* (Gaelic, meaning 'speckled, peaked one'), probably dates from the 8th century and is linked with St **Columba**; it is now in the **Museum of Scotland**.

**Moon, Lorna** (**Nora Helen Wilson Low**) (1886–1930) Author and screenwriter, b. Strichen, near Fraserburgh, she married William Hebditch and went to Canada with him. She later married Walter Moon. She went to Hollywood and became a scriptwriter and her film credits include *The Affairs of Anatol* (1921) starring Gloria Swanson, and *Upstage* (1926) starring Norma Shearer. She horrified her Scottish family and neighbours by publishing *Doorways in Drumorty* (1925), short stories exposing the drawbacks of life in a small Scottish village. Her other books include *Dark Star* (1929). She had a child by William De Mille, brother of Cecil B De Mille, who was brought up by the film magnate. *The Collected Works of Lorna Moon* was published in 2002.

**Moore, Sir John** (1761–1809) Soldier, b. Glasgow. A much-travelled soldier, Moore served in the British army in America, France, Holland and Egypt, being particularly successful in the Peninsular Wars against Napoleon. His final victory was won in desperate circumstances at Corunna in northwest Spain, where he was killed, but immortalised in the poem by Charles Wolfe, 'The Burial of Sir John Moore at Corunna'.

**Moorfoot Hills** A range of hills to the south of **Edinburgh**, a continuation of the **Lammermuir Hills**, source of the River South **Esk**.

**Morar** A peninsula in the southwest **Highlands**, with a beach of fine white sand, which has been used for the manufacture of optical instruments. Loch Morar, an inland loch, is the deepest loch in Britain at 296m (971ft), and home to Morag, a smaller relative of the **Loch Ness** monster. The River Morar, on the other hand, is Britain's shortest river, tumbling into the sea; a hydro-electric scheme was constructed in 1948.

**Moray** Area south of the **Moray Firth**, once of great extent and whose local rulers, such as **Macbeth**, could challenge for the Scottish crown. The earldom of Moray was suppressed by **David I** in 1130, but re-established by **Robert I** in 1312. A former county

(also called Morayshire and earlier Elginshire), from 1975–96, with enlarged extent, it was a district of **Grampian Region**. As Moray Council, it is now a unitary local authority. See maps on pp.394–5 and **local government**. The administrative centre is **Elgin** and other towns include **Forres**, **Lossiemouth** and **Buckie**.

**Moray, James Stewart, Earl of** (1531–70) Regent of Scotland in the minority of **James VI**. One of several illegitimate sons of **James V**, thus half-brother to **Mary, Queen of Scots**, he became a powerful figure in the Protestant government of Scotland. Implicated, at least by foreknowledge, in the murders of **Rizzio** and **Darnley**, his gift for diplomatic absences frequently served him well. Although victorious for the regency against the forces of Mary and the Hamiltons at the Battle of Langside, the majority of the nobles turned against him, and he was assassinated at **Linlithgow** by a Hamilton.

**Moray, James Stewart, Earl of** (c.1560–92) Son of Sir James Stewart of Doune, his title came from his marriage to a daughter of the above earl. He was involved in a feud with the Earl of Huntly and his killing by Huntly inspired the ballad 'The Bonnie Earl of Moray'.

**Moray, John Randolph, 3rd Earl of** see **Randolph, John, 3rd Earl of Moray**

**Moray, Thomas Randolph, 1st Earl of** see **Randolph, Thomas, 1st Earl of Moray**

**Moray District** see **Moray, Grampian Region**

**Moray Firth** An arm of the North Sea, about 56km (35mi) long, extending northeast from **Inverness** to create over 800km (500mi) of coastline. A haven for wildlife, dolphins, porpoises and whales, but also important for **fishing** and the **oil** industry. See also **Beauly Firth**.

**Moray House College of Education** see **Edinburgh University**

**Morayshire** see **Moray**

**More, Jacob** (1740–93) Artist, b. Edinburgh. During his lifetime he enjoyed a wide reputation as a landscape painter, first recognised for his scenes of the Falls of **Clyde**, painted in the early 1770s. The success of these encouraged him to move to Rome, where he remained for the rest of his life, making paintings of the Italian landscape (from which he prospered) and becoming a central figure amongst the Scottish community there.

**Morgan, Edwin** (1920– ) Poet, translator and critic, b. Glasgow. He was educated at **Glasgow University** and taught there after war service; now Emeritus Professor of English. He served in the

275

Middle East in World War II, an area which inspired some of his poetry. Among his many collections of poetry are *The Second Life* (1968), *From Glasgow to Saturn* (1973), *Sonnets from Scotland* (1984), *Sweeping Out the Dark* (1994) and *A Love of Life* (2003). His translations include *Beowulf* (1952) and poems by Boris Pasternak and Federico Garcia Lorca, among others, in *Rites of Passage* (1976). He has translated Myakovsky (*Wi the Haill Voice*, 1972), *Cyrano de Bergerac* (1992) and Racine's *Phèdre* into Scots. His *Collected Poems* were published in 1990 and *Collected Translations* in 1996. One of his many honours is that of Glasgow City Laureate, and in 2004 he was appointed Scots **Makar** (equivalent to the UK Poet Laureate).

**Morison, Roderick** see **Clarsair Dall**

**Morlich, Loch** see **Loch Morlich**

**mormaer** A governor of a Celtic, originally Pictish, province, the title giving way to 'earl' (in Latin *comes*) from c.1100. Probably from Gaelic *mor* 'great' and *maer* 'steward'. See also **toiseach**.

**Mormond Hill** Hill 234m (768ft) high, overlooking the village of Strichen, Aberdeenshire. A white horse has been cut into the side nearest the village (c.1800) and on another a stag. Now the site of radio and telecommunications masts.

**Morningside** Later Victorian and Edwardian residential area of south **Edinburgh**, famed for its supposed gentility and the refined accent of its inhabitants.

**Morris, Margaret** (1891–1980) Dancer, choreographer, teacher, b. London. She founded a school of dancing in London and a summer school in Devon and, later, schools in French and other British towns. In 1939 she settled in Glasgow with J D **Fergusson**, and founded the Celtic Ballet Club. Her dancing technique, known as the Margaret Morris Movement, is now an international dance and exercise organisation.

**Morris, Thomas, 'Old Tom'** (1821–1908) Golfer, b. St Andrews. Nicknamed the 'Nestor of Golf', but originally a **golf** ball maker and greenkeeper, he turned professional and won the British Championship belt in 1861, 1862, 1864 and 1866.

**Morris, Thomas, 'Young Tom'** (1851–75) b. St Andrews. Golfer, son of 'Old Tom' Morris. Won the British championship belt outright (after 3 successive wins, 1868–1870) and won the championship a fourth time in 1872, when his name was the first to be inscribed on the claret jug. See also **golf**.

**Morrocco, Alberto** (1917–98) Artist, b. Aberdeen. He was for many years Head of Painting at Duncan of Jordanstone College of Art, **Dundee**. His Italian parentage and his extensive travels helped inspire his landscapes, still lifes and interiors, vivid in shape, colour and pattern. He was also a successful portrait painter, his sitters including Her Majesty the Queen Mother.

**Mortimer's Deep** Stretch of water between **Inchcolm** and Braefoot Bay, **Firth of Forth**. Allegedly named after the 12th-century William de Mortimer, a loose-living noble who bought himself a burial place at **Inchcolm Abbey**. However, on its way over the water, his coffin slid over the edge of the boat and was lost, implying that his wicked life made him unfit to rest on Inchcolm. (The story is vividly portrayed in a novel by Simon Taylor, *Mortimer's Deep* (1995)).

**Mortlach Kirk** see **Dufftown**

**Morton, Alan Lauder** (1893–1971) Footballer, b. Glasgow. Played throughout his career for **Rangers**, when he was not collecting his 31 caps for Scotland, one of which was won for participating in the 1928 defeat of England at Wembley. Known as the 'wee blue devil'.

**Morton, James Douglas, 4th Earl of** (c.1516–81) Regent of Scotland. A leader in the assassination of **Rizzio**, he was pardoned by **Mary, Queen of Scots**, was then implicated in the murder of **Darnley**, and was a member of the group of nobles who defeated Mary and **Bothwell** at **Carberry Hill**. Elected regent in 1572, he tried to draw Scotland closer to England, particularly in regard to the Church. Although his firm control of lawless factions was welcomed, his nepotism was not, and he was eventually brought down by Captain James Stewart, allegedly for his part in Darnley's killing. Ironically he was beheaded in the Grassmarket in **Edinburgh** by the **maiden**, whose introduction he had engineered.

**Morton Castle** Ruined 14th-century hunting seat of the Douglases in Nithsdale, to the north of **Thornhill**, with a gatehouse similar to that of **Caerlaverock**. In the care of **Historic Scotland**.

**Moruisg** A mountain, a **Munro** of 928m (3045ft), south of Glen Carron in Glencarron and Glenuig Forest.

**Morven** Hill on **Deeside**, 871m (2857ft), 8km (5mi) north of **Ballater**; it was climbed by Queen Victoria in 1859.

**Morven** Hill in **Caithness**, 706m (2316ft), 14km (9mi) north of **Helmsdale**.

**Morvern** (Gaelic **Marbhainn**) Peninsula in the southwest **Highlands**, bounded by **Loch Sunart**, **Loch Linnhe** and the Sound of **Mull**.

**Moss Morran** see **Cowdenbeath**

**Mossgiel** Farm near **Mauchline**, Ayrshire, farmed by Robert

Burns and his brother from 1783. Though Robert was not a good farmer, this was a period of relative prosperity, and he was able to work seriously on his poetry. It was during this period of his life that he met his future wife Jean **Armour**.

**Motherwell** (pop. 30,311) Industrial town of the **Clyde** valley, near **Glasgow**, it took its name from an early 'healing well'. Until 1975 it had joint **burgh** status with its near neighbour **Wishaw**. An agricultural area till the Industrial Revolution, its heavy industry is now giving way to electronics and call centres. It was the centre of Scotland's steel industry (see David **Colville**), and also had structural engineering and crane-building firms. It is the administrative centre of **North Lanarkshire** Council. The Motherwell Heritage Centre gives a good overview of its history. See also **Dalziel**.

**Motherwell District** see **Strathclyde Region**

**Motherwell Football Club** Founded 1886, their home ground is Fir Park. They were twice winners of the Scottish Cup (1952 and 1991) and league champions in 1932.

**Motherwell, William** (1797–1835) Poet and anthologist, b. Glasgow. His own poetry was rather sentimental, but he made important collections of songs and ballads, notably *Minstrelsy: Ancient and Modern* (1827), which brought him the friendship of Sir Walter **Scott** and James **Hogg**.

**Moulin** near Pitlochry. Once an important waypoint in the **Highlands** – the Moulin Inn opened in 1695 – it declined once **Wade**'s military road took a route through **Pitlochry** in the 1720s. A settlement of very ancient origin, as shown by the numerous standing stones and hut circles in the locality, and the fine medieval stones in the kirkyard.

**Mound, the** Causeway and dam carrying the road across the mouth of the River **Fleet**, reclaiming land upstream, to the southwest of **Golspie**, in **Sutherland**. It was built in 1813–16 to a design by Thomas **Telford**. The Mound Alderwoods National Nature Reserve is nearby.

**Mound, the** see **Edinburgh**

**mountaineering** see p.278

**Mount Benger** Yarrow, near **St Mary's Loch**. A farm leased by James **Hogg**, an unsuccessful venture financially, perhaps partly due to his renowned hospitality. The Gordon Arms here was the scene of his last meeting with Sir Walter **Scott**.

**Mount Oliphant** Farm near Alloway, rented by Robert **Burns**'s father William from 1765–77, when Robert was a young boy.

**Mount Stuart House** see **Bute**

**Mounth** Mountainous country south of the **Cairngorms**, stretch-

*Mousa Broch, Shetland.*

ing from **Drumochter** almost to the east coast. Comprises a large number of **Munros** and includes the **Lochnagar** massif, **Glen Esk** and **Glen Clova**. The glens are linked by the Mounth Roads, ancient drove roads such as Capel Mounth, which runs from Glen Clova to **Ballater**. It effectively cut off the northeast of Scotland from the area to the south, hence the development of the Northeast's distinctive character. In the past the name probably referred to a wider area, stretching further west.

**Mousa, Broch of** A broch on a small island off the east coast of mainland **Shetland**, the best-preserved in Scotland, dating probably from the 1st century BC to the 3rd AD. It figures in two Icelandic sagas as a refuge for Viking-Age lovers.

**Moy** Village near **Inverness**, the seat of the Clan Mackintosh, who now have the most modern chief's house in Scotland, built in the 1950s. On 16 February 1746, Hanoverian troops, led by Lord Loudon, sallied out of Inverness to try to capture Charles Edward **Stewart**, who was staying at Moy Hall, but were ambushed and routed by **Jacobite** forces.

**MSP** Member of the **Scottish Parliament**

**Muchalls** Fishing village on the northeast coast, 7km (4mi) north of **Stonehaven**, with an Episcopal church of 1831. Nearby is Muchalls House, built 1619–27 by Alexander Burnett of Leys, and remarkably complete and unaltered, still with its barmkin. The interior has rich plasterwork dated 1624.

**Muck** (Gaelic **Eilean nam Muic**, meaning 'island of the pigs') Smallest of the **Small Isles** in the Inner **Hebrides**, southwest of **Eigg**. A very fertile island, it is home to many birds and surrounded by marine life. Visited by **Boswell** and Johnson, who recorded that the owner at the time was so embarrassed by the name that he tried to change it to Monk.

# MOUNTAINEERING AND HILLWALKING

In the late 19th and early 20th century, mountainering was a leisure activity of the upper classes, stemming from developments in the Alps and the founding of the Alpine Club; the Scottish Mountaineering Club (SMC) was founded in 1889. Early climbers are commemorated in the names of some of the peaks of the **Cuillins**: Sgurr Alasdair (Alexander **Nicolson**); Sgurr Thormaid (Norman Collie: (1859–1942) a London Professor of Chemistry who was an outstanding early climber); Sgurr Mhic Choinnich (John Mackenzie (1856–1933), a local guide and expert climber).

During the Depression of the interwar period many unemployed workers from Clydeside escaped from the deserted shipyards to the hills and a whole new working-class climbing culture developed, notably with the Craigdhu Club. After World War II, mountaineering became an increasingly popular sport, ranging from world-class rock-climbing (see Dougal **Haston**) to plain enjoyment of the hills without undue risk. Scottish mountains should not be underestimated; climbing, especially in winter, is highly valued by expert climbers. And conditions can be arctic rather than alpine, at altitudes which would classify them as mere hills in the Alps. Voluntary mountain-rescue teams in the various areas are supported by the Air-Sea Rescue service at RAF **Kinloss**.

The attraction of the sport is increased for many by classification of the hills and the aim to climb all those in one category, especially **Munros** (hills above 3000ft (917m), known as Munro-bagging. **Corbetts** are hills over 2500ft (762m) and **Donalds** are hills in the Lowlands over 2000ft (610m). Lists of these, altered from time to time, are published by the SMC's Scottish Mountaineering Trust, which also publishes a range of detailed guidebooks. The classic account of the sport is W H Murray's *Mountaineering in Scotland* (1947).

Before mountaineering became an organised sport, however, many people climbed the hills for all sorts of reasons: hunters, keepers, ghillies; soldiers (Sgurr nan Spainteach in **Kintail** is named for the Spanish soldiers who fought in the 1719 **Jacobite rising**); mapmakers; surveyors (see William **Roy**). See also **skiing**.

*Ben Nevis from the east.*

**Muckle Flugga** Uninhabited island, north of **Unst, Shetland**, the northernmost point of Britain, on the same latitude as the southernmost point of Greenland. Its **lighthouse** was built in 1858 by David Stevenson.

**Muckle Skerry** see **Pentland Skerries**

**Mugdock** see **Milngavie**

**Muick, Loch** see **Loch Muick**

**Mùideart** see **Moidart**

**Muir, Edwin** (1887–1959) Poet, critic and translator, b. Deerness, Orkney. His early poetry (and indeed much of his later work) was infused by his socialist principles and interest in Europe; collections include *Chorus of the Newly Dead* (1926), *The Narrow Place* (1943) and *The Labyrinth* (1949). Along with his wife, Willa **Muir**, he translated contemporary European literature, including works by Kafka and Feuchtwanger. His critical works include a study of John Knox. He was criticised by supporters of the Scots language for his belief, expressed in *Scott and Scotland* (1936), that use of English was essential for a national literature. After World War II he worked for the British Council in Prague and Rome, and he was for a time Warden of **Newbattle Abbey** College.

**Muir, John** (1838–1914) Naturalist, b. Dunbar, East Lothian. Moved with his family to the USA in 1849, becoming an inventor until an industrial accident cost him an eye in 1867. He then explored the wild areas of the west, developing his interest in many aspects of natural history. He led a campaign to establish Yosemite National Park in 1890 and helped to form the Sierra Club in 1892. His books include *My First Summer in the Sierra* (1911) and *The Yosemite* (1912). He is regarded as one of the first environmentalists and the father of ecology. The John Muir Trust was founded in Scotland in 1983 to further his ideals and now has care of 7 large areas of wild land, including **Knoydart, Schiehallion, Ben Nevis** and parts of **Skye**. His birthplace in **Dunbar** is now a museum.

**Muir, Thomas** (1765–99) **Advocate** and parliamentary reformer, b. Glasgow. Supporting the extension of the vote to all men over 21, he was also involved in radical and even revolutionary politics, and was arrested in 1793, escaping to France. He returned to **Edinburgh** to stand trial and was deported to Australia. He again escaped, but while on a Spanish ship he was wounded in a clash with the British, and died in France of his wounds.

**Muir, Willa** née **Anderson** (1890–1970) Novelist, poet and

*John Muir (1907).*

translator, b. Montrose, of Shetland parents. Married to Edwin **Muir**, and co-translator of Kafka and Feuchtwanger. Her novel *Imagined Corners* (1935), is an analysis of Scottish small-town life. She wrote on the role of women in society, notably in *Mrs Grundy in Scotland* (1936).

**Muiravonside Country Park** Large park on the River **Avon**, 5km (3mi) southwest of **Linlithgow**, with gardens, woodland and parkland, the latter including a disused mine shaft.

**Muirfield Links** Golf course in **Gullane**, East Lothian. Home of the Honourable Company of Edinburgh Golfers, the world's earliest **golf** club. Opened in 1891, it is one of the finest and most testing golf courses in the world, and is regularly host to the Open Championship.

**Muir of Ord** Sizeable village in **Ross and Cromarty**, 4km (3mi) north of **Beauly**, developed alongside the railway in the late 19th century. Its church and congregation were burnt by the Macdonalds in 1603. In the 1960s and 70s it was the headquarters of the Logan engineering firm.

**Mull, Isle of** (Gaelic **Muile, An t-Eilean Muileach**) One of the largest of the Inner **Hebrides**, to the west of **Oban**. Its main settlement is **Tobermory**, a late 18th-century **fishing** village. The narrow-gauge Mull and West Highland Railway runs from **Craignure** to **Torosay Castle**. Other places of interest include **Duart Castle**, the 13th-century home of the Macleans, MacKinnon's Cave, many standing stones and a stone circle at Lochbuie. To the west are the islands of **Iona** and **Staffa**. Ferries run from **Oban** to Craignure and from **Lochaline** to Fishnish on the northeast coast.

**Mullach an Rathain** see **Liathach**

**Mullach Coire Mhic Fhearchair** Remote mountain, a **Munro** (1019m/3342ft) in **Wester Ross**, 11km (7mi) north of **Kinlochewe**.

**Mullardoch, Loch** A large, very remote loch, to the north of **Glen Affric**, surrounded by mountains, many of them (**Munros**), now dammed as part of a hydroelectric scheme.

**Mullen, Jim** (1945– ) Jazz guitarist, b. Glasgow. Formed Morrissey Mullen with Dick Morrissey in 1975, later worked with several groups including Vinegar Joe, as well as with the jazz vocalist Claire Morton.

**Mull of Galloway** see **Galloway**

**Mull of Kintyre** see **Kintyre**

**multure** (pronounced **moo**ter) A duty, originally a proportion of the grain ground, payable to the owner of the mill. The word derives ultimately from Latin *molere,* 'to grind'.

**Muness Castle** see **Unst**

**Mungo, St** see **Kentigern, St**

**Munro** Name given to mountains in Scotland over 914.4m (3000ft) high: the list is frequently revised, but currently 284 peaks are considered to be Munros. The original *Munro's Tables* were compiled by Sir Hugh Thomas **Munro** (1856–1919). In 1891 Munro surveyed Scottish mountains above 3000ft (914.4m) and catalogued 236 as Munros. Collecting Munros or 'Munro-bagging' – by climbing them – is now a popular sport. See also **Corbett, mountaineering.**

**Munro, Donnie** see **Runrig**

**Munro, Sir Hector, of Novar** (1725–1805) Soldier, b. Ross and Cromarty. In the service of the East India Company, in 1764 he won the Battle of Buxar, which confirmed the Company's grip on Bengal and Bihar. He fared less well 16 years later in South India against Tipu Sultan of Mysore, but finished his career as an effective corps commander under Eyre Coote.

**Munro, Sir Hugh Thomas** see **Munro**

**Munro, Neil** (1864–1930) Journalist and novelist, b. Inveraray. Editor of the Glasgow *Evening News,* his novels include historical romances such as *John Splendid* (1898) and *The New Road* (1914). He is most remembered for his comic stories about a Clyde puffer, collected as *Para Handy and Other Tales* (1931), originally published in the *Evening News.*

**Murchison, Sir Roderick Impey** (1792–1871) Geologist, b. Tarradale, near Muir of Ord. He established portions of the geological timeline: the Silurian system and, with Adam Sedgwick, the Devonian system. He participated in a major geological survey of Russia, and his interest in Australian geology resulted in the naming after him of the Murchison River. The Murchison Falls in Uganda are also named after him. He became Director of the Geological Survey in 1855.

**Murchison, Revd Thomas Moffat** (1907–84) Minister and Gaelic writer, b. Govan. Brought up on a croft at Kylerhea, **Skye**, he was active in the Church of Scotland in **Glenelg** and at St Columba, Copland Rd, **Glasgow**. He was Chairman of the Highland Development League, established in 1936 by himself and Dr Lachlan Grant, Ballachulish, and was a formative influence on modern **Highland** economic development. He was a prolific writer in **Gaelic** and edited numerous Gaelic journals, notably the Gaelic Supplement of **Life and Work**.

**Murdock, William** (originally **Murdoch**) (1754–1839) Engineer, b. Lugar, Ayrshire. He developed many innovations for the mining industry in Cornwall, in association with Matthew Boulton and James **Watt**, but his greatest achievement was the adaptation of coal gas for lighting, first in his own home at Redruth, Cornwall.

**Mure, Elizabeth, of Rowallan** (c.1315–c.1355) First wife of **Robert II**, she gave birth to the future **Robert III**, Robert, Duke of Albany and Alexander Stewart, 'Wolf of **Badenoch**'. A papal dispensation regularising her marriage was only secured in 1347, casting possible doubt on the legitimacy of her offspring.

**Mure, Sir William** (1594–1657) Poet, b. Rowallan, Ayrshire. A Royalist and Protestant, he fought at Marston Moor. His poetry was largely religious – *Psalms* (1630), *The True Crucifixe for True Catholikes* (1629) – except for a fine translation of parts of Virgil's *Aeneid.*

**Murray, Charles** (1864–1961) Poet and engineer, b. Alford, Aberdeenshire. He spent much of his life in South Africa, where he wrote nostalgic but not excessively sentimental poems about the countryside of his Scottish home, in the dialect of the Northeast. His major collection is *Hamewith* (1900); it enjoyed success on its republication in the 1980s.

**Murray, Chic** (1919–85) Comedian, b. Greenock. After working as a double act with his wife Maidie Dickson, he became known as a solo performer for his surreal humour and his 'bunnet'. Also an actor, he appeared in films such as *Casino Royale* (1967) and *Gregory's Girl* (1981).

**Murray, Lord George** (c.1700–60) Soldier. Fought on the **Jacobite** side in 1715 and 1719, was pardoned in 1726, but fought as a lieutenant general for Charles Edward **Stewart** in the 1745 Rising, winning victories at **Prestonpans** and **Falkirk**. He disapproved of the decision to give battle at **Culloden**, but fought gallantly in the action, before escaping abroad. He died in exile in the Netherlands.

**Murray, Sir James Augustus Henry** (1837–1915) Lexicographer, b. Denholm near Hawick. He spent 36 years editing the *Oxford English Dictionary*, which was only finished in 1928, after his death. It was the first dictionary based on historical principles, tracing each word from its earliest known use. His other works included *The Dialect of the Southern Counties of Scotland* (1873). See also **dictionaries**, p.108.

**Murray, Sir John, of Broughton** (1715–77) Soldier, b. Broughton, near Peebles. Secretary to Prince Charles Edward **Stewart**, he was captured at **Culloden** and saved himself by betraying his **Jacobite** comrades.

**Murray, John** Publishing company established in London by John Murray (1745–93), b. Edinburgh, and run by successive John Murrays until 2002, till then one of the few family-run publishers remaining. The second Murray (1778–1843) was Byron's publisher, also issuing the travels of Mungo **Park**, Belzoni and others. His son (1808–92) published David **Livingstone** and Samuel **Smiles**.

**Murray, Sir John** (1841–1914) Marine zoologist, b. Ontario, Canada, of Scottish parents. He was one of the naturalists on the Challenger Expedition (1872–6) and became editor of the *Reports* of its results. In 1910, along with Lawrence Pullar, he produced (in 5 volumes) the first and only survey of the Scottish freshwater lochs, providing bathymetric and biological details of 568 lochs. Surveyors included many leading European scientists of the age. It was funded by Pullars of Perth (dry-cleaners and dyers) and dedicated to the memory of Frederick Pullar, who drowned while saving skaters when ice gave way on Airthrey Loch, **Bridge of Allan**.

**Murray, John** (1938– ) Gaelic poet and short-story writer, b.

*Chic Murray, smoking a large pipe given to him by Hugh MacDiarmid, which once belonged to Sir Harry Lauder.*

Barvas, Lewis. Formerly Editorial Officer, Gaelic Books Council, and Director of the Bilingual Project, **Western Isles**, he is best known for his collection of stories, *An Aghaidh Choimheach* (1973), in which he employs symbolist and stream-of-consciousness techniques.

**Murray-Mooney, Yvonne** (née **Murray**) (1964– ) Athlete, b. Edinburgh. She won a bronze medal for the 3000m at the Commonwealth Games in **Edinburgh** in 1986, and also at the Olympics (1988), gold at the European Championships (1990) and gold at the 1994 Commonwealth Games for 10,000m.

**Murrayfield** Scotland's national rugby stadium, **Edinburgh**, built 1924–5. In 1959 it was the first stadium to have electric undersoil heating. Completely rebuilt in the 1990s it now has a capacity of 67,500.

**Murthly Castle** Castle on the banks of the River **Tay**, near **Dunkeld**. Originally a 15th-century tower house remodelled in the late 16th, and early 17th century, with a wing and pedimented entrance hall in the **Adam** manner c.1730. The castle has some sumptuous interior work, intended for the never finished New Castle, built 1827–32 by Gillespie **Graham** and A W N Pugin and demolished 1949. Within the beautiful park is the Chapel of St Anthony the Eremite by Gillespie Graham and Pugin (1836), with murals by Alexander Christie.

**Museum of Flight** Museum portraying aviation over the century of its history. It is based at East Fortune Airfield in **East Lothian**, which was established in 1915 as a fighter base to protect Scotland from Zeppelin attacks in World War I. It was also used in World War II and the hangars of that period house a very wide collection of aircraft and engines, including a Concorde aircraft. One of the **National Museums of Scotland**.

**Museum of Scotland** Opened in 1998 in an impressive modern building, designed by Benson and Forsyth, adjoining the **Royal Museum** in Chambers Street, Edinburgh, it covers Scotland's history, its land and its people, from the earliest times to the present. One of the **National Museums of Scotland**.

**Museum of Scottish Country Life** Museum, designed by Page and Park, based at Wester Kittochside Farm near **East Kilbride**, portraying rural life in Scotland through the centuries. It is set in 68 hectares (170 acres) of farmland which was gifted to the **National Trust for Scotland** in 1992; they worked with the **National Museums of Scotland** to provide this rich resource which includes events and activities, as well as exhibits. It replaced the former Scottish Country Life Museum at **Ingliston**, near **Edinburgh**.

**Musgrave, Thea** (1928– ) Composer, b. Edinburgh. Her music, inspired by Scotland and Scottish material, includes: *Suite o Bairnsangs* (1953), *Scottish Dance Suite* (1959) and the opera *Mary, Queen of Scots* (1977). Her later work includes the operas *A Christmas Carol* (1979) and *An Occurrence at Owl Creek Bridge* (1981), *Simón Bolivar* (1993) and the orchestral *Phoenix Rising* (1997).

**Musselburgh** Former fishing and market town at the mouth of the River **Esk**, 9km (6mi) east of **Edinburgh**, former **burgh**, taking its name from the mussel beds along the Firth of **Forth**. An ancient settlement, there are Roman remains at nearby Inveresk. It boasts the oldest racecourse in Scotland (1816), moved to Musselburgh when racing stopped on the sands of **Leith**. It has a **tolbooth** built in 1590 and a 16th-century bridge. Pinkie House incorporates a 16th-century tower house of the Abbots of **Dunfermline**, but was chiefly built by Alexander Seton, Earl of Dunfermline and Chancellor of Scotland, who bought the estate in 1597. It contains important painted ceilings of that time, particularly that in the gallery. It is now part of Loretto School, a boarding school that was founded in 1778, originally for boys, now co-educational; it takes its name from the shrine of Our Lady of Loretto,

a medieval hermitage and pilgrimage centre to the east of the town. See also Battle of **Pinkie**. The town was formerly noted for the making of paper, fishing nets and wire ropes. (Yvonne **Murray-Mooney** worked in the net factory for a number of years.) The nickname the 'Honest Toun' derives from the town's refusal to accept reward for its care of the Earl of Moray, who died there in the 14th century. Its week-long annual festival in July is led by the Honest Lad and Honest Lass.

**mutchkin** see **weights and measures**, pp.382-4

**Muthil** (pronounced **mew**thil) Picturesque and very unaltered village 5km (3mi) south of **Crieff**. Destroyed by the **Jacobite** forces in 1716, rebuilt along the route of the military road soon afterwards. Its ruined medieval church, mainly 15th century with a Romanesque tower, is in the care of **Historic Scotland**. The very handsome neo-perpendicular new church is by Gillespie **Graham** (1826). The village has a museum of local history and folklife. **Drummond Castle** is nearby.

**Myllar, Andrew** Bookseller and printer. In 1507 he set up Scotland's first printing press with Walter **Chapman** in the Cowgate, Edinburgh, having a patent granted by **James IV** to print law books, mass books and Acts of Parliament.

**Mylne family** Family of royal master masons and architects of whom the most important were **John** (1611–67), who built the Tron Kirk in **Edinburgh** and Cowane's Hospital at **Stirling** and the vanished great house at Panmure; his nephew **Robert** (1633–1710), who was the main contractor for Holyroodhouse, built Mylne's Court, Lawnmarket in Edinburgh and planned the rebuilding of **Drumlanrig** with his son-in-law James **Smith**; and **Robert** (1733–1811), his great grandson who practised in London, mainly as a bridge builder, but was also responsible for the lavish interior work at **Inveraray** Castle and for the double church and other works in Inveraray.

**Mylne, Walter** (d.1558) Priest and Protestant martyr, burnt at the stake after returning from exile, believing he was safe, after the death of Cardinal **Beaton**. The death of this elderly priest inspired strong anti-Catholic feeling: he was the last Protestant martyr in Scotland.

**Myres Castle** Small castle to the southeast of Auchtermuchty, Fife, built c.1540 by John Scrymgeour, the King's macer and master of works at Holyroodhouse and **Falkland** Palace, remodelled in 1611 for John Paterson, sheriff clerk of Fife, further extended 1825.

**Myreton Motor Museum** see **Aberlady**

**Nairn** (pop. 8418) Town on the south coast of the **Moray Firth**, which was one of the earliest northeast royal **burghs**. The original **fishing** village expanded into a popular Victorian holiday resort. Still primarily a holiday town with sandy beaches, many hotels and two championship **golf** courses.

**Nairn** Also **Nairnshire**. Former county on the south coast of the **Moray Firth**. From 1975 to 1996 it was a district of **Highland Region** and it is now part of **Highland** local authority.

**Nairn, Nick** (1959– ) Chef and television presenter, b. Stirling. Chef/Director of award-winning restaurants in **Glasgow** and **Aberfoyle**. Since 1996 he has presented many television cookery programmes, including *Ready, Steady, Cook* and *Wild Harvest*.

**Nairn, Tom** (1932– ) Sociologist, b. Freuchie, Fife. A lecturer in social philosophy and sociology, he has written extensively on nationalism and leftist politics. His publications include *The Break-up of Britain; crisis and neo-nationalism* (1977); *The Enchanted Glass: Britain and its monarchy* (1994*); Modern Janus: Nationalism in the Modern World* (1990); *After Britain: New Labour and the Return of Scotland* (2000) and *Pariah: Misfortunes of the British Kingdom* (2002).

**Nairn District** see **Nairn** and **Highland Region**

**Nairnshire** see **Nairn**

**Nairne, Lady Carolina** (née **Oliphant**) (1766–1845) Songwriter, b. Gask, near Auchterarder, a member of the once staunchly **Jacobite** Oliphant family. She set many of her nostalgic songs to old Scots tunes and published them under a pseudonym.

Her songs included 'Charlie is my darling', 'Land o' the Leal' and 'Caller Herrin'.

**Napier, David** (1790–1869) One of the most innovative of the early marine engineers, he built the boiler for Henry **Bell**'s pioneering steamship *Comet*. Vessels engined by him made cross-channel navigation practicable, and developed water-borne excursion traffic on the **Clyde**. He invented the surface condenser, which later became a universal feature of steamship propulsion, and is still used in steam-driven power stations. He went to London where the firm he founded, much later, became famous for motor cars and aero-engines.

**Napier, Sir John, of Merchiston** (1550–1617) Mathematician and inventor, b. Edinburgh. Invented logarithms and 'Napier's Bones', a calculating device for multiplication and division. A committed Calvinist, he was also a believer in astrology and divination. **Napier University** in **Edinburgh** is named after him, and his castle of **Merchiston** forms part of the campus.

**Napier, Robert** (1791–1876) River **Clyde** shipbuilder and engineer, b. Dumbarton. The international reputation of Clyde shipbuilding was largely founded on his work. He built marine steam engines and warships, and was the first Clyde shipbuilder to supply the Navy. He formed a partnership with Canadian Samuel Cunard to build steam-powered transatlantic vessels.

**Napier Commission** Parliamentary Commission that investigated the state of small tenants in the **Highlands** and Islands in the 1880s, chaired by Lord Napier (1819–98), a politician and diplomat. Napier offered crofters a courteous hearing, and by the standards of the times, a radical solution in its report of 1884, leading eventually to the Crofters' Act and to the setting up of the first **Crofters' Commission**.

**Napier University** Founded in 1964 as Napier College of Science and Technology, it became a university in 1992. It has 4 main campuses in **Edinburgh**, with **Merchiston Castle** at the core of the main one. See also **Craiglockhart**.

**Nardini, Daniela** (1968– ) Actor, b. Largs. After training at the **Royal Scottish Academy of Music and Drama**, she made her breakthrough playing the part of Anna in the TV series *This Life* (1996). She has since been a regular on TV, including roles in *Rough Treatment* (2000) and *Sirens* (2002).

**NAS** see **National Archives of Scotland**

*Distant View of Stirling by Alexander Nasmyth (1827).*

**Nasmyth, Alexander** (1758–1840) Artist, b. Edinburgh. Worked as an assistant to Allan **Ramsay** in London before setting up as a portrait painter in Edinburgh. After visiting Italy he turned increasingly to landscape painting, in which he was successful and influential (having opened an art school in 1798). A close friend of Robert **Burns**, his portrait of him (**Scottish National Portrait Gallery**) is perhaps the best-known image of the poet. Nasmyth was also a gifted and imaginative designer, responsible for several engineering and architectural projects in Scotland, including his own house in Edinburgh. Nasmyth's several children, including James **Nasmyth**, also found success as artists and in engineering.

**Nasmyth, James** (1808–90) Engineer, b. Edinburgh, son of Alexander **Nasmyth**. He moved to Manchester and established a foundry business and specialised in the production of steam-powered machine tools, including the steam hammer and steam lathe. His inventions helped to enable mass production in factories, reducing the need for skilled labour.

**National Archives of Scotland (NAS)** Public body, formerly the Scottish Record Office, which preserves public and legal records from the 12th century to the present. It also contains other collections, such as family papers, and its search rooms in **Edinburgh** are available for research.

**National Bank of Scotland** Established 1825 in **Edinburgh**, and quickly expanded. In 1864 it became the first Scottish bank to open a branch in London, and in 1946 it launched Britain's first mobile banking service, on **Lewis**. In 1959 a merger with the Commercial Bank of Scotland formed the National Commercial Bank of Scotland, which 10 years later amalgamated with the **Royal Bank of Scotland**.

**National Coal Board** Established in 1947 as a nationalised industry to take over all the larger private coal-mining concerns, at a time when there was an acute shortage of energy. To meet immediate needs it opened a number of small mines, pending the completion of large deep mines, such as Killoch (Ayrshire), Seafield and Rothes (Fife) and Bilston Glen and Monktonhall (Midlothian). Exhaustion of seams and competition from other energy sources led to a rapid run-down of the Board's activities in the 1960s and 70s. The rump was privatised in the 1990s as Scottish Coal, and the last deep mine in Scotland, Castlehill, in Fife, closed in about 2000.

**National Covenant** Drawn up in 1638, this document called for Scots to oppose the innovations in religion mandated by King **Charles I**. It was first signed in Greyfriars Churchyard, **Edinburgh**, and copies were made to allow people all across Scotland to add their signatures. Supporters of the National Covenant were known as **Covenanters**.

**National Galleries of Scotland** The collection of art belonging to the Scottish nation is housed in several galleries, including: the National Gallery of Scotland on the Mound, **Edinburgh**, with its outstanding collections of Western European art from the 14th–19th centuries, including works by Botticelli, Titian, Velázquez, van Dyke, Canova, Turner, Monet and Degas, as well the most comprehensive collection of Scottish art of the same period, with masterpieces by Allan **Ramsay**, David **Wilkie**, Henry **Raeburn** and William **McTaggart**. The building, in classical style by W H **Playfair**, was completed in 1854. The adjacent **Royal Scottish Academy** building, also by Playfair, reopened in 2003 as the principal exhibition space for the National Galleries of Scotland and for the Royal Scottish Academy and other exhibiting societies. See also **Scottish National Portrait Gallery**, **Scottish National Gallery of Modern Art** (with Dean Gallery), **Duff House**, **Paxton**.

N

**National Library of Scotland** Founded in the 1680s as the Library of the Faculty of Advocates, **Edinburgh**. Its outstanding collection is based partly on its right to a copy of every book published in the British Isles, as it is one of the 6 copyright libraries. Became a national institution in 1925, and moved to its current main site on George IV Bridge in 1956.

**National Museum of Antiquities of Scotland** Former museum in **Edinburgh** which had its origins in the collections of the **Society of Antiquaries of Scotland**, founded in 1780. It shared a building with the **Scottish National Portrait Gallery**. It merged with the **Royal Scottish Museum** in 1985 as part of the National Museums of Scotland. The collections now form the basis of the **Museum of Scotland** (see also **National Museums of Scotland**).

**National Museums of Scotland** Comprise the following publicly funded museums: the **Museum of Scotland**, in an impressive modern building in **Edinburgh** opened in 1998, covers the history of Scotland from the earliest times; see also **National Museum of Antiquities**; the **Royal Museum** (formerly Royal Scottish Museum) in the adjacent Victorian building houses varied international collections; the **National War Museum of Scotland** (formerly the Scottish United Services Museum) at **Edinburgh Castle**; the **Museum of Flight** at East Fortune Airfield, East Lothian; **Shambellie House Museum of Costume**, in a country house outside **New Abbey** near Dumfries; and the **Museum of Scottish Country Life**, recently opened in partnership with the **National Trust for Scotland** at Wester Kittochside Farm near **East Kilbride**.

**National Party of Scotland** see **Scottish National Party**

**National Piping Centre** Body, based in **Glasgow**, which promotes the study of the music and history of the Highland **bagpipe**. The Centre houses a piping school with first-class practice facilities, the piping collection of the **National Museums of Scotland**, an auditorium, hotel and restaurant. Lessons are offered for beginners through to degree level. The Centre is home to the National Youth Pipe Band of Scotland.

**National Trust for Scotland** A registered charity, founded in 1931, which conserves and interprets sites of cultural or natural significance. The many properties it cares for include castles, houses, battlefields, gardens, mountains and islands. Through its 'Little Houses' scheme, it has ensured the survival of many smaller buildings, for instance in **Culross**, **Dunkeld** and the **East Neuk of Fife**. Its headquarters are in Charlotte Square, **Edinburgh**.

**National War Museum of Scotland** Museum in **Edinburgh Castle** which houses the national collections of the Scottish armed services, comprising weapons, uniforms and insignia, art and documentary evidence. One of the **National Museums of Scotland**, it was developed from the former Scottish United Services Museum.

**Natural Philosophy** The name traditionally given to the study of physics in Scottish Universities.

**Nechtan** (d.732) King of the **Picts**, succeeding after 706. His reign saw developments in the Pictish church, including greater influence from neighbouring Northumbria and a decline in the ecclesiastical authority of **Iona**. In 724 he was forced to retire to a monastery, but emerged to briefly regain the kingship in 728.

**Nechtansmere** The usual name for the battle fought on 20 May 685 at Dunnichen Moss, near **Forfar**, where **Brude** (Bridei mac Beli), King of the **Picts**, defeated the Northumbrian King Ecgfrith. Anglian northward expansion and exercise of suzerainty over the other peoples of northern Britain were halted.

**neep** Scots word for a turnip but often refers to the swede, which was introduced into Scotland from Sweden in the late 18th century. Important as animal fodder, it is also a popular vegetable, especially as an accompaniment to **haggis**, eg at Burns Suppers (see Robert **Burns**): neeps and tatties (mashed turnip and potato). See also **clapshot**.

**Ne'erday** see **New Year('s) Day**

**Neidpath Castle** L-shaped tower house on the banks of the River **Tweed**, near **Peebles**. It was built in the 14th century, and belonged to the Hay family until the late 17th century. It now belongs to Lady Elizabeth Benson, daughter of the Earl of Wemyss, and is open to the public during the summer.

**Neil, Andrew** (1949– ) Journalist and broadcaster, b. Paisley. Editor of the *Sunday Times* 1983–94. He joined The **Scotsman** as Editor-in-Chief in 1996, and became Publisher of Press Holdings, the group owning *The Scotsman*, in 1999. He has hosted various television and radio shows, and written books on the media.

**Neill, A(lexander) S(utherland)** (1883–1973) Radical teacher, b. Forfar. An internationally famous exponent of the ideas of child-centred education, he believed that Scottish education was too authoritarian to be reformable, and set up his experimental school, Summerhill, first in Lyme Regis and then (from 1927) at Leiston in Suffolk.

**N**

**Neill, Bud** (1911–70) Cartoonist, b. Glasgow. As the creator of 'Lobey Dosser', the strip cartoon which ran in the **Glasgow** *Evening Times* from 1949, Neill celebrated Glaswegian life and humour in the setting of the Wild West. A statue of Mr Dosser astride his trusty steed was erected in Woodlands Road in 1992.

**Neill, William** (1922– ) Poet, b. Prestwick. He writes in **Scots**, English and **Gaelic**. With Sorley **MacLean**, George Campbell **Hay** and Stuart MacGregor he published *Four Points of the Saltire* (1970). His other works include *Wild Places* (1985), *Making Tracks and Other Poems* (1988) and *Tales frae the Odyssey* (1992).

**Neilson, James Beaumont** (1792–1865) Inventor and engineer, b. Shettleston, Glasgow. In 1828 he devised the hot-blast system of **iron** production, which reduced the amount of coal needed and increased efficiency. As a result, cheap iron from Scottish 'black-band' ores became more readily available and **Glasgow** emerged as a market leader in heavy engineering and the River **Clyde** as the world's largest shipbuilding area.

**Nelson, Thomas** (1780–1861) Publisher, b. Throsk, near Stirling. Founded a publishing firm in **Edinburgh** which was continued by his sons. The firm developed a reputation for publishing schoolbooks and reference works. It was sold in 1960 and is now based in Tennessee, publishing Christian and reference books.

**Neptune's Staircase** see **Caledonian Canal**

**Ness** (Gaelic **Nis**) The most northerly settlement in the **Western Isles**, a crofting community on the Isle of **Lewis** consisting of a number of small villages. At the northernmost point the Butt of Lewis **lighthouse** was built in 1862. Dun Eistein, a small uninhabited island, was the stronghold of the Clan Morrison.

**Ness, River** Flows from **Loch Ness** through the centre of **Inverness** and into the **Moray Firth**. It is popular for salmon fishing. Part of it is used by the **Caledonian Canal** to reach **Loch Ness**. The Ness Islands form a picturesque wooded public park within Inverness.

**Nethy Bridge** On the edge of **Abernethy Forest**, this village in **Strathspey** has attracted tourists since the 19th century. It is well placed for outdoor activities, including walking, cycling, skiing and fishing. The ruined Castle Roy, on the edge of the village, dates from the 13th century.

**Neville's Cross, Battle of** Fought on 17 October 1346. **David II** had invaded England in support of Philip VI of France. An English army defeated the larger Scots force at the site now known as Neville's Cross, near Durham. David was captured, and remained a prisoner of the English for 11 years.

**Nevis, River** Flows west and then northwest through **Glen Nevis**, below the slopes of **Ben Nevis**, and enters the sea at **Fort William**.

**New Abbey** Village 10km (6mi) south of **Dumfries**, dominated by the ruins of **Sweetheart Abbey**. The village also contains an 18th-century oatmeal mill which has been restored to working order (in the care of **Historic Scotland**). Nearby is the **Shambellie House Museum of Costume**.

**Newark Castle** Splendid Renaissance house in **Renfrewshire**, to the east of **Port Glasgow**, with symmetrical frontage to the River **Clyde**, built 1597–1599 by Patrick Maxwell, incorporating 2 earlier towers; in the care of **Historic Scotland**.

**Newark Castle** Massive rectangular tower house on the **Yarrow Water** to the west of **Selkirk**, built as a royal castle in 1467; besieged by the English 1547–48; and occupied by Cromwell 1650; later an occasional residence of Anna, Duchess of Buccleuch, after the execution of her husband.

**Newbattle Abbey** Near **Dalkeith**. Founded in 1140 by **David I**, the abbey was 3 times burned by the English. After the **Reformation** it became the home of the Earls (later Marquesses) of Lothian. The mansion house is largely 17th and 18th century with impressive Victorian interiors by W E Nesfield and Thomas Bonnar, but incorporates a 14th-century crypt. It is now Scotland's only residential adult education college.

**Newbery, Francis** (1855–1946) Artist and educationalist, b. Membury, Devon. Best known as the dynamic and reforming Director of **Glasgow School of Art** from 1885 to 1918, under whom a generation of talented students flourished, many of whom contributed to the development of the so-called 'Glasgow Style'. Newbery's most important single act of patronage was to award the young Charles Rennie **Mackintosh** the commission to design the now famous building for the School.

**Newburgh** (pop. 1954) Fife town on the Firth of **Tay**, founded as a **burgh** in the 12th century. It had become one of the main ports for the area by the 18th century. Industries in the 19th century included textiles and linoleum manufacture, and the arrival of pleasure steamers brought tourists from **Dundee**. The ruins of **Lindores Abbey** are on its edge.

**Newburgh** Aberdeenshire village with a harbour, near the mouth of the River **Ythan**, 7km (4mi) southeast of **Ellon**.

**New College** Built in 1845–50 as the Free Church College, in

Tudor style by W H **Playfair** (to group with Gillespie **Graham**'s Tolbooth St John's Church), this building has been the home of **Edinburgh University**'s Faculty of Divinity since 1935. Its Assembly Hall is used for the annual **General Assembly** of the **Church of Scotland**, and from 1999 it provided a temporary location for the **Scottish Parliament**.

**New Galloway** Town near **Kirkcudbright** built on the River Ken in the mid-17th century, the smallest royal **burgh** in Scotland. It is at the centre of the Galloway hydroelectric scheme.

**Newhailes** Classical mansion house near **Musselburgh**, built in 1686 by James Smith for himself; in 1709 it was bought by Sir David Dalrymple (Lord **Hailes**). It has early 18th-century additions, and remarkably rich interiors, with important portraits by Allan **Ramsay** and others. Set in a designed landscape, it was recently acquired and restored by the **National Trust for Scotland**. See also **Hailes Castle**.

**Newhaven** Village on the Firth of **Forth**, now a district of **Edinburgh**. It was founded in 1500 as a royal dockyard by **James IV**. The *Great Michael*, an outstanding ship of its time, was built there and launched in 1511. Newhaven later became a **fishing** port, and Newhaven fishwives sold their wares in Edinburgh streets. There is a small museum in the former fishmarket.

**New Lanark** Very completely preserved village built around water-powered cotton-spinning mills on the banks of the River **Clyde**. Founded by David **Dale** and Richard Arkwright in 1784 and developed by Robert **Owen**. Innovative social and educational provision was introduced for workers and their families. From the 1880s to 1968 fishing nets and cotton canvas were made. It is now a World Heritage Site and is run as an industrial heritage centre and hotel.

**New Lichts** (**New Lights**) see **Presbyterian churches**

**Newliston** see **Kirkliston**

**Newmilns** (pop. 3057) Town near **Kilmarnock**, a former **burgh**. It was a centre of **Covenanting** activity, and various Covenanting martyrs are buried or commemorated in the parish church. In the

*New Lanark, aquatint by John Clark (1825).*

19th century Newmilns became a centre of muslin weaving and lace-making. Newmilns Tower was built in 1530, and has been restored as a house.

**New Pitsligo** Aberdeenshire village 16km (10mi) southwest of **Fraserburgh**, founded around the settlement of Caik (in modern usage 'Cyaak') by Sir William **Forbes** of Pitsligo in 1787. In the 19th century it became well known for lace production.

**Newport-on-Tay** (pop. 4214) Town on the banks of the River **Tay**, which was the ferry-port for crossing from **Fife** to **Dundee** until the Tay Road Bridge was built in 1966. Most of the town's houses and churches are Victorian, and several of the largest were built for Dundee's **jute** barons.

**newspapers** see p.288

**New Statistical Account** see **Statistical Accounts**

**Newstead** Site, in the Borders, near **Melrose**, of a major base for the Roman army in the late 1st and 2nd centuries AD, strategically located beside the River **Tweed**. Although little survives above ground, excavation has revealed the superimposed remains of at least 4 forts, together with some spectacular finds, including parade helmets and face-masks.

**Newtongrange** see **Scottish Mining Museum**

**Newtonmore** (Gaelic **Bail' Ùr an t-Sléibh**) Village 74km (46mi) south of **Inverness**. A popular tourist centre, it has a successful **shinty** team. The Highland Folk Museum site includes a reconstructed 18th-century township and an early 20th-century schoolhouse.

N

# NEWSPAPERS

Newspaper publishing in Scotland began with reprints of London papers, for example *Diurnall Occurrances touching the Dailie Proceedings in Parliament* of 1641. A few years later, the *Mercurius Scoticus* of Leith became the first paper both edited and printed in Scotland, but it remained the norm for some time that Scots periodicals were largely dependent on reprints from the English press.

When a genuine Scottish voice began to be heard in newspapers, it spoke with an **Edinburgh** accent: the press there thrived because the city was first with the news from London, whereas until 1788 mail from the English capital for **Glasgow** went via Edinburgh.

Many early titles were short-lived because of lack of funds or interest, but the *Caledonian Mercury*, founded in 1720, bucked that trend thanks to its consistently high standard of editorial. In the North east, the *Aberdeen Journal* (known initially as *The Aberdeen's Journal*) was founded in 1748, and would go on to become the longest-lived title in the land: a merger and a slight name change later, it is still available today as the **Press & Journal**.

The *Glasgow Advertiser*, too, is still with us in altered guise. When it began in 1783 it was by no means the first newspaper in the city, but it set new standards of professionalism; 19 years later it changed its name to *The Glasgow **Herald***, under which name it continued until a recent decision to remove the city's name from the title.

*The **Scotsman*** – founded in 1817, and no relation to a short-lived newspaper of the same name from earlier in that decade – also quickly earned a reputation for quality journalism. And on Tayside, from 1816, the *Dundee **Courier*** grew into a role similar to its counterparts in the 3 other cities.

The state of the Scottish broadsheet market has been relatively stable ever since. Each of the 4 main titles prints British and international news, and both *The Scotsman* and *The Herald* like to style themselves as national newspapers. Compared to the UK nationals, however, they are perhaps under-resourced, and more professional circulation drives by the former Fleet Street papers have affected sales of the Scottish titles. Indeed, if the Scottish broadsheet market were to be represented in military terms, the image would have to show 4 city states besieged by larger, more well-equipped English armies. Even the tabloid *Daily Record*, which for long enough boasted by far the biggest daily sale in the country, now finds that some of its sales are being gradually eroded by the Scottish edition of *The Sun*.

Sunday newspapers are in a similar situation. The once-unassailable **Sunday Post**, whose sales approached saturation levels for a time, now faces a similar challenge from the English titles as the dailies do. The *Post*, with iconic figures such as Oor Wullie and Francis Gay, was once a mirror into which the nation peered to see a somewhat flattering image of itself. Today it, like other papers, has to keep pace with changing times and audiences.

Newspapers continue to play an important role in national life. The Scottish market is among the most competitive in the world, and, while evening papers may be in a long-term decline, there is sure to be a multiplicity of morning dailies and weeklies for some time to come. Which titles survive, and who they are owned and controlled by, is an altogether different matter, one which is far harder to predict.

---

**N**

**Newton Stewart** Small town 10km (7mi) north of **Wigtown**, built from 1701 onwards, known for a time as Newton Douglas, on the site of an ancient ford over the River **Cree**, now crossed by a fine granite bridge, designed by John **Rennie** (1812–13). The town had a thriving wool market.

**New Town** see **Edinburgh**

**New Towns** Reordering of population and industries away from overcrowded towns and cities into new settlements under legislation of 1946. **East Kilbride** was the first, designated 1947, followed by Glenrothes (1950), **Cumbernauld** (1956), **Livingston** (1962), and **Irvine** (1968). The New Town Corporations were abolished in 1996, at the same time as **local-government** reorganisation.

**Newtown St Boswells** Market town 5km (3mi) from **Melrose**, which developed around a now-closed railway junction. The headquarters of the **Scottish Borders Council** is based here, in a towered modern building of considerable merit, designed by Peter Womersley in 1966–8.

**New Year('s) Day, Ne'erday** Until recently, the main public holiday of the festive season in Scotland. (Christmas Day did not become a public holiday until the 1960s.) See **Hogmanay**.

**Nicol, James** (1810–79) Geologist, b. Traquair, near Peebles. He studied in **Edinburgh**, Berlin and Bonn and became interested in geology. He began a survey of Scotland and published a *Guide to the Geology of Scotland* (1844). He became Secretary to the Geological Society of London in 1847, Professor of Geology in Cork in 1849 and Professor of **Natural Philosophy** in **Aberdeen** in 1853.

**Nicol, William** (1744–97) Schoolmaster at the High School, Edinburgh, and friend and travelling companion of Robert **Burns**. Burns named one of his sons after him, and wrote an 'Epitaph for William Nicol'.

**Nicolson, Alexander** (1827–93) Sheriff and Gaelic scholar, b. Skye. He collected **Gaelic** proverbs and revised the Gaelic Bible. In 1873 he made the first recorded ascent of the highest peak on **Skye**, **Sgurr Alasdair**, which is named after him. He was a member of the Argyll Education Commission and the **Napier Commission**.

**Niddry Castle** L-plan tower house to the southeast of Winchburgh, **West Lothian**, built around 1500 by George, 3rd Lord Seton. **Mary, Queen of Scots** spent the night here after her escape from **Loch Leven** Castle in 1568. Niddry Castle was abandoned in the 17th century. It was partially restored in the 1990s and is now a private residence.

**Nigg** Village between the **Dornoch** and **Cromarty Firths**, it expanded with **oil** developments in the 1970s; see **Cromarty Firth**. Nigg church, dating from 1626, contains an important 9th-century Pictish cross-slab.

**Ninian, St** Bishop at **Whithorn** in Galloway, probably in the early 6th century. He is said by Bede to have converted the southern **Picts**, but reliable information on his activities is very limited. His tomb at Whithorn became a popular pilgrimage destination.

**Nith, River** Rises in South Ayrshire, and flows through southwest Scotland and the town of **Dumfries** to the **Solway Firth**.

**Nithsdale** The valley of the River **Nith**, extending from South Ayrshire to the **Solway Firth**. **Dumfriesshire** was divided into 3 areas, of which Nithsdale lay furthest west. In 1975 the area became a district of **Dumfries and Galloway Region** and it is now part of Dumfries and Galloway unitary local authority; see maps on pp.394-5 and **local government**.

**Niven, Frederick** (1878–1944) Novelist, b. Chile. He lived in Scotland from age 5, and emigrated to British Columbia in 1920. He wrote novels set in both Scotland and Canada, and also published short stories and poetry.

**non-jurors** Ministers and their supporters who refused to take an oath of allegiance to **William** and **Mary** and their successors and would not support the re-introduction of exclusively presbyterian

*North Berwick, on the Firth of Forth, East Lothian.*

government of the **Church of Scotland**. These ministers, who were deprived of their parishes, created a tradition which eventually led to the formation of the **Scottish Episcopal Church**.

**Norn** see **language**, p.220

**North, Christopher** see **Wilson, John**

**North Ayrshire Council** (pop. 139,175) Local authority in central Scotland created in 1996 by the amalgamation of the former **Strathclyde Region** districts of Cunninghame and Inverclyde and including the islands of **Arran**, Great **Cumbrae** and Little Cumbrae. The administrative centre is **Irvine** and other towns include **Kilwinning**, **Saltcoats**, **Largs**, and **Kilbirnie**. It is mainly agricultural with fishing and tourism. See maps on pp.394-5, **local government** and see also **Ayrshire**, **East Ayrshire**, **South Ayrshire**.

**North Berwick** (pop. 6223) East Lothian seaside town on the Firth of **Forth**, originally centred on the Cistercian nunnery founded before 1177. It is popular with golfers and visitors. Tourism has replaced the traditional industries of **fishing** and trade and it became an upmarket dormitory town for **Edinburgh** after the railway came, with major Edwardian houses and gardens by Robert **Lorimer**, J M Dick Peddie and others. The Scottish Seabird Centre opened here in 2000, with trips to the **Bass Rock** and the Isle of **May**. The town is also associated with the 'North Berwick witch trials' of 1591, when the Earl of **Bothwell** and a group of women were accused of using witchcraft in an attempt to sink King **James VI**'s ship as he returned from Denmark with his bride.

**N**

**North British Locomotive Company** In 1903, 13 companies merged to create the largest locomotive engineering company in Europe. The firm, which supplied domestic and overseas markets, closed in 1962.

**North British Railway** see **railways** p.312

**North-East Fife District** see **Fife**

**Northern Isles** see **Orkney** and **Shetland**

**Northern Meeting** Established in 1788 as an annual event in **Inverness**, to encourage social life in the aftermath of the **Jacobite** Risings. Piping competitions have been an important part of it and it is one of the 2 major solo piping competitions. From 1841 to 1886 it awarded the Prize Pipe for **Piobaireachd**; winners of the Prize Pipe then competed for the Former Winners' Medal. From 1887 to date it has awarded the Highland Society of London Gold Medal and winners then compete for the Clasp.

**North Esk** River in Angus which flows southeast for a distance of 47km (29mi). It flows through Glen Esk and enters the North Sea 5km (3mi) north of **Montrose**.

**Northfield House** see **Preston**

**North Lanarkshire Council** Local authority formed in 1996 from the Cumbernauld and Kilsyth, Motherwell, and Monklands Districts of **Strathclyde Region**, with slightly increased area. The administrative centre is **Motherwell** and other towns include **Coatbridge**, **Airdrie**, **Cumbernauld**, and **Kilsyth**. See maps on pp.394-5 and **local government** and see also **Lanarkshire**, **South Lanarkshire**.

**North of Scotland Hydro-Electric Board** Established 1943 by Tom **Johnston**, Secretary of State for Scotland. The Board undertook a programme of construction which would harness the power of running water to supply electricity to homes throughout the **Highlands**. It lasted until privatisation in 1991.

**North Queensferry** Village in Fife, on the shores of the Firth of **Forth**, dominated by the **Forth Bridges**. Its name is said to come from the ferry established here in the 11th century by Queen Margaret to carry pilgrims on their way to **St Andrews**. There was a car ferry here until the Forth Road Bridge was opened in 1964. Deep Sea World is a popular tourist attraction. See also **South Queensferry**.

**North Rona** Uninhabited island in the Outer **Hebrides**, 71km (44mi) north of **Lewis**. Remains of an early Celtic church building survive. The island is part of the North Rona and Sula Sgeir National Nature Reserve and is an important breeding ground both for a variety of seabirds and a large colony of grey seals.

**North Ronaldsay** Northernmost of the **Orkney** Islands, location of many prehistoric sites and home to a celebrated breed of sheep. A remarkable survival, these northern Orcadian sheep are a remnant of the dun-faced stock once common over much of the Scottish mainland. In their particular habitat, they are adapted to eating seaweed for part of the year, being kept from farmland by a drystone wall which surrounds the island.

**North Uist** (Gaelic **Uibhist a Tuath**) (pop. 1271) Island south of **Harris**, linked by ferry to **Skye** and Harris (via **Berneray**, to which it has been linked by a causeway since 1999), and by causeway to **Benbecula**. It has numerous lochs, popular with anglers, sea lochs and small offshore islands. The main port is **Lochmaddy**. The principal occupations are **fishing**, crofting and tourism. Historic sites include a neolithic chambered cairn (Barpa Langass) and a medieval church site at Carinish. Evictions at Sollas in 1850 were an infamous episode in the Highland **Clearances**.

**not-proven verdict** Unique to Scots **law**, this controversial verdict may be used when judge or jury doubt that the guilt of the accused has been proven, but do not want to pass a 'not guilty' verdict. It has attracted much criticism, mainly from the families of victims.

**Nova Scotia** Province of Canada. From 1629 Sir William Alexander, Earl of Stirling, tried to establish a Scottish colony here, but in 1632 **Charles I** abandoned the small colony to gain peace with France. It was ceded to Britain in 1713, when the concept of Nova Scotia was revived. In the 18th and 19th centuries many Scots emigrated to Nova Scotia, and aspects of Scottish culture such as music and the **Gaelic** language survive there.

**Nova Scotia Baronets** Hereditary knights of an order created by **James VI** to raise money to fund the colony of **Nova Scotia**. The honour was bought by many with no interest in the colony and became prestigious.

**Nunraw Abbey/Castle** Nunraw Castle, to the east of Garvald, near **Haddington**, East Lothian, is a large later 16th-century Z-plan tower house built by Patrick Hepburn, convincingly enlarged in the same style in 1860-4 by Maitland **Wardrop** for Robert Hay. In 1946 it became Santa Maria Abbey, a Cistercian monastery, with massive new cloister buildings designed by Peter Whiston, begun in 1951.

N

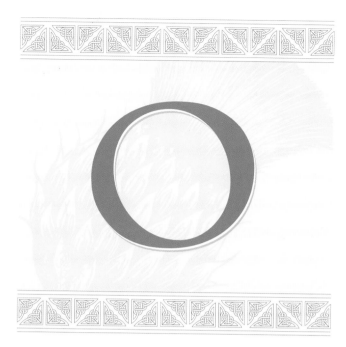

**oats** A staple food in Scotland (where it is often known as corn), especially from the time it ousted **barley** as the main staple crop around the 17th century until improved milling processes allowed the cheap production of white (wheat) flour in the 19th. The resulting change in diet, to white bread, was detrimental to health, a fact made even clearer by recent research revealing the health-giving properties of oats. Until after World War II some farm servants were paid partly in oatmeal. Oatmeal is generally ground in 4 main grades: pinhead, rough, medium and fine, and is also produced in the form of oatflakes or porridge oats, a process developed in America. It is used in many different ways, principally as the main ingredient of **porridge** and **brose**, and also features in **haggis** and other dishes. See also **Atholl brose, cranachan, meal and ale, oatcake, skirlie, sowans.**

**oatcake** A thin, flat, crisp biscuit made of oatmeal, water, salt and a little fat (sometimes with the addition of wheat flour), traditionally baked on a **girdle** in a large round cut in 4, now also baked in small rounds. So prevalent was the oatcake as a food in the past that the word 'cake' in **Scots** normally referred to oatcake, as in the poem by Robert **Burns**: 'Hear, Land o' Cakes and brither Scots...'

**Oban** (Gaelic **An t-Oban**) (pop. 8120) Town and port in **Argyll**, opposite **Mull**. It developed in the 19th century with the establishment of steamer services to the Inner and Outer **Hebrides** and the advent of the **railways**, becoming a popular summer resort, with impressive mid to late 19th-century hotels. The incomplete, Colosseum-like McCaig's Tower above the town (known as McCaig's folly), was begun in 1897 as a project to help the unemployed and celebrate the family of John Stewart McCaig, a local banker. The finest individual building is the Roman Catholic Cathedral of St Columba on Corran Esplanade, built 1932–53 to designs by Sir Giles Gilbert Scott. The **Argyllshire Gathering** is held here annually in late summer.

**O'Brien, Cardinal Keith Michael Patrick** (1938– ) Roman Catholic clergyman, b. Ballycastle, N Ireland. A schoolteacher and then assistant priest, he became Spiritual Director of St Andrews College, Drygrange, near **Melrose** and Rector, **Blairs College**, Aberdeen. Archbishop of **St Andrews** and **Edinburgh** since 1985, he became a cardinal in 2003.

**Ochil Hills** Range of hills extending from just north of **Stirling** northeastward to **Newburgh** on the Firth of **Tay**. The highest point is Ben Cleuch (720m/2363ft).

**Ochiltree** Village of late 18th- and early 19th-century cottages in east Ayrshire where the Burnock Water joins Lugar Water. Its name came from Ochiltree House (of which nothing remains), home of the Stuarts, lords of Ochiltree, into whose family both John **Knox** and Viscount **Dundee** married. The village was the birthplace of George Douglas **Brown**.

**Octavians** Eight officials whom **James VI** appointed in 1596 to reorganise the handling of the royal finances. They were David Carnegie, James Elphinstone (1st Lord Balmerino), Sir Thomas Hamilton, John Lindsay, Alexander Seton (1st Earl of Dunfermline), Sir John Skene, Walter Stewart (Lord Blantyre) and Sir Peter Young. Though soon dismissed, many of the Octavians went on to serve the king in other capacities.

**Oengus** (King of the Picts) see **Unuist**

**og(h)am** A linear alphabet based on Latin used in the early Middle Ages in Ireland, Wales and Scotland, and surviving mainly on stone monuments. Frequently it was cut on a straight edge. Interpretation is fraught with difficulties, and Scotland's 'Pictish Ogams' are surrounded in controversy.

**Ogilvie, James** see **Seafield, 1st Earl of**

**Ogilvie, St John** (c.1579–1615) Priest and martyr, b. Banffshire. He was educated by Jesuits in Germany and ordained in Paris before returning to Scotland. He was arrested and hanged for his defence of papal supremacy. He was beatified in 1927 and canonised in 1976.

**Ogilvie, John** (1733-1813) Minister and poet, b. Aberdeen; minister at Midmar, Aberdeenshire. His poetic works, including *Paradise* (1769) and *The Fame of the Druids* (1787), were

O

admired by James **Boswell** but not by Dr Johnson, who, when Ogilvie praised Scotland's 'many noble wild prospects', replied, 'But, Sir, let me tell you, the noblest prospect a Scotchman ever sees, is the high road . . . to England.'

**O-Grades** The name by which Ordinary Grade examinations were commonly known. These were introduced in 1962, replacing the **Lowers**. They were largely taken by pupils in their 4th year, providing both a recognised qualification for those who left school at this stage and a preliminary to the **Higher** Grades. They have been replaced by **Standard Grades**.

**Oich, Loch** see Loch Oich

**oil and gas** see p.293

**Old Aberdeen** see Aberdeen p.9

**Old Lights (Auld Lichts)** see **Presbyterian Churches**

**Oldmeldrum** (pop. 2003) Town in Aberdeenshire, 7km (4mi) northeast of **Inverurie**, a former **burgh**, with a central square dominated by a classical town house (1877) by William Smith of **Balmoral** fame. To the north is **Meldrum House**, now a hotel, the oldest part of which dates from the 13th century with 17th- and 19th-century additions. To the south is the impressive turreted **Barra Castle** near the site of a battle in 1307 when **Robert the Bruce** defeated the Comyns.

**Old Mills** An ancient oatmeal mill to the west of **Elgin**, now restored to full working order.

**Old Pretender** see **Stewart, James Francis Edward**

**Old Town** see **Edinburgh**, pp.130-3

**Oliphant, Laurence, of Gask** (1691-1767) **Jacobite** laird and father of Carolina, Lady **Nairne**. Worshipped at Old St Paul's Church, Jeffrey Street, **Edinburgh**. He brought to the city the good news of the victory at **Prestonpans**.

**Oliphant, Margaret** (née **Wilson**), (1828-97) Writer, b. Wallyford, Midlothian. Widowed early with a family to support she became a prolific author. Her best-known novels include *The Chronicles of Carlingford* series – *The Rector and the Doctor's Family* (1863), *Salem Chapel* (1863), *The Perpetual Curate* (1864), *Miss Majoribanks* (1866) and *Phoebe Junior* (1876), earning her the soubriquet of the 'female Trollope'. She also wrote biographies and travel books.

**Oliphant, Sir William** (d.1329) Soldier. He led a staunch defence of **Stirling** Castle against Edward I in 1304 well after the general Scottish submission of that year. His defence of **Perth** in English service in 1313 illustrates the crisis of loyalties, for supporters of the **Balliol** claim, brought about by Robert I's seizure

of the throne in 1306. By 1317 he was in Robert I's allegiance.

**Onich** A village spreading along the shore at the entrance to **Loch Leven**, 4km (2.5mi) west of **Ballachulish**. It has a monument to Dr Alexander Stewart, a **Gaelic** scholar and one of the founders of the **Mod**, who was minister here 1851–1901.

**òran mòr** Gaelic term, meaning 'great song', often used to refer to songs of the 17th and 18th centuries, by known poets to traditional tunes, about historical people and events. Many are in praise of or lamenting for clan chieftains and other notables of Highland society.

**Orchardson, Sir William Quiller** (1832–1910) Artist, b. Edinburgh. A pupil of Robert Scott **Lauder**, Orchardson moved to London early in his professional career. His paintings of social situations, in historical period settings or drawing attention to 19th-century morality, combined sophisticated observation with a mastery of technique which made him one of the most successful Scottish artists of the late Victorian period. Among his best-known works are his *Mariage de Convenance* series and his *Master Baby* (National Gallery of Scotland).

**Orchardton Tower** A 15th-century round tower house, the only such in Scotland, to the south of Palnackie in Dumfriesshire; in the care of **Historic Scotland**.

**Orchy** see **Glen Orchy**

**Order of the Thistle** see **thistle**

**Ord of Caithness** High granite ridge (244m/800ft) on the border of **Caithness** and **Sutherland** overlooking the North Sea. The A9 road from **Inverness** to **Thurso** crosses it just south of Berriedale.

**Ordinary Grades** see **O-Grades**

**Original Secession** see **Secessions**

**Orkney** (pop. 19,245) An island group lying 32km (20mi) north of northeastern Scotland from which it is separated by the **Pentland Firth**. Made up of 67 islands, about one third of which are inhabited, Orkney, with **Shetland**, belonged to the Norwegian kingdom and became part of Scotland only in 1469 as part of a pledge for the dowry of Margaret, daughter of Christian I of Denmark and Norway, who married **James III**. In the late 16th and early 17th century the islands were ruled by the Stewart Earls of Orkney; see Patrick and Robert **Stewart**. A former county, Orkney became an island authority in 1975, and is now, as Orkney Islands Council, one of the 33 unitary local authorities; see **local government**. The administrative centre is **Kirkwall** on the east of Mainland; on the west is **Stromness**, the only other

# OIL AND GAS

The distillation of coal to produce tar and naphtha (a light oil) was patented in 1781 by Archibald **Cochrane**, 9th Earl of Dundonald, and introduced by him in 1782 at **Culross**, and in 1787 at Muirkirk, Ayrshire. The tar was used to preserve the hulls of wooden ships, and the naphtha as a solvent in varnish making. Gas was produced as a by-product, but was not used commercially. William **Murdock** is said to have experimented with making coal gas when a boy, in a cave near his home in Lugar, Ayrshire. After he had moved to Birmingham, to work for Boulton and Watt, he developed practical equipment for making and purifying gas for lighting factories. Within a very few years the use of gas for street, shop and domestic lighting had been developed and by 1820 the larger Scottish towns all had their own gas works. The demand for gas grew rapidly, and by the 1850s gas lighting was almost universal in Scotland's towns and larger villages. From the 1880s electric lighting competed, and the gas industry responded by the development of appliances such as cookers, fires, water-heaters and domestic irons, and by developing more efficient ways of making gas. The making of coal gas was phased out from the 1960s to the early 1980s, and supplanted in large measure by natural gas.

In areas where it was uneconomic to install gas works, people had to rely on oil lamps and candles. Until the 1850s the oils and waxes used were of vegetable or animal origin. In 1856 James **Young** patented a method of making lighting oil and candle wax from a mineral known as torbanite. The techniques he used to refine the crude oil made by heating this mineral were later used in refining crude petroleum in the United States and elsewhere. When deposits of torbanite ran out, oil shale was used instead, and a large industry based on this developed in **West Lothian** and **Lanarkshire** in the later 19th century. The red heaps (bings) of shale waste still dominate the West Lothian landscape.

The importation and refining of crude petroleum began in Scotland in about 1920, and the shale-oil industry then declined, closing in the 1950s. The **Grangemouth** refinery grew massively after 1945, responding to demand for motor spirit, diesel fuel and heavy fuel oils. Exploration of the North Sea for oil and natural gas began in the 1950s, and sufficient gas was found to justify phasing out coal gas production. In the early 1970s oil was discovered east of **Shetland**, and an oil boom began, with **Aberdeen**, **Peterhead** and **Montrose** the main bases for supplying the drilling rigs and production platforms. The building of the steel and concrete 'jackets' for production platforms began at **Nigg** and **Ardersier** in 1972, and there were also platform yards at Ardyne and **Hunterston** on the **Clyde**; **Kishorn**, Wester Ross; **Stornoway**; and at **Methil** on the **Forth**. A yard built at Portavadie, also on the Clyde, never went into production. Drilling rigs and semi-submersible support vessels were, briefly, built at **Port Glasgow**, and **Dundee** and **Invergordon** have been used for the repair of exploration rigs.

At first the oil produced was brought to shore by tanker, but soon pipelines were laid to shore bases, at **Sullom Voe**, Shetland; **Flotta**, Orkney; Nigg, and near Peterhead at St Fergus (gas), linked by pipeline to a refining plant at Mossmorran, near **Cowdenbeath**. The refinery at Grangemouth was enlarged, and linked to the Forties oilfield (and later to the Brae field) by pipeline, and to a base for exporting oil constructed at Hound Point, near Queensferry. A large gas-fired power station was built at **Boddam**, near Peterhead. The industry has now passed its peak of production, and Shetland and Orkney, in particular, are making plans to compensate for the loss of oil-based prosperity.

*Oil Rig in the North Sea.*

O

town. The islands are mostly low-lying with steep cliffs on the western side. **Fishing** and farming are the main industries, but there is an **oil** terminal on the island of Flotta, and an oil service base on Mainland. During both World Wars **Scapa Flow** was an important naval base. In World War II causeways were built to deter submarine attack; see **Churchill Barriers**. Other industries include **whisky** distilling, tourism, knitwear and jewellery making. The main airport is at Grimsetter, near Kirkwall, and most of the populated islands have airstrips. Ferries also operate from the Scottish mainland and between the islands. The islands' history long predates their membership of both the Norse and Scottish kingdoms. Their unique prehistoric and archaeological remains (notably at **Skara Brae** and **Maes Howe** on Mainland, on **Rousay** and on **Papa Westray**) are evidence of Stone Age, Iron Age, Pictish and Celtic inhabitants. See also **Burray, Eday, Egilsay, Flotta, Hoy, North Ronaldsay, Papa Westray, Rousay, Sanday, Shapinsay, South Ronaldsay** and **Stronsay**.

**Orkneyinga Saga** or **Earls' Saga** An Icelandic history, dating from the early 13th century, of the Norse rulers of **Orkney** and **Caithness** from the 9th to the 12th centuries. Some of the stories it tells are mythical, but it also provides important information on the Scotland and Norway of that time.

**Orkney sheep** see **North Ronaldsay**

**Ormiston** Village in East Lothian near **Tranent**, with a pre-Reformation market cross now in the care of **Historic Scotland**. It was 'improved' in the 18th century by the agricultural reformer John Cockburn of Ormiston (1685–1758). He granted generous long-term leases to his tenants, but on condition that they follow new and methodical methods of land use. Sadly, he went bankrupt in the process. He also rebuilt Ormiston Hall in 1745, the earlier house being the place where George **Wishart**, the martyr, was captured in 1546 by the Earl of **Bothwell**.

**Ormiston Hill** A hill (237m/777ft) in Fife near **Newburgh**.

**Oronsay** (Gaelic **Orasaigh**) Sparsely inhabited tidal island in the Inner Hebrides that is joined at low tide to the island of **Colonsay** to the north. It has remains of Stone Age shellmounds, an Iron Age fort, Dun Domhnuill, and the ruins of a 14th-century Augustinian priory, notably the Oronsay Cross.

**Orphir** A settlement on the south coast of Mainland **Orkney** that has the remains of the 12th-century Orphir Round Church, the only medieval round church in Scotland, and the Earl's Bu, a Norse building, both now in the care of **Historic Scotland**.

**Orr, John Boyd** see **Boyd Orr, John**

**Orr, Robin** (1909– ) Composer, b. Brechin. He was Professor of Music at **Glasgow University** (1956–65) and at Cambridge University (1965–76) and co-founded **Scottish Opera** in 1962. His works include operas, e.g. *Hermiston* (1975), 3 symphonies, choral works, songs and chamber music.

**osprey** A fish-eating bird that regularly visited sites in Scotland to breed until these visits were jeopardised by the activities of fishermen and egg collectors. Modern conservationist attitudes have led to a resurgence in breeding and there are now over 50 pairs, at **Boat of Garten** and other sites.

**Ossian** Allegedly the son of the Gaelic warrior, Fionn mac Cumhaill

*Hoy Sound from Outertown, Stromness, Orkney.*

(otherwise **Fingal**), who is said to have lived in the third century AD. He was believed to have been a poet, celebrating the activities of the Fian warriors, but achieved particular fame in James **Macpherson**'s translations of Gaelic 'epics' in the 1760s, from which the adjective 'Ossianic' is derived.

**Oswald, James** (1703–93) Philosopher, b. Dunnet. He inherited the parish of **Dunnet** from his father before moving to **Methven** in 1750. He was **Moderator** of the **General Assembly** in 1765. He published *Appeal to Common Sense on Behalf of Religion* (1766–72), which argues that it is common sense that leads to revelation.

**Oswald, James** (c.1711–96). Publisher, composer, violinist and dancing master, b. probably in Stirling area. His compositions combined Scots and baroque Italian elements. In *The Caledonian Pocket Companion* (15 volumes, 1745–70) he employed Italianate violin techniques which were assimilated by Scottish fiddlers. He moved to London in 1741, and in 1761 became Chamber Composer to George III.

**Otterburn, Battle of** Defeat of the English under Henry Percy, 'Hotspur', on 5 August 1388 by invading Scots under James, 2nd Earl of Douglas, who was killed. The encounter had major repercussions for Anglo-Scottish relations and in domestic politics in both realms. One episode in a national war, the misconception that the battle was merely part of a Douglas/Percy feud owes much to the Border **ballads** which the clash inspired. See **Borders**.

**Outer Hebrides** see **Western Isles**

**Outer House** see **Court of Session**

**Outer Isles** see **Western Isles**

**outfield** Before agricultural improvements, the poorer part of the cultivated ground of a farm. It was generally cropped for 3 or 4 years until the yield did not repay the seed or the effort, then left fallow for several years to recover. It was also a general resource area, quarried for sods for building, dyking and thatching purposes. See also **infield**.

**Out Skerries** or **Skerries** An island group, the most easterly group in **Shetland**, of some 25 small islands and rocks forming

*An osprey plucks a fish from the water.*

a natural almost landlocked harbour, which led to the development of a fishing industry. The two main inhabited islands, Housay and Bruray, are connected by a road bridge. There is a Stevenson **lighthouse** on the eastern most island, Bound Skerry, an airstrip on Bruray and a roll-on/roll-off ferry to **Lerwick**.

**Out Stack** The most northerly point in the British Isles, a rock just north of **Muckle Flugga** to the north of **Unst** in **Shetland**.

**Owen, Robert** (1771–1858) Welsh social reformer, b. Newtown, Montgomeryshire. In 1799 he married the eldest daughter of David **Dale** from whom he bought the cotton mills at **New Lanark**, where he successfully implemented his ideas on progressive reform. He published *A New View of Society* (1813) and after leaving New Lanark founded several co-operative communities, including one at New Harmony in Indiana (1825–8), but none of these succeeded. He also established the Grand Consolidated Trade Union, the first large-scale trade union.

**Oyne** Village northwest of **Inverurie** in Aberdeenshire. To the southeast is the Z-plan castle of Harthill, dating from 1601, once the home of the tubulent Leith family. It was deliberately unroofed by the last Leith owner. Restored in the 1970s as a private home. To the north is Westhall, a 16th-century L-plan tower house built by the rival Abercrombies. Further south is the 16th-century L-plan tower house, Place of Tillyfour, restored and extended in 1884 by Robert **Lorimer**.

**oxgang** see **weights and measures**, p.384

**oysters** Historically, the European oyster, *Ostrea edulis*, was plentiful in the estuaries and sea lochs of Scotland and oysters were an important part of the diet, even featuring in a poem by Robert **Fergusson**. In the 1850s, however, stocks began to fall because of overfishing and (on the east coast) pollution and now there are only a few oyster beds on the west coast. In the 20th century the Pacific oyster, *Crassostrea gigas*, was introduced into fish farms on the west coast, leading to a new oyster industry, notably on **Loch Fyne**.

O

**Pabbay** (Gaelic **Pabaigh**) Uninhabited island in the Outer **Hebrides**, northeast of **Mingulay**, part of the group known as the Bishop's Isles. A symbol stone and cross slab survive from the early Christian hermitage here.

**Pabbay** Island northwest of **North Uist** and **Berneray**, separated from Berneray by the Sound of Pabbay. It has been completely uninhabited since the 1970s. The Morrison clan motto '*Teaghlach Phabaig*' or 'family of Pabbay' refers to their origins on this island.

**P & O** Initials by which the Peninsular and Oriental Steam Navigation Co Ltd became familiarly known, and which are now the identity of the modern trading company. The company was founded in 1837 as the Peninsular Steam Navigation Company, to operate the mail services from England to the Iberian Peninsula, which had previously been provided by the Royal Navy. The promoter of the concern, which started with a fleet of 7 paddle steamers, was Arthur **Anderson**, a Shetlander. Subsequently the company secured the mail contract for India, and added Oriental to its name. P & O became one of the largest and most prestigious shipping companies in the world, but like other passenger liner concerns lost most of its business after the proliferation of long-distance jet airliners in the late 1950s. The firm then developed cruise liner services, and took over a number of other businesses, including the Orkney and Shetland Shipping Co. They continued to operate ferry services to the North Isles until 2002.

**Paisley** (pop. 74,170) Town 11km (7mi) west of **Glasgow**, and at one time the fourth-largest settlement in Scotland. A former **burgh**, it is now the administrative centre of **Renfrewshire** Council. Since the 18th century it has been known for its textile industry, particularly the production of cotton thread and of **Paisley pattern** shawls. The 2 major thread firms, **Coats** and Clarks, merged in the 1890s, and are now Coats Paton, though thread-making ended in Paisley in 1984. It was also an important centre of shipbuilding and engineering. Paisley Abbey, on the east bank of the **White Cart** River, was a Cluniac house, founded as a priory in 1163. The present church is 15th century, with a choir and central tower rebuilt, mainly by Robert **Lorimer** in the 1920s. It contains the tomb of Marjory **Bruce**. It is still in use as a church. An earlier Celtic monastery was dedicated to St Mirren, and this name is now used by Paisley's **football** team. Paisley has remarkable public buildings, mainly the result of Coats and Clark generosity: the Clark Town Hall by W H Lyon of Belfast (1879–82), the Greek Library and Museum (1868) and Observatory (1883) by John **Honeyman** for the Coats family, and the cathedral-like Coats Memorial Church, by Hippolyte Jean Blanc (1886–94).

**Paisley, Janet** (1948– ) Poet, short-story writer and playwright, who lives in Falkirk. She has published collections, including poetry in *Pegasus in Flight* (1989) and *Wildfire* (1993), poetic monologues in *Ye Cannae Win* (2000), and short stories in **Scots** in *Not for Glory*. She won the Peggy Ramsay Award for her play, *Refuge*, in 1996.

**Paisley pattern/shawl** Scots and English soldiers who reached Kashmir in the service of the East India Company were the first to bring back a distinctive style of shawl in an elaborate pattern based on Hindu and Arabic motifs. Demand for imitations grew in the west, and after a brief period of production in **Edinburgh**, **Paisley** became the main centre for production. Already a weaving community, it had sufficient skilled labour to meet the demand, and the pattern became known as the Paisley pattern. For 70 years, the Paisley shawl was a highly popular fashion item and the mainstay of the Paisley economy, and the pattern has remained popular.

**Paisley University** Founded in 1897 as Paisley Technical College and School of Art, it was granted university status in 1993 and has 3500 students. Its main campus is in the centre of **Paisley**, but it also has 2 others, in **Ayr** (the former Craigie College of Education) and **Dumfries**, as a result of mergers with other colleges. Its emphasis is on vocational courses in subjects including business, engineering and science.

**pancake** Small round flat cake made by allowing thick batter to drop onto a **girdle**, smaller and thicker than an English pancake, and usually eaten cold with butter, jam etc. Also called a dropped scone.

**pan drop** A round flat white peppermint sweet, a mint imperial, often eaten in church. The ideal length of a sermon was once described as: 'twa pan drops, weel sookit and nae crunchit'.

**pan loaf** A loaf of bread with a hard smooth crust, baked in a pan or tin, in contrast to the plain loaf, a batch loaf with a hard black crust on top and a floury brown crust at the bottom. As the pan loaf was more expensive, the term has come to mean an affected and ultra-refined way of speaking designed to impress others.

**Paolozzi, Eduardo** (1924– ) Artist, b. Leith. The son of Italian immigrants, Paolozzi studied briefly in **Edinburgh** before moving to London. Influenced at first by Surrealism, his early collages and sculptures (incorporating images from popular culture and utilising found objects) were among the first expressions of British Pop Art, of which he is considered a father figure. Known in particular for his large-scale metal sculpture, he has produced work in a wide variety of media (including decorative schemes for buildings). A large collection of his work, including a reconstruction of his studio, is in the Dean Gallery, Edinburgh (see **Scottish National Gallery of Modern Art**).

**Papa Stour** (pop. 23) Island just off the west coast of **Shetland** Mainland, reached by boat from West Burrafirth. With spectacular sea caves and stacks, it is home to many seabirds. It holds much archaeological evidence of previous inhabitants, including Norse settlers. The island is fertile and in the 19th century had a population of around 300; it continues to support a small community.

**Papa Westray** (pop. 65) Island in **Orkney**, northeast of **Westray**, also known as Papay. A Neolithic farm building at Knap of Howar, built around 3500 BC, is the oldest standing house in Europe. To the north of the island is an RSPB Nature Reserve. The population has fallen dramatically since the 19th century, but a community co-operative encourages settlement and works to keep the island viable.

**Paps of Jura** see **Jura**

**Paraffin Young** see **Young, James**

**Park, Mungo** (1771–1806) Explorer, b. Foulshiels, near **Selkirk**. In 1795 he travelled to Africa, leading an expedition to find the source of the River Niger. His accounts of his travels were later published as *Travels into the Interior of Africa*. He returned to Scotland in 1801, and practised as a doctor in **Peebles**. In 1804 he led another expedition in Africa, attempting to continue his exploration of the Niger, but he was drowned in Nigeria.

**Parkhead** District of **Glasgow**, noted as the location of Celtic Park, the home stadium of **Celtic** Football Club. The Parkhead stadium was rebuilt as an all-seater stadium in the 1990s. See also **football**. It was also the site of William **Beardmore** & Co's Parkhead Forge, notable for its early adoption of steelmaking, and for its role as an armaments works in both World Wars.

**Parliament** see **Scottish Parliament**

**Parliament Hall** see **Edinburgh**

**parliamentary** Used to describe insitutions, etc, enacted, established or financed by parliament: parliamentary roads/bridges, built by the **Commission for Highland Roads and Bridges** in the early 19th century; parliamentary churches, created by Acts of Parliament in 1810 and 1824, with public funds, when larger parishes were divided; parliamentary schools, set up in the mid 19th century with government funding to pay salaries.

**parritch** see **porridge**

**partan bree** A soup made with crab, rice, cream etc; partan is a **Scots** word for crab, deriving from **Gaelic**, and bree means liquid in which something has been boiled.

**Partick Thistle Football Club** Glasgow club founded 1876, their home ground is at Firhill on the west side of the city. Traditionally a refuge for Glaswegian fans eager to avoid the religious connotations of supporting Rangers or Celtic, Thistle have a reputation for romantic inconsistency punctured by mere moments of success. They won the Scottish Cup in 1921, then 50 years later won the League Cup, defeating Celtic in a memorable final. They are nicknamed the Jags.

**Pass of Brander** see **Brander, Pass of**

**Paterson, Bill** (1945– ) Actor, b. Glasgow. His early career was associated with the theatre group 7:84. His film and television credits include *Comfort and Joy* (1984), *The Killing Fields* (1984), *The Crow Road* (1996), *Wives and Daughters* (1999) and *Darien: Disaster in Paradise* (2003).

**Paterson, Don** (1963– ) Poet and musician, b. Dundee. He began his career as a musician in popular music but soon began writing poetry, which has won several prestigious awards, including his latest collection *Landing Lights* (2003). He has also written plays for radio and for the **Dundee** Rep.

**Paterson, James** (1854–1932) Artist, b. Glasgow. Paterson is known in particular for his paintings of the landscape around the Dumfriesshire village of Moniaive, where he lived from 1884 to 1905 (after which he lived in **Edinburgh**). As a student in Paris he had met some of the future **Glasgow Boys**, and he helped establish the journal, *The Scottish Art Review*, which expressed the ideas of the School.

P

**Paterson, William** (1658–1719) Banker, b. Tynwald, Dumfriesshire. He was one of the first directors of the Bank of England in 1694, and a leading supporter of the **Darien** Expedition. He took part in the first voyage to Darien, but lost his wife and son and much of his fortune on the disastrous expedition. A supporter of the **Union**, he became MP for **Dumfries** in 1707.

**Paton, Sir Joseph Noel** (1821–1901) Artist and antiquarian, b. Dunfermline. Known for his highly detailed, ambitious paintings of historical and mythological scenes, in particular *The Quarrel of Oberon and Titania* (**National Gallery of Scotland**). He was appointed Her Majesty's Limner in Scotland in 1865 and received commissions from her to paint the royal family.

**Patrick, James McIntosh** (1907–98) Artist, b. Dundee. He first found success while still a student at **Glasgow School of Art**, producing minutely observed etchings. In the 1930s he began to work predominantly in oil, producing detailed, panoramic paintings of the rural landscape, a subject he rarely veered from and for which he became enormously popular. After World War II he worked increasingly out-of-doors, painting in watercolour.

**Pattack, Loch** see **Loch Pattack**

**Paul, John** see **Jones, John Paul**

**Paxton** Village near the English border, 7km (4mi) west of **Berwick-upon-Tweed**. Paxton House is a Palladian mansion on the north bank of the River **Tweed** built in 1758 by John and James **Adam**. It belonged to the Homes, and now displays part of the collection of the **National Galleries of Scotland**, including important paintings and furniture.

**pease brose** see **brose**

**peat** Semi-carbonised vegetable matter found under the surface of boggy moorland, long an important source of fuel, in the form of dried, brick-shaped pieces, especially in the **Highlands** and Islands. Also used in horticulture.

**Peat Inn** Small former coal-mining village, 10km (6mi) southwest of **St Andrews**. Its name comes from its coaching inn, now a hotel and restaurant, run by David Wilson, with an outstanding reputation.

**peck** see **weights and measures**, pp.382-4

**Peddie & Kinnear** Architectural partnership, formed 1856, comprising John Dick Peddie (1824–91) b. Edinburgh, and Charles George Hood Kinnear (1830–94) b. Kinloch, Fife. Work as architects to the Royal Bank from 1856 and the Bank of Scotland from 1859, included the iron dome of the Royal Bank's head office in **Edinburgh** (1857), together with the Gothic Morgan Academy, **Dundee** (1863–68) and **Aberdeen** Municipal Buildings (1867–74), numerous country houses and the hydropathics at **Dunblane** and at **Craiglockhart**, Edinburgh. Peddie, co-founder of the Scottish American Trust and the Scottish Investment Trust, became a New Worlds investment manager in 1878 and a Liberal MP in 1880, campaigning for Disestablishment; Kinnear was the inventor of the first bellows camera.

**Peden, Alexander** (c.1626–86) Covenanting minister, b. Sorn, Ayrshire. Minister at New Luce from 1660 to 1662, he was declared a rebel for preaching at **conventicles**, and spent many years evading capture in the countryside. He was imprisoned on the **Bass Rock** from 1673 to 1678, but was later released and continued his preaching. After his death his body was exhumed by government troops, and was buried beneath the **Cumnock** gallows (where they had intended to hang it in chains). After the Revolution of 1688, the people of **Cumnock** moved their burial place to beside Peden's grave as a mark of their respect. A mask he wore to disguise himself is in the **Museum of Scotland**.

**Peebles** (pop. 8065) Town on the north bank of the River **Tweed**, 37km (23mi) south of **Edinburgh**, a former royal **burgh** and county town of **Peeblesshire**. The ruined nave and west tower of the 13th-century Cross Kirk can still be seen. In the 19th and 20th centuries Peebles was a centre of wool and textile production, and it is now primarily a tourist centre and dormitory town. **Neidpath Castle** is nearby. Peebles **Common Riding** festival, the Peebles Beltane, takes place in June (but see **Beltane**). The main male participant is the Cornet and ceremonies include the crowning of the Beltane Queen.

**Peeblesshire** Former county in southeast Scotland. From 1975–96 it was the Tweeddale District of **Borders** Region and it is now part of **Scottish Borders** local authority; see maps on pp.394-5 and **local government**.

**peel** Name given to a **tower house**, particularly in the **Borders**.

**Pencaitland** Village 10km (6mi) southwest of **Haddington**. It is divided into Easter and Wester Pencaitland by the River **Tyne**, spanned by a 16th-century bridge. The parish church, dating in part from the 13th century, is in Easter Pencaitland. Nearby is Winton House, dating from 1620, built by William Wallace for the Earl of Winton and notable for its splendid plasterwork. It belongs to Sir Francis and Lady Ogilvy and is open for guided tours and for hospitality events.

P

Tulips and Fruit *by S J Peploe (c.1919)*.

**pend** Large (arched) entrance or passageway leading through the ground floor of a **tenement** building or between buildings, to give access to ground to the rear.

**Penicuik** (pop. 14,759) Town on the North **Esk**, 14km (9mi) southwest of **Edinburgh**, laid out in 1770 by Sir James Clerk, son of Sir John **Clerk** of Penicuik, and known for its papermills and for the first cotton-spinning mill. Industry today includes the Edinburgh Crystal factory. Penicuik House, built in 1761, was reduced to a shell by fire in 1899, and the Clerks of Penicuik now live in the converted stable block of 1768, set in a landscape park with ornamental buildings of the same vintage. There is a replica of Arthur's Oon (see **Stenhousemuir**) above an arch on the courtyard.

**Peninsular and Oriental Steam Navigation Co** see **P & O**

**Penkill** Small Ayrshire village, 5km (3mi) east of **Girvan**. Penkill Castle is a partly ruined 16th-century tower house reconstructed and extended in 1857 by the painter Spencer Boyd and his sister Alice in association with William Bell Scott as a pre-Raphaelite retreat. The turnpike stair was painted as a continuous mural, the King's Quair, by Scott.

**Pennan** Former fishing village at the foot of red sandstone cliffs, on the Aberdeenshire coast, west of **Fraserburgh**. It was used as a location for the 1983 film *Local Hero*.

**penny** see **weights and measures**, pp.382-4

**Pennymuir** Well-preserved Roman camps on the northern edge of the Cheviot Hills 10km (6mi) southeast of **Jedburgh**. A large temporary marching camp is enclosed by an earthen rampart, and a smaller and later camp was built in its southeast corner. They lie beside **Dere Street**, which descends the Cheviots past a large native hillfort on Woden Law.

**penny wedding** Wedding celebration at which all the guests traditionally contributed a small sum of money, or occasionally food or drink, towards the cost of the entertainment; any surplus was given to the couple as a gift.

**Pentland Firth** Channel between the northeast headland of Scotland and **Orkney**. Ferries cross from **Scrabster** to **Stromness** on Mainland Orkney, and from **John o' Groats** to **St Margaret's Hope** and Burwick on **South Ronaldsay**. Only 11km (7mi) wide, it is notorious for its tidal streams which run at speeds higher than at almost any other part of the Scottish coast. The main tide race, known as the 'Merry Men of Mey', runs from Tor Ness on **Hoy**, Orkney, to St John's Point on the **Caithness** coast.

**Pentland Hills** Range of hills lying southwest of **Edinburgh**. The highest point is Scald Law, 579m (1900ft). Since 1984 the area has been designated the Pentland Hills Regional Park. A range of walks cross the hills, and several reservoirs within the area provide much of Edinburgh's water supply. The Midlothian Ski Centre at **Hillend** lies on the northern slopes.

**Pentland Rising** In 1666 an army of **Covenanters** from the southwest advanced towards **Edinburgh**. They did not gain the support for which they had hoped, and were defeated by Royalist troops under General Tam **Dalyell** at the Battle of Rullion Green on the slopes of the **Pentland Hills**.

**Pentland Skerries** A group of uninhabited islands in the **Pentland Firth**, 5km (3mi) south of **South Ronaldsay**, known as Muckle Skerry, Little Skerry, Louther Skerry and Clettack Skerry. The **lighthouse** on Muckle Skerry was built in 1794.

**Peploe, Samuel John** (1871–1935) Artist, b. Edinburgh. One of the **Scottish Colourists**, Peploe worked in **Edinburgh** before moving to Paris at the encouragement of his friend J D **Fergusson**, where his still lifes and landscapes took on a distinctly modern note, influenced by Post-Impressionism and Fauve art. He returned to Edinburgh in 1912 and from 1920 he regularly painted on the island of **Iona**, alongside F C B **Cadell**. Towards the end of his career he taught briefly at **Edinburgh College of Art**.

**Perth** (pop. 43,450) Town on the River **Tay**, former royal **burgh** and county town of **Perthshire**, known as the 'Fair City' (from its ancient status as a cathedral city), it is now the administrative centre of **Perth and Kinross** Council and an important focus for the surrounding countryside. The Romans had a camp to the north of the city. In 1266 the Treaty of Perth, signed here, saw Magnus IV of Norway concede the **Hebrides** and the Isle of Man to **Alexander III**. Perth was the scene of a famous judicial conflict between rival clans before **Robert III** in 1396, and later a favourite residence of **James I**, who held parliaments here and was ultimately murdered here. The oldest building in the town is the largely 15th-century St John's Kirk, built on an earlier site. It gives the town its alternative name, St John's Toun, which is today borne by the local **football** team, St Johnstone. It was in St John's Kirk that John **Knox** preached a sermon which helped to begin the **Reformation** in Scotland. The County Buildings are Greek revival by Sir Robert Smirke of 1819–22 and the remarkable domed waterworks (1830–2) by Adam Anderson are now the J D **Fergusson** Gallery. Perth Prison, housing male prisoners, was built in 1810–12 for French prisoners of war

*The Pictish carved stone at Aberlemno, Angus.*

and rebuilt as a general prison in 1839–57. Pullars of Perth pioneered large-scale dyeing, laundering and dry-cleaning; its works now house local-authority offices. To the east is Kinnoull Hill, 222m (728ft).

**Perth and Kinross Council** Local-authority area formed in 1996 from the Perth and Kinross District of **Tayside** Region, with altered boundaries; see maps on pp.394-5 and **local government**. The administrative centre is **Perth** and other towns include **Blairgowrie**, **Kinross**, **Auchterarder**, **Crieff** and **Pitlochry**. Much of the land is richly agricultural, and known particularly for its fruit-growing. Tourism is important.

**Perthshire** Former large county, with **Highland** and **Lowland** areas. In 1975 a large part of it became the **Perth and Kinross** District of **Tayside** Region. See maps on pp.394-5 and **local government**.

**Peterhead** (pop. 17,947) Red-granite **fishing** town on the **Aberdeenshire** coast, founded 1587, the most easterly town on the Scottish mainland. In the late 18th century it was owned by the Merchant Maiden Company of Edinburgh and replanned on formal lines around Broad Street by a committee of feuars. It was then a spa and a leading whaling port, and by the 19th century it was dominating the herring fishing industry. Today it is Europe's leading white-fish port, with a busy fish market. The nearby prison, which now specialises in the housing and treatment of male sex offenders, was under threat of closure but has been reprieved. It was established in 1884 to build the national harbour of refuge using convict labour.

**petticoat tails** see **shortbread**

**Phantassie Doocot** Beehive **doocot** on farmland lying east of **East Linton**. It contains nest boxes for over 500 pigeons, which would have been kept for their meat and eggs. It is in the care of the **National Trust for Scotland**.

**Philiphaugh, Battle of** Battle on 13 September 1645, at Philiphaugh, near **Selkirk**. A Royalist army under the command of the Marquis of **Montrose** was surprised and defeated by the regular cavalry of the **Covenanting** General David **Leslie**.

**Philipson, Sir Robin** (1916–92) Artist, b. Broughton-in-Furness, Cumbria. Studied and worked in **Edinburgh**, where he became central to the artistic establishment in his positions as Head of Painting at **Edinburgh College of Art** and President of the **Royal Scottish Academy**. He first became known in the 1950s for his paintings of cock-fights and subsequently produced work on a wide range of subjects, including cathedral interiors, crucifixions and World War II.

**Physicians, Royal College of** see **Royal College of Physicians**

**pibroch** see **piobaireachd**

**Piccolomini, Aeneas Silvius** (1405–64) Ambassador, later Pope Pius II, b. near Siena, Italy. He wrote a colourful description of his visit to Scotland in 1435, which included a barefoot pilgrimage to **Whitekirk** and an eventful journey through the **Borders**.

**Pictish Chronicle** Chronicle which was probably written during the reign of **Kenneth II** (971–95), but only exists in several later copies. It tells of the origins of the **Picts** and lists the kings of both Picts and Scots.

**Picts** People who lived in the northern part of Scotland, equated with Cruithne in Gaelic. They were probably descended from Celtic tribes and were described by the Romans as 'Picti' (painted ones). Material evidence, such as intricately carved stones and place names, point to their society stretching from the **Northern Isles** throughout north and east Scotland, as far south as **Fife**. The separate Pictish kingdom came under great pressure from Viking attack in the 9th century, and the Gaelic kingdom of Alba, ruled by the descendants of **Kenneth mac Alpin**, had emerged in its place by c.900. See also **language**.

**Piggott, Stuart** (1910–96) Archaeologist, b. Petersfield, Hampshire. He made his name in the archaeology of southern England and India, before becoming Abercrombie Professor of Prehistoric Archaeology at **Edinburgh University** (1946–75). He excavated at **Cairnpapple** and elsewhere in Scotland and encouraged his students to view Scottish archaeology within its European context. He was President of the **Society of Antiquaries of Scotland** 1967–72 and was widely honoured outside Scotland.

**Pineapple, the** see **Airth**

**Pinkerton, Allan** (1819–84) Detective, b. Glasgow. He emigrated to America in 1842, where he set up a private detective agency in Chicago. In 1861 he prevented an assassination attempt on President Lincoln.

**Pinkerton, John** (1758–1826) Historian and writer, b. Edinburgh. He lived in London and Paris and wrote numerous books, including two histories of Scotland, the more important of which was his *History of Scotland from the accession of the House of Stuart to that of Mary* (1797). He supported Lowland Scottish culture as being vastly superior to the Highland (Celtic).

**Pinkie, Battle of** On 10 September 1547 the Scots army, under the 2nd Earl of **Arran**, was defeated by an invading English army near **Musselburgh**. The English troops were commanded by the Duke of Somerset. The battle was part of the **Rough Wooing**.

**Pinkie House** see **Musselburgh**

**pint** see **weights and measures**, pp.382–4

**piobaireachd** (often anglicised as '**pibroch**'). A style of bagpipe music considered to be one of the great musical art forms of Europe. Its origins are obscure but it appears to have been developed in or introduced to the **Highlands** of Scotland in the 16th century possibly by the **MacCrimmons**.

**Piobaireachd Society** Based in **Glasgow**, it was founded in 1903 to encourage the study and playing of **piobaireachd** and has published 15 collections of piobaireachd. It founded the Army School of Piping and supplied the instructors for it until 1957. It holds an annual conference and recommends tunes for competition at the **Northern Meeting** and the **Argyllshire Gathering**.

**pipe band** A musical group of pipers and drummers who often perform while marching on ceremonial occasions and compete on the basis of judged performances. All the Scottish regiments have a pipe band, the leader and musical director of which is known as the pipe major; this designation is now also used by non-military pipe bands.

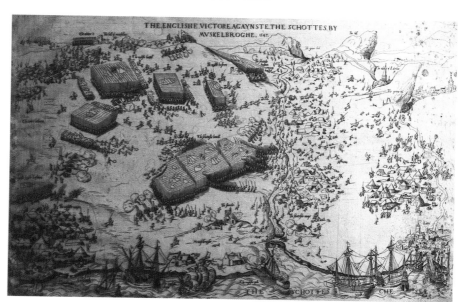

*A contemporary view of the Battle of Pinkie (1547).*

**P**

**Piper Alpha** Disaster on an offshore oil- and gas-platform in the North Sea in July 1988, when the Piper Alpha oil rig was destroyed by a fire resulting from an explosion on board, with the loss of 167 lives.

**Pitcairne, Archibald** (1652–1713) Doctor, Latinist and Jacobite propagandist, b. Edinburgh. He was a leading figure in the early **Scottish Enlightenment**. Professor of Medicine in Leyden and **Edinburgh**, he was one of the founders of the **Royal College of Physicians**. He is also remembered for his play *The Assembly* (1692), a satire on the **Church of Scotland**.

**Pitcaithly bannock** A round of thick **shortbread** flavoured and decorated with almonds, caraway seed and orange and/or lemon peel. Also spelled Pikeathly; see also **Bridge of Earn**.

**Pitcaple** Village 7km (4mi) northwest of **Inverurie**. Pitcaple Castle is a 15th-century tower, reconstructed in the early 17th century by the Leslies as a round-towered Z-plan castle, augmented by a new wing by William **Burn** in 1830.

**Pitfichie Castle** Late 16th-century tower house 11km (7mi) southwest of **Inverurie**, home of the Civil War General Sir John Urry who changed sides several times and was eventually hanged by the Marquis of **Montrose** in 1650. Picturesquely composed with circular entrance tower, unroofed in 1769, but rebuilt in 1977.

**Pitkerro House** Early 17th-century house to the northeast of **Dundee**, attractively restored and enlarged in 1902–4 for Col. Douglas Dick by Sir Robert **Lorimer**; it is now divided into flats.

**Pitlessie** Village in the **Howe of Fife**, 6km (4mi) southwest of **Cupar**. It is associated with the painting *Pitlessie Fair*, by David **Wilkie**, who was born nearby.

**Pitlochry** (Gaelic **Baile Chloichridh**) (pop. 2564) Town on the River **Tummel**, 11km (8mi) north of **Dunkeld**. It developed as a tourist resort after a visit from Queen Victoria in 1844, the arrival of the railway in 1863, reaching its climax with the building of the chateau-like Atholl Hydropathic by Andrew Heiton (1875–78), now the Atholl Palace Hotel. The town's facilities and scenic yet accessible location continue to make it popular with tourists. The Pitlochry Festival Theatre, founded in 1951, is open during the summer; the Scottish Plant Collectors' Garden is being developed here. **Loch Faskally**, lying to the north, is part of a hydroelectric scheme and includes a salmon ladder with an observation chamber.

**Pitmedden** Village with a notable walled garden near **Old Meldrum**, Aberdeenshire. Pitmedden House was destroyed by fire in 1818, but in 1952 the **National Trust for Scotland** acquired the garden, originally laid out by Sir Alexander Seton in 1675. It has been recreated as an intricate 17th-century formal garden, and includes 4 symmetrical parterres, a fountain and 27 sundials. There is also a Museum of Farming Life.

**Pitmuies** see **House of Pitmuies**

**Pitscottie** see **Lindsay, Robert**

**Pitsligo, Alexander Forbes, 4th Lord** (1678–1762) A Jacobite. He took part in both the 1715 **Jacobite Rising**, and the 1745 (at the age of 67). His estate was forfeited and he later lived there in disguise.

**Pitsligo Castle** Ruined tower house near Rosehearty, built in 1424 and extended in the 16th century. The last Lord **Pitsligo** was Alexander Forbes, 4th Lord, a **Jacobite** whose lands were forfeited after **Culloden**. It is now owned by a local trust. The magnificent Pitsligo loft of 1634 is now in the Hill Church of Rosehearty.

**Pittencrieff** see **Dunfermline**

**Pittenweem** Fishing village in the **East Neuk of Fife**, east of **St Monans**. A royal **burgh** since 1541, it was a thriving trading port and remains an active **fishing** community with a busy fish market. Several buildings dating from the 16th and 17th centuries have been restored by the **National Trust for Scotland**. Kelly Lodging in the High Street dates mainly from the late 16th century and was the town residence of the Earls of Kellie. The Augustinian Priory moved here from the Isle of **May** in the 13th century, and the remains of its church are incorporated in the present parish church which incorporated the Tolbooth Tower of 1588. The monastic buildings partly survive, the 15th-century gatehouse, the dormitory and the Great House, and the Priors Lodging, remodelled as the rectory in 1840. There is a cave associated with St **Fillan**.

**Pittodrie** see **Aberdeen Football Club**

**place names** see p.303

**plaid** A long piece of woollen, usually **tartan**, cloth formerly worn as an outer garment. In the **Highlands** it was worn round the middle and over the shoulder and held in place with a belt (belted plaid); this garment was the forerunner of the modern **kilt**. A plaid worn over the shoulder is part of **Highland dress**, especially of pipe bands (see **bagpipes**) and the word also refers to a tartan shawl formerly worn by women, and to the tartan cloth of which these are made.

**plain loaf** see **pan loaf**

**Playfair, Sir Hugh Lyon** (1786–1861) Provost of **St Andrews**,

# PLACE NAMES

Scotland has place names from many different sources. Some, especially some river names, originate from so far back in the past that one can only speculate as to their origins. But most of them mirror the country's population over the last two millennia. The majority are from **Gaelic** or English/**Scots**, but other waves of inhabitants have also left their mark. Early inhabitants of southern Scotland spoke a language related to modern Welsh, sometimes called Cumbric; reminders of their time include Penpont ('end of the bridge') and Tranent ('farmstead of the streams'). The **Picts** in the north have left only meagre linguistic trace, but their occupancy is identified from the **Forth** northwards, most clearly with Pit- names such as Pitreavie, Pitlochry. In most cases the second element is Gaelic, with *pit*, meaning 'portion (of land)', reminding us of the Pictish past.

In the Northern and Western Isles and along the adjoining seaboard, the Norse occupations from the 9th century into the medieval period have left a strong legacy in names such as Lerwick ('mud bay'), Kirkwall ('churchfield'), some in Gaelicised forms, for example Sildeag ('herring bay'; anglicised as Shieldaig), Dibidail ('deep valley'; anglicised as Dibidale).

Gaelic and Cumbric are Celtic languages, as is Pictish (but see **language**), while Scots, English and Norse are Germanic. The different structures of these families of languages lead to very frequent mispronunciation of Scottish place-names: in the Celtic languages, the naming element comes first, the describing element second, whereas in the Germanic family,

the other way round. Place-names naturally put the stress on the describing element, thus Gaelic Beinn an **Eòin** (literally mountain of the bird) would become in English **Bird** Mountain. Frequently Celtic (-origin) names are thus pronounced with the wrong stress, for example **Cairn**gorms, instead of Cairn**gorms**, **Ab**erdeen, instead of Aber**deen,** **Avie**more, instead of Avie**more.**

The great majority of names in the Highlands are of Gaelic origin and follow this pattern, but sometimes people fail to spot the exceptions, many from Norse, and will use pronunciations such as Mall**aig** and As**synt**, instead of **Mall**aig and **Ass**ynt. Further confusion is caused by the early recording of names by people who had no knowledge of the underlying language of the names, leading to frequent misspellings and gross mispronunciations.

South of the Forth-Clyde line, there are many more English/Scots names, alongside the underlying Cumbric layer, including some of Old English origin, such as Tyninghame, Berwick. But Gaelic names are to be found throughout Scotland. Edinburgh for example has the Calton Hill from Gaelic *calltainn* meaning 'hazel' and in Midlothian there is Garvald, from Gaelic *garbh allt* meaning 'rough stream'.

This rich tapestry has been the subject of much research, notably in **Edinburgh University**, and there are opportunities for anyone interested in the subject to take part. See also **language**.

---

b. Meigle, Perthshire. He was a lieutenant-colonel in the Bengal Horse Artillery. He sponsored the formation of the **Royal and Ancient** Golf Club, and as Provost (1842-6) he ran a slum-clearance and building programme to make St Andrews an upmarket holiday resort.

**Playfair, James** (1755–1794) Architect, b. Benvie near Dundee, brother of John **Playfair**. He became familiar with Paris through his inventor brother William who had settled there, and was a protégé of Henry **Dundas** for whom he built **Melville Castle** 1786-91. His Cairness House, Aberdeenshire (1791-7) is a remarkable piece of French neoclassicism with a strong emphasis on pure geometrical forms.

**Playfair, John** (1748–1819) Geologist and scientist, b. Benvie, near Dundee, brother of James **Playfair**. A minister, he became Professor of Mathematics in **Edinburgh** in 1785, and Professor of **Natural Philosophy** in 1805. He was a keen geologist and a close friend of James **Hutton**, whose work he publicised in

*Illustrations of the Huttonian Theory of the Earth* in 1802.

**Playfair, Lyon, 1st Baron** (1818-98) Scientist, teacher and politician, b. Chunar, Bengal, nephew of Sir Hugh Lyon **Playfair**. He served on the Royal Commissions on sanitation and on the potato famine in Ireland. He had a role in the Great Exhibition of 1851 and in the setting up of the Royal Scottish Museum in 1861. He was Professor of Chemistry at **Edinburgh University** from 1858, a Liberal MP from 1867, and made a peer in 1892. He was influential in Scottish university reform in the late 19th century.

**Playfair, William Henry** (1789-1857) Architect, b. London, son of James **Playfair**. He is responsible for many of **Edinburgh's** outstanding Greek-revival buildings, including the National Monument and Observatory on Calton Hill, the **Royal Scottish Academy**, the **National Gallery of Scotland**, the **Royal College of Surgeons** and the New Town streets of Royal Terrace, Carlton Terrace and Regent Terrace. He also designed the Tudor **New College** on the Mound and the Elizabethan Donaldson's School.

**P**

The Porteous Mob *by James Drummond (1855), see John Porteous.*

**Plockton** (Gaelic **Ploc Loch Aillse**, locally **Am Ploc**) Village on an inlet of the south shore of **Loch Carron**. Its scenic location attracts tourists, and it is known particularly for its palm trees, growing in the sheltered climate. It was the location for filming the television series *Hamish Macbeth* in the 1990s.

**ploughgate** see **weights and measures**, pp.382-4

**Pluscarden** Monastery lying 10km (6mi) southwest of **Elgin**. The abbey was originally founded in 1230 by **Alexander II** for Valliscaulian monks, and later became Benedictine. It was attacked by the 'Wolf of **Badenoch**', an event recorded in the chronicle composed there, the *Book of Pluscarden*. The abbey fell into ruin after the **Reformation**. In 1943 it was given to the Benedictine monks of Prinknash, Gloucestershire, by the family of the Marquess of Bute. The monks welcome visitors to the restored building.

**poinding** (pronounced 'pind ing') A legal process whereby the goods of a debtor are seized for the benefit of the creditor.

**Poker Club** Society set up in **Edinburgh** in 1762 to poke up the fires of agitation for a Scottish militia. Its founder members included Adam **Fergusson** and Adam **Smith**.

**Pollok House** Mansion house in Pollok Country Park, **Glasgow**, perhaps designed by William **Adam** and completed in 1752. It was extended by Sir Robert Rowand **Anderson** (1892–1908), when formal gardens were added. The house and grounds belonged to the Maxwell family, later Stirling-Maxwell, who gifted them to the City of Glasgow in 1966. It is now run by the **National Trust for Scotland**, and has an outstanding collection of Spanish paintings, including works by El Greco, Murillo and Goya. The **Burrell** Collection is also housed in the Park.

**Polmont** Growing dormitory town 5km (3mi) east of **Falkirk**, with a station on the **Edinburgh** to **Glasgow** railway line. It was formerly a centre of coal mining. Polmont Young Offenders' Institution is the largest in Scotland, and provides secure accommodation for male young offenders between the ages of 16 and 21.

**Pont, Timothy** (c.1565–1614) Mapmaker. He was minister of **Dunnet**, Caithness, from 1601 to 1614. He carried out an extensive survey of Scotland, and his maps were later revised by Robert **Gordon** of Straloch and published in **Blaeu**'s *Atlas Novus*. His manuscript maps have recently been made available on the Internet by the **National Library of Scotland**.

**Pontius Pilate's Bodyguard** see **Royal Scots**

**Poolewe** see **Loch Ewe**

**porridge** (in Scots **parritch**) A dish of oatmeal (or oatflakes) boiled in salted water, now a popular breakfast dish in many parts of the world, formerly an important part of the Scottish diet.

**port** A gate in a town wall.

**port-a-beul** Gaelic term for mouth music: a tune, usually a **reel**, to which repetitive words have been added to make it easier to sing, often used as an accompaniment to dancing in the absence of instrumental music.

**Port Askaig** (Gaelic **Port Ascaig**) Village on **Islay**, on the shore of the Sound of Islay. Ferries cross to here from **Jura** and from Kennacraig on the **Kintyre** coast.

**Port Charlotte** Attractive planned village on **Islay**, on the western shore of Loch Indaal, established in 1828 by Walter

Frederick Campbell and named after his mother. It includes the Museum of Islay Life and a Wildlife Information Centre.

**Port Dundas** see **Glasgow**

**Port Ellen** (Gaelic **Port Ilin**) Village on the southern shore of **Islay** which was founded by Walter Frederick Campbell in 1821 and named after his wife. In summer there is a ferry service to Kennacraig on the **Kintyre** coast. Nearby is Carraig Fhada **lighthouse**, an unusual, square building erected in 1823. There is a large distillery maltings supplying all the Islay distilleries.

**Portencross** Village on the shore of the **Firth of Clyde**, 8km (5mi) northwest of **Ardrossan**. Portencross Castle is said to have been the last resting place of kings of Scots before they were taken to **Iona** for burial. The present ruined building, which dates from the 14th century, belonged to the Boyds of Kilmarnock. It now belongs to British Nuclear Fuels Limited.

**Porteous, John** (d.1736) Soldier, b. Canongate, Edinburgh. As Captain of the **Edinburgh** City Guard, he ordered his men to fire on an angry crowd at the execution of a smuggler. Many people were killed or wounded. Captain Porteous was sentenced to death but when his execution was delayed an angry mob broke into the **tolbooth**, seized him and hanged him in the events known as the Porteous Riots.

**Port Glasgow** (pop. 16,617) Town on the Firth of **Clyde**, 32km (20mi) northwest of **Glasgow**. It was originally known as Newark but in the late 17th century it was acquired by the town council of Glasgow and changed its name to serve as a deep-water port for Glasgow merchants. The ships trading with America stopped here until the **Clyde** was deepened in Glasgow in the late 18th century. Industries which grew up included sugar refineries and particularly shipbuilding. Until the 1970s it was the home of the Gourock Ropework Co, the largest ropemaking business in the world. The **Comet** was built here, and **Newark Castle** is nearby.

**Portknockie** Former **fishing** village built on the cliffs overlooking the **Moray Firth** between **Buckie** and **Cullen**. It was established in 1677 by Cullen fishermen. There is a Pictish fort on Green Castle promontory.

**Portlethen** Town on the North Sea coast, 10km (6mi) south of **Aberdeen**. Formerly a **fishing** village, it has expanded as a commuter town for Aberdeen, with a large industrial estate.

**Portmahomack** Former **fishing** village on the **Dornoch Firth**, 3km (2mi) southwest of Tarbat Ness headland, now a holiday village. There are a number of important **Pictish** standing stones in the area. The old parish church, medieval in origin, reconstructed in the 18h century, is now the Tarbat Discovery Centre, which explores local Pictish archaeology and the site of an early Christian monastery.

**Portobello** Town east of **Edinburgh**, on the Firth of **Forth**, now a suburb of the city. The name comes from a British victory at Portobello in Panama in the 18th century. It was a popular seaside resort for Edinburgh residents particularly in the late 19th and early 20th centuries. Leading industries included glass production, brickworks and potteries. Portobello ware was produced here from the late 18th century. The factory belonged to the Buchan family from 1867 until 1972, when it moved to **Crieff**. The old kilns can still be seen in Portobello.

**Portpatrick** Village on the southwest coast, a former **burgh**, 13km (8mi) southwest of **Stranraer**. It was the main port for travel to Ireland from the 17th to the early 19th century, but was superseded by Stranraer and is now principally an attractive holiday resort. The ruins of **Dunskey Castle** stand on the cliffs nearby.

**Portrack** see **Maggie's Centres**

**Portree** (pop. 1917) The only town and main tourist centre on the Isle of **Skye**, 32km (20mi) northwest of **Kyleakin**. On the outskirts is the Aros Experience, a large visitor centre with many facilities as well as information on the history and natural history of the area.

**Portsoy** Former **fishing** village between **Banff** and **Cullen**, now a tourist resort, once an important mercantile port. Its harbour and buildings are very completely preserved and many of its 17th- and 18th-century buildings have been restored. It is known for Portsoy marble, a green and pink stone, which was used to make 2 chimney pieces for Louis XIV's palace at Versailles.

**potato** (in Scots **tattie**) A garden crop from the 1660s, in the 18th century the potato became a major field crop, becoming the staple food throughout much of the **Highlands** and Islands. The failure of the crop in the mid 1840s brought hunger and disaster to many communities, and was a major contributory factor in the large-scale emigration of the period. The potato has remained an important part of the Scottish diet; see also **clapshot, rumbledethump, stovies.**

**pottit hough** A traditional dish made of meat from the hough (the shin), boiled, shredded and served cold in a jelly made from the stock.

**pound** see **weights and measures**, pp.382-4

**Powderhall** Area of **Edinburgh** best known for the stadium which was first built here in the late 19th century. It was used for athletics, **rugby** and **football**, and in latter years it became a venue for greyhound racing and speedway. It was demolished in 1995 and has been replaced by new housing. Powderhall Waste Transfer Station, originally a refuse destructor, now processes much of Edinburgh's waste for movement to landfill sites.

**precentor** In the **Presbyterian churches**, now in the smaller denominations where instrumental music is not permitted, a person appointed to lead the singing by singing the line for the congregation to repeat.

**Presbyterian churches** see p.307

**presbytery** In the **Presbyterian churches**, the church court above the **kirk session** and below the synod (or in some denominations, the **General Assembly**), covering a specified geographical area. Ministers and elders represent each parish or congregation in the presbytery at meetings.

**Press and Journal** An **Aberdeen**-based newspaper which owes its origins to a report written on the Battle of **Culloden**, and is the country's oldest daily newspaper. It covers national and international events, but also focuses on northern Scotland. The popular tale that reportage of the sinking of the *Titanic* was headlined 'Aberdeen man dies at sea' is untrue. It has a sister paper, the *Evening Express*, and its parent company is Aberdeen Journals, part of the Northcliffe Newspapers Group Ltd.

**Preston** Village on the edge of **Prestonpans**. Among its interesting historic buildings is the mercat cross of 1617, now in the care of **Historic Scotland**. Preston Tower is a tall 15th-century tower house, with early 17th-century upper storeys. Hamilton House is a 2-storey U-plan house, with fine Renaissance detail and an enclosed court, built by John Hamilton in 1626. Northfield House is an exceptionally well-preserved house, **doocot** and garden of 1611, built for Joseph Marjoribanks, rich in painted ceilings and late 17th-century panelling.

**Preston, Battle of** A Scottish army, under the 1st Duke of Hamilton, entered England in 1648 in support of **Charles I** and the **Engagement**. They were defeated by Cromwell's troops near Preston in Lancashire between 17 and 19 August.

**Preston Hall** Symmetrical classical mansion in Midlothian, to the east of **Dalkeith**, built by the Aberdonian London architect Robert Mitchell for the retired nabob, Alexander Callender. It has a magnificent Corinthian-columned central hall with decorative painting in the manner of David **Roberts** and a fine landscaped park.

**Preston Mill** Attractive mill northeast of **East Linton**, in the care of the **National Trust for Scotland**. The buildings date from the 18th century, although there is believed to have been a mill on the site since the 16th century. The machinery is relatively modern and is in working condition. **Phantassie Doocot** is nearby.

**Prestonfield House** Now a hotel, this **Edinburgh** mansion was built in 1687 for Sir James Dick, Lord Provost; it contains original furnishings and paintings. The original house, called Priest Field, was burnt down in 1681 by a group of students opposed to the attempts of the owner, Sir James Dick, to further the Catholic cause of the Duke of York (later **James VII**).

**Prestongrange** Site of a former colliery, near **Prestonpans**, which opened around 1852. It is now the location for the Prestongrange Industrial Heritage Museum, which looks at the local **coal** industry and the other industries which developed around it, including brick making, pottery, salt and soap works. The tall beam pumping engine of the colliery was built by a Cornish firm in 1874; it is open to the public.

**Prestonpans** (pop. 7153) Coastal town in **East Lothian**, southwest of **Cockenzie**. Its name comes from the salt pans used in **salt** production. In 1749 the world's first modern sulphuric-acid works was built there. The other main industry was **coal** mining, which ceased in 1952. The parish church dates from 1596 and was recast in 1774 when the spire was added. The town's historic significance dates to September 1745, when the **Jacobite** army under Prince Charles Edward **Stewart** defeated government troops commanded by General **Cope** in the Battle of Prestonpans. The flight of the Hanoverians inspired the song 'Hey Johnnie Cope'.

**Prestwick** (pop. 14,934) Town on the Firth of **Clyde**, between **Ayr** and **Troon**, a former **burgh** now best known as the site of an international airport, valuable because of its fog-free situation. After World War II it became an important link with North America, but this declined when the range of aircraft became greater and Glasgow Airport gained international status. Passenger traffic has now increased and there is a rail link to **Glasgow**. There is also an important air traffic control centre, due to be expanded. It grew as a resort town in the mid 19th century, attracting holidaymakers from Glasgow. The Scottish Aviation Works beside the airport was for many years Scotland's only aircraft factory. Bruce's Well is said to be a site from which water flowed from the ground for **Robert I**, who sought healing for leprosy.

Prior to the revolution of 1689, the **Church of Scotland** had presbyterian and episcopalian elements, but in 1690 a purely presbyterian system was set up in the Kirk by Law Established. Since then schisms, splits and reunitings have produced a complex pattern of opposing groups; in earlier years most of the disputes were over the issue of patronage, ie of the right of a landowner to appoint a minister to a church against the wishes of its congregation. The process began in 1733 with the **Secession** under Ebenezer and Ralph **Erskine** and has continued to the present, latterly more on theological grounds, with recent divisions in both the **Free Church** and the **Free Presbyterian Church**.

Further splits took place from 1747 on, over adherence to the Burgess Oath, required by anyone who wished to become a burgess of one of the major royal **burghs**. The Burgher Seceders agreed that the oath could be signed with a clear conscience, while the Antiburgher Seceders refused on the grounds that the oath implied the upholding of the Church of Scotland (and with it the landowner's right of patronage). Both

groups had further divisions into Auld Lichts (stricter and more conservative, evangelical) and New Lichts (more liberal, moderate). In 1820 the New Lichts from both combined to form the United Secession Church, and the Auld Licht groups joined in 1842 as the Synod of Original Seceders.

In the 18th and early 19th century the Church of Scotland had developed evangelical and moderate wings. In 1843 a large evangelical group left the Church of Scotland, again over patronage, to form the **Free Church**; see **Disruption**. In 1893 a small group, largely of conservative Highland congregations, left the Free Church to form the Free Presbyterian Church. In 1900 the Free Church joined with the **United Presbyterian**, to form **the United Free Church**, which in turn reunited with the Church of Scotland in 1929 (the patronage issue having been long since solved). A small number of Highland congregations remained out of the 1900 union to form the Free Church of Scotland (known colloquially as the Wee Frees).

Further splits and joinings are shown in the chart below:

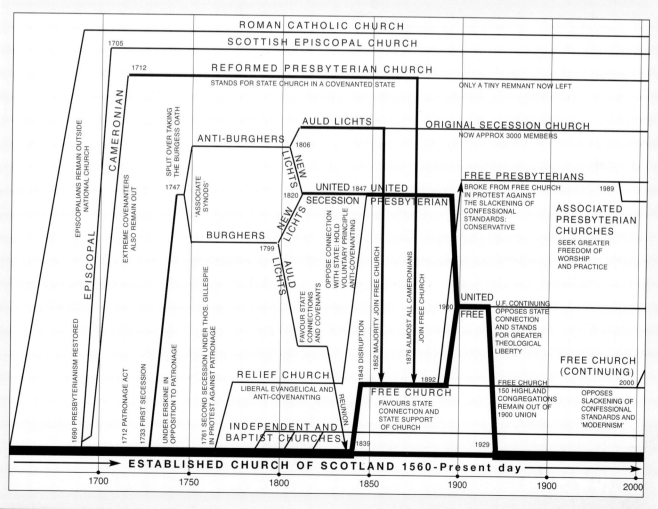

**Primus** Title given to the presiding bishop of the **Scottish Episcopal Church,** selected by the bishops themselves.

**Pringle, John Quinton** (1864–1925) Artist, b. Glasgow. He was by profession an optician but also an enthusiastic and highly able artist. Influenced by the work of the **Glasgow Boys** and familiar with the avant-garde in France, he developed an idiosyncratic style, producing painstakingly executed pictures of back-yards, street scenes and more poetically observed landscapes frequently occupied by children, using a mosaic-like style of rich colour. A large collection of his work is in Glasgow Art Gallery.

**Proclaimers, The** Pop duo formed in 1983 by Charlie and Craig Reid (1962– ), twins, b. Leith, brought up in Auchtermuchty, Fife. They recorded their first album, *This Is The Story* in 1986. *Sunshine On Leith* followed in 1988. They have remained popular both in Scotland and in the USA. After some gap they produced *Persevere* in 2001, and *Born Innocent* in 2003 and continue to tour the world.

**procurator fiscal** Lawyer whose responsibility it is to decide whether or not a criminal case should be brought to trial, and to carry out prosecutions on behalf of the crown in **sheriff courts** and **district courts**. He or she also prepares cases for the **High Court**. Informally referred to as 'the fiscal'. The procurator fiscal service is under the direction of the Crown Office.

**Prosen** see **Glen Prosen**

**proven** see **not-proven verdict**

**provost** Civic leader elected by the council of a **burgh** from their own number, equivalent to a mayor in England. The priest in charge of an episcopal cathedral. The term also applied to the head of a collegiate church.

**Pryde, James** (1866–1941) Artist, b. Edinburgh. Known both for his collaboration during the 1890s with his brother-in-law, William Nicholson, under the name 'J & W Beggarstaff', with him producing innovative and bold poster designs, and for his own paintings of sombre architectural and interior scenes.

**Ptarmigan Hill** Just to the southeast of Ben Lomond, a popular route from Loch Lomond to the Ben.

**Ptarmigans** Range of craggy hills above **Loch Tay**, to the north of **Killin**, popular with hillwalkers. The highest is Meall nan Tarmachan (Gaelic, meaning 'hill of the ptarmigans', 1044m/3421ft).

**puddin(g)** A kind of sausage made from the stomach or entrails of a sheep, pig etc, stuffed with suet, onion, oatmeal, seasoning (white or mealie pudding), or with the addition of the animal's blood (black pudding).

**puffer** Small cargo boat which carried goods, especially coal, from the Clyde to various ports in the West Highlands and Western Isles in early and mid 20th century. The puffer was immortalised in Neil Munro's Para Handy stories (1931), televised in the 1960s and 70s as The Vital Spark.

**Pullar, Lawrence** see **Murray, Sir John** (1841–1914)

**Pulteneytown** see **Wick**

**pupil** see **minor**

**Purdie, Thomas** (1843–1916) Organic chemist, b. Biggar, Lanarkshire. He became independently wealthy as a result of many years' involvement ranching in Argentina and in mining. He studied chemistry in London and in Germany. In 1884 he became Professor of Chemistry at **St Andrews** where he built chemistry labs for the university. A pioneer in the investigation of the molecular structures of carbon compounds, he owed much to the technique based on silver oxide reactions, discovered by his assistant W Pitkeathly. He arranged for his protégé, James Colquhoun **Irvine,** to succeed him.

**Purser, John** (1942– ) Composer, broadcaster and writer, b. Glasgow. His major opus is a 30-programme series for BBC Radio Scotland with accompanying book under the title *Scotland's Music* (1992). For this wide-ranging history of Scotland's traditional and classical music much early material was recorded or printed for the first time.

**pursuer** In Scots law, the equivalent of English plaintiff in a civil case.

*The Proclaimers.*

**quaich** (From Gaelic *cuach* a cup, bowl) A shallow 2-handled bowl, now usually of silver or pewter, originally used as a drinking cup. Often given as a gift or as a prize in sporting events, eg the Millennium Quaich, competed for annually by the **rugby** union teams of Scotland and Ireland. The 'Keepers of the Quaich' are a group of leading supporters of the Scotch **whisky** industry.

**Quakers** see **Friends, Religious Society of**

**Quarrier, William** (1829–1903) Philanthropist, b. Greenock. Fatherless from the age of 5, he established a shoemaking business, then used the proceeds to set up a model village near **Bridge of Weir**, Renfrewshire. Quarrier's Orphan Homes provided residential care for orphans, and were a great improvement on other attempts at poor relief; the children were placed in small 'family' groups with house 'parents'. Quarrier also worked to improve the lot of discharged prisoners and the homeless. With fewer children in residential care, Quarrier's Village now provides a range of services, especially for children and young people in need and for the disabled.

**quarter days** see **term days**

**Queen Elizabeth Forest Park** Run by the Forestry Commission, a park of 30,353 hectares (75,000 acres) in the **Trossachs**, set up in 1953 to mark the coronation of Queen Elizabeth. The David Marshall Lodge visitor centre, just to the north of **Aberfoyle**, includes information on walks, climbs and other activities. The park includes **Loch Ard**, Loch Achray and Loch Lubnaig, as well as **Ben A'an**, **Ben Ledi** and **Ben Venue**.

**Queen of the South** see **Dumfries**

**Queensberry, James Douglas, 2nd Duke of** (1662–1711) Politician, b. Sanquhar Castle, Dumfriesshire. One of the first Scots to support the revolution of **William II** and **III**, he later became a key player in the **Union of Parliaments**. As the *éminence grise* behind the commissioner to the Scottish Parliament, the Duke of Argyll, he was instrumental in bringing about the completion of the Act of Union. Rewarded with a state pension for his efforts, he was vilified by Scots nationalists for generations thereafter. He is buried in **Durisdeer** church, where there is a splendid monument to him.

**Queensberry, Sir John Sholto Douglas, 8th Marquis of** (1844–1900) Scottish nobleman, after whom the rules of boxing are known. They were largely codified by John Chambers, an English sportsman, the marquis's name being attached to them as a sign of high-born approval. The father of Lord Alfred Douglas, he was instrumental in bringing about the trial and imprisonment of Oscar Wilde, Douglas's lover.

**Queensberry House** see **Edinburgh**, p.132

**Queensferry** see **North Queensferry, South Queensferry**

**Queen's Own Cameron Highlanders** Regiment of the British Army originally founded in 1793 by Sir Alan **Cameron** of Erracht as the 79th Regiment of Foot. It was renamed the Queen's Own Cameron Highlanders in 1881. In 1961 it merged with the **Seaforth Highlanders** to form the **Queen's Own Highlanders** and in 1994 a further merger produced the **Highlanders (Seaforths, Gordons and Camerons)**.

**Queen's Own Highlanders** (Seaforths and Camerons) Regiment formed in 1961 by amalgamation of the **Seaforth Highlanders** and the **Queen's Own Cameron Highlanders**.

**Queen's Park Football Club** see **football**

**Quinag** (Gaelic **Cuinneag**) An isolated peak in **Assynt** with several subsidiary summits, to the southwest of **Kylesku**. At 809m (2653ft) it is by no means the highest in the area, but is among the most spectacular.

**Quiraing, the** (Gaelic **Cuithe-Fraing**) Expanse of mountainous landslips and peaks in the far north of **Skye**'s Trotternish peninsula. Formerly a notorious hiding place for stolen cattle, it is now a popular walking area. It also includes, in outcrops such as The Prison, some challenging climbs.

**Quoich, Loch** see **Loch Quoich**

**R & A** see **Royal and Ancient**

**Raasay** (Gaelic **Ra'arsa**) (pop. 192) Long narrow island off the east coast of **Skye**; the highest point is Dùn Caan, 443m (1456ft), with caves on the south side. It was for long the property of the Macleods of Raasay, a branch of the Macleods of **Lewis**. In 1773 they entertained Dr Johnson and James **Boswell** at the Georgian Raasay House in the southwest of the island. (It is now an outdoor centre.) The sale of the island in 1843 led to an extensive **Clearance**; even today the population is less than 200. Just before World War I an ironstone mine was opened here. It was worked during the war by German prisoners of war; the village built to house them now houses most of the island's inhabitants. Raasay was the birthplace of the poet Sorley **Maclean**.

**Rab Ha (Robert Hall)** (d.1843) Celebrated vagrant gourmand, known as 'the Glasgow Glutton'. Born in what is now known as the Merchant City, in the centre of town, he grew to become one of the best-known habitués of the area's coffee houses and hostelries. His feats of over-indulgence are said to have included the consumption, at a single sitting, of a whole calf.

**Rae, John** (1813-93) Arctic explorer, b. **Stromness**, Orkney. After qualifying as a surgeon in 1833, he joined the Hudson's Bay Company, and made his first journeys as an employee of the firm. He was an expert in survival methods, being able to live for long periods in the Arctic without external supplies. In 1847 he surveyed 1130km (700mi) of coastline around Committee Bay, then the following year he set out in search of Sir John Franklin. He was the first person to bring back information about the true fate of the Franklin expedition. He died in London and was buried in **Kirkwall**.

**Raeburn, Sir Henry** (1756-1823). Artist, b. Edinburgh. He worked first as a jeweller before his outstanding talent as a painter was recognised and cultivated by the Scottish portraitist David Martin. After a visit to Italy, Raeburn established himself in **Edinburgh** and quickly attained a reputation as the country's leading portraitist. Numerous eminent figures sat for him in his York Place studio, including leading figures of the **Scottish Enlightenment** such as David **Hume** and Adam **Smith**; his 1822 portrait of Sir Walter **Scott** (**Scottish National Portrait Gallery**) (see p.334) is arguably the best known of the author.

**Raehills** Picturesque castellated house 14km (9mi) northwest of **Lockerbie**, with colonnaded elevations built in 1782 by Alexander Stevens for the Earl of Hopetoun, subsequently the home of the Johnstones of Annandale.

**Ragman Rolls** List of over 1500 property-holders, dated 28 August 1296 at **Berwick-upon-Tweed**, who recognised the overlordship of Edward I after his conquest of Scotland. Submissions were collected throughout the kingdom, rather than a mass of Scots turning up in person at Berwick.

**railways** see p.312

**Rainy, Robert** (1826-1906) Minister, b. Glasgow. **Free Church** minister in **Huntly** and **Edinburgh**, he became Professor of Church History in New College, Edinburgh and later its Principal. He was involved in various campaigns within the church and was a prime mover in its union with the **United Presbyterian Church** in 1900.

**Rait** Picturesque thatched village 12km (7mi) northeast of **Perth**, of 18th-century date, a surprisingly complete pre-improvement **ferm toun** with the ruin of a pre-**Reformation** church.

**Rait Castle** Roofless hall house to the south of **Nairn**, with fine Gothic details built c.1300 for Sir Gervase de Rait, Constable of Nairn.

**Rammerscales** Classical mansion in Dumfriesshire, to the south of **Lochmaben**, built 1768 by Dr James Mounsey, Chief Director of the Medical Chancery of Russia; open to the public.

**Ramsay, Allan** (1686-1758) Poet, born in Leadhills, Lanarkshire. Apprenticed to an **Edinburgh** wig-maker, he turned first to writing poetry and then to bookselling. His circulating library, begun in 1725, was probably the first in Britain. He defended the use of **Scots** language and was important in reviving interest in Scottish literature, notably in his 2-volume

*The Evergreen* (1724), an anthology of 'Scots poems wrote by the ingenious before 1600' – and in the 5-volume *The Tea-Table Miscellany* (1724–37). His most popular work, *The Gentle Shepherd: A Pastoral Comedy*, was published in 1725. He made an unsuccessful attempt to establish a permanent theatre in Edinburgh. He retired from writing at a relatively early age in 1730.

**Ramsay, Allan** (1713–84) Artist, b. Edinburgh, eldest son of Allan **Ramsay** the poet. He studied in **Edinburgh**, London and Rome, returned to Edinburgh, but then moved to London where he won acclaim for his portraiture, one of the few Scots to do so outside their own country.

*Willie Johnston of Rangers Football Club heads the second goal in the Cup Winners' Cup Final against Dynamo Moscow, 1972.*

Appointed Painter-in-Ordinary to George III, his subjects also included many of the best-known figures of the time (Edward Gibbon, David **Hume**, and Jean-Jacques Rousseau, who sat for Ramsay on his visit to Britain in 1766). A serious injury to his right arm late in his life curtailed his painting career prematurely.

**Ramsay, Edward (Dean Ramsay)** (1793–1872) Theologian, b. Aberdeen. Educated at Cambridge, he became a Somerset curate in 1817. He moved to **Edinburgh** in 1824, where he became the pastor of St John's Church, and Dean of the diocese from 1846. He wrote widely on religious matters, and also produced *Reminiscences of Scottish Life and Character* (1858), which went through 21 editions in his lifetime.

**Randolph, John, 3rd Earl of Moray** (d.1346) Soldier and politician. Succeeding to the earldom on the death of his brother Thomas, 2nd Earl, in 1332, he defeated the pretender Edward **Balliol** at **Annan** in December of that year. In 1334, as joint Guardian with Robert the Steward, he was involved in a successful campaign to expel English forces from the south and west of Scotland, but in 1335 he was captured by the English. On his release in 1340 he continued to campaign against Balliol and Edward III and was an important member of **David II**'s court circle before he was killed at the battle of **Neville's Cross**.

**Randolph, Sir Thomas, 1st Earl of Moray** (d.1332) Soldier and politician. A nephew of **Robert I**, he was one of the king's most important lieutenants, active in both warfare and diplomacy. Made Earl of Moray in 1312, he recaptured **Edinburgh** Castle in 1314 and was a commander at **Bannockburn**. He became Guardian on Robert's death in 1329 but died preparing to resist the renewed threat of English invasion. He was succeeded by his son Thomas, who died in the battle of **Dupplin** in the same year.

**Ranfurly** see **Bridge of Weir**

**Rangers** Glasgow football club, formed in 1872 (though the date is often given as 1873). Joint winners (with Dumbarton) of the first Scottish League championship in 1891, they soon became one of the biggest clubs in the country. Ibrox, their home stadium in Edmiston Drive, has been awarded 5-star status by UEFA for its state-of-the-art facilities. It is now completely enclosed and has a capacity of 50,500. Perennial trophy-winners in the domestic game, Rangers have found European success elusive, though they did win the now-defunct Cup Winners' Cup in 1972. See also **football** p.151.

**Rankin, Ian** (1960– ) Crime writer, b. Cardenden, Fife. He wrote about his home town in his first novel, *The Flood* (1986). His series of books featuring the **Edinburgh**-based Inspector Rebus began with his second novel, *Knots And Crosses* (1987), and has grown in popularity and won many awards. Drawing on the image of Edinburgh's past, the Rebus novels examine the seedy, sinister side of the city which lies behind the respectable veneer.

# RAILWAYS

Early Scottish railways were horse-worked, with wooden rails, carrying coal to navigable water, for transport in ships. In 1721 the first ran from **Tranent** to **Cockenzie**, East Lothian. By the late 18th century there were several in Central Scotland and iron rails were replacing wood. In 1812 the Kilmarnock and Troon was opened as Scotland's first public railway. It had a passenger service, as did the Elgin Railway in west Fife. The first modern railway in Scotland was the Monkland and Kirkintilloch (1826), a coal line built with wrought-iron rails. The Edinburgh and Dalkeith (1831) was similar. The first loco-motive-worked line was the Garnkirk and Glasgow (1831). The success of the Liverpool and Manchester Railway (1830) led to a vogue for locomotive-worked lines carrying passengers and general freight between significant centres of population. Early Scottish examples ran from **Dundee** to **Arbroath** and **Forfar**, and from **Glasgow** to **Greenock**, **Ayr** and **Edinburgh**, all opened by 1842. Longer-distance routes followed, of which the first was the North British Railway, from Edinburgh to **Berwick** (1846). The profitability of these early main-line railway companies led to a 'Railway Mania' with investors speculating in railway shares. This led to the construction of a network of railways linking Carlisle to Glasgow (via **Lockerbie** and via **Dumfries**), to Edinburgh, Aberdeen and Dundee. There were also routes from Edinburgh to Dundee, with ferries across the **Forth** and **Tay**, and to **Hawick**. Anglo-Scottish services operated via Berwick and Carlisle. The boom collapsed in 1849, and during the 1850s few railways were built, apart from some 'cheap railways', for instance from **Stirling** to **Balloch**, and from **Leuchars** to **St Andrews**.

During the 1850s the commercial and operating problems of running railway networks were largely solved. Track and sig-nalling were improved, and more powerful locomotives and better rolling stock developed. In the late 1850s confidence returned, and lines were built between then and the mid 1860s from **Dunkeld** to **Inverness** and **Bonar Bridge**, from Dumfries to **Portpatrick**, and from Aberdeen to **Peterhead**, **Fraserburgh**, **Banff**, **Macduff** and Inverness. In the mid 1860s most of Scotland's railways were amalgamated into 4 companies, the North British, Caledonian, Glasgow and South Western, and Great North of Scotland railways. These companies built new stations in the city centres, and rebuilt existing stations to cope with increasing traffic.

Rising living standards in the 1880s and 90s made leisure travel popular. Suburban lines were also built, especially in Edinburgh and Glasgow. The popularity of the Clyde estuary resorts led to the development of rail-linked steamer services by the Caledonian, North British and Glasgow and South Western railways, with new piers at **Wemyss** Bay, Craigendoran, **Greenock** and **Ardrossan**. In Glasgow underground lines were built serving suburban, and in the case of the North British, Clyde Coast traffic. The Caledonian and the Glasgow and South Western both expanded their city-centre stations for Clyde Coast and suburban traffic. Construction of suburban lines was however halted after 1901 by the electrification and extension of the Glasgow and **Paisley** street tramways.

During World War I Britain's railways were controlled by Government. The advantages of this were such that in 1921 an Act was passed grouping most of Britain's companies into 4 large concerns. Scotland's railways were split between the London, Midland and Scottish (Caledonian and Glasgow and South Western), and London, and North Eastern (North British and Great North of Scotland) railways. The weakness of the British economy, and increasing road competition, meant that the new companies struggled. The railways were nationalised in 1948, and some line closures followed in the early 1950s. In 1955 a programme of modernisation began, replacing steam by diesel traction on most lines. The Glasgow suburban routes were electrified. The 1960s saw a drastic rationalisation of the network. Social considerations saved lines to **Wick** and **Thurso**, **Kyle of Lochalsh**, **Mallaig** and **Oban**, but the Borders lines, the **Dumfries**-Stranraer route, and the direct line from **Perth** to **Montrose** via **Forfar** all closed. Wagon-load freight also ended, with the closure of many freight-only lines. Within a very short time the railways ceased to offer a comprehensive transport service.

Since the 1960s the east coast and west coast Anglo-Scottish routes, and the Glasgow-Ayr line have been electrified. Locomotive haulage of all passenger trains, except the main-line electric ones, has ended. Since the 1980s, however, several lines closed to passengers have reopened, notably the electrified Argyle Line from Rutherglen to Partick, the Edinburgh-**Bathgate** route, and lines from Glasgow to Paisley (Canal), Maryhill, and Whifflet. Further reopenings were delayed by the fragmentation of the railways at denationalisation in 1996, but are now being actively pursued. Lines from Stirling to **Alloa**, Edinburgh to **Galashiels**, and Bathgate to **Airdrie** are likely to reopen. After nearly three centuries railways are still alive and well, and vital to Scotland.

**Rankine, William John McQuorn** (1820–72)
Scientist and engineer, b. Edinburgh. He trained as a civil engineer, working in Ireland and on railways in central Scotland. He designed the St Rollox Stalk, a 137m (450ft) chimney, the largest in the world at the time. In 1855 he was appointed the first Professor of Civil Engineering and Mechanics at **Glasgow** University, where he produced a theoretical basis for the design of ships' hulls. He published a number of influential text-books, on shipbuilding, applied mechanics, and steam engines. He developed a theory of thermodynamics as applied to heat engines, and one of the 'ideal' heat engine cycles is still known as the 'Rankine Cycle'.

**Rannoch** (Gaelic **Raineach**) Area in the central **Highlands** including Rannoch Moor, a bleak, boggy area surrounded by mountains, which has a certain austere charm. The northeast corner is a nature reserve. See also **Loch Rannoch**.

**Rashiecoat** A version of the Cinderella story, it tells of a beautiful young girl who is ill-treated by her parents and ugly older sister. Aided by a magic calf, she finds employment in the king's kitchen. When the royal household attend church on Christmas Day she is unable to attend as her clothes – the coat of rushes of the title – are not grand enough. The calf conjures up some finery and Rashiecoat goes to church, where the prince falls in love with her. She goes home early, leaving a slipper behind. Eventually the prince discovers to whom the slipper belongs, and they marry.

**Ratagan** Area in the northwest **Highlands**, on the south shore of **Loch Duich**. The many mountains in the area that are **Munros** make its youth hostel popular with climbers. The road from **Shiel Bridge** to **Glenelg** goes over the pass of Bealach Ratagan at a height of 390m (1116ft).

**Ratho** Midlothian village to the west of **Edinburgh**, on south bank of **Union Canal**. Boat trips are run from the Bridge Inn. Its church, dedicated to the Virgin Mary, is 12th century with 17th-century aisles. Ratho Park, a neo-Tudor house by William **Burn** (1824), is now a **golf** club.

**Rattray** Ruined settlement in Aberdeenshire, 12km (7mi) north of **Peterhead**. Created a royal **burgh** by **Mary, Queen of Scots** in 1564, it flourished briefly as a minor port until, in 1720, a storm blew a sand hill into the navigation channel and landlocked the

*British Railways (Scottish Region) poster of the 1950s by Terence Cuneo.*

Loch of Strathbeg on which it stood. The only remnants of the place are a ruined chapel and graveyard. Rattray Head **lighthouse**, on a large drum base, is on a rock called The Ron, just offshore.

**Rattray** Perthshire village, separated from **Blairgowrie** by the river **Ericht**. The present settlement is a little to the east of an ancient fort. Old Rattray Kirk, completed in 1170, is the oldest extant building. On a cliff above the River Ericht, 3km (2mi) to the north, is Craighall Castle, home of the Rattray family since the 16th century, which was largely rebuilt in the 19th century.

**Ravenscraig** Former steel plant outside **Motherwell**. It was built by Colvilles Ltd after 1954, with government encouragement, as an integrated steelworks and strip steel mill. As heavy industry went into a sharp decline in the 1980s, Ravenscraig took on an iconic status as the last great work-place in the country. Continual financial losses meant it was frequently under threat of closure by its owners, British Steel, a threat eventually realised in 1992. The site is being redeveloped as a new suburb of Motherwell.

*Demonstration in George Square, Glasgow, 31 January 1919, which turned into the 'Bloody Friday Riot'. See 'Red Clydeside'.*

R

**Ravenscraig Castle** see **Kirkcaldy**

**Reay** Village in Caithness near **Dounreay**, close to the buried ruins of an 18th-century village, once part of the extensive land holdings of the Clan Mackay. It has a white-harled church built in 1739 and the old churchyard has a worn cross-slab within the ruin of the old church.

**Reay** Also known as **Reay's Country** (Gaelic **Dùthaich Mhic Aoidh** 'Mackay's country'). Area of northwest **Sutherland**, part of an estate sold by the 7th Lord Reay, Chief of Clan Mackay, in 1829 to the Duke of Sutherland, since sold to the Duke of Westminster. The Reay deer forest lies inland from **Scourie** to the northwest of Loch More.

**rector** Originally a high-ranking university official, the office varying in the 4 older Scottish universities; now a public figure elected by the students (or students and staff) for 3 years, representing them on the university court, which he or she chairs. The term is also applied to the head teacher of some secondary schools, according to local custom, and in the **Scottish Episcopal Church** to a clergyman in full charge of a congregation.

**Redcastle** Small village on the north shore of the **Beauly Firth**, with a large, now derelict, mansion house. Built in the 17th century on the site of a 12th-century castle, it was altered by William **Burn** in 1840.

**Red Castle** Conspicuous red sandstone ruin on the shores of **Lunan Bay**, to the south of **Montrose**. It was originally built during the reign of King **William the Lion** in the 13th century as a hunting lodge and fortification.

**'Red Clydeside'** An often exaggerated term associated with the rise of industrial and political militancy in **Glasgow** and other Clydeside industrial towns during and after World War I. Attempts by skilled engineers to protect their wages and craft position, in the face of government pressure for dilution by unskilled male and female labour, led in 1915 to industrial action coordinated by an unofficial group of shop stewards known as the Clyde Workers' Committee, several of whom were in 1916 deported from the west of Scotland after a clash with the government in the person of Lloyd George. Members of the Committee, like Willie Gallacher, Arthur McManus and John Muir, were connected with the Socialist Labour Party, but the issues were basic to many livelihoods, as was a rent-strike against steep increases in 1915. By 1918 the Independent Labour Party, strongly Glasgow-based, had tripled its membership from 1915 figures, and the conservative Scottish establishment had become worried about subversion as a result of the 1917 Bolshevik Revolution in Russia. When the Scottish TUC supported a strike for shorter working hours in 1919, and 100,000 people demonstrated in its support in George Square, the police and the government were heavy-handed. This particular 'Bloody Friday' started with baton charges and ended with virtual military occupation of the city. With the collapse of the Liberals and the transfer of many voters to Labour, Glasgow returned 10 Labour MPs in 1922, some, like James **Maxton**, David **Kirkwood**, Emmanuel **Shinwell** and John **Wheatley**, were leaders of the previous struggles. They raised expectations of dramatic change, but could not completely deliver it.

**Red Comyn** see **Comyn, John, of Badenoch**

**Red Douglases** Magnate family which became a focus of opposition to the senior line of **Black Douglases** from the 1390s. Heads of the family were earls of Angus, one of whom, Archibald, 5th Earl, was prominent in opposition to **James III** and is popularly known by the sobriquet 'Bell the Cat'. Archibald, 6th Earl's marriage to **James IV**'s widow **Margaret Tudor** in 1514 gave the Red Douglases greater clout in Scottish politics until **James V** engineered the destruction of the family.

Several of the Scottish regiments have a long history going back to 17th-century precursors, though they usually began under a different name and saw many changes over the years. Regiments were originally raised by individuals and were known by their names. For example the **Royal Scots** regiment was raised in 1633 as Sir John Hepburn's Regiment, and the **Scots Guards** began in 1642 as Argyll's Regiment. The **Cameronian Regiment** has an interesting origin in a strict presbyterian sect in southwest Scotland during the **Covenanting** period.

In the late 17th century, these regiments were used in British campaigns abroad under **William of Orange**, and from 1707 they were integrated as line regiments of the British army where they were to play an important role, mainly in Europe, but also in colonial warfare.

In the course of the 18th century entrepreneur colonels were phased out. After 1707 all regiments of the British army were royal and known by numbers, and occasionally also by nicknames, for example the 42nd were known as the **Black Watch**, from their dark **tartan**.

Highland regiments were particularly prominent in wars from the late 18th century onwards, but only one (the Black Watch) was founded before the 1745 **Jacobite Rising**. During the Seven Years' War (1756–63) the Elder Pitt adopted a policy of deliberately recruiting Highland regiments from former Jacobite areas. By cooperating in this, the forfeited Jacobite families secured the return of their estates after the War of the American Revolution (1775–83). Several Highland regiments were therefore founded by landowners mainly from their own territory: see **Cameron Highlanders**, **Gordon Highlanders**, **Seaforth Highlanders**.

In the 19th century Scots, along with the Irish, formed a disproportionately large part of the small regular British army. In the late 19th century reforms which introduced two-battalion regiments, with one battalion normally serving overseas and the other barracked in its main recruiting area, reinforced the territorial identities of the Scottish regiments. With R B **Haldane**'s creation of the Territorial Army after 1905, this territorial identity was further strengthened, and it was deliberately emphasised to encourage recruiting after the terrible losses during the early campaigns of World War I.

Scottish regiments had a distinguished role in both World Wars, but reductions in the defence budget in the 1960s led to amalgamations, such as the formation of the **Queen's Own Highlanders (Seaforths and Camerons)**; a further joining with the Gordons in 1994 produced The **Highlanders (Seaforths, Gordons & Camerons)**. In 1971 the **Royal Scots Greys** merged with the 3rd Carabiniers to form the **Royal Scots Dragoon Guards**.

All the Scottish regiments, Highland or Lowland, wear tartan, some in the form of trews rather than kilts; see **tartan**, and all have **pipe bands**. These, originally Highland, features have come to be regarded as emblems of Scottish identity in general.

*The Thin Red Line, October 1854 by Robert Gibb, 1881, depicts the 93rd (Highlanders) Regiment at the Battle of Balaclava, 1854.*

**Redpath, Anne** (1895–1965) Artist, b. Galashiels. Studied in Edinburgh then lived in France for much of the inter-war period, painting little until after her return to Scotland in 1934. Bringing to her still-life painting an exceptional ability with colour and understanding of decorative design, her reputation grew steadily. After World War II her extensive travels (in Spain, France, Italy and elsewhere) provided her with new subjects for her painting, and she became well-known for her richly worked scenes of church interiors. In 1952 she was the first woman painter to be elected to the **Royal Scottish Academy.**

**Redpath, Jean** (1937– ) Singer, b. Edinburgh, brought up in Fife. She has had a distinguished career as a singer and interpreter of Scottish music and has spent considerable time in the USA. She was Artist-in-Residence at Wesleyan University, Connecticut 1972–6 and became the first Artist-in-Residence at **Stirling University** in 1979. She has made highly acclaimed recordings of the songs of Robert **Burns**, 323 in arrangements by the American composer Serge Hovey, and others in collaboration with Dr Donald Low of Stirling University.

**reel** Lively traditional Scottish country dance, now usually danced in sets of 3, 4 or 5 couples; the tune to which it is danced. See also **eightsome reel, strathspey, Royal Scottish Country Dance Society.**

**Reformation** In Scotland the Reformation was carried through despite the opposition of the Crown. The climactic act was the passing by the Parliament in August 1560 of Acts which ended state links with the Papacy, banned the Mass and authorised a Protestant confession of faith. These measures by the so-called Reformation Parliament were the culmination of several decades of agitation, in which Lutheran, Zwinglian and Calvinist preaching were increasingly common, and support for Protestantism was becoming more widespread. Through John **Knox**, Calvinism became the dominant influence on Scottish Protestantism. The return of **Mary, Queen of Scots** in 1561 saw no attempt by the Crown to reverse the 1560 reforms and the **Kirk** by Law Established flourished, technically continuous with the medieval one, using its canon law, as modified in 1560.

**Reformed Presbyterian Church** see **Cameronians**

**regalia** see **Honours of Scotland**

**regality** A **barony** with fuller judicial and administrative powers conceded by the Crown, to a lay or, until the **Reformation**, ecclesiastical subject. The judicial powers never included the right to try treason, but usually covered all other criminal cases. Regalities were abolished with the **Heritable Jurisdictions** 1748.

**Regent Moray** see **Moray, James Stewart, Earl of**

**Regent Morton** see **Morton, James Douglas, 4th Earl of**

**Regiam Majestatem** Compilation of Scots **law**, made around 1200 and recognised as authoritative a little over 2 centuries later.

**regiments** see p.315

**Register House** Traditional name for the building which houses the **National Archives of Scotland**, first applied to a part of **Edinburgh** Castle in the mid 16th century. Old Register House, begun at the east end of Princes Street, Edinburgh, in 1774, to a design by Robert **Adam**, was supplemented by the adjacent New Register House by Robert Matheson in 1859. The former St George's Church in Charlotte Square became West Register House in 1971.

**region** see **local government**, p.233

**Regulus, St** see **St Rule**

**Reiach, Alan** (1910–92) Architect b. London. He trained with Robert **Lorimer**, travelled in America, Russia and Scandinavia as a young man and in the prewar and postwar years was an important polemicist for good modern design. His most important work in independent practice was the Appleton Tower, **Edinburgh** University (1963). He merged his practice with that of Eric Hall in 1964.

**Reid, Alastair** (1926– ) Writer and translator, b. Whithorn. A staff writer on the *New Yorker*, the magazine in which his first poems were published in the early 1950s, he has also been influential in spreading the popularity in the English-speaking world of Hispanic poets such as Pablo Neruda.

**Reid, Charlie and Craig** see **Proclaimers**

**Reid, Jimmy** (1932– ) Trade unionist and politician, b. Glasgow. A former member of the Communist Party, he became a national figure during the 1971 work-in by the **Upper Clyde Shipbuilders**, where he was a shop steward. He was **Rector** of **Glasgow University** 1971–4. He left the Communist Party, and stood as the Labour candidate for Dundee East in the general election of 1979. Also a journalist and broadcaster, his publications include *Reflections of a Clyde-Built Man.*

**Reid, John** (1655–1723) Horticulturist, b. Niddry Castle, West Lothian, where his father and grandfather were gardeners. Following his apprenticeship he moved around the big gardens of the day, including **Drummond Castle** and **Lawers**, both in Perthshire. He is accredited with the first gardening book in Scotland, *The Scots Gard'ner* (1683) but, even before publication, he emigrated with his family to New Jersey where he eventually became Surveyor-General of the Province.

**Reid, General John** (1721–1807) Composer and soldier. He took part in the 1745 **Jacobite Rising**, being taken prisoner at **Prestonpans**, and also fought in France and North America. He composed 12 flute sonatas which are still popular. His 'The Garb of Old Gaul' is the slow march for all Scottish battalions. He left his money to endow a chair of music in **Edinburgh University**, with a concert, including some of his own music, to be held on his birthday.

**Reid, Robert** (1774–1856) King's Architect in Scotland from 1808 to 1839. He rebuilt Parliament Square, **Edinburgh**, in an **Adam**-derived manner between 1803 and 1840 and designed St George's Church, Charlotte Square, Edinburgh (now West Register House) (1811–14) and Leith Customhouse (1811–12).

**Reid, Robert** (1895–1965) Piper, b. Slamannan, Stirlingshire. Pupil of John MacDougall **Gillies**, he won many awards. He was Pipe Major in the **Highland Light Infantry**. He was a pipe maker and teacher, and published *The Piper's Delight* (1933).

**Reid, Thomas** (1710–96) Philosopher, b. Strachan, Kincardineshire, and educated in Aberdeen. After nearly 3 decades as a professor, first at **Aberdeen** and then at **Glasgow**, he left academia to devote himself to writing. Father of the 'Common sense' school of philosophy, he argued against the contention of **Hume** that the existence of anything outwith the mind cannot be proved. Reid's viewpoint became dominant in Scotland and very influential in England and in the US. His works include *Essays on the Intellectual Powers of Man* (1785).

**Reith, John, 1st Baron Reith of Stonehaven** (1899–1971) First General Manager of the BBC in 1922, and Director General 1927–38, b. Stonehaven. A pioneering figure in broadcasting, his censoriousness set the tone within the BBC for decades. The Minister of Works and Buildings 1940–42, he went on to become chairman of the Commonwealth Telecommunications Board in the immediate post-war years.

**reivers** Term used to describe criminal raiders, especially on the Scottish-English **Border** in the 16th and early 17th century. Large bands of riders made forays both across the Border and into the territory of rival families; these included Armstrongs, Elliots, Grahams, Johnstones, Kerrs, Maxwells, Nixons and Scotts.

**Relief Church** A presbyterian church formed in 1761, largely under the leadership of Thomas Gillespie of Dunfermline, Thomas **Boston** of Jedburgh and Thomas Colier, an English dissenting minister in Fife. Known as the Relief Secession, it split from the **Church of Scotland** over the patronage issue, but placed more emphasis on religious liberty than the Original **Secession**. It later became involved in missionary activities and opposition to the slave trade. In 1847 it joined with the United Secession Church to form the **United Presbyterian Church**.

**Renfrew** Town on the River **Clyde**, to the west of **Glasgow**, now adjacent to **Paisley**, a former royal **burgh** and county town of **Renfrewshire**. Once a busy port, it then became a centre of shipbuilding and boilermaking; it now relies on a range of industries. Glasgow's first airport was at Renfrew. Until 1984, the Renfrew Ferry was an important link across the Clyde; it now carries passengers only. (One of the old car ferries is now moored at a quay in central Glasgow and used as an entertainment venue). Immediately to the east is the massive Braehead shopping centre, built partly on land formerly occupied by a power station.

**Renfrew District** see **Strathclyde Region**

**Renfrew Ferry** see **Renfrew**

**Renfrewshire** Former county on the Firth of **Clyde** to the west of **Glasgow** which in 1975 became the Renfrew and Inverclyde and Eastwood Districts of **Strathclyde Region**. In 1996, most of Renfrew District became a unitary local authority as Renfrewshire Council; see maps on pp.394-5 and **local government** and see also **East Renfrewshire**. The administrative centre is **Paisley** and other towns include **Renfrew**, **Kilmacolm** and **Port Glasgow**.

**Rennie, John** (1761–1821) Civil engineer, b. **East Linton**, East Lothian. After studying at **Edinburgh** he moved to London in 1791 and found fame as a bridge-builder. He planned London Bridge, and built Southwark and Waterloo Bridges in addition to many others throughout the land. He also made canals, drained fens, and improved many harbours. His major works in Scotland were **Kelso** Bridge (1800–3) and **Leith** Docks, now filled in, begun 1799. His son, Sir John, was also a notable civil engineer.

**reset** In Scots law, to receive goods known to be stolen, usually with the intention of reselling; the act of doing this. The English equivalent is receiving.

**Restalrig** Village, now part of **Edinburgh**, with a 15th-century church to which is attached the hexagonal St Triduana's aisle, built 1477–87 for **James III**.

**R**

**Rest and be Thankful** Summit of the pass from Glen Croe to **Loch Fyne**, Argyll. Its steep road was originally constructed after the 1745 **Jacobite Rising**, as a military road from **Dumbarton** to **Inveraray**. It was popular in the early days of motoring, when hill climbs were used in sporting tests of vehicles' reliability. The old road was superseded by the present one in the early 1930s.

**Rhind, David** (1808–83) Architect, b. Edinburgh. Primarily a classical and Renaissance designer, he was responsible for the Scott Monument, in George Square, **Glasgow** (1838), the former Commercial Bank in George Street, **Edinburgh** (1843) and that in Gordon Street, Glasgow (1855); and as a neo-Jacobean designer, Daniel Stewart's Hospital in Edinburgh (1848–53).

**Rhinns (of Galloway)** Hammerhead-plan peninsula stretching from Corsewall Point in the north to the Mull of **Galloway** in the south. **Portpatrick** and Drummore are the most important villages and it also contains the **Logan Botanic Garden**. There are 3 **lighthouses** on its coast: Corsewall Point, Killantringan and Mull of Galloway.

**Rhinns (of Islay)** (Gaelic **Na Rannan Íleach**) Western promontory of **Islay**, originally an island and still largely separated from the mainland by Loch Indaal.

**Rhu** Village on the east shore of the **Gare Loch**, near **Helensburgh**. The haunt of **whisky** smugglers in the 18th and early 19th centuries, it became a fashionable area for marine villas in early Victorian times and has been a popular place for yachting and boating since the mid 19th century.

**Rhum** see **Rum**

**Rhynie** Picturesque Northeast village, 13km (8mi) south of **Huntly**, lying in a deep geological fault. A **Jacobite** stronghold, in 1746 its inhabitants put a Hanoverian army to flight. Nearby is the large vitrified fort of Tap o' Noth, dating from soon after 1000 BC. It is famous for the Rhynie Chert, a silicified peat bog of Devonian times, showing intimate detail of early land plants and insects.

**RIAS** see **Royal Incorporation of Architects in Scotland**

**Riccarton** Former estate to the southwest of **Edinburgh** close to **Currie**, now home to the main campus of **Heriot-Watt University**.

**Riccarton** Suburb to the south of **Kilmarnock**. It is the site of the former Massey-Harris agricultural-implement factory. Its Georgian parish church is a notable landmark.

**Riccio** see **Rizzio, David**

**Richey, James E** (1886–1969) Geologist, b. Co. Tyrone, Northern Ireland. He spent most of his life with the Geological Survey and demonstrated many of the features of the igneous rocks of the **Hebrides** and west coast, above all the **Mull** and **Ardnamurchan** areas. He was consulting geologist for most of the hydroelectric dams built in Scotland after World War II.

**Riddon, Loch** see **Loch Riddon**

**Riding of the Marches** Traditional ceremony of riding round the boundaries of common land, to inspect landmarks, boundary stones etc; in recent times revived as the focus of an annual local festival in certain towns, especially in the **Borders**, where in some towns it is known as the **Common Riding**. The festival often lasts for a number of days, involving various principal characters and traditional ceremonies.

**Rifkind, Sir Malcolm** (1946– ) Politician, b. Edinburgh. Elected Conservative MP for Edinburgh Pentlands in 1974, he was originally on the liberal, pro-**devolution** wing of his party, but later came to a pragmatic accommodation with Thatcherism. A minister in the Scottish Office (1979–82) and Foreign Office (1982–6), he then became Secretary of State for Scotland, holding the post for 4 years. He remained in the Cabinet as Transport Minister (1990–2), Defence Minister (1992–5), and then Foreign Secretary (1995–7), but lost his seat at the 1997 general election. In 2004 he was selected as the prospective parliamentary candidate for Kensington and Chelsea.

**rig** In pre-improvement farming, a unit of cultivation. Specifically it denoted a ploughing technique that mounded the soil into a curving strip up to over 9m (30ft) wide, with a dividing bauk or depression where the surface water could run off down the fall-line of the slope. Early improvers straightened the rigs to a standard 5 or 6m (15 or 18ft) wide, and after 1833 the spread of sub-soil drainage steadily did away with the need for them. See also **runrig**.

**Rinns** see **Rhinns**

**Rizzio** or **Riccio, David** (c.1533–66) Private secretary to **Mary, Queen of Scots**, b. Turin, Italy. Initially employed as a singer, his advancement provoked rumour and resentment, and he was murdered at Holyrood in front of the pregnant queen by a group of nobles, including the queen's husband, Lord **Darnley**.

**Rob Donn** (Robert Mackay) (1714–78) Gaelic poet, b. Strathmore, northern Sutherland. His wide-ranging oral poetry and social satire gives a vivid picture of Highland life as it was changing for ever at the time of the 1745 **Jacobite Risings**.

## Robert I, the Bruce (1274–1329)

King of Scots from 1306, hero of the **Wars of Independence**, probably b. Turnberry, Ayrshire. Though he initially supported Edward I of England in 1296, he took part in the uprising led by Sir William **Wallace** and was appointed one of the **Guardians** of Scotland in 1298. Back in English allegiance by 1302, Bruce seized the throne after killing his domestic rival John **Comyn** in 1306. He was crowned at **Scone** in April of that year. Initially a fugitive in his own land, he became a master of guerrilla warfare, and in the 8 years following his accession conducted campaigns which culminated in victory over a large English army at **Bannockburn**. Having liberated Scotland, Bruce took the fight into the north of England and Ireland, eventually securing English acknowledgement of his right to be monarch of an independent Scotland. Died at Cardross, possibly of leprosy.

*Statue of Robert I at Edinburgh Castle.*

## Robert II (1316–90) King of Scots from 1371, succeeding **David II**.

His mother was Marjory Bruce, daughter of **Robert I**, and his father Walter the Steward; he thus became first monarch of the Stewart dynasty. Considerable political tranquillity in the early part of the reign gave way to tensions within the royal family in the 1380s, with the future **Robert III** clashing with his younger brother Robert, later Duke of **Albany**. An aggressive, largely successful approach was taken towards England in foreign policy.

## Robert III (c.1337–1406) King of Scots from 1390, son of

**Robert II**. Christened John, he assumed his father's name on becoming king. Much influence during his reign was wielded by his younger brother, Robert, Duke of **Albany**, who became more powerful still after the death in captivity, probably of starvation, of the king's elder son, David, Duke of Rothesay, in 1402. Fearful of Albany's ambition, he sent his younger son, the future **James I**, to France, and died shortly after hearing of James's capture by the English.

## Robert Burns World Federation

International organisation, formerly known as the Burns Federation, based in **Kilmarnock**, aiming to encourage interest in Robert **Burns** and in Scottish literature and culture more widely. Established in 1885, it now has over 80,000 members worldwide, with affiliated Burns clubs in 16 countries. It organises competitions, especially for schoolchildren, and publishes the annual *Burns Chronicle* and a quarterly newsletter *The Burnsian*.

## Robert Gordon University

Founded as Robert Gordon's Hospital in **Aberdeen** in 1750 from a legacy left by Robert Gordon (1665–1752), a wealthy Aberdeen merchant who traded with the Baltic countries. Under the name of Robert Gordon's College, it became both a school for boys and a technical college. The latter became a university in 1992 and it now incorporates Gray's School of Art. It has 11,500 students.

## Roberts, David (1796–1864) Artist, b. Edinburgh. Worked first

as a house and theatrical painter, from the mid 1820s travelling extensively abroad, turning his sketches of architectural subjects into paintings back in his studio in London. He is best known for his panoramic scenes of the grand architecture and landscape of the Middle East, and in particular of Egypt, which were reproduced widely as lithographs and which brought him success in his own lifetime.

## Robertson, Anne Strachan (1910–97) Archaeologist

and numismatist, b. Glasgow. Professor of Roman Archaeology at **Glasgow University**, she curated the Roman collections in the Hunterian Museum, including the famous Hunter Coin Cabinet. She was an expert on the **Antonine Wall** and excavated Roman forts along the Wall and elsewhere in Scotland. Her books include *The Roman Imperial Coins in the Hunter Coin Cabinet* and *Romano-British Coin Hoards*.

R

*A romantic depiction of Rob Roy MacGregor.*

**Robertson, Belinda** (1959– ) Fashion designer, b. Glasgow. After some years in teaching and marketing, she turned to fashion design, specialising in cashmere. She now has her own collection, with outlets in Edinburgh, London and Birmingham, and her clothes have won international acclaim and many awards.

**Robertson, George, Lord Robertson of Port Ellen** (1946– ) Politician, b. Port Ellen, Islay. Elected Labour MP for **Hamilton** in 1978, he became his party's spokesman on European affairs in 1984, and held the post for 9 years before moving to the Shadow Cabinet, where he had responsibility for Scottish matters. Became Secretary of State for Defence on Labour's return to power in 1997, then 2 years later was made Secretary General of NATO, a post he held until 2003. Also in 1999, he was made a life peer.

**Robertson, James** (1958– ) Poet and novelist, b. Sevenoaks, Kent, brought up in Bridge of Allan. He has published collections of poetry and short stories and his first novel *The Fanatic* was published in 2000. His second, *Joseph Knight* (2003) won the Saltire Book of the Year Award. He has a small pamphlet-publishing project, Kettilonia, and is the general editor of Itchy Coo, a project to produce **Scots**-language texts aimed especially at schools.

**Robertson, Jeannie** (1908–75) Folksinger, b. **Aberdeen**. Little known outside the northeast until her mid-40s, she was then discovered by Hamish **Henderson**. She was one of the biggest influences of the folk revival of the late 1950s onwards, bringing to it her rich repertoire of traditional material.

**Robertson, William** (1721–93) Minister, educator and historian, b. Borthwick Manse, Midlothian. Following his father into the ministry, he was ordained as minister of Gladsmuir at the age of 22, and was minister of Greyfriars Kirk in **Edinburgh** from 1751. He served as **Moderator** of the **General Assembly** and was the leader of the **Moderate** party. His *History of Scotland 1542–1603* was widely acclaimed when published in 1759; 10 years later his *History of Charles V* met with even greater success. He became Principal of **Edinburgh University** in 1762, and Historiographer Royal 2 years later. In 1777 he published the first part of a history of America, devoted to Hispanic America, but was prevented by his mixed feelings about the American Revolution from completing the second volume. Finally he wrote with distinction on India. He was a central figure of the **Scottish Enlightenment**.

**Robert the Bruce** see **Robert I**

**Robinson Crusoe** see **Selkirk, Alexander**

**Robison, Dr John** (1739–1805) Physicist, b. Boghall, Stirlingshire. Lecturer in chemistry in the University of **Glasgow** in 1766–9, and a friend of James **Watt**, then an instrument maker in the University. In 1769 he became Professor of **Natural Philosophy** in **Edinburgh University**. There his pupils included John **Rennie**. He contributed a supplement on mechanics to the second edition of the *Encyclopaedia Britannica*.

**Rob Roy** (1671–1734) Nickname of Robert MacGregor, outlaw and rebel, b. Loch Katrine. He was a cattle dealer based at **Inversnaid** on **Loch Lomond** and provided safe passage for the (black) cattle through the Lowlands as an insurance or protection racket. Turned out of his lands in **Balquhidder** by the Duke of Montrose in 1712 after reneging on a debt, he embarked on a guerrilla campaign against his persecutor. Patronised by the Duke of **Argyll** and often calling himself Campbell, he participated unenthusiastically in the **Jacobite Risings** of 1708 and 1715. He has since been highly romanticised, largely due to Sir Walter Scott's 1818 novel *Rob Roy*.

**Rochead, John Thomas** (1814–78) Architect b. Edinburgh. Based in **Glasgow**, he was primarily an Italian Renaissance architect as at the former **Bank of Scotland** in St Vincent Place in Glasgow. He is best known as the architect of the **Wallace Monument** at **Stirling** (1861–9).

**Rockall** Uninhabited rock in the Atlantic Ocean 306km (190mi) west of **St Kilda**. It has long been disputed territory, probably because of the possibility of minerals below sea level. It was claimed by Britain in 1955 and incorporated into the United Kingdom (as part of **Inverness-shire**) by a 1971 Act of Parliament.

**Rockcliffe** Village on the Rough Firth, Kirkcudbrightshire, notable for its clement climate and rock gardens. **National Trust for Scotland** properties in the area include Rough Island bird sanctuary and the Mote of Mark, an ancient hill fort dating back to the 5th century, and associated with the King Mark of the Tristan and Isolde romance.

**Rodel** (Gaelic **Roghadal**) Village at the southern tip of **Harris**. The Church of St Clement was built in the early 16th century, but abandoned after the **Reformation**; it was restored in the late 18th century and again in the late 19th. It contains some remarkable monuments, notably the tomb of Alastair Crotach (Hunchbacked Alexander, the Macleod Chief who founded it), with its unique detailed image of a West Highland birlinn (galley).

**Rogart** (Gaelic **Rogairt**) Sutherland village on the River Fleet, focal point of the surrounding crofting community. It had a small woollen mill, serving local needs.

**Rogie Falls** (Gaelic **Eas Roagaidh**) Waterfall near the southeast end of Loch Garve, 3km (2mi) west of **Strathpeffer**. Spanned by a suspension bridge.

**Rolls Royce Ltd** Aero-engineering company, based in Derby. In the late 1930s it was directed by Government to build a large new factory at Hillington, near **Glasgow**, as a 'shadow factory' to allow production of aero engines to be increased rapidly in the event of World War II. It was fully used during World War II and afterwards was adapted to make jet engines. A second factory was built in the early 1950s, at **East Kilbride**. Both are still in operation.

**Roman Catholic Church in Scotland** After the **Reformation** of 1560, the Catholic Church survived in some areas, notably the northeast and the southwest, especially in some landed families. From 1619 Irish Franciscans began missionary work in the Gaelic-speaking **Highlands** and **Western Isles** and certain of these areas remain strongly Catholic to this day, notably **South Uist**, **Barra** and parts of western **Inverness-shire**, as well as pockets in the eastern Highlands. Apart from the brief interlude of the reign of the Catholic **James VII** (1685–8), there was considerable opposition until the late 18th century, ended officially by Catholic Emancipation in 1829. Numerous Irish immigrants swelled the numbers in towns in the west of Scotland, increased to a lesser extent by Italian immigrants later in the 19th century. Since 1878 there has been an Archbishop of **St Andrews** and **Edinburgh** and Bishops of **Aberdeen**, **Argyll** and the Isles, **Dunkeld**, and **Galloway**, and since 1947 also an Archbishop of **Glasgow** and Bishops of **Motherwell** and **Paisley**. See also **Scots Colleges**.

**Rona** Small island to the north of **Raasay**, between **Skye** and the mainland. It has had a **lighthouse** at the north end since 1857, where there is now also a marine testing station. See also **North Rona**.

**Ronaldsay** see **North Ronaldsay, South Ronaldsay**

**Rootes Ltd** Motor-car makers, builders of Hillman cars, were persuaded by Government to build a new factory at Linwood, near **Paisley**, to alleviate unemployment caused by the contraction of heavy engineering and shipbuilding on Clydeside. The factory opened in 1963, and made a light car known as the Hillman 'Imp'. It proved difficult for workers used to one-off production to adapt to mass-production, and distance from components' manufacturers and markets also made the plant uncompetitive. It was taken over by Chrysler in the 1970s, and then by Peugeot, who closed it in 1981.

**Rosebery, Archibald Primrose, 1st Earl of** (1661–1723) Politician. A strong supporter of the government, he became one of the commissioners of the 1707 Treaty of **Union** of the Scottish and English parliaments. He became Viscount Rosebery, Lord Primrose and Dalmeny in 1700 and Earl of Rosebery in 1702.

**Rosebery, Archibald Primrose, 5th Earl of** (1847–1929) Liberal politician. Born and educated in England, he succeeded to his grandfather's title in 1868 and later married into the Rothschild family. He successfully agitated for the

R

*Dolly, the first living sheep cloned from another, at the Roslin Institute, 1997.*

re-establishment of the Scottish Secretaryship, but was denied the post himself. Foreign Secretary in 1886 and again 1892–94, he became Prime Minister in 1894 on the resignation of Gladstone. His short period in office was marked by controversies over Irish Home Rule and the House of Lords; he lost the general election of 1895 and resigned the Liberal leadership the following year.

**Rosemarkie** Small town on the **Moray Firth**, on the south shore of the **Black Isle**. Now part of a conservation area, it was once the seat of the Bishops of Ross, though its church, said to have been founded in the 7th century by St Boniface, was moved to the adjacent **Fortrose** in the 13th century. A new parish church was built in 1821. There is also a museum of Pictish carved stones.

**Roslin** Small village to the south of **Edinburgh**, site of the **Rosslyn** Chapel. Rising in importance with the construction of the chapel, it was created a **burgh** by **James II** in 1456. Roslin Castle, on a cliff above the North **Esk**, was the home of the Sinclair family, early Masters of the Scottish Freemasons. Long ruined, it was restored in the late 20th century.

**Roslin Institute** One of the world's leading research institutes on farm and other animals, based at the village of **Roslin**. Its main research areas are genomics and bioinformatics, transgenics and biotechnology, animal breeding, and animal welfare and behaviour. Public interest was aroused in recent years by 'Dolly the sheep', the first mammal to be successfully cloned, in 1997. (She was named after the American singer Dolly Parton). She developed arthritis and had to be put down in 2003 because of illness; her body is on display at the **Royal Museum**.

**Rosneath** Former seat of the Dukes of Argyll and village on the **Gare Loch**, a popular boating centre; it is the site of St Modan's Well, which marks the spot of the church founded by the saint in the 7th century. Its boatbuilding yard, Silvers', pioneered the building of luxury motor yachts. The former inn is an important work by Sir Edwin Lutyens, built (1896–7) for Princess Louise, Duchess of Argyll.

**Ross, Sir John** (1777–1856) Sailor and explorer, b. Inch Manse, Wigtownshire. Having joined the navy as a boy, he served in the Napoleonic Wars, and then from 1812 led surveys of the White Sea and the Arctic. He also conducted expeditions in search of the Northwest Passage, and discovered King William Land, the Gulf of Boothia and Boothia Peninsula.

**Ross, Thomas** see **MacGibbon, David**

**Ross, William** (Gaelic **Uilleam Ros**) (1762–c.91) Gaelic poet, b. Skye. Educated in **Forres**, he later lived in **Gairloch**, working as a schoolteacher and catechist. He is regarded as one of the greatest of Gaelic love poets, much of his verse inspired by his unrequited love of Mór Ros (Marion Ross) from **Lewis**.

**Ross, William** (1879–1966) Piper, b. Camsorrie, Glen Strathfarrar. Taught by his parents and relatives, he won many awards. He was Pipe Major in the **Scots Guards** and **Lovat Scouts** and was **Piobaireachd** Society instructor to the Army School 1920–57. He was a composer and arranger of pipe music, and published *Pipe Major William Ross's Collection of Highland Bagpipe Music* Books 1 to 5 between 1923 and 1950.

**Ross and Cromarty** Former county in northern Scotland, also known as Ross-shire. In 1975 most of it became the Ross and Cromarty district of Highland Region; see maps on pp.394–5 and **local government**. Since 1996 it has been part of **Highland** local authority, but Ross and Cromarty retains a *de facto* existence as a historic part of the country. See also **Wester Ross**.

**Rossdhu** Classical mansion on **Loch Lomond** side to the south of **Luss**, built 1772–4, with a portico added c.1820. The site was the home of the Colquhoun family from the 14th century, but part of the estate is now the exclusive **Loch Lomond** Golf Club and the house is the clubhouse.

**Rossend Castle** see **Burntisland**

**Rosslyn Chapel** Architectural masterpiece in **Roslin** village, founded in 1446 by Sir William Sinclair, 3rd Earl of Orkney and later 1st Earl of Caithness. Damaged by rioters in the late 17th century, it was partially restored in 1882, then comprehensively in the 1950s. Its most striking feature is the Apprentice Pillar, very distinct from the other 15 pillars and said to have been carved, in the absence of his superior, by an inspired apprentice, whom the master mason killed out of jealousy on his return. There are many unsubstantiated beliefs about the mystical and masonic associations of the building, which is a **Scottish Episcopal Church**.

**Ross of Mull** Long southwestern peninsula of **Mull**, with formerly important red granite quarries; **Iona** is just off its western end; see **Fionnphort**.

**Ross-shire** see **Ross and Cromarty**

**Rosyth** Fife town on the Firth of **Forth**, to the south of **Dunfermline**, a garden-city development of 1915–25, associated with the Royal Naval Base or dockyard, sited there since 1909. Though closed from 1925 to 1938, it was a vital fleet base in both World Wars. More recently it has been a training base and the refitting dock for Britain's nuclear submarines. It is also the home of the Scotland Band of the Royal Marines. Inside the dockyard is the 15th-century tower house of Rosyth Castle. A ferry now runs from Rosyth to Zeebrugge.

**Rothesay** (Gaelic **Baile Bhòd**) Seaside resort on the east side of the isle of **Bute**, former royal **burgh** and a holiday destination for generations of Glaswegians, for whom a splendid modernist pavilion was built in 1936–8. The winter garden of 1923–4 also survives and the Pier has splendidly restored Victorian men's lavatories. It was a cotton-spinning town from the late 18th century until the mid 19th. The circular Rothesay Castle dates from the 12th century with later additions. It was a favourite residence of the Stewart kings and the title Duke of Rothesay has been held by the eldest son of the monarch since the 15th century. The castle suffered heavy damage by Cromwellian troops and in the Earl of Argyll's rebellion, but was partially restored in the late 19th century by the Marquess of Bute, its hereditary keeper; now in the care of **Historic Scotland**.

**Rothiemurchus** (Gaelic **Ràta Mhurchais**) Estate and large deer forest just to the north of the **Cairngorms**. It is now part of the **Cairngorms National Park**. The recently restored Doune of Rothiemurchus, mainly of 1797–1803, was the home of Elizabeth **Grant** of Rothiemurchus.

**Rough Bounds** (Gaelic **Na Garbh Criochan**) Wild, remote southwestern corner of the **Highlands**, stretching from **Loch Sunart** in the south to **Loch Hourn** in the north.

**Rough Wooing** Term applied to the greatly damaging Anglo-Scottish warfare between 1543 and 1550 in response to the Scots' repudiation of the Treaty of Greenwich (1543). The treaty had stipulated the marriage of **Mary, Queen of Scots** to Prince Edward (later Edward VI), and envisaged a union of the English and Scottish kingdoms. Heavy-handed military action ensured that the Scots eventually turned to France for a match for Mary.

**Rouken Glen** Large park in Eastwood, just outside **Glasgow**, containing a boating pond, walled garden and other amenities.

**roup** Scots term for a sale or let by public auction.

**Rousay** (pop. 212) One of the **Orkney** Islands, northeast of Mainland, with a wealth of sites of archaeological interest, including Midhowe **Broch** and the neolithic Midhowe and Taversöe Tuick Chambered Cairns (all in the care of **Historic Scotland**).

**Rowallan** Two sides of this Renaissance courtyard castle remain, 6km (4mi) north of **Kilmarnock**, built c.1560, and the entrance side of its outer court, remarkable for its twin-towered forework and high-quality detail. The new house was built by Sir Robert **Lorimer** in 1901 for the Corbetts, and was the home of Lord Rowallan.

*The interior of Rosslyn Chapel.*

*The Royal Scottish Academy, Edinburgh, built in Greek Doric style in the 19th century.*

**Rowardennan** Village on the eastern shore of **Loch Lomond**, close to **Ben Lomond**, and the start of the 'official' path up the mountain.

**Rowett Research Institute** Scientific establishment in **Aberdeen**, founded in 1913 as an independent charitable organisation with government funding, to carry out research on nutrition and its importance in the prevention of disease. Its director from 1942–5 was John **Boyd Orr**. It has carried out important studies on genetically modified crops.

**Rowling, J(oanne) K(athleen)** (1965– ) Author, b. Chipping Sodbury, Avon. Originally a teacher, she moved to **Edinburgh** and took to writing. Her first novel, *Harry Potter and the Philosopher's Stone* (1997), the tale of a boy's adventures at Hogwarts School for wizards, was a huge success, combining the appeal of the magical with the reassuring solidity of the traditional boarding-school story. Subsequent volumes of the Potter saga have been equally well received, as have the film versions of the books. She is now Scotland's wealthiest woman.

**Roxburgh** Small **Borders** village, once a royal **burgh**, on the River **Teviot**, just north of **Kelso**. Prior to the **Wars of Independence** it was one of the most important urban centres in Scotland, but after 1296 its fortunes declined and it changed hands frequently in Anglo-Scottish wars. **James II** was killed at the 1460 siege of the now ruined Roxburgh Castle.

**Roxburgh District** From 1975 to 1996 a district of **Borders Region**, in 1996 it became part of **Scottish Borders**; see **Roxburghshire**, maps on pp.394–5 and **local government**.

**Roxburghshire** Former county in southern Scotland, also known as Roxburgh. In 1975 most of it became the Roxburgh District of

**Borders Region**. Since 1996 it has been part of **Scottish Borders** local authority; see maps on pp.394–5 and **local government**.

**Roy, Archie** (**Archibald Edmiston**) (1924– ) Astronomer, b. Glasgow. A lecturer in astronomy at **Glasgow University** and Professor from 1982. His publications include *The Foundations of Astrodynamics* (1965), and he has also written and lectured on parapsychology and science fiction.

**Roy, William** (1726–90) Military surveyor, b. Carluke, Lanarkshire. Engaged on the survey of Scotland from 1747, he received a commission in the army in 1755, eventually rising to be Major-General. His technically accomplished maps constitute a unique detailed cartographic record of much of Scotland, especially the **Highlands**. He also studied Roman remains in Scotland, and his *Military Antiquities of the Romans in Britain* was published 3 years after his death.

**Royal and Ancient Golf Club,** also known as the **R & A.** Founded as the Society of St Andrews Golfers in 1754, it changed to its present name in 1834 on being granted the patronage of King William IV. It is now, with the United States Golf Association, one of the two world governing bodies for the rules of golf.

**Royal Bank of Scotland** Founded in 1727 as an offshoot of the Equivalent Company, set up with compensation granted in the 1707 **Treaty of Union** to sufferers from the **Darien** disaster. It was originally based in **Edinburgh**'s Old Town and sponsored by pro-Hanoverian politicians. It grew to breach the monopoly and to become the main rival of the older, **Jacobite**-linked **Bank of Scotland**. In 1825 it moved its headquarters to a splendid 18th-century mansion in the New Town (see Sir William **Chambers**). After many mergers and takeovers, it acquired the National Westminster Bank in 2002, making it the 2nd largest bank in Europe (and 5th largest in the world). It is one of the 3 Scottish banks permitted to issue banknotes.

**Royal Botanic Garden** Garden in Inverleith, **Edinburgh**, open to the public. It was established in 1670 by Sir Robert **Sibbald** and Dr Andrew Balfour to grow medicinal herbs, originally on a small plot of land near **Holyrood**. After several moves, it came to its present site in the 1820s. Now a 28-hectare (70-acre) site incorporating several impressive glasshouses, notably the Palm House of 1856–8 by Robert Matheson and the New Glass Houses by George Pearce and John Johnson (1965–7). It is an important research centre and specialises in plants from China and the Himalayas. It has 3 specialist gardens: **Benmore** (near **Dunoon**), **Logan** (near **Stranraer)** and **Dawyck** (near **Peebles)**.

**Royal Burgess Golfing Society** Begun on Bruntsfield Links, **Edinburgh**, in 1735, one of the first organisations devoted to the nascent sport; now a prestigious club at Barnton, a northwest suburb of Edinburgh.

**royal burgh** see **burgh**

**Royal College of Physicians** Regulatory body for the profession, established in **Edinburgh** in 1681, now based in a classical building with interiors of exceptional grandeur in Queen Street (1844 Thomas **Hamilton**).

**Royal College of Science and Technology** see **Strathclyde University**

**Royal College of Surgeons** Founded 1505 and granted a royal charter the following year, the regulatory body for the profession, based at the imposing classical Surgeons' Hall in central **Edinburgh**, designed by W H **Playfair** (1829–32). The building includes museums of surgery and dentistry.

**Royal Commission on the Ancient and Historical Monuments of Scotland** Independent non-departmental government body based in **Edinburgh**, founded in 1908 to record and interpret the sites, monuments and buildings of Scotland's past.

**Royal Company of Archers** The monarch's bodyguard in Scotland, founded 1676, given a charter from Queen Anne in 1707. Their hall in Buccleuch Street, built in 1776 and reconstructed in 1900, has archery butts behind it.

**Royal Highland Fusiliers** (**Princess Margaret's Own Glasgow and Ayrshire Regiment**) Regiment of the British Army formed in 1959 by the merger of the **Highland Light Infantry** and **Royal Scots Fusiliers**.

**Royal Highland Show** Annual agricultural exhibition now held in June at **Ingliston**, to the west of **Edinburgh**; it was previously held at different venues throughout Scotland. It is run by the Royal Highland and Agricultural Society, founded in 1784 to promote Scottish agriculture. It is the biggest annual farming event in Scotland and the north of England.

**Royal Incorporation of Architects in Scotland** (RIAS) Professional body for architects in Scotland, founded 1840, based in **Edinburgh**.

**Royal Institution** see **Royal Scottish Academy**

**Royal Museum** Opened in 1866, a wide-ranging museum in Chambers Street, **Edinburgh**, especially strong in natural history, geology, technology, Egyptology and Far Eastern antiquities. Designed by Captain Francis Fowke, it is one of the most impressive iron-framed structures surviving from early Victorian times. One of the **National Museums of Scotland**, it was formerly known as the Royal Scottish Museum. The **Museum of Scotland** is next to it and linked to it.

**Royal Observatory Edinburgh** Originally sited on Calton Hill in 1776, it moved in 1893 to its current handsome buildings by W W Robertson on Blackford Hill, also Edinburgh. It now includes the Institute for Astronomy of Edinburgh University and the UK Astronomy Technology Centre of the Particle Physics and Astronomy Research Council.

**Royal Scots** (**The Royal Regiment**) 1st Regiment of Foot, the oldest in the British Army. Originally raised in 1633 as Sir John Hepburn's Regiment, they fought in the Thirty Years' War and the Franco-Spanish War before returning to Britain. The core of the regiment were survivors from much earlier regiments, going back to an obscure past and giving it the nickname of 'Pontius Pilate's Bodyguard'. It recruits from **Edinburgh** and southeast Scotland and is based in Edinburgh Castle.

**Royal Scots Dragoon Guards** (**Carabiniers and Greys**) Regiment of the British Army formed in 1971 by the amalgamation of the **Royal Scots Greys** with the 3rd Carabiniers (Prince of Wales Dragoon Guards). It is based in **Edinburgh** Castle and recruits throughout Scotland.

**Royal Scots Fusiliers** Founded as the Earl of Mar's Regiment in 1678 to counter the **Covenanters**, they became the 21st Regiment of Foot in 1751 and were renamed Royal Scots Fusiliers in 1877. They joined with the **Highland Light Infantry** in 1959 to form the **Royal Highland Fusiliers**.

**Royal Scots Greys** Mounted regiment raised in 1681 by General Tam **Dalyell**, formerly known, *inter alia*, as the Royal Regiment of Scots Dragoons. Long distinguished by their grey horses, they were finally mechanised in India in 1938, and were merged 30 years later with the 3rd Carabiniers to become the **Royal Scots Dragoon Guards**.

**Royal Scottish Academy** Society of artists based in **Edinburgh**, founded 1826. Its first annual exhibition was held in 1827, and in 1838 it merged with the Royal Institution under the new, fuller title of Royal Scottish Academy of Painting, Sculpture and Architecture. The Greek Doric building, at the foot of the Mound, was built in the 1820s and 30s to a design by W H **Playfair** for several other organisations. It was radically adapted for the RSA in 1909–11, and sensitively updated as a venue for major exhibitions in 2001–3 as part of the Playfair Project.

R

*Scotland's 13–7 victory over England at rugby in 1990 gave them the Grand Slam (victory over the other 4 competing nations) for the third time.*

**Royal Scottish Academy of Music and Drama** An important degree-granting institution, originally founded as a music school in the 19th century; in the 1880s, as the Glasgow Atheneum, it moved to a classical building by J J **Burnet**, in central **Glasgow**. The College of Drama was founded in 1950. Its present title dates from 1968. Since 1987 it has been housed in a modern building in the north of the city centre and the Alexander **Gibson** Opera School was opened there in 1998.

**Royal Scottish Corporation** Charitable body founded by London-based Scots in 1611, granted a royal charter in 1655. It continues to help Scots in need in London and is a focus for Scottish societies there.

**Royal Scottish Country Dance Society** Organisation founded in 1923 to promote standards in Scottish country dancing (social dancing usually performed in sets of 3, 4 or 5 couples). Based in **Edinburgh**, it now has branches worldwide. It holds a Summer School in **St Andrews** and a Winter School in **Pitlochry**, as well as many other courses and events. See also **reel**, **strathspey**.

**Royal Scottish Museum** see **Royal Museum**

**Royal Scottish National Orchestra** The Scottish National Orchestra became a full-time body, based in **Glasgow**, in 1950, but its antecedents reach back to 1844. 'Royal' was added to the title in 1991. The orchestra has won many awards, toured and recorded extensively, premiered many compositions, supported **Scottish Opera** for its first 20 years, and supported a wide range of educational projects. Important conductors have included Sir Alexander **Gibson**, Neeme Järvi and Bryden Thomson.

**Royal Society of Edinburgh** Founded in Edinburgh in 1783 as a vehicle for literary and scientific debate. The scientific side of the Society soon became dominant, but the literary wing was revived in the 1970s. It occupies a palazzo-like building at 22–24 George Street, built by David **Bryce** in 1843 for the Edinburgh Life Assurance Co.

**Roybridge** Small village 5km (3mi) east of **Spean Bridge** at the southern end of **Glen Roy**, site of the 18th-century Keppoch House, and location of one of the last clan battles, between the MacDonnells of Keppoch and the MacIntoshes, in 1688.

**Ruddiman, Thomas** (1674–1757) Publisher, librarian, philologist, editor, **Jacobite**, b. Boyndie, Banffshire. He became Principal Keeper of the Advocates' Library in **Edinburgh**, (see **National Library of Scotland**), and he also ran printing and auctioneering businesses. Published works of Allan **Ramsay** and George **Buchanan**, as well as his own *Rudiments of the Latin Tongue* (1714).

**rugby** see p.327

**Rule, St** Also known as St Regulus, said by legend to have brought the relics of St **Andrew** from the Mediterranean to **Kilrimont**, the Pictish ecclesiastical complex on the headland east of **St Andrews**.

**Rullion Green, Battle of** see **Pentland Rising**

**rumbledethump** A dish of cooked potato and cabbage mixed together, sometimes with grated cheese added and browned under the grill.

**Rumbling Bridge** Gorge and falls on River Devon, 7km (4mi) northeast of **Dollar**. The name comes from the noise of the river when in spate.

Although the English schoolboy William Webb Ellis is credited with the act of picking up the ball and running with it, which distinguished rugby from other forms of football, the reality was that the traditional ball games of Scotland and England had long included elements which contributed to the sport as we know it today. Ellis's act of 1823 did, however, symbolise the parting of the ways with football, and the rules subsequently drawn up by his school, Rugby, were instrumental in establishing the game which eventually became known as rugby football. The first Scottish rugby club, Edinburgh Academy, was founded in 1857, and in the following year they played Merchiston Castle School in what is probably the oldest fixture which is still played today. They also played host, at their Raeburn Place ground, to the world's first rugby international: on 27 March 1871, with 20 men on either team, Scotland beat England by a try and a goal to a try. It was agreed to play the fixture annually, and from 1879 the teams have competed for the Calcutta Cup.

Thereafter the sport spread swiftly. The Scottish Rugby Football Union (now simply called the Scottish Rugby Union, SRU) was founded in 1873, and annual fixtures were soon established with Ireland (from 1877) and Wales (from 1883). In the latter year Ned Haig, a Melrose butcher, invented 7-a-side rugby, the abbreviated version of the game.

While a dispute over professionalism eventually led to the establishment in England of rugby league (1895), Scotland remained resolutely amateur. Indeed, a century later, some SRU officials were among the most prominent opponents of a move which led to rugby union's becoming professional in 1995.

Scotland enjoyed considerable success in the early decades of the sport, and in 1907 took the Triple Crown (a hypothetical prize for victory in the same season over the other 3 international sides) for the fifth time. Four years later, however, they also became the first home nation to lose to France, who had entered the international arena in 1910. Test matches apart, rugby was, and would remain for some time, a game with few official tournaments or trophies. Nonetheless, matches between the leading Scottish sides attracted 5-figure crowds in the inter-war years, and newspapers printed unofficial league tables.

In 1925, the SRU opened their new ground at **Murrayfield**, Edinburgh, and the stadium had a happy christening when victory over England gave Scotland their first Grand Slam (victory over the other competing nations in the same season). Thirteen years later the Scots won the Triple Crown. The post-war years were a lean period internationally, and Scotland were more commonly candidates for the Wooden Spoon than contenders for the title. It was not in fact until 1984 that a second Grand Slam was won, secured by a home victory over France. A third soon followed, and the 1990 Calcutta Cup match which clinched it is probably not the most celebrated game in the history of the sport in Scotland. England, the strong favourites, were stunned by the Scots' aggressive, self-confident performance, and although the margin of victory was a mere 6 points, the demoralising effect of the result remained with many of the English side for years to come.

The Scots teams of 1984 and 1990 were blessed with many gifted individuals, but it was also recognised that the formation of official leagues in the 1970s had helped the country steal a march on its rivals. **Hawick** were the dominant club in the first decade or so of the league, although from the late 1980s onwards their position was usurped by their **Border** rivals **Melrose**.

The more organised structure of the game at home was mirrored globally, and in 1987 the first Rugby World Cup was held. Scotland reached the quarter-finals, which also represented the limit of their achievements in 1995 and 1999. In 1991, when the tournament was held in Britain, they reached the semi-finals, losing narrowly to England at Murrayfield, the venue which had witnessed their triumph of a year earlier.

Since the advent of professionalism following the 1995 World Cup, the domestic game has undergone considerable upheaval. After much debate, the SRU went ahead with their decision to field centrally controlled professional teams, not clubs, in cross-border competitions such as the European Cup and the Celtic League. The nature and number of these teams changed several times before settling down at the present 3: the Borders, Edinburgh and Glasgow. A fourth, Caledonia, representing the north of the country, is to be re-established when finances permit.

The number of players of the sport, always small compared to most other major rugby-playing countries, has declined of late, although the SRU has succeeded in reintroducing it into many schools. There is also now a national women's team, who achieved their own Grand Slam in 1998 just a few years after being established. Traditionally reliant on private schools and Borders towns for most of its playing strength, rugby maintains its position as the preferred sport of a significant section of the establishment.

R

*Runrig's lineup, 30 years after they were founded.*

**Rumbling Bridge** Falls on the River Bran, 4km (2mi) south of **Dunkeld**.

**Runciman, Alexander** (1736–85) and **John** (1744–68/69) Artists, b. Edinburgh. Trained as decorative house painters. Alexander Runciman's most important work is considered to be the ambitious series of murals he painted at Penicuik House in the 1770s (destroyed by fire in 1899), which demonstrated his knowledge of the antique and Renaissance, applied to the subjects of St **Margaret** and **Ossian**. These were produced following his visit to Rome with his brother John, whose career ended abruptly when he died in Naples, aged 24; John's few surviving works, in particular his *King Lear in the Storm* (**National Gallery of Scotland**), show he was an artist of promise. Alexander worked principally as a history and landscape painter and was Master of the Trustees Academy.

**runrig** Also known as **rundale**. A generic term denoting a pre-improvement farming system, where a farm had several joint-tenants, each having so many **rigs** or cultivation strips. The allocation of these rigs might vary from year to year, determined by the drawing of lots, so each tenant got a chance of the best land. Used from medieval times and, in the **Highlands** and Islands, into the 20th century.

**Runrig** Celtic Band, founded by brothers Rory and Calum MacDonald on Skye in 1973, that merges Celtic / Gaelic influences with modern Rock. Since 1978 they have released 12 studio and several compilation and live albums reaching No 2 in the National Charts in 1993 with Amazing Things. In 1991 they played outdoors at Loch Lomond before 50,000 fans. In 1997, lead singer Donnie Munro left to take up a political career, and his place was taken by Cape Breton singer Bruce Guthro. They continue to perform in the UK and Europe, and in 2003 celebrated their 30th anniversary at Stirling Castle before a sellout crowd.

**Rusco** Rectangular tower house of 1500 near **Gatehouse of Fleet**, built by Robert Gordon who had married Mariota Carson; restored and reoccupied by R. Graham Carson (1975–9).

**Rutherford, Samuel** (c.1600–61) Theologian, b. Nisbet, near **Jedburgh**. A controversial figure from his early days as a professor at **Edinburgh University**, he won a sizeable following with the publication in 1636 of *Exercitationes Apologeticae Pro Divina Gratia*, a collection of his correspondence with some like-minded friends. Forbidden to preach for a time and banished to **Aberdeen** because of the views expressed therein, he later held posts in **St Andrews**. His *Lex Rex* (1661), a denial of the divine right of kings, was burned in public, and he would have been tried for high treason had not death intervened.

**Rutherglen** Industrial town to the southeast of **Glasgow**, a former royal **burgh**, now a suburb of the city (though part of **South Lanarkshire**). From 1975–96 it was part of Glasgow District of **Strathclyde Region**. It was for many years the head of the **Clyde** navigation, and had a shipyard, a large tube works, a chemical works and a paper mill.

**Ruthven, Sir Patrick** (c.1573–1651) Royalist soldier, probably b. Ballendean, Perthshire. Knighted by Gustavus Adolphus for services to the Swedish army, he returned to Scotland in 1638 and fought for **Charles I**. He was exiled to France in 1646 but came back a year before his death.

**Ruthven Barracks** see **Kingussie**

**Ruthven Castle** see **Huntingtower**

**Ruthven Raid** The 1582 detention of King **James VI** in **Ruthven Castle** for 10 months by a party of ultra-Protestants under the 1st Earl of **Gowrie**.

**Ruthwell** Small village 14km (9mi) southeast of **Dumfries**. Within the parish church is the 5m (18ft) high Ruthwell Cross, which dates from the early 8th century. Its intricate carvings include not only Latin texts relating to sculpted scenes from the New Testament, but also Anglo-Saxon runic inscriptions, often regarded as one of the earliest pieces of writing in any form of the English language. The runes record part of a poem known as 'The Dream of the Rood'. A Ruthwell minister, Dr Henry **Duncan**, founded the savings bank movement in a cottage in the village in 1810.

**Sabhal Mòr Ostaig** (Gaelic, meaning 'the big barn of Ostaig') Gaelic college near Armadale, Isle of **Skye**, founded in 1973 by Sir Iain Noble as part of scheme to regenerate the **Gaelic** language. Now part of the **UHI** Millennium Institute; it teaches Gaelic language and runs courses in other subjects (taught in Gaelic). It has a fine library of Gaelic books and other resources.

**Saddell** Village on the east coast of **Kintyre**, with an early 16th-century tower house and the ruins of a 12th-century abbey founded by **Somerled**, King of the Isles, or his son Reginald.

**Saddle, The** Mountain, a **Munro**, to the southwest of **Glen Shiel**, an impressive peak of 1010m (3314ft) and part of a long ridge.

**Sadowitz, Gerry** (1961– ) Comedian and magician, b. New Jersey, USA. Brought up in **Glasgow**, he came to the fore in the comedy boom of the 1980s, by shocking liberal audiences with his vitriolic style. Since 1990 he has appeared in a plethora of TV shows, many of them dealing primarily with his first love, conjuring.

**Sage, Donald** (1789–1869) Minister and author, b. Kildonan, Sutherland. After some years in **Lochcarron**, Achness in **Sutherland** and at the Gaelic Chapel in **Aberdeen**, he became minister at Resolis on the **Black Isle** in 1822, joining the **Free Church** at the **Disruption**. His *Memorabilia Domestica, or Parish Life in the North of Scotland* (1889) gives a vivid picture of the social and religious life in the **Highlands** in his time, not least of the **Clearances** in **Strathnaver**, which he witnessed at first hand.

**St Abb's** A picturesque fishing village and holiday resort on the southeast coast, northeast of **Eyemouth**. Nearby, the cliffs of St Abb's Head were once the site of a convent built by Ebba, a Northumbrian princess, and later burnt by the Vikings. The ruins of a priory built as a replacement by King Edgar survive next to the church. There is a **lighthouse** on the head.

**St Andrews** (pop. 14,209) Town on the northeast coast of Fife. It was an early centre of Christianity and of the Pictish cult of St **Andrew**, who became the national saint. A seat of bishops and, from 1472, of archbishops, its huge cathedral fell into ruins in the early 17th century, due to disuse, and was used as a quarry by the townspeople. In the museum in its precincts is an outstanding collection of medieval sculpture, including a spectacular Pictish sarcophagus. The 13th–16th-century ruins of the bishops' castle/palace stand on a promontory overlooking the sea; the site is much older, probably a Pictish royal fortress. In 1546 it was the scene of the murder of Cardinal **Beaton**. All of these are in the care of **Historic Scotland**. Holy Trinity Parish Church dates from 1411 and was sensitively restored by P MacGregor **Chalmers** in 1907–9. The St Andrews Preservation Trust has preserved and restored

*St Andrews Cathedral, with the town beyond.*

many of the historic buildings of the town. St Andrews is also famed for golf. The **Royal and Ancient Golf Club** was created in the 19th century by an amalgamation of other clubs. The Old Course is the most famous links. St Andrews Botanic Garden, owned by the University, is now managed by Fife Council and still used for University teaching and research as well as adult and school education. The layout comprises peat, rock and water features, bulb and herbaceous borders and a large collection of tender plants under glass. See also **St Andrews University**.

**St Andrew's College** see **Glasgow University**

**St Andrew's Day** The feast day of St **Andrew**, patron saint of Scotland, is 30 November, today celebrated less by Scots at home than Scots abroad.

**St Andrews University** The oldest university in Scotland, founded in 1411 by Bishop Henry **Wardlaw**, confirmed by papal bull in 1413. It was the university of choice for the Scottish aristocracy in the 17th century. Tainted with Jacobitism, it went into decline in the 18th, due to loss of government favour and funding. Its close association with the **Dundas** regime ensured marginalisation in liberal post-1832 Scotland. From the late 19th century it recovered by attracting private endowment and allying with University College Dundee. After the establishment of a separate **Dundee University** in 1967, it continued to expand. St Andrews remains the smallest of the ancient Scottish universities, but with a cosmopolitan tradition and a particularly strong North American connection. See also Kate **Kennedy**.

**St Blane's Church** A 12th-century Romanesque chapel at the south end of the Isle of **Bute**; in the care of **Historic Scotland**. This was the site of an early Christian monastery.

**St Boswells** see **Newtown St Boswells**

**St Cuthbert's Way** Long-distance trail from **Melrose** to Lindisfarne off the Northumbrian coast, linking places associated with St **Cuthbert**. It goes via St Boswells, Harestanes, Morebattle, **Yetholm** (where it meets the end of the Pennine Way), before crossing the border to Wooler, Fenwick and Lindisfarne.

**St Fillans** Village at the eastern end of **Loch Earn**, a favourite centre for walking and sports holidays. It has an underground hydroelectric power station. A ruined medieval chapel stands on the site of St Fillan's cell.

**St John's Toun** see **Perth**

**St Kilda** see p.359

**St Margaret's Hope** Village on the north coast of the **Orkney** island of **South Ronaldsay**. It was the island's port until the construction of the **Churchill Barriers** during World War II, and it is still a fishing and ship-repair centre. There is now a car ferry to Gills Bay near **John o' Groats** in Caithness.

**St Margaret's Hope** Anchorage in the **Firth of Forth**, 2km (1mi) northwest of **North Queensferry**, used by the **Rosyth** naval dockyard.

**St Mary's Loch** At the head of the **Yarrow** valley, surrounded by steep hills, a wild and romantic place, with excellent fishing. Tibbie Shiel's inn, between St Mary's Loch and the **Loch of the Lowes**, was a meeting place of Sir Walter **Scott** and James **Hogg**, and frequented by other writers such as Thomas **Carlyle** and R L **Stevenson**.

**St Monans** Pretty fishing village in the **East Neuk of Fife**, with two harbours and a fine church with an octagonal spire, built 1362–70. It had a celebrated boat-building industry from the 18th century until the 1990s.

**St Ninian's Isle** An 'island' linked by a natural causeway to the southwest coast of mainland **Shetland**, with the ruins of a 12th-century chapel, and scant remains of an earlier church. Excavations here uncovered a splendid hoard of 8th and 9th-century silver, perhaps buried to protect it from Viking raids. It is now in the **Museum of Scotland**, **Edinburgh**.

**St Ronan's Well** see **Innerleithen**

**St Vigean's** Small village on the north edge of **Arbroath**. It has an early 16th-century parish church, restored 1871, on a hillock surrounded by cottages, one of which contains an important museum of early Christian stones, dating from the 8th to the 10th century; in the care of **Historic Scotland**.

**Sair sanct for the croun** see **David I**

**salmon** Salmon has been fished in Scotland since the earliest times, for food, for export, and more recently also for sport. Wild Atlantic salmon still return to Scottish rivers to spawn, notably on the Rivers **Dee**, **Tay**, **Tweed** and **Spey**. Most of the former commercial salmon fisheries have closed, many of the rights bought up by the Atlantic Salmon Trust to conserve fish for rod fishermen. Most salmon sold commercially is now farmed, raised in cages. Salmon farming, an important industry in the **Highlands** and Islands in recent decades, is blamed for a reduction in the numbers of wild salmon and other marine animals including shellfish, as a result of disease and pollution caused by intensive methods.

**Salmon, James Junior** (1873–1924) Architect, b. Glasgow. Pupil of William **Leiper**. With his partner John Galt Gillespie (1870–1926), he developed an innovative art nouveau sculpturesque style at Mercantile Chambers (1896–8) and the 'Hatrack' (1899), both in **Glasgow**. At Lion Chambers on Hope Street (1906), they pioneered the use of thin-walled reinforced concrete high-rise construction. They designed several highly original Arts and Crafts houses at **Kilmacolm**.

**Salmond, Alex** (1954– ) Politician, b. Linlithgow. Trained as an accountant, he has been MP for Banff and Buchan since 1987, leader of the **Scottish National Party** 1990–2000 and subsequently its leader at Westminster.

**salt** A salt industry based on evaporation of sea water by heat existed across Scotland from prehistoric times, and from medieval times salt was a major export. **Prestonpans** (its name deriving from its salt pans) was given a charter to produce salt in the 12th century, and saltworks proliferated along the Firth of **Forth**, in **Fife** and **Ayrshire**, and elsewhere. Although salt was used in pottery, metallurgy and the textile and leather industries, it was primarily used for preserving fish and meat. Until 1825 Scottish sea salt paid a lower rate of duty than English salt. The removal of the salt duties in that year led to a rapid collapse of the Scottish trade.

**Saltcoats** A tourist resort on the west coast of Ayrshire, opposite the Isle of **Arran**. Its name derives from salt production here from medieval times until 1890. Its harbour was used to export locally mined coal to Ireland. In the 1960s, some fossilised tree stumps were discovered on the shore; they can be seen at low tide.

**saltire** The white X-shaped cross of St **Andrew**, adopted in medieval times as the symbol of Scotland, and used on a blue ground as Scotland's flag. Legend has it that **Unuist**, King of the **Picts**, was inspired to beat the Northumbrians by a vision of the cross against a blue sky, at the Battle of Athelstaneford in East Lothian; see **Athelstaneford**.

**Saltire Society** A charitable body set up in 1936 to promote awareness of Scottish culture; it makes awards in the fields of art, history, literature, music and architecture.

**Saltoun** Two villages in East Lothian, East and West Saltoun, a short distance apart, East Saltoun being the larger; once a textile production centre and noted for its lime industry. It was the first place in Scotland where pot barley was produced, by the local landowner; see Andrew **Fletcher**. Saltoun Hall, the Fletcher house, was reconstructed as a great Tudor Gothic mansion from 1817 onwards; it is now flatted. Saltoun Parish Church (John Fletcher Campbell, 1805) is one of the earliest Gothic Revival churches in Scotland.

**Salvesen, Christian** In 1846 Christian and Theodore Salvesen set up a shipping agent and shipbroking business in **Edinburgh**, incorporated as Christian Salvesen in 1872. It concentrated on shipping and whaling till after World War II, then moved into distribution and is now a major European transport and distribution company.

**Sanday** One of **Orkney**'s northern islands; archaeological sites include a large neolithic burial cairn at Quoyness.

**Sandeman, Robert** (1718–71) Son-in-law of John **Glas**, he moved to London in 1860; his branch of the Glasite sect became known as Sandemanians. In 1864 he went to the USA and founded Sandemanian congregations there. The family were also noted importers of port wine.

**Sandemanians** see **Sandeman, Robert**

**Sandwood Bay** Lovely and isolated bay on the northwest coast between **Kinlochbervie** and **Cape Wrath**.

**Sandyknowe** see **Smailholm**

**sang schules** Schools of music attached to churches and other religious foundations from the early medieval period to the **Reformation**.

*An Atlantic Salmon makes its way upstream to spawn.*

*Looking north over Scapa Flow, with Churchill Barrier No.4 to the right.*

**Sanquhar** Small town on the River **Nith**, a former royal **burgh**, featuring in **Covenanting** history for the Sanquhar Declarations by Richard Cameron in 1680, in which the **Cameronians** not only renounced allegiance to **Charles II** and his heir James Duke of York, but also declared Charles deposed as King of Scots and declared war on him. There is a fine **tolbooth**, designed by Willam **Adam** and built 1735–37. Just outside the town is Sanquhar Castle, largely 17th and 18th century.

**sasine** The process of giving possession of feudal property, originally by symbolic delivery of earth and stones, latterly by registry in the General Register of Sasines in Edinburgh.

**Satyre of the Thrie Estaitis** see **Lyndsay, Sir David**

**Sauchieburn, Battle of** Defeat of royal force under James III by rebellious nobles led at least nominally by his son, later **James IV**, on 11 June 1488 at Sauchieburn, about 5km (3mi) southwest of **Stirling**. The king was murdered after the battle, but few facts are known. There is a story that after he fell from his horse he was killed by one of the rebels disguised as a priest.

**Sauchie Tower** Great rectangular tower house built by Sir James Schaw, begun 1430; re-roofed by Clackmannanshire Heritage Trust 2000; see also William **Schaw**.

**Scald Law** see **Pentlands**

**Scalloway** (pop. 812) Small town on the west coast of mainland **Shetland**, once the capital of the islands, and a base for the Norwegian Resistance in World War II. Above the harbour, which was much enlarged in the 20th century for the **fishing** industry, is the ruin of Earl Patrick Stewart's castle, built in 1600 and abandoned at the Earl's execution in 1615. In the care of **Historic Scotland**.

**Scalpay** (Gaelic **Scalpaidh**). Small island in the **Minch** at the mouth of Loch Tarbert, Isle of **Harris**, now linked to Harris by a bridge. It was visited by Prince Charles Edward **Stewart** in his travels after the collapse of the 1745 **Jacobite Rising**.

**Scalpay** (Gaelic **Scalpaidh**). An island off the east coast of **Skye**, in the **Inner Sound**.

**Scapa Flow** A huge area of sheltered water almost entirely enclosed by the islands of **Orkney**. It was the main fleet base for the Royal Navy in World War I. The German High Seas Fleet was brought here after surrender but scuttled itself off Lyness in 1919. During World War II, Scapa Flow's eastern side was closed by the **Churchill Barriers** after the sinking of HMS *Royal Oak* by a German submarine. Since the 1970s there has been a large oil terminal on the island of Flotta. There is a Scapa Flow Visitor Centre at Lyness on the island of **Hoy**.

**Scarba** (Gaelic **Sgarba**) Island in the Inner **Hebrides**, separated from its larger neighbour **Jura** by the Gulf of **Corrievrechan**.

**Schaw, William, of Sauchie** (d.1602) Royal Master of Works from 1583. In 1584 he visited Paris with Lord Seton. He spent the winter of 1589–90 at the Danish court and returned to organise the ceremonial for the return of **James VI** with his new queen and carry out major rebuilding and additions at **Dunfermline** palace. In 1594 he rebuilt the chapel royal at **Stirling** and organised the banquet and musical ceremonial for the birth of Prince Henry. He substantially rebuilt Seton Palace in a Franco-Danish manner, and although it has not survived it clearly set the style of the Danish-inspired Scots Renaissance manner seen at Heriot's Hospital in **Edinburgh** and the north range of **Linlithgow** Palace. He was also effectively the founder of **freemasonry** in Scotland, drafting its first statutes.

**Schiehallion** (Gaelic **Sidh Chaillean**, meaning 'fairy hill of the Caledonians') An isolated and splendidly beautiful mountain (1083m/3547ft) to the southeast of **Loch Rannoch**, much of it now owned by the **John Muir Trust**. In the 18th century it was the location for experiments to calculate the earth's mass.

**scone** A semi-sweet cake of wheat flour, milk or buttermilk and raising agent, traditionally baked on a **girdle** in a large round and cut into 4. Now often baked in the oven in small rounds (with a little butter rubbed into the flour). Other ingredients may be added, giving treacle scones, bran scones, cheese scones etc.

**Scone** (Pronounced 'scoon') (pop. 4430) Town just to the northeast of **Perth**, ancient royal inaugural site and early centre of Christianity. An Augustinian monastery was established in c.1120 but burnt in 1559. In the early 19th century the Earl of Mansfield removed most of Old Scone to provide a parkland around Scone Palace, rebuilt as a great Gothic pile by William Atkinson (1803-12), now open to the public; the adjoining chapel contains a splendid memorial to Viscount Stormont (1618-19). The population was moved to New Scone to the east; in 1997 it was renamed Scone; it is the site of Perth racecourse. A nearby airfield was used for many years for training airline pilots. See also **Stone of Destiny** (Stone of Scone).

**Scotch** see **Scots**

**Scotch broth** A soup made with mutton or beef, barley, peas, onion, leeks, carrots and parsley, or other vegetables. Recipes exist from the 18th century onwards.

**Scotch bun** see **black bun**

**Scotch pie** A small round pie filled with minced mutton, with a hard raised crust, which leaves room for gravy, mashed potatoes, etc.

**Scotch whisky** see **whisky**

**Scotia** The name Scotia was first used, in Latin, in the early 11th century for the kingdom ruled by the successors of **Kenneth mac Alpin**, which was known as Alba from 900. After the southward expansion of this kingdom, the region north of the **Forth** continued to be called 'Scotia' for administrative purposes. A medieval myth claimed that the Scots were descended from 'Scota', daughter of a pharaoh of Egypt.

**Scotichronicon** see **Bower, Walter**

**Scotland on Sunday** see **Scotsman**

**Scotlandwell** Village near **Leven**, with natural springs, and a picturesque Victorian timber well-head by David **Bryce** still to be seen in the main street.

**Scotrail** see **railways** p.312

**Scots** The Scots **language** (see p.220); the people of Scotland. Also used as an adjective, along with Scottish and Scotch, to describe Scotland and things Scottish. The word 'Scotch' fell out of favour in the late 19th century, though it is still used as a vernacular form and in certain locutions, especially for food and drink: **Scotch broth**, Scotch **whisky** (often known simply as Scotch).

**Scots Brigade** Formation of the Dutch army recruited after 1568 among Scots to fight for Dutch independence against Spain. Its officers and many of its soldiers retained their Scottish identity, despite increasing numbers of other nationalities in the ranks. Strongly Protestant, the Brigade formed part of **William of Orange**'s army in 1688, but remained part of the Dutch army until its officers refused to fight against Britain in the 4th Anglo-Dutch War (1780-84), and mostly returned home. In the 1790s some of the former officers re-formed a regiment in the service of the British army, with the title Scots Brigade. In 1802 it became the 94th Regiment of Foot, serving in the Napoleonic Wars.

**Scots Colleges** After the **Reformation**, Scottish Roman Catholic priests were mainly trained in the new seminaries set up in western Europe. Scots Colleges were established in Paris (where there were Scottish students from the 14th century until 1793), Douai (1580), Rome (1600) and Madrid (1627, later in Valladolid and now in Salamanca), and other major cities.

**Scots Confession** Confession of faith of the Scottish Reformers accepted by the **Reformation** Parliament in 1560 and later by the **Church of Scotland**, superseded but not abrogated by the **Westminster Confession** in 1647.

**Scots Guards** Raised under **Charles I** in 1642 as Argyll's Regiment, to put down rebellion in Ulster, they became known as the Scots Guards in 1688. They have fought in many overseas campaigns. The band of the Scots Guards, established since at least 1716, is particularly well known, and has entertained the troops in the World Wars and the Gulf War. In 1993 the 2nd Battalion was placed in 'suspended animation' for the 2nd time.

**Scots language** The speech of Lowland Scotland; see **language**, p.220.

S

*Sir Walter Scott by Sir Henry Raeburn, 1822.*

**Scots Magazine** First published in 1739 as a patriotic alternative to London's *Gentleman's Magazine*, it was extremely popular through the 18th century, for a few years edited by William **Smellie**. In 1804, having been bought by Archibald **Constable**, it was amalgamated with the *Edinburgh Magazine*, and subsequently lost circulation to the *Edinburgh Review* and *Blackwood's*, ceasing publication on Constable's bankruptcy in 1826. D C **Thomson**'s version of *the Scots Magazine* has been published since 1927.

**Scotsman** First published in 1817 by Charles Maclaren and William Ritchie to propound Whig politics, it is now one of the main Scottish national daily papers. From 1905–99 it occupied massive buildings on North Bridge, **Edinburgh**, and is now based in new premises near the **Scottish Parliament**. For a long period after the 1950s it was owned by the Canadian Lord Thomson of Fleet; now by the reclusive Barclay brothers. It has sister papers, the *Evening News* and *Scotland on Sunday*.

**Scotstarvit** A 5-storey tower house near **Cupar**, Fife, built by the Inglis family c.1500 and later home to Sir John **Scott** who partly remodelled it. Now owned by the **National Trust for Scotland**, but in the care of **Historic Scotland**. See also **Hill of Tarvit**.

**Scott, Alexander** (1525-84) Poet, landowner and musician who wrote some charming short love poems as well as didactic verses.

**Scott, Alexander** (1920-89) Poet, writer and teacher. A lecturer in English at **Edinburgh** and **Glasgow Universities**, and one of the founders of the **Association for Scottish Literary Studies**, most of his writing is in **Scots**. His poetry collections include *Mouth Music* (1954) and *Cantrips* (1968) and he wrote a biography of William **Soutar** (1958).

**Scott, Francis George** (1880-1958) Composer, b. Hawick. An early association with Hugh **MacDiarmid**, during which Scott set many of the poet's early works to music, led to a lifetime's composing music for Scottish poetry, much of it, including the lyrics of William **Dunbar**, Robert **Burns** and William **Soutar**, published in *Scottish Lyrics Set to Music* (1922-39).

**Scott, Sir John, of Scotstarvit** (1585-1670) Statesman and anthologist. A patron of Timothy **Pont**, he contributed financially to **Blaeu's Atlas**, and editorially to *Delitiae Poetarum Scotorum* (1637) a major collection of Scottish Latin poetry. His work *The Staggering State of the Scots Statesman*, not published till 1754, exposes the greed of Scottish nobility.

**Scott, Michael** (d. c.1235) Scholar and astrologer, possibly born in Durham but strongly associated with southern Scotland. His studies at universities in Europe gained him the reputation of being a magician, and later writers, including Sir Walter **Scott**, developed this theme. He is allegedly buried in **Melrose** Abbey.

**Scott, Tom** (1918-95) Poet, b. Glasgow. Writing largely in **Scots**, his poems take up social and moral concerns. His most famous work is *Brand the Builder* (1975).

**Scott, Sir Walter** (1771-1832) Novelist and poet, b. Edinburgh. Suffering from polio as a child, he spent much of his time in the **Borders**, absorbing the impressions that colour much of his writings and developing an affection for the ballads which became one of his literary styles. He qualified as **advocate** and became **Sheriff** of Selkirkshire in 1799. He collected and 'improved' ballads he published in *The Minstrelsy of the Scottish Border* (1802-3). His own epic ballads, *The Lay of the Last Minstrel* (1805), *Marmion* (1808) and *The Lady of the Lake* (1810) were immensely popular, but later ventures into this field were less successful and he turned to novel writing, initially publishing anonymously. His historical knowledge and his facility with **Scots** speech, combined with an evenhanded approach to historical issues and a real talent for developing minor characters, resulted in novels which were both hugely popular and of high literary quality. *Waverley* (1814), *Guy*

*Mannering* (1815), *The Antiquary* (1816), *The Black Dwarf* (1816), *Old Mortality* (1816), *Rob Roy* (1818), *The Heart of Midlothian* (1818), *The Bride of Lammermoor* (1819), *Ivanhoe* (1820) and *Redgauntlet* (1824) were all written before his bankruptcy in 1826 (see Archibald **Constable**), after which Scott's writing efforts were doubled as he struggled to pay off his debts, inevitably reducing the quality of his work. His later works include *The Fair Maid of Perth* (1828), *Tales of a Grandfather* (1828–30) and *Letters on Demonology and Witchcraft* (1832). His influence in Europe and North America, especially on the Romantic movement, was immense though he was no Romantic. His values were those of the **Enlightenment**, but he created a neo-feudal lifestyle for himself at **Abbotsford** which ruined him financially. His orchestration of the visit of George IV to **Edinburgh** in 1822 did much to establish the perception of Scotland that has since persisted.

**Scott, Willie** (1897–1989). Scots singer, b. Canonbie. A shepherd and crook-maker whose impressive repertoire of **Border** ballads and songs made him a favourite at folk festivals, and a source for younger singers of fine but little-known songs.

**Scottish** see **Scots**

**Scottish and Newcastle Breweries Ltd** Formed in 1960 by amalgamating **Scottish Brewers** and Newcastle Breweries Ltd. Earlier in 1960 Scottish Brewers had absorbed 3 smaller Edinburgh brewers. The new company was the largest of its kind in Scotland. A further amalgamation has recently created Scottish Courage.

**Scottish Arts Council** Body which invests government and National Lottery funding in the arts in Scotland, funding institutions, projects and individuals in the areas of drama, dance, literature, visual arts, crafts and music.

**Scottish Assembly** see **Scottish Parliament**

**Scottish Ballet** Formed in 1957 as Western Theatre Ballet, it moved to Glasgow in 1969 as Scottish Theatre Ballet.

**Scottish baronial** see **baronial**

**Scottish Borders Council** Local authority in southeast Scotland created in 1996 from the former **Borders Region**. The administrative centre is **Newtown St Boswells** and other towns include **Duns**, **Galashiels**, **Hawick**, **Jedburgh** and **Selkirk**. See maps on pp.394–5 and **local government**.

**Scottish Brewers** Originally formed by the merger of the brewery companies William Younger and William **McEwan** in 1931, it is now the Scottish trade arm of Scottish Courage (owned by **Scottish and Newcastle**).

**Scottish Certificate of Education Examination Board** see **Scottish Qualifications Authority**.

**Scottish Chamber Orchestra** Formed 1974, it is based in **Edinburgh**. The orchestra has toured widely, and made over 140 recordings. It has commissioned more than 60 new works, including *Veni, Veni Emmanuel* by James **MacMillan** and *Ten Strathclyde Concertos* by Sir Peter Maxwell Davies. It is very active in music education.

**Scottish Civic Trust** Organisation formed in 1967 to encourage the quality of built environment in Scotland, both urban and rural, including the preservation of old buildings and the encouragement of good design in new. It is based in **Glasgow** and works with other organisations, including local groups. Its first director was Maurice **Lindsay**.

**Scottish Colourists** Collective name given to the 4 Scottish artists, F C B **Cadell**, John Duncan **Fergusson**, George Leslie **Hunter** and Samuel John **Peploe**. All spent extended periods in France in the early years of the 20th century, where they were influenced by Post-Impressionism and in particular by the expressiveness and vivid colour of Fauve painting, which they applied to the traditional subject matter of figure-painting, still-life and landscape. They all knew each other, and although they were never a formal group, their work was exhibited together during the 1920s.

**Scottish Conservative and Unionist Party** The Scottish arm of the Conservative Party. The party has recently suffered a decline in popularity, retaining no seats in Westminster in the election of 1997 and only 1 in 2001, though it has a small number of MSPs in the Scottish Parliament.

**Scottish Constitutional Convention** Multi-party body formed in 1988 to work towards a new Scottish Parliament. Its report in 1995 formed the basis of government proposals put to a referendum in 1997; see **Scottish Parliament**.

**Scottish Cooperative Wholesale Society** (SCWS) Founded in 1868 to supply Scotland's numerous retail cooperative societies with goods for resale. Initially it did this by bulk buying, but it soon developed its own plant for making a wide range of goods. By 1914 it was making many of the goods sold by the retail societies in its large complex at Shieldhall, near **Govan**, and in other places in Scotland and Northern Ireland. It had flour and oatmeal mills in **Edinburgh**. Decline in retail co-operation in the 1950s and 60s led to the closure of many of these units, and in 1973 the residue of the society was absorbed by the Cooperative Wholesale Society, its English equivalent.

# SCOTTISH ENLIGHTENMENT

The term 'Scottish Enlightenment' was invented later for the remarkable outburst of creative energy in the arts and the sciences (including social sciences) in 18th-century Scotland. The precise chronological limits of the phenomenon will always be debatable. Its roots clearly lay in Restoration Scotland after 1660, when vigorous legal, scientific and architectural developments were linked to a consensus in the ruling classes that there was an imperative need for growth to bring Scotland closer to the norms of the most advanced European countries. This vision seemed to perish in the political turmoil, famine and economic collapse of the 1690s, but re-emerged in the early 18th century. The outer limits of the Scottish Enlightenment proper may be taken as dating from 1729, when the Ulsterman and Irish Whig Francis **Hutcheson** became Professor of Moral Philosophy in **Glasgow University**, to teach among others the young Adam **Smith**, to 1832. That year saw the death of Sir Walter **Scott**, whose core values were pure Enlightenment ones, and the arrival in **Glasgow** from Belfast

of the young William Thompson, later Lord **Kelvin** and a giant of late-Victorian Scotland.

The United Kingdom of Great Britain provided the framework within which the Scottish Enlightenment developed. At first, economic stagnation and the political instability generated by the **Union** of 1707, which peaked in the 1715 **Jacobite Rising**, seemed to present the possibility of a nationalist vernacular humanism dominating the cultural agenda. With economic growth after 1740, a limited number of Whig noblemen, like the Marquess of **Bute** and the Earl of **Islay**, were able to implement a Whig Hanoverian, and secularising unionist agenda that used English rather than Scots as its main vehicle. Lay patronage in the **Church of Scotland** enabled them to buttress the ascendancy of the **Moderates**, a key group of clergymen who both played an active role in Enlightenment thought, and maintained an atmosphere of tolerance that protected even their heterodox friends like Adam Smith and David **Hume**. Lawyers, whose unique legal culture had been guaranteed by the Treaty of **Union**, were another major creative force, as well as the main administrators at local level. With growing wealth and urbanisation, the late 18th century offered unprecedented patronage for the visual arts, from portrait painting to architecture, while the Scottish universities flourished at a time when those of England and the rest of Europe were at a low ebb.

Based on a delicate balance between aristocracy and the middling orders; between unionism and national self-awareness; and between order and often chaotic growth, the Scottish Enlightenment could not last for ever, though its influence is still potent. The huge franchise extension of 1832, the growth of dissenting religious groups, the rise of the bourgeoisie, and the parallel collapse of the **Dundas** political machine that had provided the framework of political and social order in the later 18th century, effectively drew a line under the neo-classical cultural hegemony of the Enlightenment. An age of Romanticism and populist politics was dawning. Nevertheless the Enlightenment had accelerated the much-desired Improvement of Scotland. It had laid the foundations of modern rational thought in many fields, from economics and sociology to history, philosophy, geology, chemistry and literary criticism. It also left behind works of art of enduring appeal, and remarkable imaginative literature, ironically much of it in the Scots vernacular. See also Joseph **Black**, William **Cullen**, Adam **Ferguson**, James **Hutton**, Lord **Kames**, Lord **Monboddo**, Alexander **Monro**, William **Robertson**.

*Adam Smith, from a copper engraving by John Kay, 1790.*

**Scottish Council for Development and Industry** Independent organisation set up in 1946 to help to promote and develop Scotland's economy by influencing government policies. It is based in **Edinburgh** and has area offices in **Inverness** and **Aberdeen**.

**Scottish Cultural Resources Access Network** see **SCRAN**

**Scottish Development Agency** see **Scottish Enterprise**

**Scottish Education Department** (**SED**) Government department dealing with Scottish education from 1872, with considerable influence on all aspects. Known as the Scotch Education Department until 1918, it had other changes of name in the 1990s and since 1999 has been the Scottish Executive Education Department.

**Scottish Enlightenment** see p.336

**Scottish Enterprise** The major economic development agency in Lowland Scotland, funded by the **Scottish Executive** to help businesses with support and training. It is the centre of a network with 12 local enterprise companies. It is a successor to the Scottish Development Agency. See also **Highlands and Islands Enterprise**.

**Scottish Episcopal Church** The Church, like all the major Scottish denominations, traces its origins back many centuries to **Ninian**, bishop in Whithorn, and to the early Celtic church. Episcopalianism was disestablished in 1690, when Presbyterianism became the legal form of government for the established church in Scotland. During the 18th century, the Scottish Episcopalians were persecuted because they were largely **Jacobite**, but they regarded themselves as the true church of Scotland. Today they are a distinct denomination and part of the worldwide Anglican communion. There are around 53,000 members. The church has its own Scottish Liturgy (1982) and consists of 7 dioceses, each under the authority of a bishop. The **Primus** is the leading bishop who presides over the General Synod.

**Scottish Executive** The devolved government for Scotland, established in **Edinburgh** in 1999 after the first elections to a **Scottish Parliament** since 1707, taking over the administrative functions of the **Scottish Office**. It is responsible for justice, education, health, environment, economic development, transport and rural affairs, and is led by a **First Minister** nominated by the Executive; he or she appoints the other ministers. It is based mainly at Victoria Quay in **Leith** and at Old St Andrews House in the city centre.

**Scottish Fisheries Museum** see **Anstruther**

**Scottish Football Association** Scottish football's regulatory body, established in 1872 after the first international match between Scotland and England.

**Scottish Genealogy Society** Established in 1953 to promote research into Scottish family history and encourage the collection and publication of relevant material.

**Scottish Green Party** Originally the Ecology Party, and focused on environmental concerns, one of its members, Robin Harper, was elected MSP in 1999, becoming the first Green to enter a parliament in Britain; he was joined by 6 more in the 2003 election.

**Scottish Labour Party** Scots were prominent in founding the Labour Party. The **Highland Land League** was the first working people's party to achieve MPs in Westminster. After his rejection by the Liberals, Keir **Hardie** stood as an independent Labour candidate; the Scottish Labour Party was founded in 1888 and merged with the UK-wide Independent Labour Party in 1893. In 1922 Labour became Scotland's largest single party, and in 1924 the first Labour government took power at Westminster. Scottish Labour support has remained strong even when Labour has been out of favour in the UK as a whole, and the party controls the Scottish Parliament in partnership with the **Scottish Liberal Democrats**.

**Scottish Land Court** Established in 1911 to resolve disputes about agricultural and crofting holdings.

**Scottish Language Dictionaries** see **Dictionaries** p.108

**Scottish Liberal Democrats** A left-of-centre party formed from the Scottish Liberal Party and the Social Democratic Party in Scotland, part of the UK federation of Liberal Democrats, with a substantial number of MSPs. Shares control of the **Scottish Parliament** with the **Scottish Labour Party**.

**Scottish Literary Studies, Association for** see **Association for Scottish Literary Studies**

**Scottish Maritime Museum** see **Irvine**

**Scottish Mining Museum** Museum of mining history at the former Lady Victoria Colliery at Newtongrange, a former mining village to the south of **Dalkeith**, Midlothian. It has Scotland's largest steam engine.

**Scottish National Dictionary** see **Dictionaries** p.108.

*The Scottish National Gallery of Modern Art. The Landform garden in front of the gallery, designed by Charles Jencks, won the Gulbenkian Prize for Museum of the Year in 2004.*

**Scottish National Gallery of Modern Art** One of the **National Galleries of Scotland**, it houses the Scottish collections of modern and contemporary art in all media, as well as international collections. The gallery moved in 1984 from Inverleith House in the **Royal Botanic Garden** to the Greek Doric building of John Watson's School, **Edinburgh** (William **Burn** 1825). In the 1990s the nearby Dean Gallery was added, partly to house works by Eduardo **Paolozzi**. The impressive building by Thomas **Hamilton** (1831–3) began as the Dean Orphanage and was more recently the Dean Education Centre.

**Scottish National Orchestra** see **Royal Scottish National Orchestra**

**Scottish National Party** (SNP) The first distinct Scottish nationalist political party, the National Party of Scotland, was founded in 1928, but it had little success in the 1929 elections and was internally divided. In 1934 it merged with a group who had separated from the Conservatives to form the Scottish National Party. Its first MP was Robert McIntyre in 1945. The election of Winnie **Ewing** in the **Hamilton** by-election in 1967 marked the beginning of a rise in power, its continuation seen in 1973 in **Govan** in a massive victory by Margo **MacDonald** over Labour. It was a major force in the campaign for **devolution** and it had success in the 1999 **Scottish Parliament** elections, gaining 35 seats, but losing some in 2003.

**Scottish National Portrait Gallery** A collection of portraits of Scots by artists from all nations, housed in a neo-Gothic building designed by Sir Robert Rowand **Anderson**, built 1885–90, also home to the Scottish National Photography Collection. For many years the building also housed the **National Museum of Antiquities**.

**Scottish National War Museum** see **National War Museum of Scotland**

**Scottish Natural Heritage** A publicly funded body, formed in 1991 from the Nature Conservancy Council and the Countryside Commission. It aims to preserve and enhance the natural environment of Scotland, and to promote awareness of and access to it. It has responsibility for Protected Areas such as National Nature Reserves.

**Scottish Office** Government department set up in 1885 on a small scale in Dover House in London, under a Secretary for Scotland; see also **Secretaries of State**. In the 1930s 4 departments were moved to St Andrews House, a massive new building in central **Edinburgh** on the site of the old Calton jail: Agriculture and Fisheries, Education, Home and Health. In the 1970s a new headquarters was built (known as New St Andrews House) and in the 1990s there was a further move to Victoria Quay in **Leith**. With the opening of the new **Scottish Parliament** in 1999, its functions were transferred to the **Scottish Executive**, with an office for the Secretary of State, known as the Scotland Office, in Edinburgh and London; in 2003 it became part of the Department for Constitutional Affairs.

**Scottish Official Board of Highland Dancing** see **Highland dancing**

**Scottish Opera** Founded in 1962 by Sir Alexander **Gibson**, it is based at **Glasgow's** opera house, the Theatre Royal, and tours Scotland with large and small productions.

**Scottish Parliament** see pp.340-1

**Scottish Poetry Library** With a substantial collection of Scottish and international poetry, for free browsing and borrowing, the library also hosts poetry events. It has educational resources and provides a mobile poetry van, to bring poetry to all parts of Scotland. It is based in an award-winning building (Malcolm Fraser Architects 1999) in the Canongate, **Edinburgh**.

**Scottish Power** Scotland's largest electricity supplier, successor to the **South of Scotland Electricity Board**.

**Scottish Qualifications Authority** (SQA) Body which administers Scottish school examinations. It was set up in 1997, replacing the Scottish Certificate of Education Examination Board, established in 1965 to administer 'O-Grades' and 'Highers'. See also **Standard Grades**.

**Scottish Record Office** see **National Archives of Scotland**

**Scottish Renaissance** The resurgence of interest in Scottish literature and **language** inspired by Hugh **MacDiarmid** and other writers in **Scots** from the 1920s. Many writers joined in using Scots as a literary language, including William **Soutar**, Marion **Angus** and Helen B **Cruikshank**, as well as later writers such as Robert **Garioch**, Alexander **Scott** and Sydney Goodsir **Smith**. The impetus gained for Scots during this period still continues.

**Scottish Rights of Way and Access Society (Scot Ways)** Established in 1845 to safeguard Scottish rights of way against the interference of landowners, the society has won many landmark legal cases. It also campaigns for wider rights of access to privately owned land.

**Scottish Rugby Union** see **Rugby**, p.327

**Scottish Screen** A publicly funded body, formed in 1997 from several other bodies, to promote film and television production and appreciation in Scotland. It runs its own archive, which collects film produced by both professionals and amateurs.

**Scottish Seabird Centre** see **North Berwick**

**Scottish Socialist Party** Recently formed political party which campaigns vociferously for socialist change. Its leader Tommy **Sheridan** was elected to the Scottish Parliament in 1999 and was joined by 5 more members in the 2003 elections.

**Scottish Sports Council** see **sportscotland**

**Scottish Tartans Society** Organisation established in 1963, it has an online register of tartans, a Hall of Records in **Pitlochry**, and museums in **Keith**, Aberdeenshire and Franklin, North Carolina, USA. It publishes a journal, *Tartans*.

**Scottish Television (STV)** Holder of the franchise for broadcasting to central Scotland since 1957, STV was set up by Roy Thomson, the Canadian media magnate, and floated in 1965. It is now part of SMG plc (Scottish Media Group). The north and south of Scotland are served respectively by Grampian Television, based in **Aberdeen**, and Border Television, based in Carlisle.

**Scottish Tourist Board** see **VisitScotland**

**Scottish Trades Union Congress** The body that supports the trade unions and workers in Scotland, representing them in dealings with government and employers' bodies.

**Scottish United Services Museum** see **National War Museum of Scotland**

**ScotWays** see **Scottish Rights of Way and Access Society**

**Scrabster** A harbour in Thurso Bay, from where the ferry leaves for **Orkney**. Its cliffs have intriguing rock formations. It is also a **fishing** port. Holburn Head **lighthouse** is immediately adjacent.

**SCRAN** The Scottish Cultural Resources Access Network, a website providing online resources from many Scottish museums, galleries and media sources.

**SCWS** see **Scottish Cooperative Wholesale Society**

**Seafield, James Ogilvie, 1st Earl of and 4th Earl of Findlater** (1644–1730) Lawyer and politician. Appointed Lord Chancellor in 1702, he became one of the Scottish commissioners for the Union with England. He remarked on the end of the Scottish parliament as the 'end of ane old song', but despite preferment in the united parliament, by 1713 he was advocating the end of the Union.

**Seaforth Highlanders** Regiment of the British army, originally raised as 78th (later 72nd) Regiment of Foot by Kenneth Mackenzie, last Earl of Seaforth, in 1778. In 1793 the number 78th was assigned to another regiment raised by a Mackenzie, known as the Rosshire Buffs. In 1881 the two amalgamated to form the Seaforth Highlanders. Amalgamations in the 20th century produced the **Queen's Own Highlanders** (Seaforths and Camerons) in 1961 and the **Highlanders** (Seaforths, Gordons and Camerons) in 1994.

**sea loch** see **loch**

**sean triubhas** see **Highland dancing**

**Seceder** Formerly, a member of any of the branches of the **Secession** Church; now an informal name used in some parts of the **Highlands** and Islands for a member of the **Free Presbyterian Church**.

**Secessions** A succession of splits from the **Church of Scotland**, caused by concerns about the relationship between Church and State. The Original Secession occurred in 1733 (see Ebenezer **Erskine**), the Relief Secession in 1761, and the largest, in 1843, resulted in the formation of the **Free Church** of Scotland. See also **Presbyterian Churches** p.307

**Secretaries of State** Prior to the Union of the Parliaments in 1707, there were 2 Secretaries of State, but after the Union these offices soon disappeared and were replaced by a 3rd 'Secretary for Great Britain' (in addition to 2 already existing in England), with responsibility for Scotland. This office too was done away with in 1744. In 1885 a Secretary for Scotland was appointed, with a seat in the Cabinet from 1892; in 1926 the post became Secretary of State for Scotland, with increased responsibilities; see also **Scottish Office**. With the opening of the new **Scottish Parliament** in 1999, the Secretary's powers were much diminished, but continued in the Scotland Office in London. In 2003 it became part of the Department for Constitutional Affairs, and the Secretaryship is held jointly with another Cabinet post.

**S**

## TO 1707

The Scottish parliament can probably be traced back to 1235, when Alexander II held a 'colloquium' at **Kirkliston**. Little is known of its business or procedure before the reign of John **Balliol** (1292–96), when records show it being involved in justice and in the king's power-struggle with Edward I of England. From the reign of **Robert I** parliament played an increasingly important role in any business that touched the crown and community of the realm, and deliberated on treaties with foreign powers, war, taxation, law and order, trade and the administration of the realm.

The original membership of parliament had been made up of bishops and abbots (the first estate) and the king's lay tenants-in-chief (earls, barons and lords, or the second estate). By 1326 these members been joined by the '**burgh** commissioners', together forming the 'three estates' that were the main characteristic of parliament for much of its history. Parliament met in a single chamber, not separate houses of commons and lords, and was itinerant until the late 16th century, probably sitting in churches when at **Scone**, **St Andrews** or Holyrood, and usually in the **burgh** tolbooth when at **Edinburgh**, **Perth** or **Stirling**. A purpose-built parliament house was built behind St Giles' Kirk, Edinburgh, in **Charles I**'s reign, where parliament sat until 1707.

From the mid 15th century much parliamentary business was delegated to a drafting committee called the 'lords of the articles'. The committee took the business agenda of parliament and created legislation which the full assembly then voted to accept or reject. Recent research suggests that the committee was open to lobbying by interested parties and usually did not prevent parliament exerting influence over the monarch. Indeed from the late 14th century parliament was often able to oppose the king and defeat unpopular royal policies. In theory at least, the king was not meant to alter statutes without parliamentary consent after 1445, and in practice parliament exerted extensive power over taxation, legislation and foreign policy.

After 1560 the **lairds** became increasingly important to parliament, and achieved their own estate of shire commissioners after 1587, while the number of burghs in attendance also steadily increased. Problems were caused, however, by the attendance of the bishops after the **Reformation**, as they were perceived by many as tools in the hands of the monarchy. Certainly in **James VI**'s reign it was felt that the crown was exerting too much influence over parliamentary business and the lords of the articles, and it is usually argued that parliament's independence was seriously eroded in the years before 1638. This process was reversed in the **Covenanting** period (1638–51) when parliament wrested executive power from the crown, setting a precedent for the English Long Parliament. With the fall of the Covenanting regime after the invasion of Oliver Cromwell in 1651, a brief parliamentary union was forced on Scotland in 1657–1660.

Parliament was restored in 1660, and enjoyed one of its most influential periods in the decades before 1707. The final ejection of the clergy in 1689, and abolition of the lords of the articles in 1690 coincided with a period of considerable parliamentary independence, and saw the evolution of political 'parties' and vigorous electoral politics. The crown, unsurprisingly, sought to undermine this situation by corruption and political management. Robert **Burns**'s memorable claim that the Incorporating Union of England and Scotland (1707), which dissolved the first Scottish parliament, was brought about by the members being 'bought and sold for English gold' is an oversimplification, but nevertheless bribery and parliamentary division played a role, alongside wider economic imperatives resulting from the **Darien** Scheme, and some genuine enthusiasm for the creation of a British state among the political elite. The general public outside the parliament chamber felt very differently. See **Union of Parliaments**.

## REVIVAL

Though there was widespread resentment in Scotland in 1707, by the time of the Union with Ireland in 1800, it seemed unlikely that a Scottish national legislature would ever re-emerge. With the rise of pressure for Irish home rule, it was natural that the dominant Scottish Liberal Party would embrace home rule for Scotland after 1886. The collapse of Scottish Liberalism after 1919, and the gradual shift of the Labour Party away from its previous support for home rule, were only partially counter-bal-

*The new Scottish Parliament Building: MSPs' offices and Queensberry House.*

*Detail, new Scottish Parliament Building.*

anced by the founding in 1928 of the National Party of Scotland, later the **Scottish National Party** (SNP). 35 Home Rule Bills were put before the Westminster Parliament in just over 100 years, 34 in vain. Following the rise in support for the SNP in the late 1960s, the Kilbrandon Report on the constitution of 1973 recommended devolved government. But in 1979 a referendum on a Scottish assembly failed: a small favourable majority was frustrated by a ruling that it had to have the approval of 40% of the electorate. Campaigning continued in the 1980s, as the Labour party recovered its earlier commitment, and in 1988 the multi-party **Scottish Constitutional Convention** was formed to work towards this aim; see **Campaign for a Scottish Assembly, Claim of Right**.

In 1997 the Scots voted with a clear majority both for their own parliament and for giving it significant tax-raising powers; the passing of the Scotland Act 1998 led to its setting up. On 1 July 1999 the new Parliament was opened by the Queen to great

rejoicing. It has 129 members (MSPs): 73 constituency members elected on a first-past-the-post system and 56 regional members elected to bring the overall share of the seats held by each party broadly in line with the overall share of votes won. Certain areas, such as foreign affairs, are reserved matters and continue to be dealt with by the UK Parliament.

A building for the new Parliament has caused much controversy, especially over spectacularly escalating costs. Several sites were considered before it was decided that it should be built at Holyrood, at the foot of Edinburgh's Royal Mile. An innovative design by a partnership between the Catalan architects Enric Miralles and Benedetta Jugliabuie and RMJM architects was chosen. It was due to be officially opened by the Queen in October 2004. Until completion of the new building, a temporary home for the Parliament was found at the former **Lothian Region** building in George IV Bridge, with a debating chamber in the Assembly Hall of the Church of Scotland, nearby on the Mound.

*The new Scottish Parliament Building: windows of MSPs' offices.*

**Security, Act of** Legislation which became effective in 1704 when Queen Anne, having no surviving children, reluctantly signed a bill passed by the Scottish Parliament in 1703. It provided for the possibility that on Anne's death the Scottish throne would go to a Protestant of the Stewart line, but not of the Hanoverian dynasty nominated in the English Act of Succession of 1702. A gambit to force renegotiation of the Anglo-Scottish relationship, the 1704 Act helped precipitate the Act of **Union** of 1707.

**SED** see **Scottish Education Department**

**Seil** (Gaelic **Saoil**) Island off the west coast, southwest of **Oban**, southeast of **Mull**. It is linked to the mainland by a bridge over its narrow sound (often known as 'the bridge over the Atlantic'). See **slate**.

**Selkirk** (pop. 5742) Now a handsome market town by the **Ettrick**

Water in the **Borders**, a former royal **burgh**, and once a centre of conflict with the English in the Border wars. From its spired courthouse of 1803, Sir Walter **Scott** dispensed justice as **Sheriff**, 1803–32. Textiles and footwear manufacture were important industries, but both have declined in recent years. The latter gave rise to the nickname for a native of the town: 'Souter', a **Scots** word for cobbler. The main street has statues to Sir Walter Scott (1839) and Mungo **Park** (1859). Its **Common Riding** festival commemorates the loss of 80 men at the Battle of **Flodden**. Only one survived, returning with an English flag, and the festival's main participant is known as the Standard Bearer.

**Selkirk, Alexander** (or **Selcraig**) (1676–1721) Sailor, b. Lower Largo, Fife. Probably the inspiration for Daniel Defoe's *Robinson Crusoe*: on a voyage in 1704 he quarrelled with his captain William Dampier and asked to be put ashore on the uninhabited island of Juan Fernández. He was rescued after more than 4 years by Thomas Dover.

**Selkirk, Thomas Douglas, 5th Earl of** (1771–1820) Philanthropist, b. St Mary's Isle, Kirkcudbrightshire. He settled Highland emigrants on Prince Edward Island in 1803, and later in the Red River Settlement in Manitoba, on land bought from the Hudson's Bay Company. The colony was eventually ruined by the rivalry of the North West Fur Company.

**Selkirk bannock** A round glazed fruit loaf with sultanas and (often) candied peel, first made in 1859 by Robbie Douglas, a **Selkirk** baker.

**Selkirkshire** Former county in southeast Scotland around the Rivers **Yarrow** and **Ettrick**. In 1975 it became part of the Ettrick and Lauderdale District of **Borders Region**, and since 1996 it has been part of the **Scottish Borders** local authority. See maps on pp.394–5 and **local government**.

**Sellar, Patrick** (1780–1851) Estate factor, b. Moray, responsible, in the employment of the Countess of **Sutherland**, for evicting tenant families from **Strathnaver** during the Highland **Clearances**. His brutality was such that he was put on trial for arson in **Inverness**, but acquitted.

**Sempill, Robert, of Beltrees** (c.1595–c.1669) Cavalier gentleman and poet from Renfrewshire. He probably fought on the Royalist side in the Civil Wars, and is principally known for his elegy, 'The Life and Death of Habbie Simson, the Piper of Kilbarchan', which was written in the poetic form that came to be known as Standard Habbie and was used to best effect later by Robert **Burns**.

**Senators of the College of Justice** see **Court of Session**

**Session, Court of** see **Court of Session**

**Seton** A hamlet near **Aberlady**, East Lothian, with a fine 15th- to 16th-century Collegiate Church (in the care of **Historic Scotland** and open to the public), and a castle designed by Robert **Adam** in 1790 and built on the site of Seton Palace, where **Mary, Queen of Scots** took refuge after the murders of both **Rizzio** and **Darnley**.

**Seton, Mary** see **'four Marys'**

**sett** see **tartan**

**sgian dubh** From Gaelic meaning black knife, a short dagger worn in the stocking by Highlanders, now as part of **Highland dress**. See also **dirk**.

**Sgurr Alasdair** The highest mountain in the **Cuillin**, Skye, a **Munro** (992m/3255ft). It is named after Alexander **Nicolson**.

**Sgurr Dearg** Mountain in the **Cuillin**, Skye, a **Munro** (986m/3235ft). Its summit is known as the Inaccessible Pinnacle, as it requires a rock climb to reach it.

**Sgurr Fhuaran** A mountain, a **Munro** (1067m/3501ft), the principal peak of the **Five Sisters of Kintail** in Glen Shiel.

**Sgurr nan Gillean** Mountain in the **Cuillins**, Skye, a **Munro** (964m/3162ft) with a splendid ridge.

**shale** A fine-grained sedimentary rock from which oil can be distilled, exploited in Scotland in the 19th century to provide lamp oil, paraffin, lubricating oil and combustible gas. James **Young** led the industry, in **West Lothian**, notably in **Bathgate**, **Broxburn**, Addiewell and **West Calder**. In spite of imports of cheaper oil, the industry continued, bringing both prosperity and pollution to the area, until 1955, when a preferential duty on shale oil was ended. The shale-oil refinery at Pumpherston processed crude oil from Nottingham until 1964.

**Shambellie House Museum of Costume** Museum housed in a country house at **New Abbey**, Dumfriesshire, gifted to the **National Museums of Scotland** in 1977 by its owner Charles Stewart, along with his extensive costume collection. The museum also has events and activities. The house, designed by David **Bryce**, was built for the Stewart family in 1856.

**Shand, Sir James (Jimmy)** (1908–2000) Accordionist, b. East Wemyss, Fife. He left the mines at 18 to work in a music shop and became a professional player, gaining acclaim after appearing on programmes such as the White Heather Club. He toured the world and continued playing in his later years. He was knighted in 1999.

**Shankly, Bill** (1913–81) Footballer and manager, b. Glenbuck, East Ayrshire. As a wing-half he played successfully for Preston North End and for Scotland, but his greatest achievements were as manager of Liverpool from 1959 to 1974. He is alleged to have said that while some people see football as a matter of life and death, it is more important than that.

**Shapinsay** (pop. 300) **Orkney** island off **Kirkwall**. The Scots **baronial** mansion of Balfour Castle was the centre of a successful 19th-century venture in agricultural improvement, which transformed the island landscape into a neat grid of small fields and roads. The Iron Age **Broch** of Burroughston is in the care of Orkney Islands Council.

**Sharp, Alan** (1934– ) Novelist and screenwriter, b. Alyth near **Blairgowrie**. Though his first novel, *A Green Tree in Gedde* (1965) was successful, he left London for Hollywood, where he scripted

*The Hired Hand* (1971), *Ulzana's Raid* (1972) *Night Moves* (1975) and *Rob Roy* (1995). He has several children, one by Beryl Bainbridge, who wrote about Sharp in *Sweet William*.

**Sharp, James** (1613–79) Churchman, b. **Banff**. A **Covenanter**, he was imprisoned briefly in London, and in 1657 he negotiated with and impressed Cromwell. After 1660 he pragmatically recognised that both **Charles II** and the Scots nobles were determined to reimpose episcopacy and he accepted the archbishopric of **St Andrews**. Ruthless persecution of the Covenanters and feuds with **Fife** lairds led to his murder by Fife Covenanters led by John Balfour at Magus Moor, near St Andrews.

**Sharp, William** (pen name **Fiona MacLeod**) (1855-1905) Writer, b. Paisley. He travelled widely throughout his life and wrote on various subjects, but is best known for his poetry and short stories associated with the 'Celtic twilight' of the very end of the 19th century, giving a spurious picture of the Gaelic world as a dreamy mythological realm. His use of the name 'Fiona' has subsequently made it a very popular girl's name.

**Shaw, Margaret Fay** see **Campbell, John Lorne, Canna**

**Shaw, Richard Norman** (1831–1912) Architect, b. Edinburgh. A pupil of William **Burn** and G E Street, he practised in London. He did not build in Scotland, but was the premier architect of the 'Old English' domestic revival, and from the very early 1870s he paralleled J J **Stevenson** in introducing the 'Queen Anne' and, later, neo-Caroline and Georgian, to English domestic, and later, public and commercial architecture. His best-known building is the former New Scotland Yard (1887–90) on London's Embankment, which had a profound effect on Scottish commercial architecture in the 1890s.

**Shaw, William** see **Dictionaries**, p.108

**sheep's heid** A dish of a whole sheep's head boiled slowly with vegetables in water and producing a soup (also known as pow-sowdie).

**sheltie** see **Shetland**

**shenachie** (Gaelic **seanchaidh**) Originally, a professional recorder and reciter of family history, genealogy etc.; now a teller of traditional **Gaelic** heroic tales.

**Shepherd, Nan (Anna)** (1893–1981) Novelist, b. Deeside. A lecturer in English Literature at **Aberdeen** College of Education, she wrote *The Quarry Wood* (1928), *The Weatherhouse* (1930) and *A Pass in the Grampians* (1933), as well as poetry and non-fiction, and was a friend to writers like Jessie **Kesson**

*Sir Jimmy Shand, MBE.*

and Neil **Gunn**. Her novels are forward-looking, often focusing on the obstacles in the way of female independence.

**Sheridan, Tommy** (1964– ) Socialist campaigner and politician, b. Pollok, Glasgow. Scottish Socialist Party MSP for **Glasgow** from 1999, he was a leading campaigner against the poll tax in Scotland. He has been jailed for several of his protests.

**sheriff** At the present time, a local judicial officer who acts as judge in a **sheriff court**, dealing with civil and criminal cases. (Until 1971 the office was known as sheriff substitute – see below.) The sheriff court towns are grouped into sheriffdoms (currently 6), each with a sheriff principal at its head (acting as an appeal judge from the sheriffs in civil cases). Most sheriffs are assigned to a particular court, but floating and part-time sheriffs may deal with cases in any part of Scotland. Honorary sheriffs (who need not be legally qualified) can be appointed by the sheriff principal to help out as required. Until 1748 (see **heritable jurisdictions**), the sheriff, usually a hereditary office, was a chief officer of the Crown in a county, with civil and criminal jurisdiction in his area; he also had some administrative powers.

He was sometimes referred to as a sheriff principal and in practice his judicial duties were usually performed by a sheriff depute; the term 'sheriff depute' was still used after 1748 to refer to the sheriff principal (as above). Sheriff substitutes were formerly appointed by the sheriff depute and this term also continued to be used until 1971, long after it ceased to be appropriate. All sheriffs, except honorary sheriffs, are now appointed by the Crown.

**sheriff court** The lower court in Scotland for civil and criminal offences. Cases are heard before a judge called a **sheriff**. See also **Court of Session** and **High Court of Justiciary**.

**sheriff officer** A person licensed by a **sheriff** to carry out the warrants of a court.

**Sheriffmuir, Battle of** In November 1715 the forces of the Duke of Argyll made a pre-emptive strike on the **Jacobites** under the Earl of Mar on this isolated upland northeast of **Dunblane**. The battle was indecisive despite the Jacobites' greater numbers; many of them deserted on the retreat to **Perth**.

**Sherriff, George** (1898–1967) Soldier, diplomat, plant collector, b. Larbert, near Stirling. With Frank Ludlow he collected plants over a period of 30 years with 7 expeditions in Bhutan and Tibet. Many new species of rhododendron and primulas were introduced during this time. One of their more productive expeditions included Sir George **Taylor** and led to the introduction of *Meconopsis sherriffii*. In 1943 Sherriff succeeded Ludlow as British Resident in Lhasa before retiring to Angus in 1950 to develop the garden at Ascreavie.

*Aith Voe, Shetland.*

**Shetland** A group of almost 100 islands, about 20 of which are inhabited, 96km (60 miles) north of **Orkney**. A former county, also known as Zetland, it became an island authority in 1975, and since 1996, as Shetland Islands Council, it has been one of the 33 unitary local authorities; see maps on pp.394-5 and **local government**. The main town and administrative centre, **Lerwick**, is on mainland Shetland, as is its most ancient town, **Scalloway**. Inhabited since prehistoric times, as testified by houses, tombs and fields of the 4th millennium bc, and the Iron Age **brochs** of **Jarlshof** and **Mousa**, Shetland was a Norse dominion until 1469, when the islands became a dowry pledge for Margaret, daughter of Christian I of Norway, on her betrothal to **James III**. For the next 100 or so years they were administered by stewards. At the end of the 16th century it became the fief of an illegitimate branch of the royal family; see Robert **Stewart**. Shetland is famous for its breed of small, hardy ponies or 'shelties', used in coal mines throughout Britain and now popular for young children to ride, and for its small brown and black sheep, yielding the wool also known as 'Shetland', still made into delicate shawls. Like most remote areas, the islands have suffered from depopulation in the last two centuries, but since the 1970s North Sea oil has brought considerable prosperity. There is an important fishing industry, based mainly in Lerwick and on Whalsay. There is a ferry service from **Aberdeen** and in summer to the Faroe Islands, and there are airports at **Sumburgh** (used by the oil industry) and Tingwall. There is a large oil terminal at **Sullom Voe**, whose trade is shrinking as the output of oil declines. See also **Bressay, Fetlar, Papa Stour, Unst, Whalsay** and **Yell**.

**Shetland Islands Council** see **Shetland**

**Shetland pony** see **Shetland**

**Shetland sheep** see **Shetland**

**Shetland wool** see **Shetland**

**Shiant Islands** Group of small islands, Garbh Eilean, Eilean an Tighe and Eilean Mhuire, about 6km (4mi) off the east coast of **Lewis**.

**Shiel, Tibbie** see **St Mary's Loch**

**Shieldaig** Fishing village on the sea loch of the same name at the north edge of the **Applecross** peninsula. The small Shieldaig

Island, in the care of the **National Trust for Scotland**, is covered with Scots pines, a remnant of the ancient **Caledonian forest**.

**shieling** (in Gaelic **àiridh**) Spring and summer pasture, once a part of the pre-industrial system of land use. There people stayed in temporary stone and turf dwellings, tending and milking the livestock. The ruins of old shieling huts can often be spotted by the surrounding patches of green ground, still fertile from the beasts' muck.

**Shin** (Gaelic **Sin**) River in **Sutherland**, flowing south from Loch Shin at **Lairg** to Invershin at the head of the Kyle of Sutherland. It is one of the great salmon rivers of Scotland, and the spectacular Falls of Shin, just to the south of Lairg, have a salmon leap. Loch Shin is a long wide moorland loch flowing southeast to Lairg and is part of a large hydroelectric scheme, with power stations at its northwest end, at Lairg and on the river.

**shinty** (Gaelic **camanachd**) A fast, lively stick sport of Gaelic origin, played with the caman, a stick with a head of triangular section, and a leather ball. The sport's governing body is the Camanachd Association, formed in 1893, which runs the championship competition.

**Shira, Glen** see **Glen Shira**

**shortbread** A kind of biscuit made of a short dough of flour, butter and sugar, and baked in various shapes, sometimes in thin rounds cut into triangles, known as petticoat tails; this name is thought by some to come from French *petites gatelles*, but their similarity to the edge of a 19th-century petticoat is probably the more likely derivation. See also **Pitcaithly bannock**.

**Shorter Catechism** After the signing of the **Solemn League and Covenant** in 1643, the Churches of England and Scotland began to work towards uniformity, and decided on 2 forms of catechism, one full and one for 'beginners'. The Shorter Catechism, approved by the **Church of Scotland** in 1648 and the **Scottish Parliament** in 1649, is remarkable for its simplicity and clarity, and it continued to be used well into the 20th century.

**Shotts** A moorland town near **Motherwell**, once an important ironmaking centre with many coal mines; the slogan 'Shotts lights the world' derived from its manufacture of gas lamp standards. After World War II a large diesel-engine works was built, but has now closed. A prison was opened nearby in 1987.

**Sibbald, Sir Robert** (1641–1722) Naturalist and physician, b. Edinburgh. He helped to found a botanic garden near Holyrood Palace (which eventually became the **Royal Botanic Garden**) and also the **Royal College of Physicians of Edinburgh**. He was

*Glenmorangie Camanachd (shinty) Cup Final, Bught Park, Inverness. Inveraray v. Kingussie, June 2002.*

Geographer Royal and wrote on natural history, medicine and on historical subjects, including a *History of Fife* (1710).

**Sidlaw Hills** Range of hills northwest of **Dundee**, one of the 4 in the Central Lowlands, running parallel to the Firth of **Tay**. One of the highest is Dunsinane.

**Signet, Writers to the** see **Writers to the Signet**

**Signet Library** see **Writers to the Signet**

**Sigurd, Earl of Orkney** (d.1014) Sigurd 'the Stout', Lord of the **Western Isles** as well as Earl of **Orkney**, married a daughter of **Malcolm II** and fathered **Thorfinn**. A warlord of the Scandinavian tradition, he died at the Battle of Clontarf in Ireland.

**Sileas na Ceapaich** (**Julia** or **Cicely MacDonald of Keppoch**) (c.1660–c.1729) Gaelic poet. A daughter of the chief of the MacDonalds of Keppoch, she married Alexander Gordon of Camdell, near **Tomintoul**. Her poetry covers a wide range, including religious and political poems (on the **Union of Parliaments** and the 1715 **Jacobite Rising**). Her best-known poems are 'Alasdair Gleanna Garadh', an elegy for the chief of Glengarry and 'Cumha Lachlainn Daill', a lament for Lachlan Dall, a blind harper.

**'Silicon Glen'** see **Glenrothes**

**Sillars, Jim** (1937– ) Politician, b. Ayrshire. Labour MP for South Ayrshire from 1970, he helped found the **Scottish Labour Party** in 1976 but lost his seat in 1979. He later joined the **Scottish National Party** and was MP for Govan (1988–92), playing a leading role in the left wing of the party. He is married to Margo **MacDonald**.

*Sir James Young Simpson (1811-1870).*

**silver** Small quantities of silver have been mined in Scotland from early times, usually recovered from silver-bearing lead ores. Scottish silversmiths matched the finest in Europe in the Renaissance era, especially in the simplicity of Jacobean communion silver of the early 17th century. This tradition of simple elegance reached new heights in the 18th century, especially in **Edinburgh**.

**Sim, Alastair** (1900-76) Actor, b. Edinburgh. A versatile film actor, ranging from the sinister detective in *Green for Danger* (1946) to the outrageous headmistress in *The Belles of St Trinians* (1954), he was also at home on the stage, particularly in the plays of James **Bridie**.

**Simple Minds** Rock group from **Glasgow**, with key members singer Jim Kerr and guitarist Charlie Burchill. Originally influenced by glam-rock, they gradually moved into the mainstream to become one of the biggest stadium acts of the 1980s. Their 1982 album *New Gold Dream* marked the start of their most successful period, while they eventually broke through in the USA 3 years later with the single 'Don't You Forget About Me'.

**Simpson, Archibald** (1790-1847) Architect, b. Aberdeen. Trained in London, he was a sophisticated Greek revival designer. His works in **Aberdeen** included the Music Hall (1820-22), the Athenaeum (1822), the old Royal Infirmary (1832-40). His Marischal College (Tudor 1837-44) has since been enlarged; see **Aberdeen University**.

**Simpson, Sir James Young** (1811-70) Obstetrician, b. Bathgate. After pioneering the use of ether as an anaesthetic in childbirth in 1847, he tested chloroform on himself to see if it would be an improvement. Once Queen Victoria had used it, it was guaranteed acceptance despite opposition from the medical establishment. He was also a pioneer of gynaecology and hospital reform. He gave his name to the Simpson Memorial Maternity Pavilion, opened in Edinburgh in 1979, now part of Edinburgh Royal Infirmary.

**Simson, Habbie** see **Sempill, Robert**

**Sinclair, Sir John, of Ulbster** (1754-1835) Agricultural reformer, b. Thurso. As the 1st Secretary of the Board of Agriculture after 1793, he was responsible for the compilation of the **Statistical Account of Scotland**. His research into crop rotation and sheep farming was published in *Code of Agriculture* (1817).

**Singing Kettle** see **Fisher family**

**Skaill, Bay of** see **Skara Brae**

**Skara Brae** The impressive remains of a neolithic village on the Bay of Skaill, on the west coast of the **Orkney** Mainland. Stone houses inhabited between 3200 and 2200 BC still contain stone beds, cupboards and dressers. It was rediscovered after storms swept away part of the coast in the 1850s and is now in the care of **Historic Scotland**.

**Skelmorlie** A seaside residential village on the Firth of **Clyde** adjacent to Wemyss Bay, overlooked by the 16th-century Skelmorlie Castle.

**Skene, William** (1809-92) Historian, b. Knoydart, son of James Skene of Rubislaw, a friend of Sir Walter Scott. A solicitor, he spent his spare time researching Scottish historical documents, producing several books including *Celtic Scotland* (1876-80). In 1881 he became Historiographer Royal.

**Skerryvore** (from Gaelic *sgeir mhór* meaning 'big rock') An isolated rock to the southwest of **Tiree**, ringed by hazardous reefs, and with one of the most wave-battered lighthouses in the world, built 1838-44 to a design by Alan Stevenson. See also **lighthouses, Tiree**.

**Skibo Castle** Castle on the Dornoch Firth near **Dornoch**, in heavy **baronial** style, it was greatly extended by Andrew **Carnegie** in 1903. In the 1990s it became home to the exclusive Carnegie Club.

**skiing** Skiing began in Scotland in the early 20th century; the Scottish Ski Club was founded in 1907. Skiing was then part of the mountaineering scene, as it was necessary to climb every inch of the way for the descent. This was facilitated by skins, now usually synthetic material, fastened to the soles of the skis to avoid slipping. From the 1950s one or two ski-tows were erected, in **Glenshee** and on **Ben Lawers**, but it was not until the 1960s that skiing became a commercial enterprise in Scotland, with ski lifts and other facilities in the **Cairngorms**, Glenshee and **Glencoe** and later on a more modest scale at the **Lecht**. In the 1990s a further important centre was opened on Aonach Mor, near **Ben Nevis**. Ski mountaineering and Nordic/cross-country skiing continued, but all these activities have been hampered in recent years by climate change, causing lack of snow, and in 2003 facilities in Glencoe were closed after 50 years. See also **mountaineering and hillwalking**.

**Skinner, James Scott** (1843–1927) Fiddler and composer, b. Banchory. From an early age he was exceptionally talented in both Scots and classical playing, his concert appearances earning him the title of the 'Strathspey King'. His hundreds of original works include 'The Bonnie Lass o' Bon Accord' and 'The Miller o' Hirn'.

**Skipness** Village on Skipness Bay on the east coast of **Kintyre**. To the east is the 13th- and 14th-century Skipness Castle of the McSween family, a courtyard plan with tower house remodelled in the 16th century, hall-house, and gatehouse. Nearby is the now roofless Kilbrannan Chapel, built in the 16th century.

**skirlie** A dish of oatmeal and onions fried together.

**Skye** (Gaelic **An t-Eilean Sgitheanach**) Most northerly of the Inner **Hebrides**, and one of the most beautiful of Scottish islands, Skye is now easily reached by a toll bridge from the mainland. It has several mountain ranges: the **Cuillins** to the south, and Trotternish, with the Old Man of Storr, in the north, and many sea lochs. The main town is **Portree**. For many years a possession of Norway, it was lost to **Alexander III** by Haakon of Norway after the Battle of **Largs**, and came under the control of the Macleods of **Dunvegan** (in the north) and the Macdonalds of **Sleat** (in the south). Violent resistance in Skye to the later stages of the **Clearances** helped to force legal recognition of crofters' rights (see **Braes**).

**Skye and Lochalsh District** see **Highland Region**

**Slains Castle** Substantial ruin on the cliffs north of **Cruden Bay** of the house built by the 17th Earl of Errol in 1836–7, incorporating part of that built by the 9th Earl to replace an earlier castle sacked by **James VI** in 1594, a fragment of which remains. It is said to have inspired Bram Stoker to write *Dracula*.

**slate** Slate quarries providing roofing materials operated in Scotland from the 15th century to the 20th. Most famous were **Ballachulish** and the Slate Islands: **Seil**, **Easdale** and **Luing**, near **Oban**, where the economy revolved around slate until storms destroyed much of the quarries in the 19th century. Other quarries included **Huntly** and **Aberfoyle**. Recently the restarting of quarrying has been suggested to supply the building industry.

**Slater, Oscar** (1873–1948) Subject of the wrongful conviction of the murder of Marion Gilchrist in 1909. Fortunately his death sentence was commuted to life imprisonment, allowing Sir Arthur **Conan Doyle**, among others, to campaign against the verdict, although it took 19 years to obtain his release.

*Slains Castle, Aberdeenshire.*

**Sleat** (pronounced 'slate'; Gaelic **Sléibhte**) Peninsula at the south end of **Skye**, separated from the mainland by the Sound of Sleat. See also **Armadale**.

**Slessor, Mary** (1848–1915) Missionary, b. Aberdeen. A millworker and Sunday School teacher in **Dundee**, she became a missionary in Calabar, Nigeria. She was unusual in her respect for tribal customs, while working to eliminate real cruelty and hardship, adopting many African orphans herself, though she never married.

**Slezer, John** (c.1645–1717) Dutch military engineer and engraver who is thought to have produced the *Theatrum Scotiae* (1693), an important collection of topographical engravings of Scottish landscapes and townscapes.

**Sligachan** (Gaelic **Sligeachan**) Centre on **Skye**, with a hotel and campsite, for climbing, walking and fishing holidays, conveniently situated near Loch Sligachan and the **Cuillins**.

**Slochd** The highest point of the Highland road and rail links between **Aviemore** and **Inverness**, at 362m/1189ft and 401m/1315ft respectively.

**Sloy, Loch** see **Loch Sloy**

**Sma Glen** Steep-sided valley of a stretch of the River **Almond**, 9km (6mi) north of **Crieff**.

**Smail, Robert, Printing Works** see **Innerleithen**

**Smailholm** Village near **Kelso**, with a 13th-century church remodelled in the 17th and 18th centuries. Nearby Smailholm Tower, on a rocky hillock, is a fine example of a 16th-century Border tower (see p.372); in the care of **Historic Scotland**. Sir Walter **Scott** spent some time, as a small child recovering from polio, at nearby Sandyknowe, his grandfather's farm, where he heard many Border tales.

**Small, James** He started as a joiner at Blackadder Mount, Berwickshire, and worked for a while at Rotherham in Yorkshire, where he saw a Dutch design of plough; returning to Scotland in the 1760s he developed the curved cast-iron mould-board still seen on a modern tractor plough.

**Small Isles** (Gaelic **Na h-Eileanan**) Group of islands in the Inner **Hebrides**, south of **Skye**: **Rum**, **Eigg**, **Muck** and **Canna**.

*Mary Slessor.*

**Smellie, William** (1740–95) Printer and editor, b. Edinburgh. He set up as a printer in 1765, producing the first edition of the *Encyclopaedia Britannica* (1768–71) with 2 colleagues, and writing much of it himself. A close friend of Robert **Burns**, he printed the first edition of Burns's poetry. He assisted Sir John **Sinclair** with the *Statistical Account of Scotland* and was a founder member of the **Society of Antiquaries of Scotland**.

**Smiles, Samuel** (1812–1904) Writer and social reformer, b. Haddington, East Lothian. Smiles became editor of the *Leeds Times* and sat on the boards of several railways, leading to a meeting with George Stephenson, of whom he wrote a biography. His best-known books are *Self-Help* (1859), a moral tract detailing the examples set by great men, and *Lives of the Engineers* (1861–2); he wrote several related works and a number of other biographies.

**Smith, Adam** (1723–90) Political economist and moral philosopher, b. Kirkcaldy, Fife. In his mid twenties he became friends with members of the **Edinburgh** intelligentsia including David **Hume**, John **Home** and William **Robertson**, and from 1751 he held the chair of logic at **Glasgow**, transferring to moral philosophy in 1755. His *Theory of Moral Sentiments* (1759) argued for an innate sympathy with others as the basis of social morality. In 1776 he published *Inquiry into the Nature and Causes of the Wealth of Nations*, a brilliant synthesis of concepts such as the division of labour, market mechanisms and credit structures. He endorsed freer trade and consumer sovereignty but he believed in enlightened self-interest as well as moral sympathy. An 18th-century man and socially conservative, he had to be reinterpreted to become the high priest of Victorian capitalism, and more recently of Thatcherite free-market economics.

**Smith, Alexander McCall** (1948– ) Writer and academic, b. Southern Rhodesia (now Zimbabwe). Professor of Law in **Edinburgh University**, he has written important works on medical ethics, but he is well-known for his series of detective stories set in Botswana and featuring the private detective, Mma Ramotswe, beginning with *The No.1 Ladies' Detective Agency* (1998). He has also written numerous children's books and short stories.

**Smith, Ali (Alison)** (1962– ) Novelist and short-story writer, b. Inverness. After lecturing in **Strathclyde** University, she turned to writing and gained immediate acclaim with her short-story collection, *Free Love and Other Stories* (1995). Later collections of stories followed, *Other Stories and Other Stories* (1999) and *The Whole Story and Other Stories* (2003). Her novels are *Like* (1997) and *Hotel World* (2001), which won Scottish Arts Council awards and was shortlisted for the Booker Prize and the Orange Prize.

**Smith, Elaine C** (1958– ) Actress and comedian, b. Baillieston. Renowned for her portrayal of tough Scottish women, she has appeared on stage (including pantomime), film and television, but is probably still most famous for her role as Mary, wife of Rab C Nesbitt in the TV series of the same name.

**Smith, George** (1824–1901) Publisher, son of George Smith (1789–1846) b. Elgin, founder of Smith, Elder & Co, a London publishing house. The son took over the publishing business in 1843, publishing the Brownings, Trollope, Thackeray and Charlotte Brontë. He established the *Cornhill Magazine*, the *Pall Mall Gazette*, and initiated the massive work of the *Dictionary of National Biography* (1st edn, 1882–1901).

**Smith, George** see **Glenlivet**

**Smith, Iain Crichton** (Gaelic **Iain Mac a' Ghobhainn**) (1928–98) Poet and novelist, b. Lewis. He taught English in **Clydebank**, **Dumbarton** and **Oban** until 1977. He wrote poetry in both **Gaelic** and English and also excelled as a translator from Gaelic, both of his own and others' works. He wrote short stories in both languages and many novels in English, the best known of which is *Consider the Lilies* (1968) on the Highland **Clearances**. His writing in Gaelic includes the poems and short stories in *Burn is Aran* (Bread and Water 1960) and *Eadar Fealla-dhà is Glaschu* (Fun and Glasgow 1974). *Murdo and other stories* (1981) brings out his comically surreal attitudes.

**Smith, James** (c.1645–1731) Architect, b. Tarbat, Ross-shire. He studied for the priesthood at the **Scots College** in Rome but became an architect instead, marrying the daughter of the King's master mason, Robert **Mylne**. He designed the great palaces of **Drumlanrig** (1680–90), **Hamilton** (1693–1701), **Melville**, Fife (1697–1700), Yester (1700–15) and **Dalkeith** (1702–10); and in **Edinburgh** Canongate Kirk (1688–90).

**Smith, James** (1789–1850) Agricultural reformer. A wealthy cotton mill manager at Deanston, near **Doune** in Perthshire, he developed good sub-soil drainage in the 1830s, which was effective enough to be deemed 'the second Agricultural Revolution'.

**Smith, John** (1724–1814) Bookseller, b. Strathblane, Stirlingshire. He founded the firm of John Smith and Son in **Glasgow**. He also established Glasgow's first circulating library in 1753. The company now has 27 shops in Scotland, England and Botswana, most of them on university campuses.

**Smith, John** (1781–1852) and **William** (1817–91) Architects, **Aberdeen**. The father was responsible for Aberdeen's Greek revival North Church (1830) and many Tudor Gothic churches and houses in Aberdeenshire, and the son for **Balmoral** (1853–55).

**Smith, John** (1938–94) Politician, b. Dalmally, Argyll. An **advocate**, he became MP for Lanarkshire North in 1970, and from 1983 for Monklands East. After Neil Kinnock's resignation in 1992 he became Leader of the Labour Party, and until his untimely death was widely regarded as a potential future Prime Minister. He is buried on **Iona**.

**Smith, Madeleine** (1835–1928) b. Glasgow, stood trial in 1857 for the murder by poison of her lover Pierre L'Angelier. Though she was shown to have purchased arsenic, the verdict was 'not proven' and she was forced by public opinion to move to London, where she married George Wardle and joined William Morris's circle. Later she moved to the USA and married again.

**Smith, Sydney Goodsir** (1915–75) Poet, b. Wellington, New Zealand, moved to **Edinburgh** in 1928. Writing in **Scots** with vocabulary borrowed from the medieval **makars**, his works include the love poems *Under the Eildon Tree* (1948), *Figs and Thistles* (1959) and *Kynd Kittock's Land* (1965), a hymn to Edinburgh.

**Smith, Sir William** see **Boys' Brigade**

**Smith, William Wright** (1875–1956) Botanist, b. Lochmaben. He took charge of the Government Herbarium in the Calcutta Botanic Garden in 1902 and was Director of the Botanical Survey of India, gaining knowledge in the Indo-Burmese plants. In 1911 he became Deputy Keeper of the **Royal Botanic Garden, Edinburgh** and in 1922 Regius Keeper, as well as Regius Professor of Botany in **Edinburgh University**. He classified the ever increasing new plants from southeast Asia. His specialities were rhododendrons and primulas and, with Harold Fletcher, he produced the first monograph on the Genus *Primula*, establishing Edinburgh as the botanical centre for Sino-Himalayan research.

**smokie** see **Arbroath smokie**

**Smollett, Tobias** (1721-71) Novelist, b. Vale of Leven, he moved to London in 1740, hoping for success in the literary and medical fields. Never financially secure, he nevertheless aspired in the *Critical Review* to shape a standard British prose. *Roderick Random* (1748), his first novel, an entertaining story of a Scot in London, was followed by *Peregrine Pickle* (1751). Less successful novels forced him into translating from French and Spanish. Ill-health led to his spending much of the rest of his life abroad, but his final and very successful novel *Humphry Clinker* (1771) is a fond, if acerbic, tale of a tour of Britain, which undertook to bring an awareness and understanding of Scotland to English readers.

**Smoo Caves** Three massive interconnected caves in the cliffs to the west of **Loch Eriboll**, on the north coast, close to **Durness**.

**Smout, Thomas Christopher** (1933- ) Historian, b. Birmingham. After many years in **Edinburgh University**, he was Professor of Scottish History in **St Andrews University** (1980-91). An economic and social historian, he is best known for *A History of the Scottish People 1560-1830* (1969), which successfully applied many new approaches to the period. In recent years he has specialised in environmental and conservation issues and has pioneered environmental history in Scotland; in 1991 he became Deputy Chairman of **Scottish Natural Heritage**. He is Historiographer Royal in Scotland.

**Soay** Small island just southwest of **Skye**. It was a centre of shark-fishing for a few years in the 1940s. Most of the residents left in 1953.

**Soay, Soay sheep** see **St Kilda**, p.359

**Sobieski Stuarts** Brothers John Sobieski Stolberg Stuart (1795-1872) and Charles Stolberg Stuart (1799-1880) were sons of naval lieutenant Thomas Allen, who claimed to be the son of Prince Charles Edward **Stewart**. They exploited their assumed royal connections to great advantage, and published *Vestiarium Scotorum* (1842), claiming to be based on old manuscripts on clan **tartans**, and *The Costume of the Clans* (1845).

**Society in Scotland for Propagating Christian Knowledge (SSPCK)** A society founded in 1709 to further education in the **Highlands** and Islands and especially to encourage the Presbyterian faith and the English language. They eventually found it necessary to keep **Gaelic** as a first step towards their goals and, paradoxically, they were the first to produce a Gaelic New Testament, in 1767.

**Society of Antiquaries of Scotland** Society founded in 1780 by the 11th Earl of Buchan. It gathered collections which eventually became the basis of the **National Museum of Antiquities of Scotland**. Its proceedings have been published since 1851, as the Scottish archaeological journal of record.

**Sole, David** (1962- ) Rugby player, b. Aylesbury. A fiercely competitive prop forward, he was capped 44 times by Scotland between 1986 and 1992. As captain in the 1990 Grand Slam decider against England, he led his team on Scottish rugby's greatest afternoon.

**Solemn League and Covenant** The agreement between some of the **Covenanters** and the English Parliament signed at Westminster in 1643, during the Civil Wars, providing that Scotland should supply troops to assist the Parliament against Charles I, while the English parliamentarians would support the reform of the Anglican Church in a presbyterian direction. The Scots sought to safeguard their own revolution by exporting it to the larger kingdom, but English resentment was inevitable and the whole scheme collapsed, leaving the **Westminster Confession** as its sole monument.

**Solicitor General** A senior **advocate** who, as a member of the government, is the deputy and chief assistant of the **Lord Advocate**, appointed by the **First Minister**.

**Solway Firth** The arm of the sea that separates southwest Scotland from northwest England, running inland almost as far as **Gretna**. From the 1860s to the 1920s it was bridged by the Solway Viaduct, south of **Annan**, which was closed for safety reasons and demolished in the 1930s.

**Solway Moss, Battle of** In 1542 the forces of **James V** under the command of Robert, Lord Maxwell were routed at Solway Moss, near Longtown, Cumbria, just over the Scottish border, by a numerically inferior force under Sir Thomas Wharton. The extent to which the Scots were undermined by internal disagreements is debated. James died a few days later, allegedly of grief.

**Somerled** (Gaelic **Somhairle**) (d.1164) Norse-Celtic chieftain who established himself as King of the Isles, including Man, and Lord of Argyll. He was an important focus of resistance to **Malcolm IV**, rising against him in 1153 and dying at the head of a powerful invasion of the Scottish mainland at **Renfrew** in 1164. Prominent local kindreds, the MacDougalls, MacDonalds and MacRuairies, claimed descent from Somerled.

**Somerville, Jimmy** (1961- ) Singer and songwriter, b. Glasgow. His first hit, 'Smalltown Boy' with Bronski Beat in 1984, showed off his piercingly high but attractive voice; shortly afterwards he formed the Communards, where his biggest hit was 'Don't Leave Me This Way'.

**Somerville, Mary** (neé **Fairfax**) (1780–1872) Scientist, b. Jedburgh, with an impressive ability to explain scientific theory in a comprehensible manner. An advocate of rights for women, Somerville College, Oxford, is named after her.

**Soor Ploom** Nickname for a native of **Galashiels**; also (soor ploom) a kind of round, green, tart-flavoured boiled sweet, originally associated with Galashiels.

**Souness, Graeme** (1953– ) Footballer and football manager, b. Edinburgh. A midfielder with a successful career including **Rangers** and Liverpool and many Scottish internationals, he managed Rangers from 1986–91, and is currently manager of Blackburn Rovers.

**Soutar, William** (1898–1943) Poet, b. Perth. Although bedridden from 1930, he lived a productive life as a writer. His reputation rests on his poetry, much of it in Scots. It includes fine verses for children, as in *Seeds in the Wind* (1933), but it was his thoughtful lyrical mature poetry that made him a key figure in the 20th-century Scottish Renaissance. His thoughts on life, poetry and politics were published in *Diaries of a Dying Man* (1954).

**Souter** see **Selkirk**

**Souter, Brian** see **Stagecoach**

**Souter Johnnie** see **Kirkoswald**

**South Ayrshire** (pop. 114,000) Local authority in southwest Scotland created in 1996 from the Kyle and Carrick district of **Strathclyde Region**; see maps on pp.394-5 and **local government** and see also **Ayrshire, East Ayrshire, North Ayrshire**. The administrative centre is **Ayr** and other towns include **Troon, Prestwick, Girvan** and **Maybole**. It is mainly agricultural in the south with aerospace and technological industries in the north near **Prestwick** International Airport. Tourism is also important: both **Robert I** and Robert **Burns** were born in the area.

**Southend** Village at the southern tip of **Kintyre**, popular for its sandy beaches. Legend has it that nearby Keil was the landing place of St **Columba**; his 'footsteps' are to be seen on a rock near the chapel ruins. Fragments of Dunaverty Castle, a stronghold of the **Lords of the Isles**, lie nearby, the scene of a terrible massacre of Royalist forces by **Covenanters** in 1647.

**Southern Uplands** The rolling hills of southern Scotland, between the **Forth-Clyde** valley and the English Border, a geologically complex area created from ancient ocean flow sediments (420–430 million years old). The area can now be walked on the Southern Uplands Way, running 340km (212mi) from **Portpatrick** on the west coast to **Cockburnspath** on the east, via **Dalry, St Mary's Loch, Melrose** and **Lauder**. There are 80 hills over 610m (2000ft) along its route.

**Southern Uplands Fault** Major geological feature running from **Girvan** on the west coast to **Dunbar** on the east coast. It marks the southern margin of the Midland Valley of Scotland. See **Highland Boundary Fault**.

**South Lanarkshire** Local authority formed in 1996 from the Clydesdale, Hamilton and East Kilbride Districts of **Strathclyde Region**, with slightly increased area, including part of the former Glasgow District; see maps on pp. 394-5 and **local government** and see also **Lanarkshire, North Lanarkshire**. The administrative centre is **Hamilton** and other towns include **East Kilbride, Lanark** and **Rutherglen**.

**South of Scotland Electricity Board (SSEB)** Formed, after the nationalisation of the electricity supply industry in 1948, to serve customers in the south of Scotland; see **North of Scotland Hydro-electric Board**. The SSEB inherited a rag-bag of small and medium-sized generating stations, mostly coal-fired, from municipalities and area supply companies. As demand for electricity increased rapidly, it enlarged existing stations and built a handful of new ones, prior to building very large new coal-fired power stations at **Kincardine, Cockenzie** and **Longannet**, and nuclear power stations at **Hunterston** (2) and **Torness**, allowing the older stations to be closed. The company was privatised in the 1990s, as Scottish Power.

**South Queensferry** Village on the south shore of the Firth of **Forth** dominated by the Forth bridges, formerly the site of a ferry; see **North Queensferry**. It hosts an annual procession by the Burry Man. It is also the site of the Hawes Inn, which features in R L **Stevenson**'s *Kidnapped*. Its small harbour, and the nearby Port Edgar, are now yacht havens.

**South Ronaldsay** Most southerly of the **Orkney** islands, linked to **Burray** by one of the **Churchill Barriers**. The only village is **St Margaret's Hope**, which now has a car ferry to the mainland. There is a summer-only passenger ferry from Burwick to **John o' Groats**. The Tomb of the Eagles is a neolithic chambered cairn.

**South Uist** (Gaelic **Uibhist a Deas**) (pop. 1818) Island in the Outer **Hebrides**, between **Benbecula** and **Barra**, linked by ferry to **Oban** and **Barra** and by causeway to **Benbecula**. The main port is **Lochboisdale**. It has numerous lochs and several sea lochs on the east coast. The principal occupations are **fishing**, crofting and tourism. As in **Barra**, a majority of the population is Roman Catholic.

351

**Soutra** Hill between the **Moorfoot** and **Lammermuir** Hills, on a major road to the **Borders**, it is the site of Soutra Aisle, all that remains of a hospital founded for pilgrims by **Malcolm IV** in the 12th century. Excavation of the site has provided evidence of medieval medical practice. Nearby is a well-preserved stretch of Dere Street Roman road.

**sowans** A dish of oatmeal husks (and fine oatmeal) steeped in water for about a week, then strained and left to ferment. The solid matter at the bottom is eaten like **porridge**, boiled with water and salt.

**Sow of Atholl** see **Boar of Badenoch**

**Spark, Muriel** (née **Camberg**) (1918– ) Writer, b. Edinburgh. *The Prime of Miss Jean Brodie* (1961) tells the story of an **Edinburgh** girls' school teacher with advanced ideas and a peculiarly strong influence on her pupils. Her other novels include *The Ballad of Peckham Rye* (1960), *The Girls of Slender Means* (1963), *The Abbess of Crewe* (1974), *A Far Cry from Kensington* (1988) and *Reality and Dreams* (1996) and *The Finishing School* (2004). She has also written numerous short stories and poetry; her autobiography, *Curriculum Vitae*, was published in 1992.

**Spean Bridge** (pronounced **spee**an) Village northeast of **Fort William** on the River Spean, it saw the first skirmish of the 1745 **Jacobite** Rising. An 1819 bridge by Thomas **Telford** replaced **Wade**'s High Bridge over the River Spean, built in 1736, the remains of which survive. A spectacular memorial 2km (1mi) to the west commemorates commando training in the area during World War II.

*Spynie Palace, ruined castle of the bishops of Moray.*

**Spear, Shirley** see **Three Chimneys**

**Spedlins** Tower house of the Jardines of Applegarth, to the north of Applegarth, 5km (3mi) northwest of **Lockerbie**, built c.1500 and remodelled in 1605, remarkable for its deep plan; reroofed in 1988–9.

**Spence, Alan** (1947– ) Writer, b. Glasgow. A reflective, perceptive and compassionate writer, his works include novels: *The Magic Flute* (1990), and *Way to Go* (1998); short stories: *Its Colours They Are Fine* (1977) and *Stone Garden* (1995); his poetry collections include *Seasons of the Heart* (2000) and *Glasgow Zen* (2002).

**Spence, Sir Basil** (1907–76) Architect, b. India of Scottish parents, educated in **Edinburgh** and London. One of the foremost architects of the later 20th century, he designed university buildings at Cambridge, Sussex and Southampton, and housing estates in Berkshire; his masterwork was the new Coventry Cathedral (1951). His Queen Elizabeth Square high flats in **Glasgow** were not a success, and have been demolished.

**Spey** (Gaelic **Spé**) The second-longest river in Scotland, renowned for its salmon. Rising near **Loch Laggan**, it joins the River Truim at **Newtonmore**, then runs between the **Cairngorms** and **Monadhliaths** to Spey Bay. In the 18th and 19th centuries rafts of timber were floated down the Spey. See **Speyside, Strathspey**.

**Speyside** The valley of the River **Spey** is renowned for its **whisky** distilleries and salmon as much as its fine scenery; its upper end is a busy tourist area, especially for skiers, hillwalkers and mountaineers. 135km (84mi) can now be walked along the Speyside Way from **Buckie** or Spey Bay to **Aviemore**, passing the Craigellachie Forest, **Aberlour**, **Ballindalloch** and **Nethy Bridge**. Speyside is often used to describe some malt whiskies, produced at its lower end, which are not markedly peaty and have a rounded, fruity flavour. See also **Strathspey, Cairngorms**.

**Spittal of Glenshee** Small village where Glen Beg joins Glen Lochy, on the road to the **Cairnwell** Pass, perhaps deriving its name from a hospice for travellers; now a centre for walking and **skiing** holidays.

**sporran** From Gaelic *sporan*, a purse,

*Staffa. The columnar rock formations were formed from cooling volcanic lava.*

refers to a leather pouch, often ornamented, for holding money, worn in front of the **kilt**.

**sportscotland** Government-funded body, formerly known as the Scottish Sports Council, established in 1972 to encourage sport in Scotland. It has 3 national centres: Inverclyde, Glenmore Lodge and Cumbrae.

**Spottiswoode, John** (1565–1639) Churchman. Archbishop of **Glasgow** and later **St Andrews**, Chancellor of Scotland in 1635. Conciliatory by nature, he reluctantly supported **Charles I**'s ecclesiastical innovations, and became a target for the **Covenanters**, deposed and excommunicated in 1638. He wrote a *History of the Church of Scotland* (1655).

**Springbank** Distillery in **Campbeltown**, founded in 1828 by the Mitchell family, who still own it. It is a survivor of the once-thriving distillery industry in the town, and it produces 3 single malt whiskies, Springbank, Hazelburn and Longrow, the last 2 named after long-closed Campbeltown distilleries.

**Springburn** Suburb to the northeast of **Glasgow**. The first railway works was built here in 1842 and there were eventually 4 large works. Two of them, the Hyde Park Works of Nelson, Reid and Co, and the Atlas Works of Sharp, Stewart and Co, joined with another Glasgow works in 1903 to form the North British Locomotive Co Ltd. Part of the St Rollox Works still maintains electric trains.

**Spynie** Village near **Elgin**, on the River Lossie, in medieval times a harbour, later cut off from the sea, and the land drained in the 19th century. Spynie Palace is the ruined castle of the bishops of Moray (in the care of **Historic Scotland**). Its massive David's Tower

was built in the 15th century by Bishop David Stewart as protection against the Earl of Huntly, whom he had excommunicated.

**Squadrone Volante** The name (meaning the flying squadron) of a loose political group, originally led by John Hay, 2nd Marquis Tweeddale (1645–1713), which held an independent stance during discussion of the proposed Treaty of **Union**. However, they came to support the Treaty, and their 25 votes proved decisive in its acceptance. They then became the alternative to and opponents in Scotland of the **Argathelians**.

**srath** see **strath**

**SSEB** see **South of Scotland Electricity Board**

**SSPCK** see **Society in Scotland for Propagating Christian Knowledge**

**Stack Polly** (Gaelic **Stac Pollaidh**) Isolated small but conspicuous mountain (612m/2009ft) with a very rocky summit ridge, in the National Nature Reserve at Inverpolly, **Wester Ross**.

**Staffa** Uninhabited island of the Inner **Hebrides**, west of **Mull**, famous for **Fingal's Cave** and other cliffs and caves of hexagonal columnar basalt, only recognised as a geological wonder in 1772, becoming a magnet for tourists including Sir Walter **Scott**, Mendelssohn, Tennyson and Jules Verne. Its Norse name means 'island of pillars'.

**Stagecoach** Originally a bus company, set up in 1980 in **Perth** by brother and sister Brian Souter and Ann Gloag, it has developed into an international transport concern, with railway franchises and bus operations. The company was one of the prime beneficiaries of the privatisation of public transport and of the deregulation of bus services in the 1980s by the Thatcher government.

**Stair, James Dalrymple, 1st Viscount** (1619–95) Politician and jurist. He was Lord President of the **Court of Session** from 1671 to 1681 and again from 1689–98. After a successful legal and political career, he left **Edinburgh** on the arrival of **James VII** (then Duke of York) and wrote *Institutions of the Law of Scotland* (1681), the definitive work on Scots **law**. Running foul of Viscount **Dundee** in support of the **Covenanters** he left for Holland, returning with **William of Orange**.

**Stair, John Dalrymple, 1st Earl of** (1648–1707) Politician and judge, son of the 1st Viscount. Like his father, as the Master of Stair, he opposed the regime of **James VII and II**, resulting in his imprisonment. After the Revolution of 1689, he became Lord Advocate under **William III**, and Secretary of State in 1691. He was responsible for the last-minute retargeting of a punitive expedition which led to the massacre of **Glencoe**. He had to resign in 1695, but continued to wield political influence, latterly in support of the Treaty of **Union**.

**Stair, John Dalrymple, 2nd Earl of** (1673–1747) Soldier and diplomat, b. Edinburgh. Aged 8, he accidentally shot his elder brother dead, and was exiled to Holland by his parents. He fought under **William III** in Flanders in the 1690s and later, with great distinction, under Marlborough in the War of the Spanish Succession. A staunch supporter of the Hanoverian succession, he became ambassador in Paris under George I. There his intelligence operation enabled him to do much to frustrate the intrigues of the **Jacobites**. Recalled in 1720, he became a notable agricultural improver.

**Standard, Battle of the** Battle near Northallerton, Yorkshire, in 1138 in which **David I**'s invading army was defeated by an English defensive force. David was nominally fighting for Matilda in her civil war with Stephen, but also had an expansionist motive and defeat did not stop him gaining possession of much of northern England.

**Standard Grades** School courses taken by the majority of pupils in their 3rd and 4th years. They were introduced in the 1980s, replacing **O-Grades**, and can be taken at 3 levels, Foundation, General and Credit. Grades are awarded for a combination of coursework and examinations.

**Standard Life Assurance Co** Last of the large independent mutual insurance companies established in Scotland in the 19th century; it was founded in 1825. There have been repeated attempts by some policy-holders to 'demutualise' it and float it on the stock market.

**Stanley** Planned village on the River **Tay** near **Perth**, built to serve cotton mills built from 1785 onwards. Two of them have been converted to housing by the Phoenix Trust, a building preservation trust set up by the Prince of Wales. The Bell Mill is the best-preserved water-powered cotton spinning mill associated with Richard Arkwright; in the care of **Historic Scotland**. The former company church was built in 1828.

**staple** A legal and commercial arrangement with a town in the Low Countries with which Scotland traded certain exports exclusively, from the 14th to the 18th centuries. The staple moved from Bruges to Middelburg, Holland, and in the 16th century to Campvere (now Veere), where it remained.

**starrie rock** A kind of thin rock-type sweet from **Angus**, with a cross-section showing a star shape and a very distinctive flavour, still made in **Kirriemuir**.

**Statistical Accounts of Scotland** Parish-by-parish surveys based on economic and social information, provided by over 900 parish ministers, who wrote most of the accounts. The Old (First) Statistical Account (1791–99) was directed by Sir John **Sinclair** of Ulbster; the New (Second) was published in 1845. Their special importance lies in their record, at given points in time, of the impact of the agricultural and industrial revolutions. The *Third Statistical Account* was begun after World War II but not completed; published between 1951 and 1952, it is much less useful than its predecessors in giving a picture of Scottish life in its day, not least because the parish had ceased to be an important unit. The Statistical Accounts are now available on the Internet.

**Statutes of Iona** Terms imposed, on Iona in 1609 by Bishop Knox of the Isles, on several, virtually kidnapped, West Highland and island chiefs, aimed at bringing the **Highlands** more into line with **Lowland** ways of life. They included the setting up of inns, schools and Protestant churches, and an obligation on chiefs to send their sons to the Lowlands for education. Most of these provisions were unenforceable, but the important ones were honoured. These involved an obligation on the chiefs to have an **Edinburgh** lawyer and to visit Edinburgh periodically. As a result, especially during the tactful and sympathetic rule of **James VI**'s great minister Lord Dunfermline, even the most remote Hebridean chiefs were finally incorporated into the Scottish body politic.

**steel** New technology allowed the production of steel on a large scale in the later 19th century, and supported the establishment of the Steel Company of Scotland in 1872, and of other companies from about 1880. Steel rapidly took over from iron in supplying

*The Stones of Stenness, Orkney.*

the shipbuilding and railway industries, and became a boom industry until shortly after World War I, when cheaper competition and the exhaustion of local iron-ore sources started a long decline. Depression after 1929 forced rationalisation, with most of the industry being brought under the control of **Colvilles Ltd**. Though World War II and postwar reconstruction saw a revival, nationalisation, denationalisation and renationalisation took their toll, and in 1978 British Steel closed all the major steelworks in Scotland apart from **Ravenscraig**, as part of the phasing out of the Open Hearth process. Ravenscraig closed in 1992.

**Steel, Sir David, Lord Steel of Aikwood** (1938- ) Politician, b. Kirkcaldy, elected MP for Roxburgh, Selkirk and Peebles in 1965, holding the seat till 1983. Sponsor of the Abortion Reform Bill, he became the last leader of the Liberal Party in 1976, and helped form the alliance with The Social Democratic Party. In 1997 he became a life peer as Lord Steel of Aikwood; and from 1999 to 2003, Liberal Democrat MSP for Lothians and the first Presiding Officer of the new **Scottish Parliament**. See also **Aikwood**.

**Steell, Sir John** (1804–91) Artist, b. Aberdeen. The pre-eminent sculptor of the Victorian period in Scotland, Steell produced numerous monumental figures, including the marble of Sir Walter **Scott** at the base of the Scott Monument in Princes Street, **Edinburgh**, 'Queen Victoria' on the Royal Institution, Edinburgh (now the **Royal Scottish Academy**), and the equestrian monument to the Duke of Wellington, in front of Register House, Edinburgh.

**Stein, Jock (John)** (1922–85) Football manager, b. Burnbank, near Hamilton. After a footballing career, he became one of Scotland's finest managers, driving otherwise unsuccessful clubs (**Dunfermline** and, briefly, **Hibernian**) to high levels of achievement. At **Celtic** from 1965, he created an almost invincible club, winning championships, the League Cup and becoming the first British team to win the European Cup. As manager of Scotland he achieved the side's qualification for the World Cup Finals in 1982. His last years were overshadowed by the effects of a serious car crash. He died from a heart attack during an international match against Wales.

**Stenhousemuir** (pop. with Larbert 16,311) With **Larbert**, forming a town to the northwest of **Falkirk**. In the late 18th century it became the main site of the **Falkirk** Tryst, largest cattle market in Scotland. The tower house of Stenhouse, built in 1622, was the last to be built in Scotland. In its grounds till 1743 stood Arthur's Oon, a Roman shrine or memorial.

**Stenness, Stones of** Remains of a stone circle and henge on **Orkney** Mainland, at the southern end of the **Loch of Stenness**. Four of the original 12 upright stones survive, dating from 2900 BC; in the care of **Historic Scotland**.

**Stevenson, Alan, Charles, David, David A, Robert, Thomas** see **lighthouses**, p.229

**Stevenson, John James** (1831–1908) Architect, b. Glasgow. A pupil of David **Bryce** and G G Scott, he practised in **Glasgow** in partnership with Campbell Douglas (1860–69), and introduced the Continental Gothic revival to Scotland at his Botanic Gardens Church in 1862. In 1871, by which date he had settled in London, he built the Red House at Bayswater which inaugurated the 'Queen Anne' movement in architecture in England. In Scotland he pioneered the revival of late Scots Gothic forms, notably at

S

St Leonard's in the Fields, **Perth** (1883), and the Stevenson Memorial Church at Belmont Bridge, Glasgow (1900).

**Stevenson, Robert Louis** (1850–94) Writer, b. Edinburgh, son of Thomas Stevenson of the 'Lighthouse Stevensons' and Margaret Isabella Balfour. An only and often ill child, he took refuge in stories which fuelled his imagination. As a young man he investigated the seedier side of **Edinburgh**, and was often abroad, meeting his future wife, Fanny Osbourne (1840–1914), in France. They were married in California in 1880. After 7 years in Europe they returned to America. Stevenson spent the last 6 years of his life voyaging in the Pacific in search of a climate kind to his frail health; he finally settled in Samoa. Stevenson's first novel, *Treasure Island* (1883), was an immediate success, and others in the adventure genre include *Kidnapped* (1886) and *Catriona* (1893), tales of the aftermath of 1745. Darker interests emerged in the sinister *Strange Case of Dr Jekyll and Mr Hyde* (1886), *The Master of Ballantrae* (1888), *The Ebb-Tide* (1894) and the unfinished *Weir of Hermiston* (1896), and in some of his highly accomplished short stories. As a poet he is remembered most for *A Child's Garden of Verses* (1885) but also wrote strikingly for adults. Often categorised as a children's writer, he is now seen as a subtle and innovative commentator on the late-Victorian scene.

**Stevenson, Ronald** (1928– ) Composer, b. Blackburn, Lancashire. Prolific and internationally recognised, Stevenson's fertile output includes many pieces that draw on aspects of traditional Scottish music, including **pibroch** and dance forms. His *Passacaglia on DSCH* is an 80-minute single-movement work for piano. He has spent most of his adult life in Scotland.

**Steward of Scotland** A hereditary office bestowed on the family of Walter (d.1177), grandson of Alan (d. c.1114), a Breton in the service of Henry I of England, by **David I** and confirmed by **Malcolm IV**. David I gave Walter estates in Scotland, and the family surname Stewart, that of a long line of Scottish and 5 British monarchs, is derived from the title 'steward'. The office is now held by the heir apparent to the throne. See also Walter **Stewart**.

**Stewart, Alan Breck** (d.1789) Adventurer and foster brother of James **Stewart** of the Glens. A **Jacobite**, with James he was falsely

*Robert Louis Stevenson by Count Girolamo Nerli, 1892.*

accused of the **Appin murder**, but escaped to France, where he died. He is a major character in R L **Stevenson**'s *Kidnapped* and *Catriona*.

**Stewart, Alexander** see **Badenoch, Wolf of**

**Stewart, Belle** see **Stewart family**

**Stewart, Prince Charles Edward** (1720–88) Also known as the Young Pretender, and popularly as Bonnie Prince Charlie and the Young Chevalier. Son of James Francis Edward **Stewart**, the Old Pretender, and Maria Clementina Sobieska, he was born and educated in Rome, where his father was exiled. In 1745, in an attempt to restore his father to the British throne, he landed on the small west coast island of **Eriskay**, and on 19 August, raised the standard at **Glenfinnan**, thus beginning the last **Jacobite Rising**. Good looks and an attractive personality brought him much support, but the clans did not turn out in expected numbers and unrealistic aims and policies ended in disaster. On 16 April 1746, his army was heavily defeated at **Culloden** and he spent the following summer being hunted by government troops with a price of £30,000 on his head, suffering danger and hardship such as the rebellion had inflicted on his followers. His lucky escapes included his rescue by Flora **Macdonald**, who allowed him to travel with her from **Benbecula** to **Skye**, disguised as her maid, Betty Burke. In September he was safely conveyed to France. His later life went into decline and drunkenness. His ill-treated mistress, Clementina **Walkinshaw**, bore him a daughter, Charlotte, whom he created Duchess of Albany, who cared for him at the end of his life. His marriage to Louisa von Stolberg was short-lived and he died in misery in Rome.

**Stewart, David, of Garth** (1772–1829) Historian and soldier, a friend of Sir Walter **Scott**. After a career with the **Black Watch** he researched and published *Sketches of the Character, Manner and Present State of the Highlanders of Scotland, with Details of the Military Service of the Highland Regiments* (1822), praising the traditional patriarchal values of Gaelic society. He was appointed Governor-General of St Lucia in 1829, and died there.

**Stewart, Dugald** (1753–1828) Philosopher, b. Edinburgh. Professor of Moral Philosophy at **Edinburgh**, he was an admired teacher and writer, though his work was more derivative (after Thomas **Reid**) than original. A massive monument to his memory stands on Calton Hill in Edinburgh.

**Stewart, Henry Benedict, Cardinal, Duke of York** (1725–1807) b. Rome. The younger son of James Francis Edward **Stewart**, and the brother of Prince Charles Edward **Stewart**. He became a Cardinal in 1747, and did not actively pursue the Stewart claim to the throne after his brother's death.

**Stewart, Sir Jackie (John Young)** (1939– ) Racing driver, b. Dunbartonshire. A successful competitor in Grand Prix racing from 1965, he won the world title in 1969, 1971 and 1973, after which he retired. He was also an Olympic-standard clay-pigeon shooter.

**Stewart, James Francis Edward** (1688–1766) b. London, known as the 'Old Pretender'. Only son of **James VII and II** by his second wife Mary of Modena. In the exiled court at St Germain, near Paris, he was proclaimed James VIII and III by French heralds on his father's death in 1701. During the abortive 1708 **Jacobite Rising** he approached Scotland but failed to land. His part in the 1715 Rising was brief and unsuccessful. Forced to leave France in 1713, he spent the rest of his life in exile, mainly in Rome. His unhappy marriage to Princess Clementina Sobieska produced 2 sons, Prince Charles Edward **Stewart**, and Henry Benedict **Stewart**, Duke of York, later Cardinal.

**Stewart, James, of the Glens** (d.1752) **Jacobite**, evicted from his home by Colin Campbell of Glenure. With Alan Breck **Stewart**, falsely accused of Campbell's murder, he was hanged at **Ballachulish**. He features in **Stevenson**'s *Kidnapped* and *Catriona*. See **Appin murder**.

**Stewart, J(ohn) I(nnes) M(acintosh)** (pen name **Michael Innes**) (1906–94) Novelist and academic, b. Edinburgh. A Fellow of Christ Church, Oxford, he used the Oxford setting for many of his 'straight' novels, including the quintet *A Staircase in Surrey*, but ranged more widely for his huge output (as Michael Innes) of intelligent detective stories, usually featuring Inspector Appleby, starting with *Death at the President's Lodging* (1937).

**Stewart, John Roy** (Gaelic **Iain Ruadh Stiubhart**) (1700–52) Gaelic poet, b. **Badenoch**. A popular commander in the **Jacobite** army, he escaped to France after the Battle of **Culloden**. His few surviving poems include post-Culloden laments.

**Stewart, Mary** (1916– ) Novelist, b. England, but spending much of her life in Scotland, a bestselling suspense writer who later turned to historical fiction and fantasy. She is most famous for her Arthurian trilogy *The Crystal Cave* (1970), *The Hollow Hills* (1973) and *The Last Enchantment* (1979).

**Stewart, Patrick, 2nd Earl of Orkney** (d.1615) Son of Robert **Stewart, 1st Earl**, he acted like a tyrant to the people of **Orkney**. His behaviour was so outrageous it led to periods of imprisonment and eventually his castles were seized. He sent his illegitimate son Robert to recover them, but he was defeated and hanged for treason. Earl Patrick was executed in 1615 for instigating his son's rebellion. His Earl's Palace in **Kirkwall** is a spectacular ruin of a Renaissance building.

**Stewart, Robert, 1st Earl of Orkney** (1533–93) Illegitimate son of **James V** (and thus a half-brother of **Mary, Queen of Scots**), he gained power over the **Orkney** and **Shetland** Islands, being created Earl of Orkney in 1581. His rule was tyrannical, but he left a more positive legacy in the Earl's Palace at Birsay on Orkney mainland.

**Stewart, Rod** (1945– ) Rock singer, b. London. He worked with various blues and rock groups throughout the 1960s before finding success as a solo artist, and with The Faces. His 1971 album, *Every Picture Tells A Story*, was a huge success in both the UK and USA and produced the hit single 'Maggie May'. He left The Faces in 1975 and began a successful solo career with such hits as 'Sailing' and 'Do Ya Think I'm Sexy'. Scottish on his father's side, he has long been a high-profile supporter of the national football team.

**Stewart, Walter** (1293–1326) Sixth hereditary Steward of Scotland. In 1315 he married **Robert I**'s daughter Marjory, and their son became **Robert II**, first of the long line of Stewart kings.

**Stewart family of Blairgowrie: Belle** (1906–97) b. Caputh, Perthshire was the matriarch of a musical family of Scottish travellers with an unrivalled richness of oral tradition in song, story and piping. Family members became well known and respected at folk festivals, and their repertoire was extensively documented by Ewan **MacColl** and Peggy Seeger. Belle's daughter **Sheila** Stewart is an impressive storyteller and ballad singer.

**Stewartry** see **Kirkcudbrightshire**

**Stewartry District** see **Dumfries and Galloway Region**

**Stewarts and Lloyds Ltd** Company formed in 1903 by amalgamating several Scottish and Welsh tube-making firms, which dominated tube-making in Britain for many years. In the early 1930s it established an integrated iron, steel and tube-making plant at Corby, Lincolnshire, to reduce costs, and many Scots employees moved there. When the steel industry was nationalised in 1967 the company lost its identity. The residue in Scotland is now French-owned, with works at Coatdyke and New Stevenston.

**Stirling** see p.358

357

# STIRLING

Stirling (pop. 32,673) Historic town on the River **Forth**, in a strategic position to the northeast of **Glasgow** and to the northwest of **Edinburgh**, controlling access by land from the **Lowlands** to the **Highlands**, not least because it was the lowest bridging point on the Forth until comparatively recent times. The medieval bridge, dating from the late 15th or early 16th century (now a footbridge, in the care of **Historic Scotland**), can still be seen to the north of the modern bridge; in 1905 the remains of an earlier wooden bridge were found a little upstream. A former royal **burgh** and county town of **Stirlingshire**, it is now the administrative centre of **Stirling** local authority; see **local government**. The old town is on a steep volcanic rock crowned by Stirling Castle (in the care of Historic Scotland); in medieval and early modern times it was one of the main royal residences. The principal buildings comprise the Great Hall, completed in 1503 and recently restored; the Palace, built 1537–52; and the Chapel Royal, built in 1594. During the 14th-century **Wars of Independence**, the Castle was twice captured by the English and recaptured, first by William **Wallace** in 1297 after the Battle of **Stirling Bridge**; it was the last stronghold to capitulate to Edward I in 1304 and was retrieved by **Robert I** in 1314 after the Battle of **Bannockburn** nearby. William Wallace is commemorated in the National Wallace Monument, a tall baronial tower on Abbey Craig to the northeast, by J T Rochead (1861–9). **Mary, Queen of Scots** was crowned in the Castle as an infant in 1543 and **James VI** was baptised there, as was his firstborn son, Prince **Henry**. From the 18th century until the 1950s Stirling was an army base, with a garrison in the Castle and a depot beside the railway.

Much medieval and 17th- and 18th-century building survives in the town. The 15th- and 16th-century Church of the Holy Rude, where James VI was crowned, was divided into two in the 17th century, much altered in the 19th, further restored in the 20th, being reunited as one church in the 1930s. Mar's Wark is the remains of a mansion built 1570–2 by the Earl of Mar, Regent for James VI (in the care of Historic Scotland). Argyll's Lodging is a well-preserved Renaissance town house at the top of Castle Wynd, begun in 1630 by Sir William **Alexander**, Earl of Stirling, and completed in 1666 by the 9th Earl of **Argyll**. In 1799 it became a military hospital and later a youth hostel; now in the care of Historic Scotland. Cowane's Hospital was built in the mid 17th century as an almshouse, designed by John **Mylne**; it was converted for use as a Guildhall in 1852; it is now used for music and arts events. The Old High School (1854–6, by J W H and J M Hay) was converted and extended in 1990–1 by Coleman, Ballantine to become the Stirling Highland Hotel. The Tolbooth or Town House in Broad Street was built 1703–5 to a design by Sir William **Bruce**; it is now used as a venue for music and arts events. The Old Town Jail (1845–7, by Thomas Brown Jun) was restored as a visitor centre in the 1990s, giving a vivid picture of prison life then and now.

Stirling developed in the 19th century as an industrial and commercial centre, alongside the railway, and has handsome and substantial Victorian suburbs, notably in the King's Park area. The Smith Art Gallery and Museum by John Lessels (1871–4), in classical style, was founded by the painter and collector Thomas Stewart Smith. **Cambuskenneth Abbey** is nearby. See also **Stirling University**.

*Stirling Castle.*

**Stirling** Local authority in central Scotland created in 1996 from Stirling District, the main part of **Central Region**; see maps on pp.394–5 and **local government**. The administrative centre is **Stirling** and other towns include **Dunblane** and **Bridge of Allan**, but most of the area is rural.

**Stirling Bridge** Victory of Scottish insurgents, led by William **Wallace** and Andrew Murray, over an English army in 1297. This was the first significant reverse for Edward I and his occupation of Scotland quickly collapsed thereafter. A lengthy struggle ensued before Scottish independence was ultimately asserted.

**Stirling family of engineers** Begun by **Robert** Stirling (1790–1878), Church of Scotland minister of Galston, who invented a hot-air engine, recognised today as having commercial potential. His sons Patrick and James, and Patrick's son Matthew, were all notable locomotive engineers. **Patrick** (1820–95), who worked for the Glasgow and South Western and Great Northern railways, was the most successful. **James** (1835–1917) succeeded his brother on the Glasgow and South Western, and then went to the South Eastern Railway in England. **Matthew** (1856–1931) became the locomotive engineer of the Hull and Barnsley Railway. Patrick's 'eight-foot' single-driver express locomotives were among the most beautiful ever built.

**Stirlingshire** Former county in central Scotland. In 1975 it mostly became part of **Central Region**; see map on p.395, **Stirling** (local authority) and **local government**.

**Stirling University** Founded in 1967, the campus is on the old Airthrey estate near **Bridge of Allan**, and includes Airthrey Castle, designed 1790–91 by Robert **Adam** for Robert **Haldane**, much altered in the 1890s. Within the campus is the MacRobert Arts Centre, with cinema, gallery and performance space.

**Stirling, Sir William Alexander, Earl of** see **Alexander, Sir William**

**St Kilda** (Gaelic **Hirt**) Group of remote small islands and sea stacks 70km (40mi) west of **North Uist**. It is likely that the name St Kilda dervies from a copyist's error of the Old Icelandic *Skildir*. No Saint Kilda has ever been recorded. Hirta, the largest island, was inhabited from prehistoric times until 1930; its massive cliff, Conachair, is the highest in Britain (425m/1394ft). The cliffs of Boreray are almost as tall, flanked by the rock pillars of Stac an Armin and Stac Lee. The island of Soay was home to the Soay sheep, a primitive

*St Kilda: looking towards Village Bay.*

breed still found there and on Hirta, but now also worldwide as a specialist breed. The islands are home to seabirds such as puffins, fulmars and gannets, which provided food and oil for the inhabitants. There is a defence installation on Hirta, now run by civilians. The islands are owned by the **National Trust for Scotland** and leased to **Scottish Natural Heritage**, and have been designated a World Heritage Site.

**Stob Binnein** Mountain, a **Munro** (1165m/3821ft), just to the south of **Ben More**, near **Crianlarich**.

**Stob Ghabhar** Mountain, a **Munro** (1090m/3576ft), to the northwest of **Bridge of Orchy**.

**Stobhall** Estate to the northeast of **Perth**, with a magical group of 17th-century buildings on a steep hillside site, built by the 2nd Earl of Perth, comprising gatehouse, house, brewhouse, chapel and library. It is still owned by the Earls of Perth and was restored in the 1960s.

**Stobo** Tiny hamlet in the **Tweed** valley, near **Peebles**, with an essentially Romanesque church with later features. The 19th-century Stobo Castle is now a health clinic. In the grounds there is a splendid Japanese-style water garden.

**Stoer** (pronounced 'store') Remote Highland coastal village between **Lochinver** and **Kylesku**; nearby are a small **lighthouse** and the ruins of a substantial **broch**. The Stoer Group of rocks in the area are the oldest non-metamorphosed sediments in Scotland.

**Stonehaven** (pop. 9577) Former **fishing** town 21km (13mi) south of **Aberdeen**, now mainly a commuter area. Old Stonehaven was founded by George Keith, 5th Earl Marischal,

S

who also built the Old Tolbooth at the harbour. New Stonehaven was created by the Barclays of Ury in the 18th century, and developed into a base for herring fishing. Its winter fire festival, involving the swinging of balls of fire, takes place at **Hogmanay**.

**Stone of Destiny** **Kenneth mac Alpin** is said to have brought the Stone of Destiny, also known as the Stone of **Scone**, symbol of sovereignty and, according to legend, the stone used by Jacob as a pillow, from **Dunstaffnage** to the Moot Hill at Scone, the seat of government. Edward I took the stone to Westminster Abbey in 1297, but all Scottish kings were inaugurated at Scone until **James I**. Some allege that the real stone was hidden in a cave and a replica taken to London. The stone was removed from Westminster in 1950 by Scottish Nationalists and was found on the altar of **Arbroath** Abbey Church in 1951. It was finally returned to Scotland in 1996, and is kept in **Edinburgh** Castle.

**Stornoway** (Gaelic **Steornabhagh**) Main town and port of the Isle of **Lewis**, on the east coast, the administrative centre of the **Western Isles** Council. No more than a village until the later 18th century, the town retains some Georgian elegance. It was a centre of the herring industry, then a **tweed**-weaving town, and now depends largely on oil and tourism. The 19th-century Lews Castle, built by Sir James **Matheson**, was presented by Lord **Leverhulme** to the town; a college stands in its grounds. It is linked to the mainland by a ferry to **Ullapool** and air services to **Inverness**, **Glasgow** and to other islands from its airport at Melbost, both of which have recently begun Sunday services against opposition from local churches.

**Storr, Old Man of** (Gaelic **Bod Stòrr** or **Bodach Stòrr**) A rock pinnacle (49m/160ft) on the ridge of Storr in Trotternish, **Skye**. A Viking-Age silver hoard was found at its foot and is now in the **Museum of Scotland**.

**stovies** A dish of sliced onion and potato lightly fried and then stewed in water or stock, sometimes with the addition of cooked meat.

**Stracathro** Village near **Brechin**, site of the most northerly known Roman fort. It features in the *Chronicles of Fordun* as the scene of the defeat of Angus, Earl of Moray by **David I** in 1130. The churchyard at Stracathro was one of the places where John, **Balliol**, King of Scots, submitted to Edward I in 1296 and, in 1452, the Earl of Crawford, fighting for the Douglases, was defeated on the Hill of Stracathro by the Earl of Huntly leading the king's supporters. A World War II hospital was built in the park of Stracathro House, a magnificent Greek-revival mansion

of 1827–8. It was kept going to serve RAF Edzell.

**Strachur** Small village on the **Cowal** peninsula close to the east side of Loch **Fyne**. The Creggans Inn was run for many years by Sir Fitzroy **Maclean**, whose Strachur House was built c.1780.

**Strange, Sir Robert** (1721–92) Artist, b. near Kirkwall, Orkney. Strange's career was inextricably linked with Prince Charles Edward **Stewart**, whose portrait he engraved, and whom he fought alongside at **Culloden**. He spent most of his subsequent life in London or on the Continent, and achieved an international reputation for his line engravings.

**Stranraer** Port at the head of Loch Ryan, a former royal **burgh**, with regular ferries to Belfast (formerly to Larne). It took over from **Portpatrick** as the ferry port in the 1870s. A holiday resort, with pleasant beaches and other sporting facilities, it has the remains of the 16th-century Castle of St John; it was restored as a visitor centre in 1988–90. Nearby Craigcaffie Tower was built in 1570; it has superb gargoyles.

**strath** A river valley, especially when broad and flat, from Gaelic *srath*. Often found in place names; see below, and see also **glen**.

**Strathaven** (pronounced 'stray ven') Small town near **Hamilton**, established as a weaving town, with the ruins of 15th-century Avondale Castle. Sir Harry **Lauder** latterly lived here, in 'Lauder Ha'. Dungavel House, formerly a shooting lodge of the Dukes of Hamilton, was the landing place aimed for by Nazi leader Rudolf Hess when he bailed out of an aircraft over Scotland in 1941. In recent years it has been used as a prison and as a centre for asylum seekers.

**Strathblane** Village northwest of **Glasgow**, at the foot of the **Campsie Fells**, now a commuter suburb. Nearby is restored Duntreath Castle, with a fine 16th-century gatehouse. It has belonged to the Edmonstone family since 1434.

**Strathcarron** Valley of the River Carron which flows east to the Kyle of **Sutherland** at **Bonar Bridge**.

**Strathcarron** Small village near the head of **Loch Carron**, with a station on the **Inverness** to **Kyle of Lochalsh** railway.

**Strathclyde** British kingdom from at least the 5th century whose authority at times reached into northwestern England. A significant force among the warring kingdoms of North Britain, the power of Strathclyde was greatly reduced by the Norse invasion which saw the capital, **Dumbarton**, sacked in 871. Closely tied with the kingdom of the Scots thereafter, Strathclyde's independent existence finally came to an end in the early 11th century. See also **Strathclyde Region**.

**Strathclyde Region** The largest (in population) of the 9 regions forming the upper tier of local government from 1975 to 1996, formed from the former counties of **Bute**, **Dunbartonshire**, **Lanarkshire**, **Renfrewshire**, **Ayrshire**, most of **Argyll** and parts of **Stirlingshire**, and the City of **Glasgow**. It included the following districts: Argyll and Bute, Bearsden and Milngavie, Clydebank, Clydesdale, Cumbernauld and Kilsyth, Cumnock and Doone Valley, Cunninghame, Dumbarton, East Kilbride, Eastwood, Glasgow, Hamilton, Inverclyde, Kilmarnock and Loudon, Kyle and Carrick, Monklands, Motherwell, Renfrew, Strathkelvin. See maps on pp.394–5 and **local government**.

**Strathclyde University** This university, with strong links with industry, traces its origins to Anderson's University, founded in 1796 (see John **Anderson**). In 1887 it became the Glasgow and West of Scotland Technical College, in 1912 the Royal Technical College, and in 1956 the Royal College of Science and Technology. The University received its charter in 1964, incorporating the Scottish College of Commerce, and in 1993 Jordanhill College of Education. Its main campus is in the centre of **Glasgow**; one of the main buildings is the massive Royal College Building, designed by David Barclay and built in 1903–10. There are 13,000 students.

**Strathcona, Donald A Smith, Lord** (1820–1914) Canadian financier and politician, b. Forres. A clerk in the Hudson's Bay Company, he rose to become its governor, and he was a driving force behind the Canadian Pacific Railway. He became a Canadian MP and from 1896, High Commissioner for Canada in London. He gave from his great wealth to charitable and educational bodies.

**Strathdon** Aberdeenshire village where the Water of Nochty meets the River **Don**. Billy **Connolly** owns Candacraig House to the southwest.

**Strathearn** The fertile valley of the River Earn, extending from Loch **Earn** in the west to the Firth of **Tay**, through **Comrie**, **Crieff** and **Bridge of Earn**.

**Strathkelvin District** see **Strathclyde Region**

**Strathmore** Wide fertile valley, running from **Methven** to **Brechin** between the Sidlaw Hills and the **Grampians**.

**Strathnaver** Fertile valley extending 30km (19mi) from Loch Naver to the north coast. It was the scene of wholesale eviction from 1812 to 1819 in the **Clearances**, and these events are reviewed in the Strath Naver Museum at **Bettyhill** village.

**Strathpeffer** This town near **Dingwall** had been in the 19th century a celebrated spa with mineral springs, and a new spa facility was opened in 1989. It is an important tourist centre, with several large hotels. Nearby is Castle Leod, seat of the Earls of **Cromartie**, built in 1619, and extended in Victorian times; the Strathpeffer **Highland Games** are held in its grounds.

**Strathspey** The broad central valley of the River **Spey**, between **Aviemore** and **Craigellachie**. The traditional home of Clan Grant, whose seat is **Castle Grant** near **Grantown-on-Spey**. In 1978 the Strathspey Steam Railway reopened an old line as a tourist attraction; it is based at **Aviemore** station and runs north via **Boat of Garten** to Broomhill (which has been used as Glenbogle Station in the BBC's *Monarch of the Glen* television series). See also **Speyside**.

**strathspey** A traditional Scottish country dance, slower than a **reel**, now usually danced in sets of 3, 4 or 5 couples; the tune to which it is danced. See also next and **Royal Scottish Country Dance Society**.

**strathspey and reel societies** Also known as accordion and fiddle clubs or box and fiddle clubs. There are over 70 such groups throughout Scotland. Although they organise occasional concerts, their primary purpose is to meet to celebrate together through performance the instrumental element of Scotland's dance music.

**Stroma** Island in the **Pentland Firth**, 4km (2.5mi) off **John o' Groats**, inhabited until the 1950s, and now used as pasture.

**Stromeferry** (Gaelic **Port an t-Sròim**) Village near the mouth of **Loch Carron** in **Wester Ross**, on the south side of the loch, where it narrows. There was a car ferry across the loch until 1973 when a new road was opened on the east shore of the loch. Strome Castle, on a rocky promontory on the north shore, was once a major fortress of the MacDonells of Glengarry, but was destroyed in 1602 during a feud with the Mackenzies of Kintail; in the care of the **National Trust for Scotland**.

**Stromness** (pop. 1609) Town (formerly called Hamnavoe) on southwest of **Orkney** Mainland, with a sheltered harbour protected by the island of **Hoy**. Once a major trading centre with the Baltic ports and North America, it still has buildings with Scandinavian features. It is the ferry port for services from **Scrabster** and a base for maintaining the Orkney **lighthouses**. It was the birthplace and home of George Mackay **Brown**.

**Stronsay** (pop. 343) One of the northern isles of **Orkney** and a centre of the 19th-century herring industry. There are remains of an Early Christian monastery on Papa Stronsay off the east coast.

**Strontian** (pronounced strontyeean) (Gaelic **Sròn an t-Sithein**) Village in **Morvern** near the head of **Loch Sunart**. After the **Disruption** of 1843, the local landlord refused permission for

*Easter Sugar House, Gallowgate, Glasgow, drawn by William Simpson. It was the second of 6 sugar refineries set up by the merchants of Glasgow; it was demolished around 1850.*

the building of a **Free Church** and the congregation set up a floating church in the Loch, which was used till 1873. Lead mining took place here intermittently in the 18th and 19th centuries and the element strontium was isolated by Sir Humphry Davy in 1808, from Strontianite, mined in this area.

**Struth, Bill** (1875–1956) Football manager and administrator, b. Glasgow. Manager of **Rangers** from 1920 to 1954, he was also on the club's board from 1947. A stern disciplinarian, he presided over one of the most successful teams in Rangers' history, the side which won 5 consecutive championships from 1927.

**Stuart** alternative spelling of **Stewart**.

**Stuart, John McDouall** (1815–66) Explorer, b. Dysart, Fife, after whom Mount Stuart in Australia is named. He joined Charles Stuart's last expedition, made several explorations of the interior, and crossed Australia from south to north in 1860.

**STV** see **Scottish Television**

**Sueno's Stone** see **Forres**

**sugar** Trade between the River **Clyde** and the West Indies brought sugar cane to Scotland and with it a sugar-refining industry, especially in **Greenock** and **Glasgow**. There were also sugar houses in **Leith**, **Burntisland** and **Aberdeen**. The making of sugar machinery was a West of Scotland speciality. Abram Lyle (1820–91), of the sugar company Tate and Lyle, was born in Scotland, but moved to London to set up a refinery, taking with him his workers from Greenock. He introduced golden syrup (known as treacle in England) as a spreadable form of sugar. Especially in **Fife**, sugar beet is grown for animal fodder and for sugar production. Scotland's only sugar-beet factory operated in **Cupar**, Fife from 1926 till the 1970s.

**Suilven** (Gaelic **Sula-bheinn**) An unusually shaped 3-peaked ridge (731m/2399ft), with sheer rock walls, in the northwest **Highlands** near **Lochinver**. The Bealach Mor, or Great Pass, provides a way up for most climbers.

**Sula Sgeir** Remote small island 65km (41mi) north of the Butt of **Lewis**, where the men of Ness, Lewis, now under licence, go in late summer to collect young gannets (solan geese), a local delicacy, known in Gaelic as the **guga**. Now part of the North Rona and Sula Sgeir National Nature Reserve with seal and gannet colonies.

**Sullom Voe** A deep sea inlet off Yell Sound in the north of the **Shetland** Mainland. Near the entrance to the Voe, on the peninsula of Calback Ness, is the largest British oil terminal, fed by the Brent and Ninian pipelines.

**Sumburgh** Small village at the south end of **Shetland** Mainland and the site of Shetland's airport; it has a helicopter base for the North Sea oil industry. In January 1993 the oil-tanker *Braer* sank just off the coast and broke up, causing a massive oil spill. Its potentially devastating effects were mitigated by circumstances, including the weather conditions. **Sumburgh** Head, at the southern tip of Shetland, has a **lighthouse** dating from 1821, designed by Robert Stevenson. Just off the Head is the Sumburgh Roost, a savage tidal current whose noise can be heard well inland. Nearby is **Jarlshof** archaeological site.

**Summer Isles** (Gaelic **Na h-Eileanan Samhraidh**) Group of small islands at the mouth of **Loch Broom** in **Wester Ross**. Only one, Tanera Mor, has been inhabited in recent times. Sir Frank Fraser **Darling** lived there in the late 1930s and early 1940s, as an experiment in island living.

**Sunday Herald** see **Herald**

**Sunday Mail** A tabloid Sunday paper, sister paper of the **Daily Record**. Launched in 1917, it now belongs to Trinity Mirror Group.

**Sunday Post** A popular family-oriented weekly paper published by D C **Thomson** from 1919, it once boasted that it was read by

95% of the Scottish population. Its readers are devoted to the long-lived comic strips portraying the large family 'The Broons' and the hapless innocent 'Oor Wullie'.

**superintendent** In 1560 the first **General Assembly** of the **Church of Scotland** divided the country into 10 districts; the superintendent was the minister in charge of a district, who travelled between parishes instituting ministers. Though their districts corresponded roughly to the old dioceses, their powers were more those of a dean than of a bishop.

**superior** A feudal overlord who granted heritable estates or entitlements to another who thereby became a **vassal**, owing payments or services in return. The system continued until recently in Scots property law; see **feu**.

**Surgeons, Royal College of** see **Royal College of Surgeons**

**Sutherland** (Gaelic **Cataibh**) Former county in the northern **Highlands**; in 1975 a slightly larger area became the Sutherland District of **Highland Region** and in 1996 it became part of **Highland** local authority.

**Sutherland, Duke and Duchess of** George Leveson-Gower, Marquis of Stafford (1758-1833) married Elizabeth Sutherland (1765-1839), Countess of Sutherland in her own right, and they became 1st Duke and Duchess of Sutherland in 1832. In carrying out improvements on their Sutherland estates, they were among the most notorious figures of the Highland **Clearances**. She was blamed even more fiercely, especially for her callous comments on the plight of the homeless. It is estimated that 15,000 tenants were evicted, of whom some died of hunger and exposure; they were replaced by 200,000 sheep. The improvements they made in east Sutherland have, however, had lasting benefits. See also Patrick **Sellar**.

**Sutherland, Robert Garioch** see **Garioch, Robert**

**Sutherland District** see **Sutherland**

**Sutors of Cromarty** Two prominent headlands on the north and south sides of the **Cromarty Firth**. The name also refers to a hamlet near the south Sutor.

**Swan, Annie S(hepherd)** (1859-1943) Novelist, b. near Coldingham in the **Borders**. A prolific writer of romantic novels and stories for women's magazines.

**Sween, Loch** see **Loch Sween**

**Sweetheart Abbey** In the village of **New Abbey**, south of Dumfries, the beautiful red sandstone ruins of a Cistercian abbey church founded in 1273 by **Devorguilla**, who was buried here with the heart of her husband John **Balliol**; fragments

of her tomb remain. The church was saved from destruction in the 1790s, and is now in the care of **Historic Scotland**.

**sword dance** see **Highland dancing**

**Symington** A commuter village between Prestwick and Kilmarnock, with a Romanesque church.

**Symington** Small village in Lanarkshire, 5km (3mi) southwest of **Biggar**.

**Symington, William** (1763-1831) Inventor, b. Leadhills. He devised improvements in mine-pumping engines and patented a steam-powered road vehicle in 1787, and built a steam-driven paddle-wheeler boat in 1788 for Patrick **Miller**, tested on **Dalswinton** Loch. In 1802 he built the *Charlotte Dundas*, one of the earliest working steamboats. Sadly his ideas were not immediately taken up, and he died in poverty.

**synod** In the **Presbyterian churches**, the church court intermediate between the **Presbytery** and the **General Assembly**. In the smaller churches with no general assembly, the synod is the supreme court.

**Synod of Original Seceders** see **Presbyterian Churches**

*Sweetheart Abbey, New Abbey, Dumfries and Galloway.*

363

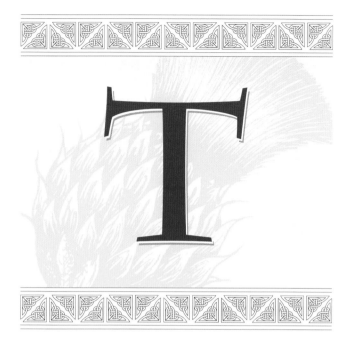

**tablet** A sweet made of sugar, butter and condensed milk, resembling, but harder than, fudge.

**tacksman** A tenant or lessee, specifically in the **Highlands** from the 16th to the 19th century, a chief tenant, often a relative of the landowner, who leased land directly from him and sub-let it to lesser tenants.

**taigh geal** see **black house**

**Tail of the Bank** Safe anchorage on the Firth of **Clyde**, off **Greenock** and **Gourock**, where large ships prepared for trial, large liners anchored to pick up passengers, and wartime convoys assembled.

**Tain** (Gaelic **Baile Dhuthaich**) (pop. 3511) Small but architecturally impressive town on the south shore of the **Dornoch Firth**, 15km (10mi) northeast of Invergordon, a former **burgh**, and once a pilgrimage centre to the shrine of St Duthac, who was born here around 1000 AD. Having fled to the shrine for safety, female relatives of **Robert I** were captured by the Earl of Ross in 1306. The Tolbooth was rebuilt (1706–8) in an older style, and there are 3 medieval churches dedicated to St Duthac. Tain Through Time is a visitor centre illustrating the town's long history, including its role as a pilgrimage centre. Highland Fine Cheeses was established in the 1960s and the **Glenmorangie** Distillery is nearby. A wartime aerodrome has recently been used as a firing range.

**Tait, Archibald Campbell** (1811–82) Clergyman, b. Edinburgh. Brought up a presbyterian, he entered the Church of England in 1836. In 1842 he succeeded Dr Arnold as headmaster of Rugby School. He became Dean of Carlisle in 1849 and Bishop of London in 1856. In 1868 he became the first Scottish Archbishop of Canterbury.

**Tait, Thomas Smith** (1882–1954) Architect b. Paisley. He was a partner of Sir John **Burnet** from 1919 and successor to his practice as Burnet, Tait and Lorne, London. A classical-modern designer, he was responsible for St Andrews House, **Edinburgh** (1934–9) and the **Glasgow** Empire Exhibition of 1938.

**Talisker** The only distillery on the Isle of **Skye**, at Carbost on the shores of Loch Harport. Established in 1830, it produces a single malt and has a visitor centre. The village and bay of the same name are some distance away on the west coast of the island.

**Tamdhu Distillery** see **Knockando**

**Tam o' Shanter** see **Burns, Robert**

**Tanera Mor** see **Summer Isles**

**Tannadice** see **Dundee United**

**Tannahill, Robert** (1774–1810) Poet, b. Paisley. A weaver without formal education, he collected traditional songs and wrote sentimental songs and poems including 'Gloomy Winter's noo awa' and 'Jessie the Flower o' Dunblane'. He drowned himself in the Glasgow, Paisley and Johnstone Canal, believing that his work was not valued, but it became posthumously very popular.

**Tannahill Weavers** Band formed in **Paisley** in 1968. Their hard-driving approach to Scots traditional song and tune, incorporating old and newer instruments, has made them highly popular as they constantly tour and record abroad. Dougie **MacLean** is a former member.

**Tantallon Castle** On a clifftop between **North Berwick** and **Dunbar**, in East Lothian, a powerful ruin partly in red sandstone, virtually one huge curtain wall, built in the late 14th century. For years a Douglas stronghold, it was destroyed by General Monck in 1651. In the care of **Historic Scotland**.

**Tap o' Noth** see **Rhynie**

**Taransay** (Gaelic **Tarasaigh**) Small island just off the west coast of South **Harris**, used in 2000 by the BBC as the setting for *Castaway*, which isolated a number of people on the uninhabited island for a year. See also **Luskentyre**.

**Tarbat** see **Portmahomack**

**Tarbat House** Classical late 18th-century mansion on the shores of the **Cromarty Firth**, 8km (5mi) northeast of **Invergordon**, designed by James McLeran (1790). It belonged to the Earls of Cromartie until 1962, and is now derelict.

**Tarbat Ness** Headland between the **Dornoch** and **Moray Firths**. Its **lighthouse** was built by Robert Stevenson in 1830 and altered in 1892.

**Tarbert** (Gaelic **An Tairbeart**). Village, once a herring port, on East Loch Tarbert, the northernmost and narrowest point of **Kintyre**. It is said that in 1098 Magnus Barelegs, King of Norway, had himself dragged across the isthmus in his ship to prove that Kintyre was an island and therefore a Norse possession. The remains of Tarbert Castle, a royal castle, overlook the small harbour and the oval vitrified fort of Dun Skeig is nearby. The very sheltered harbour is now much used by yachts.

**Tarbert** (Gaelic **An Tairbeart**), The main village, port and car ferry for **Harris** in the Outer **Hebrides**, on the narrow link between North Harris and South Harris.

**Tarbolton** Small former mining village between **Prestwick** and **Mauchline**, with a tall-spired church of 1821; it is associated with Robert **Burns**, who found inspiration for some of his poems here; the cottage where he founded the Bachelors' Club in 1780 is now in the care of the **National Trust for Scotland**. There is a fine Georgian parish church.

**tartan** Originally woollen cloth in a pattern of different coloured stripes at right angles to each other, in arrangements known as setts, now referring also to such a pattern used for many different purposes, from carpets to ties and ribbons. Uses include high fashion as well as everyday wear in many parts of the world. Used by Highlanders from early times, tartan was forbidden in the Disarming Act of 1746 as part of the attempts to destroy the Highland way of life in the aftermath of the 1745 **Jacobite Rising**; the Act was not repealed until 1782. Exempted from the ban were the Highland regiments, by then part of the British army. They wore Highland dress in tartan known as 'government pattern', squares of black, dark green and blue (still worn by the **Black Watch**); each of the other regiments had its own distinctive overcheck of red, white or yellow. The belief formerly prevailed that each **clan** had developed its own tartan from early times, but the concept of clan tartans is now known to have been created in the early 19th century, principally by a weaving company, Wilson of **Bannockburn**, encouraged by the preparations for the visit of King George IV to **Edinburgh** in 1822. Tartans are popular worldwide and special patterns have been developed for districts, societies, organisations, as well as clans. See also

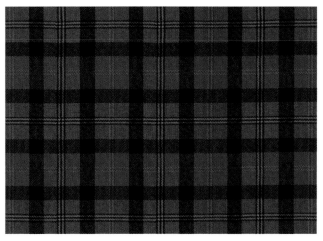

*The Malcolm tartan.*

**balmoral**, **dirk**, **Highland dress**, **kilt**, **plaid**, **sgian dubh**, **Sobieski Stuarts**, **sporran**, **trews** and **Scottish Tartans Society**.

**Tarves** A mainly 19th-century village near **Ellon**, Aberdeenshire, distinguished by the strange 19th-century folly known as Prop of Ythsie. Nearby are **Haddo House** and Tolquhon Castle; Tarves kirkyard has a fine medieval tomb commemorating William Forbes of Tolquhon.

**Tarvit** see **Hill of Tarvit**

**Tassie, James** (1735–99) Artist, b. Pollokshaws, Glasgow. By the late 18th century Tassie had become the most important portrait and antique-gem modeller in Scotland, using a special paste, which he had co-invented while working in Dublin. His portrait medallions were of numerous prominent people of the age; there is a large collection in the **Scottish National Portrait Gallery**. In 1792 he was famously commissioned by Catherine the Great of Russia to produce 12,000 pastes, housed in a specially made, highly adorned cabinet.

**tattie** see **potato**

**tatties and herrin** Dish of salt herring, lightly boiled, and boiled potatoes. Traditionally the herring were cooked briefly on top of the potatoes.

**tattie scone** A thin flat scone of mashed potato, milk and flour.

**Taversöe Tuick Chambered Cairn** see **Rousay**

**tawse** A leather strap with thongs at one end, formerly used to administer discipline in Scottish schools, until corporal punishment was banned by the European Court of Human Rights in 1982. See **Lochgelly**.

**Tay** (Gaelic **Tatha**) The River Tay flows from the eastern end of **Loch Tay** at **Kenmore** to the **Firth of Tay** at **Dundee**. It is famous for its salmon and trout.

**Tay, Firth of** The sandbank-filled estuary of the River **Tay**, from the confluence of the Rivers **Earn** and Tay, past **Dundee**, where it narrows, to the headland of Buddon Ness which juts into the North Sea.

**Tay, Loch** see **Loch Tay**

**Tay Bridges** The railway bridge across the River **Tay** at **Dundee**, 3km (2mi) long, was built 1882-8 by the engineers W H and Crawford Barlow and was the longest bridge in Britain. It replaced the earlier bridge (1878) by Thomas Bouch, destroyed in a gale in 1879, with the loss of a train and 75 lives. This was one of the most disastrous structural failures in the UK. The event was immortalised in a poem by William **McGonagall**. The road bridge, by engineers W A Fairhurst and Partners, completed in 1966, is over 2km (1.4mi) long.

**Taylor, Sir George** (1904-93) Botanist, b. Edinburgh. From assistant Keeper of Botany in 1928 he became Keeper of the British Museum (Natural History) in 1950 and Director at the Royal Botanic Garden Kew from 1956 to 1971. During this time he transformed Kew and acquired Wakehurst Place as its specialist garden. In 1938 he joined Ludlow and George **Sherriff** on an expedition to southeast Tibet. On his retirement he was Director of the Stanley Smith Horticultural Foundation, helping many budding gardeners and financing good projects and plant expeditions. His monograph on *Meconopsis* (1934) is still the standard work.

**Taylor, James** (1835-92) Tea planter, b. Laurencekirk, Kincardineshire. He went to work on the coffee estates in Ceylon (now Sri Lanka) in 1851, just before the coffee fungus destroyed the industry. He was involved in the earliest experiments with tea planting, set up the first tea factory on the island and invented a tea-rolling machine. Ceylon tea soon outstripped China in popularity, and the take-over of the industry by big business led to his dismissal, but he never returned to Scotland.

**Taylor, Sir Teddy** (1937- ) Politician, b. Glasgow. Conservative MP for Glasgow Cathcart from 1964-79, when he lost his seat to Labour, he has been MP for Rochford and Southend East since 1980.

**Taymouth, Black Book of** A collection of materials made between 1598 and 1648, covering the history and genealogy of the Campbells of Glenorchy. An important historical source, it was published in the 19th century, edited by Cosmo **Innes**.

**Taymouth Castle** Huge castellated mansion near **Kenmore**, Perthshire, on the site of an earlier castle (known as Balloch Castle) of the Earls of **Breadalbane**. It was built by Archibald and James Elliot (1802-10) and spectacularly enlarged by James Gillespie **Graham** and A W N Pugin (1838-42) with painted decoration by J G Crace. It was later a hotel, hospital, civil defence college and a school. Now privately owned, the estate offers golf and fishing to the public.

**Taynuilt** (Gaelic **Taigh an Uillt**) Village east of **Oban**, close to **Loch Etive**, where it is joined by the River **Awe**, with nearby the impressive hydroelectric Inverawe power station by James Shearer (1959-65). It was once an iron-smelting centre (see **Bonawe**), now a holiday base for anglers and climbers.

**Tayport** Village on the south bank of the Firth of **Tay**, a former **burgh** and railway ferry port to **Broughty Ferry**. It has a quaint parish church of 1794 and 1825 with a tower, and a simple but sophisticated RC Church of Our Lady Star of the Sea by Reginald Fairlie (1938-9), with sculpture by Hew **Lorimer**.

**Tayside Region** One of the 9 regions forming the upper tier of local government from 1975 to 1996, formed from the former counties of **Angus**, **Kinross**, part of **Perth** and **Dundee** City. It consisted of the districts of **Perth and Kinross**, **Angus** and **Dundee** City, which are now unitary local authorities (with slightly altered boundaries). See maps on pp.394-5 and **local government**.

**Tayvallich** (Gaelic **Taigh a' Bhealaich**) Village on an inlet of **Loch Sween**, near the **Knapdale** Forest, with a very sheltered harbour, popular for yachting.

**teabread** Semi-sweet buns, **scones**, **pancakes** etc, often eaten with tea.

**Tealing** Village to the north of **Dundee** with a remarkable **doocot** built in 1595. Nearby is a substantial Iron Age earthhouse with a cup and ring marked stone, discovered in 1871. Both in the care of **Historic Scotland**. John **Glas**, founder of the Glasites, was minister here until he was deposed in 1726. Sandstone from Tealing provided building and paving stones widely used in Dundee in the 19th century.

**Teallach, An** (Gaelic, meaning 'the forge') Mountain massif in **Wester Ross** near the head of Little Loch Broom. It has 3 ridges and 2 of its peaks are **Munros**: Bidein a' Ghlas Thuill (1062m/3484ft) and Sgurr Fiona (1060m/3478ft).

**Tedder, Arthur W, Lord** (1890-1967) Airforce commander, b. Glenguin, Stirlingshire. He joined the Royal Flying Corps in World

War I, and later became Director-General of Research and Development at the Air Ministry. During World War II he commanded the Middle East Air Force, cooperating closely with the 8th Army in North Africa. He later became Eisenhower's deputy supreme commander. In 1945 he was made Marshal of the RAF.

**Teenage Fanclub** Rock group formed in Glasgow in 1989, based around the trio of singer-songwriters, Norman Blake, Gerard Love and Raymond McGinley. Their guitar-based melodies are reminiscent of 1960s American groups. Their love and mastery of the genre is shown to best effect on their albums *Bandwagonesque* and *Grand Prix*.

**teinds** The tenth portion of the produce of a parish (known as 'tithe' in England) and anciently claimed by the church. At the **Reformation** the right to collect teinds became a 'property' which could be bought and sold to individuals called 'titulars' (with the minister's stipend being a burden on the teinds). By the terms of the 1925 Church Act, landowners, known as **heritors**, have paid specified sums to the **Church of Scotland**, effectively from what were formerly the parish teinds.

**Teith** River running from **Loch Venachar** in the **Trossachs**, through **Callander**, where it is joined by the River Leny, and past **Doune** to join the River **Forth** near **Stirling**.

**Telfer, Jim** (1940– ) Rugby player and coach, b. Pathhead, Midlothian. A hardworking, uncompromising forward for **Melrose** and Scotland, he successfully applied those qualities to his coaching career. He made his club the strongest in the country, and then took over as national coach, taking Scotland to the Grand Slam in 1984. He was assistant to Ian **McGeechan** when the team repeated the feat 6 years later, and also twice coached the British Lions. He became Scotland's Director of Rugby in 1999, retiring 4 years later.

**Telford, Thomas** (1757–1834) Civil engineer, b. Westerkirk near Langholm. One of the most outstanding 19th-century civil engineers in the UK, he was first apprenticed to a stonemason. He became surveyor of works for Shropshire in 1787 and designed many features of the Ellesmere Canal (now known as the Llangollen canal). After reporting on the need for public works in Scotland he built the **Caledonian Canal** (1803–23),

*An early 20th-century advertisement for Templeton's Carpets, Glasgow. The façade of the factory was designed by William Leiper, modelled on the Doge's Palace in Venice.*

many roads and harbours and hundreds of bridges; see **Commission for Highland Roads and Bridges**. Outside Scotland he built the Menai suspension bridge, St Katherine's Docks, London, and contributed to drainage projects in the Fens. He was the main designer for the Gota Canal which links the west and east coasts of Sweden. He was the first President of the Institution of Civil Engineers in London.

**Temperley, Joe** (1929– ) Jazz musician, b. Lochgelly, Fife. His career as a saxophonist began in the late 1940s with a succession of English bands, then in 1965 he moved to New York. He has been based in the USA since, and has worked with many of the great names of the genre.

**Templars** see **Knights Templars**

**Temple** Picturesque village in Midlothian, 4km (3mi) southwest of **Gorebridge**, headquarters of the **Knights Templars** until their suppression in 1312. Their buildings have gone but there is a fine roofless parish church of c.1300 and a handsome new church of 1832, now a house. The artist Sir William **Gillies** lived in the village for many years. **Arniston House** is nearby.

**Templeton, James and Co Ltd** Carpet makers, founded in 1839 by James Templeton and John Quiglay, initially specialised in their invention of the chenille axminster carpet. The firm later made wilton carpets, and from about 1890 spool axminster carpets. It became the largest of its kind in Scotland, and a major exporter. In the 1960s its business was badly hit by cheap imports and it closed in about 1980. The so-called 'Doge's Palace' building of 1888–90 facing Glasgow Green, built for spool axminster carpet weaving, is an iconic Victorian factory of international repute.

**Temple Wood Stone Circles** see **Kilmartin**

**tenement** In Scotland the term usually refers to a large building, usually of 3 or more storeys, divided into flats; it also refers to the section of such a building served by one stair.

**Tennant, Charles** (1768–1838) Industrialist, b. Ochiltree, Ayrshire. His exploitation of his (and other inventors') experiments with bleaching textiles made him a fortune, particularly his patenting of a chlorine-based powder bleach invented by Charles **Macintosh**. His St Rollox Chemical Works was the largest in the world by the 1830s.

**Tennant, Emma** (1937– ) Novelist, b. London. She worked as a journalist on women's fashion magazines before beginning to publish novels, often with a particular women's slant, which include revisionary treatments of classic texts, for example, *The Bad Sister* (1978), *Two Women of London* (1989), *Tess* (1993) and *Emma in Love* (1996). Some of her most recent works have focused on her own life and family, such as *Strangers: a family romance* (1998) and *Girlitude* (1999); she is a daughter of Lord Glenconner and spent some of her childhood on the family estate near **Peebles**.

**Tentsmuir** Area of consolidated and growing sand dunes on the northeast **Fife** coast, just to the north of **Leuchars**, mainly covered by Scots and Corsican pine plantations. It has a fine recreational beach.

**term days** The 4 days of the year, the quarter days, on which certain payments, e.g. rent or interest, become due, leases begin and end and, formerly, contracts of employment, especially on farms, began and ended. See **Candlemas**, **Lammas**, **Martinmas**, **Whitsunday**.

**Terpersie** Pioneer Z-plan house with circular towers, 5km (3mi) northwest of **Alford**, Aberdeenshire, built by the

*Desperate Dan, a cartoon character in the* Dandy, *published by D C Thomson.*

Gordons (1561), repaired after it was burnt in 1665 and re-roofed from ruins in 1983–9.

**Teviot** River in the **Borders** famed for its trout and salmon fishing. It rises in **Eskdalemuir** forest and flows northeast through **Hawick** to join the **Tweed** at **Kelso**.

**Teviotdale** The valley of the **Teviot**, stretching from Teviothead through **Hawick** to near Ancrum.

**thane** In the medieval period a Crown officer, often of noble rank, with fiscal and judicial responsibility for a district ranging from one to 3 or 4 parishes. Some **mormaers** (earls) and bishops were served by thanes. See **toiseach**.

**Theatrum Scotiae** see **Slezer, John**

**Thenew** see **Kentigern**

**Thin, James** (1824–1915) Bookseller, opened his first eponymous shop in **Edinburgh** in 1848 with great success; he became a friend of many authors including R L **Stevenson** and Thomas **Carlyle**. His company continued, with much recent expansion, until 2002, when the shops were taken over by Blackwells and Ottakars.

**Third Lanark Football Club** Founded in 1872 as an offshoot of the Third Regiment of the Lanarkshire Rifle Volunteers. Based at Cathkin Park in Glasgow, Thirds were champions in 1904 and Scottish Cup winners in 1889 and 1905. After a protracted decline they fell into financial trouble and were closed by court order in 1967.

**Thirlestane Castle** Long towered and turreted house in the **Borders**, on the **Leader** Water, to the northeast of **Lauder**. Built 1590 for Lord Maitland, it was remodelled (1670–7) by Sir William **Bruce** for the Duke of **Lauderdale**, with spectacular plasterwork by Houlbert and Dunsterfield; remodelled again by William **Burn** and David **Bryce** (1840–1). Still home to the Maitland family, it is owned by a trust and open to the public, with many visitor amenities; it incorporates the Borders Country Life Museum.

**thistle** Emblem of Scotland since the late Middle Ages; it appears on coins of **James III** in 1470. The Order of the Thistle is Scotland's senior order of chivalry. Though something similar may have existed earlier, it was established in 1687 by **James VII**, consisting of the sovereign and 12 knights (all sympathetic to the king's religious and political principles). After the Revolution of 1688 it fell into desuetude but was revived by Queen Anne in 1703. It now has 16 knights. Originally for landowners, after 1945 military and naval figures entered, and more recently political figures.

**Thom, Alexander** (1894–1985) Engineer and archaeological theorist, b. Argyll. Educated at **Glasgow University**, he was Professor of Engineering Science at Oxford. From the mid 1930s he studied the megalithic monuments of Brittany and Britain. His theories of astronomical calendars and megalithic measuring units have not been widely accepted, but his surveys have provided a good base for subsequent research. His publications include *Megalithic Sites in Britain* (1967) and *Megalithic Rings* (1980).

**Thomas the Rhymer** (*fl.* c.1270) Seer and poet, also known as Thomas of Erceldoune (see **Earlston**). His prophecies, published in 1602, included the Battle of **Bannockburn** and the accession of **James VI** to the English throne. His knowledge allegedly came from time spent in Elfland with a fairy mistress. He is the subject of a famous Border ballad.

**Thomason Charles S** (1833–1911) Piper and soldier, b. India, partly brought up on his grandfather's estate at Elchies, Moray, where pipers were employed. He collected and preserved many old manuscripts of pipe music and published *Ceol Mor, a Collection of Piobaireachd* (1900). He was the first President of the **Piobaireachd** Society.

**Thomson, Alexander** ('Greek' Thomson) (1817–75), b. Balfron, Stirlingshire. Internationally known architect who developed an individual style from pure Greek, Egyptian, Assyrian and Indian elements. His most important surviving works are St Vincent Street Church (1857–9); the Egyptian Halls, Union St (1873); Moray Place (1859); Great Western Terrace (1869); and Holmwood (1857), in the care of the **National Trust for Scotland**, all in **Glasgow**.

**Thomson, D C** Dundee newspaper firm built up by David Couper

*Dennis the Menace and Gnasher, cartoon characters in the Beano, published by D C Thomson.*

Thomson (1861–1954). Established under this name in 1905, the firm's 'serious' publications – the *Dundee Courier*, *Sunday Post*, *Scots Magazine* and *People's Friend* – are complemented by its comics, including the *Beano* and *Dandy*; many of the original cartoon characters created by the staff of D C Thomson, were illustrated by the English cartoonist, Dudley D Watkins (1906-69). Based in Dundee, D C Thomson is one of the few newspaper firms still to have an office in Fleet Street, London. They publish over 200 million magazines, comics and newspapers every year.

**Thomson, Derick** (**Ruaridh MacThomais**) (1921– ) Poet, b. Stornoway. Professor of Celtic at **Glasgow University** (1963–91) he was editor of **Gairm** and helped found the Gaelic Books Council in 1968. His poems are collected in *Creachadh na Clarsaich* (*Plundering the Harp*, 1982) and *Meall Garbh* (*Rugged Mountain* 1995) and he has written and edited many books on **Gaelic** culture and literature, including *An Introduction to Gaelic Poetry* (1974); he edited *The Companion to Gaelic Scotland* (1994).

**Thomson, George** (1757–1851) Publisher and editor, b. Limekilns, Fife. A musical enthusiast who collected together songs of Scotland and Ireland and harpers' tunes of Wales, commissioned lyrics from Robert **Burns**, Sir Walter **Scott**, James **Hogg** and others, and then engaged Haydn, Beethoven, Weber and other leading composers to write accompaniments for his *Select Collection of Original Scotish Airs* (6 volumes, 1793–1841).

**Thomson, Sir Godfrey Hilton** (1881–1955) Educationist and psychologist, b. Carlisle. Together with William **McClelland** he promoted the use of tests to select pupils for secondary education. These became known as the 'Thomson's Moray House Tests'. He was Professor of Education at **Edinburgh University** (1925–51), and head of Moray House, the Edinburgh teacher training centre.

**Thomson, James** (1700–48) Poet, b. Ednam, near Kelso. In 1725 he moved to London. A writer with an orotund style, he wrote (largely unsuccessful) plays, but is chiefly remembered for his long poem *The Seasons* (1730) and for the words of 'Rule Britannia'.

**T**

**Thomson, James** (1834–82) Poet, b. Port Glasgow. Also known by the pseudonym B V (Bysshe Vanolis, from the middle name of the poet Shelley and an anagram of Novalis, the German Romantic poet). Suffering from depression and alcoholism, he had several occupations, including journalism, mainly in London. He is best known for the poem 'City of Dreadful Night', a despairing portrayal of modern urban life.

**Thomson, John, of Duddingston** (1778–1840) Artist, b. Dailly, Ayrshire. Minister at Duddingston, **Edinburgh**, from 1805, Thomson is best known for his paintings of the Scottish landscape. Although considered an amateur artist, Thomson brought a romantic sensibility to his art (differentiating it from the neo-classical work of many of his more established contemporaries), which helped set the pattern for landscape painting in Scotland in the 19th century. He was a close friend of Sir Walter **Scott** and, along with J M W Turner, produced illustrations for Scott's *Provincial Antiquities of Scotland*.

**Thorfinn, Earl of Orkney** (d. c.1060). Known as 'the Mighty', he ruled **Orkney** and mainland Scotland as far as the **Moray Firth**. A powerful figure in the north, he defeated **Macbeth** in battle and was secure enough to make a pilgrimage to Rome in around 1050. His widow Ingibjorg married **Malcolm III**.

**Threave** Gigantic tower house built in the later 14th century by Archibald the Grim, Earl of Douglas, on a small island in the River **Dee** near **Castle Douglas**. Gutted by **Covenanters** in the 1640s, it remains as a forbidding ruin; in the care of **Historic Scotland**. Nearby are Threave House, a baronial mansion by **Peddie & Kinnear** (1871) for a Liverpool merchant, and its gardens, in the care of the **National Trust for Scotland**, whose school of horticulture has developed them over 45 years by student projects. The garden exhibits peat, rock and water features and shrub borders set in mature woodland. The classical walled garden, with its glass range, grows fruit and vegetables and has herbaceous borders.

**Three Chimneys** Award-winning restaurant near **Dunvegan** in the northwest of **Skye**. Run by Shirley and Eddie Spear, it specialises in local produce. It also has accommodation.

**Thurso** A town on the north coast, on Thurso Bay 32km (20 miles) west of **John o' Groats**, a former **burgh** and once a major trading port for Scandinavia. It has 17th- and 18th-century merchants' and fishermen's houses and some fine Georgian buildings. The River Thurso flows through the town with salmon and trout fishing, and the town is now popular as a surfing centre. With the development of the **Dounreay** nuclear power station in the 1950s and 60s, the population more than doubled. Nearby **Scrabster** has a ferry service to Stromness in **Orkney**. Thurso Heritage Museum presents the local history.

**Tibbie Shiels Inn** see **St Mary's Loch**

**Tighnabruaich** Small tourist resort of the Cowal peninsula, on the Kyles of **Bute**, popular for yachting, and for many years a destination for steamer trips from other piers on the River **Clyde**. At nearby **Kames** there was a gunpowder works.

**Tillicoultry** (pop. 5400) Town, a former **burgh**, at the base of the **Ochil Hills**, between **Dollar** and **Alva**. It was once an important centre of the textile industry, using water from local burns, and it had paper-coating industry in the 20th century. The largest surviving mill is now a retail furniture warehouse.

**Tillycairn** Tall classic 16th-century L-plan house, 8km (5mi) southwest of **Kemnay**, Aberdeenshire, built or completed by Matthew Lumsden (who wrote *A Genealogical History of the House of Forbes*); re-roofed for David Lumsden (1980–84).

**Tillyfour, Place of** see **Oyne**

**Tilquhillie Castle** Unturreted Z-plan house, to the southeast of **Banchory**, with rounded angles corbelled to the square, built 1576 for John Douglas, reoccupied in recent years.

**Tilt** River which runs southwest from the **Cairngorms** to meet the River Garry at **Blair Atholl**.

**Tinto Hill** Prominent hill (707m/2319ft) to the southwest of **Biggar**, from which, on a clear day, the **Bass Rock** can be seen in one direction, and as far as Ireland in the other.

**Tinwald House** Gibbsian villa to the northeast of **Dumfries**, flanked by detached stable and office pavilions built in 1738–40 by William **Adam** for Charles Erskine, then Lord Advocate.

**Tioram, Castle** see **Castle Tioram**

**Tiree** (Gaelic **Tir-iodh**) (pop. 770) Island furthest from the mainland of the Inner **Hebrides**, a popular tourist destination, with splendid beaches and excellent opportunites for windsurfing; it often has the highest annual levels of sunshine in the UK. It is linked by ferry from Scarinish, the main village, to **Oban** and **Coll**, and there is an air connection to **Glasgow**. It has an impressive **broch** at Dun Mor Vaul on the north coast. Hynish, at the southern end, was the land base of the **Skerryvore** lighthouse, and the Signal Tower has recently been restored and converted into the Skerryvore Lighthouse Museum.

**TMSA** see **Traditional Music & Song Association of Scotland**

**tobacco industry** Developed in the late 18th century, making spun tobacco (plug, for pipe smoking) and snuff. In the late 19th century cigarette making began on a large scale, Stephen Mitchell's 'Prize Crop' being a noted brand. In the interwar years Dobie's 'Four Square' brand, made in **Paisley**, was popular. In about 1950 W D and H O Wills built a large factory in **Glasgow**. The industry is now virtually extinct in Scotland.

**Tobacco Lords** Contemporary term used to describe the leading **Glasgow** merchants involved in the tobacco trade, especially in the generation before the American Revolution. They were a small, closely intermarried group, whose social origins lay in wealthy business families. By c.1750 tobacco was just under half of all Scottish imports from outside the United Kingdom and all but 2% of this was coming in through **Port Glasgow** and **Greenock** on the account of a tiny group of Glasgow merchants. Their town mansions underlined how much richer they were than any other businessmen, and they invested in estates near Glasgow as well as in a wide range of banking, import-export, and manufacturing enterprises. Three groups of interlocked partnerships that prefigured the future joint-stock company structure dominated the trade by the 1770s: the Cunningham, Speirs and Glassford groups. Other family names were Buchanan, Berrie, Bogle, Gray and Kippen. Though they survived the Revolution better than was once thought, their ascendancy was inevitably eroded by economic change and the rise of new industrial dynasties.

**Tobermory** (Gaelic **Tobar Mhoire**) (pop. 980) Chief town of the island of **Mull**, it was a planned **fishing** village built in 1788 by the **British Fisheries Society** to take advantage of the safe natural harbour for the herring trade. It is now largely a tourist centre. Its colourful buildings are a main feature of the town. It has a malt-**whisky** distillery. A large Spanish ship, probably the galleon *Florida*, remnant of the Spanish Armada, was sunk in Tobermory Bay in 1588. The town is the location for the popular children's TV programme *Balamory*.

**toiseach** In the early Middle Ages, the head of a family group in the **Gaelic**-speaking areas of Scotland. From the 13th to the 16th century toiseach was often treated as an equivalent to **thane**. (The name Mac(k)intosh means 'son of the thane'.)

**tolbooth** Originally a place where tolls and market dues were collected; later the administrative headquarters of a town, often combining council chamber, court and town jail; now applied in some towns to the building which served these functions. See also **town house**.

**Tomatin** (Gaelic **Tom-Aitinn**) Village on the River **Findhorn**, south of **Inverness**, famous for its distillery, the largest in Scotland, established in 1897. It has a visitor centre. There are 2 notable viaducts on the **Aviemore-Inverness** railway, opened in 1897.

**Tomintoul** (Gaelic **Tom an t-Sabhail**) Highest village in the **Highlands** (at 340m/1160ft), 21km (13mi) southeast of **Grantown-on-Spey**, overlooking the valley of the River **Avon**. It was expanded in the late 18th century by the Duke of Gordon. It has a distillery (founded in 1964) and tourism has been helped by the nearby ski area at the **Lecht**.

**Tongland** Small village on the River **Dee**, to the northeast of **Kirkcudbright**. It has the largest power station of the **Galloway** hydroelectric scheme, built in the 1930s in Art Deco style by Sir Alexander Gibb and Partners, and the whole scheme is controlled from Tongland. Tongland Bridge over the River **Dee** was built by Thomas **Telford**, with help from Alexander **Nasmyth**, in 1804–8. Tongland Abbey was founded in 1218; all that remains of it is a re-used arched door in the old Parish Church.

**Tongue** (Gaelic **Tunga**) Village on the north coast, on the east side of the Kyle of Tongue, 50km (31mi) north of **Lairg**. The Kyle of Tongue was spanned by a bridge and causeways in 1971. The House of Tongue, dating from the late 17th to the 19th century, was the seat of the Mackay clan.

**Torhouse Stone Circle** 5km (3mi) west of **Wigtown**, a circle of 19 low standing stones, with the highest stones to the southeast and the lowest to the northwest, perhaps aligned upon the midwinter sunrise. There is a ring-cairn within the circle. In the care of **Historic Scotland**.

**Torness** Nuclear power station on the east coast 8km (5mi) southeast of **Dunbar**, East Lothian, commissioned in 1988. It has a visitor centre.

**Torosay Castle** Mansion to the southeast of **Craignure**, Isle of **Mull**, built in baronial style (1856–8) by David **Bryce**. Three garden terraces were later created in Italianate style with rococo statuary, contrasting with the informal woodland plantings, rock and water gardens. It is now linked to Craignure by a narrow-gauge railway.

**Torphichen** Village near **Bathgate**, West Lothian, site of the Scottish base of The Knights of St John of Jerusalem (or Knights Hospitallers). The nave of the Preceptory Church, dating from the 12th century and later, was used as the parish church until 1756, when it was replaced by the present church alongside. The transepts of the Preceptory Church survive; in the care of **Historic Scotland**.

*Smailholm Tower, near Kelso, Borders, a fine example of a 16th-century tower house.*

**Torrance, Sam** (1953– ) Professional golfer, b. **Largs**. Represented Scotland in many World and Dunhill Cups; captained winning Ryder Cup team in 2002.

**Torridon** (Gaelic **Toirbheartan**) Scenic area in **Wester Ross**, between **Loch Maree** and **Loch Torridon**, a popular climbing centre as it encompasses the peaks of **Beinn Eighe**, Beinn Alligin and **Liathach**. Much of the land is in the care of the **National Trust for Scotland**. The Torridon red sandstones and conglomerates which provide typical stepped landscape features bury an ancient land surface of metamorphic rocks.

**Torrington, Jeff** (1935– ) Writer, b. Gorbals, **Glasgow**. His vivid and powerful 'working-class' novel *Swing Hammer Swing!* won the Whitbread Prize for a first novel in 1992. It was followed by *The Devil's Carousel* (1996), a brutally honest picture of a moribund car factory.

**Torry Research Institute** Founded in 1930 as a Government-funded fishery research base. Situated at Torry, on the south side of **Aberdeen** Harbour, it developed a world reputation in its field. It was privatised in the 1990s, but still operates, giving advice on such issues as conservation of fish stocks.

**Torwoodlee** Borders village near **Galashiels**, with a renowned **golf** course. Nearby is a ruined Iron Age hillfort overlain by a late **broch** of around AD 100, which appears to have been deliberately demolished, perhaps by the Roman army. Torwoodlee House was built in 1784 to replace the tower house built by the Pringles in 1601.

**Touch House** Pedimented mansion to the west of Cambusbarron, near **Stirling**, built 1757–62 for the Seton family, incorporating a 16th- and 17th-century Z-plan house. It has fine woodwork and plasterwork and the interior was sensitively modified by Sir Robert **Lorimer** (1927–8).

**Toward** Small village near Toward Point at the southern tip of the **Cowal** peninsula. Castle Toward is a neo-Tudor house by David **Hamilton** (1820–1) for Kirkman **Finlay** as a safe refuge from civil unrest in Glasgow. It was greatly enlarged in the 1920s for the Coats family, and is now an outdoor activity centre. Nearby is Toward Castle, the ruined 15th-century tower house of the Lamonts, which the Marquis of Argyll destroyed in 1646 before massacring its garrison.

**tower house** A tall narrow tower built both for domestic living and military security; most of them date from the 14th century until well into the 17th (when their defensive purpose was no longer effective). They often had a surrounding enclosure or barmkin with out-houses to provide shelter for tenants and stock in a brief emergency. See also **peel**.

**Towie Barclay** A rib-vaulted L-plan tower house south of **Turriff**, built in 1593 by the Barclays of Tolly, a family which became Russian. It was restored from a ruinous state in the 1970s by Marc Ellington; it is privately owned.

**town guard** or **city guard** Group of men raised to protect and keep order in the city of **Edinburgh**. Possibly originating in the reign of **James V**, it was remodelled in the 17th century and continued until the early 19th century. Many of the men were former Highland soldiers, and they gained a reputation for drunkenness and incompetence.

**town house** Former name for the administrative headquarters of a town, equivalent to English town hall (which in Scotland usually refers to a large hall for public events). See also **tolbooth**.

**Townsend, Gregor** (1973– ) Rugby player, b. Edinburgh. First capped in 1993 while playing for his home town club Gala (Galashiels), he went on to set a record for appearances for Scotland. When **rugby** went professional he moved to Northampton, and then to the French clubs Brive and Castres, before returning to join the revived **Borders** team. Blessed with an intuitive understanding of the game, he prefers to play at stand-off but has also been used at centre.

## Traditional Music & Song Association of Scotland

(TMSA) Society founded in 1966 to encourage and preserve Scotland's traditional music. It runs concerts, festivals, workshops and competitions, as well as providing information. Based in **Edinburgh**, it has 10 branches throughout Scotland.

**tramways** Electric tramways developed in Scotland from about 1900, replacing horse and steam tramways. Most large towns and cities had electric tramways, and there were also some 'inter-urban' tramways, mostly in Fife and on Clydeside. They offered cheap, fast and frequent services, and proved very popular. Their routes stimulated linear development of housing and shopping in a manner still clearly visible. They competed effectively with railways, halting expansion of suburban rail systems in the early 1900s. After World War I they in turn were badly hit by competition from motor buses, and by 1939 only the systems in the **four cities** were still working. **Glasgow**'s was the last to close, in 1962. A short electric tramway now operates at Summerlee Heritage Park in **Coatbridge**.

**Tranent** Town near **Prestonpans**, East Lothian, a centre of coal mining since the 13th century, now a business and market town. In the 'Massacre of Tranent' in 1797, 11 miners were killed and many more injured resisting **militia** recruitment. The Tranent-Cockenzie Railway was the first in Scotland (1721). The site of the Battle of **Prestonpans** is nearby.

**Tranter, Nigel** (1909–2000) Novelist and historian, b. Glasgow. A prolific writer of history, fictionalised history and fiction, with a substantial interest in architecture (*The Fortified House in Scotland* 1962–71), he lived most of his life in **East Lothian**. His studies of Scottish heroes include *The Young Montrose* (1972) and *The Wallace* (1975); as Nye Tredgold he wrote several Western novels.

**Traprain Law** A prominent hill near **Haddington**, East Lothian, with an Iron Age fort and a long history of habitation dating from the Neolithic period to early Christian times. It was most important under the Votadini (see **Gododdin**) during the Roman occupation when it was a large and prosperous settlement. Dating from this period is the Traprain treasure, a hoard of silver found in 1919 and now in the **Museum of Scotland**. The nearby Loth Stone is alleged to mark the burial place of the legendary King Loth, after whom the Lothians were supposedly named.

**Traquair** Hamlet near **Innerleithen**, with probably the oldest inhabited home in Scotland, Traquair House (open to the public; privately owned), built before 1107 as a hunting lodge for Scottish kings. The house was progressively enlarged from the 15th century and was given its present form in 1641 by the first Earl of Traquair, a formal courtyard being added in 1695 when the interior was modernised. The Bear Gates at the entrance were allegedly closed after the flight of Prince Charles Edward **Stewart** in 1746 and will not be reopened till another Stewart is crowned. The 18th-century brewhouse produces some highly regarded Traquair ales.

**Traquair, Phoebe Anna** (1852–1936) Artist, b. Dublin, settled in **Edinburgh** where her husband, Ramsay Traquair, was Keeper of Natural History at the **Royal Scottish Museum**. Painter of murals, enameller and embroiderer, frequently of religious subjects. With John **Duncan** she was central to the Celtic Revival in Scotland and a founder of the Scottish Society of Arts and Crafts. Her decorative schemes include the Song School of St Mary's Cathedral Choir School, Edinburgh, and murals for the

*Trams in Sauchiehall Street, Glasgow, 1957.*

373

Catholic Apostolic Church, Edinburgh, recently rescued from decay and now known as the Mansfield Traquair Centre.

**Traverse Theatre** Founded in 1963 as a private theatre club in tiny premises in **Edinburgh**'s Lawnmarket, it continues to encourage experimental work, including new plays by Scottish playwrights. It moved to the West Bow close by in 1969 and in 1992 to premises in Saltire Court, a modern office block in the West End.

**Treaty of Union** see **Union of Parliaments**

**Treig, Loch** see **Loch Treig**

**Treshnish Isles** Line of now uninhabited islands in the Inner **Hebrides**, west of **Mull**. The main islands are: Fladda to the north; Lunga, the largest, a haven for seals, birds and rabbits; its summit, Cruachan (337ft/103m) is the highest point in the chain; and Bac Mòr, also known as the Dutchman's Cap, from its central flattish hill, 85m (278ft) high, surrounded by a lowland 'brim', so resembling a hat.

**trews** From Gaelic *triubhas* (meaning 'trousers'), originally close-fitting, usually **tartan** trousers with the legs covering the feet; the term is now also used to refer to tartan trousers worn by some Scottish regiments and to short tartan trunks worn under the **kilt**.

**Trinity House** see **Leith**

**Trocchi, Alexander** (1925–84) Novelist, b. Glasgow. He lived consecutively in Paris, New Mexico, New York and London, latterly suffering the results of his heroin addiction. Perhaps best known for the controversial *Cain's Book* (1960) and *Young Adam* (1954), an existential thriller (filmed in 2003), Trocchi also wrote poetry and reviews.

**tron** A public weighing-machine for merchandise in a market place; hence, the market place, or town centre. The name survives in the Tron Kirk in **Edinburgh** and **Glasgow**, and in the Trongate in Glasgow.

**Trool, Loch** see **Glen Trool**

**Troon** (pop. 14,776) Town north of **Ayr** on the Firth of **Clyde**, a former **burgh** and once a coal port and shipbuilding centre; a dormitory town for **Glasgow** and a holiday resort, with very grand early 20th-century houses and hotels, beaches and several golf courses. A high-speed car ferry from Troon to Belfast was opened in 2000.

**Trossachs** (Gaelic **Na Tròiseachan**) Scenic area between **Loch Lomond** and **Callander**, formerly applied specifically to the beautiful wooded gorge between **Loch Achray** and **Loch Katrine**, made famous by Sir Walter **Scott** in 'The Lady of the Lake'. It is now part of the **Loch Lomond and the Trossachs National Park**.

**Trustee Savings Bank** (TSB) The savings-bank movement developed from the founding of a bank in **Ruthwell**, Dumfriesshire, in 1810 by the Rev Henry **Duncan**. By 1818 there were 465 savings banks in Britain, including 182 in Scotland. The Trustee Savings Bank Association was set up in 1887 to help cooperation between the banks and, after many changes in status, Lloyds TSB Group plc was formed in 1995, now one of the largest groups in domestic banking.

**Tulla, Loch** see **Loch Tulla**

**Tulliallan** Just north of **Kincardine on Forth**, Fife, site of a Forestry Commission nursery and Tulliallan Castle, designed by William Atkinson (1817–20) for Admiral Lord Keith, now the Scottish Police College. Nearby are the ruins of a 14th-century hall-house, recently consolidated.

**Tullibardine** Village to the northwest of **Auchterarder**, Perth and Kinross. It has a well-preserved Collegiate Chapel founded in 1445, once the burial place of the dukes of **Atholl** (one of whose titles is Marquess of Tullibardine), later of the earls of **Perth**, and now in the care of **Historic Scotland**. (The Tullibardine distillery is in nearby **Blackford**.)

**Tullibody** Small village to the northwest of **Alloa**, which prospered in the 19th century as a result of textiles and **whisky** distilling. It had the largest tannery in Scotland, now demolished. The former parish church dates from early medieval times, it was reconstructed in the 16th century but lost its roof when supporters of **Mary of Guise** used the wood to make a bridge over the River Devon. Short-lived coalmining in the 1940s–60s at nearby Glenochil was followed by the opening of a prison in 1979.

**Tullibole** Picturesque house of the 16th- and early 17th centuries, near Crook of Devon, to the west of **Kinross**, with a stepped roofline, comprising a tall plain tower built by the Herings to which the Halidays added a turreted T-plan wing shortly after acquiring the estate in 1598.

**Tummel** (Gaelic **Teimheil**) River which flows east from Dunalastair Water (near **Loch Rannoch**), through **Loch Tummel**, and then southeast through **Loch Faskally** and past **Pitlochry** to join the **Tay** near **Logierait**. It has good trout and salmon fishing. It is part of the very large Tummel Garry hydroelectric power scheme, with 9 power stations over a wide area.

**Tummel, Loch** see **Loch Tummel**

T

**Tummel Bridge** Village on the River **Tummel**, near the west end of **Loch Tummel**. The military bridge built by General **Wade** in 1730 is accompanied by a modern bridge on the road from **Aberfeldy**.

**Turgot** (d. 1115) Confessor to Queen **Margaret** and her hagiographer. Under **Alexander I** he was made Bishop of **St Andrews**.

**Turnberry** Golfing and beach resort in Ayrshire, 9km (6mi) north of **Girvan**. The 5-star Turnberry Hotel, built from 1904 for the Glasgow and South Western Railway by James **Miller**, is often reckoned to be the best in Scotland. It now has the Colin **Montgomerie** Golf Academy. Turnberry has been the venue for the Open Golf Championship. Turnberry Castle, fragments of which remain, is alleged to be the birthplace of **Robert I**, and was a centre for his campaigns. Turnberry Lighthouse is built over it.

**Turnhouse** see **Edinburgh**, pp.130-3

**Turriff** Aberdeenshire market town, a former **burgh**, on the River **Deveron**, 14km (9mi) south of **Banff**, with a ruined medieval church, of which only the tower and belfry survive. In 1639 it saw the first major skirmish of the Civil War, when the Royalists beat the **Covenanters** in the 'Trot of Turriff'. The town is the centre for a large agricultural area, and had sizeable agricultural implement works and cornmills. Nearby is Delgatie Castle, a tower house built 1570–9 by the Hay family, with fine painted ceilings, and extended in 1768; it now has the Clan Hay Centre, is open to the public and has self-catering accommodation. Craigston Castle, seat of the Urquharts, built in 1604 and memorable for its sculpture and carved woodwork of that date, is 7km (4mi) northeast of the town. The Turriff Show is the largest agricultural show in northeast Scotland.

**tweed** A hard-wearing woollen cloth, often in natural colours, produced in the **Borders** from **Cheviot sheep** and, famously, in the **Hebrides** from **Blackface sheep**; see **Harris tweed**. Its name is said to come from a misreading of 'tweel' (twill) in a letter to a London merchant, but may be from 'tweeled' (meaning woven), perhaps influenced by the River **Tweed** which runs through much of the textile-making country. Tweed was washed and shrunk to give it a waterproof, felt-like surface, providing weatherproof

*Weaving tweed on a handloom, Kirriemuir, c.1904.*

long-lasting clothing, especially for country wear. In the later 19th and early 20th centuries fine tweeds, made from imported merino and other wools, became fashionable and were widely exported.

**Tweed** The largest river in the **Borders**, 155km (96 mi) long, flowing from Tweed's Well near **Moffat**, then northeast through **Peebles**, then east to **Melrose** and **Kelso** and from **Coldstream** northeast to **Berwick-upon-Tweed**, forming part of the border with England on the way. It is fed by the **Teviot** and the **Ettrick** and **Leader** Waters, and is famed for its salmon fishing. In the past it provided power for the textile mills in the Borders.

**Tweeddale District** see **Borders Region**

**Tyndrum** (Gaelic **Taigh an Droma**) Just north of **Crianlarich** and now a tourist resort, the village was the site of leadmining in the 18th and 19th centuries. There was briefly some goldmining in the 1980s. Nearby is Ben Lui National Nature Reserve.

**Tynecastle** Off Gorgie Road, **Edinburgh**, Tynecastle Stadium was built by **Heart of Midlothian** (Hearts) football club in 1886, and was substantially rebuilt to provide all-seated accommodation in the 1990s.

**Tyninghame** An attractive estate village near **Dunbar**, East Lothian, replacing an original village moved in 1761 from around Tyninghame House where it obstructed the Earl of Haddington's country views. Tyninghame House is a **baronial** mansion, remodelled by William **Burn** in 1829 from a much older house; now converted into apartments.

**Ubiquitous Chip** Award-winning restaurant in the west end of **Glasgow**, founded in 1969 by its owner and chef Ronnie Clydesdale. It specialises in traditional Scottish food, using local produce.

**UCS** see **Upper Clyde Shipbuilders**

**Uddingston** (pop. 5576) Small town on the River **Clyde** to the southwest of **Coatbridge**, with the remains of **Bothwell Castle**. It has had various industries, notably Tunnock's bakery, producing popular sweets and biscuits, and an important Victorian agricultural implement works.

**Udny Castle** Tall rectangular tower house 21km (13mi) northwest of **Aberdeen**, with a remarkable wall-chambered plan and turreted parapets, built in the mid to late 16th century for the Udnys; famed for the family's legendary 'feel' or jester, Jamie Fleeman (1713–78).

**UHI Millennium Institute** (formerly **University of the Highlands and Islands Project**) Higher-education institution providing university-level courses and research opportunities throughout the **Highlands** and Islands and beyond, aiming to achieve university status in 2007. A partnership of different institutions, it offers wide-ranging courses in over 50 centres and also has courses on-line.

**Uig** A group of dwellings on the west coast of **Lewis**, by the sandy bay where the Lewis Chessmen were found.

**Uig** Village on Uig Bay at the west of Trotternish, **Skye**, with car ferries to **Lochmaddy** in **North Uist** and **Tarbert** in **Harris**. Prince Charles Edward **Stewart** and Flora **Macdonald** landed nearby at Kilbride Bay in their flight after the 1745 Rising.

**Uist** see **North, South Uist**

**Ullapool** (Gaelic **Ullapul**) Once the main herring port on the west coast, developed by the **British Fisheries Society** in 1788, this **Wester Ross** village on **Loch Broom**, with charming whitewashed buildings, is now a tourist centre. It has a car ferry to **Stornoway**. In the 1970s and 80s the fishing trade was boosted by factory ships from eastern Europe, which bought mackerel for processing on board; see **klondykers**. The former **Parliamentary** church is now a local museum.

**Ulva** (Gaelic **Ulbha**) Island off the west coast of **Mull**, birthplace of Lachlan **MacQuarie**, whose family owned it. In the mid 19th century it suffered from the potato famine and **clearances** by a new owner. It is now only sparsely populated but encouraging tourism.

**unco guid** Expression used to refer to the self-righteously moral or pious, after Robert **Burns**'s poem 'Address to the Unco Guid'.

**unicorn** The unicorn has appeared as a supporter on royal seals and coins from medieval times. Though the lion was the Stewart's heraldic animal, the unicorn became the national heraldic symbol, and after 1603 **James VI**'s coat of arms included the Scottish unicorn and the English lion.

**Union Canal** Built by Hugh Baird with help from Thomas **Telford** and finished in 1822, it runs between **Edinburgh** and **Falkirk** and was originally linked to the **Forth and Clyde Canal** by 11 locks. It fell into disuse in the 1930s but has very recently been restored, and the locks replaced by the **Falkirk** Wheel, a boatlifting system, as part of the **Millennium Link**. See also **Linlithgow**.

**Union of the Crowns** In 1603, on the death of Queen Elizabeth, **James VI** acceded to the linked crowns of England and Ireland as James I. Though James VI and I and his successors were

*Ullapool, Wester Ross.*

thereafter rulers of 3 kingdoms, the Scottish Crown and state remained distinct until the **Union of Parliaments** in 1707.

**Union of Parliaments** On 1 May 1707, against the wishes of many Scots, an Act of Union was passed by the **Scottish Parliament**, suspending its own existence and agreeing to terms for a Treaty of Union with England, including a new joint parliament, thus creating the United Kingdom of Great Britain. In exchange for the Scottish agreement to the Treaty of Union and the Hanoverian succession, Scotland received assurance of freedom of trade, and the promise of a sum of money, known as the 'Equivalent', to offset their liability for a share of the English national debt and to compensate stockholders in the Company of Scotland who had lost their money in the **Darien** disaster. The Treaty of Union guaranteed the continuation of the distinctive Scottish legal system. It also contained guarantes of the right and autonomy of the **burghs**. Separate legislation guaranteed the **Church of Scotland** in its Presbyterian form. In practice the distinctive Scottish **education** system, in both schools and universities, also survived.

**United Free Church** The **Free Church of Scotland** was formed at the **Disruption** of 1843. In 1900 most of it united with the **United Presbyterian Church** to form the United Free Church; see also **Free Church**. In 1929 the bulk of the United Free Church joined with the **Church of Scotland**, leaving a minority of United Free Church members (the 'continuers') adhering to their principles of autonomy, equality and voluntary contribution.

**United Presbyterian Church** Formed by the union of the **Secession** Church and the **Relief Church** in 1847, in 1900 it merged with the **Free Church** to form the **United Free Church**.

**United Secession Church** see **Presbyterian churches**

**United Turkey Red Co Ltd** Company formed in 1897 by amalgamating 6 calico-printing works on the River **Leven**, from the late 18th until the early 20th century the centre of the calico-printing industry in Scotland. The firm's printed cottons were mainly exported, to India and the Middle East. It was the last firm of its kind in Scotland, closing in 1961, though by that time it was operating at a very low level.

**University of the Highlands and Islands** see **UHI Millennium Institute**

*A barge heading east from the Almond aqueduct on the Union Canal, c.1900.*

**Unna, Percy** (1878–1950) English civil engineer, philanthropist, environmentalist. President of the Scottish Mountaineering Club in the 1930s, he was one of the first to recognise the need to protect the mountain environment and formulated 'Unna's Rules'. His generous donations and bequests helped the **National Trust for Scotland** to purchase and maintain mountain properties, notably **Glencoe** and **Ben Lawers**.

**Unst** Northernmost inhabited island of Scotland, in the **Shetland** group, northeast of Yell, with a population of fishermen and crofters, it is accessible by air, or by ferry from Yell. The port of Baltasound is its chief settlement. Its attractions include a seabird sanctuary at Hermaness, and the rare dunite-serpentine headland of the Keen of Hamar, which has a unique flora including the rare endemic Shetland mouse-ear (*Cerastium nigrescens*). Some of the land is in the care of the **National Trust for Scotland**. The remains of St Olaf's church at Lunda Wick date originally from the 12th century. Muness Castle, a very grand and complete, though roofless, Z-plan house, was built in 1598 by Lawrence Bruce of Cultmalindie (uncle of Patrick **Stewart, Earl of Orkney**). The most northerly castle in Britain, it is in the care of **Historic Scotland**.

**Unuist** (or **Oengus, Angus**) (d. 761) King of the **Picts**. The son of Uurguist (Fergus), he was one of the most powerful of Pictish kings, leading campaigns against the Britons of **Strathclyde** and the Scots, whose kingdom he subjugated. He probably founded **St Andrews**, although the tale that this was inspired by the miraculous intervention of the saint before the battle of **Athelstaneford** is legendary.

*Workers at Upper Clyde Shipbuilders at the gates of the Clydebank branch, 1971.*

**Uphall** Village near Broxburn, **West Lothian**. The parish church has a 12th-century tower, nave and chancel, with later additions. The core of Houston House Hotel is a tower house built around 1600, enlarged in 1737 by Thomas Shairp, an Edinburgh advocate. Nearby quarries provided stone for many prominent Edinburgh buildings, and Uphall had shale-mining and paraffin-oil works.

**Up Helly Aa** Fire festival held in **Lerwick**, Shetland on the last Tuesday in January, begun in the 19th century, reminiscent of Shetland's Viking past. A procession of guisers follow the Guiser Jarl to the burning site where their flaming torches are thrown into a model Viking ship.

**Upper Clyde Shipbuilders** (UCS) Company formed in 1968 as part of a Government-sponsored rationalisation of British shipbuilding. It was an amalgamation of the yards of **Fairfield** (Glasgow) Ltd, Alexander Stephen and Sons Ltd, John **Brown** and Co Ltd, and Charles Connell and Co Ltd, initially with **Yarrow** and Co as an associate. UCS failed in 1971, and a 'work-in' by employees ensued. The action succeeded and the government injected a futher £35 million into it. However, the success was short-lived. The Clydebank yard was sold for oil-rig construction, and the Fairfield yard continued until 1977 when it was nationalised. (It was sold to Kvaerner, a Norwegian firm, in 1988 and survives as part of **BAE Systems.**)

**Upper Largo** Village near the south coast of Fife, to the northeast of **Lower Largo**. Its parish church has a 17th-century chancel and central steeple, and was restored and extended

1816–17 by Alexander Leslie.

**uppies and doonies** see **handba**

**upset price** At auction, a price which will be acceptable to the seller; (for property) a price below which bids will not be accepted.

**Ure, Midge** (1953– ) Musician, b. Cambuslang, **Glasgow**. First a member of 'bubblegum' band Slik, he achieved his greatest success with new-wave Ultravox ('Vienna' 1981) and later Visage. He contributed substantially to the Band Aid charity success and now performs as a solo artist.

**Urquhart, Fred** (1912–95) Writer, b. Edinburgh. Primarily known for his many short stories, often of the supernatural (*Seven Ghosts in Search*, 1983), he was also a novelist, anthologist, literary agent and publisher's reader. *Time Will Knit* (1938) depicts a changing fishing village near **Edinburgh** and *Palace of Green Days* (1979) is autobiographical.

**Urquhart, Sir Thomas** (c.1611–60) Writer and translator, b. **Cromarty**. Something of a polymath, he published a study of trigonometry, an attack on the Scottish church, a largely imaginary history of his own family, and a superbly lively and colloquial translation of Rabelais' *Gargantua and Pantagruel*. A lifelong Royalist, he is said to have died in a fit of laughter on hearing of the Restoration.

**Urquhart Castle** Ruins of a sizeable castle on a defensive site on the north shore of **Loch Ness**, mostly dating from the 13th century with a 16th-century tower. It was built on the site of an early historic fort and played a significant role in the Wars of Independence. In the care of **Historic Scotland**, with a new visitor centre.

**Usher, Andrew** (1826–98) Whisky distiller and blender, b. Edinburgh. He is traditionally credited with introducing, in about 1860, the practice of blending Scotch malt and grain whiskies to make a standard product, which he marketed as 'Old Vatted Glenlivet'. The practice of blending was the foundation of the subsequent international success of the Scotch **whisky** industry. Usher made a considerable fortune, part of which he used to fund the building of the Usher Hall, **Edinburgh**'s main concert hall.

**usquebaugh** see **whisky**

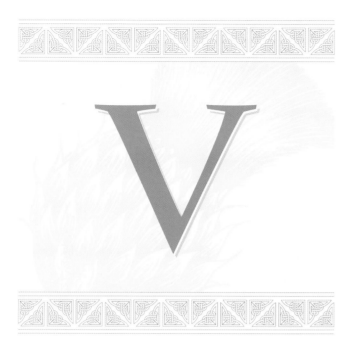

**Valentine, James** (1815-80) Photographer and publisher, studied the daguerrotype process and opened a studio in **Dundee** in the 1850s. A founder member of the Edinburgh Photographic Society, his fine landscape photographs contributed to the success of his eponymous photographic company, which began making postcards in the 1890s. The company's photographic collection is in **St Andrews University** Library.

**Vale of Leven** Valley of the River **Leven**, which flows south from **Loch Lomond** to **Dumbarton**, with the former textile towns of **Alexandria**, Bonhill, Jamestown, Renton and **Balloch**.

**Valladolid** see **Scots Colleges**

**vassal** An owner holding heritable property in **feu** from a **superior**.

**Veere** see **staple**

**Venachar, Loch** see **Loch Venachar**

**Vettriano, Jack** (1951- ) Painter, b. Kirkcaldy. A self-taught artist; his stylised, nostalgic paintings command high prices and are popular as prints and greetings cards.

**VisitScotland** Scotland's main national tourist board, founded by government in 1969 as the Scottish Tourist Board to provide information and promote tourism throughout Scotland.

**vitious intromission** Scots **law** term for unwarranted interference with the moveable estate of a deceased without legal title, whereby liability for all the debts of the deceased may be incurred.

**Voil, Loch** see **Loch Voil**

**Votadini** see **Gododdin**

**Waddell, Willie** (1921-92) Football player and manager, b. Forth, Lanarkshire. A speedy and powerful winger for **Rangers** 1938-56, with 17 national caps, he managed **Kilmarnock** before returning to Rangers as manager in 1969. He redeveloped the stadium after the **Ibrox** disaster of 1971 and guided the team to success in league and competitions, remaining on the board for many years.

**Wade, General George** (1673-1748) Soldier and road-builder, b. West Meath, Ireland. He was given the task of the disarmament of the Highland clans after the 1715 **Jacobite Rising** and from 1726-37 constructed a network of military roads and bridges in the **Highlands**, some of which are still known by his name. In the Rising of 1745 he commanded an army based in northeast England, but failed to cross the Pennines in time to intercept the Jacobite army's thrust down the west of England.

**Walker, Helen** see **Deans, Jeanie**

**Walkinshaw, Clementina** (c.1720-1802) Mistress of Prince Charles Edward **Stewart**, whom she met, probably at **Bannockburn** House, in 1745 and followed to the Low Countries in 1752, leaving him in 1760 because of his cruelty. She bore him a daughter, Charlotte (1753-89), whom Charles later created Duchess of Albany, and who cared for him in his final years in Italy.

**Wallace, Sir William** (d. 1305) Soldier and national icon, perhaps b. at Elderslie near Paisley, son of Sir Malcolm Wallace. A leader of the resistance movement against English occupation,

V

W

*Sir William Wallace, from the Scottish National Portrait Gallery.*

he defeated an English army with Sir Andrew Murray at **Stirling Bridge** in 1297. In the following year an army led by Edward I defeated Wallace at **Falkirk.** Wallace continued to resist the English at home and abroad where he sought to enlist French help, until his capture in 1305 by Sir John **Menteith** and execution for treason in London. The Hollywood blockbuster **Braveheart** has increased the prominence of Wallace as a national hero in modern Scottish consciousness.

**Wallace, William** (d.1631) Master Mason to the Crown from 1617, he was associated with the Anglo-Danish Renaissance of the remodelling of the King's Lodging at Edinburgh Castle (1615–17), the north range of **Linlithgow Palace** (1618–20), **Winton House** (1620–7) and Heriot's Hospital, **Edinburgh**, begun 1628.

**wallie** Scots word meaning, fine, pleasant, ornamental, often applied to porcelain, as in **wallie dugs**, tall ornamental porcelain dogs displayed in pairs; **wallie close**, a tiled close, in Glasgow regarded as a sign of social superiority. Wallies are false teeth.

**Walton, Cecile** see **Walton, Edward Arthur**

**Walton, E(dward) A(rthur)** (1860–1922) Artist b. Renfrewshire. Along with his close friends James **Guthrie** and Joseph **Crawhall**, Walton was one of the most prominent of the **Glasgow Boys**. His paintings of the 1880s (during the Boys' heyday) were of the rural landscape or of intimate village life (his watercolours of **Helensburgh** of 1883 are regarded as amongst

the finest output of the Glasgow School). His daughter Cecile Walton (1891–1956) was a talented painter and illustrator and was married to the artist Eric Robertson; his brother George Walton (1867–1920), also an artist and designer, worked on designs for Miss **Cranston**'s Tea Rooms in **Glasgow**.

**Walton, George** see **Walton, Edward Arthur**

**Wanlockhead** One of the highest villages in Scotland, at 450m (1500ft) above sea level, in the **Lowther Hills**, southwest of **Abington**, just to the southwest of **Leadhills**, once a centre of mining for lead, gold and silver. There is a lead-mining museum there. Like Leadhills it had an early subscription library, founded by the miners in 1756, with contributions from the mining companies. Its 1851 building can still be seen.

**wappinschaw** Formerly a periodical review of the men under arms in a particular district. Later a shooting competition.

**Wardlaw, Henry** (d. 1440) Churchman, tutor to **James I**. As Bishop of **St Andrews**, he helped found **St Andrews University**, and was its first chancellor.

**Wardrop, James Maitland** (1824–82) Architect, b. London. Principal rival to David **Bryce** as a country-house architect, he initially worked in partnership with Thomas Brown, designing handsome courthouses at **Wigtown**, **Alloa**, **Forfar** and **Stirling**. He designed the great Scots baronial houses of Lochinch (1864), **Nunraw** (1868) and Beaufort (1880) and remodelled **Callendar House** as a French chateau (1869–77). In later years he sometimes worked in an unturreted 17th-century manner, as at **Kinnordy** (1879).

**Wark, Kirsty** (1955– ) Journalist and presenter, b. Dumfries. She joined BBC Radio Scotland in 1976 and later appeared on *Reporting Scotland* and current affairs programmes. After a few years on BBC *Breakfast Time* she joined *Newsnight* in 1993, becoming a respected political commentator and interviewer. With her husband, Alan Clements, she runs an independent production company, Wark Clements, now joined with Muriel **Gray** and Hamish Barbour's Ideal World to form IWC Media.

**Warner, Alan** (1964– ) Novelist, b. Oban. A writer of darkly humorous books including *Morvern Callar* (1995), *The Sopranos* (1998) and *The Man Who Walks* (2002), he is distinguished by his pictorially descriptive style, which makes him popular with film directors.

**Wars of Independence** The death of **Alexander III** in 1286 precipitated a crisis in the Scottish succession. His infant heir, (**Margaret Maid of Norway**), was betrothed to Edward, Prince

**W**

of Wales, eldest son of Edward I of England, but she died on her way to Scotland, leaving the throne open to several claimants. Edward I, in the **Great Cause**, adjudicated in favour of John **Balliol**, who was compelled to recognise the English king's overlordship. When the Scots rejected this and allied with France against England, Edward invaded in 1296, sacked **Berwick-upon-Tweed** and crushed the Scots at **Dunbar**. John Balliol was deposed, but William **Wallace** and others fought on. When **Robert I** seized the throne in 1306 he eventually established his authority in Scotland against domestic opponents still loyal to Balliol, and Edward II, who succeeded his father in 1307. The victory at **Bannockburn** in 1314 was a significant part of this process. It was raiding of northern England that finally forced recognition of Scottish independence in the treaty of Edinburgh-Northampton of 1328, the traditional terminal date of the Wars of Independence. Edward III, however, made renewed and intensive efforts to subdue Scotland in the 1330s and intermittent Anglo-Scottish warfare would continue throughout the later Middle Ages.

**Water of Leith** River that rises in the **Pentland Hills** and runs northeast through Balerno, Currie and **Edinburgh** to join the **Firth of Forth** at **Leith**. It formerly powered many paper- and cornmills.

**Watkins, Dudley D** see **Thomson, D C**

**Watson, Thomas Lennox** (1850–1920) Architect, b. Glasgow. Trained in London with Alfred Waterhouse but designed Wellington Church, **Glasgow** (1882–4) (known as 'The United Presbyterian Madeleine'), and some very stylish 'Old English' and Arts and Crafts buildings, notably the Clyde Yacht Club (Royal Marine Hotel), Hunters Quay (1888).

**Watson, W(illiam) J(ohn)** (1865–1948) Gaelic scholar, b. Easter Ross. Professor of Celtic at **Edinburgh University**, he specialised in the history of place names, and his major work, *History of the Celtic Placenames of Scotland* (1926), has not yet been superseded. His other works include anthologies, *Rosg Gàidhlig* (1915) and *Bàrdachd Ghàidhlig* (1918).

**Watt, Alison** (1965– ) Artist, b. Greenock. Winner of the National Portrait Gallery's annual portrait competition in 1987 (which led to a commission to paint Her Majesty the Queen Mother), she is recognised for her enigmatic paintings of the figure, and in particular of the female nude. Most recently she has produced works which dispense with the figure altogether, concentrating instead on the meticulous depiction of folded fabric.

**Watt, James** (1736–1819) Inventor, b. Greenock. Trained as a mathematical instrument maker, he became involved in surveys of the Scottish waterways, designed the **Monkland Canal**, at the same time studying the capacity of steam as a source of power. He developed the concept of the separate condenser and air pump among other improvements to the steam engine, and went into partnership with Matthew Boulton in Birmingham in 1774, continuing his innovations until his retirement. The introduction of the Watt beam engine for pumping water from coal mines was a major contribution to the industrial revolution. The watt, a unit of electrical energy, is named after him.

**waulking songs** Highly rhythmic **Gaelic** songs used by groups of Hebridean women for the strenuous process of shrinking wet **tweed** by hand. The songs may have elements of Ossianic legends or sly current social comment. They have outlasted their purpose and feature in the repertoires of modern Gaelic singers and groups.

**Wedderburn** Giant castellated mansion to the southeast of **Duns**, Berwickshire, built (1771–5) by Robert and James **Adam** and the local architect James Nisbet for Patrick Horne of Billie; interiors have chimneypieces acquired on his Grand Tour, including one by Piranesi.

*Chalk drawing of James Watt by John Henning, 1809.*

W

# WEIGHTS AND MEASURES

Scotland had a different system of weights and measures from that of England, and these were used for all forms of trade, taxation assessment and contract. When the Scottish **burghs** were first established as trading centres, the early Scottish units were based on existing English practice, but the two systems evolved separately and subsequent Scottish units were strongly influenced by trading contacts with the Low Countries (particularly Flanders) and France. A number of the Scottish units have familiar names (pound, stone, pint, gallon, etc) also found in England, but others are distinctly Scottish (such as the grain firlot and boll).

Several varieties of these units were often in use at the same time for different commodities (for example, there were distinct gallons for wine and ale) although individual references may not make this clear. On a number of occasions the legislation changed the permitted sizes of measures.

. The Jeddart Jug: the standard ale pint measure for Jedburgh, 1563.

Market practice also allowed the measures to be used with various types of traditional allowances (or 'charities'), which had the effect of increasing their sizes within controlled limits. For all these reasons, it may not be possible to give a clear equivalent in modern units of the quantity of goods being described.

The Scottish administration controlled the unit sizes through definitions given in particular Acts of Parliament (assizes) or other forms of legislation. The administration also retained physical standards, which were accurately made and adjusted vessels and weights designed to be the principal authorised reference standards for the kingdom. The principal burghs also held particular secondary standards and were given authority to issue more accessible copies to other burghs for the regulation of ordinary trade. Thus, **Stirling** held the commercial pint standard, **Linlithgow** held the firlot (for dry measure), **Edinburgh** had the ell (linear measure) and **Lanark** the stone (of weight). Some of these early standards, such as the old Stirling Joug pint of c.1510, still survive in museum collections. In addition, **Perth** is associated with a subsidiary linear standard for thread (the reel), and **Aberdeen** held the salmon barrel.

Scottish units were theoretically replaced by English units at the **Union of the Parliaments** in 1707, when new sets of English standards were issued to the main Scottish burghs. However, this had very little effect on the internal markets of the burghs, and the traditional units remained in almost exclusive use until the mid 19th century, when they were progressively replaced by the new British 'Imperial' system. Before this, the self-contained nature of these local and regional trading areas, and the lack of effective central control after 1707, meant that some geographical variation became established in the later sizes of the traditional Scottish units.

## LIQUID CAPACITY

The standard unit of liquid capacity was the pint.

1 pint = 2 chopins, 4 mutchkins, or 16 gills (or 'jowcats')

Initially, the ale gallon was 6 ale pints, and there was a wine gallon, also of 6 pints, which was half as big again. However, ale and wine were both sold with an allowance of 1/16 added, so that the retail vessels were enhanced by this amount. The 1563 **Jedburgh** standard for testing retail pints is shown left.

The basic pint of the legislation (without the extra $\frac{1}{16}$) formed the basis of the dry measure series, and for burghs this may have been the principal purpose for holding standards of this size. This statutory pint was the size of the basic ale pint, but was increased by a half to match the basic wine pint in 1426, and by a further third in about 1500, remaining subsequently at this size (about 1.70 litres), with some minor adjustment in the late 16th century. From at least 1550, the enhanced versions of this larger pint (about 1.80 litres) and its chopin were the usual vessels for the sale of ale. Indirect evidence suggests that the liquid gallon was considered to be 8 pints from about 1450.

## DRY CAPACITY

The standard of dry capacity, for grain, oatmeal, etc., was the firlot (which was the Scots equivalent of the English bushel). The firlot was a shallow cylindrical wooden coopered vessel, which was defined in the legislation by its dimensions and also as the volume of a set number of pints of grain. Its volume was progressively increased over several assizes (by a process of engrossing allowances in the use of the measure), until it reached 21¼ dry pints (34.6 litres) at the 1618 Assize. Barley and malt, which were previously measured as 3 fills of the wheat firlot for 2 firlots of barley or malt, were from 1618 measured in a separate series of larger measures, where the barley firlot was 31 dry pints (49.5 litres). The theoretical relationships between the volume sizes is:

    1 firlot  = 4 pecks, each of 4 lippies or forpets
    4 firlots = 1 boll
    16 bolls  = 1 chalder

In practice, however, the relationships were different, because heaping allowances were provided for the merchants conducting transactions and the permitted trade measures were enlarged to incorporate these allowances.

An allowance of $\frac{1}{16}$ in the firlot was first officially admitted in 1426 (although it presumably pre-dated this), and by about 1500 an additional charity of $\frac{1}{16}$ for trading in bolls (the 'peck to the boll') was also being taken at the firlot level. The combined increase of $\frac{1}{8}$ was the amount by which the firlot was increased at the major assizes until 1618. An extra allowance was taken in trading in chalders, and an equivalent amount for all dry produce imported by sea (and measured by the larger 'water metts'). Only $\frac{1}{16}$ seems to have been sanctioned for the 1618 firlots, implying trading volumes of about 36.8 and 52.6 litres, but

*Standard trone stone weight, by Hans Cochran, 1553.*

quantities were still liable to increases from charities allowed on trading in bolls and chalders.

By the late 18th century the Linlithgow firlots were described (incorrectly) as by water fill, from the 1618 specifications, which should have resulted in capacities of 36.0 and 52.5 litres, approximately matching the earlier correct usage. However, they were typically found in the burghs at about 37 and 54 litres, and in the 1820s the standards were officially determined to be 36.3 and 52.9 litres.

## WEIGHT

From the late 16th century, the relationship of the various parts of the weight series was:

    1 ounce  = 16 drops (or 24 deniers, each of 24 grains,
               for bullion weight)
    1 pound  = 16 ounces
    16 pounds = 1 stone

Before 1563, the merchant and market stones each comprised 15 pounds (although the sub-division of the former before the mid-15th century is more complex). A fine example of a 1553 standard 15-pound trone stone is shown above.

The weights defined in the assizes are the bullion or merchant weights, for fine materials. The heavier trone weight series, used for most market produce, is mentioned in the legislation only once, at an unsuccessful attempt to suppress it in 1618. The trone weights were maintained at $1^1/4$ times the merchant weights. The standards of the burghs was the Lanark trone stone (about 9.80 kg for the 16-pound stone) until 1618, when a revised merchant ('troye' or later 'Dutch') stone of about 7.89 kg was substituted. From the 1680s, oatmeal was measured by weight rather than volume, reckoned at 8 troye stone per boll of meal = 140 avoirdupois pounds or 63 kg.

## LENGTH AND AREA

The Scottish and English inches were identical, and in Scottish use:

    1 foot  = 12 inches
    1 ell   = 37 inches (0.940 m), not divided in inches,
              but in $^1/_2$, $^1/_4$, $^1/_8$, etc.

A longer ell of 37.2 inches (0.945m), and therefore equivalent to 37 over-sized inches, is found in the 18th century. It appears to arise from a late 17th-century re-measurement of the yarn reel, but instead of being restricted to textile use it was also inappropriately applied from the late 18th century in land measurement. In markets for coarse and unbleached cloth, 'plaiding' ells and yards were used, which incorporated a shrinkage allowance of approximately $^1/_{16}$, and were therefore usually of about 39-40 inch and $38^1/_4$-$38^1/_2$ inch (about 1.00 and 0.98m) respectively.

## FOR LAND MEASUREMENT:

1 (lineal) fall, raip (rope) or rod = 6 ells or $18^1/_2$ feet (5.64 m) but initially (to about the 14th century) the rod for measuring plots in burghs was 20 feet.

1 (Scots) chain (late 16th century) = 4 falls or 24 ells (74 feet or 22.5 m), with 100 links to the chain. (The link was also the same as the small foot, of about 9 inches or 0.22 m long, used by tradesmen and for measuring material such as glass.)

1 (Scots) furlong = 40 falls, also considered as the length that could be ploughed by a team of oxen without a rest.

1 (Scots measured) mile (from 16th century) = 8 furlongs (1.12 English statute miles, 1.80 km), but the older Scots common mile of 1500 paces (each of 5 feet) was 1.42 English miles or 2.29 km.

## LAND AREA:

1 rood (earlier, 'particate') of land = 40 square falls

1 (Scots) acre = 4 roods, 160 square falls or 10 (Scots) square chains (0.509 hectares), and an acre strip of arable land was a furlong in extent and 4 falls wide (the 'acre's breadth')

1 ploughgate (earlier 'carrucat') = 8 oxgangs, taken as 104 (Scots) acres (53 hectares), being the area that could be ploughed by an 8-ox team in a ploughing season.

## WORK AREA:

1 square fall = 36 square ells (31.8 square m): the 'rood of work' or 'small rood' for measuring the work of craftsmen such as masons, slaters or wrights.

## YARN MEASURE

Linen and woollen yard were measured on the reel, a winding frame with a circumference of $2^1/_2$ ells ('long' or 'ten quarter' reel) or occasionally of $1^1/_4$ ells ('short' or 'five quarter' reel) for doubled yarn, analogous to the English $1^1/_4$ yard cloth ell of 45 inches. Seventeenth-century regulations describe how one turn of the reel took up a 'thread'; the yarn was cut after 120 turns on the reel, and sold (by weight) in 'hesps' or hanks of 12 'cutts'. The ell is the late 17th-century version of 37.2 inches, hence the thread is 93 inches (2.36 m), the cutt is 300 ells (282 m), and the hesp 3600 ells (3.38 km). A yard-based circumference of 90 inches is normally found on 19th-century reels.

## COINAGE

Prices must be considered in terms of Scottish currency, based from the 1130s on silver pennies of identical weight and value to those of England, at 20 pennies (20d) to the ounce. Shillings, merks (or marks) and pounds were currencies of account at 12d, 160d (or 13s 8d) and 240d (20s) until the later introduction of higher value coins. Although Scots currency exchanged at parity with that of England until 1367, it subsequently depreciated more rapidly, with an exchange rate set at 2:1 in 1390, 3:1 in 1452, 6:1 in 1565, 8:1 in 1579, 10:1 in 1597 and finally 12:1 in 1601. This last rate was maintained when the currencies came under single control at the Union of the Crowns in 1603; so from that time 12 pounds Scots = 1 pound Sterling, and 1 pound Scots = 1s 8d Sterling.

Separate Scots coins were last minted in 1709.

**Wee Frees** see **Free Church of Scotland**

**Weem** (Gaelic **Uaimh**) Small village near **Aberfeldy** dominated by the tall and handsome 18th-century inn. The old parish church (1609) has an elaborate sculptured mural monument of 1616 to the Menzies family and a remarkable collection of hatchments; nearby is **Castle Menzies**.

**Weights and measures** see pp.382–4

**Weir, Judith** (1954– ) Composer, b. Cambridge of Scottish parents. Her music has a wide range, much of it influenced by her interest in worldwide folklore and theatre. Her operas include *A Night at the Chinese Opera* (1987); she has also composed song cycles and orchestral work such as *The Welcome Arrival of Rain* (2001).

**Weir, Major Thomas** (1599–1670) Soldier and warlock, b. **Carluke**, Lanarkshire. A **Covenanter**, on his retirement from the military he became Captain of the **Town Guard** in **Edinburgh** and a respected preacher. One day, however, he revealed his participation in witchcraft and incest, and after a trial was strangled and burned at the stake. His sister was convicted of witchcraft and hanged. It was long believed that his ghost haunted the area of his home in the West Bow, Lawnmarket, Edinburgh.

**Weir, Tom** (1914– ) Climber, journalist and photographer, b. Glasgow. He climbed in the Himalayas, Atlas, Kurdistan and elsewhere, and has written evocatively on nature and environmental issues. He was presenter of the long-running Scottish Television series *Weir's Way*.

**Weir, William Douglas, 1st Viscount Weir of Eastwood** (1877–1959), b. Glasgow, son of James Weir, one of the founders of G and J Weir, engineers, of the Holm Foundry, Cathcart. He rose to prominence in World War I, when the company made military aircraft and shell cases on a large scale. In 1918 he became Secretary of State for Air, and was responsible for the creation of the RAF. Between the wars he served as a Government adviser, recommending the creation of the National Grid for the distribution of electricity, and being instrumental in the direction of re-armament after 1936, especially the re-equipment and expansion of the RAF from 1936. Weirs again contributed to the war effort in World War II. The Weir Group is one of largest pump-making concerns in the world.

**Wellins, Bobby** (1936– ) Jazz musician, b. Glasgow. After learning clarinet at the RAF School of Music in the early 1950s,

*Alan Wells winning the men's 100m final at the Moscow Olympics, 1980.*

he worked with a number of London dance bands, but by the end of the decade he had turned largely to improvisation. He worked with the Stan Tracey Quartet in the 1960s, playing on the album *Under Milk Wood*, and has also worked extensively as a teacher and composer.

**Well of the Seven Heads** (Gaelic **Tobar nan Ceann**) An elegant monument by the roadside on **Loch Oich**-side commemorates an act of revenge against the 7 kinsmen who murdered the young MacDonald of Keppoch and his brother in the late 17th century. The murderers were killed and their severed heads were rinsed in the well by the poet **Iain Lom** before he presented them to the MacDonnell of Glengarry (who had refused to avenge Keppoch).

**Wells, Alan** (1952– ) Athlete, b. Edinburgh, concentrated on sprinting, winning gold in the 100m at the 1978 Commonwealth Games and 1980 Olympics, and the 100m and 200m at the 1982 Commonwealth Games.

**Welsh, Alex** (1929–82) Jazz musician, b. Edinburgh. His early career was in Scotland, where he played cornet and trumpet. In the 1950s he moved to London, and became one of the key members of the trad jazz revival. He also toured extensively in the UK and Europe.

**Welsh, Irvine** (1958– ) Novelist, b. Leith. After a number of dead-end jobs, he gained huge success with *Trainspotting* (1993), a brutal but often comic story of the drug scene, partially based on his own experiences, and filmed in 1996. His output since includes *The Acid House* (short stories, 1995) and *Porno* (2002).

**W**

**Welsh, Jane** see **Carlyle, Jane Welsh**

**Wemyss** An area along the Fife shore of the Firth of Forth, notable for its caves (weems, from Gaelic *uamh* a cave), some of which contain Pictish art.

**Wemyss Bay** Attractive Victorian residential village on the Firth of **Clyde**, with a railway pier, formerly a hub for Clyde coast steamer services and now terminus of the ferry to **Rothesay**.

**Wemyss Castle** Clifftop castle of the Wemyss family, near West **Wemyss** on the Fife coast, its nucleus a 15th-century tower incorporated into a long U-plan house by Robert **Mylne** (1669), plain externally but with fine 17th- and 18th-century interiors.

**Wemyss ware** Colourful pottery, often in unusual forms, such as the characteristic pigs and other eccentric animals covered in cabbage roses, which originated in Robert Heron's pottery in **Ceres** in Fife in the late 19th century. His best-known designer was Karel Nekula. After some years in Devon and more out of production, it is once more made in Fife, but it is the early items that have become highly valued.

**West Calder** Town southwest of Edinburgh, an old village with a ruined church of 1643, which became a centre of the oil shale industry in the 19th century. Nearby is Hermand House, a handsome classical house built in 1757 for George Fergusson, the law lord Lord Hermand.

**West Dunbartonshire** Local authority formed in 1996 from parts of Dumbarton District and Clydebank District of **Strathclyde Region**; see maps on pp. 394-5 and **local government** and see also **Dunbartonshire** and **East Dunbartonshire**. The administrative centre is **Dumbarton** and other towns include **Clydebank** and **Alexandria**.

**Wester Ross** Scenic area in the northwest **Highlands**, formerly the western mainland part of the country of **Ross and Cromarty**. It includes **Lochbroom**, **Gairloch**, **Torridon** and **Kintail**.

**Western Isles** (Gaelic **na h-Eileanan Siar**) Also known as the Outer **Hebrides**, a long island group of some 200 islands off the west coast of Scotland from which it is separated by the **Minch**. The crescent of islands stretches 209km (130mi) from the Butt of Lewis in the north to Barra Head in the south. In 1975 a new island authority was formed, with the Western Isles Council (Comhairle nan Eilean Siar) covering **Lewis** (previously part of **Ross and Cromarty**), **Harris**, **North Uist**, **Benbecula**, **South Uist** and **Barra** (all previously part of **Inverness-shire**). The area has continued as a local-authority unit after 1996; see maps on pp.394-5 and **local government**.

The largest island is divided between **Lewis** in the north and **Harris** in the south. The only town is **Stornoway**, on Lewis. The inlands of the islands are made up of rolling peat moorland with many lochs. The highest hills are in North Harris. The eastern shores are barren and rock-strewn but the western shores have long white beaches fringing a **machair** of fertile grassland. The main industries are **fishing**, crofting and **tweed** manufacture. **Gaelic** is still spoken throughout the islands. There are airfields on Lewis, Benbecula and Barra and ferry services to **Ullapool** and **Oban** on the mainland and to Uig on **Skye**. The islands have many prehistoric remains, the best known being the standing stones at **Calanais** and the **broch** at **Carloway**, both on Lewis.

**Westhall** see **Oyne**

**West Highland Free Press** Weekly newspaper published in **Skye** since 1972. It campaigns for land reform and supports the Gaelic language, with the slogan of the 19th-century **Highland Land League**: *An Tir, An Cànan, 'sna Daoine* – 'The Land, the Language, the People'.

**West Highland Way** A long-distance trail 156km (95mi) long, established in 1980, it runs along old drove roads, military roads and disused railways from **Milngavie** near **Glasgow** to **Fort William** in the **Highlands**, past **Loch Lomond**, **Crianlarich**, **Bridge of Orchy** and **Kinlochleven**.

**West Kilbride** Ayrshire village 7km (4mi) northwest of **Ardrossan**. A popular retirement area with lavish Edwardian and interwar houses, it has spread to include the shore hamlet of Seamills. Nearby is Law Castle and the **Hunterston** nuclear power station.

**West Linton** Large village on the Lyne Water below the **Pentland Hills**, 12km (7mi) southwest of **Penicuik**, once a silver- and leadmining area and a busy sheep market. The Gifford Stones are 3 panels of stone carvings rescued from the house of James Gifford, a 17th-century farmer and stonemason; they are now in the wall of a house standing on the same site.

**West Lothian** Former county south of the Firth of **Forth** (formerly Linlithgowshire); in 1975, with a somewhat enlarged area, it became a district of **Lothian Region** and, as West Lothian Council, since 1996 it has been a unitary local authority; see maps on pp.394-5 and **local government**. The administrative centre is **Livingston** and other towns include **Linlithgow** and **Bathgate**. It was the centre of the **shale**-oil industry and later industries have included engineering and electronics.

**Westminster Confession** Confession of faith drawn up in the 1640s by the Westminster Assembly, which was set up by the English parliament and consisted of English divines, with Scottish members in an advisory capacity. The Confession is Calvinist in essence, and was accepted by the **Church of Scotland** after 1688 as its principal subordinate standard of faith. It is now even more strongly adhered to by the **Free Church** and the **Free Presbyterian Church**.

**Westray** One of the North Islands of **Orkney**, with 2 early medieval churches and the substantial ruins of the Z-plan Noltland Castle, built in the 1570s by Gilbert Balfour with artillery fortifications, never fully completed and burnt by the **Covenanters** (in the care of **Historic Scotland**). Westray is now a centre of the **fishing** industry.

**Wet (Witt), James (Jacob) De** (1640–97) Artist, b. Haarlem, brought to Scotland in the mid 1670s by the architect Sir William **Bruce** to work at the Palace of Holyroodhouse, **Edinburgh**, where in 1684 he painted a sequence of the Scottish Kings for the Long Gallery. He also produced portraits and decorations for other Scottish houses, including **Glamis** Castle, returning finally to the Netherlands in 1691.

**Wet Wet Wet** Pop group formed in 1982 by Graeme Clark, Neil Mitchell, Marti Pellow and Tom Cunningham, which had chart success with light soul in the late 1980s and early 1990s. Their biggest hit was their cover of the Troggs' 'Love is all Around', the theme song for the film *Four Weddings and a Funeral*, in 1994.

**Whalsay** (pop. 1034) Island east of **Shetland** Mainland, important for its **fishing** industry, it has a church of 1733 and a 17th-century Hanseatic trading booth, restored in 1984. Its port is Symbister. The poet Hugh **MacDiarmid** spent some years there in the 1930s.

**Wheatley Report** A Royal Commission on Local Government in Scotland (1969), under the chairmanship of Lord Wheatley, a **Court of Session** judge, which resulted in the 1973 Local Government (Scotland) Act, implemented in 1975, creating a 2-tier system of local government; see **local government**.

**Wheeler, Sir H(arry) Anthony** (1919– ) Architect, b. Stranraer. With his partner Frank Sproson he was responsible for some remarkably innovative local authority housing in **Glenrothes**, **Dysart**, Buckhaven and elsewhere, and was architect of the Hunter Building at **Edinburgh College of Art** (1972–76).

**Whigs** Originally a term of derision directed at **Covenanters** who participated in the Whiggamore Raid of 1648 and later opposed the succession of the Catholic **James VII**, it described those who were opposed to the absolutist pretensions of late Restoration monarchy. The English Whig party merged with the Liberals in the mid 19th century. In Scotland Whigs supported the Hanoverians against the **Jacobites** and were largely supportive of union with England, but the Whig-Tory polarisation of political factions never really happened in Scotland where, Jacobites apart, the 2 political parties in the 18th century, at least until 1763, were **Argathelians** (supporters of the Duke of Argyll), and the **Squadrone Volante**.

**Whiggamore Raid** Political coup in 1648 provoked by the bankruptcy of the Engagers' policy of alliance with **Charles I** and war with the English parliament after the defeat of their army at Preston by Cromwell. With strong popular support, a force of poorly armed Whiggamores from the western **Lowlands**, led by Lord Eglinton, but with the tacit support of the Marquis of **Argyll**, who grasped the folly of the **Engagement**, marched on **Edinburgh** and compelled a politically isolated Committee of Estates, which fled to **Stirling**, to install a regime led by Argyll and commited to coexistence with England.

**whisky** see p.388

**Whistlebinkies** Group formed in **Glasgow** in late 1960s. Named after a 19th-century collection of Scottish poetry, the group's instrumental emphasis combines respect for the acoustic music of Scotland with a willingness to collaborate with such classical performers as Yehudi Menuhin and **Capella Nova**. Key members are piper Robert Wallace, instrumentalist and composer Eddie MacGuire and concertina player Stuart Eydmann.

**Whitby, Synod of** When Christianity came to Britain, missionaries from Rome visited the south and missionaries from Ireland the north. This led to differing traditions, for instance in the observance of Easter. In 663 or 664 the two traditions met in a conference at Whitby in Northumbria, the northern or Celtic tradition represented by King Oswy and the bishops Colman and Chad, and the southern or Roman by Oswy's son and bishops Agilbert and Wilfrid (the engineer of the conference). Oswy's feeling that he could not oppose the tradition of St Peter led to a decision for Rome. Colman left Lindisfarne, with the bones of St Aidan, for **Iona**, where Roman traditions were finally accepted in 716.

**White, Kenneth** (1936– ) Poet and essayist, b. Gorbals, Glasgow. He lived and travelled widely before settling in Brittany. His large body of writing combines international influences with

Scotch whisky is essentially made by malting barley, extracting the sugars from the malt with hot water, fermenting the 'sweet worts', to form 'wash', and distilling this twice or three times. The resulting spirit has to be matured for at least 3 years in oak casks before it can legally be called Scotch whisky. A great deal of this malt whisky is blended with grain whisky, made using unmalted cereal, usually maize, as well as barley. Most commercially available whisky is blended.

A drink of this kind has been distilled in Scotland from early times. The word whisky itself derives from Gaelic *uisge beatha*, meaning 'water of life'. In the past the name has also appeared in Scots as *usquebaugh*, and the Latin equivalent, *aqua vitae*, is recorded earlier, used for distilled spirits of various kinds, including whisky. The monasteries were the first large-scale producers of malt spirit, which otherwise remained largely a domestic process up until the later 18th century. In the Highlands in particular production was widespread but small-scale, and often became illicit, as taxation of the product gradually increased, and the privilege of distilling at home was withdrawn.

Technical innovations in the 19th century, and improvements in transport and shipping, led to a growth in the whisky industry. The traditional pot-still method of production, still used for making malt whisky, involves two separate distillations. The patent still, of which one version was invented in 1826 by Robert Stein and a much improved one 4 years later by Aeneas Coffey of Dublin, allows for continuous and faster production. This method is used to produce grain whisky in large quantities, though both Stein and Coffey stills were formerly used for making malt whisky. The later 19th century saw the introduction of blended whiskies. Although the term first meant a mixture of malts, it soon took on its present meaning of a combination of malt and grain whiskies.

Barely 5% of the malt whisky produced in Scotland today is bottled as single malts, the rest going into blends. Although appreciation of malt whisky has grown significantly in recent decades, it is the sale of blends which accounts for most of the industry's income at home and overseas. The Famous Grouse has been the leading brand domestically for over 20 years, while Johnnie Walker Red Label is the world best-seller.

Despite being manufactured by a relatively simple process, and containing few ingredients, whisky is probably the most complex of spirits. Every malt whisky in the land is essentially composed of water and barley, yet the same ingredients can produce a great array of flavours. The main factors in the flavour are the water, which varies widely in the different whisky regions; the peat which provides smoke to dry the malt (though nowadays other fuels are also used); the size and shape of the stills; and the type of cask used and the length of the maturing process. The great majority of casks used in maturing whisky nowadays are Bourbon casks from the USA, but some malt whisky is matured in sherry casks from Spain, producing a different flavour. **Speyside** is famous for its distilleries, and there are several scattered around the **Lowlands**. **Campbeltown** in Kintyre once had 34 distilleries; it now has only 3. There are also distilleries on **Arran**, **Islay**, **Jura**, **Mull**, **Skye** and the Mainland of **Orkney**. Grain whisky is made in **Glasgow**, **Edinburgh**, **Fife** and **Invergordon**.

Popular on the world market, Scotch has to compete not only with other alcoholic beverages, but also with other types of whisky, some of them crude imitations. It is a tough market, yet **Scotch** retains a prestigious reputation. While much of this is due to the inherent quality of the product, astute marketing also plays its part, and many distilleries encourage consumer interest with visitor centres and guided tours. Much of the industry is now owned by international firms.

*Onion-shaped whisky stills at Fettercairn Distillery.*

innovative philosophical insights. He has a high reputation in France, where he was Professor of 20th-Century Literature at the Sorbonne (1983–96). He was long unrecognised in his native land but since the publication of a poetry collection, *The Bird Path*, in 1989, others works have followed, including *The Blue Road* (1990) and *House of Tides* (2002), about his life in Brittany. His *Open Worlds: Collected Poems 1960–2000* was published in 2003. His idea of 'geopoetics' has developed and he set up the International Institute of Geopoetics in France in 1989; it now has related centres in other countries, including Scotland.

**White Cart Water** see **Cart**

**white cockade** A white rosette worn by **Jacobites** to represent the **white rose** as an emblem of the Stewart cause.

**Whitekirk** Tiny village between **Dunbar** and **Tantallon**, East Lothian, distinguished by a huge church, originally 12th-century and rebuilt in the 15th century (burned by suffragettes in 1914 and restored by Robert **Lorimer**). Nearby is a tithe barn, almost unique in Scotland, built as a tower house in 1540 and extended as a barn in the 17th century, now converted to a house. Whitekirk was once a major pilgrimage centre to its holy well, and the custom has recently been revived.

**Whitelaw, William** (1918–99) Politician, b. Nairn. MP for Penrith and the Borders division of Cumbria from 1955–83, when he was made Viscount Whitelaw. He was the first Northern Ireland Secretary (1972). His family were iron- and coal-masters.

**white rose** A Jacobite symbol (see **white cockade**), the **Jacobite** rose is usually regarded as *Alba Maxima*, also the white rose of York.

**Whithorn** Small **Galloway** town of early 19th-century houses, a former royal **burgh**, 15km (9mi) south of **Wigtown**. St **Ninian** is credited with having established a church here, known to Bede as Candida Casa (the White House), traditionally believed to have been the first Christian settlement in Scotland. Extensive excavations in the 1990s show that the site was continuously occupied from c.500, although little is actually known about Ninian or when he flourished. The now-ruined 12th-century cathedral-priory was an important pilgrim destination in the later Middle Ages. The Whithorn museum contains several important carved stones, including the 10th-century Monreith Cross.

**Whithorn, Isle of** see **Isle of Whithorn**

**Whitsun(day)** 15 May, one of the Scottish **term days**, though the date for removals and employment was later changed to 28 May. It was used as the name for the summer term in some of the

Scottish universities. The Christian festival of Whitsun or Pentecost is not on a fixed date, but varies with the date of Easter.

**Whittinghame** Little is left of this **East Lothian** village, to the south of **East Linton**, other than the parish church of 1821 and the schoolhouse. Whittinghame House is a great classical mansion by Sir Robert Smirke (1817); it belonged to the Balfours, including the Prime Minister Arthur **Balfour**, and is now divided. Whittinghame Tower, allegedly the scene of James **Bothwell**'s conspiracy to murder Lord **Darnley**, of late 15th-century date with fine 17th-century interiors, is now the home of the Balfours.

**Whyte, Christopher** (1952– ) Poet, novelist and academic, b. Glasgow. He taught in Italy for 12 years before returning to Scotland where he now lectures at **Glasgow University**. He has written **Gaelic** verse and edited collections of Gaelic poetry, notably Sorley **MacLean**'s *Dain do Eimhir* (2002). His novels include *Euphemia McFarrigle and the Laughing Virgin* (1995) and *The Cloud Machinery* (2000).

**Wick** Town at the northeastern tip of Scotland, a former royal **burgh**, with an airport with connections to **Orkney**, **Aberdeen** and **Edinburgh**. It was once the most important centre of the herring industry, with a harbour built by Thomas **Telford** (1824–31) and enlarged by the Stevensons (1862–67). Its new town (Pulteneytown) was laid out by Thomas Telford in 1808. The Caithness Glass factory is nearby. Wick Heritage Centre preserves items from the town's past. The Sinclair Aisle by the parish church contains monuments to the Earls of Shetland. Southeast of the town is the clifftop stronghold of Old Wick, probably originally a Norse house, in the 17th century a seat of the Earls of Caithness.

**Wigtown** Small **Galloway** town, a former royal **burgh**, 11km (7mi) south of **Newton Stewart**, still medieval in layout, with the ruins of the Old Parish Church (rebuilt in 1560 and 1730). Its churchyard contains gravestones of the **Wigtown Martyrs**. Their fate and even their existence has long been disputed, but Robert **Wodrow** records that the **Covenanters** Margaret Wilson and Margaret McLachlan were executed in 1685 for their refusal to take the oaths required by the Test Act, being tied to stakes below the high water mark in Wigtown Bay and left to drown. An obelisk monument was erected to their memory in 1858. The town is now predominantly late Georgian with a central square dominated by the Gothic County Buildings by Maitland **Wardrop** (1862). Wigtown has recently become Scotland's first Book Town, with many (second-hand) bookshops and literary events; see also **Dalmellington**.

The Chalmers Bethune Family, *portrait by David Wilkie, 1804.*

**Wigtown District** see **Dumfries and Galloway Region, Wigtownshire**

**Wigtownshire** Former county, the southwesternmost point of Scotland, known locally as 'the Shire', as opposed to the Stewartry (of **Kirkcudbright**); in 1975, with slight changes to its boundaries, it became Wigtown District and since 1996 it has been part of **Dumfries and Galloway.**

**Wilkie, Sir David** (1785–1841) Artist, b. Cults, Fife. Highly accomplished as an artist from his youth, Wilkie became one of the most influential artists of the early 19th century. He received instant recognition when his *Village Politicians* was exhibited at the Royal Academy in 1806, and he continued to excel at producing Scottish and other genre scenes, filled with rich incident. He was also an exceptional portraitist. Latterly he worked as a history painter and travelled extensively in Spain and the Middle East. His death at sea, near Malta, inspired his friend J M W Turner to paint *Peace: Burial at Sea.*

**William I** (1143–1214) King of Scots, succeeding his brother **Malcolm IV** in 1165. His long reign saw the extension and consolidation of royal power in the peripheries of Scotland and the continued spread, notable since the reign of **David I**, of Anglo-French influences in government and society. Attempting to seize the northern counties of England, William was captured at Alnwick in 1174 and forced to pay homage to Henry II of England in the Treaty of Falaise. Richard I later released William from the terms of this treaty for a cash payment (the Quitclaim of Canterbury, 1189). Though known by later chroniclers as 'the Lion', the reason for the epithet is unknown.

**William II and III** (1650–1702) King of Scotland, England and Ireland, b. The Hague. William, Prince of Orange, grandson of **Charles I**, married Mary, eldest daughter of the Duke of York (**James VII and II**) in 1677. James's Catholic policies led to an invitation to William to protect the Protestant religion and to the Glorious Revolution of 1688. James fled from the throne and William and Mary were proclaimed joint king and queen in 1689. James's Scottish supporters were victorious at **Killiecrankie**, but were later defeated at the Haughs of **Cromdale**. William was not popular in Scotland or England and, after his death when his horse stumbled on a molehill, a favourite Jacobite toast was 'To the little gentleman in black velvet'. He was succeeded by Mary's sister, Anne, as he had no children.

**William and Mary** see **William II and III**

**William of Orange** see **William II and III**

**Williamson, Duncan** (1928– ) Traveller, storyteller and singer, b. in a tent near Furnace, Argyll. Bearer of an enormous wealth of orally transmitted traditional lore. Scotland's best-known storyteller, he became well known through several books of stories collected during his travelling life, edited by his then wife Linda. His books include *The Horsieman*, *The Broonie*, *Silkies and Fairies*, and *Fireside Tales of the Traveller Children.*

**Williamson, Roy** see **Corries**

**Wilson, Brian** (1948–) Politician and journalist, b. **Dunoon**. He has been Labour MP for Cunninghame North since 1987 and Minister of State for various departments since 1997, latterly the Prime Minister's Special Representative for Trade and Reconstruction. He founded and edited the **West Highland Free Press**.

**Wilson, Charles** (1810–63) Architect. b. Glasgow. He was responsible for the planning of the Park area including the design of Trinity College (1856–61), the 3 hilltop towers which are the great landmarks of Glasgow's West End. He also designed the domed Neilson Institution (1849–50) which similarly dominates the **Paisley** skyline, and the neo-Tudor mental hospital at Gartnavel, **Glasgow** (1841–3).

**W**

**Wilson, Sir Daniel** (1816–92) Archaeologist and historian, b. Edinburgh. A multi-faceted scholar and artist, professor and later president at Toronto University, he published many books on Scottish archaeology, including *The Archaeology and Prehistoric Annals of Scotland* (1851), *Prehistoric Man* (1862), *Memorials of Edinburgh in Olden Times* (1847) and *The Lost Atlantis* (1892).

**Wilson, David** see **Peat Inn**

**Wilson, George Washington** (1823–93) Photographer, b. Alvah, Banffshire. Began his artistic career as a painter, but in the early 1850s started to use photography, with which he had considerable commercial success. His published photographs include views of **Aberdeen** and of Scottish and English scenery, and he was patronised by Queen Victoria.

**Wilson, James** (1742–89) Politician, b. near Ceres, Fife, moved to Philadelphia as a young man, where he campaigned for independence; he signed the Declaration of Independence in 1776. A conservative Federalist who believed in the need for a stronger central government for the new US, he is seen as a co-author with James Madison of the American Constitution of 1787.

**Wilson, Jocky** (1951– ) Darts professional, b. Kirkcaldy. Formerly a miner at Seafield Colliery, he was unemployed when he won his first big competition, and quickly became a popular figure, winning the world championship in 1982 and 1989.

**Wilson, John** (pen name **Christopher North**) (1785–1854) Writer and critic, b. Paisley. With J G **Lockhart**, he was an early editor of *Blackwood's Magazine*. His main contribution, under the name of Christopher North, was *Noctes Ambrosianae* (1822–35), lively imaginary conversations set in an **Edinburgh** tavern; they feature a caricature of James **Hogg**, as 'the Shepherd', the simple countryman, and Thomas de Quincey makes appearances as 'the Opium-eater'. They were published in 4 volumes in 1885. A political appointee to the chair of Moral Philosophy at Edinburgh, he managed to overcome his lack of qualifications with his charismatic lectures.

**Wilson, Thomas Brendan** (1928–2001) Composer, b. USA. Resident in Scotland nearly all his life. His work is deeply serious, and includes a number of impressive religious works. His opera *The Confessions of a Justified Sinner* (1976) is considered an outstanding work.

**Winning, Thomas, Cardinal** (1925–2001) Churchman, b. Wishaw. A career priest, he became Archbishop of Glasgow in 1974 and was made a cardinal in 1994. A conscientious Christian, and much loved for his championship of the poor, he also provoked debate with some of his hardline views.

**Winter Queen** see **Elizabeth of Bohemia**

**Winton House** see **Pencaitland**

**Winzet, Ninian** (1518–92) Churchman, b. Renfrew. A Catholic priest who resisted the **Reformation**, he was a witty opponent of John **Knox**, publishing several pamphlets against him in **Scots**.

**Wishart, George** (c 1513–46) Protestant martyr, b. Angus. After charges of heresy, he was forced into exile in England and on the Continent, but returned in 1543. An inspiration to John **Knox**, with his preaching of Lutheran doctrines, Wishart was burnt at the stake at **St Andrews** on the orders of Cardinal David **Beaton**.

**Wishaw** Industrial town southeast of **Glasgow**, near **Motherwell**, with which it had joint **burgh** status until 1975, formerly a major centre of the iron, steel and coal industries.

**Witherspoon, John** (1723–94) Theologian, b. Gifford, East Lothian. He became President of the College of New Jersey (now Princeton) in 1768, where he taught future US President James Madison. His teaching helped to entrench the influence of **Common Sense philosophy** in North American education. He contributed to the shaping of the American Declaration of Independence in 1776.

**Witt, Jacob de** see **Wet, James de**

**Wodrow, Robert** (1679–1734) Church historian, b. Glasgow. He wrote histories of the **Covenanters**, including a *History of the Sufferings of the Church of Scotland* (1721–2).

**Wolf of Badenoch** see **Stewart, Alexander**

**Wolfson, Sir Isaac** (1897–1992) Businessman and philanthropist, b. Glasgow. Starting at the bottom, Wolfson became managing director of Great Universal Stores and made a fortune. The Wolfson Foundation, which he established in 1955, continues to support charitable aims, particularly Jewish causes. He founded Wolfson College, Oxford, in 1966, and was a major benefactor to **Glasgow University**.

**wolves** Once quite common in the forests of the north, until destroyed by hunting and trapping, the wolf was the last large predator to become extinct in Scotland, probably in the late 17th century. Recently efforts have been made to reintroduce it, but these seem unlikely to succeed, although there is little evidence that the Scottish wolf was ever a danger to humans. A small pack lives in captivity at Kincraig Highland Wildlife Park.

**W**

**Wood, Sir Andrew** (c.1455–1539) Naval commander, b. Largo, Fife. A trader and shipowner, he was knighted by **James III** after service at sea against the English. He also served **James IV**, his naval exploits recounted in sometimes questionable detail by the later chronicler Robert **Lindsay** of Pitscottie. Wood was later made captain of the royal flagship, the **Great Michael**. After the Battle of **Flodden**, he did diplomatic service in France.

**Wood, Stanley Purdie** (1939– ) Fossil collector, b. Edinburgh. After some years in the Merchant Navy, he worked with an insurance company. He became interested in fossils after finding fossil fish on the shore near **Edinburgh**, and he discovered a Carboniferous fossil shark on a housing estate in **Bearsden**, Glasgow. At East Kirkton, near **Bathgate**, he discovered the earliest known amphibian and reptile, known as Lizzie.

**Wood, Wendy** (Gwendoline Meacham) (1892–1981) Political activist, b. Maidstone. By blood one quarter Scots, in her heart wholly, she was a founder member of the National Party of Scotland (later the SNP) in 1928, but found it rather restrictive. She was popular for her energy, commitment and imagination, leading a march on **Stirling** Castle in 1932, and replacing the Union flag with the Lion Rampant, and was an inspiring speaker and broadcaster, often working with young people.

**woollen manufacture** The most widely distributed of the textile industries in Scotland. Wool from locally reared sheep was initially hand-spun and woven or knitted on a domestic scale. Knitting frames were introduced in the 17th century, and in the late 18th century first carding, and then weaving, were mechanised. Power-loom weaving supplanted handlooms in the mid 19th century, and later power-operated knitting machines were introduced. With power came concentration, in the **Borders** in **Galashiels**, **Innerleithen**, Walkerburn and **Peebles** (tweed) and in **Hawick** (hosiery). Other centres of the industry were in **Dumfries (tweed)**, **Clackmannanshire** and **Stirling**shire (woollens and **tartans**) and **Aberdeen** (woollens). In the **Western Isles** hand-spinning and weaving survived, and were organanised in the 1890s as the **Harris Tweed** industry. This survives, as does part of the Borders hosiery industry.

**Worcester, Battle of** The final battle in the Civil War was fought near Worcester on 3 September 1651. The largely Scottish army fighting for **Charles II** was defeated by the Parliamentary forces, but Charles escaped to France to await the Restoration. The defeat opened the way for the English under General **Monck** to crush remaining resistance in Scotland.

Most of the captured Scots were sent as slaves to the West Indies.

**Wrath, Cape** see **Cape Wrath**

**Wright, Frances** (Fanny) (1795–1852) Social reformer, b. Dundee. A wealthy and influential woman, she emigrated to the US in 1818 and campaigned for female suffrage and the abolition of slavery. She produced, with Robert Dale Owen (1801–77), grandson of David **Dale**, the socialist paper, *Free Enquirer*.

**Wright, John Michael** (1617–94) Artist, possibly b. London of Scottish parents. By 1636 Wright was in **Edinburgh** studying under George **Jamesone**, and then Rome. In much demand as a portrait painter, his sitters included King **Charles II**, Sir William **Bruce**, and the wonderfully stylish *Lord Mungo Murray* in Highland dress (**Scottish National Portrait Gallery**).

**Wright, Revd Kenyon Edward** (1932– ) Episcopal clergyman, b. Paisley. After many years as a missionary in India, he returned to the UK, to Coventry Cathedral, where he was canon (1974–81). From 1981 to 1990 he was General Secretary of the Scottish Churches Council. In the political arena he played a leading role in the **Scottish Constitutional Convention.**

**Writers to the Signet (W.S.)** One of the legal bodies for Scottish solicitors (the others include the Society of Solicitors in the Supreme Court) deriving its name from those authorised to use the private seal (signet) of the king. The Signet Library houses a fine collection of law books in an elegant Georgian building adjoining Parliament House in **Edinburgh**.

**Wylie, Edward Grigg** (1884/5–1954) Classical-modern architect, b. Glasgow. He designed the Glasgow Dental Hospital and the Scottish Legal Life Building, Bothwell Street, both **Glasgow** (1927–31) and was architect to the Scottish Industrial Estates, designing those at Hillington, Carfin, Larkhall and Newhouse.

**Wylie, George** (1921– ) Artist, b. Glasgow. He worked as a customs officer before taking up art. His works, generally on a large scale, such as the giant floating paper boat *Origami*, have achieved wide popularity with both critics and the public.

**Wyntoun, Andrew** (c.1355–1420) Historian, prior of the monastery of St Serf, Loch Leven. His *Orygynal Cronykil of Scotland* is a lengthy verse history strongly nationalistic in flavour. It is a valuable resource, often drawing on earlier sources which have now been lost.

**Wyre** One of the North Islands of **Orkney**, to the southeast of **Rousay**, with Cubbie Roo's Castle, the ruined 12th-century stronghold of a Norse pirate, now in the care of **Historic Scotland**.

**Wyvis, Ben** see **Ben Wyvis**

**Yarrow** The Yarrow Water runs from **St Mary's Loch** and meets the **Ettrick** valley at **Philiphaugh**. The **ballads** of the area and its scenery were a source of inspiration to Walter **Scott**, James **Hogg** and R L **Stevenson**.

**Yarrow, Sir Alfred Fernandez** (1842–1932) Shipbuilder, b. London. Alfred Yarrow moved his shipbuilding business from the Isle of Dogs to Scotstoun, on the River **Clyde** to the west of **Glasgow**, in 1907 bringing many workers up from London, and established Yarrow's Shipyards. He prospered during World War I, manufacturing torpedo boats and destroyers, and after 1918 manufactured lifejackets and disability aids such as artificial limbs. His son Sir Harold succeeded him and developed his father's philanthropic projects. The yard is now run by BAE Systems.

**Yell** Island of the **Shetland** group, lying immediately north of the Mainland. Its ferry port is Ulsta. The Old Haa of Burravoe, built 1672 for Robert Tyrie and recently restored, contains a local history exhibition.

**Yester House/Castle** see **Gifford**

**Yetholm** Southeast of **Kelso** near the Border, the twin villages of Kirk and Town Yetholm are separated by the Bowmont Water. Kirk Yetholm was well known as a base of the Scottish gypsies until the 19th century. It is northern end of the Pennine Way, which meets the **St Cuthbert's Way** there.

**York, Cardinal** see **Stewart, Henry Benedict, Cardinal, Duke of York**

**Young, Douglas** (1913–73) Poet and dramatist, b. Tayport, Fife. A member (later chairman) of the SNP, he was imprisoned for refusing to serve in World War II because there was no independent Scottish army. He taught classics at **Dundee** and **St Andrews**, and later at Canadian and US universities. He wrote poetry in **Scots** and oustanding Scots versions of Aristophanes' plays: *The Burdies* (1959) and *The Puddocks* (1957).

**Young, James** (1811–83) Industrial chemist, b. Glasgow. Manager of chemical works in northeast England, he developed various cost-saving processes, but it was his experiments with paraffin production that developed the **shale** industry in Scotland (and gave him the nickname of 'Paraffin' Young). He endowed a chair of chemical technology in what is now **Strathclyde University**.

**Younger, George, 1st Viscount Younger of Leckie** (1851–1929) Brewer and politician, b. Alloa. A nephew of William

*James 'Paraffin' Young.*

McEwan, he ran the Younger brewing firm (which merged with McEwan's in 1931) before becoming MP for **Ayr**. His great-grandson, George Younger (1931–2003), also MP for Ayr (1964–92), was Secretary of State for Scotland from 1979 to 1986, and served as Defence Secretary, 1986–9.

**Young Pretender** see **Stewart, Charles Edward**

**Ythan** River in Aberdeenshire which flows, mainly in an easterly direction, from Ythanwells (to the east of **Huntly**), passing **Fyvie** and **Ellon**, where it widens and flows south to the sea near **Newburgh**.

**Yule** The pagan celebration of the winter solstice was transformed by the early Christian Church into the festival of Christmas; it extended from Christmas Eve until Twelfth Night. After the **Reformation** the Church disapproved of the festival, perhaps looking back to its origins, but the term is still used for Christmas in some parts of Scotland.

**Zetland** see **Shetland**

# Scotland's Current Unitary Authorities

Shetland Islands

Orkney Islands

Na h-Eileanan Siar

Highland

Moray

Aberdeenshire

Aberdeen
City

Perth and
Kinross

Angus

Dundee
City

Argyll and Bute

Stirling

Clackmannanshire

Fife

1 Inverclyde
2 Renfrewshire
3 East Renfrewshire
4 Glasgow City
5 Edinburgh City

West
Dunbartonshire

East
Dunbartonshire

Falkirk

1

2   4

3

North
Lanarkshire

West
Lothian

5

East
Lothian

Midlothian

North
Ayrshire

South
Lanarkshire

Scottish
Borders

East
Ayrshire

South
Ayrshire

Dumfries and Galloway

0        40 kilometres

0     20 miles

N

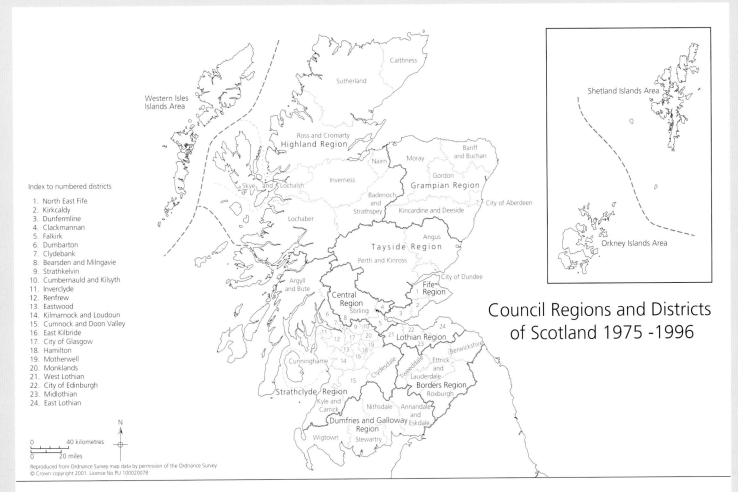

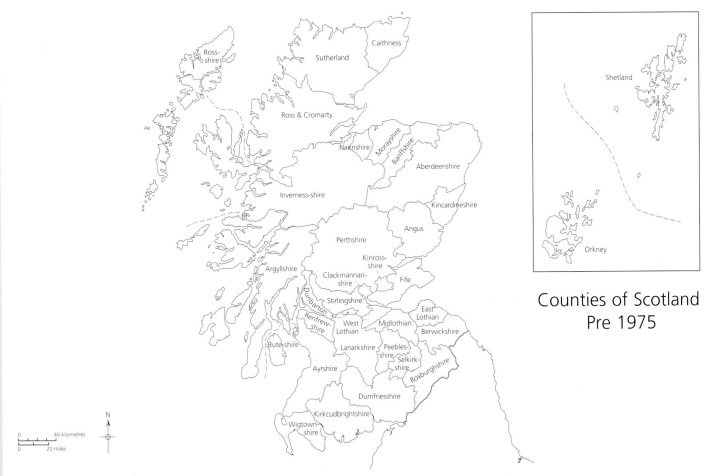

Index to numbered districts

1. North East Fife
2. Kirkcaldy
3. Dunfermline
4. Clackmannan
5. Falkirk
6. Dumbarton
7. Clydebank
8. Bearsden and Milngavie
9. Strathkelvin
10. Cumbernauld and Kilsyth
11. Inverclyde
12. Renfrew
13. Eastwood
14. Kilmarnock and Loudoun
15. Cumnock and Doon Valley
16. East Kilbride
17. City of Glasgow
18. Hamilton
19. Motherwell
20. Monklands
21. West Lothian
22. City of Edinburgh
23. Midlothian
24. East Lothian

Western Isles
Islands Area

Caithness

Sutherland

Shetland Islands Area

Orkney Islands Area

Ross and Cromarty
Highland Region

Banff
and Buchan

Nairn    Moray

Gordon

Grampian Region

Inverness

Skye and Lochalsh

Badenoch
and
Strathspey

Kincardine and Deeside

City of Aberdeen

Lochaber

Angus

Tayside Region

Perth and Kinross

City of Dundee

Argyll
and Bute

Fife
Region

Central
Region

Stirling

1

2

Lothian Region

22

24

21

23

Berwickshire

Ettrick
and
Lauderdale

Clydesdale

Tweeddale

Cunninghame

Roxburgh

Borders Region

Strathclyde Region

Kyle and
Carrick

Nithsdale

Annandale
and
Eskdale

Dumfries and Galloway
Region

Wigtown    Stewartry

## Council Regions and Districts
## of Scotland 1975 -1996

N

0    40 kilometres

0    20 miles

Ross-
shire

Caithness

Sutherland

Shetland

Ross & Cromarty

Nairnshire

Morayshire

Banffshire

Aberdeenshire

Orkney

Inverness-shire

Kincardineshire

Angus

Perthshire

Kinross-
shire

Argyllshire

Clackmannan-
shire

Fife

Dunbarton

Stirlingshire

East
Lothian

Renfrew-
shire

West
Lothian

Midlothian

Berwickshire

Bute-shire

Lanarkshire

Peebles-
shire

Selkirk-
shire

Ayrshire

Roxburghshire

Dumfriesshire

Kirkcudbrightshire

Wigtown-
shire

## Counties of Scotland
## Pre 1975

N

0    40 kilometres

0    20 miles

# CALENDAR OF ANNUAL FESTIVALS

**JAN 1: NE'ERDAY.** New Year's Day is the largest traditional holiday in Scotland. It became the central winter holiday in 1560 when the Protestant reformers banned Yule.

**JAN 25: BURNS NIGHT.** Anniversary of the birth of Robert Burns, celebrated with a dinner of haggis etc, and speeches, songs and recitations; the main speech is known as the Immortal Memory.

**JAN** (last Tuesday): **UP HELLY AA.** Major holiday in Shetland at which the islands' Viking history is celebrated, including in Lerwick the burning of a Viking longship.

**FEB** (moveable): **FASTERN'S E'EN.** The Scots Shrove Tuesday, the day before the beginning of Lent. This was once a major holiday but today it is marked only by folk football matches in the Borders.

**MARCH 1: WHUPPITY STOORIE** (or **SCOORIE**), Lanark, when at 6 o' clock in the evening boys run or walk three times round the parish church, each swinging round a ball of paper on a string. It is supposed to be a way of greeting spring.

**APR 1: HUNTYGOWK,** meaning 'look who's a cuckoo' – the Scots April Fool.

**APR 6: TARTAN DAY.** Started in Canada in the 1980s. It achieved a high profile when the first major American event was held in 1998, and it now has its focus in Manhattan. It is on the anniversary of the Declaration of Arbroath, one of the sources for the constitution of the United States of America.

**APRIL** (middle): **LINKS MARKET,** Kirkcaldy. An annual market at Easter was established in the burgh in 1305 and it seems to have been held without major interruptions since then. It is now regarded by touring showmen in Scotland as the start of their season.

**MAY 1: BELTANE,** a quarter-day in the Celtic calendar and the most important Celtic holiday after Samhuinn, which occurs six months later. People greet the dawn, particularly on Arthur's Seat in Edinburgh, visit holy wells and light bonfires.

**JUNE: HAWICK COMMON RIDING** is held on the Friday and Saturday which fall between 5/6 and 11/12 June. It dates from a skirmish with the English in 1514, the year after the disastrous Battle of Flodden. Other ancient common ridings are held at Selkirk and Lauder. They all feature a ride on horseback round the boundaries of the town.

**JUNE** (on the Thursday between 6 and 12 June): **LANIMER DAY,** Lanark. 'Lanimer' is a Scots word meaning 'land boundary': before about 1800 many burghs made an annual check of their boundaries. At Lanark, this in now part of the burgh's summer holiday.

**JUNE** (first Friday after the second Monday): **SELKIRK COMMON RIDING.**

**JUNE** (first Tuesday after the second Thursday): Riding of the Marches at Linlithgow.

**JUNE** (midsummer): **CERES GAMES.** A holiday is said to have been held at this Fife village since 1315, the first anniversary of the Battle of Bannockburn.

**JULY** (various dates): **THE TRADES,** the trades holidays at various burghs, originally the period when tradesmen took their summer week, or later fortnight, but now largely forgotten.

**JULY** (middle): **GLASGOW FAIR** dates from the late 12th century and until about 1820 was a general fair for trading and the sale of horses and cattle. By 1840 it had completely changed, becoming a huge and varied collection of shows at the foot of the Saltmarket, spilling onto Glasgow Green. Then people started to leave the city by railway and steamboat – going 'doon the watter' – and the Fair became identified with the Firth of Clyde and with towns like Rothesay and Dunoon. Around 1960 it collapsed because car ownership enabled Glasgow people to travel further, and cheap flights to Spain allowed them to enjoy better weather.

**JULY** (last Friday): **LANGHOLM COMMON RIDING.**

**AUG 1: LAMMAS FAIR** to mark one of the Scottish term days, still held in St Andrews and Inverkeithing, where it includes the Hat and Ribbon Race.

**AUG** (first Saturday): **LAUDER COMMON RIDING.**

**AUG: MARYMASS,** Irvine. Originally held on 15 August, the Feast of the Assumption of the Virgin (Mary-mass), the holiday now focuses on a week in the middle of the month. In 1928 the holiday was reorganised so that it now commemorates a visit to Irvine made by Mary, Queen of Scots.

**AUG: RED HOSE RACE,** Carnwath. A foot race for the prize of a pair of red hose has been held here at least since 1456.

**OCT: THE MOD.** The festival of the Gaelic language, arts and culture is held annually in October, at a different venue each year.

**OCT 31: HALLOWEEN.** The evening before All Hallows' Day, now more usually called All Saints' Day. Traditional activities such as guising and dooking for apples are now being supplanted by imports from America such as 'trick or treat'.

**NOV 1: SAMHUINN.** The beginning of the Celtic Year, and also All Saints' Day.

**NOV 30: ST ANDREW'S DAY.** Since 1560 it has been celebrated only rarely, though now more popular with Scots abroad than at home.

**DEC 25: YULE.** The Protestant reformers abolished Christmas in 1560, although it survived in a limited form in various places, particularly the northeast. In the 1840s English Christmas started to be imported and after World War I it became quite an important festival.

**DEC 31: HOGMANAY** see Jan 1: Ne'erday and p.285.

# SCOTTISH SOCIETIES AND ORGANISATIONS

*indicates entry in text*

**\*ASSOCIATION FOR SCOTTISH LITERARY STUDIES (ASLS)**
c/o Department of Scottish History,
University of Glasgow,
9 University Gardens,
Glasgow G12 8QH
Tel 0141 330 5309
www2.arts.gla.ac.uk/ScotLit/ASLS

**\*BÒRD NA GÀIDHLIG (ALBA)**
Ness Horizons, Kintail House,
Beechwood Park, Inverness IV2 3BW.
Tel 01463 732570
www.bord-na-gaidhlig.org.uk

**\*CLI GAIDHLIG**
North Tower, The Castle, Inverness IV2 3EE
Tel 01463 226710   www.cli.org.uk

**\*COLLEGE OF PIPING**
16-24 Otago Street, Glasgow G12 8JH
Tel 0141 334 3587
www.college-of-piping.co.uk

**\*COMUNN GAIDHEALACH, AN**
109 Church Street, Inverness IV1 1EY
Tel 01463 231226   www.the-mod.co.uk

**\*HISTORIC SCOTLAND**
Longmore House, Salisbury Place,
Edinburgh EH9 1SH
Tel 0131 668 8600
www.historic-scotland.gov.uk

**MOUNTAINEERING COUNCIL OF SCOTLAND**
The Old Granary, West Mill Street,
Perth PH1 5QP
Tel 01738 638 227
www.mountaineering-scotland.org.uk

**\*NATIONAL ARCHIVES OF SCOTLAND**
H M General Register House,
2 Princes Street, Edinburgh EH1 3YY
Tel 0131 535 1334   www.nas.gov.uk

**\*NATIONAL GALLERIES OF SCOTLAND**
The Mound, Edinburgh EH2 2EL
Tel 0131 624 6200
recorded information 0131 332 2266
www.natgalscot.ac.uk

**\*NATIONAL LIBRARY OF SCOTLAND**
George IV Bridge, Edinburgh EH1 1EW
Tel 0131 226 4531   www.nls.uk

**\*NATIONAL MUSEUMS OF SCOTLAND**
Chambers Street, Edinburgh EH1 1JF
Tel 0131 225 4422   www.nms.ac.uk

**\*NATIONAL TRUST FOR SCOTLAND (NTS)**
28 Charlotte Square, Edinburgh EH2 4ET
Tel 0131 243 9300   www.nts.org.uk

**\*ROBERT BURNS WORLD FEDERATION**
Dean Castle Country Park, Kilmarnock,
Ayrshire KA3 1XB
Tel 01563 572469   www.worldburnsclub.com

**ROYAL HIGHLAND AND AGRICULTURAL SOCIETY**
Royal Highland Centre, Ingliston,
Edinburgh EH28 8NF
Tel 0131 335 6200   www.rhaas.org.uk

**\*ROYAL INCORPORATION OF ARCHITECTS IN SCOTLAND**
15 Rutland Square, Edinburgh EH1 2BE
Tel 0131 229 7545   www.rias.org.uk

**\*ROYAL SCOTTISH ACADEMY**
The Mound, Edinburgh EH2 2EL
Tel 0131 225 6671
www.royalscottishacademy.org

**\*ROYAL SCOTTISH COUNTRY DANCE SOCIETY**
12 Coates Crescent, Edinburgh EH3 7AF
Tel 0131 225 3854   www.rscds.org

**\*ROYAL SOCIETY OF EDINBURGH**
22-26 George Street, Edinburgh EH2 2PQ
Tel 0131 240 5000   www.ma.hw.ac.uk/RSE

**\*SALTIRE SOCIETY**
9 Fountain Close, 22 High Street,
Edinburgh EH1 1TF
Tel 0131 556 1836
www.saltiresociety.org.co.uk

**SCOTCH MALT WHISKY SOCIETY**
The Vaults, 87 Giles Street, Edinburgh EH6 6BZ
Tel 0131 554 3451   www.smws.com

**SCOTS LANGUAGE RESOURCE CENTRE**
A K Bell Library, York Place, Perth PH2 8EP
Tel 01738 440199   www.scotsyett.com

**SCOTS ANCESTRY RESEARCH SOCIETY**
8 York Road, Edinburgh EH5 3EH
Tel 0131 552 2028   www.scotsanc.co.uk

**\*SCOTTISH ARTS COUNCIL**
12 Manor Place, Edinburgh EH3 7DD
Tel 0131 226 6051   www.sac.org.uk

**\*SCOTTISH BALLET**
261 West Princes Street, Glasgow G4 9EE
Tel 0141 331 2931   www.scottishballet.co.uk

**SCOTTISH BOOK TRUST**
Sandeman House, Trunk's Close,
55 High Street, Edinburgh EH1 1SR
Tel 0131 524 0160
www.scottishbooktrust.com

**SCOTTISH COMMUNITY DRAMA ASSOCIATION**
5 York Place, Edinburgh EH1 3EB
Tel 0131 557 5552   www.scda.org.uk

**\*SCOTTISH FOOTBALL ASSOCIATION**
Hampden Park, Glasgow G42 9AY
Tel 0141 616 6000   www.scottishfa.co.uk

**\*SCOTTISH GENEALOGY SOCIETY**
15 Victoria Terrace, Edinburgh EH1 2JL
Tel 0131 220 3677   www.scotsgenealogy.com

**SCOTTISH LANGUAGE DICTIONARIES**
27 George Square, Edinburgh EH8 9LD
Tel 0131 650 4149   www.sldl.org.uk

**SCOTTISH MUSIC CENTRE**
1 Bowmont Gardens, Glasgow G12 9LR
Tel 0141 334 6393
www.scottishmusiccentre.com

**\*SCOTTISH NATURAL HERITAGE**
12 Hope Terrace, Edinburgh EH9 2AS
Tel 0131 447 4784   www.snh.org.uk

**SCOTTISH OFFICIAL BOARD OF HIGHLAND DANCING**
Heritage House, 32 Grange Loan,
Edinburgh EH9 2NR
Tel 0131 668 3965
www.scottishhighlanddancing.org

**\*SCOTTISH OPERA**
39 Elmbank Crescent, Glasgow G2 4PT
Tel Box Office 0141 332 9000
enquiries 0141 248 4567
www.scottishopera.org.uk

**SCOTTISH PIPE BAND ASSOCIATION**
45 Washington Street, Glasgow G3 8AZ
Tel 0141 221 5414   wwwrspba.org

**SCOTTISH PLACE-NAME SOCIETY**
(Comann Ainmean-Aite na h-Alba)
c/o School Of Scottish Studies,
University of Edinburgh,
Edinburgh EH8 9LD
www.st-andrews.ac.uk/institute/sassi/spns

**\*SCOTTISH POETRY LIBRARY**
5 Crichton's Close, Canongate,
Edinburgh EH8 8DT
Tel 0131 557 2876   www.spl.org.uk

**SCOTTISH PUBLISHERS ASSOCIATION**
Scottish Book Centre, 137 Dundee Street,
Edinburgh EH11 1BG
Tel 0131 228 6866
www.scottishbooks.org

**\*SCOTTISH RUGBY UNION**
Murrayfield, Edinburgh EH12 5PJ
Tel 0131 346 5000   www.sru.org.uk

**\*SCOTTISH SCREEN**
2nd Floor, 249 West George Street,
Glasgow G2 4QE
Tel 0141 302 1700
www.scottishscreen.com

**\*SCOTTISH TARTANS SOCIETY**
www.scottish-tartans-society.co.uk

**SCOTTISH YOUTH HOSTELS ASSOCIATION**
7 Glebe Crescent, Stirling FK8 2JA
Tel 01786 891400   www.syha.org.uk

**\*SCOTWAYS**
(Scottish Rights of Way and Access Society)
24 Annandale Street, Edinburgh EH7 4AN
Tel 0131 558 1222   www.scotways.com

**\*SCRAN SCOTTISH CULTURAL RESOURCES ARCHIVE**
Abden House, 1 Marchhall Crescent,
Edinburgh EH16 5HP
Tel 0131 662 1211   www.scran.ac.uk

**\*SOCIETY OF ANTIQUARIES OF SCOTLAND**
Royal Museum, Chambers Street,
Edinburgh EH1 2JL
Tel 0131 247 4115/4113
www.socantscot.org

**\*SPORTSCOTLAND**
Caledonia House, South Gyle,
Edinburgh EH12 9DQ
Tel 0131 317 7200
www.sportscotland.org.uk

**\*TRADITIONAL MUSIC AND SONG ASSOCIATION OF SCOTLAND (TMSA)**
95-97 St Leonard's Road, Edinburgh EH8 9QY
Tel 0131 667 5587   www.tmsa.info

**\*VISITSCOTLAND**
23 Ravelston Terrace,
Edinburgh EH4 3TP
Tel 0131 332 2433
www.visitscotland.com

# FURTHER READING

*Mainly readily available standard works*

**GENERAL/GENERAL HISTORY** see also Politics

Daiches, David ed
   *The New Companion to Scottish Culture* Edinburgh 1993.
Devine, T M *The Scottish Nation 1700-2000* London 1999.
Devine, T M and Finlay, R J eds
   *Scotland in the Twentieth Century* Edinburgh 1996.
Donaldson, Gordon and Morpeth, Robert S
   *A Dictionary of Scottish History* Edinburgh 1977.
Donnachie, Ian and Hewitt, George
   *Collins Dictionary of Scottish History* new edn Glasgow 2003
Ferguson, William *The Identity of the Scottish Nation:*
   *An Historic Quest* Edinburgh 1998.
Houston, R A and Knox, W W J eds
   *The New Penguin History of Scotland* London 2001.
Keay, John and Keay, Julia
   *Collins Encyclopaedia of Scotland* new edn London 2000.
Lynch, Michael *Scotland: A New History* London 1992.
Lynch, Michael ed
   *The Oxford Companion to Scottish History* Oxford 2001.
McCrone, David *Understanding Scotland:*
   *the Sociology of a Stateless Nation* 2nd edn London 2001.
Menzies, Gordon ed *Who are the Scots? and The Scottish Nation*
   Edinburgh 2002.
Menzies, Gordon ed *In Search of Scotland* Edinburgh 2001.
Smith, Robin *The Making of Scotland: A Comprehensive Guide to the*
   *Growth of its Cities, Towns and Villages* Edinburgh 2001.
Smout, T C *A History of the Scottish People, 1530-1860* London 1969.
Smout, T C *A Century of the Scottish People, 1830-1950* London 1986.
Tabraham, Chris *The Illustrated History of Scotland* Edinburgh 2003.
Thomson, Derick S *The Companion to Gaelic Scotland* Oxford 1983.


New History of Scotland (Edinburgh)
   Smyth, Alfred *Warlords and Holy Men: Scotland AD 800-1000* 1989.
   Barrow, Geoffrey *Kingship & Unity: Scotland 1000-1306* new edn
   2003.
   Grant, Alexander *Independence & Nationhood:*
      *Scotland 1306-1469* 1991.
   Wormald, Jennifer *Court, Kirk and Community:*
      *Scotland 1470-1625* 1991.
   Mitchison, Rosalind *Lordship to Patronage: Scotland 1603-1745* 1990.
   Lenman, Bruce *Integration and Enlightenment:*
      *Scotland 1745-1832* 1990.
   Checkland, O and Checkland, S *Industry & Ethos:*
      *Scotland 1832-1914* 1989.
   Harvie, Christopher *No Gods and Precious Few Heroes:*
      *Twentieth-Century Scotland* new edn 1998.


**SCOTLAND TODAY** (annual publications)
*The Complete Scotland.*
*Who's Who in Scotland.*
*Whitaker's Scottish Almanack*


**AGRICULTURE**
Fenton, Alexander *Scottish Country Life: Our Rural Past* Edinburgh 1987.
Sprott, Gavin *Agriculture* Edinburgh 1995
Symon, J A *Scottish Farming, Past and Present* (1959)


**ARCHAEOLOGY**
Ritchie, Anna and Graham *Oxford Archaeological Guide:*
   *Scotland* Oxford 1998.
Armit, Ian *Scotland's Hidden History* Stroud 1998.
Exploring Scotland's Heritage series (Series Editor Anna Ritchie)
   Baldwin, John *Edinburgh, Lothian and the Borders* Edinburgh 1997.
   Close-Brooks, Johanna *The Highlands* Edinburgh 1996.
   Ritchie, Anna *Orkney* Edinburgh 1996.
   Ritchie, Anna *Shetland* Edinburgh 1997.

   Ritchie, Graham and Harman, Mary *Argyll and the Western Isles*
      Edinburgh 1996.
   Shepherd, Ian *Aberdeen and North-East Scotland* Edinburgh 1996.
   Stell, Geoffrey *Dumfries and Galloway* Edinburgh 1996.
   Stevenson, Jack *Glasgow, Clydeside and Stirling* Edinburgh 1995.
   Walker, Bruce and Ritchie, Graham *Fife, Perthshire and Angus*
      Edinburgh 1996.


**ARCHITECTURE**
The Buildings of Scotland series (London and New Haven)
   Gifford, John *Dumfries and Galloway* 1996.
   Gifford, John *Fife* 1988.
   Gifford, John *Highlands and Islands* 1992.
   Gifford, John, McWilliam, Colin and Walker, David *Edinburgh* 1984.
   Gifford, John and Walker, Frank Arneil
      *Stirling and Central Scotland* 2002.
   McWilliam, Colin *Lothian Except Edinburgh* 1978.
   Walker, Frank Arneil *Argyll and Bute* 2000.
   Williamson, Elizabeth, Riches, Anne and Higgs, Malcolm *Glasgow* 1990.

The Rutland Press, publishing arm of the Royal Incoporation of
Architects in Scotland, publishes an extensive series of Illustrated
Architecural Guides to various part of Scotland; see their website at
www.rias.org.uk


Dunbar, John G *Scottish royal palaces: the architecture of the royal*
   *residences during the late medieval and early Renaissance periods*
   East Linton 1999.
Fawcett, Richard *Scottish medieval churches: an introduction to the*
   *ecclesiastical architecture of the 12th to the 16th centuries in the*
   *care of the Secretary of State for Scotland* Edinburgh 1985.
Fenton, Alexander and Walker, Bruce *The Rural Architecture of Scotland*
   Edinburgh 1981.
Glendinning, Miles, MacInnes, Ranald and MacKechnie, Aoghnus
   *A History of Scottish Architecture* Edinburgh 1996.
Macaulay, James *The classical country house in Scotland 1660-1800*
   London 1987.
Stell, Geoffrey, Shaw, John and Storrier, Susan eds *Scotland's Buildings:*
   *Scottish Life and Society*, vol.3, Edinburgh 2004.


**ART**
Billcliffe, Roger *The Glasgow Boys* London 1985.
Brown, Katrina *et al Here and Now – Scottish Art 1990-2001*
   Dundee 2001.
Harris, Paul and Halsby, Julian
   *The Dictionary of Scottish Painters 1600-1960* Edinburgh 1990.
Hartley, Keith *et al Scottish Art since 1900* London 1989.
Holloway, James *Patrons and Painters: Art in Scotland 1650-1760*
   Edinburgh 1989.
Long, Philip and Cumming, Elizabeth
   *The Scottish Colourists 1900-1930* Edinburgh 2000.
Macdonald, Murdo *Scottish Art* London 2000.
McEwen, Peter *Dictionary of Scottish Art and Architecture*
   Woodbridge 1994.
Macmillan, Duncan *Painting in Scotland: The Golden Age* Oxford 1986.
Macmillan, Duncan *Scottish Art 1460-1990* Edinburgh 1990.
Thomson, Duncan *Painting in Scotland 1570-1650* Edinburgh 1975.


**CLANS**
Macinnes, Allan I *Clanship, commerce and the House of Stuart,*
   *1603-1788* East Linton 1996.
Moncreiffe of that Ilk, Sir Iain *The Highland Clans: the dynastic origins,*
   *chiefs and background of the Clans and of some other families*
   *connected with Highland history* revised edn London 1982.
Munro, R W *Highland Clans and Tartans* London 1977.

## CLEARANCES

Richards, Eric *The Highland Clearances:
    people, landords and rural turmoil* Edinburgh 2000.

## DANCE

Flett, J F and T M *Traditional Dancing in Scotland* London 1964.
Goodwin, Noël *Ballet for Scotland:
    the first ten years of the Scottish Ballet* Edinburgh 1979.

## DRESS

Cheape, Hugh *Tartan: The Highland Habit* Edinburgh 1991.
Dunbar, J Telfer *History of Highland Dress* London 1979.
Grange, R M D *A Short History of Scottish Dress* London 1966.
Marshall, Rosalind K *Costume in Scottish Portraits, 1560-1830*
    Edinburgh 1986.
Maxwell, Stuart and Hutchison, Robin
    *Scottish Costume 1550-1850* London 1958.

## EDUCATION

Anderson, R D, *Education and Opportunity in Victorian Scotland*
    Edinburgh 1983.
Anderson, R D *Education and the Scottish People, 1750-1918*
    Oxford 1995.
Bryce, T G K and Humes, W eds *Scottish Education*
    2nd edn Edinburgh 2003.
Davie, G E *The Democratic Intellect* Edinburgh 1961.
Holmes, Heather ed *Education*: *Scottish Life and Society*, vol. 11,
    Edinburgh 2000.
Paterson, L *Scottish Education in the Twentieth Century*
    Edinburgh 2003.
Withrington, Donald J *Going to School* Edinburgh 1997.

## ENLIGHTENMENT

Broadie, Alexander *The Scottish Enlightenment: the historical age of the
    historical nation* Edinburgh 2001.
Broadie, Alexander ed *Cambridge Companion to the Scottish
    Enlightenment* Cambridge 2003.

## ENVIRONMENT

Paterson, Anna *Scotland's Landscape: Endangered Icon* Edinburgh 2002.
Cramb, Auslan *Fragile Land: The State of the Scottish Environment*
    Edinburgh 1998.
Dunion, Kevin *Troublemakers: The Struggle for Environmental Justice in
    Scotland* Edinburgh 2003.
Slesser, Malcolm, King, Jane and Crane, David *Searching for a
    Sustainable Scotland* Edinburgh 1995.
Smout, T C *Nature Contested: Environmental History in Scotland and
    Northern England since 1600* Edinburgh 2000.

## FISHING INDUSTRY

Anson, P *Fishing Boats and Fisher Folk on the East Coast of Scotland*
    London 1930.
Dunlop, J *The British Fisheries Society 1786-1893* Edinburgh 1978.
Gray, M *The Fishing Industries of Scotland, 1790-1914* Oxford 1978.
Gunn, N *The Silver Darlings* London 1941.
Martin, A *Fishing and Whaling* Edinburgh 1995.
Martin, A *The Ring-Net Fishermen* Edinburgh 1981.

## FOOD/DRINK

Brown, Catherine *Scottish Cookery* new edn Edinburgh 1999.
Bruce-Gardyne, Tom *The Scotch Whisky Book* Edinburgh 2002.
Daiches, David *Scotch Whisky: Its Past and Present* 3rd edn London
    1978.
Gunn, Neil M *Whisky and Scotland: A Practical and Spiritual Survey*
    London 1935.
Kay, Billy and Maclean, Cailean *Knee Deep in Claret: A Celebration of
    Wine in Scotland* Edinburgh 1983.
McNeill, F Marian *The Scots Kitchen: Its Traditions and Lore with Old-
    time Recipes* Glasgow 1929.

McNeill, F Marian *The Scots Cellar: Its Traditions and Lore*
    Edinburgh 1956.

## FORESTRY

Anderson, M L *History of Scottish Forestry* 2 vols 1967.
Ryle, George *Forest Service: The first forty-five years of the Forestry
    Commission of Great Britain* Newton Abbot 1969.
Smout, T C *People and Woods in Scotland: A History* Edinburgh 2002.

## GARDENS

Burbidge, Brinsley *The Scottish Garden* Edinburgh 1989.
Coats, Alice *The Plant Hunters* London 1969.
Fletcher, Harold R. and Brown, William *The Royal Botanic Garden,
    Edinburgh 1670-1970* Edinburgh 1970.
Hadfield, Miles, Harling, Robert, and Highton, Leonie *British Gardeners;
    A Biographical Dictionary* London 1980.
King, Peter *The Good Gardens Guide 2003* London.
Little, Allen ed *Scotland's Gardens* Edinburgh 1981.

## GEOLOGY

Trewin, Nigel H *The Geology of Scotland* 4th edn London 2002.

## HERALDRY

Burnett, Charles J and Dennis, Mark D *Scotland's Heraldic Heritage:
    the lion rejoicing* Edinburgh 1997.

## INDUSTRY

Hamilton, Henry *The Industrial Revolution in Scotland* Oxford 1932.
Hume, John R *Industrial Archaeology of Scotland* Vol 1 *The Lowlands
    and Borders* London 1976; Vol 2 *The Highlands and Islands*
    London 1977.

## JACOBITE RISINGS

Lenman, Bruce *The Jacobite Risings in Britain 1689-1746* London 1980.
Lenman, Bruce *The Jacobite Cause* Glasgow 1986.
Prebble, John *Culloden* London 1961.

## LANGUAGES:

Scots
See introductions to the following dictionaries:
*Concise Scots Dictionary* Aberdeen 1985.
*Dictionary of the Older Scottish Tongue* 12 vols, Chicago and Oxford
    1931-2002.
*Scottish National Dictionary* 10 vols, Edinburgh 1931-76.

The last two major works are now available together on the Internet:
www.dsl.ac.uk

Corbett, John *Language and Scottish Literature* Edinburgh 1997.
Corbett, John, McClure, J Derrick and Stuart-Smith, Jane eds *The
    Edinburgh Companion to Scots* Edinburgh 2003.
Jones, Charles ed *The Edinburgh History of the Scots Language*
    Edinburgh 1997.
McClure, J Derrick *Why Scots Matters* revised edn Edinburgh 1997.

Gaelic
*A Fresh Start for Gaelic: Cothrom Ùr Don Ghàidhlig* Edinburgh 2002.
Thomson, Derick S *The Companion to Gaelic Scotland* Oxford 1983.

## LAW

Walker, David M *The Scottish Legal System: An Introduction to the
    Study of Scots Law* 8th edn 2001.

## LITERATURE

Craig, Cairns general ed *The History of Scottish Literature*
    4 vols Aberdeen 1987-8.
    Vol 1 *Origins to 1660* ed R D S Jack.
    Vol 2 *1660-1800* ed Andrew Hook.
    Vol 3 *Nineteenth Century* ed Douglas Gifford.

Vol 4 *Twentieth Century* ed Cairns Craig.
Watson, Roderick *The Literature of Scotland* London 1984.

### English and Scots
Craig, Cairns *The Modern Scottish Novel; Narrative and the National Imagination* Edinburgh 1999.
Gifford, Douglas, Dunnigan, Sarah and MacGillivray, Allan eds *Scottish Literature in English and Scots* Edinburgh 2002.
Lyle, Emily *Scottish Ballads* Edinburgh 1994.

### Gaelic
Thomson, Derick *The Companion to Gaelic Scotland* Oxford 1983.
Thomson, Derick *An Introduction to Gaelic Poetry* Edinburgh 1990.

And introductions to the following:
Black, Ronald ed *An Lasair: Anthology of 18th Century Scottish Gaelic Verse* Edinburgh 2001.
Black, Ronald I M ed *An Tuil: Anthology of 20th Century Scottish Gaelic Verse* Edinburgh 1999.
Meek, Donald ed *Caran an t-saoghail = The wiles of the world: anthology of 19th century Scottish Gaelic verse* Edinburgh 2003.

## MEDICINE
Comrie, John D *A History of Scottish Medicine to 1860.* 2 vols London 1932.
Dingwall, Helen M *A History of Scottish Medicine: Themes and Influences* Edinburgh 2002.
Hamilton, David *The Healers: A History of Medicine in Scotland* Edinburgh 1981.

## MILITARY
Henderson, Diana M *The Scottish Regiments* 2nd edn Glasgow 1996.
MacDougall, Norman *Scotland at War: AD 79-1918* Edinburgh 1991.
Wood, Stephen *The Scottish soldier: an illustrated social and military history of Scotland's fighting men through two thousand years* Edinburgh 1987.

## MUSIC See also Literature
Alburger, Mary Ann *Scottish Fiddlers and their Music* Edinburgh 1996.
Cannon, Roderick D *The Highland bagpipe and its music* 2nd edn Edinburgh 2002.
Cheape, Hugh *The Book of the Bagpipe* Belfast 1999
Collinson, Francis M *The Traditional and National Music of Scotland* London 1966.
Davie, Cedric Thorpe *Scotland's Music* Edinburgh 1980.
Emmerson, George S *Ranting Pipe and Trembling String* London 1971.
Farmer, Henry George *A history of music in Scotland* London 1947.
Munro, Ailie *The Democratic Muse: Folk Music Revival in Scotland* Aberdeen 1996.
Purser, John *Scotland's Music: A history of the traditional and classical music of Scotland from earliest times to the present day* Edinburgh 1992.
Sanger, Keith and Kinnaird, Alison *Tree of Strings = Crann nan Teud: a history of the harp in Scotland* Temple 1992.

## PLACE-NAMES
Drummond, Peter *Scottish Hill and Mountain Names: The origin and meaning of the names of Scotland's hills and mountains* Glasgow 1991.
Nicolaisen, W F H *Scottish place-names: their study and significance* London 1976
Watson, William J *The History of the Celtic Place-names of Scotland* Edinburgh 1926.

## POLITICS See also General History
Paterson, Lindsay *The Autonomy of Modern Scotland* Edinburgh 1994.
Lynch, Peter *Scottish Government and Politics: an Introduction* Edinburgh 2001.

Nairn, Tom *The Break-Up of Britain* 2nd edn London 1981.
Taylor, Brian *The Road to the Scottish Parliament* Edinburgh 2002.

## RELIGION
Cameron, Nigel M de S ed *Dictionary of Scottish Church History and Theology* Edinburgh 1993.
Maclean, Colin *Going to Church* Edinburgh 1997.

## SPORT
Burnett, John *Riot, Revelry and Rout: sport in Lowland Scotland before 1860* East Linton 2000
Jarvie, Grant and Burnett, John eds *Sport, Scotland and the Scots* East Linton 2000.

### CURLING
Murray, W H *The Curling Companion* Glasgow 1981.
Smith, David B *Curling: an illustrated history* Glasgow 1981.

### FOOTBALL
Archer, Ian and Royle, Trevor eds *We'll support you evermore: the impertinent saga of Scottish 'fitba'* London 1976.

### GOLF
Hamilton, David *Golf: Scotland's Game* Kilmacolm 1998.

### HIGHLAND GAMES
Webster, David *Scottish Highland Games* Edinburgh 1973.

### MOUNTAINEERING/MOUNTAINS
Bearhop, Derek A *Munro's Tables* new edn Glasgow 1997.
Bennet, Donald J *The Munros* 2nd edn Glasgow 1991.
Milne, Rob and Brown, Hamish *The Corbetts and other Scottish hills* Glasgow 1990.
Murray, W H *Mountaineering in Scotland* London 1947.
Simpson, Myrtle *Skisters: the story of Scottish skiing* Carrbridge 1982.

The Scottish Mountaineering Club publishes a series of guidebooks to various parts of Scotland: district guides for hillwalkers and climbers, very practical climbers' guides; see their website:smc.org.uk

### RUGBY
Massie, Allan *A Portrait of Scottish Rugby* Edinburgh 1984.

### SHINTY
Hutchinson, Roger *Camanachd!:The Story of Shinty* Edinburgh 1989.
MacLennan, Hugh Dan *Shinty!* Nairn 1993.

## THEATRE
Bruce, Frank *Scottish Showbusiness: music hall, variety and pantomime* Edinburgh 2000.
Findlay, Bill ed *A history of Scottish theatre* Edinburgh 1998.
Maloney, Paul *Scotland and the Music Hall, 1850-1914* Manchester 2003.

## TRANSPORT
Gordon, George and Dicks, Brian eds *Essays in Scottish Urban History* Aberdeen 1983.
Haldane, A R B *The Drove Roads of Scotland* London 1952.
Haldane, A R B *New Ways through the Glens: Highland Road, Bridge and Canal Makers of the Early Nineteenth Century* London 1962.
Lindsay, Jean *The Canals of Scotland* Newton Abbot 1968.
Taylor, William *The Military Roads in Scotland* Newton Abbot 1976.
Thomas, John *A Regional History of the Railways of Great Britain* Vol 6 *Scotland: The Lowlands and the Borders* Newton Abbot 1971.
Thomas, John and Turnock, David *A Regional History of the Railways of Great Britain* Vol 15 *The North of Scotland* Newton Abbot 1989.

## WEIGHTS AND MEASURES
Connor, R D and Simpson, A D C with Morrison-Low, A D *Weights and Measures in Scotland: A European Perspective* Edinburgh 2004.